Algebraic, Analytic,
and Computational Number Theory
and Its Applications

Algebraic, Analytic, and Computational Number Theory and Its Applications

Editors

Diana Savin
Nicusor Minculete
Vincenzo Acciaro

Basel • Beijing • Wuhan • Barcelona • Belgrade • Novi Sad • Cluj • Manchester

Editors

Diana Savin
Mathematics and
Computer Science
Transilvania University
of Brasov
Brasov, Romania

Nicusor Minculete
Mathematics and
Computer Science
Transilvania University
of Brasov
Brasov, Romania

Vincenzo Acciaro
Economic Studies
Chieto-Pescara University
Pescara, Italy

Editorial Office
MDPI
St. Alban-Anlage 66
4052 Basel, Switzerland

This is a reprint of articles from the Special Issue published online in the open access journal *Mathematics* (ISSN 2227-7390) (available at: https://www.mdpi.com/journal/mathematics/special_issues/algebraic_analytic_computational_number_theory).

For citation purposes, cite each article independently as indicated on the article page online and as indicated below:

Lastname, A.A.; Lastname, B.B. Article Title. *Journal Name* **Year**, *Volume Number*, Page Range.

ISBN 978-3-0365-9859-8 (Hbk)
ISBN 978-3-0365-9860-4 (PDF)
doi.org/10.3390/books978-3-0365-9860-4

© 2024 by the authors. Articles in this book are Open Access and distributed under the Creative Commons Attribution (CC BY) license. The book as a whole is distributed by MDPI under the terms and conditions of the Creative Commons Attribution-NonCommercial-NoDerivs (CC BY-NC-ND) license.

Contents

About the Editors vii

Preface ix

Diana Savin, Nicuşor Minculete and Vincenzo Acciaro
Algebraic, Analytic, and Computational Number Theory and Its Applications
Reprinted from: *Mathematics* **2024**, *12*, 10, doi:10.3390/math12010010 1

Dorin Andrica and Ovidiu Bagdasar
On Generalized Lucas Pseudoprimality of Level k
Reprinted from: *Mathematics* **2021**, *9*, 838, doi:10.3390/math9080838 9

Eva Trojovská and Pavel Trojovský
On Fibonacci Numbers of Order r Which Are Expressible as Sum of Consecutive Factorial Numbers
Reprinted from: *Mathematics* **2021**, *9*, 962, doi:10.3390/math9090962 27

Busakorn Aiewcharoen, Ratinan Boonklurb and Nanthiya Konglawan
Global and Local Behavior of the System of Piecewise Linear Difference Equations $x_{n+1} = |x_n| - y_n - b$ and $y_{n+1} = x_n - |y_n| + 1$ Where $b \geq 4$
Reprinted from: *Mathematics* **2021**, *9*, 1390, doi:10.3390/math9121390 37

Nicuşor Minculete and Diana Savin
Some Properties of Euler's Function and of the Function τ and Their Generalizations in Algebraic Number Fields
Reprinted from: **2021**, *9*, 1710, doi:10.3390/math9151710 65

Jukkrit Daengsaen and Sorasak Leeratanavalee
Regularities in Ordered n-Ary Semihypergroups
Reprinted from: *Mathematics* **2021**, *9*, 1857, doi:10.3390/math9161857 75

Wenjing Ding, Huafeng Liu and Deyu Zhang
New Zero-Density Results for Automorphic L-Functions of $GL(n)$
Reprinted from: *Mathematics* **2021**, *9*, 2061, doi:10.3390/math9172061 97

Nazlıhan Terzioğlu, Can Kızılateş and Wei-Shih Du
New Properties and Identities for Fibonacci Finite Operator Quaternions
Reprinted from: *Mathematics* **2022**, *10*, 1719, doi:10.3390/math10101719 111

Dana Piciu and Diana Savin
Residuated Lattices with Noetherian Spectrum
Reprinted from: *Mathematics* **2022**, *10*, 1831, doi:10.3390/math10111831 125

Antanas Laurinčikas and Renata Macaitienė
A Generalized Bohr–Jessen Type Theorem for the Epstein Zeta-Function
Reprinted from: *Mathematics* **2022**, *10*, 2042, doi:10.3390/math10122042 139

Kwang-Seob Kim
Some Remarks on the Divisibility of the Class Numbers of Imaginary Quadratic Fields
Reprinted from: *Mathematics* **2022**, *10*, 2488, doi:10.3390/math10142488 151

Avinash Vijayarangan, Veena Narayanan, Vijayarangan N and Srikanth R
Novel Authentication Protocols Based on Quadratic Diophantine Equations
Reprinted from: *Mathematics* **2022**, *10*, 3136, doi:10.3390/math10173136 161

Ying Wang, Muhammad Ahsan Binyamin, Iqra Amin, Adnan Aslam and Yongsheng Rao
On the Classification of Telescopic Numerical Semigroups of Some Fixed Multiplicity
Reprinted from: *Mathematics* **2022**, *10*, 3871, doi:10.3390/math10203871 . . . . **171**

Ayşe Zeynep Azak
Pauli Gaussian Fibonacci and Pauli Gaussian Lucas Quaternions
Reprinted from: *Mathematics* **2022**, *10*, 4655, doi:10.3390/math10244655 . . . . **181**

Alaa Altassan and Murat Alan
Almost Repdigit k-Fibonacci Numbers with an Application of k-Generalized Fibonacci Sequences
Reprinted from: *Mathematics* **2023**, *11*, 455, doi:10.3390/math11020455 . . . . **191**

Artūras Dubickas
Density of Some Special Sequences Modulo 1
Reprinted from: *Mathematics* **2023**, *11*, 1727, doi:10.3390/math11071727 . . . . **207**

Teerapat Srichan
A Bound for a Sum of Products of Two Characters and Its Application
Reprinted from: *Mathematics* **2023**, *11*, 2507, doi:10.3390/math11112507 . . . . **217**

Muh Nur, Mawardi Bahri, Anna Islamiyati and Harmanus Batkunde
A New Semi-Inner Product and p_n-Angle in the Space of p-Summable Sequences
Reprinted from: *Mathematics* **2023**, *11*, 3139, doi:10.3390/math11143139 . . . . **225**

Dorin Andrica and Ovidiu Bagdasar
Remarks on the Coefficients of Inverse Cyclotomic Polynomials
Reprinted from: *Mathematics* **2023**, *11*, 3622, doi:10.3390/math11173622 . . . . **239**

Lhoussain El Fadil
On Indices of Septic Number Fields Defined by Trinomials $x^7 + ax + b$
Reprinted from: *Mathematics* **2023**, *11*, 4441, doi:10.3390/math11214441 . . . . **255**

Zakariae Cheddour, Abdelhakim Chillali and Ali Mouhib
Generalized Fibonacci Sequences for Elliptic Curve Cryptography
Reprinted from: *Mathematics* **2023**, *11*, 4656, doi:10.3390/math11224656 . . . . **267**

Elif Tan, Diana Savin and Semih Yılmaz
A New Class of LeonardoHybrid Numbers and Some Remarks on Leonardo Quaternions over Finite Fields
Reprinted from: *Mathematics* **2023**, *11*, 4701, doi:10.3390/math11224701 . . . . **285**

About the Editors

Diana Savin

Diana Savin is an Associate Professor at the Faculty of Mathematics and Computer Science, Transilvania University of Brașov, Romania. Diana Savin graduated from the Faculty of Mathematics and Computer Science of the University of Bucharest in 1996. She obtained a PhD in Mathematics (namely in algebraic number theory) at Ovidius University of Constanta, Romania, in 2004. Her research directions are algebraic number theory (especially ramification theory in algebraic number fields), associative algebra, computational number theory and combinatorics. She has written several research articles on these areas. Alone, or jointly with V. Acciaro, M. Taous and A. Zekhnini, she has studied quaternion algebra over some algebraic number fields, using ramification theory in algebraic number fields.

Nicusor Minculete

Nicusor Minculete is An associate Professor and Head of Department at the Faculty of Mathematics and Computer Science, Transilvania University of Brașov, Romania. Nicușor Minculete has earned the following degrees: Mathematics at University of Bucharest (1994); Ph.D. in Mathematics at Institute of Mathematics of the Romanian Academy (2012). Nicușor Minculete has the following research interests: mathematical inequalities and its applications; number theory; and Euclidean geometry. Nicușor Minculete is a Member of the Editorial Board at the following journals: *European Journal of Mathematics and Applications*, *International Journal of Geometry*, *Bulletin of the Transilvania University of Brasov*, *General Mathematics*, *Octogon Mathematical Magazine*.

Vincenzo Acciaro

Vincenzo Acciaro is an Associate Professor at the Department of Economic Studies of the University of Pescara, Italy. In 1987, he graduated in Computer Science at the University of Bari, Italy. In 1991, he earned his master's degree in Computer Science at Carleton University, Ottawa, Canada, with a thesis about the generation of random elements in permutation groups. In 1995, he earned his Ph.D. in Computer Science at Carleton University, Ottawa, Canada, with a thesis about local global methods in number theory. His research interests are mainly in the fields of algebraic number theory, associative algebra and computational number theory.

Preface

Analytic number theory is a branch of number theory which uses methods from mathematical analysis in order to solve difficult problems about integers.

Analytic number theory can be split into two major areas: multiplicative number theory and additive number theory. Bernhard Riemann made some very important contributions to the field of analytic number theory; among others, he investigated the Riemann zeta function, and he established its importance for understanding the distribution of prime numbers. A typical problem of analytic number theory is the enumeration of number-theoretic objects like primes, solutions of Diophantine equations, etc.

Algebraic number theory on the other hand studies the arithmetic of algebraic number fields, i.e., the ring of integers of arbitrary number fields. It embraces, among others, the study of the ideals and of the group of units in the ring of integers and the extent to which unique factorization holds.

Algebraic number theory has become an important branch of pure mathematics, on par with algebraic geometry. There are two standard ways to approach algebraic number theory, one by means of ideals and the other by means of valuations. Factorization in a field makes sense only with respect to a subring, and so, we must resurrect the ring of integers in a number field in order to define it.

The class number of a number field is by definition the order of the ideal class group of its ring of integers—it measures how far the ring of integers is from being a unique factorization domain. The divisibility properties of class numbers are very important for the investigation of the structure of ideal class groups of number fields. There has been considerable investigation in the past on the divisibility of the class numbers of quadratic number fields. Lastly, since any factorization of an algebraic integer is defined up to multiplicative units, we need to understand the structure of the group of units in the ring of integers in order to fully understand the arithmetic of the number field.

The purpose and scope of this "Special Issue" are to collect new results in algebraic number theory and analytic number theory (namely in the areas of ramification theory in algebraic number fields, class field theory, arithmetic functions, L-functions, modular forms and elliptic curves) and in some similar research areas (namely elementary number theory, associative algebras, logical algebras, combinatorics, difference equations and algebraic hyper-structures).

These papers have been written by scientists working in leading universities or leading research centers in China, the Czech Republic, Korea, Lithuania, Romania, Taiwan, Thailand, Turkey, the United Kingdom, India, Pakistan, Saudi Arabia, Indonesia and Morocco.

Diana Savin, Nicusor Minculete, and Vincenzo Acciaro
Editors

Editorial

Algebraic, Analytic, and Computational Number Theory and Its Applications

Diana Savin [1,*], Nicusor Minculete [1] and Vincenzo Acciaro [2]

1. Faculty of Mathematics and Computer Science, Transilvania University of Brașov, Iuliu Maniu Street, 50, 500091 Brașov, Romania; minculete.nicusor@unitbv.ro
2. Department of Economic Studies, G. d'Annunzio University of Chieti-Pescara, Viale Pindaro, 42, 65127 Pescara, Italy; vincenzo.acciaro@unich.it
* Correspondence: diana.savin@unitbv.ro

Citation: Savin, D.; Minculete, N.; Acciaro, V. Algebraic, Analytic, and Computational Number Theory and Its Applications. *Mathematics* **2024**, *12*, 10. https://doi.org/10.3390/math12010010

Received: 15 December 2023
Accepted: 18 December 2023
Published: 20 December 2023

Copyright: © 2023 by the authors. Licensee MDPI, Basel, Switzerland. This article is an open access article distributed under the terms and conditions of the Creative Commons Attribution (CC BY) license (https://creativecommons.org/licenses/by/4.0/).

Analytic number theory is a branch of number theory which inherits methods from mathematical analysis in order to solve difficult problems about the integers. Analytic number theory can be split into two major areas: multiplicative number theory and additive number theory. Bernhard Riemann made some very important contributions to the field of analytic number theory: among others, he investigated the Riemann zeta function and he established its importance for understanding the distribution of prime numbers. Some of the most useful tools in multiplicative number theory are the Dirichlet series and the technique of partial summation, which can be used to characterize the coefficients of the Dirichlet series [1]. A typical problem of analytic number theory is the enumeration of number-theoretic objects like primes, solutions of Diophantine equations, etc.

Algebraic number theory, on the other hand, studies the arithmetic of algebraic number fields, i.e., the ring of integers of arbitrary number fields. It embraces, among others, the study of the ideals and of the group of units in the ring of integers, the extent to which unique factorization holds, and so on [2–4]. Algebraic number theory has become an important branch of pure mathematics, on a par with algebraic geometry. There are two standard ways to approach algebraic number theory, one by means of ideals and the other by means of valuations [5]. Factorization in a field makes sense only with respect to a subring, and so we must resurrect the ring of integers in a number field in order to define it. Since the unique factorization property will fail in general, we need a way to measure how much it fails. The class number of a number field is, by definition, the order of the ideal class group of its ring of integers—it measures how far our ring of integers is from being a unique factorization domain. The divisibility properties of class numbers are very important for the investigation of the structure of ideal class groups of number fields. There has been considerable investigation in the past on the divisibility of the class numbers of quadratic number fields [6–14].

Lastly, since any factorization of an algebraic integer is defined up to multiplicative units, we need to understand the structure of the group of units in the ring of integers in order to fully understand the arithmetic of the number field.

Some important properties of associative algebra can be studied by employing the standard tools of algebraic number theory, elementary number theory, computational number theory, and combinatorics (see [15–20]). Three papers of this Special Issue deal with sequences of special numbers and special quaternions [21–23].

The purpose and scope of this Special Issue is to collect new results in algebraic number theory and analytic number theory (namely, in the areas of ramification theory in algebraic number fields, class field theory, arithmetic functions, *L*-functions, modular forms, and elliptic curves) and in some close research areas (namely, associative algebra, logical algebra, elementary number theory, combinatorics, difference equations, group rings, and algebraic hyperstructures).

In the following part of this Editorial, we discuss the manuscripts which have been selected for publication in this Special Issue. These papers were written by scientists working in leading universities or leading research centers in China, Czech Republic, Korea, Lithuania, Romania, Taiwan, Thailand, Turkey, United Kingdom, India, Pakistan, Saudi Arabia, Indonesia, and Morocco. The contributions are listed in the List of Contributions.

Contribution 1 is from D. Andrica and O. Bagdasar. In the paper titled "On Generalized Lucas Pseudoprimality of Level k", they investigate the Fibonacci pseudoprimes of level k. They disprove a statement concerning the relationship between sets of different levels and prove a counterpart of this result for the Lucas pseudoprimes of level k. They use some recently found properties of the generalized Lucas pseudoprimes and generalized Pell–Lucas sequences to define new kinds of pseudoprimes of levels k^+ and k^- and parameter a. For these novel pseudoprime sequences, they investigated some basic properties and computed several associated integer sequences, which were added to the Online Encyclopedia of Integer Sequences.

Contribution 2 is from E. Trojovská and P. Trojovský. In the paper "On Fibonacci Numbers of Order r Which Are Expressible as Sum of Consecutive Factorial Numbers", they investigate the sequence of the generalized Fibonacci number of order r. Let $(t_n^{(r)})_{n \geq 0}$ be the sequence of the generalized Fibonacci number of order r, which is defined by the recurrence $t_n^{(r)} = t_{n-1}^{(r)} + \ldots + t_{n-r}^{(r)}$ for $n \geq r$, with initial values $t_0^{(r)} = 0$ and $t_i^{(r)} = 1$, for all $1 \leq i \leq r$. In 2002, Grossman and Luca searched for terms of the sequence $(t_n^{(2)})_n$ which are expressible as a sum of factorials. In this paper, the authors continue this program by proving that, for any $l \geq 1$, there exists an effectively computable constant $C = C(l) > 0$ (only depending on l), such that, if (m,n,r) is a solution of $t_m^{(r)} = n! + (n+1)! + \ldots + (n+l)!$, with r even, then $\max\{m,n,r\} < C$. As an application, they solve the previous equation for all $1 \leq l \leq 5$.

Contribution 3 is from B. Aiewcharoen et al. In the paper "Global and Local Behavior of the System of Piecewise Linear Difference Equations $x_{n+1} = |x_n| - y_n - b$ and $y_{n+1} = x_n - |y_n| + 1$, where $b \geq 4$", they study the system of piecewise linear difference equations $x_{n+1} = |x_n| - y_n - b$ and $y_{n+1} = x_n - |y_n| + 1$ where $n \geq 0$. The global behavior at $b = 4$ shows that all solutions become the equilibrium point. For a large value of $|x_0|$ and $|y_0|$, they prove that (i) if $b = 5$, then the solution becomes the equilibrium point, and (ii) if $b \geq 6$, then the solution becomes the periodic solution of prime period 5.

Contribution 4 is from N. Minculete and D. Savin. In the paper "Some Properties of Euler's Function and of the Function τ and Their Generalizations in Algebraic Number Fields", they prove some inequalities which involve Euler's function, the extended Euler's function, the function τ, and the generalized Euler's function τ in algebraic number fields, thus extending the results they obtained in [24,25].

Contribution 5 is from J. Daengsaen and S. Leeratanavalee. In the paper "Regularities in Ordered n–Ary Semihypergroups", they approach a class of hyperstructures called ordered n–ary semihypergroups and study them using j-hyperideals for all positive integers $1 \leq j \leq n$ and $n \geq 3$. They first introduce the notion of (softly) left regularity, (softly) right regularity, (softly) intra-regularity, complete regularity, and generalized regularity of ordered n–ary semihypergroups and investigate their related properties. They present several of their characterizations in terms of j-hyperideals. Finally, they also establish the relationships between various classes of regularities in ordered n–ary semihypergroups.

Contribution 6 is from W. Ding et al. In the paper "New Zero-Density Results for Automorphic L–Functions of $GL(n)$", they study the automorphic L-function of $GL(n)$. Let $L(s, \pi)$ be an automorphic L-function of $GL(n)$, where π is an automorphic representation of group $GL(n)$ over the rational number field $\mathbb{Q}$. They study the zero-density estimates for $L(s, \pi)$. If $N_\pi(\sigma, T_1, T_2) = \sharp\{\rho = \beta + i\gamma : L(\rho, \pi) = 0, \sigma < \beta < 1, T_1 \leq \gamma \leq T_2\}$, where $0 \leq \sigma < 1$ and $T_1 < T_2$; then, they establish an upper bound for $N_\pi(\sigma, T, 2T)$ when σ is close to 1. They restrict the imaginary part γ into a narrow strip $[T, T + T^\alpha]$ with $0 < \alpha \leq 1$ and prove some new zero-density results on $N_\pi(\sigma, T, T + T^\alpha)$ (under specific conditions), thus improving the previous results when σ is near 34 and 1, respectively. Their proofs rely on the zero-detecting method and the Halász-Montgomery method.

Contribution 7 is from N. Terzioğlu et al. In the paper "New Properties and Identities for Fibonacci Finite Operator Quaternions", they define a new family of quaternions whose components are the Fibonacci finite operator numbers. They also prove some properties of this new family of quaternions. Moreover, by using their matrix representation, they present many identities related to Fibonacci finite operator quaternions.

Contribution 8 is from D. Piciu and D. Savin. In the paper "Residuated Lattices with Noetherian Spectrum", they characterize the residuated lattices for which the topological space of prime ideals is a Noetherian space. They introduce the notion of i-Noetherian residuated lattice and investigate its properties. They prove that a residuated lattice is i-Noetherian if and only if every ideal is principal. Moreover, they show that a residuated lattice has the spectrum of a Noetherian space if and only if it is i-Noetherian. In the last section of the paper, the authors compare ideals in residuated lattices with ideals in unitary commutative rings. They prove that if $(R, +, \cdot)$ is a Boolean ring, then any ideal of R is idempotent. Additionally, the authors prove that any Boolean ring is a Bezout ring with zero divisors.

Contribution 9 is from A. Laurinčikas and R. Macaitienė. In the paper "A Generalized Bohr-Jessen Type Theorem for the Epstein Zeta-Function", they study some properties of the the Epstein zeta function. Let Q be a positive defined $n \times n$ matrix and $Q[\underline{x}] = \underline{x}^T Q \underline{x}$. The Epstein zeta function $\zeta(s; Q)$, $s = \sigma + it$, is defined for $\sigma > \frac{n}{2}$ by the meromorphic continuation of the series $\zeta(s; Q) = \sum_{\underline{x} \in \mathbb{Z}^n - \{\underline{0}\}} (Q[\underline{x}])^{-s}$ to the whole complex plane. Suppose that $n \geq 4$ is even and $\phi(t)$ is a differentiable function with a monotonic derivative. They prove that $\frac{1}{T} \text{meas}\{t \in [0, T] : \zeta(\sigma + i\phi(t); Q) \in A\}; A \in B(\mathbb{C})$, converges weakly to an explicitly given probability measure on $(\mathbb{C}, B(\mathbb{C}))$ as $T \to \infty$.

Contribution 10 is from K.-S. Kim, S. In the paper "Some Remarks on the Divisibility of the Class Numbers of Imaginary Quadratic Fields" [6], he investigates, for a given integer n, some families of imaginary quadratic number fields of the form $\mathbb{Q}(\sqrt{4q^2 - p^n})$ whose ideal class group has a subgroup isomorphic to $\mathbb{Z}/n\mathbb{Z}$, thus continuing the work of K. Chakraborty, A. Hoque, Y. Kishi, and P.P. Pandey, who studied the more restricted family $\mathbb{Q}(\sqrt{q^2 - p^n})$ with p and q as distinct odd prime numbers and $n \geq 3$ as an odd integer (see Theorem 1.2 of [8]).

Contribution 11 is from A. Vijayarangan, V. Narayanan, V. Natarajan, and S. Raghavendran. In the paper "Novel Authentication Protocols Based on Quadratic Diophantine Equations", they determine some geometric properties of positive integral solutions of the quadratic Diophantine equation $x_1^2 + x_2^2 = y_1^2 + y_2^2$. Moreover, in the same paper, the authors develop a new authentication protocol based on the geometric properties of the solutions of this quadratic Diophantine equation. The paper successfully depicts the role of number theory—especially Diophantine equations—in cryptography.

Contribution 12 is from Y. Wang, M.A. Binyamin, I. Amin, A. Aslam, and Y. Rao. In the paper "On the Classification of Telescopic Numerical Semigroups of Some Fixed Multiplicity", they expand on the results of Suer and Ilhan [26–28] for telescopic numerical semigroups of multiplicities 8 and 12 with embedding dimension four. Moreover, the authors compute the Frobenius number and genus for these classes in terms of the minimal system of generators.

Contribution 13 is from A.Z. Azak. In the paper "Pauli Gaussian Fibonacci and Pauli Gaussian Lucas Quaternions", she investigates the Pauli–Fibonacci quaternions (resp. Pauli–Lucas quaternions) whose coefficients consist of Gaussian–Fibonacci numbers (resp. Gaussian–Lucas numbers). Gaussian–Fibonacci numbers and Gaussian–Lucas numbers were introduced by Jordan in [29]. In [30], S. Halici introduced complex Fibonacci quaternions. Recently, the investigation of Gaussian–Lucas numbers has become an active research topic, and many of their properties have been exploited [31,32]. In the paper published in this Special Issue, the authors prove the Binet formulas for Pauli–Gaussian–Fibonacci and Pauli–Gaussian–Lucas quaternions and they also prove the Honsberger's, Catalan's and Cassini's identities for Pauli–Gaussian–Fibonacci quaternions.

Contribution 14 is from A. Altassan and M. Alan. In the paper "Almost Repdigit k-Fibonacci Numbers with an Application of k-Generalized Fibonacci Sequences", they introduce the notion of *almost repdigit*. In Theorem 1, which is the main result of this paper, the authors determine all the terms of the k-generalized Fibonacci sequence, which are almost repdigits. In order to prove this theorem, the authors make use of linear forms in the logarithms of algebraic numbers, Matveev's Theorem [33], some results from Baker and Davenport [34], the reduction algorithm from Dujella and Pethö [35], and various properties of k-Fibonacci numbers.

Contribution 15 is from A. Dubickas. In the paper "Density of Some Special Sequences Modulo 1", he explicitly describes all the elements of the sequence of fractional parts $\left\{ a^{f(n)}/n \right\}$ where $f \in \mathbb{Z}[X]$ is a non constant polynomial with a positive leading coefficient and $a \geq 2$ is an integer. The author proves that this sequence is dense everywhere in $[0,1]$, thus expanding on the result of Cilleruelo, Kumchev, Luca, Rué, and Shparlinski [36], who required f to be the identity function and used a very different method. The author then proved that the result still holds true for the sequence of fractional parts $\left\{ a^{f(n)}/n^d \right\}$ if we impose suitable condition on d, i.e., if $d \geq 1$ has no prime divisors other than those of a. In particular, this implies that for any pair of integers $a \geq 2$ and $b \geq 1$, the sequence of fractional parts $\left\{ a^n / \sqrt[b]{n} \right\}$ is dense everywhere in $[0,1]$.

Contribution 16 is from T. Srichan. In the paper "A Bound for a Sum of Products of Two Characters and Its Application", he obtains a nice bound on the sum $\sum_{m^a n^b \leq x} \chi_1^a(m) \chi_2^b(n)$, where χ_i is the primitive Dirichlet character modulus q_i; the numbers a and b are fixed positive integers; and χ^a and χ^b are not principal characters. The main result of this paper is Theorem 1. In the last section of the article, the author presents an interesting application of this theorem, namely, a nice estimate of the error term in the problem of finding an asymptotic estimate of the number of full-square integers simultaneously belonging to two arithmetic progressions.

Contribution 17 is from M. Nur, M. Bahri, A. Islamiyati, and H. Batkunde. In the paper "A New Semi-Inner Product and p_n-Angle in the Space of p-Summable Sequences", they define a semi-inner product in the space of p-summable sequences equipped with an n-norm. The authors also introduce some concepts of functional analysis with connections to number theory, namely, the concept of p_n-orthogonality, a p_n-angle between two vectors in the space of p-summable sequences (resp. p_n-orthogonality, p_n-angle between one-dimensional subspaces and arbitrary-dimensional subspaces). They also obtain some interesting results involving these concepts.

Contribution 18 is from D. Andrica and O. Bagdasar. In the paper "Remarks on the Coefficients of Inverse Cyclotomic Polynomials", they study some properties of the n-th inverse cyclotomic polynomial, i.e., those polynomials whose roots are exactly all the non-primitive n-th roots of unity. These polynomials, which have been an object of investigation recently, are defined as the ratio of the polynomial $x^n - 1$ to the n-th cyclotomic polynomial $\Phi_n(x)$, and they satisfy some very nice properties (e.g., while a cyclotomic polynomial is palindromic, an inverse cyclotomic polynomial is anti-palindromic). After reviewing some known formulae for the calculation of the coefficients of cyclotomic polynomials, the authors derive two new recursive formulas for the coefficients of inverse cyclotomic polynomials (Theorems 4 and 6). These formulas are expressed in terms of Ramanujan sums and provide counterparts to similar formulae that were obtained by the same authors for cyclotomic polynomials. In the last section of the paper, the authors apply these recursive formulas to compute the coefficients of some ternary and quaternary inverse cyclotomic polynomials, i.e., when n is a product of three or four distinct primes.

Contribution 19 is from L. El Fadil. In the paper "On Indices of Septic Number Fields Defined by Trinomials $x^7 + ax + b$", he computes, for every prime integer p, the highest power $\nu_p(i(K))$ of p by dividing the index $i(K)$ of the number field K generated by the root of an irreducible trinomial $x^7 + ax + b$. This allowed him to compute the index $i(K)$ of the number field K, which is defined as the greatest common divisor of the indices of all the integral primitive elements of K. In particular, when the index of K is not trivial, then we can assert that K is not monogenic, i.e., its ring of integers cannot be generated by a single integral element. The monogenity of number fields is a classical problem of algebraic number fields, going back to Dedekind, Hasse, and Hensel. Recently, the monogenity of a number field and the construction of all possible generators of power integral bases have been intensively studied among others, such as Gaál, Nakahara, Pohst, and their collaborators. In the classical algebraic number theory book [37], Narkiewicz asked for an explicit formula to compute $\nu_p(i(K))$ for a given p. The method employed by the author of the paper in this Special Issue, who solves the problem posed by Narkiewicz in a very special case, is based on the study of the factorization of the prime ideals in the ring of integers of the septic field K.

Contribution 20 is from Z. Cheddour, A. Chillali, and A. Mouhib. In the paper "Generalized Fibonacci Sequences for Elliptic Curve Cryptography", they propose a generalization of the Fibonacci sequence based on elliptic curves. The study of repeating sequences in algebraic structures began with the early work of Wall, who studied regular Fibonacci sequences in cyclic groups. In this paper, the authors continue along this path and explore the concept of Fibonacci sequences for groups generated by points on an elliptic curve. They propose an encryption system which makes use of this sequence, and it is based on the discrete logarithm problem on elliptic curves. The authors compare the memory consumption of the proposed elliptic-curve-based cryptosystem with the Cramer–Shoup signature scheme relying on a strong RSA, and they show that in the proposed cryptosystem, it is significantly lower. Moreover, a notable advantage of the proposed scheme lies in its ability to generate a larger number of points with the same prime order p of the finite field.

Contribution 21 is from E. Tan, D. Savin, and S. Yılmaz. In the paper "A New Class of Leonardo Hybrid Numbers and Some Remarks on Leonardo Quaternions over Finite Fields", they introduce the generalized Leonardo hybrid numbers. Moreover, the authors define a new class of Leonardo hybrid numbers called q-generalized Leonardo hybrid numbers. Some properties of Leonardo numbers were studied by Catarino and Borges [38,39], by Alp and Kocer [40], and by Tan and Leung [41]. In this Special Issue paper, the authors obtain many important properties of generalized Leonardo hybrid numbers and q-generalized Leonardo hybrid numbers, including recurrence relations, the Binet formula, the exponential generating function, Vajda's identity, and the summation formulas. In [42], Savin determined which of the Fibonacci quaternions are invertible (resp. divisors of zero) in quaternion algebra over finite fields, namely, in quaternion algebra $Q_{\mathbb{Z}_p}(-1,-1)$. In [43] Mangueira, Alves, and Catarino introduced the notion of Leonardo Quaternions. In this Special Issue paper, the authors determine the Leonardo quaternions which are divisors of zero in the quaternion algebras $Q_{\mathbb{Z}_3}(-1,-1)$ and $Q_{\mathbb{Z}_5}(-1,-1)$. Moreover, the authors identify certain Leonardo quaternions that are invertible in the quaternion algebra $Q_{\mathbb{Z}_p}(-1,-1)$ for a prime integer $p \geq 7$.

In conclusion, we think that this Special Issue will be of great interest to all mathematicians specializing in algebraic, analytic, and computational number theory and their applications. The techniques employed in the papers of this Special Issue can prove to be very effective in obtaining new results in these areas of mathematics.

Acknowledgments: We are pleased to thank Christopher Goodrich, Adolfo Ballester-Bolinches, Alexander Felshtyn, Jiyou Li, Abdelmejid Bayad, Patrick Solé, Clemente Cesarano, Li Guo, and Carsten Schneider, who kindly accepted to be the academic editors for some of the papers published in this Special Issue.

Conflicts of Interest: The authors declare no conflict of interest.

List of Contributions

1. Andrica, D.; Bagdasar, O. On Generalized Lucas Pseudoprimality of Level k. *Mathematics* **2021**, *9*, 838. https://doi.org/10.3390/math9080838.
2. Trojovská, E.; Trojovský, P. On Fibonacci Numbers of Order r Which Are Expressible as Sum of Consecutive Factorial Numbers. *Mathematics* **2021**, *9*, 962. https://doi.org/10.3390/math9090962.

3. Aiewcharoen, B.; Boonklurb, R.; Konglawan, N. Global and Local Behavior of the System of Piecewise Linear Difference Equations $x_{n+1} = |x_n| - y_n - b$ and $y_{n+1} = x_n - |y_n| + 1$, Where $b \geq 4$. *Mathematics* 2021, 9, 1390. https://doi.org/10.3390/math9121390.
4. Minculete, N.; Savin, D. Some Properties of Euler's Function and of the Function τ and Their Generalizations in Algebraic Number Fields. *Mathematics* 2021, 9, 1710. https://doi.org/10.3390/math9151710.
5. Daengsaen, J.; Leeratanavalee, S. Regularities in Ordered n–Ary Semihypergroups. *Mathematics* 2021, 9, 1857. https://doi.org/10.3390/math9161857.
6. Ding, W.; Liu, H.; Zhang, D. New Zero-Density Results for Automorphic L–Functions of $GL(n)$. *Mathematics* 2021, 9, 2061. https://doi.org/10.3390/math9172061.
7. Terzioğlu, N.; Kızılateş, C.; Du, W.-S. New Properties and Identities for Fibonacci Finite Operator Quaternions. *Mathematics* 2022, 10, 1719. https://doi.org/10.3390/math10101719.
8. Piciu, D.; Savin, D. Residuated Lattices with Noetherian Spectrum. *Mathematics* 2022, 10, 1831. https://doi.org/10.3390/math10111831.
9. Laurinčikas, A.; Macaitienė, R. A Generalized Bohr–Jessen Type Theorem for the Epstein Zeta-Function. *Mathematics* 2022, 10, 2042. https://doi.org/10.3390/math10122042.
10. Kim, K.-S. Some Remarks on the Divisibility of the Class Numbers of Imaginary Quadratic Fields. *Mathematics* 2022, 10, 2488. https://doi.org/10.3390/math10142488.
11. Vijayarangan, A.; Narayanan, V.; Natarajan, V.; Raghavendran, S. Novel Authentication Protocols Based on Quadratic Diophantine Equations. *Mathematics* 2022, 10, 3136. https://doi.org/10.3390/math10173136.
12. Wang, Y.; Binyamin, M.A.; Amin, I.; Aslam, A.; Rao, Y. On the Classification of Telescopic Numerical Semigroups of Some Fixed Multiplicity. *Mathematics* 2022, 10, 3871. https://doi.org/10.3390/math10203871.
13. Azak, A.Z. Pauli Gaussian Fibonacci and Pauli Gaussian Lucas Quaternions. *Mathematics* 2022, 10, 4655. https://doi.org/10.3390/math10244655.
14. Altassan, A.; Alan, M. Almost Repdigit k-Fibonacci Numbers with an Application of the k-Generalized Fibonacci Sequence. *Mathematics* 2023, 11, 455. https://doi.org/10.3390/math11020455.
15. Dubickas, A. Density of Some Special Sequences Modulo 1. *Mathematics* 2023, 11, 1727. https://doi.org/10.3390/math11071727.
16. Srichan, T. A Bound for a Sum of Products of Two Characters and Its Application. *Mathematics* 2023, 11, 2507. https://doi.org/10.3390/math11112507.
17. Nur, M.; Bahri, M.; Islamiyati, A.; Batkunde, H. A New Semi-Inner Product and p_n-Angle in the Space of p-Summable Sequences. *Mathematics* 2023, 11, 3139. https://doi.org/10.3390/math11143139.
18. Andrica, D.; Bagdasar, O. Remarks on the Coefficients of Inverse Cyclotomic Polynomials. *Mathematics* 2023, 11, 3622. https://doi.org/10.3390/math11173622.
19. El Fadil, L. On Indices of Septic Number Fields Defined by Trinomials $x^7 + ax + b$. *Mathematics* 2023, 11, 4441. https://doi.org/10.3390/math11214441.
20. Cheddour, Z.; Chillali, A.; Mouhib, A. Generalized Fibonacci Sequences for Elliptic Curve Cryptography. *Mathematics* 2023, 11, 4656. https://doi.org/10.3390/math11224656.
21. Tan, E.; Savin, D.; Yılmaz, S. A New Class of Leonardo Hybrid Numbers and Some Remarks on Leonardo Quaternions over Finite Fields. *Mathematics* 2023, 11, 4701. https://doi.org/10.3390/math11224701.

References

1. Apostol, T. *An Introduction to Analytic Number Theory*; Springer: New York, NY, USA, 1976.
2. Lemmermeyer, F. *Reciprocity Laws, from Euler to Eisenstein*; Springer: Heidelberg, Germany, 2000.
3. Milne, J.S. Algebraic Number Theory, Course Notes. 2008. Available online: https://www.jmilne.org/math/CourseNotes/ANT.pdf (accessed on 1 January 2023).
4. Ribenboim, P. *Classical Theory of Algebraic Numbers*; Springer: New York, NY, USA, 2001.

5. Swinnerton-Dyer, H.P.F. *A Brief Guide to Algebraic Number Theory*; Cambridge University Press: Cambridge, UK, 2001.
6. Kim, K.-S. Some Remarks on the Divisibility of the Class Numbers of Imaginary Quadratic Fields. *Mathematics* **2022**, *10*, 2488. [CrossRef]
7. Ankeny, N.; Chowla, S. On the divisibility of the class numbers of quaddratic fields. *Pac. J. Math.* **1955**, *5*, 321–324. [CrossRef]
8. Chakraborty, K.; Hoque, A.; Kishi, Y.; Pandey, P.P. Divisibility of the class numbers of imaginary quadratic fields. *J. Number Theory* **2018**, *185*, 339–348. [CrossRef]
9. Cohn, J.H.E. On the class number of certain imaginary quadratic fields. *Proc. Am. Math. Soc.* **2002**, *130*, 1275–1277. [CrossRef]
10. Gross, B.H.; Rohrlich, D.E. Some results on the Mordell–Weil group of the Jacobian of the Fermat curve. *Invent. Math.* **1978**, *44*, 201–224. [CrossRef]
11. Ishii, K. On the divisibility of the class number of imaginary quadratic fields. *Proc. Jpn. Acad. Ser. A* **2011**, *87*, 142–143. [CrossRef]
12. Murty, M.R. Exponents of class groups of quadratic fields. In *Topics in Number Theory; Mathematics and Its Applications*; Kluwer Academic Publishers: University Park, PA, USA; Dordrecht, The Netherlands, 1999; Volume 467, pp. 229–239.
13. Soundararajan, K. Divisibility of class numbers of imaginary quaddratic fields. *J. Lond. Math. Soc.* **2000**, *61*, 681–690. [CrossRef]
14. Yamamoto, Y. On unramified Galois extensions of quadratic number fields. *Osaka J. Math.* **1970**, *7*, 57–76.
15. Gille, P.; Szamuely, T. *Central Simple Algebras and Galois Cohomology*; Cambridge University Press: Cambridge, UK, 2006.
16. Lam, T.Y. *Introduction to Quadratic Forms over Fields*; AMS: Providence, RI, USA, 2004.
17. Voight, J. *Quaternion Algebras*; Springer: Berlin/Heidelberg, Germany, 2021.
18. Flaut, C.; Savin, D. Some examples of division symbol algebras of degree 3 and 5. *Carpathian J. Math.* **2015**, *31*, 197–204. [CrossRef]
19. Savin, D. About division quaternion algebras and division symbol algebras. *Carpathian J. Math.* **2016**, *32*, 233–240. [CrossRef]
20. Acciaro, V.; Savin, D.; Taous, M.; Zekhnini, A. On quaternion algebras over the composite of quadratic number fields. *Glas. Mat.* **2021**, *56*, 63–78. [CrossRef]
21. Terzioğlu, N.; Kızılateş, C.; Du, W.-S. New Properties and Identities for Fibonacci Finite Operator Quaternions. *Mathematics* **2022**, *10*, 1719. [CrossRef]
22. Azak, A.Z. Pauli Gaussian Fibonacci and Pauli Gaussian Lucas Quaternions. *Mathematics* **2022**, *10*, 4655. [CrossRef]
23. Tan, E.; Savin, D.; Yılmaz, S. A New Class of Leonardo Hybrid Numbers and Some Remarks on Leonardo Quaternions over Finite Fields. *Mathematics* **2023**, *11*, 4701. [CrossRef]
24. Minculete, N.; Savin, D. Some Properties of Extended Euler's Function and Extended Dedekind's Function. *Mathematics* **2020**, *8*, 1222. [CrossRef]
25. Minculete, N.; Savin, D. Some generalizations of the functions τ and $\tau^{(e)}$ in algebraic number fields. *Expo. Math.* **2021**, *39*, 344–353. [CrossRef]
26. Suer, M.; Ilhan, S. On telescopic numerical semigroup families with embedding dimension 3. *J. Sci. Technol.* **2019**, *12*, 457–462. [CrossRef]
27. Suer, M.; Ilhan, S. On triply generated telescopic semigroups with multiplicity 8 and 9. *Bulg. Acad. Sci.* **2020**, *72*, 315–319.
28. Suer, M.; Ilhan, S. Telescopic numerical semigroups with multiplicity Ten and embedding dimension three. *J. Univers. Math.* **2022**, *5*, 139–148. [CrossRef]
29. Jordan, J.H. Gaussian Fibonacci and Lucas Numbers. *Fibonacci Quart.* **1965**, *3*, 315–318.
30. Halici, S. On Complex Fibonacci Quaternions. *Am. Math. Mon.* **2013**, *23*, 105–112. [CrossRef]
31. Halici, S. On Quaternion-Gaussian Lucas Numbers. *Math. Meth. Appl. Sci.* **2021**, *44*, 7601–7606. [CrossRef]
32. Halici, S.; Cerda-Morales, G. On Quaternion-Gaussian Fibonacci Numbers and Their Properties. *An. Ştiinţ. Univ. Ovidius Constanta* **2021**, *29*, 71–82. [CrossRef]
33. Matveev, E.M. An explicit lower bound for a homogeneous rational linear form in the logarithms of algebraic numbers, II. *Izv. Ross. Akad. Nauk Ser. Mat.* **2000**, *64*, 125–180; Translation in *Izv. Math.* **2000**, *64*, 1217–1269. [CrossRef]
34. Baker, A.; Davenport, H. The equations $3x^2 - 2 = y^2$ and $8x^2 - 7 = z^2$. *Quart. J. Math. Oxford Ser.* **1969**, *20*, 129–137. [CrossRef]
35. Dujella, A.; Pethö, A. A generalization of a theorem of Baker and Davenport. *Quart. J. Math. Oxford Ser.* **1998**, *49*, 291–306. [CrossRef]
36. Cilleruelo, J.; Kumchev, A.; Luca, F.; Rué, J.; Shparlinski, I.E. On the fractional parts of a^n/n. *Bull. Lond. Math. Soc.* **2013**, *45*, 249–256. [CrossRef]
37. Narkiewicz, W. *Elementary and Analytic Theory of Algebraic Numbers*; Springer: New York, NY, USA, 2004.
38. Catarino, P.; Borges, A. On Leonardo numbers. *Acta Math. Univ. Comen.* **2019**, *89*, 75–86.
39. Catarino, P.; Borges, A. A note on incomplete Leonardo numbers. *Integers* **2020**, *20*, 1–7.
40. Alp, Y.; Kocer, E.G. Some properties of Leonardo numbers. *Konuralp J. Math.* **2021**, *9*, 183–189.
41. Tan, E.; Leung, H.H. On Leonardo p-numbers. *Integers* **2023**, *23*, A7.
42. Savin, D. About Special Elements in Quaternion Algebras Over Finite Fields. *Adv. Appl. Clifford Algebr.* **2017**, *27*, 1801–1813. [CrossRef]
43. Mangueira, M.C.S.; Alves, F.R.V.; Catarino, P.M.M.C. Hybrid Quaternions of Leonardo. *Trends Comput. Appl. Math.* **2022**, *23*, 51–62. [CrossRef]

Disclaimer/Publisher's Note: The statements, opinions and data contained in all publications are solely those of the individual author(s) and contributor(s) and not of MDPI and/or the editor(s). MDPI and/or the editor(s) disclaim responsibility for any injury to people or property resulting from any ideas, methods, instructions or products referred to in the content.

Article

On Generalized Lucas Pseudoprimality of Level k

Dorin Andrica [1] and Ovidiu Bagdasar [2],*

[1] Faculty of Mathematics and Computer Science, Babeș-Bolyai University, 400084 Cluj-Napoca, Romania; dandrica@math.ubbcluj.ro
[2] School of Computing and Engineering, University of Derby, Derby DE22 1GB, UK
* Correspondence: o.bagdasar@derby.ac.uk

Abstract: We investigate the Fibonacci pseudoprimes of level k, and we disprove a statement concerning the relationship between the sets of different levels, and also discuss a counterpart of this result for the Lucas pseudoprimes of level k. We then use some recent arithmetic properties of the generalized Lucas, and generalized Pell–Lucas sequences, to define some new types of pseudoprimes of levels k^+ and k^- and parameter a. For these novel pseudoprime sequences we investigate some basic properties and calculate numerous associated integer sequences which we have added to the Online Encyclopedia of Integer Sequences.

Keywords: generalized lucas sequences; legendre symbol; jacobi symbol; pseudoprimality

MSC: 11A51; 11B39; 11B50

1. Introduction

Let a and b be integers. The **generalized Lucas** sequence $\{U_n(a,b)\}_{n\geq 0}$ and its companion, the **generalized Pell–Lucas** sequence $\{V_n(a,b)\}_{n\geq 0}$, denoted by U_n and V_n for simplicity, are defined by

$$U_{n+2} = aU_{n+1} - bU_n, \quad U_0 = 0, U_1 = 1, \quad n = 0,1,\ldots \qquad (1)$$

$$V_{n+2} = aV_{n+1} - bV_n, \quad V_0 = 2, V_1 = a, \quad n = 0,1,\ldots. \qquad (2)$$

The general term of these sequences is given by the following Binet-type formulae

$$U_n = \frac{\alpha^n - \beta^n}{\alpha - \beta} = \frac{1}{\sqrt{D}}(\alpha^n - \beta^n), \quad V_n = \alpha^n + \beta^n, \quad n = 0,1,\ldots, \qquad (3)$$

where $D = a^2 - 4b \neq 0$ and $\alpha = \frac{a+\sqrt{D}}{2}$, $\beta = \frac{a-\sqrt{D}}{2}$ are the roots of the quadratic $z^2 - az + b = 0$. By Viéte's relations, one has $\alpha + \beta = a$ and $\alpha\beta = b$, while $\alpha - \beta = \sqrt{D}$.

Using bivariate cyclotomic polynomials, the relations (3) can be written [1] (p. 99) in terms of α and β, as

$$U_n = \prod_{d|n, d\geq 2} \Phi_d(\alpha, \beta),$$

where

$$\Phi_d(\alpha, \beta) = \prod_{j=1, \gcd(j,n)=1}^{n} (\alpha - \zeta^j \beta),$$

and ζ is a primitive n-th root of unity. It can be checked that $\Phi_d(\alpha, \beta)$ is an integer for any $d \geq 2$, and this feature can highlight arithmetic properties of the integers U_n.

If ω is an n-th root of -1, the following formula for can be written for V_n as

$$V_n = \prod_{d|n} \Phi_d(\alpha, \omega\beta),$$

However, the use of this formula is limited since $\Phi_d(\alpha, \omega\beta)$ is not always an integer.

The formulae (3) also extend naturally to negative indices. For any integer $n \geq 0$ one has

$$U_{-n} = \frac{1}{\sqrt{D}}(\alpha^{-n} - \beta^{-n}) = -\frac{1}{b^n}U_n, \quad V_{-n} = \alpha^{-n} + \beta^{-n} = \frac{1}{b^n}V_n.$$

Clearly, U_n and V_n are integers for all $n \in \mathbb{Z}$ if and only if $b = \pm 1$, and for this reason we shall focus on this case.

For $b = -1$, if k is a positive real number, then the k-Fibonacci and k-Lucas numbers are obtained for $F_{k,n} = U_n(k, -1)$ and $L_{k,n} = V_n(k, -1)$, in which case $D = k^2 + 4$ [2]. Clearly, for $k = 1$ we get the Fibonacci and Lucas numbers $F_n = U_n(1, -1)$ and $L_n = V_n(1, -1)$ with $D = 5$, and for $k = 2$ the Pell and Pell–Lucas numbers $P_n = U_n(2, -1)$ and $Q_n = V_n(2, -1)$, where $D = 8$.

When $b = 1$, the sequences $U_n(a, 1)$ have interesting combinatorial interpretations, while the terms $V_n(a, 1)$ can be linked to the number of solutions for certain Diophantine equations (see [3]) and to important classes of polynomials (see [4] (Chapter 2.2)).

The following results have been recently proved by the authors in [3].

Theorem 1 (Theorem 3.1, [3]). *Let p be an odd prime, k a non-negative integer, and r an arbitrary integer. If $b = \pm 1$ and a is an integer such that $D = a^2 - 4b > 0$ is not a perfect square, then the sequences U_n and V_n defined by (1) and (2) satisfy the following relations*

$$(1) \quad 2U_{kp+r} \equiv \left(\frac{D}{p}\right)U_k V_r + V_k U_r \pmod{p};$$

$$(2) \quad 2V_{kp+r} \equiv D\left(\frac{D}{p}\right)U_k U_r + V_k V_r \pmod{p},$$

where $\left(\frac{D}{p}\right)$ is the Legendre symbol (see, e.g., [5]).

Theorem 2 (Theorem 3.5, [3]). *Let p be an odd prime, and let $k > 0$ and a be integers so that $D = a^2 + 4 > 0$ is not a perfect square. If $U_n = U_n(a, -1)$ and $V_n = V_n(a, -1)$, then we have*

(1) $U_{kp-\left(\frac{D}{p}\right)} \equiv U_{k-1} \pmod{p}$;

(2) $V_{kp-\left(\frac{D}{p}\right)} \equiv \left(\frac{D}{p}\right)V_{k-1} \pmod{p}$.

Theorem 3 (Theorem 3.7, [3]). *Let p be an odd prime, and let $k > 0$ and a be integers so that $D = a^2 - 4 > 0$ is not a perfect square. If $U_n = U_n(a, 1)$ and $V_n = V_n(a, 1)$, then we have*

(1) $U_{kp-\left(\frac{D}{p}\right)} \equiv \left(\frac{D}{p}\right)U_{k-1} \pmod{p}$;

(2) $V_{kp-\left(\frac{D}{p}\right)} \equiv V_{k-1} \pmod{p}$.

Applying Theorem 1 for $k = 1$ and $r = 0$, we obtain the well known relations

$$U_p \equiv \left(\frac{D}{p}\right) \pmod{p}; \tag{4}$$

$$V_p \equiv a \pmod{p}. \tag{5}$$

Taking $k=1$ in Theorems 2 and 3, and since $U_0 = 0$ and $V_0 = 2$, one has

$$U_{p-\left(\frac{D}{p}\right)} \equiv 0 \pmod{p}; \tag{6}$$

$$V_{p-\left(\frac{D}{p}\right)} \equiv 2\left(\frac{D}{p}\right)^{\frac{1-b}{2}}. \tag{7}$$

Pseudoprimes are those composite numbers that, under certain conditions, behave similarly to the prime numbers. These have numerous applications in the factorization of large integers, primality testing, and cryptography. Some important notions of pseudo-primality are linked to the generalized Lucas sequences $\{U_n(a,b)\}_{n\geq 0}$ and $\{V_n(a,b)\}_{n\geq 0}$ given by (1) and (2), based on the relations (4), (5), (6) and (7), which were known even to Lucas (see [6]).

Definition 1. *An odd composite integer n is said to be a **generalized Lucas pseudoprime of parameters** a **and** b if $\gcd(n,b) = 1$ and n divides $U_{n-\left(\frac{D}{n}\right)}$, where $\left(\frac{D}{n}\right)$ is the Jacobi symbol.*

By relation (4), we deduce that $U_p^2 \equiv 1 \pmod{p}$. Using this, in our paper [7] we have defined a weak pseudoprimality notion for generalized Lucas sequences $U_n(a,b)$.

Definition 2. *A composite integer n for which $n \mid U_n^2 - 1$ is called a **weak generalized Lucas pseudoprime** of parameters a and b.*

This notion plays a key role in the present paper. Another weak pseudoprimality concept for generalized Pell–Lucas sequences inspired by (5) is also defined in [7].

Definition 3. *A composite integer n is said to be a **generalized Bruckman–Lucas pseudoprime** of parameters a and b if $n \mid V_n(a,b) - a$.*

Historical details and various pseudoprimality tests for generalized Lucas sequences are given in the papers by Brillhart, Lehmer, and Selfridge [8], and by Baillie and Wagstaff in [9]. Grantham [10] unified many pseudoprimality notions under the name of Frobenius pseudoprimes and several examples are listed in Rotkiewics [11]. Various strong concepts like super-pseudoprimes [12], or extensions of recurrences to more general contexts like abelian groups have been proposed [13].

Interesting divisibility results for U_n and V_n are stated in [9] (Section 2).

Proposition 1. *If n is an odd composite number such that $\gcd(n, 2abD) = 1$, then any two of the following statements imply the other two.*

(1) $U_n \equiv \left(\frac{D}{n}\right) \pmod{n}$;

(2) $V_n \equiv V_1 = a \pmod{n}$;

(3) $U_{n-\left(\frac{D}{n}\right)} \equiv U_0 = 0 \pmod{n}$;

(4) $V_{n-\left(\frac{D}{n}\right)} \equiv 2b^{\frac{1-\left(\frac{D}{n}\right)}{2}} \pmod{n}$ *(valid whenever $\gcd(n, D) = 1$).*

The structure of this paper is as follows. In Section 2 we review the notion of Fibonacci pseudoprime of level k, and propose a counterpart defined for Lucas sequences. We also disprove a statement formulated in [14] for Fibonacci numbers, which shows that the relationship between the pseudoprimes of different levels is not trivial. In Section 3 we define the generalized Lucas and Pell–Lucas pseudoprimality of level k, which involves the Jacobi symbol. For these notions we study some new related integer sequences indexed in the Online Encyclopedia of Integer Sequences (OEIS). Finally, in Section 4 we summarize the findings and suggest future directions of investigation.

The numerical simulations in this paper have been performed with specialist Matlab libraries and Wolfram Alpha (explicit formulae are indicated in OEIS). Sometimes we have provided more terms than in the OEIS (which has a limit of 260 characters), so that the readers can check the numerical examples and counterexamples.

2. Fibonacci and Lucas Pseudoprimes of Level k

In this section we present the Fibonacci pseudoprimes of level k and give a counterexample to a result from [14], about the connection between the sets of pseudoprimes on different levels. We then define the Lucas pseudoprimes of level k, for which we also explore connections between the pseudoprimes on different levels.

2.1. Fibonacci Pseudoprimes of Level k

For a prime p, the following relations follow from (4) and (6) for $a = 1$ and $b = -1$.

$$F_p \equiv \left(\frac{p}{5}\right) \pmod{p}; \tag{8}$$

$$F_{p-\left(\frac{p}{5}\right)} \equiv 0 \pmod{p}. \tag{9}$$

A composite number n is called a **Fibonacci pseudoprime** if $n \mid F_{n-\left(\frac{n}{5}\right)}$. The even Fibonacci pseudoprimes are indexed as A141137 in the OEIS [15], while the odd Fibonacci pseudoprimes indexed as A081264 start with the terms

323, 377, 1891, 3827, 4181, 5777, 6601, 6721, 8149, 10877, 11663, 13201, 13981, 15251, 17119, 17711, 18407, 19043, 23407, 25877, 27323, 30889, 34561, 34943, 35207, 39203, 40501, ...

In [14], the authors introduced the following notion. Let k be a fixed positive integer. A composite number n is called a **Fibonacci pseudoprime of level** k if it satisfies

$$n \mid F_{kn-\left(\frac{n}{5}\right)} - F_{k-1}.$$

The set of all the Fibonacci pseudoprimes of level k is denoted by $\mathcal{F}_k$. Notice that for $k = 1$ we obtain the classical Fibonacci pseudoprimes. We now state a corrected version of Proposition 1 in [14], and then discuss why the original version does not hold.

Proposition 2. *Let n be a positive integer that is coprime with 10. If $n \in \mathcal{F}_1$, then $n \in \mathcal{F}_2$ if and only if $n \mid F_n^2 - 1$.*

Proof. Notice that the conditions in the hypothesis relate to Equations (8) and (9). Clearly, $n \in \mathcal{F}_1$ is equivalent to $n \mid F_{n-\left(\frac{n}{5}\right)}$, while $n \in \mathcal{F}_2$ is equivalent to $n \mid F_{2n-\left(\frac{n}{5}\right)} - F_1$.

For all integers $m \geq r \geq 0$, Catalan's identity $F_m^2 - F_{m+r}F_{m-r} = (-1)^{m-r}F_r^2$, is valid. Using this identity for $m = n - \left(\frac{n}{5}\right)$ and $r = n$ and since $\gcd(5, n) = 1$, one has

$$F_{n-\left(\frac{n}{5}\right)}^2 + (-1)^{\left(\frac{n}{5}\right)} F_{2n-\left(\frac{n}{5}\right)} = (-1)^{-\left(\frac{n}{5}\right)} F_n^2.$$

Since $\left(\frac{n}{5}\right)$ is odd, this can be rewritten as

$$F_{n-\left(\frac{n}{5}\right)}^2 + \left(F_n^2 - 1\right) = F_{2n-\left(\frac{n}{5}\right)} - F_1. \tag{10}$$

Clearly, if $n \in \mathcal{F}_1$, then by taking the relation (10) modulo n, one obtains that $n \mid F_n^2 - 1$ is equivalent to $n \in \mathcal{F}_2$. □

Remark 1. Notice that if $n \mid F_n^2 - 1$ and $n \in \mathcal{F}_2$, then by (10) it follows that $n \mid F_{n-\left(\frac{n}{5}\right)}^2$. This may not always indicate that $n \in \mathcal{F}_1$. However, this assertion holds whenever n is square-free. We have confirmed that the numbers satisfying both $n \mid F_n^2 - 1$ and $n \in \mathcal{F}_2$ with $n \leq 39500$ are

$$323, 377, 1891, 3827, 4181, 5777, 6601, 6721, 8149, 10877, 11663, 13201, 13981, 15251,$$
$$17119, 17711, 18407, 19043, 23407, 25877, 27323, 30889, 34561, 34943, 35207, 39203,$$

which are all square-free and satisfy $n \in \mathcal{F}_1$.

We now recall Proposition 1 in [14], which states that if $n \in \mathbb{N}$ is coprime with 10, then $n \in \mathcal{F}_k$ for all $k \geq 1$ if and only if $n \in \mathcal{F}_1$ and $n \mid F_n^2 - 1$. In particular, if $n \mid F_{n-\left(\frac{n}{5}\right)}$ and $n \mid F_n - \left(\frac{n}{5}\right)$, then $n \in \mathcal{F}_k$ for all $k \geq 1$. The following example gives an integer n for which $n \in \mathcal{F}_1$ and $n \mid F_n^2 - 1$, (hence in $\mathcal{F}_2$), but which is not in $\mathcal{F}_3$. This shows that Proposition 1 in [14] does not generally hold.

Example 1. The first composite integer n for which $n \mid F_{n-\left(\frac{n}{5}\right)}$ and $n \mid F_n^2 - 1$ is $n = 323$. For this integer one can check that $n \mid F_{2n-\left(\frac{n}{5}\right)} - F_1$, but we have $F_{3n-\left(\frac{n}{5}\right)} - F_2 \equiv 321 \pmod{n}$, where $\left(\frac{n}{5}\right) = -1$. The calculations involving the large numbers below are implemented with the vpi (variable precision integer) library in Matlab®. We have

$F_{n-\left(\frac{n}{5}\right)} = 23041483585524168262220906489642018075101617466780496790573690289968 \equiv 0 \pmod{n}$

$F_{2n-\left(\frac{n}{5}\right)} = 733699527799930913528078624701375446456404924309271040434990690014584668246528603476477043108568806527592562210693671820824200536283473 \equiv 1 = F_1 \pmod{n}$

$F_{3n-\left(\frac{n}{5}\right)} = 23362861818152996537467507811299195417669439511689710925227862142275523753399638967783310781704529676533897971172191948004316934631842045065771638088947558424515687624190113122357319209227560059859345335 \equiv 322 \pmod{n}.$

We now discuss why the proof of Proposition 1 in [14] fails, but we mention that the error in the proof is not trivial as we can notice in the previous numerical example.

Remark 2. The problems appear at the induction step. When applying Catalan's identity for $m = kn - \left(\frac{n}{5}\right)$ and $r = n$ one obtains the identity

$$F_{kn-\left(\frac{n}{5}\right)}^2 - F_{(k+1)n-\left(\frac{n}{5}\right)} F_{(k-1)n-\left(\frac{n}{5}\right)} = (-1)^{(k-1)n-\left(\frac{n}{5}\right)} F_n^2.$$

Assuming $n \in \mathcal{F}_k$ and taking this relation modulo n one obtains after some steps

$$F_{(k+1)n-\left(\frac{n}{5}\right)} F_{k-2} \equiv F_{k-1}^2 + (-1)^k \pmod{n}$$
$$F_k F_{k-2} \equiv F_{k-1}^2 + (-1)^k \pmod{n},$$

from where the authors (incorrectly) claim $n \mid F_{(k+1)n-\left(\frac{n}{5}\right)} - F_k$. In fact, we only have

$$\left[F_{(k+1)n-\left(\frac{n}{5}\right)} - F_k\right] F_{k-2} \equiv 0 \pmod{n}.$$

This holds when n is coprime with F_{k-2}, but this cannot be guaranteed in general.

2.2. Lucas Pseudoprimes of Level k

From the relations (5) and (7) applied for $a = 1$ and $b = -1$ one obtains

$$L_p \equiv 1 \pmod{p}; \qquad (11)$$

$$L_{p-\left(\frac{p}{5}\right)} \equiv 2\left(\frac{p}{5}\right) \pmod{p}. \qquad (12)$$

A composite integer n satisfying the property $n \mid L_n - 1$ is called a **Bruckman–Lucas pseudoprime**. The sequence is indexed in the OEIS [15] as A005845, and begins with

$705, 2465, 2737, 3745, 4181, 5777, 6721, 10877, 13201, 15251, 24465, 29281, 34561, 35785, 51841,$
$54705, 64079, 64681, 67861, 68251, 75077, 80189, 90061, 96049, 97921, 100065, 100127, \ldots.$

In 1964 Lehmer [16] proved that Fibonacci pseudoprimes are infinite, while in 1994 Bruckman showed that the Bruckman–Lucas pseudoprimes are odd [17], and also he proved that these numbers are infinitely many [18].

For a positive integer k we define the **Lucas pseudoprimes of level** k as the composite integers n satisfying the relation

$$n \mid L_{kn-\left(\frac{n}{5}\right)} - \left(\frac{n}{5}\right) L_{k-1}.$$

The set of all the Lucas pseudoprimes of level k is denoted by $\mathcal{L}_k$.

For $k = 1$ the integers $n \in \mathcal{L}_1$ satisfy $n \mid L_{n-\left(\frac{n}{5}\right)} - 2\left(\frac{n}{5}\right)$ and define the sequence A339125 added by us to OEIS, which starts with the terms

$9, 49, 121, 169, 289, 361, 529, 841, 961, 1127, 1369, 1681, 1849, 2209, 2809, 3481, 3721,$
$3751, 4181, 4489, 4901, 4961, 5041, 5329, 5777, 6241, 6721, 6889, 7381, 7921, 9409, \ldots.$

For $k = 2$ the integers $n \in \mathcal{L}_2$ satisfy the relation $n \mid L_{2n-\left(\frac{n}{5}\right)} - \left(\frac{n}{5}\right)$, and recover a sequence we have indexed as A339517, whose first elements are

$323, 377, 609, 1891, 3081, 3827, 4181, 5777, 5887, 6601, 6721, 8149, 8841, 10877, 11663, 13201,$
$13981, 15251, 17119, 17711, 18407, 19043, 23407, 25877, 26011, 27323, 30889, 34561, \ldots.$

The following result highlights a connection between the Lucas pseudoprimes of levels 1 and 2 via the positive integers with the property $n \mid F_n^2 - 1$.

Proposition 3. *Let n be a positive integer that is coprime with 10. If $n \in \mathcal{L}_1$, then $n \in \mathcal{L}_2$ if and only if $n \mid F_n^2 - 1$.*

Proof. One can easily check (see Lemma 2.4 [19]) that for any integers m and r we have

$$L_m^2 - L_{m+r} L_{m-r} = -5(-1)^{m-r} F_r^2, \quad L_{-m} = (-1)^m L_m.$$

Using this identity for $m = n - \left(\frac{n}{5}\right)$ and $r = n$, we get

$$L_{n-\left(\frac{n}{5}\right)}^2 - L_{2n-\left(\frac{n}{5}\right)} L_{-\left(\frac{n}{5}\right)} = -5(-1)^{-\left(\frac{n}{5}\right)} F_n^2.$$

As n and 5 are coprime, we have $L_{-\left(\frac{n}{5}\right)} = (-1)^{-\left(\frac{n}{5}\right)} L_{\left(\frac{n}{5}\right)}$ and $L_{\left(\frac{n}{5}\right)} = \left(\frac{n}{5}\right)$, while since $\left(\frac{n}{5}\right) = \pm 1$, it follows that $(-1)^{-\left(\frac{n}{5}\right)} = -1$. Therefore

$$L_{n-\left(\frac{n}{5}\right)}^2 + \left(\frac{n}{5}\right) L_{2n-\left(\frac{n}{5}\right)} = 5 F_n^2. \tag{13}$$

This identity can be further written as

$$\left(L_{n-\left(\frac{n}{5}\right)}^2 - 4\right) + \left(\frac{n}{5}\right)\left(L_{2n-\left(\frac{n}{5}\right)} - \left(\frac{n}{5}\right)\right) = 5\left(F_n^2 - 1\right). \tag{14}$$

Now we take this relation modulo n. Clearly, from $n \in \mathcal{L}_1$ we $L_{n-\left(\frac{n}{5}\right)} \equiv 2\left(\frac{n}{5}\right)$ (mod n), hence the first bracket vanishes. Notice that if any of the other two brackets in (14) vanish, then the third vanishes as well, hence $n \in \mathcal{L}_2$ if and only if $n \mid F_n^2 - 1$. □

One could check that if $n \mid F_n^2 - 1$ and $n \in \mathcal{L}_2$, then it does not follow that $n \in \mathcal{L}_1$. We give an example below.

Example 2. *From Example 1, we know that for $n = 323$ we have $n \mid F_n^2 - 1$ and $\left(\frac{n}{5}\right) = -1$. One can check numerically that $n \mid L_{2n-\left(\frac{n}{5}\right)} - \left(\frac{n}{5}\right)L_1$, but $L_{n-\left(\frac{n}{5}\right)} \equiv 2 \neq 2\left(\frac{n}{5}\right)$ (mod n).*

$L_{n-\left(\frac{n}{5}\right)} = 515223235996776294967379903295286389565835483043780536155810435356 82 \equiv 2 \pmod{n}$

$L_{2n-\left(\frac{n}{5}\right)} - \left(\frac{n}{5}\right)L_1 = 1640602019220142242807174250662450257647811248912718386198074020 4184$
$6262156924015992064406990410128506570256616706671043831467653299 2880 \equiv 0 \pmod{n}.$

It can be checked that $n = 323$ is the smallest odd composite number for which $n \mid F_n^2 - 1$ and $n \in \mathcal{L}_2$ but $n \notin \mathcal{L}_1$, but as we will see later, there are (possibly infinitely) many numbers that satisfy this property.

3. Generalized Lucas Pseudoprimes of Level k

In this section we use Theorems 2 and 3 to extend the notions presented in Section 2 for generalized Lucas and Pell–Lucas sequences. We calculate the terms of the integer sequences obtained for a few particular parameter values and we formulate some conjectures.

3.1. Jacobi's Symbol

Let $n = p_1^{\alpha_1} p_2^{\alpha_2} \cdots p_k^{\alpha_k}$ be the prime factorization of an odd integer n. The Jacobi symbol is defined as

$$\left(\frac{a}{n}\right) = \left(\frac{a}{p_1}\right)^{\alpha_1} \left(\frac{a}{p_2}\right)^{\alpha_2} \cdots \left(\frac{a}{p_k}\right)^{\alpha_k},$$

where a is an integer. When n is a prime this recovers the Legendre symbol.

Jacobi's symbol is completely multiplicative in both the numerator and denominator, i.e., for m, n, m_1, m_2, n_1, n_2 integers, we have

$$\left(\frac{m_1 m_2}{n}\right) = \left(\frac{m_1}{n}\right)\left(\frac{m_2}{n}\right), \quad \text{so} \quad \left(\frac{m^2}{n}\right) = \left(\frac{m}{n}\right)^2 = 1 \text{ or } 0;$$

$$\left(\frac{m}{n_1 n_2}\right) = \left(\frac{m}{n_1}\right)\left(\frac{m}{n_2}\right), \quad \text{so} \quad \left(\frac{m}{n^2}\right) = \left(\frac{m}{n}\right)^2 = 1 \text{ or } 0.$$

The Jacobi symbol also satisfies the quadratic reciprocity law. This states that if m and n are odd positive coprime integers, then the following identity holds

$$\left(\frac{m}{n}\right)\left(\frac{n}{m}\right) = (-1)^{\frac{m-1}{2} \cdot \frac{n-1}{2}} = \begin{cases} 1 & \text{if } n \equiv 1 \pmod{4} \text{ or } m \equiv 1 \pmod{4}, \\ -1 & \text{if } n \equiv m \equiv 3 \pmod{4}. \end{cases}$$

3.2. Results for b = −1

We shortly denote $U_n = U_n(a, -1)$ and $V_n = V_n(a, -1)$. If p is prime number and a is an odd integer, then by the law of quadratic reciprocity for the Jacobi symbol with $D = a^2 + 4$ one has

$$\left(\frac{D}{p}\right)\left(\frac{p}{D}\right) = (-1)^{\frac{p-1}{2} \cdot \frac{D-1}{2}} = 1. \tag{15}$$

This implies $\left(\frac{D}{p}\right) = \left(\frac{p}{D}\right)$, hence the results in Theorem 2 can be written as

(1) $U_{kp-\left(\frac{p}{D}\right)} \equiv U_{k-1} \pmod{p}$;

(2) $V_{kp-\left(\frac{p}{D}\right)} \equiv \left(\frac{p}{D}\right) V_{k-1} \pmod{p}$.

We now investigate similar relations modulo a composite number n, where $\left(\frac{n}{D}\right)$ is the Jacobi symbol, which is well-defined for any odd composite integers n and D. These allow us to define new concepts of pseudoprimality.

Definition 4. *Let a, k, and n be non-negative integers, where a is odd. We say that the composite number n is a*

(1) **generalized Lucas pseudoprime of level k^- and parameter a** *if*

$$n \mid U_{kn-\left(\frac{n}{D}\right)} - U_{k-1}.$$

The set of all such numbers is denoted by $\mathcal{U}_k^-(a)$.

(2) **generalized Pell–Lucas pseudoprime of level k^- and parameter a** *if*

$$n \mid V_{kn-\left(\frac{n}{D}\right)} - \left(\frac{n}{D}\right) V_{k-1}.$$

The set of all such numbers is denoted by $\mathcal{V}_k^-(a)$.

In [19] we proved connections between the sets of generalized Lucas and Pell–Lucas pseudoprimes of levels 1^- and 2^-, which are linked through the property $n \mid U_n^2 - 1$ (see Definition 2). Integers having this property were called weak generalized Lucas pseudoprimes of parameters a and b and present interest in their own right. Some of their properties, associated integer sequences and conjectures have been discussed in [7].

Theorem 4. *Let $a, n > 0$ be odd integers with $\gcd(D, n) = 1$. The following statements hold*

(1) *Reference [19] (Theorem 4.3). If $n \in \mathcal{U}_1^-(a)$, then $n \in \mathcal{U}_2^-(a)$ if and only if $n \mid U_n^2 - 1$.*

(2) *Reference [19] (Theorem 4.6). If $n \in \mathcal{V}_1^-(a)$ and $\gcd(a, n) = 1$, then $n \in \mathcal{V}_2^-(a)$ if and only if $n \mid U_n^2 - 1$.*

We now present the integer sequences $\mathcal{U}_k^-(a)$, $\mathcal{V}_k^-(a)$ calculated for the values $a = 1, 3, 5, 7$ and $k = 1, 2, 3$. Most of these were added by the authors to OEIS [15]. For these values we show that the reciprocal statements in Theorem 4 do not hold, and also, the results cannot be extended directly to superior levels.

To begin with, we provide some details on weak generalized Lucas pseudoprimes.

Remark 3. *For $b = -1$, the odd integers n satisfying the property $n \mid U_n^2 - 1$ recover the weak Fibonacci pseudoprimes indexed as A337231 for $a = 1$, A337234 for $a = 3$, A337237 for $a = 5$, and A338081 for $a = 7$. The reader can use these to check the numerical examples.*

Remark 4. *As seen in Example 2, even when $n \mid U_n^2 - 1$, and $n \in \mathcal{U}_2^-(a)$ (or $n \in \mathcal{V}_2^-(a)$), it does not mean that $n \in \mathcal{U}_1^-(a)$ (or $n \in \mathcal{V}_1^-(a)$). For U_n we have the following examples:*

- $a = 1$: *None found for $n \leq 50000$ (see also, Remark 1);*
- $a = 3$: $9, 63, 99, 153, 1071, 1881, 1953, 9999, 13833, 16191$;
- $a = 5$: *None found for $n \leq 15000$;*
- $a = 7$: $49, 147, 245, 637, 833, 1127, 1225, 2499, 3185, 3479, 4753, 5537, 15925$.

For V_n we have

- $a = 1$: $323, 377, 1891, 3827, 6601, 8149, 11663, 13981, 17119, 17711, 18407, 19043$;
- $a = 3$: $1763, 3599, 5559, 6681, 12095, 12403, 12685, 14279, 15051, 19043$;
- $a = 5$: $15, 45, 91, 135, 143, 1547, 1573, 1935, 2015, 6543, 8099, 10403, 10905$;
- $a = 7$: $35, 65, 175, 391, 455, 575, 1247, 1295, 1763, 1775, 2275, 2407, 3367, 4199, 4579$.

Also the connections between the levels 2^- and 3^- are non-trivial.

Remark 5. *As seen in Example 1, even when $n \mid U_n^2 - 1$, if $n \in \mathcal{U}_1^-(a)$ (hence $n \in \mathcal{U}_2^-(a)$), it does not mean that $n \in \mathcal{U}_3^-(a)$. The following values have been found:*

- $a = 1$: $323, 377, 1891, 3827, 6601, 8149, 11663, 13981, 17119, 17711, 18407, 19043$;
- $a = 3$: $1763, 3599, 5559, 6681, 12095, 12403, 12685, 14279, 15051, 19043$;
- $a = 5$: $15, 45, 91, 135, 143, 1547, 1573, 1935, 2015, 6543, 8099, 10403, 10905$;
- $a = 7$: $35, 65, 175, 391, 455, 575, 1247, 1295, 1763, 1775, 2275, 2407, 3367, 4199, 4579$.

The following n with $n \mid U_n^2 - 1$ and $n \in \mathcal{V}_1^-(a), n \in \mathcal{V}_2^-(a)$, but $n \notin \mathcal{V}_3^-(a)$ were found:

- $a = 1$: None found for $n \leq 50000$;
- $a = 3$: None found for $n \leq 20000$;
- $a = 5$: $18901, 19601, 19951$;
- $a = 7$: None found for $n \leq 17000$.

The numerical results in Remarks 4 and 5 suggest the following conjecture.

Conjecture 1. *If $n \mid U_n^2 - 1$, then $n \in \mathcal{U}_1^-(a) \setminus \mathcal{U}_3^-(a)$ if and only if $n \in \mathcal{V}_2^-(a) \setminus \mathcal{V}_1^-(a)$.*

Example 3. *If $b = -1, a = 1, D = 5$, we obtain the classical Fibonacci and Lucas numbers.*

- The set $\mathcal{U}_1^-(1)$ recovers the odd Fibonacci pseudoprimes A081264 in [15].
- The set $\mathcal{U}_2^-(1)$ gives A340118 and its first elements are

  $323, 377, 609, 1891, 3081, 3827, 4181, 5777, 5887, 6601, 6721, 8149, 10877, 11663, 13201,$
  $13601, 13981, 15251, 17119, 17711, 18407, 19043, 23407, 25877, 27323, 28441, 28623,$
  $30889, 32509, 34561, 34943, 35207, 39203, 40501, \ldots$

- The set $\mathcal{U}_3^-(1)$ is A340235 and its first elements are

  $9, 27, 161, 341, 901, 1107, 1281, 1853, 2241, 2529, 4181, 5473, 5611, 5777, 6119, 6721,$
  $7587, 8307, 9729, 10877, 11041, 12209, 13201, 13277, 14981, 15251, 16771, 17567, \ldots$

- The set $\mathcal{V}_1^-(1)$ recovers A339125, seen in Section 2.2.
- The set $\mathcal{V}_2^-(1)$ is A339517, seen in Section 2.2.
- The sequence $\mathcal{V}_3^-(1)$ is given by A339724 and starts with the elements

  $9, 21, 161, 341, 901, 1281, 1853, 3201, 4181, 5473, 5611, 5777, 6119, 6721, 9729, 10877,$
  $11041, 12209, 12441, 13201, 14981, 15251, 16771, 17941, 20591, 20769, 20801, \ldots$

Example 4. $b = -1, a = 3, D = 13$.

- The set $\mathcal{U}_1^-(3)$ recovers pseudoprimes indexed as A327653 in [15], starting with

  $119, 649, 1189, 1763, 3599, 4187, 5559, 6681, 12095, 12403, 12685, 12871, 12970, 14041,$
  $14279, 15051, 16109, 19043, 22847, 23479, 24769, 26795, 28421, 30743, 30889, \ldots$

- The set $\mathcal{U}_2^-(3)$ gives A340119 and its first elements are

  $9, 27, 63, 81, 99, 119, 153, 243, 567, 649, 729, 759, 891, 903, 1071, 1189, 1377, 1431, 1539,$
  $1763, 1881, 1953, 2133, 2187, 3599, 3897, 4187, 4585, 5103, 5313, 5559, 5589, 5819,$
  $6561, 6681, 6831, 6993, 8019, 8127, 8829, 8855, 9639, 9999, 10611, 11135, \ldots$

- The set $\mathcal{U}_3^-(3)$ is indexed as A340236 and its first elements are

  $9, 119, 121, 187, 327, 345, 649, 705, 1003, 1089, 1121, 1189, 1881, 2091, 2299, 3553, 4187,$
  $5461, 5565, 5841, 6165, 6485, 7107, 7139, 7145, 7467, 7991, 8321, 8449, 11041, \ldots$

- The set $\mathcal{V}_1^-(3)$ recovers A339126, and starts with

  $9, 25, 49, 119, 121, 289, 361, 529, 649, 833, 841, 961, 1089, 1189, 1369, 1681, 1849, 1881,$
  $2023, 2209, 2299, 2809, 3025, 3481, 3721, 4187, 4489, 5041, 5329, 6241, 6889, 7139, \ldots$

- The set $\mathcal{V}_2^-(3)$ giving A339518, has the first elements

  $15, 75, 105, 119, 165, 255, 375, 649, 1189, 1635, 1763, 1785, 1875, 2233, 2625, 3599, 3815,$
  $4125, 4187, 5475, 5559, 5887, 6375, 6601, 6681, 7905, 8175, 9265, 9375, 9471, 11175, \ldots$

- The set $\mathcal{V}_3^-(3)$ is given by A339725 and starts with the elements

  $9, 27, 119, 133, 145, 165, 205, 261, 341, 393, 649, 693, 705, 901, 945, 1121, 1173, 1189,$
  $1353, 1431, 1485, 1881, 2133, 2805, 3201, 3605, 3745, 4187, 5173, 5461, 5841, 5945, \ldots$

Example 5. $b = -1, a = 5, D = 29$.

- The set $\mathcal{U}_1^-(5)$ recovers the entry A340095 in [15], starting with

  $9, 15, 27, 45, 91, 121, 135, 143, 1547, 1573, 1935, 2015, 6543, 6721, 8099, 10403, 10877,$
  $10905, 13319, 13741, 13747, 14399, 14705, 16109, 16471, 18901, 19043, 19109, \ldots$

- The set $\mathcal{U}_2^-(5)$ gives A340120 and its first elements are

  $9, 15, 25, 27, 45, 75, 91, 121, 125, 135, 143, 147, 175, 225, 275, 325, 375, 441, 483, 625,$
  $675, 735, 755, 1125, 1323, 1547, 1573, 1875, 1935, 2015, 2205, 2275, 2485, \ldots$

- The set $\mathcal{U}_3^-(5)$ is indexed as A340237 and its first elements are

  $9, 27, 33, 35, 65, 81, 99, 121, 221, 243, 297, 363, 513, 585, 627, 705, 729, 891, 1089, 1539,$
  $1541, 1881, 2145, 2187, 2299, 2673, 3267, 3605, 4181, 4573, 4579, 5265, 5633, 6721, \ldots$

- The set $\mathcal{V}_1^-(5)$ recovers A339127, and starts with

  $9, 25, 27, 49, 81, 121, 169, 175, 225, 243, 289, 325, 361, 529, 637, 729, 961, 1225, 1331,$
  $1369, 1539, 1681, 1849, 2025, 2209, 2809, 3025, 3481, 3721, 4225, 4489, 5041, 5329, \ldots$

- The set $\mathcal{V}_2^-(5)$ giving A339519, has the first elements

  $9, 15, 27, 39, 45, 91, 117, 121, 135, 143, 195, 287, 351, 507, 585, 741, 1521, 1547, 1573,$
  $1755, 1935, 2015, 2067, 2535, 2601, 3157, 3227, 3445, 3505, 3519, 3731, 4563, \ldots$

- The set $\mathcal{V}_3^-(5)$ is given by A339726 and starts with the elements

  $9, 25, 27, 33, 35, 45, 65, 81, 99, 117, 121, 161, 175, 221, 225, 297, 325, 363, 585, 645, 705,$
  $825, 891, 1089, 1281, 1539, 1541, 1881, 2025, 2133, 2145, 2181, 2299, 2325, 2925, \ldots$

Example 6. $b = -1, a = 7, D = 53$.

- The set $\mathcal{U}_1^-(7)$ recovers the entry A340096 in [15], starting with

  $25, 35, 51, 65, 91, 175, 325, 391, 455, 575, 1247, 1295, 1633, 1763, 1775, 1921, 2275,$
  $2407, 2599, 2651, 3367, 4199, 4579, 4623, 5629, 6441, 9959, 10465, 10825, 10877, \ldots$

- The set $\mathcal{U}_2^-(7)$ gives A340121 and its first elements are

  $25, 35, 39, 49, 51, 65, 91, 147, 175, 245, 301, 325, 343, 391, 455, 507, 575, 605, 637, 663,$
  $741, 833, 897, 903, 935, 1127, 1205, 1225, 1247, 1295, 1505, 1595, 1633, 1715, 1763, \ldots$

- The set $\mathcal{U}_3^-(7)$ is indexed as A340238 and its first elements are

  $9, 25, 27, 51, 91, 105, 153, 185, 225, 289, 325, 425, 459, 481, 513, 747, 867, 897, 925,$
  $945, 1001, 1189, 1299, 1469, 1633, 1785, 1921, 2241, 2245, 2599, 2601, 2651, 2769, \ldots$

- The set $\mathcal{V}_1^-(7)$ recovers A339128, and starts with

  $9, 25, 49, 51, 91, 121, 125, 153, 169, 289, 325, 361, 441, 529, 625, 637, 833, 841, 867, 961,$
  $1183, 1225, 1369, 1633, 1681, 1849, 1921, 2209, 2599, 2601, 2651, 3481, 3721, 4225, \ldots$

- The set $\mathcal{V}_2^-(7)$ giving A339520, has the first elements

  $25, 35, 51, 65, 75, 91, 105, 175, 203, 325, 391, 455, 575, 645, 861, 1247, 1275, 1295,$
  $1633, 1763, 1775, 1785, 1875, 1921, 2275, 2407, 2415, 2599, 2625, 2651, 3045, 3367, \ldots$

- The set $\mathcal{V}_3^-(7)$ is given by A339727 and starts with the elements

  $9, 25, 49, 51, 69, 91, 105, 143, 145, 153, 185, 221, 225, 325, 339, 391, 425, 441, 481,$
  $637, 645, 705, 805, 833, 897, 925, 1001, 1173, 1189, 1207, 1225, 1281, 1299, 1365, \ldots$

In 1964, E. Lehmer [16] proved that the sequence $\mathcal{U}_1^-(1)$ is infinite.

Conjecture 2. *If a and k are positive integers with a odd, then $\mathcal{U}_k^-(a)$ and $\mathcal{V}_k^-(a)$ are infinite.*

3.3. Results for $b = 1$

We shortly denote $U_n = U_n(a, 1)$ and $V_n = V_n(a, 1)$. If p is prime and a odd, then we have $D = a^2 - 4$, and by the law of quadratic reciprocity for the Jacobi symbol (15) we get $\left(\frac{D}{p}\right) = \left(\frac{p}{D}\right)$, hence the results in Theorem 3 can be rewritten as

(1) $U_{kp-\left(\frac{p}{D}\right)} \equiv \left(\frac{p}{D}\right) U_{k-1} \pmod{p}$;

(2) $V_{kp-\left(\frac{p}{D}\right)} \equiv V_{k-1} \pmod{p}$.

We investigate similar relations modulo a composite number n, where $\left(\frac{n}{D}\right)$ is the Jacobi symbol, which is well-defined for any odd composite integers n and D, which allow us to naturally define new pseudoprimality notions.

Definition 5. *Let a, k and n be non-negative integers, with a odd. We say that the composite number n is a*

(1) **generalized Lucas pseudoprime of level k^+ and parameter** a *if*

$$n \mid U_{kn - \left(\frac{n}{D}\right)} - \left(\frac{n}{D}\right) U_{k-1}.$$

The set of all such numbers is denoted by $\mathcal{U}_k^+(a)$.

(2) *generalized Pell–Lucas pseudoprime of level* k^+ *and parameter* a *if*

$$n \mid V_{kn-\left(\frac{n}{D}\right)} - V_{k-1}.$$

The set of all such numbers is denoted by $\mathcal{V}_k^+(a)$.

In [19] we have proved connections between the sets of generalized Lucas and Pell–Lucas pseudoprimes of levels 1^+ and 2^+, linked through the property $n \mid U_n^2 - 1$ (similarly to Theorem 4).

Theorem 5. *Let $a, n > 0$ be odd integers with $\gcd(D, n) = 1$. We have:*
(1) *Reference [19] (Theorem 4.9). If $n \in \mathcal{U}_1^+(a)$, then $n \in \mathcal{U}_2^+(a)$ if and only if $n \mid U_n^2 - 1$.*
(2) *Reference [19] (Theorem 4.12). If $n \in \mathcal{V}_1^+(a)$ and $\gcd(a, n) = 1$, then $n \in \mathcal{V}_2^+(a)$ if and only if $n \mid U_n^2 - 1$.*

We now present the integer sequences $\mathcal{U}_k^+(a)$, $\mathcal{V}_k^+(a)$ calculated for the values $a = 3, 5, 7$ and $k = 1, 2, 3$. Most of these have been added by the authors to OEIS [15]. For these values we show that the reciprocal statements in Theorem 5 do not hold, and also, the results cannot be extended directly to superior levels.

We first provide some details on weak generalized Lucas pseudoprimes.

Remark 6. *For $b = 1$, the odd integers n satisfying the property $n \mid U_n^2 - 1$ recover the sequences A338007 for $a = 3$, A338009 for $a = 5$, and A338011 for $a = 7$. The reader can use these links to check the numerical examples given below.*

We now show that the reciprocals of Theorem 5 do not hold.

Remark 7. *(1) If $n \mid U_n^2 - 1$ with $n \in \mathcal{U}_2^+(a)$, does not imply $n \in \mathcal{U}_1^+(a)$. A counterexample is given by $U_n = U_n(3, 1)$ (bisection of Fibonacci numbers), where $D = 5$. For $n = 9$ we have $U_n = 2584$, $\left(\frac{n}{5}\right) = 1$, $n \mid U_{2n-\left(\frac{n}{5}\right)} - U_1$ and $n \mid U_n^2 - 1$, but $U_{n-\left(\frac{n}{5}\right)} \equiv 6 \neq 0 \pmod{n}$.*

$$U_{n-\left(\frac{n}{5}\right)} = 987 \equiv 6 \pmod{n};$$
$$U_{2n-\left(\frac{n}{5}\right)} - U_1 = 5702886 \equiv 0 \pmod{n};$$
$$U_n^2 - 1 = 6677055 \equiv 0 \pmod{n}.$$

(2) When $n \mid U_n^2 - 1$ with $n \in \mathcal{V}_2^+(a)$, it does not imply $n \in \mathcal{V}_1^+(a)$. A counterexample is given by $V_n = V_n(3, 1) = L_{2n}$ (bisection of Lucas numbers), where $D = 5$. For $n = 21$ we get $V_n = 599074578$, one has $\left(\frac{n}{5}\right) = 1$ and

$$V_{n-\left(\frac{n}{5}\right)} = 228826125 \equiv 5 \neq 2 \pmod{n};$$
$$V_{2n-\left(\frac{n}{5}\right)} - V_1 = 137083915467899400 \equiv 0 \pmod{n};$$
$$U_n^2 - 1 = 71778070001175615 \equiv 0 \pmod{n}.$$

For the calculations we have used the **vpi** (variable precision integer) library in Matlab.

For each value $a = 3, 5, 7$ there might be infinitely many such integers n.

Remark 8. *As seen in Example 2, even when $n \mid U_n^2 - 1$, and $n \in \mathcal{U}_2^+(a)$ (or $n \in \mathcal{V}_2^+(a)$), it does not mean that $n \in \mathcal{U}_1^+(a)$ (or $n \in \mathcal{V}_1^+(a)$). For U_n we have:*
- $a = 3$: $9, 63, 423, 2871, 2961, 8001$;
- $a = 5$: $25, 275, 425, 575, 775, 6325, 6575, 9775, 13175, 17825$;
- $a = 7$: $49, 1127, 2303$

For V_n we have
- $a = 3$: $21, 329, 451, 861, 1081, 1819, 2033, 2211, 3653, 4089, 5671, 8557, 11309,$
  $13861, 14701, 17513, 17941, 19951, 20473$;
- $a = 5$: $115, 253, 391, 713, 715, 779, 935, 1705, 2627, 2893, 2929, 3281, 4141, 5191,$
  $5671, 7739, 8695, 11815, 12121, 17963$;
- $a = 7$: $1771, 7471, 7931, 15449$.

We show that for U_n one cannot make the jump from levels 1^+ and 2^+ to level 3^+, even under the extra condition $n \mid U_n^2 - 1$.

Example 7. *When $b = 1$ and $a = 3$ we have $D = 5$. The first composite integer n for which $n \mid U_{n-\left(\frac{n}{5}\right)}$ and $n \mid U_n^2 - 1$ is $n = 21$. For this integer one can check that $n \mid U_{2n-\left(\frac{n}{5}\right)} - U_1$, but we have $U_{3n-\left(\frac{n}{5}\right)} - U_2 \equiv 15 \pmod{n}$, where $\left(\frac{n}{5}\right) = 1$. The calculations with large integers are implemented with the vpi library in Matlab®. We have*

$$U_{n-\left(\frac{n}{5}\right)} = 102334155 \equiv 0 \pmod{n};$$
$$U_{2n-\left(\frac{n}{5}\right)} = 61305790721611591 \equiv \left(\frac{n}{5}\right) U_1 = 1 \pmod{n};$$
$$U_{3n-\left(\frac{n}{5}\right)} = 36726740705505779255899443 \equiv 18 \neq \left(\frac{n}{5}\right) U_2 = 3 \pmod{n};$$
$$U_n^2 - 1 = 71778070001175615 \equiv 0 \pmod{n}.$$

We now find multiple such integers for U_n, as in Remark 5.

Remark 9. *Below we present some integers n which satisfy the properties $n \mid U_n^2 - 1$ and $n \in \mathcal{U}_1^+(a) \cap \mathcal{U}_2^+(a)$, but $n \notin \mathcal{U}_3^+(a)$.*
- $a = 3$: $21, 329, 451, 861, 1081, 1819, 2033, 2211, 3653, 4089, 5671, 8557, 11309,$
  $13861, 14701, 17513, 17941, 19951, 20473$;
- $a = 5$: $115, 253, 391, 713, 715, 779, 935, 1705, 2627, 2893, 2929, 3281, 4141, 5191,$
  $5671, 7739, 11815, 12121, 17963$;
- $a = 7$: $1771, 7471, 7931, 15449$.

We conjecture that these sequences exist and are infinite for all odd integers a.

By Theorem 5 we have that whenever $n \mid U_n^2 - 1$ we have $\mathcal{V}_1^+(a) \subseteq \mathcal{V}_2^+(a)$. The following property for V_n is suggested by numerical simulations for $a = 3, 5, 7$ and $n \leq 17000$, but we do not currently have a proof.

Conjecture 3. *If $a, n \geq 3$ are odd integers such that n is composite and $n \mid U_n^2 - 1$, then we have $\mathcal{V}_2^+(a) \subseteq \mathcal{V}_3^+(a)$.*

Example 8. $b = 1, a = 3, D = 5$ *(bisection of Fibonacci and Lucas numbers).*

- The set $\mathcal{U}_1^+(3)$ recovers the entry A340097 in [15], starting with

  $21, 323, 329, 377, 451, 861, 1081, 1819, 1891, 2033, 2211, 3653, 3827, 4089, 4181, 5671,$
  $5777, 6601, 6721, 8149, 8557, 10877, 11309, 11663, 13201, 13861, 13981, \ldots.$

- The set $\mathcal{U}_2^+(3)$ recovers A340122 and its first elements are

  $9, 21, 27, 63, 81, 189, 243, 323, 329, 351, 377, 423, 451, 567, 729, 783, 861, 891, 963, 1081,$
  $1701, 1743, 1819, 1891, 1967, 2033, 2187, 2211, 2871, 2889, 2961, 3321, 3653, \ldots.$

- The set $\mathcal{U}_3^+(3)$ is indexed as A340239 and its first elements are

  $9, 49, 63, 141, 161, 207, 323, 341, 377, 441, 671, 901, 1007, 1127, 1281, 1449, 1853,$
  $1891, 2071, 2303, 2407, 2501, 2743, 2961, 3827, 4181, 4623, 5473, 5611, 5777, 6119, \ldots$

- The set $\mathcal{V}_1^+(3)$ recovers A339129, and starts with

  $9, 49, 63, 121, 169, 289, 323, 361, 377, 441, 529, 841, 961, 1127, 1369, 1681, 1849, 1891,$
  $2209, 2303, 2809, 2961, 3481, 3721, 3751, 3827, 4181, 4489, 4901, 4961, 5041, 5329, 5491,$
  $5777, 6137, 6241, 6601, 6721, 6889, 7381, 7921, 8149, 9409, 10201, 10609, 10877, 10933,$
  $11449, 11663, 11881, 12769, 13201, 13981, 14027, 15251, 16129, 17119, 17161, \ldots$

- The set $\mathcal{V}_2^+(3)$ giving A339521, has the first elements

  $21, 203, 323, 329, 377, 451, 609, 861, 1001, 1081, 1183, 1547, 1729, 1819, 1891, 2033,$
  $2211, 2821, 3081, 3549, 3653, 3827, 4089, 4181, 4669, 5671, 5777, 5887, 6601, \ldots$

- The set $\mathcal{V}_3^+(3)$ is given by A339728 and starts with the elements

  $9, 21, 27, 63, 161, 189, 207, 261, 287, 323, 341, 377, 671, 783, 861, 901, 987, 1007,$
  $1107, 1269, 1281, 1287, 1449, 1853, 1891, 2071, 2241, 2407, 2431, 2501, 2529, 2567,$
  $2743, 2961, 3201, 3827, 4181, 4623, 5029, 5473, 5611, 5777, 5781, 6119, 6601, \ldots$

Recall that $U_n(1, -1) = F_n$ and $V_n(1, -1) = L_n$, while $U_n(3, 1) = F_{2n}$ (A001906) and $V_n(3, 1) = L_{2n}$ (A001906) represent the bisection of Fibonacci and Lucas sequences, respectively. The numerical results suggest the following two conjectures.

Conjecture 4. $\mathcal{U}_1^-(1) \subset \mathcal{U}_1^+(3)$. *Notice that the terms of* $\mathcal{U}_1^-(1)$ *(Fibonacci pseudoprimes)*

$$323, 377, 1891, 3827, 4181, 5777, 6601, 6721, 8149,$$

can be found amongst the elements of $\mathcal{U}_1^+(3)$.

Conjecture 5. $\mathcal{V}_1^-(1) \subset \mathcal{V}_1^+(3)$. *One may notice that the elements of* $\mathcal{V}_1^-(1)$ *smaller than* 10000 *also belong to the set* $\mathcal{V}_1^+(3)$.

Note that for $a = 5$ and $a = 7$, the values $D = 21$ and $D = 45$ are not prime.

Example 9. $b = 1$, $a = 5$, $D = 21$.

- The set $\mathcal{U}_1^+(5)$ recovers the entry A340098 in [15], starting with

  $115, 253, 391, 527, 551, 713, 715, 779, 935, 1705, 1807, 1919, 2627, 2893, 2929, 3281,$
  $4033, 4141, 5191, 5671, 5777, 5983, 6049, 6479, 7645, 7739, 8695, 9361, 11663, \ldots$

- The set $\mathcal{U}_2^+(5)$ recovers A340123 and its first elements are

  $25, 115, 125, 253, 275, 391, 425, 505, 527, 551, 575, 625, 713, 715, 775, 779, 935, 1705,$
  $1807, 1919, 2525, 2627, 2875, 2893, 2929, 3125, 3281, 4033, 4141, 5191, 5555, \ldots$

- The set $\mathcal{U}_3^+(5)$ is indexed as A340240 and its first elements are

  $55, 407, 527, 529, 551, 559, 965, 1199, 1265, 1633, 1807, 1919, 1961, 3401, 3959, 4033,$
  $4381, 5461, 5777, 5977, 5983, 6049, 6233, 6439, 6479, 7141, 7195, 7645, 7999, \ldots$

- The set $\mathcal{V}_1^+(5)$ recovers A339130, and starts with

  25, 121, 169, 275, 289, 361, 527, 529, 551, 575, 841, 961, 1369, 1681, 1807, 1849, 1919, 2209, 2783, 2809, 3025, 3481, 3721, 4033, 4489, 5041, 5329, 5777, 5983, 6049, 6241, 6479, 6575, 6889, 7267, 7645, 7921, 8959, 8993, 9361, 9409, 9775, ...

- The set $\mathcal{V}_2^+(5)$ giving A339522, has the first elements

  95, 115, 145, 253, 391, 527, 551, 713, 715, 779, 935, 1045, 1615, 1705, 1805, 1807, 1919, 2185, 2627, 2755, 2893, 2929, 2945, 3281, 4033, 4141, 4205, ...

- The set $\mathcal{V}_3^+(5)$ is given by A339729 and starts with the elements

  25, 55, 85, 115, 155, 187, 253, 275, 341, 407, 527, 551, 559, 575, 851, 925, 1199, 1265, 1633, 1775, 1807, 1919, 1961, 2123, 2507, 2635, 2641, 2725, ...

Example 10. $b = 1$, $a = 7$, $D = 45$.

The following sequences of pseudoprimes are obtained.

- The set $\mathcal{U}_1^+(7)$ recovers the entry A340099 in [15], starting with

  323, 329, 377, 451, 1081, 1771, 1819, 1891, 2033, 3653, 3827, 4181, 5671, 5777, 6601, 6721, 7471, 7931, 8149, 8557, 10877, 11309, 11663, 13201, 13861, 13981, 14701, ...

- The set $\mathcal{U}_2^+(7)$ recovers A340124 and its first elements are

  49, 323, 329, 343, 377, 451, 1081, 1127, 1771, 1819, 1891, 2033, 2303, 2401, 3653, 3827, 4181, 5671, 5777, 6601, 6721, 7471, 7931, 8149, 8557, 9691, 10877, 11309, ...

- The set $\mathcal{U}_3^+(7)$ is indexed as A340241 and its first elements are

  161, 323, 329, 341, 377, 451, 671, 901, 1007, 1079, 1081, 1271, 1819, 1853, 1891, 2033, 2071, 2209, 2407, 2461, 2501, 2743, 3653, 3827, 4181, 4843, 5473, 5611, 5671, ...

- The set $\mathcal{V}_1^+(7)$ recovers A339131, and starts with

  49, 121, 169, 289, 323, 329, 361, 377, 451, 529, 841, 961, 1081, 1127, 1369, 1681, 1819, 1849, 1891, 2033, 2209, 2303, 2809, 3481, 3653, 3721, 3751, 3827, 4181, 4489, 4901, 4961, 5041, 5329, 5491, 5671, 5777, 6137, 6241, 6601, 6721, 6889, 7381, 7921, ...

- The set $\mathcal{V}_2^+(7)$ giving A339523, has the first elements

  91, 203, 323, 329, 377, 451, 1001, 1081, 1183, 1547, 1729, 1771, 1819, 1891, 1967, 2033, 2093, 2639, 2821, 3197, 3311, 3653, 3731, 3827, 4181, 4669, ...

- The set $\mathcal{V}_3^+(7)$ is given by A339730 and starts with the elements

  49, 161, 287, 323, 329, 341, 377, 451, 671, 737, 901, 1007, 1079, 1081, 1127, 1271, 1363, 1541, 1819, 1853, 1891, 1927, 2033, 2071, 2303, 2407, 2431, 2461, 2501, 2567, 2743, ...

Conjecture 6. *If a and k are positive integers with a odd, then $\mathcal{U}_k^+(a)$ and $\mathcal{V}_k^+(a)$ are infinite.*

4. Conclusions and Further Work

In this paper we have analyzed the Fibonacci pseudoprimes of level k, and we have formulated an analogous version of this concept for the Lucas numbers (Section 2.2).

In Section 3 we have generalized these notions for Lucas $\{U_n(a,b)\}_{n\geq 0}$, and generalized Pell–Lucas sequences $\{V_n(a,b)\}_{n\geq 0}$, obtaining the generalized Lucas and Pell–Lucas pseudoprimes of levels k^- (for $b=-1$) and k^+ (for $b=1$) and parameter a. For these concepts, it was known from [19], that under the supplementary condition $n \mid U_n^2 - 1$, the pseudoprimes of levels 1^- and 2^-, and 1^+ and 2^+, respectively, coincide.

The purpose of this paper has been threefold. First, to calculate the explicit values of these pseudoprimes for levels $k=1,2,3$, for $b=-1$ with $a=1,3,5,7$ and for $b=1$ with $a=3,5,7$. This effort led to numerous new additions to OEIS. Second, we have shown that reciprocal statements for Theorems 4 and 5 do not hold, providing a range of counterexamples (Remark 4 and Remarks 7 and 8, respectively). Thirdly, we have shown that the transition from levels 1^- and 2^- to level 3^- (and from levels 1^+ and 2^+ to 3^+, respectively) cannot be guaranteed in general, even under the supplementary condition $n \mid U_n^2 - 1$ (Remarks 5 and 7, respectively).

An interesting problem for further investigation is the connection between the generalized Lucas and Pell–Lucas pseudoprimes of levels k^- and k^+ and parameter a, and the weak pseudoprimality concepts defined in [7].

Numerous open problems remain to be solved, as seen from Conjectures 1, 2, 3, 4, 5, or 6. Another interesting direction for further study, suggested by one of the referees, was to explore whether any odd composite integer could be a pseudoprime of a given level, or to find the smallest such integer that cannot be a pseudoprime at all. We invite the readers to join us in trying to solve these problems.

Author Contributions: Conceptualization, D.A. and O.B.; Data curation, D.A.; Formal analysis, O.B.; Investigation, O.B.; Methodology, D.A.; Software, O.B.; Writing–original draft, D.A. and O.B.; Writing–review–editing, O.B. All authors claim to have contributed significantly and equally to this work. All authors have read and agreed to the published version of the manuscript.

Funding: This research received no external funding.

Institutional Review Board Statement: Not applicable.

Informed Consent Statement: Not applicable.

Data Availability Statement: Codes for all the sequences in this paper are provided in OEIS.

Acknowledgments: The authors would like to thank the referees for their valuable feedback and constructive comments, which helped to improve the quality of the manuscript. The would also wish the thank the editorial team of OEIS, who have reviewed the multiple new integer sequences mentioned in this paper.

Conflicts of Interest: The authors declare no conflict of interest.

References

1. Everest, G.; van der Poorten, A.; Shparlinski, I.; Ward, T. *Recurrence Sequences*; Mathematical Surveys and Monographs 104; American Mathematical Society: Providence, RI, USA, 2003.
2. Falcon, S. On the k-Lucas numbers. *Int. J. Contemp. Math. Sci.* **2011**, *6*, 1039–1050.
3. Andrica, D.; Bagdasar, O. On some arithmetic properties of the generalized Lucas sequences. *Mediterr. J. Math.* **2021**, *18*, 47. [CrossRef]
4. Andrica, D.; Bagdasar, O. *Recurrent Sequences: Key Results, Applications and Problems*; Springer: Berlin, Germany, 2020.
5. Andreescu, T.; Andrica, D. *Number Theory. Structures, Examples, and Problems*; Birkhauser Verlag: Boston, MA, USA; Berlin, Germany; Basel, Switzerland, 2009.
6. Williams, H.C. *Edouard Lucas and Primality Testing*; Wiley-Blackwell: Hoboken, NJ, USA, 2011.
7. Andrica, D.; Bagdasar, O.; Rassias, T.M. Weak pseudoprimality associated to the generalized Lucas sequences. In *Approximation and Computation in Science and Engineering*; Daras, N.J., Rassias, T.M., Eds.; Springer: Berlin, Germany, 2021.
8. Brillhart, J.; Lehmer, D.H.; Selfridge, J.L. New primality criteria and factorizations of $2^m \pm 1$. *Math. Comput.* **1975**, *29*, 620–647.
9. Baillie, R.; Wagstaff, S.S., Jr. Lucas Pseudoprimes. *Math. Comput.* **1980**, *35*, 1391–1417. [CrossRef]

10. Grantham, J. Frobenius pseudoprimes. *Math. Comput.* **2000**, *70*, 873–891. [CrossRef]
11. Rotkiewicz, A. Lucas and Frobenius pseudoprimes. *Ann. Math. Sil.* **2003**, *17*, 17–39.
12. Somer, L. On superpseudoprimes. *Math. Slovaca* **2004**, *54*, 443–451.
13. Marko, F. A note on pseudoprimes with respect to abelian linear recurring sequence. *Math. Slovaca* **1996**, *46*, 173–176.
14. Andrica, D.; Crişan, V.; Al-Thukair, F. On Fibonacci and Lucas sequences modulo a prime and primality testing. *Arab J. Math. Sci.* **2018**, *24*, 9–15. [CrossRef]
15. The On-Line Encyclopedia of Integer Sequences, Published Electronically. 2020. Available online: https://oeis.org (accessed on 12 March 2021).
16. Lehmer, E. On the infinitude of Fibonacci pseudoprimes. *Fibonacci Q.* **1964**, *2*, 229–230.
17. Bruckman, P.S. Lucas pseudoprimes are odd. *Fibonacci Q.* **1994**, *32*, 155–157.
18. Bruckman, P.S. On the infinitude of Lucas pseudoprimes. *Fibonacci Q.* **1994**, *32*, 153–154.
19. Andrica, D.; Bagdasar, O. Pseudoprimality related to the generalized Lucas sequences. *Math. Comput. Simul.* **2021**, in press. [CrossRef]

Article

On Fibonacci Numbers of Order r Which Are Expressible as Sum of Consecutive Factorial Numbers

Eva Trojovská and Pavel Trojovský *

Department of Mathematics, Faculty of Science, University of Hradec Králové,
50003 Hradec Králové, Czech Republic; eva.trojovska@uhk.cz
* Correspondence: pavel.trojovsky@uhk.cz; Tel.: +42-049-333-2860

Abstract: Let $(t_n^{(r)})_{n\geq 0}$ be the sequence of the generalized Fibonacci number of order r, which is defined by the recurrence $t_n^{(r)} = t_{n-1}^{(r)} + \cdots + t_{n-r}^{(r)}$, for $n \geq r$, with initial values $t_0^{(r)} = 0$ and $t_i^{(r)} = 1$, for all $1 \leq i \leq r$. In 2002, Grossman and Luca searched for terms of the sequence $(t_n^{(2)})_n$, which are expressible as a sum of factorials. In this paper, we continue this program by proving that, for any $\ell \geq 1$, there exists an effectively computable constant $C = C(\ell) > 0$ (only depending on ℓ), such that, if (m, n, r) is a solution of $t_m^{(r)} = n! + (n+1)! + \cdots + (n+\ell)!$, with r even, then $\max\{m, n, r\} < C$. As an application, we solve the previous equation for all $1 \leq \ell \leq 5$.

Keywords: diophantine equation; factorial; fibonacci r-numbers; 2-adic valuation

MSC: 11Dxx; 11B39

Citation: Trojovská, E.; Trojovský, P. On Fibonacci Numbers of Order r Which Are Expressible as Sum of Consecutive Factorial Numbers. *Mathematics* **2021**, *9*, 962. https://doi.org/10.3390/math9090962

Academic Editors: Diana Savin, Nicusor Minculete and Vincenzo Acciaro

Received: 9 April 2021
Accepted: 23 April 2021
Published: 25 April 2021

Publisher's Note: MDPI stays neutral with regard to jurisdictional claims in published maps and institutional affiliations.

Copyright: © 2021 by the authors. Licensee MDPI, Basel, Switzerland. This article is an open access article distributed under the terms and conditions of the Creative Commons Attribution (CC BY) license (https://creativecommons.org/licenses/by/4.0/).

1. Introduction

We recall that the factorial of an integer $n \geq 1$, denoted by $n!$, is the product $\prod_{j=1}^{n} j$. Along the years, several authors have considered Diophantine problems involving factorial numbers. For instance, Erdős and Selfridge [1] proved that 1 is the only perfect power in the sequence of factorials. However, the most famous and calssical among such problems was raised by Brocard [2], in 1876, and, independently, by Ramanujan [3,4] (p. 327 in ref. [4]), in 1913. The Diophantine equation

$$n! + 1 = m^2,$$

in positive integers m and n, is known as Brocard–Ramanujan Diophantine equation. There are three solutions, namely, $(n, m) = (4, 5), (5, 11)$, and $(7, 71)$, and no solution was found for $7 < n < 10^9$ (as can be see in [5]). In fact, the Brocard–Ramanujan equation remains still as an open problem.

Let $(F_n)_{n\geq 0}$ be the Fibonacci sequence that is given by $F_0 = 0$, $F_1 = 1$ and $F_{n+2} = F_{n+1} + F_n$, for $n \geq 0$. There are also several interesting problems related to Fibonacci numbers (for recent results, we refer the reader to [6,7] and references therein). For instance, the problem of the perfect powers in the Fibonacci sequence attracted much attention during some past decades. In 2003, Bugeaud et al. ([8] Theorem 1) confirmed the expectation, that 0, 1, 8, and 144 are the only perfect powers among $(F_n)_{n\geq 0}$. A generalization (for Fibonomial coefficients) of this result can be found in [9]. We still refer the reader to [8] for additional references and history.

Many mathematicians have been interested in Diophantine problems that involve both Fibonacci and factorial numbers. For instance, in 1999, Luca [10] proved that $F_{12} = 2!2!3!3!$ is the largest Fibonacci number which can be written as a product of factorials. Additionally, $F_1F_2F_3F_4F_5F_6F_8F_{10}F_{12} = 11!$ is the largest product of distinct Fibonacci numbers, which is a product of factorials (see [11]).

Moreover, Grossman and Luca [12] showed that, for any given $\ell \geq 1$, there are only finitely many positive integers n, such that

$$F_n = m_1! + m_2! + \cdots + m_\ell!$$

holds for some $m_1, m_2, \ldots, m_\ell \in \mathbb{Z}_{\geq 1}$. Moreover, they determined all of the solutions for $\ell \in \{1, 2\}$. In 2010, the case $\ell = 3$ was completely solved in [13] (for the inverse problem, i.e., factorials that are written as sum of a given number of Fibonacci numbers, we refer the reader to [14] and the references therein).

As any very well-studied object in mathematics, the Fibonacci sequence possesses many kinds of generalizations. The most well-known generalization is probably the so-called k-generalized Fibonacci sequence (or the sequence of the k-bonacci numbers), which is defined for $n \geq 2$ by the kth order recurrence

$$F_n^{(k)} = F_{n-1}^{(k)} + \cdots + F_{n-k}^{(k)}, \quad \text{with} \quad F_{-(k-2)}^{(k)} = \cdots = F_0^{(k)} = 0 \text{ and } F_1^{(k)} = 1.$$

Some interesting features of the sequence $(F_n^{(k)})_n$ we can find, e.g., in [15–19]. Here, we are interested in a sequence $(t_n^{(r)})_{n \geq 0}$ with the same recurrence relation, but with modified initial conditions. This sequence is called generalized Fibonacci numbers of order r and it is defined by

$$t_n^{(r)} = \begin{cases} 0, & \text{if } n = 0; \\ 1, & \text{if } 1 \leq n \leq r - 1; \\ \sum_{i=1}^{r} t_{n-i}^{(r)}, & \text{if } n \geq r. \end{cases}$$

For $r = 2$, we have the sequence of Fibonacci numbers and, for $r = 3$, we have the Tribonacci numbers.

We remark that the equation $F_m = n!$ may be solved by a direct application of the Carmichael Theorem about primitive divisors in the Fibonacci sequence (which asserts that for any $n > 12$, there exists a prime number p, such that $p \mid F_n$, but $p \nmid \prod_{i=1}^{n-1} F_i$). However, there is no such a result for Tribonacci numbers. Thus, Lengyel and Marques [20] provided a complete description for the 2-adic valuation $\nu_2(t_n^{(3)})$ (where $\nu_p(s) := \max\{k \geq 0 : p^k \mid s\}$) in order to solve the equation $t_n^{(3)} = m!$. After that, some authors generalized their results for $\nu_2(t_n^{(r)})$ (see [21,22]). In particular, Sobolewski [21] completely characterized $\nu_2(t_n^{(r)})$, for all $n \geq 1$ and $r \geq 4$ with r even.

In this paper, we search for terms of a generalized Fibonacci sequence of order r, which can be written as a sum of consecutive factorial numbers. In particular, we provide an explicit constant (depending only on the number of factorials), which is an upper bound for the number of the possible solutions. More precisely, we have

Theorem 1. *Let ℓ be a positive integer and let $(n, m, r) \in \mathbb{Z}_{\geq 1}^3$ be a solution of the Diophantine equation*

$$t_m^{(r)} = n! + (n+1)! + \cdots + (n+\ell)!, \tag{1}$$

with $m > r \geq 2$ even. We have

(a) *For $n \leq 3$, it holds that*

   (i) *If $m \leq 2r$, then either $(n, m, r, \ell) \in \{(1, 4, 2, 1), (1, 60, 56, 5)\}$ or*

$$(n, m, r, \ell) = \left(3, 2 + \frac{1}{2}\sum_{j=3}^{\ell+3} j!, 1 + \frac{1}{2}\sum_{j=3}^{\ell+3} j!, \ell\right), \tag{2}$$

   where ℓ is any positive integer.

   (ii) *If $m > 2r$, then*

$$m < 7.1(\ell + 4)\log(\ell + 3).$$

(b) For $n \geq 4$, it holds that

$$n < 2\log((\ell+1)\log(\ell+1)) + 105, \ m < 6(n+\ell+1)\log(n+\ell) \ and \ r \leq \frac{m-2}{2}.$$

As an application of the previous result, we found all solutions of (1) for some cases of ℓ. Actually, we prove that

Theorem 2. *All of the solutions of the Equation (1) for positive integers n, m, r and ℓ, with $r \equiv 0$ (mod 2), $m > r \geq 2$, and $\ell \leq 5$ are*

$$(n, m, r, \ell) \in \{(1,4,2,1), (1,60,56,5), (2,6,2,1), (2,10,4,3), (3,17,16,1), (3,77,76,2),$$
$$(3,437,436,3), (3,2957,2956,4), (3,23117,23116,5), (4,12,2,1)\}.$$

We organize this paper, as follows. In Section 2, we will present some helpful properties of the sequence $(t_n^{(r)})_n$. The third section is devoted to the proof of Theorems 1 and 2. The computations of this paper will be performed by using the Wolfram Mathematica software.

2. Auxiliary Results

Before proceeding further, some considerations will be needed for the convenience of the reader.

The characteristic polynomial of the sequence $(t_n^{(r)})_n$ is $\psi_k(x) = x^r - x^{r-1} - \cdots - x - 1$, which has only one root outside the unit circle, say α, which is located in the interval $(2(1-2^{-r}), 2)$ (see [23]). Furthermore, one can deduce from ([21] Lemma 4) that

Lemma 1. *For all $n \geq 1$, we have*

$$t_n^{(r)} > \alpha^{n-r-1}.$$

In particular, $t_n^{(r)} > (\sqrt{2})^{n-r-1}$, for all $n \geq 1$.

The last inequality follows because $\alpha > 2 - 1/2^{r-1} \geq 2 - 1/2 = 3/2 > \sqrt{2}$ (for all $r \geq 2$).

Another very useful tool is related to the *p-adic order* (recall that the *p*-adic order, or valuation, of s, $\nu_p(s)$, is the exponent of the highest power of a prime p, which divides s). An explicit formula for $\nu_p(F_n)$ was provided, see [24–27]. In particular, Lengyel [25] showed that

Lemma 2. *We have that*

$$\nu_2(F_n) = \begin{cases} 0, & \text{for } n \equiv 1,2 \pmod{3}; \\ 1, & \text{for } n \equiv 3 \pmod{6}; \\ \nu_2(n)+2, & \text{for } n \equiv 0 \pmod{6}. \end{cases}$$

In 2014, Lengyel and Marques [20] characterized $\nu_2(t_n^{(3)})$ and, recently, Sobolewsky [21] and Young [22] worked on a description of $\nu_2(t_n^{(r)})$, for even and odd r, respectively. In particular, the case in which r is even was completely solved:

Lemma 3. *For $r = 2k \geq 4$, we have that*

$$\nu_2(t_n^{(r)}) = \begin{cases} 0, & \text{for } n \equiv 1, 2, \ldots, 2k \pmod{2k+1}; \\ 1, & \text{for } n \equiv 2k+1 \pmod{2(2k+1)}; \\ \nu_2(n) + \nu_2(k-1) + 2, & \text{for } n \equiv 0 \pmod{2(2k+1)}. \end{cases}$$

Remark 1. We remark that the $v_2(t_n^{(r)})$ is not completely characterized for $r \geq 5$ odd. In fact, the only missing case happens if $n \equiv r+1 \pmod{2r+2}$ and $v_2(n-r-1) = v_2(r^2-1)$. Indeed, Young [22] showed that, in this case, $v_2(t_n^{(r)}) = v_2(z - (n-r-1)/(2r+2)) + 2$, for some 2-adic integer z. As will be seen after, the proof of Theorem 1 only requires an upper bound for $v_2(t_n^{(r)})$, but there is no a direct tool for providing a useful such bound for $v_2(z - (n-r-1)/(2r+2))$. Even the deep theory of linear forms in p-adic logarithms is not helpful, since it is conjectured that z is a 2-adic transcendental number.

We require one last fact about v_2 in order to complete our proof of Theorem 1.

Lemma 4. For any integer $n \geq 1$, we have

$$v_2(n!) \geq n - \left\lfloor \frac{\log n}{\log 2} \right\rfloor - 1, \tag{3}$$

where $\lfloor x \rfloor$ denotes the largest integer that is less than or equal to x. In particular, $v_2(n!) \geq n/4$, for all $n \geq 4$.

We refer the reader to ([28] Lemma 2.4) for a proof of this result.
Now, we are ready to deal with the proof of theorems.

3. The Proofs
3.1. The Proof of Theorem 1

Write

$$t_m^{(r)} = n! + (n+1)! + \cdots + (n+\ell)!$$

as $t_m^{(r)} = n! d_{n,\ell}$, where

$$d_{n,\ell} = 1 + (n+1) + (n+1)(n+2) + \cdots + (n+1) \cdots (n+\ell).$$

Note that $d_{n,\ell}$ is an integer and, moreover, the following estimate holds

$$n! d_{n,\ell} \leq (\ell+1)(n+\ell)! \leq (\ell+1)(n+\ell)^{n+\ell} < (n+\ell)^{n+\ell+1},$$

where we used that $s! \leq s^s$, for all $s \geq 1$ (we decided to use this inequality instead of the sharper $s! \leq 2(s/2)^s$, for $s \geq 3$, in order to leave the bounds notationally simpler and we observe that this choice does not change them in order).

The proof splits into two cases.

3.1.1. The Case $n \leq 3$

If $r < m \leq 2r$, then

$$t_{r+i}^{(r)} = 2^{i-1}(2r-3) + 1,$$

for $i \in [1, r]$ (this can be seen in ([22] p. 4)). If $i = 1$, then the equation becomes

$$2(r-1) = n! + (n+1)! + \cdots + (n+\ell)!$$

and so

$$r - 1 = \frac{n!}{2} + \frac{(n+1)!}{2} + \cdots + \frac{(n+\ell)!}{2}.$$

Because the left-hand side is an odd integer, then $n \in \{2, 3\}$. If $n = 2$, then

$$r - 1 = 1 + \frac{3!}{5} + (\text{sum of even terms})$$

yielding that $r = 5 +$ (sum of even terms) is odd (where we convention that (sum of even terms) is zero, for $\ell = 1$). Thus, there is no solution for $n = 2$ and $r < m \leq 2r$. When $n = 3$, we have that

$$r - 1 = \frac{3!}{2} + \frac{4!}{2} + \cdots + \frac{(\ell+3)!}{2}$$

is even. Thus, we obtain the following family of solutions

$$n = 3, \ r = 1 + \frac{3!}{2} + \frac{4!}{2} + \cdots + \frac{(\ell+3)!}{2}, \ m = r + 1 \text{ and } \ell.$$

For $i > 1$, one has that $t_m^{(r)} > 1$ is odd, which forces $n = 1$. Thus, we have

$$2^{i-1}(2r - 3) + 1 = 1! + 2! + \cdots + (\ell+1)!$$

and, so

$$2^{i-1}(2r - 3) = 2! + \cdots + (\ell+1)!. \tag{4}$$

If $r = 2$, then the equation becomes

$$2 = 2! + \cdots + (\ell+1)!,$$

where we used that $i = 2$ (since $1 < i \leq r = 2$). The previous equality only holds for $\ell = 1$, yielding the solution $(n, m, r, \ell) = (1, 4, 2, 1)$.

Supposing that $r \geq 4$, then $2r - 3$ is an odd number larger than 1. On the other hand, $2! + 3!$ and $2! + 3! + 4!$ are powers of 2 and so $\ell \geq 4$. However, if $\ell = 4$, then

$$2^{i-1}(2r - 3) = 2! + 3! + 4! + 5! = 152 = 2^3 \cdot 19$$

yielding that $2r - 3 = 19$ and, so, $r = 11$, which is odd (remember that our assumption is that r is even). Thus, we may assume $\ell \geq 5$. Because $\nu_2(s!) \geq 4$, for all $s \geq 6$, then the 2-adic valuation of right-hand side of (4) is 3 yielding that $i = 4$. Therefore, we can rewrite the previous equality as

$$2r - 3 = 19 + \frac{6!}{8} + \cdots + \frac{(\ell+1)!}{8}$$

and, then

$$r = 11 + \frac{6!}{16} + \cdots + \frac{(\ell+1)!}{16}.$$

Now, we observe that the right-hand side is only even for $\ell = 5$ (since $7!/16 = 315$ and $(\ell+1)!/16$ is even, for all $\ell \geq 7$). Therefore, $r = 11 + 6!/16 = 56$, which leads to the solution

$$t_{60}^{(56)} = 1! + 2! + 3! + 4! + 5! + 6!.$$

Therefore, let us suppose that $m > 2r$. In this case, by Lemma 1, together with $r < m/2$, one has that

$$(\sqrt{2})^{(m/2)-1} \leq 3! d_{3,\ell} \leq 6(\ell+1)(\ell+3)^{\ell+3} < 6(\ell+3)^{\ell+4}.$$

By applying the log function together with an straightforward calculation, we arrive at

$$m < \frac{4}{\log 2}(\ell + 4) \log(\ell + 3) + \frac{4 \log 6}{\log 2} + 2 < 7.1(\ell + 4) \log(\ell + 3).$$

In conclusion, we have

$$n \leq 3 \text{ and } r/2 < m < 7.1(\ell + 4) \log(\ell + 3)$$

as desired.

3.1.2. The Case $n \geq 4$

In this case, from the equation $t_m^{(r)} = n! d_{n,\ell}$, one deduces that 4 divides $t_m^{(r)}$. Accordingly, by combining Lemmas 2 and 3, we have that $2(r+1)$ divides m and

$$\nu_2(t_m^{(r)}) = \nu_2(m) + \nu_2(\widehat{k} - 1) + 2,$$

where $\widehat{k} := (1 - \delta_{2,r})k$ and $\delta_{i,j}$ is the Kronecker delta (whose value is 1 if $i = j$, and 0 otherwise).

On the other hand, since $d_{n,\ell}$ is an integer,

$$\nu_2(m) + \nu_2(\widehat{k} - 1) + 2 = \nu_2(t_m^{(r)}) \geq \nu_2(n!) \geq n/4,$$

where we used Lemma 4, since $n \geq 4$. Because $\nu_2(m) + \nu_2(\widehat{k} - 1) = \nu_2(m(\widehat{k} - 1))$, we get

$$\nu_2(m(\widehat{k} - 1)) \geq \frac{n}{4} - 2.$$

In particular, $2^{\lfloor (n/4) - 2 \rfloor}$ divides $m(\widehat{k} - 1)$ and so

$$2^{(n/4) - 3} < 2^{\lfloor (n/4) - 2 \rfloor} \leq m(\widehat{k} - 1),$$

where we used that $\lfloor x \rfloor > x - 1$. After some computations, we obtain

$$n < \frac{4}{\log 2} \log(m(\widehat{k} - 1)) + 12.$$

Because $2(2k+1)$ divides m, then $\widehat{k} - 1 \leq k - 1 < 2(2k+1) \leq m$ and, hence

$$n < \frac{8}{\log 2} \log m + 12 < 11.6 \log m + 12. \tag{5}$$

On the other hand, it follows again from Lemma 1 that

$$(\sqrt{2})^{m-r-1} \leq t_m^{(r)} \leq n! d_{n,\ell} < (n+\ell)^{n+\ell+1}.$$

Because $2(r+1) \leq m$, then $r + 1 \leq m/2$ and so

$$(\sqrt{2})^{m/2} \leq n! d_{n,\ell} < (n+\ell)^{n+\ell+1}.$$

After some manipulations, we get

$$m \leq \frac{4}{\log 2}(n+\ell+1)\log(n+\ell).$$

Now, the goal is to write the previous right-hand side in a better (product) form. For that, we shall use that $x + y \leq xy$, for all $x, y \in \mathbb{R}_{\geq 2}$. From this inequality, we have $n + \ell + 1 \leq n(\ell + 1)$ (since $n \geq 4$ and $\ell + 1 \geq 2$). For $\log(n + \ell)$, we have a more delicate issue (since ℓ may be equal to 1). However, we use the following trick

$$\begin{aligned}
\log(n + \ell) &= \log((n-1) + (\ell + 1)) \leq \log((n-1)(\ell + 1)) \\
&= \log(n-1) + \log(\ell + 1) \leq 1.9 \log(n-1) + 2.9 \log(\ell + 1) \\
&\leq 5.6 \log(n-1) \log(\ell + 1) < 5.6 (\log n) \log(\ell + 1),
\end{aligned}$$

where we used that $1.9 \log(n-1) \geq 1.9 \log 3 > 2$ and $2.9 \log(\ell+1) \geq 2.9 \log 2 > 2$. Therefore, we have

$$\begin{aligned} m &\leq \frac{4}{\log 2}(n+\ell+1)\log(n+\ell) < 32.4n(\ell+1)(\log n)\log(\ell+1) \\ &< 33n(\ell+1)(\log n)\log(\ell+1). \end{aligned} \quad (6)$$

Summarizing, we obtained that

$$m < 33n(\ell+1)(\log n)\log(\ell+1). \quad (7)$$

By combining (5) and (7), we get

$$n - \log(n \log n) < 52.6 + \log((\ell+1)\log(\ell+1)). \quad (8)$$

We claim that $\log(n \log n) < n/2$, for all $n \geq 4$. Indeed, let us consider the function $g : (1, +\infty) \to \mathbb{R}$, as defined by $g(x) := xe^{-x/2} \log x$. Thus,

$$g'(x) = e^{-x/2}\left(\log x - \frac{x \log x}{2} + 1\right).$$

However, $(x \log x)/2 > \log x + 1 = \log(ex)$, if and only if $x^{x-2} > e^2$, which is true for all $x \geq 4$. Subsequently, $g'(x) < 0$, for all $x \geq 4$ and, so, g is a decreasing function in the interval $[4, +\infty)$. In particular, for $n \geq 4$, we have

$$ne^{-n/2} \log n = g(n) \leq g(4) = \frac{4 \log 4}{e^2} < 0.75\ldots < 1,$$

which yields $n \log n < e^{n/2}$ and, finally, $\log(n \log n) < n/2$ as claimed (we point out that to use the easier inequality $e^x > 1 + x + x^2/2$, for $x > 0$, is not satisfactory, since $1 + n/2 + n^2/8 > n \log n$, only for $n > 19$).
By returning to (8), we deduce that

$$n < 2\log((\ell+1)\log(\ell+1)) + 105$$

as desired. The proof is then complete (by considering the inequality in (6)).

3.2. The Proof of Theorem 2

If $n \leq 3$ and $m \leq 2r$, then we have the following solutions that arise from (2):

$$(n, m, r, \ell) \in \{(3, 17, 16, 1), (3, 77, 76, 2), (3, 437, 436, 3), (3, 2957, 2956, 4), (3, 23117, 23116, 5)\}.$$

Furthermore, the solutions $(n, m, r, \ell) = (1, 4, 2, 1)$ and $(n, m, r, \ell) = (1, 60, 56, 5)$ were detected in the proof of Theorem 1.
For the case in which either $n \in \mathbb{Z}_{\geq 4}$ or $(n, m) \in \{1, 2, 3\} \times \mathbb{Z}_{>2r}$, we use the estimates that are provided in Theorem 1 (for $\ell \leq 5$) to infer that

$$n \leq 109, \ m \leq 3276 \text{ and } r \leq 1638.$$

For dealing with these remaining cases, we wrote two simple routines in Wolfram Mathematica software. First, the nth term of the sequence $(t_n^{(r)})_n$ can be defined as

```
t[n_, r_] :=
 t[n, r] =
  Which[n == 0, 0, 0 < n < r, 1, n >= r,
   Sum[t[n - i, r], {i, 1, r}]];
```

Afterwards, we shall use the following command to search for all solutions of

$$t_m^{(r)} = n! + (n+1)! + \cdots + (n+\ell)!$$

in the range $1 \leq n \leq 109, r < m \leq 3276$ and $2 \leq r \leq 1638$ (r even) when either $n \in \mathbb{Z}_{\geq 4}$ or $(n,m) \in \{1,2,3\} \times \mathbb{Z}_{>2r}$.

For the case $n \geq 4$, the routine

```
Catch[Do[{ n, m, r,1};
  If[t[m,r] == Sum[Factorial[n+i], {i,0,1}],
    Print[{n,m,r,1}]], {1,1,5}, {n, 4, 109},{r, 2, 1638,2}, {m,    r+1, 3276}]]
```

returns $\{4, 12, 2, 1\}$ as the only solution.

For the case $n \leq 3$ and $m > 2r$, the routine

```
Catch[Do[{ n, m, r,1};
  If[t[m,r] == Sum[Factorial[n+i], {i,0,1}],
    Print[{n,m,r,1}]], {1,1,5}, {n, 1, 3}, {r, 2, 1638,2}, {m,    2r+1, 3276}]]
```

returns $\{2, 6, 2, 1\}$ and $\{2, 10, 4, 3\}$ as solutions. This finishes the proof.

The calculation took roughly 2 h on 2.5 GHz Intel Core i5 4 GB Mac OSX. The proof is then complete.

4. Conclusions

In this paper, we work on searching for the terms of the Fibonacci sequence of order r, $(t_n^{(r)})_n$, which can be written as sum of consecutive factorials, where $t_n^{(r)} = \sum_{j=1}^{r} t_{n-j}^{(r)}$ with $t_0^{(r)} = 0$ and $t_1^{(r)} = \cdots = t_{r-1}^{(r)} = 1$. More precisely, we prove that, for any given $\ell \geq 1$, there exists a positive explicit constant C, depending only on ℓ, for which all triples $(n, m, r) \in \mathbb{Z}_{\geq 1}^3$ (with r even) of solutions of the Diophantine equation $t_m^{(r)} = \sum_{j=0}^{\ell}(n+j)!$ must satisfy $\max\{n, m, r\} < C$. The methods that are presented in this work combine upper bounds for the 2-adic valuation of $t_n^{(r)}$ together with some estimates and a computational approach. This may benefit future research concerning similar problems for other linear recurrence sequences (or even for $(t_n^{(r)})$ in the case of an odd r).

Author Contributions: P.T. conceived the presented idea, on the conceptualization, methodology, and investigation. Writing—review & editing and preparation of program procedures in *Mathematica* were done by E.T. Both authors have read and agreed to the published version of the manuscript.

Funding: The authors were supported by the Project of Specific Research PrF UHK No. 2101/2021, University of Hradec Králové, Czech Republic.

Institutional Review Board Statement: Not applicable.

Informed Consent Statement: Informed consent was obtained from all subjects involved in the study.

Conflicts of Interest: The authors declare no conflict of interest.

References

1. Erdős, P.; Selfridge, J.L. The product of consecutive integers is never a power. *Ill. J. Math.* **1975**, *19*, 292–301. [CrossRef]
2. Brocard, H. Question 166. *Nouv. Corresp. Math.* **1876**, *2*, 287.
3. Ramanujan, S. Question 469. *J. Indian Math. Soc.* **1913**, *5*, 59.
4. Ramanujan, S. *Collected Papers*; Chelsea: New York, NY, USA, 1962.
5. Berndt, B.C.; Galway, W. The Brocard–Ramanujan diophantine equation $n! + 1 = m^2$. *Ramanujan J.* **2000**, *4*, 41–42. [CrossRef]
6. Flaut, C.; Savin, D.; Zaharia, G. Some Applications of Fibonacci and Lucas Numbers. In *Algorithms as a Basis of Modern Applied Mathematics. Studies in Fuzziness and Soft Computing*; Hošková-Mayerová, Š., Flaut, C., Maturo, F., Eds.; Springer: Cham, Switzerland, 2021; Volume 404.
7. Flaut, C.; Shpakivskyi, V.; Vlad, E. Some remarks regarding $h(x)$-Fibonacci polynomials in an arbitrary algebra. *Chaos Solitons Fractals* **2017**, *99*, 32–35. [CrossRef]
8. Bugeaud, Y.; Mignotte, M.; Siksek, S. Classical and modular approaches to exponential Diophantine equations I. Fibonacci and Lucas powers. *Ann. Math.* **2006**, *163*, 969–1018. [CrossRef]
9. Marques, D.; Togbé, A. Perfect powers among Fibonomial coefficients. *C. R. Acad. Sci. Paris Ser. I* **2010**, *348*, 717–720. [CrossRef]
10. Luca, F. Products of factorials in binary recurrence sequences. *Rocky Mt. J. Math.* **1999**, *29*, 1387–1411. [CrossRef]

11. Luca, F.; Stănică, P. $F_1F_2F_3F_4F_5F_6F_8F_{10}F_{12} = 11!$ *Port. Math.* **2006**, *63*, 251–260.
12. Grossman, G.; Luca, F. Sums of factorials in binary recurrence sequences. *J. Number Theory* **2002**, *93*, 87–107. [CrossRef]
13. Bollman, M.; Hernández, H.S.; Luca, F. Fibonacci numbers which are sums of three factorials. *Publ. Math. Debr.* **2010**, *77*, 211–224.
14. Luca, F.; Siksek, S. Factorials expressible as sums of at most three Fibonacci numbers. *Proc. Edinb. Math. Soc.* **2010**, *53*, 679–729. [CrossRef]
15. Gabai, H. Generalized Fibonacci k-sequences. *Fib. Quart.* **1970**, *8*, 31–38.
16. Marques, D. On the intersection of two distinct k-generalized Fibonacci sequences. *Math. Bohem.* **2012**, *137*, 403–413. [CrossRef]
17. Bravo, J.J.; Luca, F. Coincidences in generalized Fibonacci sequences. *J. Number Theory* **2013**, *133*, 2121–2137. [CrossRef]
18. Dresden, G.P.; Du, Z. A Simplified Binet Formula for k-Generalized Fibonacci Numbers. *J. Integer Seq.* **2014**, *17*, 1–9.
19. Trojovský, P. On Terms of Generalized Fibonacci Sequences which are Powers of their Indexes. *Mathematics* **2019**, *7*, 700. [CrossRef]
20. Marques, D.; Lengyel, T. The 2-adic order of the Tribonacci numbers and the equation $T_n = m!$ *J. Integer Seq.* **2014**, *17*, 14101.
21. Sobolewski, B. The 2-adic valuation of generalized Fibonacci sequences with an application to certain Diophantine equations. *J. Number Theory* **2017**, *180*, 730–742. [CrossRef]
22. Young, P.T. 2-adic valuations of generalized Fibonacci numbers of odd order. *Integers* **2018**, *18*, A1.
23. Wolfram, A. Solving generalized Fibonacci recurrences. *Fibonacci Quart.* **1998**, *36*, 129–145.
24. Halton, J.H. On the divisibility properties of Fibonacci numbers. *Fibonacci Quart.* **1966**, *4*, 217–240.
25. Lengyel, T. The order of the Fibonacci and Lucas numbers. *Fibonacci Quart.* **2002**, *33*, 234–239.
26. Robinson, D.W. The Fibonacci matrix modulo m. *Fibonacci Quart.* **1963**, *1*, 29–36.
27. Vinson, J. The relation of the period modulo m to the rank of apparition of m in the Fibonacci sequence. *Fibonacci Quart.* **1963**, *1*, 37–45.
28. Marques, D. The order of appearance of product of consecutive Fibonacci numbers. *Fibonacci Quart.* **2012**, *50*, 132–139.

Article

Global and Local Behavior of the System of Piecewise Linear Difference Equations $x_{n+1} = |x_n| - y_n - b$ and $y_{n+1} = x_n - |y_n| + 1$ Where $b \geq 4$

Busakorn Aiewcharoen [1], Ratinan Boonklurb [2,*] and Nanthiya Konglawan [2]

[1] The Demonstration School of Silpakorn University, Faculty of Education, Silpakorn University, Nakhon Pathom 73000, Thailand; aiewcharoen_b@su.ac.th
[2] Department of Mathematics and Computer Science, Faculty of Science, Chulalongkorn University, Bangkok 10330, Thailand; nanthiya_21@hotmail.com
* Correspondence: ratinan.b@chula.ac.th

Abstract: The aim of this article is to study the system of piecewise linear difference equations $x_{n+1} = |x_n| - y_n - b$ and $y_{n+1} = x_n - |y_n| + 1$ where $n \geq 0$. A global behavior for $b = 4$ shows that all solutions become the equilibrium point. For a large value of $|x_0|$ and $|y_0|$, we can prove that (i) if $b = 5$, then the solution becomes the equilibrium point and (ii) if $b \geq 6$, then the solution becomes the periodic solution of prime period 5.

Keywords: equilibrium point; periodic solution; system of piecewise linear difference equation

MSC: 39A10; 65Q10

1. Introduction

The first order system of the piecewise difference equation of the form

$$x_{n+1} = |x_n| - ay_n - b \text{ and } y_{n+1} = x_n - c|y_n| + d \quad (1)$$

for $n \geq 0$ with a given initial condition (x_0, y_0) has been considered by several researchers. System (1) is actually motivated by the Lozi map [1,2] which is the system given by $x_{n+1} = -a|x_n| + y_n + 1$ and $y_{n+1} = bx_n$, where $a, b \in \mathbb{R}$ and a system $x_{n+1} = |x_n| - y_n + 1$ and $y_{n+1} = x_n$ given in [3,4] or, equivalently, the Devaney's Gingerbread man map $x_{n+1} = |x_n| - x_{n-1} + 1$ studied in [5]. It is known that if the sequences $(x_n)_{n=0}^{\infty}$ and $(y_n)_{n=0}^{\infty}$ satisfy (1) and the given initial conditions for all $n \geq 0$, then $(x_n, y_n)_{n=0}^{\infty}$ is called a solution of (1). Let $(x_n, y_n)_{n=0}^{\infty}$ be the solutions of (1) with a given initial condition (x_0, y_0). If there exist real numbers $\bar{x}$ and $\bar{y}$ and an integer N such that $(x_n, y_n) = (\bar{x}, \bar{y})$ for all $n \geq N$, then we say that the solution $(x_n, y_n)_{n=0}^{\infty}$ eventually becomes the equilibrium point $(\bar{x}, \bar{y})$ of (1). On the other hand, if p is the smallest positive integer such that $(x_{n+p}, y_{n+p}) = (x_n, y_n)$ for all $n \geq N$, then we say that the solution $(x_n, y_n)_{n=0}^{\infty}$ eventually becomes the solution of prime period p of (1). For more details about the system of difference equations and their solutions, one may see [6,7]. Actually, to establish the stability of the system of difference equations involves derivatives of a function. However, the system (1) contains absolute value which is not differentiable. Thus, to study the behavior of the solution of (1), one needs to consider several regions of initial conditions and gather the information to obtain the results.

In 2010, Tikjha et al. [8] considered (1) when $a = b = c = 1$ and $d = 0$. They proved that, for a given initial condition $(x_0, y_0) \in \mathbb{R}^2$, the solution of (1) either eventually becomes the solution of prime period 5 or the equilibrium point of (1). For $a = b = 1$, $c = -1$ and $d = 0$, Grove et al. [9] showed that for a given initial condition $(x_0, y_0) \in \mathbb{R}^2$, the solution of (1) is either (from the beginning) the equilibrium point or eventually becomes the solution of prime period 3 of (1). In the doctoral dissertation written by Lapierre [10], he studied some properties of solutions for 81 possible forms of (1) where $a, b, c, d \in \{-1, 0, 1\}$. Kongtan and Tikjha [11] let $a = c = d = 1$ and $b = 2$, $x_0 = 0$ and $y_0 \in \left(\frac{1}{2}, \infty\right)$ and proved that the solution of (1) eventually becomes the solution of prime period 4 of (1). With $a = 1, c = -1, d = 0$ and $b \in (0, \infty)$, Tikjha et al. [12] showed that the solution of (1) either eventually becomes the solution of prime period 3 or the equilibrium point of (1) for all initial conditions $(x_0, y_0) \in \mathbb{R}^2$. In 2017, Tikjha et al. [13] considered the case that $a = c = 1$, b and d in $(-\infty, 0)$ and proved that the solution of (1) eventually becomes the equilibrium point of (1) for all initial conditions $(x_0, y_0) \in \mathbb{R}^2$ within 6 iterations. In the same year, Tikjha [14] wrote a manuscript in Thai where, if $a = c = d = 1, b = 2$, $x_0 = 0$ and $y_0 \in \left(0, \frac{1}{2}\right)$, then the solution of (1) eventually becomes the solution of prime period 4 of (1). Recently, Tikjha and Piasu [15] considered $a = c = d = 1$ and $b = 3$ with initial condition (x_0, y_0) being in a specific region in the first quadrant and showed that the solution of (1) either eventually becomes the equilibrium point or the solution of prime period 4. Tikjha and Lapaierre [16] also studied (1) with $a = b = 1$ and $c = d = -1$ and the initial condition (x_0, y_0) is an element in the closed second or fourth quadrant. They proved that the solution of (1) either eventually becomes the solution of prime period 3 or 4. In addition, Tikjha et al. [17] proved that, if $a = c = d = 1, b \in \{2, 3\}$ and $y_0 = 0$, then under some conditions on x_0 the solution of (1) eventually becomes the solution of prime period 4.

In this paper, we let $a = c = d = 1$ and $b \geq 4$. That is, we consider the system

$$x_{n+1} = |x_n| - y_n - b \text{ and } y_{n+1} = x_n - |y_n| + 1. \tag{2}$$

Let us first establish the lemma about the equilibrium of (2).

Lemma 1. *Let $b \geq 3$.*
(i) *The equilibrium point of (2) is $(-1, -b + 2)$.*
(ii) *Let $(x_n, y_n)_{n=0}^{\infty}$ be the solution of (2). Assume that there exists a positive integer N such that $y_N = -x_N - b + 1 \leq 0$ and $x_N \leq 0$. Then, $(x_n, y_n) = (-1, -b + 2)$ for all $n > N$.*

Proof. (i) By considering four cases of $|x|$ and $|y|$, we can solve the system of equations $x = |x| - y - b$ and $y = x - |y| + 1$ and the only case that gives the solution is when x and y are negative, which is $(x, y) = (-1, -b + 2)$.
(ii) Assume that there exists a positive integer N such that $y_N = -x_N - b + 1 \leq 0$ and $x_N \leq 0$. Then,

$$x_{N+1} = |x_N| - y_N - b = -x_N - (-x_N - b + 1) - b = -1$$
$$y_{N+1} = x_N - |y_N| + 1 = x_N + (-x_N - b + 1) + 1 = -b + 2.$$

Since $b \geq 4$, $-b + 2 < 0$. Thus,

$$x_{N+2} = |x_{N+1}| - y_{N+1} - b = 1 - (-b + 2) - b = -1$$
$$y_{N+2} = x_{N+1} - |y_{N+1}| + 1 = -1 + (-b + 2) + 1 = -b + 2.$$

Therefore, by mathematical induction, we have $(x_n, y_n) = (-1, -b + 2)$ for all $n > N$. □

In Section 2 of this article, a global behavior for the case $b = 4$ is proved. We can conclude that all solutions eventually become the equilibrium point $(-1, -2)$. Local behavior for $b \geq 5$ with large values of $|x_0|$ and $|y_0|$ is studied in Section 3. It is revealed that, locally, all solutions of Equation (2) for $b = 5$ eventually become the equilibrium point. It can be seen that for $b \geq 6$, some solutions have a chance to becomes periodic.

Finally, a conclusion and discussion about our work and our conjecture are provided in the last section.

2. Global Behavior for $b = 4$

In this section, we investigate the global behavior where $b = 4$. The first four lemmas deal with the case when $x_0 = 0$ or $y_0 = 0$.

Lemma 2. *If $x_0 \geq 0$ and $y_0 = 0$, then the solution $(x_n, y_n)_{n=0}^{\infty}$ of (2) eventually becomes the equilibrium point $(-1, -2)$ of (2).*

Proof. Let $x_0 \geq 0$ and $y_0 = 0$.
Case 1 $x_0 \in \left[0, \frac{1}{8}\right)$. We have

$$x_1 = |x_0| - y_0 - 4 = x_0 - 4 < 0, \quad y_1 = x_0 - |y_0| + 1 = x_0 + 1 \geq 0$$
$$x_2 = |x_1| - y_1 - 4 = -2x_0 - 1 < 0, \quad y_2 = x_1 - |y_1| + 1 = -4$$
$$x_3 = |x_2| - y_2 - 4 = 2x_0 + 1 > 0, \quad y_3 = x_2 - |y_2| + 1 = -2x_0 - 4 < 0$$
$$x_4 = |x_3| - y_3 - 4 = 4x_0 + 1 > 0, \quad y_4 = x_3 - |y_3| + 1 = -2$$
$$x_5 = |x_4| - y_4 - 4 = 4x_0 - 1 < 0, \quad y_5 = x_4 - |y_4| + 1 = 4x_0 \geq 0$$
$$x_6 = |x_5| - y_5 - 4 = -8x_0 - 3 < 0, \quad y_6 = x_5 - |y_5| + 1 = 0$$
$$x_7 = |x_6| - y_6 - 4 = 8x_0 - 1 < 0, \quad y_7 = x_6 - |y_6| + 1 = -8x_0 - 2 = -x_7 - 4 + 1 < 0.$$

By Lemma 1, we have $(x_n, y_n) = (-1, -2)$ for all $n \geq 8$.
Case 2 $x_0 \in \left[\frac{1}{8}, \frac{3}{16}\right)$. We have the same $(x_1, y_1) - (x_7, y_7)$ as in Case 1, while, $x_7 \geq 0$ and

$$x_8 = |x_7| - y_7 - 4 = 16x_0 - 3 < 0, \quad y_8 = x_7 - |y_7| + 1 = -2$$
$$x_9 = |x_8| - y_8 - 4 = -16x_0 + 1 < 0, \quad y_9 = x_8 - |y_8| + 1 = -16x_0 - 4 = -x_9 - 4 + 1 < 0.$$

By Lemma 1, we have $(x_n, y_n) = (-1, -2)$ for all $n \geq 10$.
Case 3 $x_0 \in \left[\frac{3}{16}, \frac{1}{4}\right)$. We have the same $(x_1, y_1) - (x_8, y_8)$ as in Case 2, while

$$x_9 = |x_8| - y_8 - 4 = 16x_0 - 5 < 0, \quad y_9 = x_8 - |y_8| + 1 = 16x_0 - 4 < 0$$
$$x_{10} = |x_9| - y_9 - 4 = -32x_0 + 5 < 0, \quad y_{10} = x_9 - |y_9| + 1 = 32x_0 - 8 = -x_{10} - 4 + 1 < 0.$$

By Lemma 1, we have $(x_n, y_n) = (-1, -2)$ for all $n \geq 11$.
Case 4 $x_0 \in \left[\frac{1}{4}, 1\right]$. Then, $x_5 \geq 0$. We have the same $(x_1, y_1) - (x_5, y_5)$ as in Case 1, while

$$x_6 = |x_5| - y_5 - 4 = -5, \qquad y_6 = x_5 - |y_5| + 1 = 0.$$

Direct computation gives $x_{10} = |x_9| - y_9 - 4 = -3 < 0$ and $y_{10} = x_9 - |y_9| + 1 = -x_{10} - 4 + 1 = 0$. By Lemma 1, we have $(x_n, y_n) = (-1, -2)$ for all $n \geq 11$.
Case 5 $x_0 \in (1, 4)$. We have

$$x_1 = |x_0| - y_0 - 4 = x_0 - 4 < 0, \quad y_1 = x_0 - |y_0| + 1 = x_0 + 1 > 0$$
$$x_2 = |x_1| - y_1 - 4 = -2x_0 - 1 < 0, \quad y_2 = x_1 - |y_1| + 1 = -4$$
$$x_3 = |x_2| - y_2 - 4 = 2x_0 + 1 > 0, \quad y_3 = x_2 - |y_2| + 1 = -2x_0 - 4 < 0$$
$$x_4 = |x_3| - y_3 - 4 = 4x_0 + 1 > 0, \quad y_4 = x_3 - |y_3| + 1 = -2$$
$$x_5 = |x_4| - y_4 - 4 = 4x_0 - 1 > 0, \quad y_5 = x_4 - |y_4| + 1 = 4x_0 > 0$$
$$x_6 = |x_5| - y_5 - 4 = -5, \qquad y_6 = x_5 - |y_5| + 1 = 0.$$

Similar to Case 4, we can conclude that $(x_n, y_n) = (-1, -2)$ for all $n \geq 11$.

Case 6 $x_0 \in [4, \infty)$. Then, $x_1 \geq 0$. We have the same (x_1, y_1) as in Case 5, while $x_2 = |x_1| - y_1 - 4 = -9$ and $y_2 = x_1 - |y_1| + 1 = -4$. By direct computation, we can conclude that $(x_n, y_n) = (-1, -2)$ for all $n \geq 11$. □

Lemma 3. *If $x_0 = 0$ and $y_0 \geq 0$, then the solution $(x_n, y_n)_{n=0}^{\infty}$ of (2) eventually becomes the equilibrium point $(-1, -2)$ of (2).*

Proof. By separate cases as in Lemma 2, we can conclude the behavior of the solution in Table 1.

Table 1. Cases for $x_0 = 0$ and $y_0 \geq 0$.

If $y_0 \in A$,	Then $(x_n, y_n) = (-1, -2)$ for All $n \geq N$
$A = \left(\frac{1}{4}, \frac{1}{2}\right); \left[\frac{1}{2}, 1\right]$	$N = 6$
$A = \left[0, \frac{1}{4}\right]; \left(1, \frac{9}{8}\right)$	$N = 7$
$A = \left[\frac{9}{8}, \frac{19}{16}\right)$	$N = 9$
$A = \left[\frac{19}{16}, \frac{5}{4}\right); \left[\frac{5}{4}, \infty\right)$	$N = 10$

□

Lemma 4. *If $x_0 = 0$ and $y_0 < 0$, then the solution $(x_n, y_n)_{n=0}^{\infty}$ of (2) eventually becomes the equilibrium point $(-1, -2)$ of (2).*

Proof. By separate cases as in Lemma 2, we can conclude the behavior of the solution in Table 2.

Table 2. Cases for $x_0 = 0$ and $y_0 < 0$.

If $y_0 \in A$,	Then $(x_n, y_n) = (-1, -2)$ for All $n \geq N$
$A = \{-3\}$	$N = 1$
$A = [-4, -1) \setminus \{-3\}$	$N = 2$
$A = \left(-\frac{9}{2}, -4\right); \left[-1, -\frac{1}{2}\right)$	$N = 4$
$A = \left(-5, -\frac{9}{2}\right]$	$N = 5$
$A = \left(-\frac{21}{4}, -5\right]; \left[-\frac{1}{2}, -\frac{1}{4}\right)$	$N = 6$
$A = \left[-\frac{1}{4}, 0\right)$	$N = 7$
$A = \left(-\frac{43}{8}, -\frac{21}{4}\right]$	$N = 8$
$A = \left(-\infty, -\frac{11}{2}\right]; \left(-\frac{11}{2}, -\frac{43}{8}\right]$	$N = 9$

□

Lemma 5. *If $x_0 < 0$ and $y_0 = 0$, then the solution $(x_n, y_n)_{n=0}^{\infty}$ of (2) eventually becomes the equilibrium point $(-1, -2)$ of (2).*

Proof. By separate cases as in Lemma 2, we can conclude the behavior of the solution in Table 3.

Table 3. Cases for $x_0 < 0$ and $y_0 = 0$.

If $x_0 \in A$,	Then $(x_n, y_n) = (-1, -2)$ for All $n \geq N$
$A = \{-3\}$	$N = 1$
$A = (-4, -1) \setminus \{-3\}$	$N = 2$
$A = \left(-\frac{9}{2}, -4\right]; \left[-1, -\frac{1}{2}\right)$	$N = 4$
$A = \left(-5, -\frac{9}{2}\right]$	$N = 5$
$A = \left(-\frac{21}{4}, -5\right]; \left[-\frac{1}{2}, -\frac{1}{4}\right)$	$N = 6$
$A = \left[-\frac{1}{4}, 0\right)$	$N = 7$
$A = \left(-\frac{43}{8}, -\frac{21}{4}\right]$	$N = 8$
$A = \left(-\infty, -\frac{11}{2}\right]; \left(-\frac{11}{2}, -\frac{43}{8}\right]$	$N = 9$

□

The next four lemmas consider (x_0, y_0) in each quadrant. The only complicated cases are the second and the forth quadrants. For the first and the third quadrants we just show the regions considered without the detail of the proof.

Lemma 6. *If $b = 4$, $x_0 > 0$ and $y_0 > 0$, then the solution $(x_n, y_n)_{n=0}^{\infty}$ of (2) eventually becomes the equilibrium point $(-1, -2)$ of (2).*

Proof. If $(x, y) \in A \subset \mathbb{R}^+ \times \mathbb{R}^+$, then $(x_n, y_n) = (-1, -2)$ for all $n \geq N$, where:

- $A = \{(x, y) | x - y + 1 > 0 \text{ and } -2x + 2y - 1 \geq 0\}$; $\{(x, y) | -2x + 2y - 1 < 0 \text{ and } 4x - 4y + 1 < 0\}$ and $N = 6$.
- $A = \{(x, y) \in \mathbb{R}^+ \times \mathbb{R}^+ | 4x - 4y + 1 \geq 0 \text{ and } 4x - 4y < 0\}$; $\{(x, y) | -8x + 8y - 9 < 0 \text{ and } x - y + 1 < 0\}$ and $N = 7$.
- $A = \{(x, y) | 4x - 4y \geq 0 \text{ and } 8x - 8y - 1 < 0\}$ and $N = 8$.
- $A = \{(x, y) | -16x + 16y - 19 < 0 \text{ and } -8x + 8y - 9 \geq 0\}$ and $N = 9$.
- $A = \{(x, y) | 8x - 8y - 1 \geq 0 \text{ and } 16x - 16y - 3 < 0\}$; $\{(x, y) | -4x + 4y - 5 < 0 \text{ and } -16x + 16y - 19 \geq 0\}$; $\{(x, y) | -4x + 4y - 5 \geq 0\}$ and $N = 10$.
- $A = \{(x, y) | x - y - 4 \geq 0\}$; $\{(x, y) | 16x - 16y - 3 \geq 0 \text{ and } 4x - 4y - 1 < 0\}$; $\{(x, y) | 4x - 4y - 1 \geq 0 \text{ and } x - y - 4 < 0\}$ and $N = 11$. □

Lemma 7. *If $b = 4$, $x_0 < 0$ and $y_0 < 0$, then the solution $(x_n, y_n)_{n=0}^{\infty}$ of (2) eventually becomes the equilibrium point $(-1, -2)$ of (2).*

Proof. If $(x, y) \in A \subset \mathbb{R}^- \times \mathbb{R}^-$, then $(x_n, y_n) = (-1, -2)$ for all $n \geq N$, where:

- $A = \{(-1, -2)\}$ and $N = 0$.
- $A = \{(x, y) | -x - y - 4 < 0 \text{ and } x + y + 1 < 0\} \setminus \{(-1, -2)\}$ and $N = 2$.
- $A = \{(x, y) | -2x - 2y - 9 < 0 \text{ and } -x - y - 4 \geq 0\}$; $\{(x, y) | x + y + 1 \geq 0 \text{ and } 2x + 2y + 1 < 0\}$ and $N = 4$.
- $A = \{(x, y) | -2x - 2y - 10 < 0 \text{ and } -2x - 2y - 9 \geq 0\}$ and $N = 5$.
- $A = \{(x, y) | -4x - 4y - 21 < 0 \text{ and } -2x - 2y - 10 \geq 0\}$; $\{(x, y) | 2x + 2y + 1 \geq 0 \text{ and } 4x + 4y + 1 < 0\}$ and $N = 6$.
- $A = \{(x, y) | 4x + 4y + 1 \geq 0\}$ and $N = 7$.
- $A = \{(x, y) | -8x - 8y - 43 < 0 \text{ and } -4x - 4y - 21 \geq 0\}$ and $N = 8$.
- $A = \{(x, y) | -2x - 2y - 11 \geq 0\}$; $\{(x, y) | -2x - 2y - 11 < 0 \text{ and } -8x - 8y - 43 \geq 0\}$ and $N = 9$. □

Lemma 8. *If $b = 4$, $x_0 < 0$ and $y_0 > 0$, then the solution $(x_n, y_n)_{n=0}^{\infty}$ of (2) eventually becomes the equilibrium point $(-1, -2)$ of (2).*

Proof. Let $x_0 < 0$ and $y_0 > 0$. Then,

$$x_1 = |x_0| - y_0 - 4 = -x_0 - y_0 - 4, \qquad y_1 = x_0 - |y_0| + 1 = x_0 - y_0 + 1.$$

Case 1 $(x_0, y_0) \in \left\{(x,y) | x - y + 1 \geq 0 \text{ and } y < \frac{1}{2}\right\}$. We have $x_1 < -x_0 + y_0 - 1 \leq 0$ and $y_1 \geq 0$ and

$$x_2 = |x_1| - y_1 - 4 = 2y_0 - 1 < 0, y_2 = x_1 - |y_1| + 1 = -2x_0 - 4 < -2(x_0 - y_0 + 1) \leq 0.$$

By using the result of Lemma 7, we obtain that
- if $(x_0, y_0) \in \{(x, y) | 4x - 4y + 1 \geq 0\}$, then

$$x_6 = |x_5| - y_5 - 4 = -8x_0 + 8y_0 - 3 < -2(4x_0 - 4y_0 + 1) \leq 0,$$
$$y_6 = x_5 - |y_5| + 1 = 8x_0 - 8y_0 < -8y_0 < 0 \text{ and } y_6 = -x_6 - 4 + 1.$$

By Lemma 1, we have $(x_n, y_n) = (-1, -2)$ for all $n \geq 7$;
- if $(x_0, y_0) \in \{(x, y) | 2x - 2y + 1 \geq 0 \text{ and } 4x - 4y + 1 < 0\}$, then

$$x_5 = |x_4| - y_4 - 4 = -4x_0 + 4y_0 - 3 < -2(2x_0 - 2y_0 + 1) \leq 0,$$
$$y_5 = x_4 - |y_4| + 1 = 4x_0 - 4y_0 < 0 \text{ and } y_5 = -x_5 - 4 + 1.$$

By Lemma 1, we have $(x_n, y_n) = (-1, -2)$ for all $n \geq 6$;
- if $(x_0, y_0) \in \left\{(x, y) | x - y + 1 \geq 0, 2x - 2y + 1 < 0 \text{ and } y < \frac{1}{2}\right\}$, then

$$x_3 = |x_2| - y_2 - 4 = 2x_0 - 2y_0 + 1 < 0,$$
$$y_3 = x_2 - |y_2| + 1 = -2x_0 + 2y_0 - 4 < -2(x_0 - y_0 + 1) \leq 0 \text{ and } y_3 = -x_3 - 4 + 1.$$

By Lemma 1, we have $(x_n, y_n) = (-1, -2)$ for all $n \geq 4$.

Case 2 $(x_0, y_0) \in \left\{(x,y)\Big| x - y + 1 \geq 0, 2x + 2y - 1 < 0 \text{ and } y \geq \frac{1}{2}\right\}$. We have the same (x_2, y_2) as in Case 1, while

$$x_3 = |x_2| - y_2 - 4 = 2x_0 + 2y_0 - 1 < 0,$$
$$y_3 = x_2 - |y_2| + 1 = -2x_0 + 2y_0 - 4 < -2(x_0 - y_0 + 1) \leq 0.$$

By using the result of Lemma 7, we obtain that

$$x_4 = |x_3| - y_3 - 4 = -4y_0 + 1 < -2y_0 + 1 \leq 0,$$
$$y_4 = x_3 - |y_3| + 1 = 4y_0 - 4 < -4(x_0 - y_0 + 1) \leq 0 \text{ and } y_4 = -x_4 - 4 + 1.$$

By Lemma 1, we have $(x_n, y_n) = (-1, -2)$ for all $n \geq 5$.

Case 3 $(x_0, y_0) \in \{(x, y) | x - y + 1 \geq 0 \text{ and } 2x + 2y - 1 \geq 0\}$. We have the same (x_2, y_2) and (x_3, y_3) as in Case 2, while $x_3 \geq 0$ and

$$x_4 = |x_3| - y_3 - 4 = 4x_0 - 1 < 0, \qquad y_4 = x_3 - |y_3| + 1 = 4y_0 - 4 \leq 0.$$

By using the result of Lemma 7, we obtain that

$$x_5 = |x_4| - y_4 - 4 = -4x_0 - 4y_0 + 1 < -2(2x_0 + 2y_0 - 1) \leq 0$$
$$y_5 = x_4 - |y_4| + 1 = 4x_0 + 4y_0 - 4 < -4x_0 + 4y_0 - 4 \leq 0 \text{ and } y_5 = -x_5 - 4 + 1.$$

By Lemma 1, we have $(x_n, y_n) = (-1, -2)$ for all $n \geq 6$.

Case 4 $(x_0, y_0) \in \{(x, y) | -x - y - 4 < 0 \text{ and } x - y + 1 < 0\}$. We have $x_1 < 0$ and $y_1 < 0$. By using the result of Lemma 7, we obtain that

- if $y_0 < \frac{1}{2}$, then $x_2 = |x_1| - y_1 - 4 = 2y_0 - 1 < 0$, $y_2 = x_1 - |y_1| + 1 = -2y_0 - 2 < 0$ and $y_2 = -x_2 - 4 + 1$. By Lemma 1, we have $(x_n, y_n) = (-1, -2)$ for all $n \geq 3$;
- if $\frac{1}{2} \leq y_0 < \frac{3}{4}$, then

$$x_4 = |x_3| - y_3 - 4 = -4y_0 + 1 < -2(2y_0 - 1) \leq 0,$$
$$y_4 = x_3 - |y_3| + 1 = 4y_0 - 4 < 4y_0 - 3 < 0 \text{ and } y_4 = -x_4 - 4 + 1.$$

By Lemma 1, we have $(x_n, y_n) = (-1, -2)$ for all $n \geq 5$;
- if $\frac{3}{4} \leq y_0 < 1$, then

$$x_5 = |x_4| - y_4 - 4 = -8y_0 + 5 < -2(4y_0 - 3) \leq 0,$$
$$y_5 = x_4 - |y_4| + 1 = 8y_0 - 8 < 0 \text{ and } y_5 = -x_5 - 4 + 1.$$

By Lemma 1, we have $(x_n, y_n) = (-1, -2)$ for all $n \geq 6$;
- If $1 \leq y_0 < \frac{9}{8}$, then

$$x_6 = |x_5| - y_5 - 4 = 8y_0 - 9 < 0,$$
$$y_6 = x_5 - |y_5| + 1 = -8y_0 + 6 < -8(y_0 - 1) \leq 0 \text{ and } y_6 = -x_6 - 4 + 1.$$

By Lemma 1, we have $(x_n, y_n) = (-1, -2)$ for all $n \geq 7$;
- If $\frac{9}{8} \leq y_0 < \frac{19}{16}$, then

$$x_8 = |x_7| - y_7 - 4 = -16y_0 + 17 < -2(8y_0 - 9) \leq 0,$$
$$y_8 = x_7 - |y_7| + 1 = 16y_0 - 20 < 16y_0 - 19 < 0 \text{ and } y_8 = -x_8 - 4 + 1.$$

By Lemma 1, we have $(x_n, y_n) = (-1, -2)$ for all $n \geq 9$;
- If $\frac{19}{16} \leq y_0 < \frac{5}{4}$, then

$$x_9 = |x_8| - y_8 - 4 = -32y_0 + 37 < -2(16y_0 - 19) \leq 0,$$
$$y_9 = x_8 - |y_8| + 1 = 32y_0 - 40 < 0 \text{ and } y_9 = -x_9 - 4 + 1.$$

By Lemma 1, we have $(x_n, y_n) = (-1, -2)$ for all $n \geq 10$;
- If $y_0 \geq \frac{5}{4}$, then

$$x_5 = |x_4| - y_4 - 4 = -5, \qquad y_5 = x_4 - |y_4| + 1 = 0.$$

Similar to the proof of Case 4 of Lemma 2, we can conclude that $(x_n, y_n) = (-1, -2)$ for all $n \geq 10$.

Case 5 $(x_0, y_0) \in \left\{ (x, y) \mid -x - y - 4 \geq 0 \text{ and } x > -\frac{9}{2} \right\}$. We have $x_1 > 0$ and $y_1 < -(-x_0 - y_0 - 4) \leq 0$. Then,

$$x_2 = |x_1| - y_1 - 4 = -2x_0 - 9 < 0, \qquad y_2 = x_1 - |y_1| + 1 = -2y_0 - 2 < 0.$$

By using the result of Lemma 7, we obtain that

$$x_3 = |x_2| - y_2 - 4 = 2x_0 + 2y_0 + 7 < 2x_0 + 2y_0 + 8 \leq 0,$$
$$y_3 = x_2 - |y_2| + 1 = -2x_0 - 2y_0 - 10 < -2x_0 - 9 < 0 \text{ and } y_3 = -x_3 - 4 + 1.$$

By Lemma 1, we have $(x_n, y_n) = (-1, -2)$ for all $n \geq 4$.

Case 6 $(x_0, y_0) \in \left\{ (x, y) \mid -x - y - 4 \geq 0, -2x + 2y - 11 < 0, -2x - 2y - 10 < 0 \text{ and } -5 < x \leq -\frac{9}{2} \right\}$. We have the same (x_2, y_2) as in Case 5, while $x_2 \geq 0$ and

$$x_3 = |x_2| - y_2 - 4 = -2x_0 + 2y_0 - 11 < 0, \quad y_3 = x_2 - |y_2| + 1 = -2x_0 - 2y_0 - 10 < 0.$$

By using the result of Lemma 7, we obtain that
- if $-5 < x_0 \le -\frac{9}{2}$, then

$$x_4 = |x_3| - y_3 - 4 = 4x_0 + 17 < 4x_0 + 18 = 2(2x_0 + 9) \le 0,$$
$$y_4 = x_3 - |y_3| + 1 = -4x_0 - 20 < 0 \text{ and } y_4 = -x_4 - 4 + 1.$$

By Lemma 1, we have $(x_n, y_n) = (-1, -2)$ for all $n \ge 5$;
- if $-\frac{41}{8} < x_0 \le -5$, then

$$x_6 = |x_5| - y_5 - 4 = -8x_0 - 41 < 0,$$
$$y_6 = x_5 - |y_5| + 1 = 8x_0 + 38 < 8x_0 + 40 \le 0 \text{ and } y_6 = -x_6 - 4 + 1.$$

By Lemma 1, we have $(x_n, y_n) = (-1, -2)$ for all $n \ge 7$;
- if $-\frac{83}{16} < x_0 \le -\frac{41}{8}$, then

$$x_8 = |x_7| - y_7 - 4 = 16x_0 + 81 < 16x_0 + 82 = 2(8x_0 + 41) \le 0,$$
$$y_8 = x_7 - |y_7| + 1 = -16x_0 - 84 < -16x_0 - 83 < 0 \text{ and } y_8 = -x_8 - 4 + 1.$$

By Lemma 1, we have $(x_n, y_n) = (-1, -2)$ for all $n \ge 9$;
- if $x_0 \le -\frac{83}{16}$, then

$$x_9 = |x_8| - y_8 - 4 = 32x_0 + 165 < 32x_0 + 166 = 2(16x_0 + 83) \le 0,$$
$$y_9 = x_8 - |y_8| + 1 = -32x_0 - 168 = 8(-2x_0 + 2y_0 - 11) + 8(-2x_0 - 2y_0 - 10) < 0$$
$$\text{and } y_9 = -x_9 - 4 + 1.$$

By Lemma 1, we have $(x_n, y_n) = (-1, -2)$ for all $n \ge 10$.

Case 7 $(x_0, y_0) \in \{(x,y)| -2x + 2y - 11 < 0, \text{ and } -2x - 2y - 10 \ge 0\}$. We have the same (x_2, y_2) and (x_3, y_3) as in Case 6, while $y_3 \ge 0$ and

$$x_4 = |x_3| - y_3 - 4 = 4x_0 + 17 < 4x_0 + 4y_0 + 20 \le 0, y_4 = x_3 - |y_3| + 1 = 4y_0 > 0$$
$$x_5 = |x_4| - y_4 - 4 = -4x_0 - 4y_0 - 21 < 0,$$
$$y_5 = x_4 - |y_4| + 1 = 4x_0 - 4y_0 + 18 < 4x_0 + 4y_0 + 18$$
$$= -2(-2x_0 - 2y_0 - 9) < -2(-2x_0 - 2y_0 - 10) \le 0.$$

By using the result of Lemma 7, we obtain that
- if $y_0 < \frac{1}{8}$, then

$$x_6 = |x_5| - y_5 - 4 = 8y_0 - 1 < 0,$$
$$y_6 = x_5 - |y_5| + 1 = -8y_0 - 2 < 0 \text{ and } y_6 = -x_6 - 4 + 1.$$

By Lemma 1, we have $(x_n, y_n) = (-1, -2)$ for all $n \ge 7$;
- if $\frac{1}{8} \le y_0 < \frac{3}{16}$, then

$$x_8 = |x_7| - y_7 - 4 = -16y_0 + 1 < -16y_0 + 2 = -2(8y_0 - 1) \le 0,$$
$$y_8 = x_7 - |y_7| + 1 = 16y_0 - 4 < 16y_0 - 3 < 0 \text{ and } y_8 = -x_8 - 4 + 1.$$

By Lemma 1, we have $(x_n, y_n) = (-1, -2)$ for all $n \ge 9$;
- if $y_0 \ge \frac{3}{16}$, then

$$x_9 = |x_7| - y_7 - 4 = -32y_0 + 5 < -32y_0 + 6 \le 0,$$
$$y_9 = x_7 - |y_7| + 1 = 32y_0 - 8 = 2y_8 < 0 \text{ and } y_9 = -x_9 - 4 + 1.$$

By Lemma 1, we have $(x_n, y_n) = (-1, -2)$ for all $n \ge 10$.

Case 8 $(x_0, y_0) \in \{(x,y)| -2x + 2y - 11 \geq 0, \text{ and } -2x - 2y - 10 \geq 0\}$. We have the same (x_2, y_2) and (x_3, y_3) as in Case 6, while $x_3 \geq 0$ and $y_3 \geq 0$. By using the results of Lemmas 2, 3 and 7, we obtain that

- if $y_0 \leq \frac{1}{8}$, then

$$x_8 = |x_7| - y_7 - 4 = 16y_0 - 3 < 16y_0 - 2 \leq 0,$$
$$y_8 = x_7 - |y_7| + 1 = -16y_0 < 0 \text{ and } y_8 = -x_8 - 4 + 1.$$

  By Lemma 1, we have $(x_n, y_n) = (-1, -2)$ for all $n \geq 9$;
- if $\frac{1}{8} < y_0 < \frac{3}{16}$, then

$$x_8 = |x_7| - y_7 - 4 = -16y_0 + 1 < -16y_0 + 2 < 0,$$
$$y_8 = x_7 - |y_7| + 1 = 16y_0 - 4 < 16y_0 - 3 < 0 \text{ and } y_8 = -x_8 - 4 + 1.$$

  By Lemma 1, we have $(x_n, y_n) = (-1, -2)$ for all $n \geq 9$.
- if $\frac{3}{16} \leq y_0 < \frac{4}{16}$, then

$$x_9 = |x_8| - y_8 - 4 = -32y_0 + 5 < -32y_0 + 6 \leq 0,$$
$$y_9 = x_8 - |y_8| + 1 = 32y_0 - 8 < 0 \text{ and } y_9 = -x_9 - 4 + 1.$$

  By Lemma 1, we have $(x_n, y_n) = (-1, -2)$ for all $n \geq 10$;
- if $\frac{4}{16} \leq y_0 < \frac{9}{32}$, then

$$x_{10} = |x_9| - y_9 - 4 = 32y_0 - 9 < 0,$$
$$y_{10} = x_9 - |y_9| + 1 = -32y_0 + 6 < -2(16y_0 - 4) \leq 0 \text{ and } y_{10} = -x_{10} - 4 + 1.$$

  By Lemma 1, we have $(x_n, y_n) = (-1, -2)$ for all $n \geq 11$;
- if $\frac{9}{32} \leq y_0 < \frac{19}{64}$, then

$$x_{12} = |x_{11}| - y_{11} - 4 = -64y_0 + 17 < -2(32y_0 - 9) \leq 0,$$
$$y_{12} = x_{11} - |y_{11}| + 1 = 64y_0 - 20 < 64y_0 - 19 < 0 \text{ and } y_{12} = -x_{12} - 4 + 1.$$

  By Lemma 1, we have $(x_n, y_n) = (-1, -2)$ for all $n \geq 13$;
- if $\frac{19}{64} \leq y_0 < \frac{5}{16}$, then

$$x_{13} = |x_{12}| - y_{12} - 4 = -128y_0 + 37 < -2(64y_0 - 19) \leq 0,$$
$$y_{13} = x_{12} - |y_{12}| + 1 = 128y_0 - 40 < 0 \text{ and } y_{13} = -x_{13} - 4 + 1.$$

  By Lemma 1, we have $(x_n, y_n) = (-1, -2)$ for all $n \geq 14$.
- if $\frac{5}{16} \leq y_0 < \frac{5}{4}$, then

$$x_9 = |x_8| - y_8 - 4 = -5, \qquad y_9 = x_8 - |y_8| + 1 = 0.$$

  Similar to the proof of Case 4 of Lemma 2, we can conclude that $(x_n, y_n) = (-1, -2)$ for all $n \geq 14$;
- if $y_0 \geq \frac{5}{4}$, then

$$x_5 = |x_4| - y_4 - 4 = -9, \qquad y_5 = x_4 - |y_4| + 1 = -4.$$

  Similar to the proof of Case 6 of Lemma 2, we can conclude that $(x_n, y_n) = (-1, -2)$ for all $n \geq 14$.

Case 9 $(x_0, y_0) \in \{(x, y) | -x - y - 4 \geq 0, -2x + 2y - 11 \geq 0 \text{ and } x > -5\}$. $1 - y_0 = 5 - y_0 - 4 > -x_0 - y_0 - 4 \geq 0$. Then, $y_0 < 1 < \frac{5}{4}$. We have the same (x_2, y_2) and (x_3, y_3) as in Case 6, while $x_3 \geq 0$, $y_3 < 0$ and

$$x_4 = |x_3| - y_3 - 4 = 4y_0 - 5 < 0, \qquad y_4 = x_3 - |y_3| + 1 = -4x_0 - 20 < 0.$$

By using the result of Lemma 7, we obtain that

$$x_5 = |x_4| - y_4 - 4 = 4x_0 - 4y_0 + 21 < 4x_0 - 4y_0 + 22 \leq 0,$$
$$y_5 = x_4 - |y_4| + 1 = -4x_0 + 4y_0 - 24 < 4y_0 - 24 < 4 - 24 < 0 \text{ and } y_5 = -x_5 - 4 + 1.$$

By Lemma 1, we have $(x_n, y_n) = (-1, -2)$ for all $n \geq 6$.

Case 10 $(x_0, y_0) \in \{(x, y) | -x - y - 4 \geq 0, -2x + 2y - 11 \geq 0, -2x - 2y - 10 < 0, x \leq -5 \text{ and } y \leq \frac{5}{4}\}$. We have the same (x_2, y_2)-(x_4, y_4) as in Case 9, while $y_4 \geq 0$ and

$$x_5 = |x_4| - y_4 - 4 = 4x_0 - 4y_0 + 21 < 4x_0 - 4y_0 + 22 \leq 0,$$
$$y_5 = x_4 - |y_4| + 1 = 4x_0 + 4y_0 + 16 = -4(-x_0 - y_0 - 4) \leq 0.$$

By using the result of Lemma 7, we obtain that

- if $-\frac{41}{8} < x_0 \leq -5$, then

$$x_6 = |x_5| - y_5 - 4 = -8x_0 - 41 < 0,$$
$$y_6 = x_5 - |y_5| + 1 = 8x_0 + 38 < 8x_0 + 40 \leq 0 \text{ and } y_6 = -x_6 - 4 + 1.$$

By Lemma 1, we have $(x_n, y_n) = (-1, -2)$ for all $n \geq 7$;

- if $-\frac{83}{16} < x_0 \leq -\frac{41}{8}$, then

$$x_8 = |x_7| - y_7 - 4 = 16x_0 + 81 < 16x_0 + 82 = 2(8x_0 + 41) \leq 0,$$
$$y_8 = x_7 - |y_7| + 1 = -16x_0 - 84 < -16x_0 - 83 < 0 \text{ and } y_8 = -x_8 - 4 + 1.$$

By Lemma 1, we have $(x_n, y_n) = (-1, -2)$ for all $n \geq 9$;

- if $-\frac{84}{16} < x \leq -\frac{83}{16}$, then

$$x_9 = |x_8| - y_8 - 4 = 32x_0 + 165 < 32x_0 + 166 \leq 0,$$
$$y_9 = x_8 - |y_8| + 1 = -32x_0 - 168 = -2(16x_0 + 84) < 0 \text{ and } y_9 = -x_9 - 4 + 1.$$

By Lemma 1, we have $(x_n, y_n) = (-1, -2)$ for all $n \geq 10$;

- if $-\frac{85}{16} \leq x_0 < -\frac{339}{64}$, then

$$x_{13} = |x_{12}| - y_{12} - 4 = 128x_0 + 667 < 2(64x_0 + 339) < 0,$$
$$y_{13} = x_{12} - |y_{12}| + 1 = -128x_0 - 680 \leq 0 \text{ and } y_{13} = -x_{13} - 4 + 1.$$

By Lemma 1, we have $(x_n, y_n) = (-1, -2)$ for all $n \geq 14$;

- if $-\frac{339}{64} \leq x_0 < -\frac{169}{32}$, then

$$x_{12} = |x_{11}| - y_{11} - 4 = 64x_0 + 337 < 2(32x_0 + 169) \leq 0,$$
$$y_{12} = x_{11} - |y_{11}| + 1 = -64x_0 - 340 < 0 \text{ and } y_{12} = -x_{12} - 4 + 1.$$

By Lemma 1, we have $(x_n, y_n) = (-1, -2)$ for all $n \geq 13$;

- if $-\frac{169}{32} \leq x_0 \leq -\frac{84}{16}$, then

$$x_{10} = |x_9| - y_9 - 4 = -32x_0 - 169 \leq 0,$$
$$y_{10} = x_9 - |y_9| + 1 = 32x_0 + 166 < 2(16x_0 + 84) \leq 0 \text{ and } y_{10} = -x_{10} - 4 + 1.$$

By Lemma 1, we have $(x_n, y_n) = (-1, -2)$ for all $n \geq 11$;
- if $x_0 \leq -\frac{85}{16}$, then

$$x_9 = |x_8| - y_8 - 4 = -5, \qquad y_9 = x_8 - |y_8| + 1 = 0.$$

Similar to the proof of Case 4 of Lemma 2, we can conclude that $(x_n, y_n) = (-1, -2)$ for all $n \geq 14$.

Case 11 $(x_0, y_0) \in \left\{(x, y) \mid -x - y - 4 \geq 0, -2x - 2y - 10 < 0 \text{ and } y \geq \frac{5}{4}\right\}$. We have the same (x_2, y_2)-(x_4, y_4) as in Case 9. Since $y_0 \geq \frac{5}{4}$, $x_4 \geq 0$ and $-x_0 - \frac{5}{4} - 4 \geq -x_0 - y_0 - 4 \geq 0$. Then, $x_0 \leq -\frac{21}{4} < -5$ and $y_4 = -4(x_0 + 5) > 0$. By using the result of Lemma 6, we obtain that

- if $(x_0, y_0) \in \left\{(x, y) \mid -2x - 2y - 10 < 0, -16x - 16y - 65 \geq 0 \text{ and } y \geq \frac{5}{4}\right\}$, then

$$x_9 = |x_8| - y_8 - 4 = -5, \qquad y_9 = x_8 - |y_8| + 1 = 0.$$

Similar to the proof of Case 4 of Lemma 2, we can conclude that $(x_n, y_n) = (-1, -2)$ for all $n \geq 14$;

- if $(x_0, y_0) \in \left\{(x, y) \mid -x - y - 4 \geq 0, -16x - 16y - 65 < 0 \text{ and } y \geq \frac{5}{4}\right\}$, then

$$x_9 = |x_8| - y_8 - 4 = 32x_0 + 32y_0 + 124 < 32x_0 + 32y_0 + 128 \leq 0, y_9 = x_8 - |y_8| + 1 = 0.$$

By using the result of Lemma 5, we have $(x_n, y_n) = (-1, -2)$ for all $n \geq 11$.

Figure 1 shows region of each case presented in the proof of this lemma.

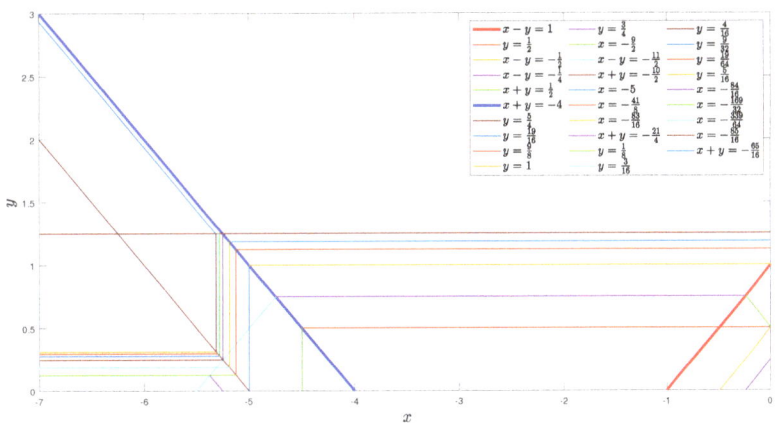

Figure 1. Regions of each case considered when $x_0 < 0$ and $y_0 > 0$. □

Lemma 9. *If $b = 4$, $x_0 > 0$ and $y_0 < 0$, then the solution $(x_n, y_n)_{n=0}^{\infty}$ of (2) eventually becomes the equilibrium point $(-1, -2)$ of (2).*

Proof. Let $x_0 > 0$ and $y_0 < 0$. Then,

$$x_1 = |x_0| - y_0 - 4 = x_0 - y_0 - 4, \qquad y_1 = x_0 - |y_0| + 1 = x_0 + y_0 + 1.$$

Case 1 $(x_0, y_0) \in \{(x, y) \mid x - y - 4 < 0 \text{ and } x + y + 1 \geq 0\}$. We have $x_1 < 0$ and $y_1 \geq 0$. By using the results of Lemmas 5 and 8, we have that

- if $(x_0, y_0) \in \{(x,y) | x + y + 1 \geq 0, 2x + 2y + 1 < 0 \text{ and } y > -2\}$, then

  $x_3 = |x_2| - y_2 - 4 = 2x_0 + 2y_0 + 1 < 0,$
  $y_3 = x_2 - |y_2| + 1 = -2x_0 - 2y_0 - 4 < -2(x_0 + y_0 + 1) \leq 0 \text{ and } y_3 = -x_3 - 4 + 1.$

  By Lemma 1, we have $(x_n, y_n) = (-1, -2)$ for all $n \geq 4$;

- if $(x_0, y_0) \in \{(x,y) | 2x + 2y + 1 \geq 0, 4x + 4y + 1 < 0 \text{ and } y \geq -2\}$, then

  $x_5 = |x_4| - y_4 - 4 = -4x_0 - 4y_0 - 3 < -2(2x_0 + 2y_0 + 1) \leq 0,$
  $y_5 = x_4 - |y_4| + 1 = 4x_0 + 4y_0 < 4x_0 + 4y_0 + 1 < 0 \text{ and } y_5 = -x_5 - 4 + 1.$

  By Lemma 1, we have $(x_n, y_n) = (-1, -2)$ for all $n \geq 6$;

- if $(x_0, y_0) \in \{(x,y) | 4x + 4y + 1 \geq 0, 4x + 4y < 0 \text{ and } y \geq -2\}$, then

  $x_6 = |x_5| - y_5 - 4 = -8x_0 - 8y_0 - 3 < -2(4x_0 + 4y_0 + 1) \leq 0,$
  $y_6 = x_5 - |y_5| + 1 = 8x_0 + 8y_0 < 0 \text{ and } y_6 = -x_6 - 4 + 1.$

  By Lemma 1, we have $(x_n, y_n) = (-1, -2)$ for all $n \geq 7$;

- if $(x_0, y_0) \in \{(x,y) | 4x + 4y \geq 0 \text{ and } 8x + 8y - 1 < 0\}$, then

  $x_7 = |x_6| - y_6 - 4 = 8x_0 + 8y_0 - 1 < 0,$
  $y_7 = x_6 - |y_6| + 1 = -8x_0 - 8y_0 - 2 < -2(4x_0 + 4y_0) \leq 0 \text{ and } y_7 = -x_7 - 4 + 1.$

  By Lemma 1, we have $(x_n, y_n) = (-1, -2)$ for all $n \geq 8$;

- if $(x_0, y_0) \in \{(x,y) | 8x + 8y - 1 \geq 0 \text{ and } 16x + 16y - 3 < 0\}$, then

  $x_9 = |x_8| - y_8 - 4 = -16x_0 - 16y_0 + 1 < -2(8x_0 + 8y_0 - 1) \leq 0,$
  $y_9 = x_8 - |y_8| + 1 = 16x_0 + 16y_0 - 4 < 16x_0 + 16y_0 - 3 < 0 \text{ and } y_9 = -x_9 - 4 + 1.$

  By Lemma 1, we have $(x_n, y_n) = (-1, -2)$ for all $n \geq 10$;

- if $(x_0, y_0) \in \{(x,y) | 16x + 16y - 3 \geq 0 \text{ and } 4x + 4y - 1 < 0\}$, then

  $x_{10} = |x_9| - y_9 - 4 = -32x_0 - 32y_0 + 5 < -2(16x_0 + 16y_0 - 3) \leq 0,$
  $y_{10} = x_9 - |y_9| + 1 = 32x_0 + 32y_0 - 8 < 0 \text{ and } y_{10} = -x_{10} - 4 + 1.$

  By Lemma 1, we have $(x_n, y_n) = (-1, -2)$ for all $n \geq 11$;

- if $(x_0, y_0) \in \{(x,y) | 4x + 4y - 1 \geq 0 \text{ and } x - y - 4 < 0\}$, then

  $x_6 = |x_5| - y_5 - 4 = -5, \qquad y_6 = x_5 - |y_5| + 1 = 0.$

  Similar to the proof of Case 4 of Lemma 2, we can conclude that $(x_n, y_n) = (-1, -2)$ for all $n \geq 11$;

- if $(x_0, y_0) \in \left\{(x,y) \middle| x - y - 4 < 0, x + y + 1 \geq 0 \text{ and } y \leq -\frac{19}{8}\right\}$, then

  $x_7 = |x_6| - y_6 - 4 = 16y_0 + 37 < 0,$
  $y_7 = x_6 - |y_6| + 1 = -16y_0 - 40 = -8(x_0 + y_0 + 1) + 8(x_0 - y_0 - 4) < 0$
  and $y_7 = -x_7 - 4 + 1.$

  By Lemma 1, we have $(x_n, y_n) = (-1, -2)$ for all $n \geq 8$;

- if $(x_0, y_0) \in \left\{(x,y) \middle| x - y - 4 < 0, x + y + 1 \geq 0 \text{ and } -\frac{19}{8} < y \leq -\frac{9}{4}\right\}$, then

  $x_6 = |x_5| - y_5 - 4 = 8y_0 + 17 < 2(4y_0 + 9) \leq 0,$
  $y_6 = x_5 - |y_5| + 1 = -8y_0 - 20 = -4(x_0 + y_0 + 1) + 4(x_0 - y_0 - 4) < 0$
  and $y_6 = -x_6 - 4 + 1.$

By Lemma 1, we have $(x_n, y_n) = (-1, -2)$ for all $n \geq 7$;

- if $(x_0, y_0) \in \left\{(x,y) \big| x+y+1 \geq 0, 2x+2y+1 < 0 \text{ and } -\frac{9}{4} < y \leq -2\right\}$, then

$$x_4 = |x_3| - y_3 - 4 = -4y_0 - 9 < 0,$$
$$y_4 = x_3 - |y_3| + 1 = 4y_0 + 6 < 4(y_0 + 2) \leq 0 \text{ and } y_4 = -x_4 - 4 + 1.$$

By Lemma 1, we have $(x_n, y_n) = (-1, -2)$ for all $n \geq 5$;

- if $(x_0, y_0) \in \left\{(x,y) \big| 2x+2y+1 \geq 0, x-y-4 < 0, x < \frac{7}{4} \text{ and } y \leq -2\right\}$, then

$$x_5 = |x_4| - y_4 - 4 = -4x_0 - 4y_0 - 3 < -2(2x_0 + 2y_0 + 1) \leq 0,$$
$$y_5 = x_4 - |y_4| + 1 = 4x_0 + 4y_0 \leq -1 < 0 \text{ and } y_5 = -x_5 - 4 + 1.$$

Since $x_0 < \frac{7}{4}$ and $y_0 \leq -2$, $y_5 = 4x_0 + 4y_0 < 7 - 8 < 0$. By Lemma 1, we have $(x_n, y_n) = (-1, -2)$ for all $n \geq 6$;

- if $(x_0, y_0) \in \left\{(x,y) \big| 2x+2y+1 \geq 0, x-y-4 < 0, x \geq \frac{7}{4} \text{ and } y \leq -2\right\}$, then

$$x_6 = |x_5| - y_5 - 4 = -8x_0 + 13 < -8x_0 + 14 = -2(4x_0 - 7) \leq 0,$$
$$y_6 = x_5 - |y_5| + 1 = 8x_0 - 16 \text{ and } y_6 = -x_6 - 4 + 1.$$

Since $x_0 - y_0 - 4 < 0$ and $y_0 \leq -2$, $x_0 < y_0 + 4 \leq 2$. Then, $y_6 = 8(x_0 - 2) < 0$. By Lemma 1, we have $(x_n, y_n) = (-1, -2)$ for all $n \geq 7$.

Figure 2 shows regions considered in the proof of Case 1 of this lemma.

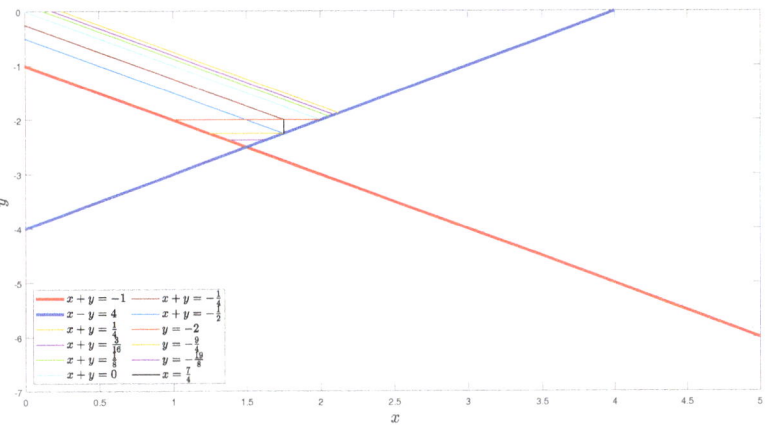

Figure 2. Regions considered in the proof of Case 1.

Case 2 $(x_0, y_0) \in \{(x,y) | x - y - 4 < 0 \text{ and } x + y + 1 < 0\}$. We have $x_1 < 0$ and $y_1 < 0$. By using the result of Lemma 7, we have that

- if $x_0 < 1$, then

$$x_2 = |x_1| - y_1 - 4 = -2x_0 - 1 < 0, \qquad y_2 = x_1 - |y_1| + 1 = 2x_0 - 2 < 0$$
$$\text{and } y_2 = -x_2 - 4 + 1.$$

By Lemma 1, we have $(x_n, y_n) = (-1, -2)$ for all $n \geq 3$;

- if $1 \leq x_0 < \frac{5}{4}$, then

$$x_4 = |x_3| - y_3 - 4 = 4x_0 - 5 < 0, \qquad y_4 = x_3 - |y_3| + 1 = -4x_0 + 2 \leq 0$$
$$\text{and } y_4 = -x_4 - 4 + 1.$$

By Lemma 1, we have $(x_n, y_n) = (-1, -2)$ for all $n \geq 5$;
- if $\frac{5}{4} \leq x_0 < \frac{11}{8}$, then

$$x_6 = |x_5| - y_5 - 4 = -8x_0 + 9 < -8x_0 + 10 = -2(4x_0 - 5) \leq 0,$$
$$y_6 = x_5 - |y_5| + 1 = 8x_0 - 12 < 8x_0 - 11 < 0 \text{ and } y_6 = -x_6 - 4 + 1.$$

By Lemma 1, we have $(x_n, y_n) = (-1, -2)$ for all $n \geq 7$;
- if $x_0 \geq \frac{11}{8}$, then

$$x_7 = |x_6| - y_6 - 4 = -16x_0 + 21 < -2(8x_0 - 11) \leq 0,$$
$$y_7 = x_6 - |y_6| + 1 = 16x_0 - 24 = 2y_6 < 0 \text{ and } y_7 = -x_7 - 4 + 1.$$

By Lemma 1, we have $(x_n, y_n) = (-1, -2)$ for all $n \geq 8$.

Figure 3 shows regions considered in the proof of Case 2 of this lemma.

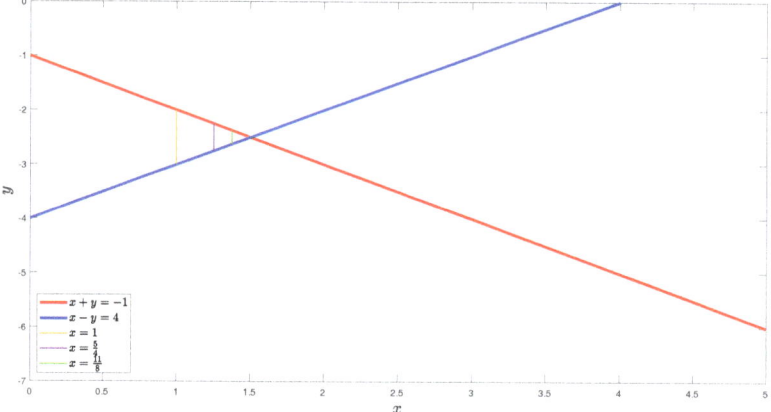

Figure 3. Regions considered in the proof of Case 2.

Case 3 $(x_0, y_0) \in \{(x, y) | x - y - 4 \geq 0 \text{ and } x + y + 1 < 0\}$. We have $x_1 \geq 0$ and $y_1 < 0$.

Case 3.1 $(x_0, y_0) \in \left\{ (x, y) \big| x - y - 4 \geq 0, x < 1 \text{ and } y > -\frac{9}{2} \right\}$. Then,

$$x_2 = |x_1| - y_2 - 4 = -2y_0 - 9 < 0, \qquad y_2 = x_1 - |y_1| + 1 = 2x_0 - 2 < 0.$$

By using the result of Lemma 7, we have that
- if $(x_0, y_0) \in \left\{ (x, y) \big| x - y - 4 \geq 0, 2x - 2y - 10 < 0, x < 1 \text{ and } y > -\frac{9}{2} \right\}$, then

$$x_3 = |x_2| - y_2 - 4 = -2x_0 + 2y_0 + 7 < -2(x_0 - y_0 - 4) \leq 0,$$
$$y_3 = x_2 - |y_2| + 1 = 2x_0 - 2y_0 - 10 < 0 \text{ and } y_3 = -x_3 - 4 + 1.$$

By Lemma 1, we have $(x_n, y_n) = (-1, -2)$ for all $n \geq 4$;
- if $(x_0, y_0) \in \left\{ (x, y) \big| 2x - 2y - 10 \geq 0, 4x - 4y - 21 < 0, x < 1 \text{ and } y > -\frac{9}{2} \right\}$, then

$$x_5 = |x_4| - y_4 - 4 = 4x_0 - 4y_0 - 21 < 0,$$
$$y_5 = x_4 - |y_4| + 1 = -4x_0 + 4y_0 + 18 \leq 0 \text{ and } y_5 = -x_5 - 4 + 1.$$

By Lemma 1, we have $(x_n, y_n) = (-1, -2)$ for all $n \geq 6$;

- if $(x_0, y_0) \in \left\{(x,y) \middle| 4x - 4y - 21 \geq 0, 8x - 8y - 43 < 0, x < 1 \text{ and } y > -\frac{9}{2}\right\}$, then

    $x_7 = |x_6| - y_6 - 4 = -8x_0 + 8y_0 + 41 < -2(4x_0 - 4y_0 - 21) \leq 0,$
    $y_7 = x_6 - |y_6| + 1 = 8x_0 - 8y_0 - 44 < 8x_0 - 8y_0 - 43 < 0 \text{ and } y_7 = -x_7 - 4 + 1.$

    By Lemma 1, we have $(x_n, y_n) = (-1, -2)$ for all $n \geq 8$;

- if $(x_0, y_0) \in \left\{(x,y) \middle| 8x - 8y - 43 \geq 0, x < 1 \text{ and } y > -\frac{9}{2}\right\}$, then

    $x_8 = |x_7| - y_7 - 4 = -16x_0 + 16y_0 + 85 < -2(8x_0 - 8y_0 - 43) \leq 0,$
    $y_8 = x_7 - |y_7| + 1 = 16x_0 - 16y_0 - 88 < 16 + 72 - 88 = 0 \text{ and } y_8 = -x_8 - 4 + 1.$

    By Lemma 1, we have $(x_n, y_n) = (-1, -2)$ for all $n \geq 9$.

Case 3.2 $(x_0, y_0) \in \left\{(x,y) \middle| x - y - 4 \geq 0, x + y + 1 < 0, x \geq 1 \text{ and } y > -\frac{9}{2}\right\}$. We have the same (x_2, y_2) as in Case 3.1, while $x_2 < 0$ and $y_2 \geq 0$. By using the results of Lemmas 5 and 8, we have that

- if $(x_0, y_0) \in \left\{(x,y) \middle| -8x - 8y - 27 \geq 0, 1 \leq x < \frac{5}{4} \text{ and } y > -\frac{9}{2}\right\}$, then

    $x_8 = |x_7| - y_7 - 4 = 16x_0 + 16y_0 + 53 < -2(-8x_0 - 8y_0 - 27) \leq 0,$
    $y_8 = x_7 - |y_7| + 1 = -16x_0 - 16y_0 - 56 < -16 + 72 - 56 = 0 \text{ and } y_8 = -x_8 - 4 + 1.$

    By Lemma 1, we have $(x_n, y_n) = (-1, -2)$ for all $n \geq 9$;

- if $(x_0, y_0) \in \left\{(x,y) \middle| -8x - 8y - 27 < 0, -4x - 4y - 13 \geq 0, 1 \leq x < \frac{5}{4} \text{ and } y > -\frac{9}{2}\right\}$, then

    $x_7 = |x_6| - y_6 - 4 = 8x_0 + 8y_0 + 25 < -2(-4x_0 - 4y_0 - 13) \leq 0,$
    $y_7 = x_6 - |y_6| + 1 = -8x_0 - 8y_0 - 28 < -8x_0 - 8y_0 - 27 < 0 \text{ and } y_7 = -x_7 - 4 + 1.$

    By Lemma 1, we have $(x_n, y_n) = (-1, -2)$ for all $n \geq 8$;

- if $(x_0, y_0) \in \left\{(x,y) \middle| -4x - 4y - 13 < 0, -2x - 2y - 6 \geq 0, 1 \leq x < \frac{5}{4} \text{ and } y > -\frac{9}{2}\right\}$, then

    $x_5 = |x_4| - y_4 - 4 = -4x_0 - 4y_0 - 13 < 0,$
    $y_5 = x_4 - |y_4| + 1 = 4x_0 + 4y_0 + 10 < -2(-2x_0 - 2y_0 - 6) \leq 0 \text{ and } y_5 = -x_5 - 4 + 1.$

    By Lemma 1, we have $(x_n, y_n) = (-1, -2)$ for all $n \geq 6$;

- if $(x_0, y_0) \in \left\{(x,y) \middle| 4x - 4y - 23 \geq 0, -2x - 2y - 6 \geq 0, \text{ and } y > -\frac{9}{2}\right\}$, then

    $x_7 = |x_6| - y_6 - 4 = -8x_0 + 8y_0 + 45 < -2(4x_0 - 4y_0 - 23) \leq 0,$
    $y_7 = x_6 - |y_6| + 1 = 8x_0 - 8y_0 - 48 < -2(-4x_0 + 4y_0 - 23) \leq 0 \text{ and } y_7 = -x_7 - 4 + 1.$

    By Lemma 1, we have $(x_n, y_n) = (-1, -2)$ for all $n \geq 8$;

- if $(x_0, y_0) \in \left\{(x,y) \middle| 4x - 4y - 23 < 0, -2x - 2y - 6 \geq 0, \text{ and } x > \frac{5}{4}\right\}$, then

    $x_6 = |x_5| - y_5 - 4 = -8x_0 + 9 < -2(4x_0 - 5) < 0,$
    $y_6 = x_5 - |y_5| + 1 = 8x_0 - 12 < 8x_0 - 11 = (4x_0 - 4y_0 - 23) - 2(-2x_0 - 2y_0 - 6) < 0$
    and $y_6 = -x_6 - 4 + 1.$

    By Lemma 1, we have $(x_n, y_n) = (-1, -2)$ for all $n \geq 7$;

- if $(x_0, y_0) \in \left\{(x,y) \mid x - y - 4 \geq 0, x + y + 1 < 0, -2x - 2y - 6 < 0 \text{ and } 1 \leq x < \frac{5}{4}\right\}$, then

$$x_4 = |x_3| - y_3 - 4 = 4x_0 - 5 < 0,$$
$$y_4 = x_3 - |y_3| + 1 = -4x_0 + 2 < -4(x_0 - 1) \leq 0 \text{ and } y_4 = -x_4 - 4 + 1.$$

By Lemma 1, we have $(x_n, y_n) = (-1, -2)$ for all $n \geq 5$;

- if $(x_0, y_0) \in \left\{(x,y) \mid x - y - 4 \geq 0, -2x - 2y - 6 < 0 \text{ and } \frac{5}{4} \leq x < \frac{11}{8}\right\}$, then

$$x_6 = |x_5| - y_5 - 4 = -8x_0 + 9 < -2(4x_0 - 5) \leq 0,$$
$$y_6 = x_5 - |y_5| + 1 = 8x_0 - 12 < 8x_0 - 11 < 0 \text{ and } y_6 = -x_6 - 4 + 1.$$

By Lemma 1, we have $(x_n, y_n) = (-1, -2)$ for all $n \geq 7$;

- if $(x_0, y_0) \in \left\{(x,y) \mid x - y - 4 \geq 0, -2x - 2y - 6 < 0 \text{ and } \frac{11}{8} \leq x < \frac{3}{2}\right\}$, then

$$x_7 = |x_6| - y_6 - 4 = -16x_0 + 21 < -2(8x_0 - 11) \leq 0,$$
$$y_7 = x_6 - |y_6| + 1 = 16x_0 - 24 = 8(2x_0 - 3) < 0 \text{ and } y_7 = -x_7 - 4 + 1.$$

By Lemma 1, we have $(x_n, y_n) = (-1, -2)$ for all $n \geq 8$;

- if $(x_0, y_0) \in \left\{(x,y) \mid x + y + 1 < 0, \frac{3}{2} \leq x < \frac{25}{16} \text{ and } y > -\frac{9}{2}\right\}$, then

$$x_8 = |x_7| - y_7 - 4 = 16x_0 - 25 < 0,$$
$$y_8 = x_7 - |y_7| + 1 = -16x_0 + 22 < -8(2x_0 - 3) \leq 0 \text{ and } y_8 = -x_8 - 4 + 1.$$

By Lemma 1, we have $(x_n, y_n) = (-1, -2)$ for all $n \geq 9$;

- if $(x_0, y_0) \in \left\{(x,y) \mid x + y + 1 < 0, \frac{25}{16} \leq x < \frac{51}{32} \text{ and } y > -\frac{9}{2}\right\}$, then

$$x_{10} = |x_9| - y_9 - 4 = -32x_0 + 49 < -2(16x_0 - 25) \leq 0,$$
$$y_{10} = x_9 - |y_9| + 1 = 32x_0 - 52 < 32x_0 - 51 < 0 \text{ and } y_{10} = -x_{10} - 4 + 1.$$

By Lemma 1, we have $(x_n, y_n) = (-1, -2)$ for all $n \geq 11$;

- if $(x_0, y_0) \in \left\{(x,y) \mid x + y + 1 < 0, \frac{51}{32} \leq x < \frac{13}{8} \text{ and } y > -\frac{9}{2}\right\}$, then

$$x_{11} = |x_{10}| - y_{10} - 4 = -64x_0 + 101 < -2(32x_0 - 51) \leq 0,$$
$$y_{11} = x_{10} - |y_{10}| + 1 = 64x_0 - 104 < 0 \text{ and } y_{11} = -x_{11} - 4 + 1.$$

By Lemma 1, we have $(x_n, y_n) = (-1, -2)$ for all $n \geq 12$;

- if $(x_0, y_0) \in \left\{(x,y) \mid x + y + 1 < 0, x \geq \frac{13}{8} \text{ and } y > -\frac{9}{2}\right\}$, then

$$x_7 = |x_6| - y_6 - 4 = -5, \qquad y_7 = x_6 - |y_6| + 1 = 0.$$

Similar to the proof of Case 4 of Lemma 2, we can conclude that $(x_n, y_n) = (-1, -2)$ for all $n \geq 12$.

Case 3.3 $(x_0, y_0) \in \left\{(x,y) \mid x + y + 1 < 0, x < 1 \text{ and } y \leq -\frac{9}{2}\right\}$. We have the same (x_2, y_2) as in Case 3.2, while $x_2 \geq 0, y_2 < 0$ and

$$x_3 = |x_2| - y_2 - 4 = -2x_0 - 2y_0 - 11 < 2x_0 - 2y_0 - 10 < 0,$$
$$y_3 = x_2 - |y_2| + 1 = 2x_0 - 2y_0 - 10 < 0.$$

By using the result of Lemma 7, we have that

- if $(x_0, y_0) \in \left\{(x,y) \big| 2x - 2y - 10 < 0, x < 1 \text{ and } y \leq -\frac{9}{2}\right\}$, then

  $x_4 = |x_3| - y_3 - 4 = 4y_0 + 17 < 2(2y_0 + 9) \leq 0,$
  $y_4 = x_3 - |y_3| + 1 = -4y_0 - 20 < 2(2x_0 - 2y_0 - 10) < 0$ and $y_4 = -x_4 - 4 + 1.$

  By Lemma 1, we have $(x_n, y_n) = (-1, -2)$ for all $n \geq 5$;

- if $(x_0, y_0) \in \left\{(x,y) \big| 2x - 2y - 10 \geq 0, 4x - 4y - 21 < 0 \text{ and } y \leq -\frac{9}{2}\right\}$, then

  $x_5 = |x_4| - y_4 - 4 = 4x_0 - 4y_0 - 21 < 0,$
  $y_5 = x_4 - |y_4| + 1 = -4x_0 + 4y_0 + 18 < -2(2x_0 - 2y_0 - 10) \leq 0$ and $y_5 = -x_5 - 4 + 1.$

  By Lemma 1, we have $(x_n, y_n) = (-1, -2)$ for all $n \geq 6$;

- if $(x_0, y_0) \in \left\{(x,y) \big| 4x - 4y - 21 \geq 0, 8x - 8y - 43 < 0 \text{ and } y \leq -\frac{9}{2}\right\}$, then

  $x_7 = |x_6| - y_6 - 4 = -8x_0 + 8y_0 + 41 < -2(4x_0 - 4y_0 - 21) \leq 0,$
  $y_7 = x_6 - |y_6| + 1 = 8x_0 - 8y_0 - 44 < 8x_0 - 8y_0 - 43 < 0$ and $y_7 = -x_7 - 4 + 1.$

  By Lemma 1, we have $(x_n, y_n) = (-1, -2)$ for all $n \geq 8$;

- if $(x_0, y_0) \in \left\{(x,y) \big| 8x - 8y - 43 \geq 0, 8x - 8y - 44 < 0 \text{ and } y \leq -\frac{9}{2}\right\}$, then

  $x_8 = |x_7| - y_7 - 4 = -16x_0 + 16y_0 + 85 < -2(8x_0 - 8y_0 - 43) \leq 0,$
  $y_8 = x_7 - |y_7| + 1 = 16x_0 - 16y_0 - 88 < 0$ and $y_8 = -x_8 - 4 + 1.$

  By Lemma 1, we have $(x_n, y_n) = (-1, -2)$ for all $n \geq 9$;

- if $(x_0, y_0) \in \{(x,y)|8x - 8y - 44 \geq 0, -2x - 2y - 11 < 0, 16x - 16y - 89 < 0$ and $x < 1\}$, then

  $x_9 = |x_8| - y_8 - 4 = 16x_0 - 16y_0 - 89 < 0,$
  $y_9 = x_8 - |y_8| + 1 = -16x_0 + 16y_0 + 86 < -2(8x_0 - 8y_0 - 44) \leq 0$
  and $y_9 = -x_9 - 4 + 1.$

  By Lemma 1, we have $(x_n, y_n) = (-1, -2)$ for all $n \geq 10$;

- if $(x_0, y_0) \in \{(x,y)|16x - 16y - 89 \geq 0, -2x - 2y - 11 < 0, 32x - 32y - 179 < 0$ and $x < 1\}$, then

  $x_{11} = |x_{10}| - y_{10} - 4 = -32x_0 + 32y_0 + 177 < -2(16x_0 - 16y_0 - 89) \leq 0,$
  $y_{11} = x_{10} - |y_{10}| + 1 = 32x_0 - 32y_0 - 180 < 32x_0 - 32y_0 - 179 < 0$
  and $y_{11} = -x_{11} - 4 + 1.$

  By Lemma 1, we have $(x_n, y_n) = (-1, -2)$ for all $n \geq 12$;

- if $(x_0, y_0) \in \{(x,y)|32x - 32y - 179 \geq 0, -2x - 2y - 11 < 0, 8x - 8y - 45 < 0$ and $x < 1\}$, then

  $x_{12} = |x_{11}| - y_{11} - 4 = -64x_0 + 64y_0 + 357 < -2(32x_0 - 32y_0 - 179) \leq 0,$
  $y_{12} = x_{11} - |y_{11}| + 1 = 64x_0 - 64y_0 - 360 < 0$ and $y_{12} = -x_{12} - 4 + 1.$

  By Lemma 1, we have $(x_n, y_n) = (-1, -2)$ for all $n \geq 13$;

- if $(x_0, y_0) \in \left\{(x,y) \big| 8x - 8y - 45 \geq 0, -2x - 2y - 11 < 0 \text{ and } x < 1\right\}$, then

  $x_8 = |x_7| - y_7 - 4 = -5, \qquad y_8 = x_7 - |y_7| + 1 = 0.$

- Similar to the proof of Case 4 of Lemma 2, we can conclude that $(x_n, y_n) = (-1, -2)$ for all $n \geq 13$;
- if $(x_0, y_0) \in \left\{(x, y) \middle| -2x - 2y - 11 \geq 0 \text{ and } x < \frac{1}{32}\right\}$, then

$$x_9 = |x_8| - y_8 - 4 = 32x_0 - 1 < 0,$$
$$y_9 = x_8 - |y_8| + 1 = -32x_0 - 2 < 0 \text{ and } y_9 = -x_9 - 4 + 1.$$

By Lemma 1, we have $(x_n, y_n) = (-1, -2)$ for all $n \geq 10$;
- if $(x_0, y_0) \in \left\{(x, y) \middle| -2x - 2y - 11 \geq 0 \text{ and } \frac{1}{32} \leq x < \frac{3}{64}\right\}$, then

$$x_{11} = |x_{10}| - y_{10} - 4 = -64x_0 + 1 < -2(32x_0 - 1) \leq 0,$$
$$y_{11} = x_{10} - |y_{10}| + 1 = 64x_0 - 4 < 64x_0 - 3 < 0 \text{ and } y_{11} = -x_{11} - 4 + 1.$$

By Lemma 1, we have $(x_n, y_n) = (-1, -2)$ for all $n \geq 12$;
- if $(x_0, y_0) \in \left\{(x, y) \middle| -2x - 2y - 11 \geq 0 \text{ and } \frac{3}{64} \leq x < \frac{1}{16}\right\}$, then

$$x_{12} = |x_{11}| - y_{11} - 4 = -128x_0 + 5 < -2(64x_0 - 3) \leq 0,$$
$$y_{12} = x_{11} - |y_{11}| + 1 = 128x_0 - 8 < 0 \text{ and } y_{12} = -x_{12} - 4 + 1.$$

By Lemma 1, we have $(x_n, y_n) = (-1, -2)$ for all $n \geq 13$;
- if $(x_0, y_0) \in \left\{(x, y) \middle| -2x - 2y - 11 \geq 0 \text{ and } \frac{1}{16} \leq x < 1\right\}$, then

$$x_8 = |x_7| - y_7 - 4 = -5, \qquad y_8 = x_7 - |y_7| + 1 = 0.$$

Similar to the proof of Case 4 of Lemma 2, we can conclude that $(x_n, y_n) = (-1, -2)$ for all $n \geq 13$.

Case 3.4 $(x_0, y_0) \in \left\{(x, y) \middle| x + y + 1 < 0, x \geq 1 \text{ and } y \leq -\frac{9}{2}\right\}$. We have the same (x_2, y_2) as in Case 3.2, while $x_2 \geq 0$ and $y_2 \geq 0$. By using the results of Lemmas 2, 3 and 6, we have that
- if $(x_0, y_0) \in \left\{(x, y) \middle| -2x - 2y - 6 \geq 0, 4x + 4y + 13 \geq 0, x \geq 1 \text{ and } y \leq -\frac{9}{2}\right\}$, then

$$x_7 = |x_6| - y_6 - 4 = -8x_0 - 8y_0 - 27 < -2(4x_0 + 4y_0 + 13) \leq 0,$$
$$y_7 = x_6 - |y_6| + 1 = 8x_0 + 8y_0 + 24 \leq 0 \text{ and } y_7 = -x_7 - 4 + 1.$$

By Lemma 1, we have $(x_n, y_n) = (-1, -2)$ for all $n \geq 8$;
- if $(x_0, y_0) \in \left\{(x, y) \middle| 4x + 4y + 13 < 0, -8x - 8y - 27 < 0, x \geq 1 \text{ and } y \leq -\frac{9}{2}\right\}$, then

$$x_7 = |x_6| - y_6 - 4 = 8x_0 + 8y_0 + 25 < 2(4x_0 + 4y_0 + 13) < 0,$$
$$y_7 = x_6 - |y_6| + 1 = -8x_0 - 8y_0 - 28 < -8x_0 - 8y_0 - 27 < 0 \text{ and } y_7 = -x_7 - 4 + 1.$$

By Lemma 1, we have $(x_n, y_n) = (-1, -2)$ for all $n \geq 8$;
- if $(x_0, y_0) \in \left\{(x, y) \middle| -8x - 8y - 27 \geq 0, -8x - 8y - 28 < 0, x \geq 1 \text{ and } y \leq -\frac{9}{2}\right\}$, then

$$x_8 = |x_7| - y_7 - 4 = 16x_0 + 16y_0 + 53 < -2(-8x_0 - 8y_0 - 27) \leq 0,$$
$$y_8 = x_7 - |y_7| + 1 = -16x_0 - 16y_0 - 56 < 0 \text{ and } y_8 = -x_8 - 4 + 1.$$

By Lemma 1, we have $(x_n, y_n) = (-1, -2)$ for all $n \geq 9$;

- if $(x_0, y_0) \in \{(x,y)| -8x - 8y - 28 \geq 0, -16x - 16y - 57 < 0 \text{ and } x \geq 1\}$, then

  $x_9 = |x_8| - y_8 - 4 = -16x_0 - 16y_0 - 57 < 0,$
  $y_9 = x_8 - |y_8| + 1 = 16x_0 + 16y_0 + 54 < -2(-8x_0 - 8y_0 - 28) \leq 0$ and $y_9 = -x_9 - 4 + 1.$

  By Lemma 1, we have $(x_n, y_n) = (-1, -2)$ for all $n \geq 10$;

- if $(x_0, y_0) \in \{(x,y)| -16x - 16y - 57 \geq 0, -32x - 32y - 115 < 0 \text{ and } x \geq 1\}$, then

  $x_{11} = |x_{10}| - y_{10} - 4 = 32x_0 + 32y_0 + 113 < -2(-16x_0 - 16y_0 - 57) \leq 0,$
  $y_{11} = x_{10} - |y_{10}| + 1 = -32x_0 - 32y_0 - 116 < -32x_0 - 32y_0 - 115 < 0$
  and $y_{11} = -x_{11} - 4 + 1.$

  By Lemma 1, we have $(x_n, y_n) = (-1, -2)$ for all $n \geq 12$;

- if $(x_0, y_0) \in \{(x,y)| -32x - 32y - 115 \geq 0, -8x - 8y - 29 < 0 \text{ and } x \geq 1\}$, then

  $x_{12} = |x_{11}| - y_{11} - 4 = 64x_0 + 64y_0 + 229 < -2(-32x_0 - 32y_0 - 115) \leq 0,$
  $y_{12} = x_{11} - |y_{11}| + 1 = -64x_0 - 64y_0 - 232 < 0$ and $y_{12} = -x_{12} - 4 + 1.$

  By Lemma 1, we have $(x_n, y_n) = (-1, -2)$ for all $n \geq 13$;

- if $(x_0, y_0) \in \{(x,y)| -8x - 8y - 29 \geq 0, -2x - 2y - 11 < 0 \text{ and } x \geq 1\}$, then

  $x_8 = |x_7| - y_7 - 4 = -5, \qquad y_8 = x_7 - |y_7| + 1 = 0.$

  Similar to the proof of Case 4 of Lemma 2, we can conclude that $(x_n, y_n) = (-1, -2)$ for all $n \geq 13$;

- if $(x_0, y_0) \in \{(x,y)| -2x - 2y - 11 \geq 0 \text{ and } x \geq 1\}$, then

  $x_4 = |x_3| - y_3 - 4 = -9, \qquad y_4 = x_3 - |y_3| + 1 = -4.$

  Similar to the proof of Case 6 of Lemma 2, we can conclude that $(x_n, y_n) = (-1, -2)$ for all $n \geq 13$;

- if $(x_0, y_0) \in \left\{(x,y)\middle| -2x - 2y - 6 < 0, 16x + 16y + 47 < 0 \text{ and } y \leq -\frac{9}{2}\right\}$, then

  $x_8 = |x_7| - y_7 - 4 = 16x_0 + 16y_0 + 47 < 0,$
  $y_8 = x_7 - |y_7| + 1 = -16x_0 - 16y_0 - 50 < 8(-2x_0 - 2y_0 - 6) < 0$
  and $y_8 = -x_8 - 4 + 1.$

  By Lemma 1, we have $(x_n, y_n) = (-1, -2)$ for all $n \geq 9$;

- if $(x_0, y_0) \in \left\{(x,y)\middle| 16x + 16y + 47 \geq 0, 32x + 32y + 93 < 0, \text{ and } y \leq -\frac{9}{2}\right\}$, then

  $x_{10} = |x_9| - y_9 - 4 = -32x_0 - 32y_0 - 95 < -2(16x_0 + 16y_0 + 47) \leq 0,$
  $y_{10} = x_9 - |y_9| + 1 = 32x_0 + 32y_0 + 92 < 32x_0 + 32y_0 + 93 < 0$
  and $y_{10} = -x_{10} - 4 + 1.$

  By Lemma 1, we have $(x_n, y_n) = (-1, -2)$ for all $n \geq 11$;

- if $(x_0, y_0) \in \left\{(x,y)\middle| 32x + 32y + 93 \geq 0, 8x + 8y + 23 < 0 \text{ and } y \leq -\frac{9}{2}\right\}$, then

  $x_{11} = |x_{10}| - y_{10} - 4 = -64x_0 - 64y_0 - 187 < -2(32x_0 + 32y_0 + 93) \leq 0,$
  $y_{11} = x_{10} - |y_{10}| + 1 = 64x_0 + 64y_0 + 184 < 0$ and $y_{11} = -x_{11} - 4 + 1.$

  By Lemma 1, we have $(x_n, y_n) = (-1, -2)$ for all $n \geq 12$;

- if $(x_0, y_0) \in \left\{ (x,y) \big| 8x + 8y + 23 \geq 0, x + y + 1 < 0 \text{ and } y \leq -\frac{9}{2} \right\}$, then

$$x_7 = |x_6| - y_6 - 4 = -5, \qquad y_7 = x_6 - |y_6| + 1 = 0.$$

Similar to the proof of Case 4 of Lemma 2, we can conclude that $(x_n, y_n) = (-1, -2)$ for all $n \geq 12$.

Figure 4 shows regions considered in the proof of Case 3 of this lemma.

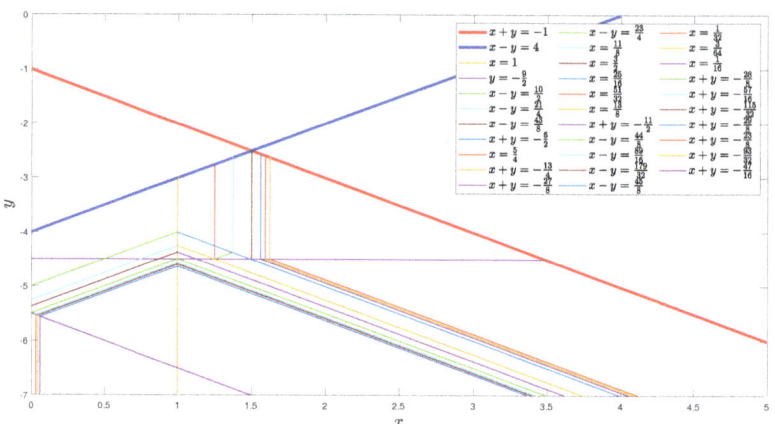

Figure 4. Regions considered in the proof of Case 3.

Case 4 $(x_0, y_0) \in \{(x,y) | x - y - 4 \geq 0 \text{ and } x + y + 1 \geq 0\}$. We have $x_1 \geq 0$ and $y_1 \geq 0$. By using the results of Lemmas 2, 3 and 6, we have that

- if $y_0 \geq -\frac{15}{8}$, then

$$x_6 = |x_5| - y_5 - 4 = -5, \qquad y_6 = x_5 - |y_5| + 1 = 0.$$

Similar to the proof of Case 4 of Lemma 2, we can conclude that $(x_n, y_n) = (-1, -2)$ for all $n \geq 11$;

- if $-\frac{61}{32} \leq y_0 < -\frac{15}{8}$, then

$$x_{10} = |x_9| - y_9 - 4 = -64y_0 - 123 < -2(32y_0 + 61) \leq 0,$$
$$y_{10} = x_9 - |y_9| + 1 = 64y_0 + 120 < 0 \text{ and } y_{10} = -x_{10} - 4 + 1.$$

By Lemma 1, we have $(x_n, y_n) = (-1, -2)$ for all $n \geq 11$;

- if $-\frac{31}{16} \leq y_0 < -\frac{61}{32}$, then

$$x_9 = |x_8| - y_8 - 4 = -32y_0 - 63 < -2(16y_0 + 31) \leq 0,$$
$$y_9 = x_8 - |y_8| + 1 = 32y_0 + 60 < 32y_0 + 61 < 0 \text{ and } y_9 = -x_9 - 4 + 1.$$

By Lemma 1, we have $(x_n, y_n) = (-1, -2)$ for all $n \geq 10$;

- if $-2 \leq y_0 < -\frac{31}{16}$, then

$$x_7 = |x_6| - y_6 - 4 = 16y_0 + 31 < 0,$$
$$y_7 = x_6 - |y_6| + 1 = -16y_0 - 34 < -16(y_0 + 2) \leq 0 \text{ and } y_7 = -x_7 - 4 + 1.$$

By Lemma 1, we have $(x_n, y_n) = (-1, -2)$ for all $n \geq 8$;

- if $-\frac{9}{4} < y_0 < -2$, then

$$x_6 = |x_5| - y_5 - 4 = -8y_0 - 19 < -2(4y_0 + 9) < 0,$$
$$y_6 = x_5 - |y_5| + 1 = 8y_0 + 16 < 0 \text{ and } y_6 = -x_6 - 4 + 1.$$

By Lemma 1, we have $(x_n, y_n) = (-1, -2)$ for all $n \geq 7$;
- if $-\frac{19}{8} < y_0 \leq -\frac{9}{4}$, then

$$x_6 = |x_5| - y_5 - 4 = 8y_0 + 17 < 2(4y_0 + 9) \leq 0,$$
$$y_6 = x_5 - |y_5| + 1 = -8y_0 - 20 < -8y_0 - 19 < 0 \text{ and } y_6 = -x_6 - 4 + 1.$$

By Lemma 1, we have $(x_n, y_n) = (-1, -2)$ for all $n \geq 7$;
- if $-\frac{20}{8} < y_0 \leq -\frac{19}{8}$, then

$$x_7 = |x_6| - y_6 - 4 = 16y_0 + 37 < 2(8y_0 + 19) \leq 0,$$
$$y_7 = x_6 - |y_6| + 1 = -16y_0 - 40 < 0 \text{ and } y_7 = -x_7 - 4 + 1.$$

By Lemma 1, we have $(x_n, y_n) = (-1, -2)$ for all $n \geq 8$;
- if $-\frac{41}{16} < y_0 \leq -\frac{20}{8}$, then

$$x_8 = |x_7| - y_7 - 4 = -16y_0 - 41 < 0,$$
$$y_8 = x_7 - |y_7| + 1 = 16y_0 + 38 < 2(8y_0 + 20) \leq 0 \text{ and } y_8 = -x_8 - 4 + 1.$$

By Lemma 1, we have $(x_n, y_n) = (-1, -2)$ for all $n \geq 9$;
- if $-\frac{83}{32} < y_0 \leq -\frac{41}{16}$, then

$$x_{10} = |x_9| - y_9 - 4 = 32y_0 + 81 < 2(16y_0 + 41) \leq 0,$$
$$y_{10} = x_9 - |y_9| + 1 = -32y_0 - 84 < -32y_0 - 83 < 0 \text{ and } y_{10} = -x_{10} - 4 + 1.$$

By Lemma 1, we have $(x_n, y_n) = (-1, -2)$ for all $n \geq 11$;
- if $-\frac{21}{8} < y_0 \leq -\frac{83}{32}$, then

$$x_{11} = |x_{10}| - y_{10} - 4 = 64y_0 + 165 < 2(32y_0 + 83) \leq 0,$$
$$y_{11} = x_{10} - |y_{10}| + 1 = -64y_0 - 168 < 0 \text{ and } y_{11} = -x_{11} - 4 + 1.$$

By Lemma 1, we have $(x_n, y_n) = (-1, -2)$ for all $n \geq 12$;
- if $-\frac{9}{2} < y_0 \leq -\frac{21}{8}$, then

$$x_7 = |x_6| - y_6 - 4 = -5, \qquad y_7 = x_6 - |y_6| + 1 = 0.$$

Similar to the proof of Case 4 of Lemma 2, we can conclude that $(x_n, y_n) = (-1, -2)$ for all $n \geq 12$;
- if $y_0 \leq -\frac{9}{2}$, then

$$x_3 = |x_2| - y_2 - 4 = -9, \qquad y_3 = x_2 - |y_2| + 1 = -4.$$

Similar to the proof of Case 6 of Lemma 2, we can conclude that $(x_n, y_n) = (-1, -2)$ for all $n \geq 13$.

Figure 5 shows regions considered in the proof of Case 4 of this lemma.

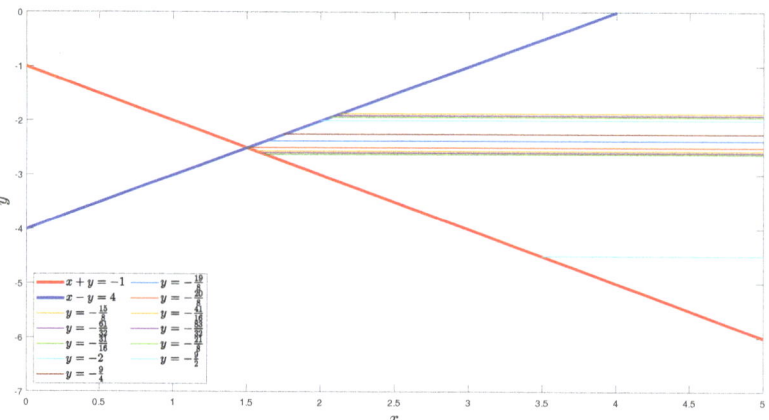

Figure 5. Regions considered in the proof of Case 4. □

Therefore, as we combine Lemmas 2–9, we can have the following theorem. It can be seen that the solutions do not show any periodic behavior. This is not the same as the other values of b considered in [11,14,15,17].

Theorem 1. *If $b = 4$, $(x_0, y_0) \in \mathbb{R}^2$, then the solution $(x_n, y_n)_{n=0}^{\infty}$ of (2) eventually becomes the equilibrium point $(-1, -2)$ of (2) within 14 iterations.*

3. Local Behavior for $b \geq 5$

In this section, we investigate local behavior for several values of $b \geq 5$.

3.1. $b = 5$

First, let us start with $b = 5$ where $x_0 = 0$ or $y_0 = 0$.

Lemma 10. *If $x_0 \geq 0$ and $y_0 = 0$, then the solution $(x_n, y_n)_{n=0}^{\infty}$ of (2) eventually becomes the equilibrium point $(-1, -3)$ of (2).*

Proof. By separate cases as in Lemma 2, we can conclude the behavior of the solution in Table 4.

Table 4. Cases for $x_0 \geq 0$ and $y_0 = 0$.

If $x_0 \in A$,	Then $(x_n, y_n) = (-1, -3)$ for All $n \geq N$
$A = \left[0, \frac{1}{8}\right)$	$N = 7$
$A = \left[\frac{1}{8}, \frac{3}{16}\right)$	$N = 9$
$A = \left[\frac{3}{16}, \frac{7}{32}\right]$	$N = 11$
$A = \left[\frac{7}{32}, \frac{1}{4}\right); \left[\frac{1}{4}, 1\right]; (1, 5); [5, \infty)$	$N = 12$

□

Lemma 11. *If $x_0 = 0$ and $y_0 \geq 0$, then the solution $(x_n, y_n)_{n=0}^{\infty}$ of (2) eventually becomes the equilibrium point $(-1, -3)$ of (2).*

Proof. By separate cases as in Lemma 2, we can conclude the behavior of the solution in Table 5.

Table 5. Cases for $x_0 = 0$ and $y_0 \geq 0$.

If $y_0 \in A$,	Then $(x_n, y_n) = (-1, -3)$ for All $n \geq N$
$A = \left(\frac{1}{4}, \frac{1}{2}\right); \left[\frac{1}{2}, 1\right]; \left(1, \frac{9}{8}\right]$	$N = 6$
$A = \left[0, \frac{1}{4}\right]$	$N = 7$
$A = \left(\frac{9}{8}, \frac{19}{16}\right]$	$N = 8$
$A = \left(\frac{19}{16}, \frac{39}{32}\right]$	$N = 10$
$A = \left(\frac{39}{32}, \frac{5}{4}\right); \left[\frac{5}{4}, \infty\right)$	$N = 11$

□

Lemma 12. *If $x_0 = 0$ and $y_0 < 0$, then the solution $(x_n, y_n)_{n=0}^{\infty}$ of (2) eventually becomes the equilibrium point $(-1, -3)$ of (2).*

Proof. By separate cases as in Lemma 2, we can conclude the behavior of the solution in Table 6.

Table 6. Cases for $x_0 = 0$ and $y_0 < 0$.

If $y_0 \in A$,	Then $(x_n, y_n) = (-1, -3)$ for All $n \geq N$
$A = \{-4\}$	$N = 1$
$A = (-5, -1) \setminus \{-4\}$	$N = 2$
$A = \left(-\frac{11}{2}, -5\right]; \left[-1, -\frac{1}{2}\right)$	$N = 4$
$A = \left(-\frac{25}{4}, -\frac{11}{2}\right]$	$N = 5$
$A = \left[-\frac{1}{2}, -\frac{1}{4}\right)$	$N = 6$
$A = \left(-\frac{51}{8}, -\frac{25}{4}\right]; \left[-\frac{1}{4}, 0\right)$	$N = 7$
$A = \left(-\frac{103}{16}, -\frac{51}{8}\right]$	$N = 9$
$A = \left(-\infty, -\frac{13}{2}\right]; \left(-\frac{13}{2}, -\frac{103}{16}\right]$	$N = 10$

□

Lemma 13. *If $x_0 < 0$ and $y_0 = 0$, then the solution $(x_n, y_n)_{n=0}^{\infty}$ of (2) eventually becomes the equilibrium point $(-1, -3)$ of (2).*

Proof. By separate cases as in Lemma 2, we can conclude the behavior of the solution in Table 7.

Table 7. Cases for $x_0 < 0$ and $y_0 = 0$.

If $x_0 \in A$,	Then $(x_n, y_n) = (-1, -3)$ for All $n \geq N$
$A = \{-4\}$	$N = 1$
$A = (-5, -1) \setminus \{-4\}$	$N = 2$
$A = \left(-\frac{11}{2}, -5\right]; \left[-1, -\frac{1}{2}\right)$	$N = 4$
$A = \left(-\frac{25}{4}, -\frac{11}{2}\right]$	$N = 5$
$A = \left[-\frac{1}{2}, -\frac{1}{4}\right)$	$N = 6$
$A = \left(-\frac{51}{8}, -\frac{25}{4}\right]; \left[-\frac{1}{4}, 0\right)$	$N = 7$
$A = \left(-\frac{103}{16}, -\frac{51}{8}\right]$	$N = 9$
$A = \left(-\infty, -\frac{13}{2}\right]; \left(-\frac{13}{2}, -\frac{103}{16}\right]$	$N = 10$

□

3.2. $b \geq 5$ with Large Value of $|x_0|$ and $|y_0|$

It can be seen from Lemmas 2–5 and 10–13 that if $(x_0$ and $|y_0|$ is large enough) or $(y_0$ and $|x_0|$ is large enough), then we can easily determine the behavior of the solutions without considering several cases. However, for these initial conditions, it possesses the periodic behavior.

Lemma 14. *If $b \geq 6$, $x_0 \geq b$ and $y_0 = 0$, then the solution $(x_n, y_n)_{n=0}^{\infty}$ of (2) eventually becomes the periodic solution of prime period 5 of (2).*

Proof. Let $b \geq 6$, $x_0 \geq b$ and $y_0 = 0$. Then,

$x_1 = |x_0| - y_0 - b = x_0 - b \geq 0,$ $y_1 = x_0 - |y_0| + 1 = x_0 + 1 \geq 0$
$x_2 = |x_1| - y_1 - b = -2b - 1 < 0,$ $y_2 = x_1 - |y_1| + 1 = -b < 0$
$x_3 = |x_2| - y_2 - b = 2b + 1 > 0,$ $y_3 = x_2 - |y_2| + 1 = -3b < 0$
$x_4 = |x_3| - y_3 - b = 4b + 1 > 0,$ $y_4 = x_3 - |y_3| + 1 = -b + 2 \leq -4 < 0$
$x_5 = |x_4| - y_4 - b = 4b - 1 \geq 23 > 0,$ $y_5 = x_4 - |y_4| + 1 = 3b + 4 > 0$
$x_6 = |x_5| - y_5 - b = -5,$ $y_6 = x_5 - |y_5| + 1 = b - 4 \geq 2 > 0$
$x_7 = |x_6| - y_6 - b = -2b + 9 \leq -3 < 0,$ $y_7 = x_6 - |y_6| + 1 = -b < 0$
$x_8 = |x_7| - y_7 - b = 2b - 9 \geq 3 > 0,$ $y_8 = x_7 - |y_7| + 1 = -3b + 10 \leq -8 < 0$
$x_9 = |x_8| - y_8 - b = 4b - 19 \geq 5 > 0,$ $y_9 = x_8 - |y_8| + 1 = -b + 2 \leq -4 < 0$
$x_{10} = |x_9| - y_9 - b = 4b - 21 \geq 3 > 0,$ $y_{10} = x_9 - |y_9| + 1 = 3b - 16 \geq 2 > 0$
$x_{11} = |x_{10}| - y_{10} - b = -5 = x_6,$ $y_{11} = x_{10} - |y_{10}| + 1 = b - 4 = y_6.$

By mathematical induction, we have $x_{n+5} = x_n$ and $y_{n+5} = y_n$ for all $n \geq 6$. □

Lemma 15. *If $b \geq 6$, $x_0 = 0$ and $y_0 \geq \frac{b}{4}$, then the solution $(x_n, y_n)_{n=0}^{\infty}$ of (2) eventually becomes the periodic solution of prime period 5 of (2).*

Proof. Let $b \geq 6$, $x_0 = 0$ and $y_0 \geq \frac{b}{4}$. Then,

$x_1 = |x_0| - y_0 - b = -y_0 - b < 0,$

$y_1 = x_0 - |y_0| + 1 = -y_0 + 1 \leq -\dfrac{-b+4}{4} \leq -\dfrac{1}{2} < 0$

$x_2 = |x_1| - y_1 - b = 2y_0 - 1 \geq \dfrac{b-2}{2} \geq 2 > 0,$

$y_2 = x_1 - |y_1| + 1 = -2y_0 - b + 2 \leq \dfrac{-3b+4}{2} \leq -7 < 0$

$x_3 = |x_2| - y_2 - b = 4y_0 - 3 \geq b - 3 \geq 3 > 0, y_3 = x_2 - |y_2| + 1 = -b + 2 \leq -4 < 0$
$x_4 = |x_3| - y_3 - b = 4y_0 - 5 \geq b - 5 \geq 1 > 0, y_4 = x_3 - |y_3| + 1 = 4y_0 - b \geq 0$
$x_5 = |x_4| - y_4 - b = -5,$ $y_5 = x_4 - |y_4| + 1 = b - 4 \geq 2 > 0.$

Similar to Lemma 14, we can conclude by mathematical induction that $x_{n+5} = x_n$ and $y_{n+5} = y_n$ for all $n \geq 5$. □

Lemma 16. *If $b \geq 6$, $x_0 \leq -\frac{3}{2}b + 1$ and $y_0 = 0$, then the solution $(x_n, y_n)_{n=0}^{\infty}$ of (2) eventually becomes the periodic solution of prime period 5 of (2).*

Proof. Let $b \geq 6$, $x_0 \leq -\frac{3}{2}b + 1$ and $y_0 = 0$. Then,

$$x_1 = |x_0| - y_0 - b = -x_0 - b \geq \frac{3}{2}b - 1 - b \geq 2 > 0,$$
$$y_1 = x_0 - |y_0| + 1 = x_0 + 1 \leq -\frac{3}{2}b + 2 \leq -7 < 0$$
$$x_2 = |x_1| - y_1 - b = -2x_0 - 2b - 1 \geq 3b - 2 - 2b - 1 \geq 3 > 0,$$
$$y_2 = x_1 - |y_1| + 1 = -b + 2 \leq -4 < 0$$
$$x_3 = |x_2| - y_2 - b = -2x_0 - 2b - 3 \geq 3b - 2 - 2b - 3 \geq 1 > 0,$$
$$y_3 = x_2 - |y_2| + 1 = -2x_0 - 3b + 2 \geq 3b - 2 - 3b + 2 = 0$$
$$x_4 = |x_3| - y_3 - b = -5, \qquad y_4 = x_3 - |y_3| + 1 = b - 4 \geq 2 > 0.$$

Similar to Lemma 14, we can conclude by mathematical induction that $x_{n+5} = x_n$ and $y_{n+5} = y_n$ for all $n \geq 4$. □

Lemma 17. *If $b \geq 6$, $x_0 = 0$ and $y_0 \leq -\frac{3}{2}b + 1$, then the solution $(x_n, y_n)_{n=0}^{\infty}$ of (2) eventually becomes the periodic solution of prime period 5 of (2).*

Proof. Let $b \geq 6$, $x_0 = 0$ and $y_0 \leq -\frac{3}{2}b + 1$. Then,

$$x_1 = |x_0| - y_0 - b = -y_0 - b \geq \frac{3}{2}b - 1 - b \geq 2 > 0,$$
$$y_1 = x_0 - |y_0| + 1 = y_0 + 1 \leq -\frac{3}{2}b + 2 \leq -7 < 0$$
$$x_2 = |x_1| - y_1 - b = -2y_0 - 2b - 1 \geq 3b - 3 - 2b - 1 \geq 2 > 0,$$
$$y_2 = x_1 - |y_1| + 1 = -b + 2 \leq -4 < 0$$
$$x_3 = |x_2| - y_2 - b = -2y_0 - 2b - 3 \geq 3b - 2 - 2b - 3 \geq 1 > 0,$$
$$y_3 = x_2 - |y_2| + 1 = -2y_0 - 3b + 2 \geq 3b - 2 - 3b + 2 = 0$$
$$x_4 = |x_3| - y_3 - b = -5, \qquad y_4 = x_3 - |y_3| + 1 = b - 4 \geq 2 > 0.$$

Similar to Lemma 14, we can conclude by mathematical induction that $x_{n+5} = x_n$ and $y_{n+5} = y_n$ for all $n \geq 4$. □

Next, if $x_0 y_0 > 0$ and $|x_0|$ and $|y_0|$ are large enough, we can conclude the following theorem about the solution of (2) when $b \geq 5$.

Lemma 18. *If $b \geq 5$ and $(x_0, y_0) \in \{(x, y) \in \mathbb{R}^+ \times \mathbb{R}^+ | x - y - b \geq 0\}$, then the solution $(x_n, y_n)_{n=0}^{\infty}$ of (2) eventually becomes (i) the equilibrium point $(-1, -3)$ of (2) for $b = 5$ and (ii) the periodic solution of prime period 5 of (2).*

Proof. (i) Let $b = 5$ and $(x_0, y_0) \in \{(x, y) \in \mathbb{R}^+ \times \mathbb{R}^+ | x - y - 5 \geq 0\}$. Then,

$$x_1 = |x_0| - y_0 - 5 = x_0 - y_0 - 5, \quad y_1 = x_0 - |y_0| + 1 = x_0 - y_0 + 1 > x_0 - y_0 - 5 \geq 0$$
$$x_2 = |x_1| - y_1 - 5 = -11, \qquad y_2 = x_1 - |y_1| + 1 = -5$$
$$x_3 = |x_2| - y_2 - 5 = 11, \qquad y_3 = x_2 - |y_2| + 1 = 15$$
$$x_4 = |x_3| - y_3 - 5 = 21, \qquad y_4 = x_3 - |y_3| + 1 = -3$$
$$x_5 = |x_4| - y_4 - 5 = 19, \qquad y_5 = x_4 - |y_4| + 1 = 19$$
$$x_6 = |x_5| - y_5 - 5 = -5, \qquad y_6 = x_5 - |y_5| + 1 = 1.$$

By direct computation, we can conclude that $(x_n, y_n) = (-1, -3)$ for all $n \geq 12$.

(ii) Let $b \geq 6$ and $(x_0, y_0) \in \{(x, y) \in \mathbb{R}^+ \times \mathbb{R}^+ | x - y - b \geq 0\}$. Then,

$$x_1 = |x_0| - y_0 - b = x_0 - y_0 - b, \quad y_1 = x_0 - |y_0| + 1 = x_0 - y_0 + 1 > x_0 - y_0 - b \geq 0$$
$$x_2 = |x_1| - y_1 - b = -2b - 1 < 0, \quad y_2 = x_1 - |y_1| + 1 = -b < 0.$$

Similar to Lemma 14, we can conclude by mathematical induction that $x_{n+5} = x_n$ and $y_{n+5} = y_n$ for all $n \geq 6$. □

Lemma 19. *If $b \geq 5$ and $(x_0, y_0) \in \{(x, y) \in \mathbb{R}^- \times \mathbb{R}^- | -x - y - \frac{3}{2}b + 1 \geq 0\}$, then the solution $(x_n, y_n)_{n=0}^{\infty}$ of (2) eventually becomes (i) the equilibrium point $(-1, -3)$ of (2) for $b = 5$ and (ii) the periodic solution of prime period 5 of (2).*

Proof. (i) Let $b = 5$ and $(x_0, y_0) \in \{(x, y) \in \mathbb{R}^- \times \mathbb{R}^- | -x - y - \frac{17}{2} \geq 0\}$. Then,

$$x_1 = |x_0| - y_0 - 5 = -x_0 - y_0 - 5 > -x_0 - y_0 - \frac{17}{2} \geq 0,$$
$$y_1 = x_0 - |y_0| + 1 = x_0 + y_0 + 1 < x_0 + y_0 + \frac{17}{2} \leq 0$$
$$x_2 = |x_1| - y_1 - 5 = -2x_0 - 2y_0 - 11 > 2\left(-x_0 - y_0 - \frac{17}{2}\right) \geq 0, y_2 = x_1 - |y_1| + 1 = -3$$
$$x_3 = |x_2| - y_2 - 5 = -2x_0 - 2y_0 - 13 > 2\left(-x_0 - y_0 - \frac{17}{2}\right) \geq 0,$$
$$y_3 = x_2 - |y_2| + 1 = -2x_0 - 2y_0 - 13 = x_3 \geq 0$$
$$x_4 = |x_3| - y_3 - 5 = -5, \quad y_4 = x_3 - |y_3| + 1 = 1.$$

Similar to the proof of Lemma 18(i), we can conclude that $(x_n, y_n) = (-1, -3)$ for all $n \geq 10$.

Case (ii) Let $b \geq 6$ and $(x_0, y_0) \in \{(x, y) \in \mathbb{R}^- \times \mathbb{R}^- | -x - y - \frac{3}{2}b + 1 \geq 0\}$. Since $b \geq 6$, $-b + \frac{3}{2}b = \frac{1}{2}b \geq 3 > 1, 2 + 1 = 3 < b = -2b + 3b$ and $3 + 1 = 4 < b = -2b + 3b$. Thus, $-b > -\frac{3}{2}b + 1, -2b - 1 > -3b + 2$ and $-2b - 3 > -3b + 1$, respectively. Then,

$$x_1 = |x_0| - y_0 - b = -x_0 - y_0 - b > -x_0 - y_0 - \frac{3}{2}b + 1 \geq 0,$$
$$y_1 = x_0 - |y_0| + 1 = x_0 + y_0 + 1 < -\frac{3}{2}b + 1 + 1 \leq -7 < 0$$
$$x_2 = |x_1| - y_1 - b = -2x_0 - 2y_0 - 2b - 1 > -2x_0 - 2y_0 - 3b + 2 \geq 0,$$
$$y_2 = x_1 - |y_1| + 1 = -b + 2 \leq -4 < 0$$
$$x_3 = |x_2| - y_2 - b = -2x_0 - 2y_0 - 2b - 3 > -2x_0 - 2y_0 - 3b + 2 \geq 0,$$
$$y_3 = x_2 - |y_2| + 1 = -2x_0 - 2y_0 - 3b + 2 \geq 0$$
$$x_4 = |x_3| - y_3 - b = -5, \quad y_4 = x_3 - |y_3| + 1 = b - 4 \geq 2 > 0.$$

Similar to Lemma 14, we can conclude by mathematical induction that $x_{n+5} = x_n$ and $y_{n+5} = y_n$ for all $n \geq 4$. □

4. Conclusions and Discussion

It is shown completely that for $b = 4$, all solutions of (2) eventually becomes the equilibrium point $(-1, -2)$. It is also suspected from Lemmas 10–13 and Lemmas 18 (i)–19 (i) that for $b = 5$, all solutions of (2) eventually becomes the equilibrium point $(-1, -3)$, while for $b \geq 6$, concerning the solutions of (2) with a chance to possess the periodic behavior of prime period 5 and for some small values of $|x_0|$ and $|y_0|$, it may also becomes the equilibrium point.

As we mentioned before that since the absolute value function is not differentiable, one needs to find an alternative method to analyze the behavior of (2). Thus, we choose to use a fundamental method to complete our full analysis. However, this give some insight to those who want to do further investigation concerning this type of problem. For example, (i) one can roughly see how many cases need to be considered for each value of b; (ii) one can see, for a big region, that the behavior of the solutions remains the same; (iii) one can estimate the maximum iteration until the behavior of the solutions become either equilibrium or periodic.

Finally, these complete results for $b = 4$ and partial results for $b = 5$, where all solutions asymptotically become equilibrium, are in contrast with the existing results concerning Equation (1) which usually involving periodic behavior. Thus, one may try to consider these cases of b and prove our conjecture that only for $b = 4$ and 5 do all solutions eventually become the equilibrium point, while for $b \geq 6$ all solutions eventually become either equilibrium or periodic of prime period 5.

Author Contributions: Conceptualization, B.A., R.B. and N.K.; methodology, B.A., R.B. and N.K.; validation, B.A., R.B. and N.K.; formal analysis, B.A.; investigation, B.A.; resources, B.A.; writing—Original draft preparation, B.A.; writing—Review and editing, R.B. and N.K.; visualization, B.A.; supervision, R.B. and N.K.; project administration, R.B. and N.K.; funding acquisition, B.A. and R.B. All authors have read and agreed to the published version of the manuscript.

Funding: This research received no external funding.

Institutional Review Board Statement: The study did not involve humans or animals.

Informed Consent Statement: The study did not involve humans.

Conflicts of Interest: The authors declare no conflict of interest.

References

1. Botella–Soler, V.; Castelo, J.M.; Oteo, J.A.; Ros, J. Bifurcations in the Lozi map. *J. Phys. A Math. Theor.* **2011**, *44*, 1–17. [CrossRef]
2. Lozi, R. Un attracteur etrange du type attracteur de Henon. *J. Phys.* **1978**, *39*, 9–10. [CrossRef]
3. Barnsley, M.F.; Devaney, R.L.; Mandelbrot, B.B.; Peitgen, H.O.; Saupe, D.; Voss, R.F. *The Science of Fractal Images*; Springer: New York, NY, USA, 1991.
4. Devaney, R.L. A piecewise linear model of the zones of instability of an area-preserving map. *Physica D* **1984**, *10*, 387–393. [CrossRef]
5. Kulenović, M.R.S.; Merino, O. *Discrete Dynamic Systems and Difference Equations with Mathematica*; Chapman and Hall/CRC: New York, NY, USA, 2002.
6. Grove, E.A.; Ladas, G. *Periodicities in Nonlinear Difference Equations*; Chapman and Hall/CRC: New York, NY, USA, 2005.
7. Kocic, V.L.; Ladas, G. *Global Behavior of Nonlinear Difference Equations of Higher Order with Applications*; Kluwer Academic: Boston, MA, USA, 1993.
8. Tikjha, W.; Lapierre, E.G.; Lenbury, Y. On the global character of the system of piecewise linear difference equations $x_{n+1} = |x_n| - y_n - 1$ and $y_{n+1} = x_n - |y_n|$. *Adv. Differ. Equ.* **2010**, *2010*, 57381. [CrossRef]
9. Grove, E.A.; Lapierre, E.; Tikjha, W. On the global behavior of $x_{n+1} = |x_n| - y_n - 1$ and $y_{n+1} = x_n + |y_n|$. *Cubo Math. J.* **2012**, *14*, 111–152. [CrossRef]
10. Lapierre, E.G. On the Global Behavior of Some Systems of Difference. Ph.D. Thesis, University of Rhode Island, Kingston, RI, USA, 2013.
11. Kongtan, T.; Tikjha, W. Prime period 4 solution of cartain piecewise linear system of difference equation $x_{x+1} = |x_n| - y_n - 2$ and $y_{n+1} = x_n - |y_n| + 1$ with initial conditions $x_0 = 0$ and $y_0 \in \left(\frac{1}{2}, \infty\right)$. *Rajabhat Math. J.* **2016**, *1*, 81–87.
12. Tikjha, W.; Lapierre, E.; Lenbury, Y. Periodic solutions of a generalized system of piecewise linear difference equations. *Adv. Differ. Equ.* **2015**, *2015*, 248. [CrossRef]
13. Tikjha, W.; Lapierre, E.; Sitthiwirattham, T. The stable equilibrium of a system of piecewise linear difference equations. *Adv. Differ. Equ.* **2017**, *2017*, 67. [CrossRef]
14. Tikjha, W. Prime period 4 solution and equilibrium point of the system of difference equation $x_{n+1} = |x_n| - y_n - 2$ and $y_{n+1} = x_n - |y_n| + 1$ where $x_0 = 0$ and $0 < y_0 < \frac{1}{2}$. *Srinakharinwirot Sci. J.* **2017**, *33*, 183–194. (In Thai)
15. Tikjha, W.; Piasu, K. A necessary condition for eventually equilibrium or periodic to a system of difference equations. *J. Comput. Anal. Appl.* **2020**, *28*, 254–260.
16. Tikjha, W.; Lapierre, E. Periodic solutions of a system of piecewise linear difference equations. *Kyungpook Math. J.* **2020**, *60*, 401–413. [CrossRef]
17. Tikjha, W.; Watcharasuntonkit, S.; Rartchapan, N. Equilibrium Point and Prime Period 4 in Certain Piecewise Linear System of Difference Equation, NU. *Int. J. Sci.* **2020**, *17*, 14–22.

Article

Some Properties of Euler's Function and of the Function τ and Their Generalizations in Algebraic Number Fields

Nicuşor Minculete * and Diana Savin

Faculty of Mathematics and Computer Science, Transilvania University, Iuliu Maniu Street 50, 500091 Braşov, Romania; diana.savin@unitbv.ro or dianet72@yahoo.com
* Correspondence: minculete.nicusor@unitbv.ro

Abstract: In this paper, we find some inequalities which involve Euler's function, extended Euler's function, the function τ, and the generalized function τ in algebraic number fields.

Keywords: arithmetic functions; algebraic number fields; Dedekind rings

MSC: primary: 11A25; 11R04; secondary: 11Y70; 13F05

1. Introduction and Preliminaries

Let the function $\varphi : \mathbb{N}^* \to \mathbb{N}^*$, $\varphi(n) = |\{k \in \mathbb{N}^* | k \leq n, (k,n) = 1\}|$, $(\forall) \, n \in \mathbb{N}^*$. φ is called *Euler's function* or *Euler's totient function*. We remark that $\varphi(n)$ is the number of invertible elements in the unitary ring $\mathbb{Z}/n\mathbb{Z}$. If $n \in \mathbb{N}, n \geq 2$, the following formula to calculate $\varphi(n)$ is known: if $l \in \mathbb{N}^*$, $n = p_1^{\alpha_1} \cdot p_2^{\alpha_2} \cdot \ldots \cdot p_l^{\alpha_l}$, where $p_1, p_2 \ldots p_l \in \mathbb{N}$ are unique distinct prime numbers and $\alpha_i \in \mathbb{N}^*$, $i = \overline{1,l}$ then $\varphi(n) = n \cdot \left(1 - \frac{1}{p_1}\right) \cdot \left(1 - \frac{1}{p_2}\right) \cdot \ldots \cdot \left(1 - \frac{1}{p_l}\right)$. A known property is that φ is a multiplicative function, but it is immediately noticed that φ is not a completely multiplicative function. An important number of monographs in number theory studied these types of functions [1–5].

Let the function $\tau : \mathbb{N}^* \to \mathbb{N}^*$, $\tau(n) = |\{k \in \mathbb{N}^* | k | n\}|$, $(\forall) \, n \in \mathbb{N}^*$. $\tau(1) = 1$. If $n \in \mathbb{N}, n \geq 2, , n = p_1^{\alpha_1} \cdot p_2^{\alpha_2} \cdot \ldots \cdot p_l^{\alpha_l}$, where $p_1, p_2 \ldots p_l \in \mathbb{N}$ are unique distinct prime numbers and $\alpha_i \in \mathbb{N}^*$, then $\tau(n) = (\alpha_1 + 1) \cdot (\alpha_2 + 1) \cdot \ldots \cdot (\alpha_l + 1)$. τ is a multiplicative function, but τ is not a completely multiplicative function.

Many analytics properties of these functions can be found in [6–8]. In [9] Rassias introduced the function

$$\phi(n, A, B) = \sum_{A \leq k \leq B, (n,k)=1} 1,$$

as a generalized totient function. He proved that:

$$\phi(n, A, B) = \sum_{d | n} \mu(d) \cdot \left(\left[\frac{B}{d}\right] - \left[\frac{A}{d}\right] \right),$$

where μ is Möbius' function (see Lemma 5.22 from [9]) and

$$\phi(n, A, B) = \frac{B - A}{n} \cdot \varphi(n) + \delta_{n,A} + O\left(\sum_{d|n} \mu(d)^2 \right),$$

for each $n, A, B \in \mathbb{N}, n > 1$, where $\delta_{n,A} = 1$ if $(n, A) = 1$, and 0 otherwise (see Proposition 5.23 from [9]).

Let n be a positive integer, $n \geq 2$, and let K be an algebraic number field, with degree $[K : \mathbb{Q}] = n$. Let $\mathcal{O}_K$ be the ring of integers of the field K, and let Spec $(\mathcal{O}_K)$ be the set of the

prime ideals of the ring $\mathcal{O}_K$. It is known that the ring of integers of an arbitrary algebraic number field K is a Dedekind domain. Let $\mathbb{J}$ be the set of ideals of the ring $\mathcal{O}_K$.

It is known that Euler's function was extended to the set $\mathbb{J}$ like this: let I be an ideal from the set $\mathbb{J}$. Taking into account that $\mathcal{O}_K$ is a Dedekind domain and the fact that in any Dedekind domain, there is a factorization theorem for ideals similar to the fundamental theorem of arithmetics in the set of integer numbers, $I = P_1^{\alpha_1} \cdot P_2^{\alpha_2} \cdot \ldots \cdot P_l^{\alpha_l}$, where $P_1, P_2, \ldots, P_l$ are unique different prime ideals in the ring $\mathcal{O}_K$ and $\alpha_i \in \mathbb{N}^*$ $i = \overline{1,l}$, and then

$$\varphi_{ext} : \mathbb{J} \to \mathbb{N}^*,$$

$$\varphi_{ext}(I) = N(I) \cdot \left(1 - \frac{1}{N(P_1)}\right) \cdot \left(1 - \frac{1}{N(P_2)}\right) \cdot \ldots \cdot \left(1 - \frac{1}{N(P_l)}\right),$$

where $N(I)$ is the norm of the ideal I. We recall the norm of an ideal I is defined as follows $N(I) = [\mathcal{O}_K : I]$. The following properties of the norm function are known:

Proposition 1.
$$N(I_1 \cdot I_2) = N(I_1) \cdot N(I_2),$$
for $(\forall)$ nonzero ideals I_1, I_2 from the set $\mathbb{J}$.

Proposition 2. *If I is an ideal from $\mathbb{J}$ with the property $N(I)$ as a prime number, then $I \in Spec(\mathcal{O}_K)$.*

Proposition 3. *If $P \in Spec(\mathcal{O}_K)$ and p is a prime positive integer such that the ideal P divides the ideal $p\mathcal{O}_K$, then $N(P) = p^f$, where $f \in \mathbb{N}^*$ is the residual degree of the ideal P.*

Proposition 4. *The norm function $N : \mathbb{J} \to \mathbb{N}^*$ is not injective.*

We recall that:

Proposition 5. *If I_1 and I_2 are nonzero ideals from $\mathbb{J}$ such that $I_1 + I_2 = \mathcal{O}_K$, then*

$$\varphi_{ext}(I_1 \cdot I_2) = \varphi_{ext}(I_1) \cdot \varphi_{ext}(I_2).$$

These results can be found in [6,10–17].

In the paper [18], the authors extended the function τ to the set $\mathbb{J}$ of the ideals of the ring $\mathcal{O}_K$. We denote this function with τ_{ext} to distinguish it from the function $\tau : \mathbb{N}^* \to \mathbb{N}^*$. Thus, $\tau_{ext} : \mathbb{J} \to \mathbb{N}^*$, $\tau_{ext}(I) =$ the number of ideals from $\mathbb{J}$, which divide the ideal I. Using the above notations, we have:

$$\tau_{ext}(I) = (\alpha_1 + 1) \cdot (\alpha_2 + 1) \cdot \ldots \cdot (\alpha_l + 1).$$

Quickly, we obtain that:

Proposition 6.
$$\tau_{ext}(I_1 \cdot I_2) = \tau_{ext}(I_1) \cdot \tau_{ext}(I_2),$$
for any I_1 and I_2 which are nonzero ideals from $\mathbb{J}$, such that $I_1 + I_2 = \mathcal{O}_K$.

In this article, we obtain certain inequalities involving the functions τ, τ_{ext}, φ, φ_{ext}.

2. Results

Popovici (in [19]) obtained the following inequality:

$$\varphi^2(a \cdot b) \leq \varphi\left(a^2\right) \cdot \varphi\left(b^2\right) \ (\forall) \ a, b \in \mathbb{N}^*,$$

where φ is Euler's function. In [20] (Proposition 3.4), Minculete and Savin proved a similar inequality, for extended Euler's function:

Proposition 7. *Let n be a positive integer, $n \geq 2$, and let K be an algebraic number field of degree $[K : \mathbb{Q}] = n$. Then:*

$$\varphi_{ext}^2(I \cdot J) \leq \varphi_{ext}(I^2) \cdot \varphi_{ext}(J^2), \ (\forall) \text{ ideals } I \text{ and } J \text{ of } \mathcal{O}_K.$$

We ask ourselves if the functions τ and τ_{ext} satisfy a similar inequality. We obtain that these functions satisfy the opposite inequality.

Proposition 8. *Let K be an algebraic number field. Then:*

$$\tau_{ext}^2(I \cdot J) \geq \tau_{ext}(I^2) \cdot \tau_{ext}(J^2), \ (\forall) \text{ ideals } I \text{ and } J \text{ of } \mathcal{O}_K.$$

Proof. Let I and J be two nonzero ideals in the ring $\mathcal{O}_K$. Applying the fundamental theorem of Dedekind rings, $(\exists !) l, r \in \mathbb{N}^*$, the different prime ideals $P_1, P_2, \ldots, P_l, P_1'', P_2'', \ldots, P_r''$ of the ring $\mathcal{O}_K$ and $\alpha_1, \alpha_2, \ldots \alpha_l, \gamma_1, \gamma_2, \ldots, \gamma_r \in \mathbb{N}^*$ such that $I = P_1^{\alpha_1} \cdot P_2^{\alpha_2} \cdot \ldots \cdot P_l^{\alpha_l} \cdot (P_1'')^{\gamma_1} \cdot \ldots \cdot (P_r'')^{\gamma_r}$ and $(\exists !) m \in \mathbb{N}^*$, the different prime ideals $P_1', P_2', \ldots, P_m'$ of the ring $\mathcal{O}_K$ and $\beta_1, \beta_2, \ldots, \beta_m, \gamma_{r+1}, \gamma_{r+2}, \ldots, \gamma_{2r} \in \mathbb{N}^*$ such that $J = (P_1')^{\beta_1} \cdot \ldots \cdot (P_m')^{\beta_m} \cdot (P_1'')^{\gamma_{r+1}} \cdot \ldots \cdot (P_r'')^{\gamma_{2r}}$. It results that

$$\tau_{ext}^2(I \cdot J) = (\alpha_1 + 1)^2 \cdot (\alpha_2 + 1)^2 \cdot \ldots \cdot (\alpha_l + 1)^2 \cdot$$

$$\cdot (\beta_1 + 1)^2 \cdot (\beta_2 + 1)^2 \cdot \ldots \cdot (\beta_m + 1)^2 \cdot (\gamma_1 + \gamma_{r+1} + 1)^2 \cdot (\gamma_2 + \gamma_{r+2} + 1)^2 \cdot \ldots \cdot (\gamma_r + \gamma_{2r} + 1)^2$$

and

$$\tau_{ext}(I^2) \cdot \tau_{ext}(J^2) = (2\alpha_1 + 1) \cdot (2\alpha_2 + 1) \cdot \ldots \cdot (2\alpha_l + 1) \cdot (2\beta_1 + 1) \cdot (2\beta_2 + 1) \cdot \ldots \cdot (2\beta_m + 1) \cdot$$

$$\cdot (2\gamma_1 + 1) \cdot (2\gamma_2 + 1) \cdot \ldots \cdot (2\gamma_r + 1) \cdot (2\gamma_{r+1} + 1) \cdot (2\gamma_{r+2} + 1) \cdot \ldots \cdot (2\gamma_{2r} + 1).$$

It immediately follows that

$$(\alpha_i + 1)^2 \geq 2\alpha_i + 1, \ (\forall) \ i = \overline{1, l},$$

$$(\beta_i + 1)^2 \geq 2\beta_i + 1, \ (\forall) \ i = \overline{1, m}$$

and

$$(\gamma_i + \gamma_{r+i} + 1)^2 \geq (2\gamma_i + 1) \cdot (2\gamma_{r+i} + 1) \Leftrightarrow (\gamma_i - \gamma_{r+i})^2 \geq 0 \ (\forall) \ i = \overline{1, r}.$$

Thus, we obtain that

$$\tau_{ext}^2(I \cdot J) \geq \tau_{ext}(I^2) \cdot \tau_{ext}(J^2), \ (\forall) \text{ ideals } I \text{ and } J \text{ of } \mathcal{O}_K.$$

□

Sivaramakrishnan (in [21]) obtained the following inequality involving Euler's function and the function τ:

Proposition 9. *For any positive integer n, the following inequality is true*

$$\varphi(n) \cdot \tau(n) \geq n.$$

Now, we generalize Proposition 9, for an extended Euler's function and the function τ_{ext}.

Proposition 10. *Let K be an algebraic number field and let $\mathcal{O}_K$ be the ring integers of the field K. Then, the following inequality is true:*

$$\varphi_{ext}(I) \cdot \tau_{ext}(I) \geq N(I), \ (\forall) \text{ a nonzero ideal } I \text{ of } \mathcal{O}_K.$$

Proof. Let I be a nonzero ideal of the ring $\mathcal{O}_K$. According to the fundamental theorem of Dedekind rings, $(\exists !) l \in \mathbb{N}^*$, the different ideals $P_1, P_2, \ldots, P_l \in Spec(\mathcal{O}_K)$ and $\alpha_1, \alpha_2, \ldots \alpha_l \in \mathbb{N}^*$ such that $I = P_1^{\alpha_1} \cdot P_2^{\alpha_2} \cdot \ldots \cdot P_l^{\alpha_l}$. Using the properties of the functions φ_{ext}, N and τ_{ext} which we specified in the introduction and preliminaries section, we have:

$$\varphi_{ext}(I) \cdot \tau_{ext}(I) = \prod_{i=1}^{l} \varphi_{ext}(P_i^{\alpha_i}) \cdot \tau_{ext}(P_i^{\alpha_i}) =$$

$$\prod_{i=1}^{l} (N(P_i))^{\alpha_i} \cdot \left(1 - \frac{1}{N(P_i)}\right) \cdot (\alpha_i + 1).$$

It results that

$$\varphi_{ext}(I) \cdot \tau_{ext}(I) = N(I) \cdot \prod_{i=1}^{l} \frac{N(P_i) - 1}{N(P_i)} \cdot (\alpha_i + 1). \tag{1}$$

It is easy to see that

$$\frac{N(P_i) - 1}{N(P_i)} \cdot (\alpha_i + 1) \geq \frac{N(P_i) - 1}{N(P_i)} \cdot 2 \geq 1, \ (\forall) \alpha_i \in \mathbb{N}^*, \ (\forall) P_i \in Spec(\mathcal{O}_K). \tag{2}$$

From (1) and (2), it results that

$$\varphi_{ext}(I) \cdot \tau_{ext}(I) \geq N(I), \ (\forall) \text{ a nonzero ideal } I \text{ of } \mathcal{O}_K.$$

□

We are giving another result involving Euler's function and the function τ.

Proposition 11. *For any positive integer n, the following inequality*

$$\frac{3\sqrt{15}}{2} \cdot \varphi(n) \geq \tau(n) \cdot \sqrt{n} \tag{3}$$

holds. The equality is obtained only for $n = 60$.

Proof. For $n = 1$, we have $\frac{3\sqrt{15}}{2} \varphi(1) = \frac{3\sqrt{15}}{2} > 1 = \tau(1)\sqrt{1}$. We take $n \geq 2$. By mathematical induction, we proved the inequality

$$\sqrt{p^d}\left(1 - \frac{1}{p}\right) \geq d + 1,$$

for every $d \geq 1$, where $p \geq 7$ is a prime number. This inequality is in fact the following:

$$\varphi(p^d) \geq \tau(p^d)\sqrt{p^d}. \tag{4}$$

We consider the decomposition in prime factors of n given by $n = 2^a 3^b 5^c \prod_{i=1}^{s} p_i^{a_i}$, $p_i \neq 2, 3, 5$. We know that if the functions φ and τ are multiplicative arithmetic functions, then the inequality of the statement becomes

$$\frac{3\sqrt{15}}{2} \varphi(2^a) \varphi(3^b) \varphi(5^c) \prod_{i=1}^{s} \varphi(p_i^{a_i}) \geq \tau(2^a)\sqrt{2^a}\tau(3^b)\sqrt{3^b}\tau(5^c)\sqrt{5^c} \prod_{i=1}^{s} \tau(p_i^{a_i})\sqrt{p_i^{a_i}}$$

$$= (a+1)(b+1)(c+1)\sqrt{2^a 3^b 5^c} \prod_{i=1}^{s}(a_i+1)\sqrt{p_i^{a_i}}.$$

It is easy to see, by mathematical induction, that for every $a, b, c \geq 1$, we have the following inequalities:

$$2^a \geq \frac{4}{9}(a+1)^2, \; 3^b \geq \frac{3}{4}(b+1)^2, \; 5^c \geq \frac{5}{4}(c+1)^2,$$

which are equivalent to

$$3\sqrt{2^a}\frac{1}{2} \geq a+1, \; \sqrt{3}\sqrt{3^b}\frac{2}{3} \geq b+1, \; \frac{\sqrt{5}}{2}\sqrt{5^c}\frac{4}{5} \geq c+1,$$

which means that

$$3\varphi(2^a) \geq \tau(2^a)\sqrt{2^a}, \; \sqrt{3}\varphi(3^b) \geq \tau(3^b)\sqrt{3^b}, \; \frac{\sqrt{5}}{2}\varphi(5^c) \geq \tau(5^c)\sqrt{5^c}.$$

Using the above inequalities and (4), we deduce the inequality of the statement. In the case when $c = 0$, we have $n = 2^a 3^b \prod_{i=1}^{s} p_i^{a_i}$, so the inequality of the statement becomes

$$\frac{3\sqrt{15}}{2}\varphi(2^a)\varphi(3^b)\prod_{i=1}^{s}\varphi(p_i^{a_i}) = \frac{\sqrt{5}}{2}3\varphi(2^a)\sqrt{3}\varphi(3^b)\prod_{i=1}^{s}\varphi(p_i^{a_i}) \geq \frac{\sqrt{5}}{2}\tau(n)\sqrt{n} > \tau(n)\sqrt{n}.$$

Analogously, the cases are treated when at least one of the numbers a, b, c is equal to 0. Therefore, the inequality of the statement is true.

Now, we prove that the equality in (3) is obtained only for $n = 60$. For this, we study the equality

$$\frac{3\sqrt{15}}{2} \cdot \varphi(n) = \tau(n) \cdot \sqrt{n}. \tag{5}$$

If $n \not\equiv 0 \pmod{15}$, then $n = 15k + r$, where $k \in \mathbb{N}, r \in \{1, \ldots, 14\}$, which means that

$$\sqrt{\frac{15}{15k+r}} = \frac{2\tau(15k+r)}{3\varphi(15k+r)} \in \mathbb{Q},$$

which is false, because $\sqrt{\frac{15}{15k+r}} \notin \mathbb{Q}$. To prove this, we assume by absurdity that $\sqrt{\frac{15}{15k+r}} \in \mathbb{Q}$, so there are $a, b \in \mathbb{N}^*, (a, b) = 1$ such that $\sqrt{\frac{15}{15k+r}} = \frac{b}{a}$. This implies the equality

$$b^2 \cdot (15k + r) = 15a^2.$$

Since $(15k+r, 15) \in \{1, 3, 5\}$, we obtain that $b \equiv 0 \pmod{15}$ when $(15k+r, 15) = 1$, $b \equiv 0 \pmod 5$ when $(15k+r, 15) = 3$, respectively, $b \equiv 0 \pmod 3$ when $(15k+r, 15) = 5$. In the first case, when $(15k+r, 15) = 1$, we find $b = 15b'$, where $b' \in \mathbb{N}$. Therefore, the above equality becomes

$$15(b')^2 \cdot (15k+r) = a^2.$$

It results that $a \equiv 0 \pmod{15}$, which is false because $(a, b) = 1$.

In the second case, when $(15k+r, 15) = 3$, we find $r = 3r'$ and $b = 5b'$, where $r \in \{3, 6, 9, 12\}, b' \in \mathbb{N}$. We obtain that

$$5(b')^2 \cdot (5k + r') = a^2.$$

It results that $a \equiv 0 \pmod 5$, which is false because $(a, b) = 1$.

Analogously, we obtain a contradiction in the third case, when $(15k+r, 15) = 5$.

If $n \equiv 0 \pmod{15}$, then we have $n = 15k$, with $k \in \mathbb{N}^*$. Replacing it in equality (5), we obtain
$$2\sqrt{k} \cdot \tau(15k) = 3\varphi(15k),$$
which can be written as
$$\sqrt{k} = \frac{3\varphi(15k)}{2\tau(15k)} \in \mathbb{Q},$$
thus, there exists $q \in \mathbb{N}^*$ such that $k = q^2$. Replacing it in the above equality, we deduce the following relation
$$3\varphi\left(15q^2\right) = 2q\tau\left(15q^2\right). \tag{6}$$
If $(15, q) = 1$, then relation (6) becomes
$$3\varphi\left(q^2\right) = q\tau\left(q^2\right). \tag{7}$$
We study equality (7) in two cases:

Case I: when q is a prime number, we obtain
$$3q(q-1) = 3q,$$
it follows that $q = 2$, so $k = 4$. Therefore, we have $n = 60$.

Case II: when q is a compose number,
$\varphi\left(q^2\right)$ is an even number and $\tau\left(q^2\right)$ is an odd number. It follows from relation (7) that q is an even number, so $q = 2^s \cdot v$, where $s, v \in \mathbb{N}^*$, v is an odd number. Relation (7) becomes
$$3\varphi\left(2^{2s} \cdot v^2\right) = 2^s \cdot v \cdot \tau\left(2^{2s} \cdot v^2\right),$$
which implies, taking into account that $(2, v) = 1$, the following inequality holds:
$$3 \cdot 2^{s-1}\varphi\left(v^2\right) = v(2s+1) \cdot \tau\left(v^2\right). \tag{8}$$
For $s \geq 2$, the term from the left part of the equality (8) is an even number and the term $(2s+1) \cdot \tau\left(v^2\right)$ is an odd number, so v is an even number, which is false, because $(2, v) = 1$. The case $q = 2v$ then remains, where $v \geq 3$ is an odd number. Relation (7) becomes
$$\varphi\left(v^2\right) = v\tau\left(v^2\right),$$
but $\varphi\left(v^2\right)$ is an even number and $\tau\left(v^2\right)$ is an odd number; thus, we deduce that the number v is an even number, which is false.

If $(15, q) \neq 1$, then $q = 3^a 5^b$ or $q = 3^a 5^b \prod_{p \text{ prime } p \geq 7} p^c$, where $a, b \in \mathbb{N}$, with $a + b \geq 1$ and $c \in \mathbb{N}^*$. We note $P = \prod_{p \text{ prime, } p \geq 7} p^c$. For $q = 3^a 5^b$, relation (6) becomes
$$3\varphi\left(3^{2a+1}5^{2b+1}\right) = 2 \cdot 3^a 5^b \tau\left(3^{2a+1}5^{2b+1}\right),$$
which is equivalent to $3^{a+1}5^b = (a+1)(b+1)$, which is false, because $3^{a+1}5^b > (a+1)(b+1)$, and it is easy to see by mathematical induction for $a, b \in \mathbb{N}$, with $a + b \geq 1$. For $q = 3^a 5^b P$, relation (6) becomes
$$3\varphi\left(3^{2a+1}5^{2b+1}P^2\right) = 2 \cdot 3^a 5^b P\tau\left(3^{2a+1}5^{2b+1}P^2\right),$$
which is equivalent to $3^{a+1}5^b \varphi(P^2) = (a+1)(b+1)P\tau(P^2)$, so we obtain
$$3^{a+1}5^b \prod_{p \text{ prime, } p \geq 7}(p^c - 1) = (a+1)(b+1)\prod(2c+1).$$

However, by mathematical induction, we have $p^c - 1 > 2c + 1$, where $p \geq 7$ and $c \geq 1$. Combining the above inequalities, we prove that $3^{a+1}5^b \prod_{p \text{ prime}, p \geq 7}(p^c - 1) > (a+1)(b+1)\prod(2c+1)$. Consequently, the statement is true. □

Now, we generalize Proposition 11, for extended Euler's function and the function τ_{ext}.

Proposition 12. *Let K be an algebraic number field of degree $[K : \mathbb{Q}] = n$, where n is a positive integer, $n \geq 2$. Then:*

$$3^{r_1} \cdot \sqrt{3}^{r_2} \cdot \left(\frac{4}{3}\right)^{r_3} \cdot \left(\frac{\sqrt{5}}{2}\right)^{r_4} \cdot \varphi_{ext}(I) \geq \tau_{ext}(I) \cdot \sqrt{N(I)}, \, (\forall) \text{ a nonzero ideal } I \text{ of } \mathcal{O}_K,$$

where r_1 is the number of prime ideals of norm 2, which divides I; r_2 is the number of prime ideals of norm 3, which divides I; r_3 is the number of prime ideals of norm 4, which divides I; and r_4 is the number of prime ideals of norm 5, which divides I.

Proof. Let I be a nonzero ideal of the ring $\mathcal{O}_K$. Applying the fundamental theorem of Dedekind rings, Propositions 3 and 4, it results that $(\exists!) r_1, r_2, r_3, r_4, l \in \mathbb{N}, l \geq 5$, the different prime ideals $P_{11}, ..., P_{1r_1}, P_{21}, ..., P_{2r_2}, P_{31}, ..., P_{3r_3}, P_{41}, ..., P_{4r_4}, P_5, P_6, ..., P_l$ of the ring $\mathcal{O}_K$ and $\alpha_{11}, ..., \alpha_{1r_1}, \alpha_{21}, ..., \alpha_{2r_2}, \alpha_{31}, ..., \alpha_{3r_3}, \alpha_{41}, ..., \alpha_{4r_4} \in \mathbb{N}, \alpha_5, ... \alpha_l \in \mathbb{N}^*$ such that

$$I = \prod_{i=1}^{r_1} P_{1i}^{\alpha_{1i}} \cdot \prod_{i=1}^{r_2} P_{2i}^{\alpha_{2i}} \cdot \prod_{i=1}^{r_3} P_{3i}^{\alpha_{3i}} \cdot \prod_{i=1}^{r_4} P_{4i}^{\alpha_{4i}} \cdot P_5^{\alpha_5} \cdot ... \cdot P_l^{\alpha_l},$$

with $N(P_{1i}) = 2, i = \overline{1, r_1}$, $N(P_{2i}) = 3, i = \overline{1, r_2}$, $N(P_{3i}) = 4, i = \overline{1, r_3}$, $N(P_{4i}) = 5, i = \overline{1, r_4}$ and $N(P_i) \geq 7, (\forall) i = \overline{5, l}$.

Applying the inequality $\sqrt{a^d} \cdot \left(1 - \frac{1}{a}\right) \geq d + 1, (\forall) d, a \in \mathbb{N}^*, a \geq 7$ for $a = N(P_i)$ we obtain:

$$\sqrt{(N(P_i))^d} \cdot \left(1 - \frac{1}{N(P_i)}\right) \geq d + 1, (\forall) d \in \mathbb{N}^*, (\forall) P_i \in \mathbb{J}, N(P_i) \geq 7.$$

The last inequality is equivalent with

$$\sqrt{(N(P_i))^{\alpha_i}} \cdot \left(1 - \frac{1}{N(P_i)}\right) \geq \alpha_i + 1, (\forall) P_i | I, (\forall) i = \overline{5, l}.$$

It results that

$$\prod_{i=5}^{l} \sqrt{(N(P_i))^{\alpha_i}} \cdot \left(1 - \frac{1}{N(P_i)}\right) \geq \prod_{i=5}^{l} \tau_{ext}(P_i^{\alpha_i}). \tag{9}$$

Applying the inequality $3\sqrt{2^d} \cdot \left(1 - \frac{1}{2}\right) \geq d + 1, (\forall) d \in \mathbb{N}^*$, for $N(P_{1i}) = 2$ and for $d = \alpha_{1i}, (\forall) i = \overline{1, r_1}$, we obtain:

$$3\sqrt{(N(P_{1i}))^{\alpha_{1i}}} \cdot \left(1 - \frac{1}{N(P_{1i})}\right) \geq \alpha_{1i} + 1, (\forall) i = \overline{1, r_1}.$$

From this last inequality, it results that

$$3^{r_1} \cdot \prod_{i=1}^{r_1} \sqrt{(N(P_{1i}))^{\alpha_{1i}}} \cdot \left(1 - \frac{1}{N(P_{1i})}\right) \geq \prod_{i=1}^{r_1} \tau_{ext}(P_{1i}^{\alpha_{1i}}). \tag{10}$$

Applying the inequality $\sqrt{3} \cdot \sqrt{3^d} \cdot \left(1 - \frac{1}{3}\right) \geq d+1$, $(\forall)\, d \in \mathbb{N}^*$, for $N(P_{2i}) = 3$ and for $d = \alpha_{2i}$, $(\forall)\, i = \overline{1, r_2}$, we obtain:

$$\sqrt{3}\sqrt{(N(P_{2i}))^{\alpha_{2i}}} \cdot \left(1 - \frac{1}{N(P_{2i})}\right) \geq \alpha_{2i} + 1,\ (\forall)\, i = \overline{1, r_2}.$$

From this last inequality, it results that

$$\sqrt{3}^{r_2} \cdot \prod_{i=1}^{r_2} \sqrt{(N(P_{2i}))^{\alpha_{2i}}} \cdot \left(1 - \frac{1}{N(P_{2i})}\right) \geq \prod_{i=1}^{r_2} \tau_{ext}\left(P_{2i}^{\alpha_{2i}}\right). \tag{11}$$

Applying the inequality $\frac{4}{3} \cdot \sqrt{4^d} \cdot \left(1 - \frac{1}{4}\right) \geq d+1$, $(\forall)\, d \in \mathbb{N}^*$, for $N(P_{3i}) = 4$ and for $d = \alpha_{3i}$, $(\forall)\, i = \overline{1, r_3}$, we obtain:

$$\frac{4}{3}\sqrt{(N(P_{3i}))^{\alpha_{3i}}} \cdot \left(1 - \frac{1}{N(P_{3i})}\right) \geq \alpha_{3i} + 1,\ (\forall)\, i = \overline{1, r_3}.$$

From this last inequality, it results that

$$\left(\frac{4}{3}\right)^{r_3} \cdot \prod_{i=1}^{r_3} \sqrt{(N(P_{3i}))^{\alpha_{3i}}} \cdot \left(1 - \frac{1}{N(P_{3i})}\right) \geq \prod_{i=1}^{r_3} \tau_{ext}\left(P_{3i}^{\alpha_{3i}}\right). \tag{12}$$

Applying the inequality $\frac{\sqrt{5}}{2} \cdot \sqrt{5^d} \cdot \left(1 - \frac{1}{5}\right) \geq d+1$, $(\forall)\, d \in \mathbb{N}^*$, for $N(P_{4i}) = 5$ and for $d = \alpha_{4i}$, $(\forall)\, i = \overline{1, r_4}$, we obtain:

$$\frac{\sqrt{5}}{2}\sqrt{(N(P_{4i}))^{\alpha_{4i}}} \cdot \left(1 - \frac{1}{N(P_{4i})}\right) \geq \alpha_{4i} + 1,\ (\forall)\, i = \overline{1, r_4}.$$

From this last inequality, it results that

$$\left(\frac{\sqrt{5}}{2}\right)^{r_4} \cdot \prod_{i=1}^{r_4} \sqrt{(N(P_{4i}))^{\alpha_{4i}}} \cdot \left(1 - \frac{1}{N(P_{4i})}\right) \geq \prod_{i=1}^{r_4} \tau_{ext}\left(P_{4i}^{\alpha_{4i}}\right). \tag{13}$$

Multiplying member-by-member inequalities (9)–(13) and applying Propositions 5 and 6, we obtain that

$$3^{r_1} \cdot \sqrt{3}^{r_2} \cdot \left(\frac{4}{3}\right)^{r_3} \cdot \left(\frac{\sqrt{5}}{2}\right)^{r_4} \cdot \varphi_{ext}(I) \geq \tau_{ext}(I) \cdot \sqrt{N(I)},$$

$(\forall)$ a nonzero ideal I of the ring $\mathcal{O}_K$. □

3. Conclusions

Regarding the Number Theory, many papers studied the properties of the Euler totient function and the function that characterizes the number of divisors of a natural number. In this paper, we have presented some arithmetic inequalities that can be extended to inequalities in the algebraic fields theory. If K is an algebraic number field, then we deduce:

$$\tau_{ext}^2(I \cdot J) \geq \tau_{ext}\left(I^2\right) \cdot \tau_{ext}\left(J^2\right),\ (\forall)\ \text{ideals}\ I\ \text{and}\ J\ \text{of}\ \mathcal{O}_K.$$

For any positive integer n, the following inequality $\varphi(n) \cdot \tau(n) \geq n$ holds. This inequality has been extended to an algebraic number field K:

$$\varphi_{ext}(I) \cdot \tau_{ext}(I) \geq N(I),\ (\forall)\ \text{a nonzero ideal}\ I\ \text{of}\ \mathcal{O}_K,$$

where $\mathcal{O}_K$ is the ring integers of the field K. Another interesting arithmetic inequality is proven, namely:

$$\frac{3\sqrt{15}}{2} \cdot \varphi(n) \geq \tau(n) \cdot \sqrt{n},$$

for any positive integer n. This generates the following inequality in an algebraic number field K with the degree $[K : \mathbb{Q}] = n, n \geq 2$:

$$3^{r_1} \cdot \sqrt{3}^{r_2} \cdot \left(\frac{4}{3}\right)^{r_3} \cdot \left(\frac{\sqrt{5}}{2}\right)^{r_4} \cdot \varphi_{ext}(I) \geq \tau_{ext}(I) \cdot \sqrt{N(I)},$$

for all nonzero ideal I of $\mathcal{O}_K$, where r_1 is the number of prime ideals of norm 2, which divides I, r_2 is the number of prime ideals of norm 3, which divides I, r_3 is the number of prime ideals of norm 4, which divides I, and r_4 is the number of prime ideals of norm 5, which divides I.

In future research, we will search for other arithmetic inequalities that can extend to an algebraic field. We can see how some calculations are transferred from the elementary number theory to algebraic fields theory. It should be mentioned that these calculations cannot always be done by analogy.

Author Contributions: Conceptualization, N.M. and D.S.; methodology, N.M. and D.S.; validation, N.M. and D.S.; formal analysis, N.M. and D.S.; investigation, N.M. and D.S.; resources, N.M. and D.S.; writing—original draft preparation, N.M. and D.S.; writing—review and editing, N.M. and D.S.; visualization, N.M. and D.S.; supervision, N.M. and D.S. All authors have read and agreed to the published version of the manuscript.

Funding: Both authors acknowledges the financial support from Transilvania University of Brașov.

Institutional Review Board Statement: Not applicable.

Informed Consent Statement: Not applicable.

Data Availability Statement: Not applicable.

Acknowledgments: The authors want to thank the anonymous reviewers and editor for their careful reading of the manuscript and for many valuable remarks and suggestions.

Conflicts of Interest: The authors declare no conflict of interest.

References

1. Andreescu, T.; Andrica, D. *Number Theory (Structures, Examples, and Problems)*; Birkhauser: Boston, MA, USA, 2009.
2. Lemmermeyer, F. *Reciprocity Laws, from Euler to Eisenstein*; Springer: Heidelberg, Germany, 2000.
3. Nathanson, M. *Elementary Methods in Number Theory*; Springer: New York, NY, USA, 2006.
4. Sierpinski, W. *Elementary Theory of Numbers*; Panstwowe Wydawnictwo Naukowe: Warsaw, Poland, 1964.
5. Subbarao, M.V. *On Some Arithmetic Convolutions in: The Theory of Arithmetic Functions*; Lecture Notes in Mathematics; Springer: New York, NY, USA, 1972.
6. Apostol, T.M. *Introduction to Analytic Number Theory*; Springer: New York, NY, USA, 1976.
7. Iwaniek, H.; Kowalski, E. *Analytic Number Theory*; American Mathematical Society, Colloquium Publications: Providence, RI, USA, 2004
8. Postnikov, A.G. *Introduction to Analytic Number Theory*; Translations of Mathematical Monographs; American Mathematical Society: Providence, RI, USA, 1988.
9. Rassias, M. From a Cotangent Sum to a Generalized Totient Function. *Appl. Anal. Discret. Math.* **2017**, *11*, 369–385. [CrossRef]
10. Albu, T.; Ion, I.D. *Chapters of the Algebraic Number Theory*; Academy Publishing House: Bucharest, Romania, 1984. (In Romanian)
11. Alexandru, V.; Goșoniu, N.M. *Elements of Number Theory*; Bucharest University Publishing House: Bucharest, Romania, 1999. (In Romanian)
12. Ireland, K.; Rosen, M. *A Classical Introduction to Modern Number Theory*; Springe: New York, NY, USA, 1992.
13. Panaitopol, L.; Gica, A. *An Introduction to Arithmetic and Number Theory*; Bucharest University Publishing House: Bucharest, Romania, 2001. (In Romanian)
14. Ribenboim, P. *My Numbers, My Friends (Popular Lectures on Number Theory)*; Springer: New York, NY, USA, 2000.
15. Ribenboim, P. *Classical Theory of Algebraic Numbers*; Springer: New York, NY, USA, 2001.

16. Sándor, J.; Crstici, B. *Handbook of Number Theory II*; Kluwer Academic Publishers: Dordrecht, The Netherlands; Boston, MA, USA; London, UK, 2004.
17. Savin, D.; Ştefănescu, M. *Lessons of Arithmetics and Number Theory*; Matrix Rom Publishing House: Bucharest, Romania, 2008. (In Romanian)
18. Minculete, N.; Savin, D. Some Generalizations of the Functions τ and $\tau^{(e)}$ in Algebraic Number Fields. *Expo. Math.* **2020**, *39*. Available online: https://www.sciencedirect.com/science/article/abs/pii/S0723086920300347 (accessed on 20 July 2021). [CrossRef]
19. Popovici, C.P. *Number Theory*; Didactic and Pedagogical Publishing House: Bucharest, Romania, 1973. (In Romanian)
20. Minculete, N.; Savin, D. Some Properties of Extended Euler's Function and Extended Dedekind's Function. *Mathematics* **2020**, *8*, 1222. [CrossRef]
21. Sivaramakrishnan, R. *Classical Theory of Arithmetic Functions, Monographs & Textbooks in Pure and Applied Mathematics No. 126*; M. Dekker: New York, NY, USA, 1989.

Article

Regularities in Ordered n-Ary Semihypergroups

Jukkrit Daengsaen [1,†] and Sorasak Leeratanavalee [2,*,†]

[1] Department of Mathematics, Faculty of Science, Chiang Mai University, Chiang Mai 50200, Thailand; daengsaen.j@gmail.com

[2] Research Center in Mathematics and Applied Mathematics, Department of Mathematics, Faculty of Science, Chiang Mai University, Chiang Mai 50200, Thailand

* Correspondence: sorasak.l@cmu.ac.th
† These authors contributed equally to this work.

Abstract: This paper deals with a class of hyperstructures called ordered n-ary semihypergroups which are studied by means of j-hyperideals for all positive integers $1 \leq j \leq n$ and $n \geq 3$. We first introduce the notion of (softly) left regularity, (softly) right regularity, (softly) intra-regularity, complete regularity, generalized regularity of ordered n-ary semihypergroups and investigate their related properties. Several characterizations of them in terms of j-hyperideals are provided. Finally, the relationships between various classes of regularities in ordered n-ary semihypergroups are also established.

Keywords: ordered semihypergroup; n-ary semihypergroup; regular element

1. Introduction

The generalization of classical algebraic structures to n-ary structures, where $n \geq 2$, was first proposed by Kasner [1] in 1904. In particular, an n-ary semigroup is the simplest n-ary structure that represents a generalization of ordinary semigroups. It is well known that ideals in semigroups play a significant role for studying the structural properties of regular semigroups. In 1963, Sioson [2] investigated remarkable properties of j-ideals in n-ary semigroups where $1 \leq j \leq n$ and $n \geq 2$. Moreover, the author introduced the concept of regular n-ary semigroups, which is an extension of the concept of regular semigroups, and characterized them in terms of principal j-ideals. We noticed that the notion of j-ideals in n-ary semigroups can be considered as a generalization of (right, left) ideals in classical semigroups. In 1979, Dudek and Groździńska [3] introduced a new concept of regular n-ary semigroups for $n \geq 3$ and discussed its related properties. On the other hand, the concept of j-ideals in n-ary semigroups was extended to considering ordered n-ary semigroups by Simueny et al. [4]. Pornsurat et al. [5] investigated the characterizations of intra-regular ordered n-ary semigroups by means of semiprime j-ideals. For a special case $n = 3$, several kinds of regularity of ordered ternary semigroups in terms of entirely ideal-theoretical characterizations have been studied by different authors. For example, the regular ordered ternary semigroup in terms of quasi-ideals and bi-ideals was described by Daddi and Pawar [6]. Some properties of left regular, right regular, completely regular, intra-regular and lightly regular ordered ternary semigroups by means of semiprime ideals were investigated by Pornsurat and Pibaljommee [7] and Kar et al. [8]. Additionally, several types of weak regularity of ordered ternary semigroups in terms of fuzzy ideals were studied by Bashir and Du [9].

The investigation of hyperstructure theory was first initiated by Marty [10] in 1934 when he introduced and studied the concept of hypergroups as a generalization of groups by using a hyperoperation (also called multi-valued operation). Since, the hyperstructure theory has been studied by many mathematicians, see the work of Corsini [11,12], Corsini and Leoreanu [13], Davvaz and Leoreanu [14], Cristea et al. [15,16], Vougiouklis [17] and Heidari et al. [18]. In 2009, Davvaz et al. [19] introduced a special class of hyperstructures called n-ary semihypergroups, which is a natural extension of semigroups, n-ary semigroups and semihypergroups. Such an n-ary hyperstructure and its generalization have been widely studied from the theoretical point of view and for application in many subjects of pure and applied mathematics—for example, applications in biology [20,21] and in chemistry [22–24]. In [25], Hila et al. introduced the concept of j-hyperideals of n-ary semihypergroups, which is a generalization of j-ideals of n-ary semigroups, and discussed the related properties. The interesting properties of j-hyperideals in ternary semihypergroups and n-ary semihypergroups can be found in [26,27]. The left regularity, right regularity, intra-regularity, and complete regularity of ternary semihypergroups in terms of various j-hyperideals were characterized by Naka et al. [28,29]. Moreover, several kinds of regularity of ordered ternary semihypergroups have been investigated by Basar et al. [30] and Talee et al. [31]. Motivated by previous works on hyperideal theory in (ordered) ternary semihypergroups, in this paper we attempt to study the regularity of ordered n-ary semihypergroups, where $n \geq 3$. We introduce the concept of (softly) left regularity, (softly) right regularity, (softly) intra-regularity, complete regularity and generalized regularity of ordered n-ary semihypergroups and study their related properties. Several characterizations of them in terms of j-hyperideals are investigated. Finally, the relationships between various classes of regularities in ordered n-ary semihypergroups are also presented. As an application of our results, the corresponding results in (ordered) n-ary semigroups and n-ary semihypergroups are also obtained.

2. Preliminaries

Let S be a nonempty set and let $\mathcal{P}^*(S)$ be the set of all nonempty subsets of S. A mapping $f : S \times \cdots \times S \to \mathcal{P}^*(S)$, where S appears $n \geq 2$ times, is called an *n-ary hyperoperation*. A structure (S, f) is called an *n-ary hypergroupoid* [32]. For simplicity of notion, we use the abbreviated symbol a_j^k to denote a sequence of elements $a_j, a_{j+1}, \ldots, a_k$ of S. For the case $k < j$, a_j^k is the empty symbol. For convenience, we write $f(a_1^n)$ instead of $f(a_1, a_2, \ldots, a_n)$, and write $f(a_1^j, b_{j+1}^k, c_{k+1}^n)$ instead of $f(a_1, \ldots, a_j, b_{j+1}, \ldots, b_k, c_{k+1}, \ldots, c_n)$. In the case where $a_1 = \ldots = a_j = a$ and $c_{k+1} = \ldots = c_n = c$, we write the second expression in the form $f(a^j, b_{j+1}^k, c^{n-k})$. For any abbreviated symbol of a sequence of subsets of S, we denote analogously. For $A_1, \ldots, A_n \in \mathcal{P}^*(S)$, we define

$$f(A_1^n) = f(A_1, \ldots, A_n) := \bigcup \{f(a_1^n) : a_j \in A_j, j = 1, \ldots, n\}.$$

If $A_1 = \{a_1\}$, then we write $f(\{a_1\}, A_2^n)$ as $f(a_1, A_2^n)$ and analogously in other cases. In the case $A_1 = \ldots = A_j = Y$ and $A_{j+1} = \ldots = A_n = Z$, we write $f(A_1^n)$ as $f(Y^j, Z^{n-j})$.

An n-ary hyperoperation f of an n-ary hypergroupoid (S, f) is called *associative* [19] if

$$f(a_1^{i-1}, f(a_i^{n+i-1}), a_{n+i}^{2n-1}) = f(a_1^{j-1}, f(a_j^{n+j-1}), a_{n+j}^{2n-1})$$

hold for all $a_1^{2n-1} \in S$ and for all $1 \leq i \leq j \leq n$. An n-ary hypergroupoid (S, f) is called an *n-ary semihypergroup* (also called an *n-ary hypersemigroup* [19,33]) if f satisfies the associative law. For any positive integer $m = k(n-1) + 1$, where $k \geq 2$, the m-ary hyperoperation g of the form

$$g(a_1^{k(n-1)+1}) = \underbrace{f(f(\ldots f(f(a_1^n), a_{n+1}^{2n-1}), \ldots), a_{(k-1)(n-1)+2}^{k(n-1)+1})}_{f \text{ appears } k \text{ times}}$$

is denoted by f_k. In this case, f_k is said to be an *m-ary hyperoperation derived from f* [32].

An *ordered n-ary semihypergroup* $(S, f, \leq)$ (also called a *partially ordered n-ary semihypergroup* or a *po-n-ary semihypergroup*) is an n-ary semihypergroup (S, f) and a partially ordered set $(S, \leq)$ such that a partial order $\leq$ is compatible with f. Indeed, for any $a, b \in S$,

$$a \leq b \text{ implies } f(c_1^{j-1}, a, c_{j+1}^n) \preceq f(c_1^{j-1}, b, c_{j+1}^n)$$

for all $c_1^n \in S$ and for all $1 \leq j \leq n$. Note that, for any $X, Y \in \mathcal{P}^*(S)$, $X \preceq Y$ means for every $x \in X$ there exists $y \in Y$ such that $x \leq y$. If H is an n-ary subsemihypergroup of an ordered n-ary semihypergroup $(S, f, \leq)$, i.e., $f(H^n) \subseteq H$, then $(H, f, \leq)$ is an ordered n-ary semihypergroup.

Throughout this paper, S stands for an ordered n-ary semihypergroup $(S, f, \leq)$ with $n \geq 3$, unless specified otherwise. Any $X \in \mathcal{P}^*(S)$ is denoted as

$$(X] = \{a \in S : a \leq b \text{ for some } b \in X\}.$$

Lemma 1 ([5]). *Let $X, Y, X_1, \ldots, X_n \in \mathcal{P}^*(S)$. Then, the following statements hold:*

(i) $X \subseteq (X]$;
(ii) $(X] = ((X]]$;
(iii) $f((X_1], (X_2], \ldots, (X_n]) \subseteq (f(X_1^n)]$;
(iv) $(X \cup Y] = (X] \cup (Y]$;
(v) $X \subseteq Y$ implies $(X] \subseteq (Y]$.

Definition 1. *For any positive integer $1 \leq j \leq n$ and $n \geq 2$, a nonempty subset A of S is called a j-hyperideal [25] of S if $f(x_1^{j-1}, a, x_{j+1}^n) \subseteq A$ for all $a \in A$, $x_1^{j-1}, x_{j+1}^n \in S$ and $(A] = A$. If A is a j-hyperideal of S, for all $1 \leq j \leq n$, then A is called a hyperideal of S.*

For any $A \in \mathcal{P}^*(S)$ and for any positive integer $1 \leq j \leq n$, we denote by $M^j(A)$ the j-hyperideal of S generated by A. In particular, we write $M^j(a)$ instead of $M^j(\{a\})$ for all $a \in S$.

Lemma 2 ([26]). *Let $A \in \mathcal{P}^*(S)$. Then, the following statements hold.*

(i) $M^1(A) = (f(A, S^{n-1}) \cup A]$;
(ii) $M^n(A) = (f(S^{n-1}, A) \cup A]$;
(iii) For any $1 < j < n$, $M^j(A) = \left(\bigcup_{k \geq 1} f_k(S^{k(j-1)}, A, S^{k(n-j)}) \cup A\right]$.

Definition 2 ([5]). *For any positive integer $1 \leq j \leq n$, a j-hyperideal A of S is called prime if, for every $x_1^n \in S$, $f(x_1^n) \subseteq A$ implies $x_i \in A$ for some $1 \leq i \leq n$. A is called semiprime if, for every $a \in S$, $f(a^n) \subseteq A$ implies $a \in A$.*

3. Regularities in Ordered n-Ary Semihypergroups

In this section, we introduce different types of regularity of ordered n-ary semihypergroups and investigate the characterization of them in terms of j-hyperideals for $1 \leq j \leq n$ and $n \geq 3$. According to the notion of regular n-ary semigroups (without order), where $n \geq 3$, which was studied by Dudek and Groździńska [3], the following definition is a generalization of such a notion on ordered n-ary semihypergroups where $n \geq 3$.

Definition 3. *Let S be an ordered n-ary semihypergroup with $n \geq 3$. An element $a \in S$ is called regular if there exist $x_2^{n-1} \in S$ such that $a \in (f(a, x_2^{n-1}, a)]$. S is called regular if every elements of S is regular, i.e., S is regular if and only if $a \in (f(a, S^{n-2}, a)]$ for all $a \in S$.*

Theorem 1. *Let S be an ordered n-ary semihypergroup with $n \geq 3$. Then, the following statements are equivalent.*

(i) S is regular;
(ii) $\bigcap_{j=1}^{n} M_j \subseteq (f(M_1, M_{n-1}, M_{n-2}, \ldots, M_2, M_n)]$ for all j-hyperideals M_j of S;
(iii) $\bigcap_{j=1}^{n} M^j(a_j) \subseteq (f(M^1(a_1), M^{n-1}(a_2), \ldots, M^2(a_{n-1}), M^n(a_n))]$ for all $a_1^n \in S$;

(iv) $\bigcap_{j=1}^{n} M^j(a) \subseteq \left(f(M^1(a), M^{n-1}(a), \ldots, M^2(a), M^n(a))\right]$ for all $a \in S$.

Proof. The proof is similar to Theroem 1 in [3]. □

Next, we introduce the concepts of left regular, right regular and intra-regular ordered n-ary semihypergroups, where $n \geq 3$. To introduce the notion of intra-regular ordered n-ary semihypergroups, the following properties are needed.

Lemma 3. *Let S be an ordered n-ary semihypergroup with $n \geq 3$. For any positive integer $1 < j < n$, the following statements are equivalent.*

(i) *For each $a \in S$ there exist $x_1^{j-1}, x_{j+1}^n \in S$ such that $a \in \left(f(x_1^{j-1}, f(a^n), x_{j+1}^n)\right]$;*
(ii) *For each $a \in S$ there exist $y_1^{2n-2} \in S$ such that $a \in \left(f(y_1^{n-1}, f(f(a^n), y_n^{2n-2}))\right]$.*

Proof. Let $a \in S$ and let j be a fixed positive integer satisfying $1 < j < n$ and $n \geq 3$.

(i) $\Longrightarrow$ (ii) Let $a \in \left(f(x_1^{j-1}, f(a^n), x_{j+1}^n)\right]$ for some $x_1^{j-1}, x_{j+1}^n \in S$. Firstly, we show that $a \in \left(f(z_1, f(a^n), z_3^n)\right]$ for some $z_1, z_3^n \in S$. For case $j = 2$ and $n \geq 3$, we are done. Suppose that $2 < j < n$ and $n > 3$, by associativity and Lemma 1, we have

$$\begin{aligned}
a &\in \left(f(x_1^{j-1}, f(a^n), x_{j+1}^n)\right] \\
&= \left(f(f(x_1^{j-1}, a^{n-j+1}), a, a^{j-2}, x_{j+1}^n)\right] \\
&\subseteq \left(f(f(x_1^{j-1}, a^{n-j+1}), f(x_1^{j-1}, f(a^n), x_{j+1}^n), a^{j-2}, x_{j+1}^n)\right] \\
&= \left(f_2(f(x_1^{j-1}, a^{n-j+1})^2, a, \{a^{j-2}, x_{j+1}^n\}^2)\right] \\
&\subseteq \ldots \\
&\subseteq \left(f_{(n-j+1)}(\{f(x_1^{j-1}, a^{n-j+1})\}^{n-j+1}, a, \{a^{j-2}, x_{j+1}^n\}^{n-j+1})\right] \\
&\subseteq \left(f_{(n-j+1)}(\{f(x_1^{j-1}, a^{n-j+1})\}^{n-j+1}, f(x_1^{j-1}, f(a^n), x_{j+1}^n), \{a^{j-2}, x_{j+1}^n\}^{n-j+1})\right] \\
&= \left(f_{(n-j+1)}(f(\{f(x_1^{j-1}, a^{n-j+1})\}^{n-j+1}, x_1^{j-1}), f(a^n), x_{j+1}^n, \{a^{j-2}, x_{j+1}^n\}^{n-j+1})\right] \\
&= \left(f_{(n-j+1)}(f(\{f(x_1^{j-1}, a^{n-j+1})\}^{n-j+1}, x_1^{j-1}), f(a^n), x_{j+1}^n, a^{j-3}, \right. \\
&\quad\left. a, x_{j+1}^n, \{a^{j-2}, x_{j+1}^n\}^{n-j})\right] \\
&= \left(f(f(\{f(x_1^{j-1}, a^{n-j+1})\}^{n-j+1}, x_1^{j-1}), f(a^n), x_{j+1}^n, a^{j-3}, \right. \\
&\quad \underbrace{f(a, x_{j+1}^n, a^{j-2}, f(x_{j+1}^n, a^{j-2}, x_{j+1}, f(\ldots f(x_{n-1}^n, a^{j-2}, x_{j+1}^n)\ldots))))}_{f \text{ appears } n-j \text{ times}}\right] \\
&= \left(f(U, f(a^n), x_{j+1}^n, a^{j-3}, V)\right]
\end{aligned}$$

where $U := f(\{f(x_1^{j-1}, a^{n-j+1})\}^{n-j+1}, x_1^{j-1})$ and $V := f(a, x_{j+1}^n, a^{j-2}, f(x_{j+1}^n, a^{j-2}, x_{j+1}, f(\ldots f(x_{n-1}^n, a^{j-2}, x_{j+1}^n)\ldots)))$.

It follows that $a \leq b$ for some

$$b \in f(U, f(a^n), x_{j+1}^n, a^{j-3}, V) := \bigcup_{c \in U, d \in V} f(c, f(a^n), x_{j+1}^n, a^{j-3}, d).$$

Then, there exist $z_1 \in U, z_n \in V$ such that $b \in f(z_1, f(a^n), z_3^n)$, where $z_3 = x_{j+1}, \ldots,$ $z_{n-j+2} = x_n, z_{n-j+3} = a, \ldots, z_{n-1} = a$. Thus, $a \in (f(z_1, f(a^n), z_3^n)]$. Next, we consider

$$\begin{aligned}
a &\in (f(z_1, f(a^n), z_3^n)] \\
&= (f_{(2)}(z_1, a, a^{n-1}, z_3^n)] \\
&\subseteq (f_{(2)}(z_1, f_{(2)}(z_1, a, a^{n-1}, z_3^n), a^{n-1}, z_3^n)] \\
&\subseteq \ldots \\
&\subseteq (f_{(2n-2)}(\{z_1\}^{n-1}, a, \{a^{n-1}, z_3^n\}^{n-1})] \\
&= (f(\{z_1\}^{n-1}, f_{(2n-4)}(f(a^n), z_3^n, \{a^{n-1}, z_3^n\}^{n-2})] \\
&= (f(\{z_1\}^{n-1}, f(f(a^n), z_3^n, \underbrace{f(f(\ldots f(f(a^{n-1}, z_3), z_4^n, a^2), \ldots), a, z_3^n)}_{f \text{ appears } 2n-5 \text{ times}})))].
\end{aligned}$$

This means that $a \leq p$ for some

$$p \in f(\{z_1\}^{n-1}, f(f(a^n), z_3^n, \underbrace{f(f(\ldots f(f(a^{n-1}, z_3), z_4^n, a^2), \ldots), a, z_3^n)}_{f \text{ appears } 2n-5 \text{ times}}))).$$

Then, there exists $y_{2n-2} \in f(f(\ldots f(f(a^{n-1}, z_3), z_4^n, a^2), \ldots), a, z_3^n)$ such that $p \in f(y_1^{n-1}, f(f(a^n), y_n^{2n-2}))$, where $y_1 = \ldots = y_{n-1} = z_1, y_n = z_3, y_{n+1} = z_4, \ldots, y_{2n-3} = z_n$. Therefore, $a \in (f(y_1^{n-1}, f(f(a^n), y_n^{2n-2}))]$.

$(ii) \implies (i)$ Let $a \in (f(y_1^{n-1}, f(f(a^n), y_n^{2n-2}))]$ for some $y_1^{2n-2} \in S$. By associativity, we have

$$\begin{aligned}
a &\in (f(y_1^{n-1}, f(f(a^n), y_n^{2n-2}))] \\
&= (f(f(y_1^{n-1}, a), a, a^{n-3}, f(a, y_n^{2n-2}))] \\
&\subseteq (f(f(y_1^{n-1}, a), f(f(y_1^{n-1}, a), a, a^{n-3}, f(a, y_n^{2n-2})), a^{n-3}, f(a, y_n^{2n-2}))] \\
&= (f(f(f(y_1^{n-1}, a), y_1^{n-1}), f(a^n), y_n^{2n-4}, f(y_{2n-3}^{2n-2}, a^{n-3}, f(a, y_n^{2n-2})))].
\end{aligned}$$

This means that $a \leq b$ for some $b \in f(z_1, f(a^n), z_3^n)$, where $z_1 \in f(f(y_1^{n-1}, a), y_1^{n-1})$ and $z_n \in f(y_{2n-3}^{2n-2}, a^{n-3}, f(a, y_n^{2n-2}))$ and $z_3 = y_n, z_4 = y_{n+1}, \ldots, z_{n-1} = y_{2n-4}$. It follows that $a \in (f(z_1, f(a^n), z_3^n)]$. Next, we show that $a \in (f(z_1^{j-1}, f(a^n), z_{j+1}^n)]$.

For case $j = 2$ and $n \geq 3$, we have $a \in (f(z_1, f(a^n), z_3^n)] = (f(z_1^{j-1}, f(a^n), z_{j+1}^n)]$.
For case $2 < j < n$ and $n > 3$, we have

$$\begin{aligned}
a &\in (f(z_1, f(a^n), z_3^n)] \\
&= (f_2(z_1, a^{j-3}, a, a^{n-j+2}, z_3^n)] \\
&\subseteq (f_2(z_1, a^{j-3}, f(z_1, f(a^n), z_3^n), a^{n-j+2}, z_3^n)] \\
&= (f(z_1, a^{j-3}, z_1, f(a^n), z_3^{n-j+1}, f(z_{n-j+2}^n, a^{n-j}, f(a^2, z_3^n)))].
\end{aligned}$$

Consequently, there exists $c \in f(x_1^{j-1}, f(a^n), x_{j+1}^n)$ such that $a \leq c$ where $x_1 = z_1 = x_{j-1}, x_2 = x_3 = \ldots = x_{j-2} = a, x_{j+1} = z_3, x_{j+2} = z_4, \ldots, x_{n-1} = z_{n+1}$ and $x_n \in f(z_{n-j+2}^n, a^{n-j}, f(a^2, z_3^n))$. Therefore, $a \in (f(x_1^{j-1}, f(a^n), x_{j+1}^n)]$. □

Without loss of generality, we introduce the notion of intra-regular ordered n-ary semihypergroups, where $n \geq 3$, as follows.

Definition 4. Let S be an ordered n-ary semihypergroup with $n \geq 3$. Let $a \in S$.
(i) a is called left regular if there exist $x_1^{n-1} \in S$ such that $a \in \left(f(x_1^{n-1}, f(a^n))\right]$;
(ii) a is called right regular if there exist $x_1^{n-1} \in S$ such that $a \in \left(f(f(a^n), x_1^{n-1})\right]$;
(iii) a is called intra-regular if it satisfies one of the equivalent conditions in Lemma 3.

Furthermore, S is said to be (left regular, right regular) intra-regular if every element of S is (left regular, right regular) intra-regular.

Clearly, the concept of an intra-regular ordered ternary semihypergroup, which was introduced in Definition 2.29 [31], is equal to Definition 4(iii) (for $n = 3$) under the condition (i) of Lemma 3. Moreover, if we consider any ordered n-ary semigroup as an ordered n-ary semihypergroup, then Definition 8 in [5] and Definition 4(iii) under the condition (ii) of Lemma 3 coincide.

Remark 1. Let S be an ordered n-ary semihypergroup with $n \geq 3$. Then, the following statements hold.
(i)   S is left regular if and only if $a \in \left(f(S, a^{n-1})\right]$ for all $a \in S$;
(ii) S is right regular if and only if $a \in \left(f(a^{n-1}, S)\right]$ for all $a \in S$;
(iii) S is intra-regular if and only if one of the following two conditions holds.
   (1) For any $1 < j < n$, $a \in \left(f(S^{j-1}, f(a^n), S^{n-j})\right]$ for all $a \in S$.
   (2) $a \in \left(f(S^{n-1}, f(f(a^n), S^{n-1}))\right]$ for all $a \in S$.

Example 1. Let $S = \{a, b, c, d, e\}$. Define a ternary hyperoperation $f : S \times S \times S \to \mathcal{P}^*(S)$ by the following table

f	a	b	c	d	e
aa	S	$\{b,c,e\}$	$\{b,c,e\}$	S	$\{b,c,e\}$
ab	S	$\{b,c,e\}$	$\{b,c,e\}$	S	$\{b,c,e\}$
ac	S	$\{b,c,e\}$	$\{b,c,e\}$	S	$\{b,c,e\}$
ad	S	$\{b,c,e\}$	$\{b,c,e\}$	S	$\{b,c,e\}$
ae	S	$\{b,c,e\}$	$\{b,c,e\}$	S	$\{b,c,e\}$

f	a	b	c	d	e
ba	$\{b,c,d\}$	b	b	$\{b,c,d\}$	b
bb	$\{b,c,d\}$	b	b	$\{b,c,d\}$	b
bc	$\{b,c,d\}$	b	b	$\{b,c,d\}$	b
bd	$\{b,c,d\}$	b	b	$\{b,c,d\}$	b
be	$\{b,c,d\}$	b	b	$\{b,c,d\}$	b

f	a	b	c	d	e
ca	$\{b,c,d\}$	b	b	$\{b,c,d\}$	b
cb	$\{b,c,d\}$	b	b	$\{b,c,d\}$	b
cc	$\{b,c,d\}$	b	b	$\{b,c,d\}$	b
cd	$\{b,c,d\}$	b	b	$\{b,c,d\}$	b
ce	$\{b,c,d\}$	b	b	$\{b,c,d\}$	b

f	a	b	c	d	e
da	$\{b,c,d\}$	b	b	$\{b,c,d\}$	b
db	$\{b,c,d\}$	b	b	$\{b,c,d\}$	b
dc	$\{b,c,d\}$	b	b	$\{b,c,d\}$	b
dd	$\{b,c,d\}$	b	b	$\{b,c,d\}$	b
de	$\{b,c,d\}$	b	b	$\{b,c,d\}$	b

f	a	b	c	d	e
ea	S	$\{b,c,e\}$	$\{b,c,e\}$	S	$\{b,c,e\}$
eb	S	$\{b,c,e\}$	$\{b,c,e\}$	S	$\{b,c,e\}$
ec	S	$\{b,c,e\}$	$\{b,c,e\}$	S	$\{b,c,e\}$
ed	S	$\{b,c,e\}$	$\{b,c,e\}$	S	$\{b,c,e\}$
ee	S	$\{b,c,e\}$	$\{b,c,e\}$	S	$\{b,c,e\}$

and define a partial order on S as follows

$$\leq := \{(a,a), (b,a), (b,b), (b,d), (b,e), (c,a), (c,c), (c,d), (c,e), (d,a), (d,d), (e,a), (e,e)\}.$$

Then, (S, f) is a left regular ordered ternary semihypergroup. Moreover, it is not difficult to show that (S, f) is also a right regular ordered ternary semihypergroup.

Example 2. Let $S = \{a, b, c, d, e\}$. Define a ternary hyperoperation $f : S \times S \times S \to \mathcal{P}^*(S)$ by the following table

f	a	b	c	d	e		f	a	b	c	d	e
aa	b	b	$\{a,b,c\}$	$\{a,b,c\}$	e		ba	b	b	$\{a,b,c\}$	$\{a,b,c\}$	e
ab	b	b	$\{a,b,c\}$	$\{a,b,c\}$	e		bb	b	b	$\{a,b,c\}$	$\{a,b,c\}$	e
ac	b	b	$\{a,b,c\}$	$\{a,b,c\}$	e		bc	b	b	$\{a,b,c\}$	$\{a,b,c\}$	e
ad	b	b	$\{a,b,c\}$	$\{a,b,c\}$	e		bd	b	b	$\{a,b,c\}$	$\{a,b,c\}$	e
ae	e	e	e	e	e		be	e	e	e	e	e

f	a	b	c	d	e		f	a	b	c	d	e
ca	b	b	$\{a,b,c\}$	$\{a,b,c\}$	e		da	b	b	$\{a,b,c\}$	$\{a,b,c\}$	e
cb	b	b	$\{a,b,c\}$	$\{a,b,c\}$	e		db	b	b	$\{a,b,c\}$	$\{a,b,c\}$	e
cc	b	b	$\{a,b,c\}$	$\{a,b,c\}$	e		dc	b	b	$\{a,b,c\}$	$\{a,b,c\}$	e
cd	b	b	$\{a,b,c\}$	$\{a,b,c\}$	e		dd	b	b	$\{a,b,c\}$	d	e
ce	e	e	e	e	e		de	e	e	e	e	e

f	a	b	c	d	e
ea	e	e	e	e	e
eb	e	e	e	e	e
ec	e	e	e	e	e
ed	e	e	e	e	e
ee	e	e	e	e	e

and define a partial order on S as follows

$$\leq := \{(a,a),(a,c),(b,b),(b,c),(c,c),(d,d),(e,e)\}.$$

Then, (S, f) is an intra-regular ordered ternary semihypergroup.

Theorem 2. *S is left regular (right regular, respectively) if and only if every n-hyperideal (1-hyperideal, respectively) of S is semiprime.*

Proof. Let A be an n-hyperideal of S. Let $a \in S$ such that $f(a^n) \subseteq A$. Since S is left regular, there exist $x_1^{n-1} \in S$ such that $a \in \left(f(x_1^{n-1}, f(a^n))\right] \subseteq \left(f(x_1^{n-1}, A)\right] \subseteq (A] = A$. Thus, A is semiprime. Conversely, suppose that every n-hyperideal of S is semiprime: let $a \in S$. Clearly, $(f(S, a^{n-1})]$ is an n-hyperideal of S. Since $f(a^n) \subseteq (f(S, a^{n-1})]$, we have $a \in (f(S, a^{n-1})]$. From Remark 1, we conclude that S is a left regular ordered n-ary semihypergroup. □

Theorem 3. *S is intra-regular if and only if $A \cap H \cap B \subseteq (f(A, H^{n-2}, B)]$ for all n-hyperideals A, 1-hyperideals B of S and $H \in \mathcal{P}^*(S)$.*

Proof. Let S be an intra-regular ordered n-ary semihypergroup with $n \geq 3$. Let A be an n-hyperideal, B be a 1-hyperideal of S and $H \in \mathcal{P}^*(S)$. Suppose that $a \in A \cap H \cap B$: since S is intra-regular, there exist $x_1^{2n-2} \in S$ such that $a \in \left(f(x_1^{n-1}, f(f(a^n), x_n^{2n-2}))\right] = \left(f(f(x_1^{n-1}, a), a^{n-2}, f(a, x_n^{2n-2}))\right]$. Since $a \in A$, we have $f(x_1^{n-1}, a) \subseteq A$. Similarly, since $a \in B$, we obtain $f(a, x_n^{2n-2}) \subseteq B$. Since $a \in H$, we have $a \in (f(A, H^{n-2}, B)]$ and then $A \cap H \cap B \subseteq (f(A, H^{n-2}, B)]$. Conversely, let $a \in S$. From Lemmas 1 and 2, we have

$$a \in M^n(a) \cap (a] \cap M^1(a)$$
$$\subseteq \left(f(M^n(a), (a]^{n-2}, M^1(a)) \right]$$
$$\subseteq \left(f(\left(\{a\} \cup f(S^{n-1}, a) \right], (a]^{n-2}, \left(\{a\} \cup f(a, S^{n-1}) \right]) \right]$$
$$\subseteq (f(a^n)] \cup \left(f(a^{n-1}, f(a, S^{n-1})) \right] \cup \left(f(f(S^{n-1}, a), a^{n-2}, a) \right] \cup$$
$$\left(f(f(S^{n-1}, a), a^{n-2}, f(a, S^{n-1})) \right]$$
$$= (f(a^n)] \cup \left(f(f(a^n), S^{n-1}) \right] \cup \left(f(S^{n-1}, f(a^n)) \right] \cup \left(f(S^{n-1}, f(f(a^n), S^{n-1})) \right].$$

Case 1: $a \in (f(a^n)]$. Then, $a \in (f(a^n)] \subseteq \left(f(a^{n-1}, f(a^n)) \right] \subseteq \left(f(a^{n-1}, f(f(a^n), a^{n-1})) \right] \subseteq \left(f(S^{n-1}, f(f(a^n), S^{n-1})) \right]$.

Case 2: $a \in \left(f(f(a^n), S^{n-1}) \right]$. Then, $a \in \left(f(f(a^n), S^{n-1}) \right] \subseteq ((f(a^{n-1}, f(f(f(a^n), S^{n-1}), S^{n-1}))] = (f(a^{n-1}, f(f(a^n), S^{n-2}, f(S^n)))] \subseteq \left(f(S^{n-1}, f(f(a^n), S^{n-1})) \right]$.

Case 3: $a \in \left(f(S^{n-1}, f(a^n)) \right]$. Using the similar proof as in Case 2, we obtain $a \in \left(f(S^{n-1}, f(f(a^n), S^{n-1})) \right]$.

From Cases 1 to 3 and Lemma 1(iii), we conclude that S is intra-regular. □

Definition 5. *Let S be an ordered n-ary semihypergroup with $n \geq 3$. S is called completely regular if S is regular, left regular and right regular.*

Example 3. *Let $S = \{a, b, c, d, e\}$. Define a ternary hyperoperation $f : S \times S \times S \rightarrow \mathcal{P}^*(S)$ by the following table*

f	a	b	c	d	e
aa	$\{a,b,e\}$	$\{a,b,e\}$	$S \setminus \{d\}$	S	$\{a,b,e\}$
ab	$\{a,b,e\}$	$\{a,b,e\}$	$S \setminus \{d\}$	S	$\{a,b,e\}$
ac	$\{a,b,e\}$	$\{a,b,e\}$	$S \setminus \{d\}$	S	$\{a,b,e\}$
ad	$\{a,b,e\}$	$\{a,b,e\}$	$S \setminus \{d\}$	S	$\{a,b,e\}$
ae	$\{a,b,e\}$	$\{a,b,e\}$	$S \setminus \{d\}$	S	$\{a,b,e\}$

f	a	b	c	d	e
ba	$\{a,b,e\}$	$\{a,b,e\}$	$S \setminus \{d\}$	S	$\{a,b,e\}$
bb	$\{a,b,e\}$	b	$S \setminus \{d\}$	S	$\{a,b,e\}$
bc	$\{a,b,e\}$	$\{a,b,e\}$	$S \setminus \{d\}$	S	$\{a,b,e\}$
bd	$\{a,b,e\}$	$\{a,b,e\}$	$S \setminus \{d\}$	S	$\{a,b,e\}$
be	$\{a,b,e\}$	$\{a,b,e\}$	$S \setminus \{d\}$	S	$\{a,b,e\}$

f	a	b	c	d	e
ca	$\{a,b,e\}$	$\{a,b,e\}$	$S \setminus \{d\}$	S	$\{a,b,e\}$
cb	$\{a,b,e\}$	$\{a,b,e\}$	$S \setminus \{d\}$	S	$\{a,b,e\}$
cc	$\{a,b,e\}$	$\{a,b,e\}$	$S \setminus \{d\}$	S	$\{a,b,e\}$
cd	$\{a,b,e\}$	$\{a,b,e\}$	$S \setminus \{d\}$	S	$\{a,b,e\}$
ce	$\{a,b,e\}$	$\{a,b,e\}$	$S \setminus \{d\}$	S	$\{a,b,e\}$

f	a	b	c	d	e
da	$\{a,b,e\}$	$\{a,b,e\}$	$S \setminus \{d\}$	S	$\{a,b,e\}$
db	$\{a,b,e\}$	$\{a,b,e\}$	$S \setminus \{d\}$	S	$\{a,b,e\}$
dc	$\{a,b,e\}$	$\{a,b,e\}$	$S \setminus \{d\}$	S	$\{a,b,e\}$
dd	$\{a,b,e\}$	$\{a,b,e\}$	$S \setminus \{d\}$	S	$\{a,b,e\}$
de	$\{a,b,e\}$	$\{a,b,e\}$	$S \setminus \{d\}$	S	$\{a,b,e\}$

f	a	b	c	d	e
ea	$\{a,b,e\}$	$\{a,b,e\}$	$S \setminus \{d\}$	S	$\{a,b,e\}$
eb	$\{a,b,e\}$	$\{a,b,e\}$	$S \setminus \{d\}$	S	$\{a,b,e\}$
ec	$\{a,b,e\}$	$\{a,b,e\}$	$S \setminus \{d\}$	S	$\{a,b,e\}$
ed	$\{a,b,e\}$	$\{a,b,e\}$	$S \setminus \{d\}$	S	$\{a,b,e\}$
ee	$\{a,b,e\}$	$\{a,b,e\}$	$S \setminus \{d\}$	S	e

and define a partial order on S as follows

$$\leq := \{(a,a), (a,c), (a,d), (b,b), (b,a), (b,c), (b,d), (c,c), (c,d), (d,d), (e,a), (e,c), (e,d), (e,e)\}.$$

Then, (S, f) is a completely regular ordered ternary semihypergroup.

Lemma 4. *S is completely regular if and only if $a \in \left(f(f(a^{n-1}, S), a^{n-1}) \right]$ for all $a \in S$.*

Proof. Let S be a completely regular ordered n-ary semihypergroup and $a \in S$. Since S is regular, we have $a \in \left(f(a, S^{n-2}, a) \right]$. Since S is left regular and right regular, by Remark 1(i) and (ii), we have $a \in \left(f(S, a^{n-1}) \right]$ and $a \in \left(f(a^{n-1}, S) \right]$. It follows that $a \in \left(f(a, S^{n-2}, a) \right] \subseteq \left(f(f(a^{n-1}, S), S^{n-2}, f(S, a^{n-1})) \right] = \left(f(f(a^{n-1}, f(S^n)), a^{n-1}) \right] \subseteq \left(f(f(a^{n-1}, S), a^{n-1}) \right]$. Conversely, let $a \in S$. Then, $a \in \left(f(f(a^{n-1}, S), a^{n-1}) \right] = \left(f(a, f(a^{n-2}, S, a), a^{n-2}) \right] \subseteq \left(f(a, S^{n-2}, a) \right]$. So S is regular. Furthermore, we have $a \in$

$(f(f(a^{n-1}, S), a^{n-1})] = (f(a^{n-1}, f(S, a^{n-1}))] \subseteq (f(a^{n-1}, S)]$. From Remark 1(ii), S is right regular. Clearly, $a \in (f(f(a^{n-1}, S), a^{n-1})] \subseteq (f(S, a^{n-1})]$. From Remark 1(ii), S is left regular. Therefore, S is completely regular. □

Next, we introduce the concept of softly left, softly right and softly intra-regular ordered n-ary semihypergroups, which are generalizations of left, right and intra-regular ordered n-ary semihypergroups, where $n \geq 3$.

Definition 6. *Let S be an ordered n-ary semihypergroup with $n \geq 3$. Let $a \in S$.*
(i) *a is called softly left regular if there exist $x_1^{2n-3} \in S$ such that*

$$a \in \left(f(x_1^{n-1}, f(a, x_n^{2n-3}, a))\right].$$

(ii) *a is called softly right regular if there exist $x_1^{2n-3} \in S$ such that*

$$a \in \left(f(f(a, x_1^{n-2}, a), x_{n-1}^{2n-3})\right].$$

(iii) *a is called softly intra-regular if there exist $x_1^{3n-4} \in S$ such that*

$$a \in \left(f(x_1^{n-1}, f(f(a, x_n^{2n-3}, a), x_{2n-2}^{3n-4}))\right].$$

Additionally, S is called (softly left regular, softly right regular) softly intra-regular if each element of S is (softly left regular, softly right regular) softly intra-regular.

Remark 2. *Let S be an ordered n-ary semihypergroup with $n \geq 3$. Then, the following statements hold.*
(i) *S is softly left regular if and only if $a \in (f(S^{n-1}, f(a, S^{n-2}, a))]$ for all $a \in S$;*
(ii) *S is softly right regular if and only if $a \in (f(f(a, S^{n-2}, a), S^{n-1})]$ for all $a \in S$;*
(iii) *S is softly intra-regular if and only if $a \in (f(S^{n-1}, f(f(a, S^{n-2}, a), S^{n-1}))]$ for all $a \in S$.*

Example 4. *Let $S = \{a, b, c, d\}$. Define a ternary hyperoperation $f : S \times S \times S \to \mathcal{P}^*(S)$ by the following table*

f	a	b	c	d
aa	a	a	a	d
ab	a	a	a	d
ac	a	a	a	d
ad	d	d	d	d

f	a	b	c	d
ba	$\{a,b,c\}$	$\{a,b,c\}$	$\{a,b,c\}$	d
bb	$\{a,b,c\}$	$\{a,b,c\}$	$\{a,b,c\}$	d
bc	$\{a,b,c\}$	$\{a,b,c\}$	$\{a,b,c\}$	d
bd	d	d	d	d

f	a	b	c	d
ca	a	a	a	d
cb	a	a	a	d
cc	a	a	a	d
cd	d	d	d	d

f	a	b	c	d
da	d	d	d	d
db	d	d	d	d
dc	d	d	d	d
dd	d	d	d	d

and define a partial order on S as follows

$$\leq := \{(a,a), (a,b), (a,c), (b,b), (c,b), (c,c), (d,d)\}.$$

Then, (S, f) is a softly left regular ordered ternary semihypergroup.

Example 5. Let $S = \{a, b, c, d, e\}$. Define a ternary hyperoperation $f : S \times S \times S \rightarrow \mathcal{P}^*(S)$ by the following table

f	a	b	c	d	e
aa	b	b	b	b	e
ab	b	b	b	b	e
ac	b	b	b	b	e
ad	b	b	b	b	e
ae	e	e	e	e	e

f	a	b	c	d	e
ca	$\{a,b,c\}$	$\{a,b,c\}$	$\{a,b,c\}$	$\{a,b,c\}$	e
cb	$\{a,b,c\}$	$\{a,b,c\}$	$\{a,b,c\}$	$\{a,b,c\}$	e
cc	$\{a,b,c\}$	$\{a,b,c\}$	$\{a,b,c\}$	$\{a,b,c\}$	e
cd	$\{a,b,c\}$	$\{a,b,c\}$	$\{a,b,c\}$	$\{a,b,c\}$	e
ce	e	e	e	e	e

f	a	b	c	d	e
ba	b	b	b	b	e
bb	b	b	b	b	e
bc	b	b	b	b	e
bd	b	b	b	b	e
be	e	e	e	e	e

f	a	b	c	d	e
da	$\{a,b,c\}$	$\{a,b,c\}$	$\{a,b,c\}$	$\{a,b,c\}$	e
db	$\{a,b,c\}$	$\{a,b,c\}$	$\{a,b,c\}$	$\{a,b,c\}$	e
dc	$\{a,b,c\}$	$\{a,b,c\}$	$\{a,b,c\}$	$\{a,b,c\}$	e
dd	$\{a,b,c\}$	$\{a,b,c\}$	$\{a,b,c\}$	d	e
de	e	e	e	e	e

f	a	b	c	d	e
ea	e	e	e	e	e
eb	e	e	e	e	e
ec	e	e	e	e	e
ed	e	e	e	e	e
ee	e	e	e	e	e

and define a partial order on S as follows

$$\leq := \{(a,a), (a,c), (b,b), (b,c), (c,c), (d,d), (e,e)\}.$$

Then, (S, f) is a softly intra-regular ordered ternary semihypergroup.

Theorem 4. *Let S be an ordered n-ary semihypergroup with $n \geq 3$. Then, the following statements are equivalent.*

(i) *S is softly left regular.*
(ii) *For any positive integer $1 < j \leq n$, $M_j \cap M_n \subseteq \left(f(M_j, S^{n-2}, M_n)\right]$ for all j-hyperideals M_j and all n-hyperideals M_n of S.*
(iii) *$M_n \subseteq \left(f(M_n, S^{n-2}, M_n)\right]$ for all n-hyperideals M_n of S.*

Proof. $(i) \Longrightarrow (ii)$ Let j be a fixed positive integer such that $1 < j \leq n$ and $n \geq 3$. Let M_j be a j-hyperideal and M_n be an n-hyperideal of S and $a \in M_j \cap M_n$. Since S is softy left regular, there exist x_1^{2n-3} such that $a \in \left(f(x_1^{n-1}, f(a, x_n^{2n-3}, a))\right]$. By associativity, we have

$$\begin{aligned}
a &\in \left(f(x_1^{n-1}, f(a, x_n^{2n-3}, a))\right] \\
&\subseteq \left(f(x_1^{n-1}, f(f(x_1^{n-1}, f(a, x_n^{2n-3}, a)), x_n^{2n-3}, a))\right] \\
&\subseteq \ldots \\
&\subseteq \left(f_{2(j-1)}(\{x_1^{n-1}\}^{j-1}, a, \{x_n^{2n-3}, a\}^{j-1})\right] \\
&= \left(f_{2(j-1)}(\{x_1^{n-1}\}^{j-1}, a, x_n^{2n-3}, a, \{x_n^{2n-3}, a\}^{j-2})\right] \\
&\subseteq \left(f_{2(j-1)}(\{x_1^{n-1}\}^{j-1}, a, x_n^{2n-3}, f(x_1^{n-1}, f(a, x_n^{2n-3}, a)), \{x_n^{2n-3}, a\}^{j-2})\right]
\end{aligned}$$

$$
\begin{aligned}
&\subseteq (f_{2(j-1)}(\{x_1^{n-1}\}^{j-1},a,x_n^{2n-3},f(x_1^{n-1},f(f(x_1^{n-1},f(a,x_n^{2n-3},a)),x_n^{2n-3},a)),\\
&\quad \{x_n^{2n-3},a\}^{j-2})]\\
&\subseteq \ldots\\
&\subseteq (f_{2(j-1)}(\{x_1^{n-1}\}^{j-1},a,x_n^{2n-3},f_{2(n-j)}(\{x_1^{n-1}\}^{n-j},a,\{x_n^{2n-3},a\}^{n-j}),\\
&\quad \{x_n^{2n-3},a\}^{j-2})]\\
&\subseteq (f_{2(n-1)}(S^{(n-1)(j-1)},a,S^{n-2},S^{(n-1)(n-j)},S^{(n-1)(n-2)},a)]\\
&= (f(\underbrace{f(S^{j-1},f(\ldots,f(S^{j-1}}_{f\text{ appears }n-1\text{ times}},a,S^{n-j}),\ldots),S^{n-j}),S^{n-2},\\
&\quad \underbrace{f(S^{n-1},f(S^{n-1},\ldots f(S^{n-1},f(S^{n-1},a))\ldots))}_{f\text{ appears }n-2\text{ times}})], \text{ since } a \in M_j \cap M_n,\\
&\subseteq \left(f(M_j,S^{n-2},M_n)\right].
\end{aligned}
$$

Consequently, $M_j \cap M_n \subseteq (f(M_j,S^{n-2},M_n)]$.

$(ii) \implies (iii)$ It is obvious.

$(iii) \implies (i)$ Let $a \in S$. Then, $a \in M^n(a) \subseteq (f(M^n(a),S^{n-2},M^n(a))] \subseteq (f(\{a\} \cup f(S^{n-1},a),S^{n-2},\{a\} \cup f(S^{n-1},a))]$. We have four cases to be considered as follows.

Case 1: $a \in (f(a,S^{n-2},a)]$. Then, we have $a \in (f(a,S^{n-2},a)] \subseteq (f(a,S^{n-2},f(a,S^{n-2},a))] \subseteq (f(S^{n-1},f(a,S^{n-2},a))]$.

Case 2: $a \in (f(a,S^{n-2},f(S^{n-1},a))]$. Then, we have $a \in (f(a,S^{n-2},f(S^{n-1},a))] \subseteq (f(f(a,S^{n-2},f(S^{n-1},a)),S^{n-2},f(S^{n-1},a))] = (f(f(a,S^{n-1}),S^{n-2},f(a,S^{n-3},f(S^n),a))] \subseteq (f(S^{n-1},f(a,S^{n-2},a))]$.

Case 3: $a \in (f(f(S^{n-1},a),S^{n-2},a)]$. Then, we have $a \in (f(f(S^{n-1},a),S^{n-2},a)] = (f(S^{n-1},f(a,S^{n-2},a))]$.

Case 4: $a \in (f(f(S^{n-1},a),S^{n-2},f(S^{n-1},a))]$. Then, we have $a \in (f(f(S^{n-1},a),S^{n-2},f(S^{n-1},a))] = (f(S^{n-1},f(a,S^{n-3},f(S^n),a))] \subseteq (f(S^{n-1},f(a,S^{n-2},a))]$.

From Cases 1 to 4 and Remark 2(i), S is softly left regular. □

Using the similar proof of Theorem 4, we obtain the following result.

Theorem 5. *Let S be an ordered n-ary semihypergroup with $n \geq 3$. Then, the following statements are equivalent.*

(i) *S is softly right regular;*
(ii) *For any positive integer $1 \leq j < n$, $M_1 \cap M_j \subseteq (f(M_1,S^{n-2},M_j)]$ for all 1-hyperideals M_1 and all j-hyperideals M_j of S;*
(iii) *$M_1 \subseteq (f(M_1,S^{n-2},M_1)]$ for all 1-hyperideals M_1 of S.*

Theorem 6. *Let S be an ordered n-ary semihypergroup with $n \geq 3$. Then, the following statements are equivalent.*

(i) *S is softly intra-regular.*
(ii) *For any positive integer $1 < i \leq n$ and $1 \leq j < n$, $M_i \cap M_j \subseteq (f(M_i,S^{n-2},M_j)]$ for all i-hyperideals M_i and all j-hyperideals M_j of S.*
(iii) *For any positive integer $1 < k < n$, $M_k \subseteq (f(M_k,S^{n-2},M_k)]$ for all k-hyperideals M_k of S.*

Proof. $(i) \implies (ii)$ Let i,j be two fixed positive integers such that $1 < i \leq n$ and $1 \leq j < n$. Let M_i be an i-hyperideal and M_j be a j-hyperideal of S and $a \in M_i \cap M_j$. Since S is softly intra-regular, there exist $x_1^{3n-4} \in S$ such that $a \in \left(f(x_1^{n-1},f(f(a,x_n^{2n-3},a),x_{2n-2}^{3n-4}))\right]$. By associativity, we have

$$
\begin{aligned}
a &\in \left(f(x_1^{n-1}, f(f(a, x_n^{2n-3}, a), x_{2n-2}^{3n-4})) \right] \\
&\subseteq \left(f(x_1^{n-1}, f(f(f(x_1^{n-1}, f(f(a, x_n^{2n-3}, a), x_{2n-2}^{3n-4})), x_n^{2n-3}, a), x_{2n-2}^{3n-4})) \right] \\
&\subseteq \ldots \\
&\subseteq \left(f_{3(i-1)}(\{x_1^{n-1}\}^{i-1}, a, \{x_n^{2n-3}, a, x_{2n-2}^{3n-4}\}^{i-1}) \right] \\
&= \left(f_{3(i-1)}(\{x_1^{n-1}\}^{i-1}, a, x_n^{2n-3}, a, x_{2n-2}^{3n-4}, \{x_n^{2n-3}, a, x_{2n-2}^{3n-4}\}^{i-2}) \right] \\
&\subseteq \left(f_{3(i-1)}(\{x_1^{n-1}\}^{i-1}, a, x_n^{2n-3}, f(x_1^{n-1}, f(f(a, x_n^{2n-3}, a), x_{2n-2}^{3n-4})), \right. \\
&\quad \left. x_{2n-2}^{3n-4}, \{x_n^{2n-3}, a, x_{2n-2}^{3n-4}\}^{i-2}) \right] \\
&\subseteq \left(f_{3(i-1)}(\{x_1^{n-1}\}^{i-1}, a, x_n^{2n-3}, \right. \\
&\quad f(x_1^{n-1}, f(f(f(x_1^{n-1}, f(f(a, x_n^{2n-3}, a), x_{2n-2}^{3n-4})), x_n^{2n-3}, a), x_{2n-2}^{3n-4})), \\
&\quad \left. x_{2n-2}^{3n-4}, \{x_n^{2n-3}, a, x_{2n-2}^{3n-4}\}^{i-2}) \right] \\
&\subseteq \ldots \\
&\subseteq \left(f_{3(i-1)}(\{x_1^{n-1}\}^{i-1}, a, x_n^{2n-3}, f_{3(n-i)}(\{x_1^{n-1}\}^{n-i}, a, \{x_n^{2n-3}, a, x_{2n-2}^{3n-4}\}^{n-i}), \right. \\
&\quad \left. x_{2n-2}^{3n-4}, \{x_n^{2n-3}, a, x_{2n-2}^{3n-4}\}^{i-2}) \right] \\
&\subseteq \left(f_{3(i-1)}(S^{(i-1)(n-1)}, a, S^{n-2}, f_{3(n-i)}(S^{(n-i)(n-1)}, a, S^{(n-i)(2n-2)}), \right. \\
&\quad \left. S^{n-1}, S^{2(n-1)(i-2)}) \right] \\
&= \left(f_{2(n-1)}(\underbrace{f(S^{i-1}, f(\ldots, f(S^{i-1}}_{f \text{ appears } n-1 \text{ times}}, a, S^{n-i}), \ldots), S^{n-i}), S^{n-2}, a, S^{(n-i)(2n-2)}, \right. \\
&\quad \left. S^{(n-1)(2i-3)} \right], \\
&\quad \text{since } a \in M_i, \\
&\subseteq \left(f_{2(n-1)}(M_i, S^{n-2}, a, S^{(n-1)(2n-3)}) \right] \\
&= \left(f_2(M_i, S^{n-2}, a, S^{n-2}, \underbrace{f(f(\ldots f(f(S^n), S^{n-1})\ldots), S^{n-1})}_{f \text{ appears } 2n-4 \text{ times}}) \right] \\
&\subseteq \left(f_2(M_i, S^{n-2}, a, S^{n-1}) \right].
\end{aligned}
$$

On the other hand, we have

$$
\begin{aligned}
a &\in \left(f_2(M_i, S^{n-2}, a, S^{n-1}) \right] \\
&\subseteq \left(f_2(M_i, S^{n-2}, f(x_1^{n-1}, f(f(a, x_n^{2n-3}, a), x_{2n-2}^{3n-4})), S^{n-1}) \right] \\
&\subseteq \left(f_2(M_i, S^{n-2}, f(x_1^{n-1}, f(f(a, x_n^{2n-3}, f(x_1^{n-1}, f(f(a, x_n^{2n-3}, a), x_{2n-2}^{3n-4}))), x_{2n-2}^{3n-4})), \right. \\
&\quad \left. S^{n-1}) \right] \\
&\subseteq \ldots \\
&\subseteq \left(f_2(M_i, S^{n-2}, f_{3(n-j)}(\{x_1^{n-1}, a, x_n^{2n-3}\}^{n-j}, a, \{x_{2n-2}^{3n-4}\}^{n-j}), S^{n-1}) \right] \\
&= \left(f_{3(n-j)+2}(M_i, S^{n-2}, \{x_1^{n-1}, a, x_n^{2n-3}\}^{n-j}, a, \{x_{2n-2}^{3n-4}\}^{n-j}, S^{n-1}) \right] \\
&= \left(f_{3(n-j)+2}(M_i, S^{n-2}, \{x_1^{n-1}, a, x_n^{2n-3}\}^{n-j-1}, x_1^{n-1}, a, x_n^{2n-3}, a, \{x_{2n-2}^{3n-4}\}^{n-j}, \right. \\
&\quad \left. S^{n-1}) \right] \\
&\subseteq \left(f_{3(n-j)+2}(M_i, S^{n-2}, S^{(2n-2)(n-j-1)}, S^{n-1}, a, S^{n-2}, a, S^{(n-j)(n-1)}, S^{n-1}) \right] \\
&= \left(f_{3(n-j)+1}(M_i, S^{n-2}, S^{(2n-2)(n-j-1)}, S^{n-1}, a, S^{n-2}, a, S^{(n-j-1)(n-1)}, S^{n-2}, \right. \\
&\quad \left. f(S^n)) \right]
\end{aligned}
$$

$$
\begin{aligned}
&\subseteq \left(f_{3(n-j)+1}(M_i, S^{n-2}, S^{(2n-2)(n-j-1)}, S^{n-1}, a, S^{n-2}, a, S^{(n-j-1)(n-1)}, S^{n-1})\right] \\
&= \left(f_{3(n-j)+1}(M_i, S^{n-2}, S^{(2n-2)(n-j-1)}, S^{n-1}, a, S^{n-2}, a, S^{(n-j)(n-1)})\right] \\
&\subseteq \left(f_{3(n-j)+1}(M_i, S^{n-2}, S^{(2n-2)(n-j-1)}, S^{n-1}, \right. \\
&\qquad f(x_1^{n-1}, f(f(a, x_n^{2n-3}, a), x_{2n-2}^{3n-4})), S^{n-2}, a, S^{(n-j)(n-1)})\right] \\
&\subseteq \left(f_{3(n-j)+1}(M_i, S^{n-2}, S^{(2n-2)(n-j-1)}, S^{n-1}, \right. \\
&\qquad f(x_1^{n-1}, f(f(a, x_n^{2n-3}, f(x_1^{n-1}, f(f(a, x_n^{2n-3}, a), x_{2n-2}^{3n-4}))), x_{2n-2}^{3n-4})), S^{n-2}, a, \\
&\qquad S^{(n-j)(n-1)})\right] \\
&\subseteq \ldots \\
&\subseteq \left(f_{3(n-j)+1}(M_i, S^{n-2}, S^{(2n-2)(n-j-1)}, S^{n-1}, \right. \\
&\qquad f_{3(j-1)}(\{x_1^{n-1}, a, x_n^{2n-3}\}^{j-1}, a, \{x_{2n-2}^{3n-4}\}^{j-1}), S^{n-2}, a, S^{(n-j)(n-1)})\right] \\
&\subseteq \left(f_{3(n-1)+1}(M_i, S^{n-2}, S^{(2n-2)(n-j-1)}, S^{n-1}, S^{2(n-1)(j-1)}, \right. \\
&\qquad a, S^{(n-1)(j-1)}, S^{n-2}, a, S^{(n-j)(n-1)})\right] \\
&= \left(f_{2n-1}(M_i, S^{n-2}, S^{(2n-2)(n-j-1)}, S^{n-1}, S^{2(n-1)(j-1)}, \right. \\
&\qquad a, S^{n-2}, \underbrace{f(S^{j-1}, f(\ldots, f(S^{j-1}}_{f \text{ appears } n-1 \text{ times}}, a, S^{n-j}), \ldots), S^{n-j}))\right],
\end{aligned}
$$

since $a \in M_j$,

$$
\begin{aligned}
&\subseteq \left(f_{2n-1}(M_i, S^{n-3}, S^{(n-1)(2n-2)}, M_j)\right] \\
&= \left(f(M_i, S^{n-3}, \underbrace{f(f(\ldots f(f(S^n), S^{n-1}), \ldots), S^{n-1}}_{f \text{ appears } 2n-2 \text{ times}}), M_j)\right] \\
&\subseteq \left(f(M_i, S^{n-2}, M_j)\right].
\end{aligned}
$$

Thus, $M_i \cap M_j \subseteq \left(f(M_i, S^{n-2}, M_j)\right]$.

$(ii) \implies (iii)$ It is obvious.

$(iii) \implies (iv)$ Let $a \in S$. Then, $a \in M^k(a) \subseteq \left(f(M^k(a), S^{n-2}, M^k(a))\right] \subseteq \left(f(\bigcup_{p \geq 1} f_p(S^{p(k-1)}, a, S^{p(n-k)}) \cup \{a\}, S^{n-2}, \bigcup_{q \geq 1} f_q(S^{q(k-1)}, a, S^{q(n-k)}) \cup \{a\})\right]$.

We consider the following cases.

Case 1: $a \in \left(f(f_p(S^{p(k-1)}, a, S^{p(n-k)}), S^{n-2}, f_q(S^{q(k-1)}, a, S^{q(n-k)}))\right] = \left(f_{1+p+q}(S^{p(k-1)}, a, S^{p(n-k)}, S^{n-2}, S^{q(k-1)}, a, S^{q(n-k)})\right]$ for some $p, q \geq 1$. Then,

$$
\begin{aligned}
a &\in \left(f_{1+p+q}(S^{p(k-1)}, a, S^{p(n-k)}, S^{n-2}, S^{q(k-1)}, a, S^{q(n-k)})\right] \\
&\subseteq \left(f_{1+p+q}(S^{p(k-1)}, f_{1+p+q}(S^{p(k-1)}, a, S^{p(n-k)}, S^{n-2}, S^{q(k-1)}, a, S^{q(n-k)}), \right. \\
&\qquad S^{p(n-k)}, S^{n-2}, S^{q(k-1)}, a, S^{q(n-k)})\right] \\
&\subseteq \ldots \\
&\subseteq \left(f_{(1+p+q)(n-1)}(S^{p(k-1)(n-1)}, a, \{S^{p(n-k)}, S^{n-2}, S^{q(k-1)}, a, S^{q(n-k)}\}^{n-1})\right] \\
&= \left(f_{n+p(n-k)+q(n-1)}(\underbrace{f(f(\ldots f(f(S^n), S^{n-1}), \ldots), S^{n-1}}_{f \text{ appears } p(k-1)-1 \text{ times}}), S^{n-2}, a, \right. \\
&\qquad \{S^{p(n-k)}, S^{n-2}, S^{q(k-1)}, a, S^{q(n-k)}\}^{n-1})\right] \\
&\subseteq \left(f_{n+p(n-k)+q(n-1)}(S^{n-1}, a, \{S^{p(n-k)}, S^{n-2}, S^{q(k-1)}, a, S^{q(n-k)}\}^{n-2}, \right. \\
&\qquad S^{p(n-k)}, S^{n-2}, S^{q(k-1)}, a, S^{q(n-k)})\right]
\end{aligned}
$$

$$
\begin{aligned}
&\subseteq \left(f_{n+p(n-k)+q(n-1)}(S^{n-1}, a, S^{(p(n-k)+(n-1)(q+1))(n-2)+p(n-k)+(n-2)+q(k-1)},\right.\\
&\quad\left. a, S^{q(n-k)})\right]\\
&\subseteq \left(f_{n+p(n-k)+q(n-1)}(S^{n-1}, a, S^{(p(n-k)+(n-1)(q+1))(n-2)+p(n-k)+(n-2)+q(k-1)},\right.\\
&\quad\left. f_{1+p+q}(S^{p(k-1)}, a, S^{p(n-k)}, S^{n-2}, S^{q(k-1)}, a, S^{q(n-k)}), S^{q(n-k)})\right]\\
&\subseteq \left(f_{n+p(n-k)+q(n-1)}(S^{n-1}, a, S^{(p(n-k)+(n-1)(q+1))(n-2)+p(n-k)+(n-2)+q(k-1)},\right.\\
&\quad f_{1+p+q}(S^{p(k-1)}, a, S^{p(n-k)}, S^{n-2}, S^{q(k-1)},\\
&\quad\left. f_{1+p+q}(S^{p(k-1)}, a, S^{p(n-k)}, S^{n-2}, S^{q(k-1)}, a, S^{q(n-k)}), S^{q(n-k)}), S^{q(n-k)})\right]\\
&\subseteq \ldots\\
&\subseteq \left(f_{n+p(n-k)+q(n-1)}(S^{n-1}, a, S^{(p(n-k)+(n-1)(q+1))(n-2)+p(n-k)+(n-2)+q(k-1)},\right.\\
&\quad\left. f_{(1+p+q)(n-2)}(\{S^{p(k-1)}, a, S^{p(n-k)}, S^{n-2}, S^{q(k-1)}\}^{(n-2)}, a, S^{q(n-k)(n-2)}), S^{q(n-k)})\right]\\
&= \left(f_{n+p(n-k)+q(n-1)+(n-1)+p(n-2)+q(k-2)}(S^{n-1}, a,\right.\\
&\quad S^{(p(n-k)+(n-1)(q+1))(n-2)+p(n-k)+(n-2)+q(k-1)},\\
&\quad \{S^{p(k-1)}, a, S^{p(n-k)}, S^{n-2}, S^{q(k-1)}\}^{(n-2)}\\
&\quad\left., a, S^{n-2}, \underbrace{f(S^{n-1}, f(\ldots, f(S^{n-1}, f(S^n))\ldots)))}_{f \text{ appears } q(n-k)-1 \text{ times}}\right]\\
&\subseteq \left(f_{n+p(n-k)+q(n-1)+(n-1)+p(n-2)+q(k-2)}(S^{n-1}, a,\right.\\
&\quad S^{(p(n-k)+(n-1)(q+1))(n-2)+p(n-k)+(n-2)+q(k-1)}, S^{((p+1)(n-1)+q(k-1))(n-2)}, a,\\
&\quad\left. S^{n-1})\right]\\
&= \left(f_{n+p(n-k)+q(n-1)+(n-1)+p(n-2)+q(k-2)}(S^{n-1}, a,\right.\\
&\quad\left. S^{(n-1)(p(n-k)+q(k-1)+(n-2)(p+q+2))+(n-2)}, a, S^{n-1})\right]\\
&= \left(f(S^{n-1}, f(f(a, S^{n-3}, \underbrace{f(S^{n-1}, f(\ldots, f(S^{n-1}, f(S^n))\ldots))}_{f \text{ appears } p(n-k)+q(k-1)+(n-2)(p+q+2) \text{ times}}, a), S^{n-1}))\right]\\
&\subseteq \left(f(S^{n-1}, f(f(a, S^{n-2}, a), S^{n-1}))\right].
\end{aligned}
$$

Case 2: $a \in \left(f(f_p(S^{p(k-1)}, a, S^{p(n-k)}), S^{n-2}, a)\right] = \left(f_{p+1}(S^{p(k-1)}, a, S^{p(n-k)}, S^{n-2}, a)\right]$ for some $p \geq 1$. Then,

$$
\begin{aligned}
a &\in \left(f_{p+1}(S^{p(k-1)}, a, S^{p(n-k)}, S^{n-2}, a)\right]\\
&\subseteq \left(f_{p+1}(S^{p(k-1)}, f_{(p+1)}(S^{p(k-1)}, a, S^{p(n-k)}, S^{n-2}, a), S^{p(n-k)}, S^{n-2}, a)\right]\\
&\subseteq \ldots\\
&\subseteq \left(f_{(p+1)(n-1)}(S^{p(k-1)(n-1)}, a, \{S^{p(n-k)}, S^{n-2}, a\}^{(n-3)}, S^{p(n-k)}, S^{n-2},\right.\\
&\quad\left. a, S^{p(n-k)}, S^{n-2}, a)\right]\\
&\subseteq \left(f_{(p+1)(n-1)}(S^{p(k-1)(n-1)}, a, \{S^{p(n-k)}, S^{n-2}, a\}^{(n-3)}, S^{p(n-k)}, S^{n-2},\right.\\
&\quad\left. f_{p+1}(S^{p(k-1)}, a, S^{p(n-k)}, S^{n-2}, a), S^{p(n-k)}, S^{n-2}, a)\right]\\
&\subseteq \ldots\\
&\subseteq \left(f_{(p+1)(n-1)}(S^{p(k-1)(n-1)}, a, \{S^{p(n-k)}, S^{n-2}, a\}^{(n-3)}, S^{p(n-k)}, S^{n-2},\right.\\
&\quad\left. f_{(p+1)(n-2)}(S^{p(k-1)(n-2)}, a, \{S^{p(n-k)}, S^{n-2}, a\}^{(n-2)}), S^{p(n-k)}, S^{n-2}, a)\right]\\
&\subseteq \left(f_{(p+1)(2n-3)}(S^{p(k-1)(n-1)}, a, \{S^{p(n-k)}, S^{n-2}, a\}^{(n-3)}, S^{p(n-k)}, S^{n-2},\right.\\
&\quad\left. S^{p(k-1)(n-2)}, a, \{S^{p(n-k)}, S^{n-2}, a\}^{(n-1)})\right]
\end{aligned}
$$

$$\subseteq \left(f_{(p+1)(2n-3)}(S^{p(k-1)(n-1)}, a, S^{n-3}, S^n, S^{(n-1)((p+1)(n-2)-2)}, \right.$$
$$\left. a, S^{(n-1)(p(n-k)+n-1)}) \right]$$
$$\subseteq (f(\underbrace{f(f(\ldots f(f(S^n), S^{n-1}), \ldots), S^{n-1})}_{f \text{ appears } p(k-1) - 1 \text{ times}}, S^{n-2}, f(f(a, S^{n-3},$$
$$\underbrace{f(f(\ldots f(f(S^n), S^{n-1}), \ldots), S^{n-1})}_{f \text{ appears } (p+1)(n-2) - 1 \text{ times}}, a), S^{n-2}, \underbrace{f(f(\ldots f(f(S^n), S^{n-1}), \ldots), S^{n-1})}_{f \text{ appears } p(n-k) + n - 2 \text{ times}})))]$$
$$\subseteq (f(S^{n-1}, f(f(a, S^{n-2}, a), S^{n-1}))].$$

Case 3: $a \in \left(f(a, S^{n-2}, f_q(S^{q(k-1)}, a, S^{q(n-k)})) \right]$. The proof is similar to Case 2.

Case 4: $a \in (f(a, S^{n-2}, a)]$. Then, $a \in (f(a, S^{n-2}, a)] \subseteq (f(a, S^{n-2}, f(a, S^{n-2}, a))] \subseteq (f(a, S^{n-2}, f(a, S^{n-2}, f(a, S^{n-2}, a)))] \subseteq (f(S^{n-1}, f(a, S^{n-2}, f(a, S^{n-1})))] = (f(S^{n-1}, f(f(a, S^{n-2}, a), S^{n-1}))].$

From Cases 1 to 4 and Remark 2(iii), we conclude that S is softly intra-regular. □

Definition 7. *Let S be an ordered n-ary semihypergroup with $n \geq 3$. An element $a \in S$ is called generalized regular if there exist $x_1^{2n-2} \in S$ such that $a \in \left(f(x_1^{n-1}, f(a, x_n^{2n-2})) \right]$. S is called generalized regular if every element of S is generalized regular, i.e., S is generalized regular if and only if $a \in (f(S^{n-1}, f(a, S^{n-1}))]$ for all $a \in S$.*

Example 6. *Let $S = \{a, b, c, d, e\}$. Define a ternary hyperoperation $f : S \times S \times S \to \mathcal{P}^*(S)$ by $f(x_1, x_2, x_3) = (x_1 \circ x_2) \circ x_3$, for all $x_1^3 \in S$, where $\circ$ is defined by the following table*

∘	a	b	c	d	e
a	a	$S \setminus \{d\}$	a	d	a
b	a	$S \setminus \{d\}$	a	d	a
c	a	$S \setminus \{d\}$	a	d	a
d	a	$S \setminus \{d\}$	a	d	a
e	a	$S \setminus \{d\}$	a	d	a

and define a partial order on S as follows

$$\leq := \{(a,a), (a,b), (a,c), (a,e), (b,b), (c,c), (c,b), (c,e), (d,d), (e,b), (e,e)\}.$$

Then, (S, f) is a generalized regular ordered ternary semihypergroup.

Theorem 7. *S is generalized regular if and only if for each $1 < j < n$, $M_j \subseteq (f(S^{n-j}, M_j, S^{j-1})]$ for all j-hyperideals M_j of S.*

Proof. Firstly, let j be a fixed positive integer satisfying $1 < j < n$. Let M_j be a j-hyperideal of S and $a \in M_j$. Since S is generalized regular, there exist $x_1^{2n-2} \in S$ such that

$$a \in \left(f(x_1^{n-1}, f(a, x_n^{2n-2})) \right]$$
$$= \left(f(x_1^{n-j}, f(x_{n-j+1}^{n-1}, a, x_n^{2n-j-1}), x_{2n-j}^{2n-2}) \right], \text{ since } a \in M_j,$$
$$\subseteq \left(f(x_1^{n-j}, M_j, x_{2n-j}^{2n-2}) \right]$$
$$\subseteq \left(f(S^{n-j}, M_j, S^{j-1}) \right].$$

Thus, $M_j \subseteq (f(S^{n-j}, M_j, S^{j-1})]$. Conversely, let $a \in S$. Then, $a \in M^j(a) \subseteq (f(S^{n-j}, M^j(a), S^{j-1})] \subseteq \left(f(S^{n-j}, \bigcup_{k \geq 1} f_k f(S^{k(j-1)}, a, S^{k(n-j)}) \cup \{a\}, S^{j-1}) \right]$. We have two cases to be considered, as follows.

Case 1: $a \in \left(f(S^{n-j}, f_k(S^{k(j-1)}, a, S^{k(n-j)}), S^{j-1})\right]$ for some $k \geq 1$.
If $k = 1$, then $a \in \left(f(S^{n-j}, f(S^{j-1}, a, S^{n-j}), S^{j-1})\right] = \left(f(S^{n-1}, f(a, S^{n-1}))\right]$.
If $k \geq 2$, then

$$\begin{aligned} a \in a &\in \left(f_{k+1}(S^{n-j}, S^{k(j-1)}, a, S^{k(n-j)}, S^{j-1})\right] \\ &= \left(f_{k+1}(S^{n-j}, S^{j-1}, S^{j-1}, S^{(k-2)(j-1)}, a, S^{(k-2)(n-j)}, S^{n-j}, S^{n-j}, S^{j-1})\right] \\ &= \left(f_{k+1}(f(S^n), S^{j-2}, S^{(k-2)(j-1)}, a, S^{(k-2)(n-j)}, S^{n-j-1}, f(S^n))\right] \\ &\subseteq \left(f_{k-1}(S^{(k-1)(j-1)}, a, S^{(k-1)(n-j)})\right]. \end{aligned}$$

By associativity, we have

$$\begin{aligned} a \in &\left(f_{k-1}(S^{(k-1)(j-1)}, a, S^{(k-1)(n-j)})\right] \\ \subseteq &\left(f_{k-1}(S^{(k-1)(j-1)}, f_{k-1}(S^{(k-1)(j-1)}, a, S^{(k-1)(n-j)}), S^{(k-1)(n-j)})\right] \\ \subseteq &\ \ldots \\ \subseteq &\left(f_{(k-1)(n-1)}(S^{(k-1)(j-1)(n-1)}, a, S^{(k-1)(n-j)(n-1)})\right] \\ = &(f(\underbrace{f(f(..f(f(S^n), S^{n-1}),...), S^{n-1})}_{f \text{ appears } (k-1)(j-1)-1}, S^{n-2}, f(a, S^{n-2}, \\ &\underbrace{f(f(..f(f(S^n), S^{n-1}),...), S^{n-1})}_{f \text{ appears } (k-1)(n-j)-1})))] \\ \subseteq &\left(f(S^{n-1}, f(a, S^{n-1}))\right]. \end{aligned}$$

Case 2: $a \in \left(f(S^{n-j}, a, S^{j-1})\right]$. Then, $a \in \left(f(S^{n-j}, a, S^{j-1})\right] \subseteq$
$\left(f(S^{n-j}, f(S^{n-j}, a, S^{j-1}), S^{j-1})\right] \subseteq \ldots \subseteq \left(f_{n-1}(S^{(n-j)(n-1)}, a, S^{(j-1)(n-1)})\right]$.
Next, we consider the following cases.
If $j = 2$ and $n = 3$, then we are done.
If $j = 2$ and $n > 3$, then $a \in \left(f_{n-1}(S^{(n-2)(n-1)}, a, S^{(n-1)})\right] = (f(\underbrace{f(f(\ldots f(f(S^n), S^{n-1}),\ldots), S^{n-1})}_{f \text{ appears } n-2 \text{ times}}, S^{n-2}, f(a, S^{n-1})) \subseteq \left(f(S^{n-1}, f(a, S^{n-1}))\right]$.
If $j > 2$ and $n > 3$, then

$$\begin{aligned} a \in &\left(f_{n-1}(S^{(n-2)(n-1)}, a, S^{(n-1)})\right] \\ = &(f(\underbrace{f(f(\ldots f(f(S^n), S^{n-1}),\ldots), S^{n-1})}_{f \text{ appears } n-j-1 \text{ times}}, S^{n-2}, f(a, S^{n-2}, \\ &\underbrace{f(f(\ldots f(f(S^n), S^{n-1}),\ldots), S^{n-1})}_{f \text{ appears } j-2 \text{ times}})))] \\ \subseteq &\left(f(S^{n-1}, f(a, S^{n-1}))\right]. \end{aligned}$$

Therefore, S is generalized regular. □

Finally, we establish the relationships between regularities in ordered n-ary semihypergroups, where $n \geq 3$, as follows.

Lemma 5. *Let S be an ordered n-ary semihypergroup with $n \geq 3$. Then, the following statements hold.*

(i)   Every left (right) regular is intra-regular;
(ii) Every regular is softly left (right) regular;
(iii) Every left (right) regular is softly left (right) regular;
(iv) Every softly left (right) regular is softly intra-regular;
(v)   Every intra-regular is softly intra-regular;

(vi) Every softly intra-regular is generalized regular.

Proof. (i) Let S be a left regular ordered n-ary semihypergroup. Then, there exist $x_1^{n-1} \in S$ such that $a \in \left(f(x_1^{n-1}, f(a^n))\right] \subseteq \left(f(x_1^{n-1}, f(f(x_1^{n-1}, f(a^n)), a^{n-1}))\right] = \left(f(f(x_1^{n-1}, x_1), x_2^{n-1}, f(f(a^n), a^{n-1}))\right] \subseteq (f(S^{n-1}, f(f(a^n), S^{n-1}))]$. Consequently, by Remark 1, we conclude that S is intra-regular.

(ii) Let S be a regular ordered n-ary semihypergroup. Then, there exist $x_2^{n-1} \in S$ such that $a \in (f(a, x_2^{n-1}, a)] \subseteq (f(a, x_2^{n-1}, f(a, x_2^{n-1}, a))] \subseteq (f(S^{n-1}, f(a, S^{n-2}, a))]$. From Remark 2(i), S is softly left regular.

The proofs of (iii)–(vi) are obvious. □

The following examples show that the converse assertions of Lemma 5 do not hold true in general.

Example 7. *We know that an ordered ternary semihypergroup (S, f), as given in Example 2, is an intra-regular ordered ternary semihypergroup. Since $f(S, a, a) = \{b, e\}$, we have $a \notin (f(S, a, a))]$. From Remark 1, we conclude that (S, f) is not a left regular ordered ternary semihypergroup. This shows that the converse statement of Lemma 5(i) does not hold.*

Example 8. *Let $S = \{a, b, c, d\}$. Define a ternary hyperoperation $f : S \times S \times S \to \mathcal{P}^*(S)$ by the following table*

f	a	b	c	d
aa	a	$\{a,b,c\}$	a	d
ab	a	$\{a,b,c\}$	a	d
ac	a	$\{a,b,c\}$	a	d
ad	d	d	d	d

f	a	b	c	d
ba	a	$\{a,b,c\}$	a	d
bb	a	$\{a,b,c\}$	a	d
bc	a	$\{a,b,c\}$	a	d
bd	d	d	d	d

f	a	b	c	d
ca	a	$\{a,b,c\}$	a	d
cb	a	$\{a,b,c\}$	a	d
cc	a	$\{a,b,c\}$	a	d
cd	d	d	d	d

f	a	b	c	d
da	d	d	d	d
db	d	d	d	d
dc	d	d	d	d
dd	d	d	d	d

and define a partial order on S as follows

$$\leq := \{(a,a), (a,b), (a,c), (b,b), (c,b), (c,c), (d,d)\}.$$

Then, (S, f) is an ordered ternary semihypergroup. Clearly, $a \in (f(f(a,a,a),a,a)]$, $b \in \{a,b,c\} = (f(f(b,a,b),a,b)]$, $c \in \{a,b,c\} = (f(f(c,a,c),a,b)]$ and $d \in (f(f(d,d,d),d,d)]$. By Definition 6, (S, f) is a softly right ordered ternary semihypergroup. On the other hand, since $c \notin (f(c, S, c)]$, by Definition 3, we conclude that (S, f) is not a regular ordered ternary semihypergroup. This shows that the reverse assertion of Lemma 5(ii) is not true.

Example 9. *We know that an ordered ternary semihypergroup (S, f) that has been given in Example 6 is a generalized regular ordered ternary semihypergroup. Clearly, $K = \{a, c, d\}$ is a 3-hyperideal of S. Looking at the table, one can immediately see that $f(K, S, K) = f(a, S, K) \cup f(c, S, K) \cup f(d, S, K) = \{a, d\}$. It follows that $K \nsubseteq f(K, S, K)$. From Theorem 4, we conclude that (S, f) is not a softly left regular ordered ternary semihypergroup.*

Example 10. *We know that an ordered ternary semihypergroup (S, f), which was given in Example 1, is a left regular and right regular ordered ternary semihypergroup. Since $c \notin \{b\} = (f(f(c,c,S), c, c)]$, by Lemma 4, we conclude that (S, f) is not a completely regular ordered ternary semihypergroup.*

Example 11. Let $S = \{a, b, c, d, e, g\}$. Define a ternary hyperoperation $f : S \times S \times S \to \mathcal{P}^*(S)$ by the following table

f	a	b	c	d	e	g
aa	a	a	a	a	e	a
ab	a	a	a	a	e	a
ac	a	a	a	a	e	a
ad	a	a	a	a	e	a
ae	e	e	e	e	e	e
ag	a	a	a	a	e	a

f	a	b	c	d	e	g
ba	a	a	a	a	e	a
bb	a	$\{a,b\}$	$\{a,d\}$	$\{a,b\}$	e	$\{a,g\}$
bc	a	a	$\{a,g\}$	$\{a,b\}$	e	a
bd	a	$\{a,b\}$	$\{a,d\}$	$\{a,b\}$	e	$\{a,g\}$
be	e	e	e	e	e	e
bg	a	a	$\{a,g\}$	$\{a,b\}$	e	a

f	a	b	c	d	e	g
ca	a	a	a	a	e	a
cb	a	a	a	a	e	a
cc	a	a	$\{a,c\}$	$\{a,d\}$	e	a
cd	a	$\{a,d\}$	$\{a,c\}$	$\{a,d\}$	e	$\{a,c\}$
ce	e	e	e	e	e	e
cg	a	a	a	a	e	a

f	a	b	c	d	e	g
da	a	a	a	a	e	a
db	a	$\{a,d\}$	$\{a,c\}$	$\{a,d\}$	e	$\{a,c\}$
dc	a	a	$\{a,c\}$	$\{a,d\}$	e	a
dd	a	$\{a,d\}$	$\{a,c\}$	$\{a,d\}$	e	$\{a,c\}$
de	e	e	e	e	e	e
dg	a	a	$\{a,c\}$	$\{a,d\}$	e	a

f	a	b	c	d	e	g
ea	e	e	e	e	e	e
eb	e	e	e	e	e	e
ec	e	e	e	e	e	e
ed	e	e	e	e	e	e
ee	e	e	e	e	e	e
eg	e	e	e	e	e	e

f	a	b	c	d	e	g
ga	a	a	a	a	e	a
gb	a	a	a	a	e	a
gc	a	a	$\{a,g\}$	$\{a,b\}$	e	a
gd	a	$\{a,b\}$	$\{a,g\}$	$\{a,b\}$	e	$\{a,g\}$
ge	e	e	e	e	e	e
gg	a	a	a	a	e	a

and define a partial order on S as follows

$$\leq := \{(a,a), (a,b), (a,c), (a,d), (a,g), (b,b), (c,c), (d,d), (e,e), (g,g)\}.$$

Then, (S, f) is an ordered ternary semihypergroup. Evidently, $A = \{a, e\}$, $B = \{a, c, d, e\}$ and S are all a 1-hyperideal of S. It is not difficult to show that $A = (f(A, S, A)]$, $B = (f(B, S, B)]$ and $S = (f(S, S, S)]$. From Theorem 5, we conclude that (S, f) is a softly right regular ordered ternary semihypergroup. Since $f(g, g, g) = \{a\} \subseteq A$ but $g \notin A$, we find that A is not a semiprime 1-hyperideal of S. From Theorem 2, (S, f) is not a right regular ordered ternary semihypergroup. This shows that the converse assertion of Lemma 5(iii) is not true in general.

Example 12. We know that an ordered ternary semihypergroup (S, f) that has been given in Example 5 is a softly intra-regular ordered ternary semihypergroup. Obviously, $K = \{a, b, e\}$ is a 1-hyperideal of S. Since $K \nsubseteq \{b, e\} = (f(K, S, K)]$, by Theorem 5, we conclude that (S, f) is not a softly right regular ordered ternary semihypergroup, which verifies that the converse statement of Lemma 5(iv) does not hold.

Example 13. Let $S = \{a, b, c, d, e, g\}$. Define a ternary hyperoperation $f : S \times S \times S \rightarrow \mathcal{P}^*(S)$ by the following table

f	a	b	c	d	e	g
aa	a	a	a	a	e	a
ab	a	a	a	a	e	a
ac	a	a	a	a	e	a
ad	a	a	a	a	e	a
ae	e	e	e	e	e	e
ag	a	a	a	a	e	a

f	a	b	c	d	e	g
ba	a	a	a	a	e	a
bb	a	$\{a,b\}$	a	$\{a,d\}$	e	a
bc	a	a	a	a	e	a
bd	a	$\{a,b\}$	$\{a,d\}$	$\{a,d\}$	e	$\{a,b\}$
be	e	e	e	e	e	e
bg	a	a	a	a	e	a

f	a	b	c	d	e	g
ca	a	a	a	a	e	a
cb	a	$\{a,g\}$	a	$\{a,c\}$	e	a
cc	a	$\{a,g\}$	$\{a,c\}$	$\{a,c\}$	e	$\{a,g\}$
cd	a	$\{a,g\}$	$\{a,c\}$	$\{a,c\}$	e	$\{a,g\}$
ce	e	e	e	e	e	e
cg	a	$\{a,g\}$	a	$\{a,c\}$	e	a

f	a	b	c	d	e	g
da	a	a	a	a	e	a
db	a	$\{a,b\}$	a	$\{a,d\}$	e	a
dc	a	$\{a,b\}$	$\{a,d\}$	$\{a,d\}$	e	$\{a,b\}$
dd	a	$\{a,b\}$	$\{a,d\}$	$\{a,d\}$	e	$\{a,b\}$
de	e	e	e	e	e	e
dg	a	$\{a,b\}$	a	$\{a,d\}$	e	a

f	a	b	c	d	e	g
ea	e	e	e	e	e	e
eb	e	e	e	e	e	e
ec	e	e	e	e	e	e
ed	e	e	e	e	e	e
ee	e	e	e	e	e	e
eg	e	e	e	e	e	e

f	a	b	c	d	e	g
ga	a	a	a	a	e	a
gb	a	$\{a,g\}$	a	$\{a,c\}$	e	a
gc	a	a	a	a	e	a
gd	a	$\{a,g\}$	$\{a,c\}$	$\{a,c\}$	e	$\{a,g\}$
ge	e	e	e	e	e	e
gg	a	a	a	a	e	a

and define a partial order on S as follows

$$\leq := \{(a,a), (a,b), (a,c), (a,d), (a,g), (b,b), (c,c), (d,d), (e,e), (g,g)\}.$$

Then, (S, f) is an ordered ternary semihypergroup. Clearly, $K = \{a, e\}$ and S are all 2-hyperideals of S. It is easy to show that $K = (f(K, S, K)]$. From Theorem 6, (S, f) is a softly intra-regular ordered ternary semihypergroup. However, (S, f) is not an intra-regular ordered ternary semihypergroup. In fact, there exist a n-hyperideal $A = \{a, b, e, g\}$, an 1-hyperideal $B = \{a, c, e, g\}$ and a nonempty subset $H = \{a, b, c, g\}$ of S such that $A \cap H \cap B = \{a, g\} \not\subseteq \{a, e\} = f(A, H, B)$. From Theorem 3, we conclude that (S, f) is not an intra-regular ordered ternary semihypergroup. This shows that the converse statement of Lemma 5(v) does not satisfy.

Example 14. Let $S = \{a, b, c, d\}$. Define a ternary hyperoperation $f : S \times S \times S \rightarrow \mathcal{P}^*(S)$ by the following table

f	a	b	c	d
aa	a	a	a	a
ab	a	a	a	a
ac	a	a	a	a
ad	a	a	a	a

f	a	b	c	d
ba	a	a	a	a
bb	a	b	b	b
bc	a	b	b	b
bd	a	b	b	b

f	a	b	c	d
ca	a	a	a	a
cb	a	b	b	b
cc	a	b	b	b
cd	a	b	b	$\{b,c\}$

f	a	b	c	d
da	a	a	a	a
db	a	b	b	b
dc	a	b	b	$\{b,c\}$
dd	a	b	$\{b,c\}$	d

and define a partial order on S as follows

$$\leq := \{(a,a), (b,b), (b,c), (c,c), (d,d)\}.$$

Then, (S, f) is an ordered ternary semihypergroup. Clearly, $\{a\}, \{a, b\}, \{a, b, c\}$ and S are all 2-hyperideals of S. It is not difficult to see that $A = (f(S, A, S)]$ for all 2-hyperideals A of S. From Theorem 7, (S, f) is a generalized regular ordered ternary semihypergroup. On the other hand, S is not a softly intra-regular ordered ternary semihypergroup. In fact, since $K = \{a, b, c\}$ is an 2-hyperideal of S and $A \nsubseteq \{a, b\} = (f(A, S, A)]$, by Theorem 6, we conclude that (S, f) is not a softly intra-regular ordered ternary semihypergroup. This shows that the reverse assertion of Lemma 5(vi) does not hold true in general.

4. Conclusions

Similar to the theory of ordered semigroups, left and right hyperideals play an important role for studying the regularity of ordered semihypergroups. In this paper, we investigated the properties of j-hyperideals, which is a generalization of a left and a right hyperideal of an ordered semihypergroup, on ordered n-ary semihypergroups, where a positive integer $1 \leq j \leq n$ and $n \geq 3$. We introduced the notions of (softly) left regularity, (softly) right regularity, (softly) intra-regularity, complete regularity and generalized regularity of ordered n-ary semihypergroups and gave the characterizations of them in terms of j-hyperideals. Finally, we obtained the relationships between various regularities in ordered n-ary semihypergroups which can be expressed by Figure 1.

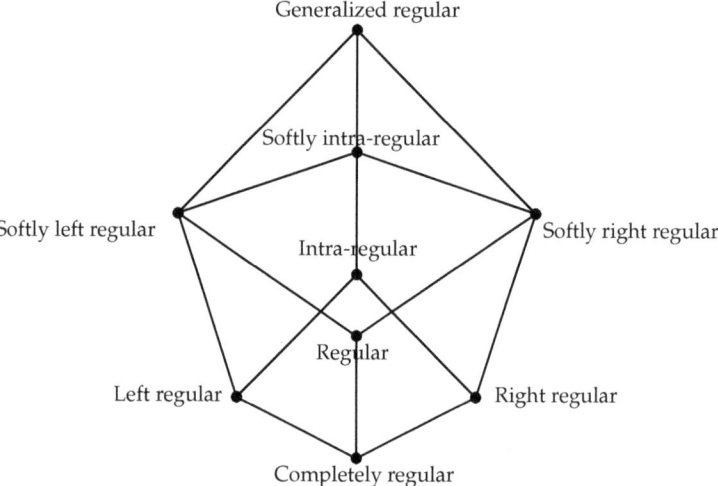

Figure 1. The relationships between various regularities in ordered n-ary semihypergroups.

As an application of the results of this paper, the corresponding results for n-ary semihypergroups can be also obtained because every n-ary semihypergroup endowed with the equality relation is an ordered n-ary semihypergroup.

Author Contributions: Conceptualization, J.D. and S.L.; Investigation, J.D. and S.L.; Supervision, S.L.; Writing–original draft, J.D.; Writing–review and editing, S.L. All two authors contributed equally to all aspects of this work. All authors have read and agreed to the published version of the manuscript.

Funding: This research received no external funding.

Data Availability Statement: Not applicable.

Acknowledgments: The authors are highly grateful to the referees for their valuable comments and suggestions for improving the article. This research was supported by Chiang Mai University, Chiang Mai 50200, Thailand.

Conflicts of Interest: The authors declare no conflict of interest.

References

1. Kasner, E. An extension of the group concept (reported by L.G. Weld). *Bull. Am. Math. Soc.* **1904**, *10*, 290–291.
2. Sioson, F.M. On regular algebraic systems. *Proc. Jpn. Acad. Ser. B* **1963**, *39*, 283–286.
3. Dudek, W.A.; Groździńska, I. On ideals in regular n-semigroups. *Mat. Bilten (Skopje)* **1979**, *3*, 35–44.
4. Simueny, A.; Petchkaew, P.; Chinramy, R. Minimal and maximal ordered n-ideals in ordered n-ary semigroups. *Thai J. Math.* **2020**, 117–125.
5. Pornsurat, P.; Ayutthaya, P.P.; Pibaljommee, B. Prime i-ideals in ordered n-ary semigroups. *Mathematics* **2021**, *9*, 491. [CrossRef]
6. Daddi, V.R.; Pawar, Y.S. On ordered ternary semigroups. *Kyungpook Math. J.* **2012**, *52*, 375–381. [CrossRef]
7. Pornsurat, P.; Pibaljommee, B. Regularities in ordered ternary semigroups. *Quasigroups Relat. Syst.* **2019**, *27*, 107–189.
8. Kar, S.; Roy, A.; Dutta, I. On regularities in po-ternary semigroups. *Quasigroups Relat. Syst.* **2020**, *28*, 149–158.
9. Bashir, S.; Du, X. Intra-regular and weakly regular ordered ternary semigroups. *Ann. Fuzzy Math. Inform.* **2017**, *13*, 539–551. [CrossRef]
10. Marty, F. Sur une generalization de la notion de group. In Proceeding of the 8th Congress Mathematics Scandenaves, Stockholm, Sweden, 14–18 August 1934; pp. 45–49.
11. Corsini, P. Binary relations and hypergroupoids. *Ital. J. Pure Appl. Math.* **2000**, *7*, 11–18.
12. Corsini, P. On the hypergroups associated with a binary relation. *Multi-Valued Log.* **2000**, *5*, 407–419.
13. Corsini, P.; Leoreanu, V. Hypergroups and binary relations. *Algebra Universalis* **2000**, *43*, 321–330. [CrossRef]
14. Davvaz, B.; Leoreanu-Fotea, V. Binary relations on ternary semihypergroups. *Commun. Algebra* **2010**, *38*, 3621–3636. [CrossRef]
15. Cristea, I. Several aspects on the hypergroups associated with n-ary relations. *An. Stiint. Univ. Ovidius Constanta* **2009**, *17*, 99–110.
16. Cristea, I.; Stefanescu, M. Binary relations and reduced hypergroups. *Discret. Math.* **2008**, *308*, 3537–3544. [CrossRef]
17. Vougiouklis, T. *Hyperstructures and Their Representations*; Hadronic Press: Palm Harbor, FL, USA, 1994.
18. Heidari, D.; Davvaz, B.; Modarres, S.M.S. Topological hypergroups in the sense of Marty. *Commun. Algebra* **2014**, *42*, 4712-4721. [CrossRef]
19. Davvaz, B.; Dudek, W.A.; Vougiouklis, T. A generalization of n-ary algebraic systems. *Commun. Algebra* **2009**, *37*, 1248–1263. [CrossRef]
20. Al Tahan, M.; Davvaz. B. Algebraic hyperstructures associated to biological inheritance. *Math. Biosci.* **2017**, *285*, 112–118. [CrossRef]
21. Al Tahan, M.; Davvaz. B. n-ary hyperstructures associated to the genotypes of F_2-offspring. *Int. J. Biomath.* **2017**, *10*, 1750118. [CrossRef]
22. Davvaz, B.; Dehghan-Nezhad, A. Dismutation reactions as experimental verifications of ternary algebraic hyperstructures. *Match-Commun. Math. Comput. Chem.* **2012**, *68*, 551–559.
23. Davvaz, B.; Dehghan-Nezhad, A.; Benvidi, A. Chain reactions as experimental examples of ternary algebraic hyperstructures. *Match-Commun. Math. Comput. Chem.* **2011**, *65*, 491–499.
24. Al Tahan, M.; Davvaz. B. Electrochemical cells as experimental verifications of n-ary hyperstructures. *Matematika* **2019**, *35*, 13–24. [CrossRef]
25. Hila, K.; Davvaz, B.; Naka, K.; Dine, J. Regularity in term of hyperideals. *Chin. J. Math.* **2013**, *2013*, 167037. [CrossRef]
26. Daengsaen, J.; Leeratanavelee, S.; Davvaz, B. On minimal and maximal hyperideals in n-ary semihypergroups. *Mathematics* **2020**, *8*, 1656. [CrossRef]
27. Naka, K.; Hila, K. Some properties of hyperideals in ternary semihypergroups. *Math. Slovaca* **2013**, *63*, 449–468. [CrossRef]
28. Naka, K.; Hila, K. On the structure of quasi-hyperideals and bi-hyperideals in ternary semihypergroups. *Afr. Mat.* **2015**, *26*, 1573–1591. [CrossRef]
29. Naka, K.; Hila, K. Regularity of ternary semihypergroups. *Quasigroups Relat. Syst.* **2017**, *25*, 291–306.
30. Basar, A.; Yaqoob, N.; Abbasi, M.Y.; Satyanrana, B.; Sharma, P.K. On characterization of regular ordered ternary semihypergroups by relative hyperideals. *Ann. Commun. Math.* **2021**, *4*, 73–88.
31. Talee, A.F.; Abbasi, M.Y.; Hila, K.; Khan, S.A. A new approach towards int-soft hyperideals in ordered ternary semihypergroups. *J. Discret. Math. Sci. Cryptogr.* **2020**. [CrossRef]
32. Davvaz, B.; Vougiouklis, T. n-ary Hypergroup. *Iran. J. Sci. Technol.* **2006**, *30*, 165–174.
33. Davvaz, B.; Dudek, W.A.; Mirvakili, S. Neutral elements, fundamental relations and n-ary hypersemigroups. *Int. J. Algebra Comput.* **2009**, *19*, 567–583. [CrossRef]

Article

New Zero-Density Results for Automorphic L-Functions of $GL(n)$

Wenjing Ding, Huafeng Liu and Deyu Zhang *

School of Mathematics and Statistics, Shandong Normal University, Jinan 250358, China; ding_wenjing@stu.sdnu.edu.cn (W.D.); huafengliu@sdnu.edu.cn (H.L.)
* Correspondence: zhangdeyu@sdnu.edu.cn

Abstract: Let $L(s,\pi)$ be an automorphic L-function of $GL(n)$, where π is an automorphic representation of group $GL(n)$ over rational number field $\mathbb{Q}$. In this paper, we study the zero-density estimates for $L(s,\pi)$. Define $N_\pi(\sigma, T_1, T_2) = \sharp \{\rho = \beta + i\gamma : L(\rho, \pi) = 0, \sigma < \beta < 1, T_1 \leq \gamma \leq T_2\}$, where $0 \leq \sigma < 1$ and $T_1 < T_2$. We first establish an upper bound for $N_\pi(\sigma, T, 2T)$ when σ is close to 1. Then we restrict the imaginary part γ into a narrow strip $[T, T + T^\alpha]$ with $0 < \alpha \leq 1$ and prove some new zero-density results on $N_\pi(\sigma, T, T + T^\alpha)$ under specific conditions, which improves previous results when σ near $\frac{3}{4}$ and 1, respectively. The proofs rely on the zero detecting method and the Halász-Montgomery method.

Keywords: zero density; automorphic L-function; automorphic representation

MSC: 11F66; 11M26; 11M41

Citation: Ding, W.; Liu, H.; Zhang, D. New Zero-Density Results for Automorphic L-Functions of $GL(n)$. *Mathematics* **2021**, *9*, 2061. https://doi.org/10.3390/math9172061

Academic Editors: Diana Savin and Alexander Felshtyn

Received: 17 June 2021
Accepted: 24 August 2021
Published: 26 August 2021

Publisher's Note: MDPI stays neutral with regard to jurisdictional claims in published maps and institutional affiliations.

Copyright: © 2021 by the authors. Licensee MDPI, Basel, Switzerland. This article is an open access article distributed under the terms and conditions of the Creative Commons Attribution (CC BY) license (https://creativecommons.org/licenses/by/4.0/).

1. Introduction

Let π be an automorphic representation of group $GL(n)$ over rational number field $\mathbb{Q}$. Then the automorphic (finite-part) L-function related to π can be defined as

$$L(s,\pi) = \sum_{n=1}^{\infty} \frac{A_\pi(n)}{n^s} \quad (\Re s > 1).$$

Furthermore, $L(s,\pi)$ satisfies the Euler product

$$L(s,\pi) = \prod_{p<\infty} \prod_{j=1}^{m} (1 - \alpha_\pi(p,j)p^{-s})^{-1} \quad (\Re s > 1), \qquad (1)$$

where $\alpha_\pi(p,j)$ are the Langlands parameters of π. The automorphic L-function $L(s,\pi)$ can be analytically continued to the whole complex plane and has a standard functional equation.

The zero estimates of $L(s,\pi)$ is an important topic in number theory and has many applications in various problems, for instance, the applications in the composition of integers and integral ideals (see [1–4], etc.) in divisor problems (see [5–8], etc.) and in mean value estimates involving Hecke eigenvalues (see [9–12], etc.). Many scholars have established zero-density estimates of $L(s,\pi)$ (see [13–15], etc.). We know that all non-trivial zeros of $L(s,\pi)$ are included in the critical strip $0 < \Re s < 1$. As we all know, the Generalized Riemann Hypothesis (GRH) conjectures that all these non-trivial zeros are on the critical line $\Re s = \frac{1}{2}$. Now the GRH is still open. Then it is natural to study the zero-density estimates of $L(s,\pi)$ in a rectangle including the critical line.

Let

$$N_\pi(\sigma, T_1, T_2) = \sharp \{\rho = \beta + i\gamma : L(\rho, \pi) = 0, \sigma < \beta < 1, T_1 \leq \gamma \leq T_2\},$$

where $0 \leq \sigma < 1$ and $T_1 < T_2$. Then the famous "density hypothesis" is

$$N_\pi(\sigma, T, 2T) \ll T^{2(1-\sigma)+\varepsilon}, \quad \frac{1}{2} \leq \sigma < 1.$$

Here we take the Riemann zeta function $\zeta(s)$ as an example of the automorphic L-function $L(s, \pi)$. To specify π by cusp forms and Maass forms, we refer to the references [16–18] and references therein. From the works of Ingham [19] and Huxley [20] we know that

$$N_\zeta(\sigma, T, 2T) \ll \begin{cases} T^{\frac{3(1-\sigma)}{2-\sigma}+\varepsilon}, & \text{if } \frac{1}{2} \leq \sigma < \frac{3}{4}, \\ T^{\frac{3(1-\sigma)}{3\sigma-1}+\varepsilon}, & \text{if } \frac{3}{4} \leq \sigma < 1. \end{cases}$$

About the results on the density hypothesis, in 1977, Jutila [21] proved that

$$N_\zeta(\sigma, T, 2T) \ll T^{2(1-\sigma)+\varepsilon}, \quad \frac{11}{14} \leq \sigma < 1.$$

In 2000, Bourgain [22] improved Jutila's result to

$$N_\zeta(\sigma, T, 2T) \ll T^{2(1-\sigma)+\varepsilon}, \quad \frac{25}{32} \leq \sigma < 1.$$

For $\frac{1}{2} \leq u \leq 1$, let

$$M(u, T) = \max_{1 \leq \gamma \leq T} |\zeta(u + i\gamma)|.$$

When σ is close to 1, Ivić (see [23], Theorem 11.3) proved that for $\frac{9}{10} \leq \sigma \leq 1$,

$$N_\zeta(\sigma, -T, T) \ll (M(5\sigma - 4, 3T))^{\frac{7}{6}} \log^{\frac{169}{12}} T.$$

In this paper, motivated by Ivić's work, we first establish an upper bound of $N_\pi(\sigma, T, 2T)$, when σ is close to 1 in the following theorem.

Theorem 1. Let $M_1(u, T) = \max_{1 \leq \gamma \leq T} |\zeta(u + i\gamma)|$ and $M_2(u, T) = \max_{1 \leq \gamma \leq T} |L(u + i\gamma, \pi)|$ for $\frac{1}{2} \leq u < 1$, $T \geq 3$. Then for $\frac{9}{10} \leq \sigma \leq 1$ we have

$$N_\pi(\sigma, T, 2T) \ll (M_1(5\sigma - 4, 3T))^{\frac{2}{3}} (M_2(5\sigma - 4, 4T))^{\frac{1}{2}} T^\varepsilon. \tag{2}$$

Remark 1. *Since $L(s, \pi)$ is a general automorphic L-function in Theorem 1, the mean value estimate now is worse than the case of the Rieman zeta function, which results in the T^ε (see the argument around (22) for details).*

Now we restrict the imaginary part γ into a narrow strip $[T, T + T^\alpha]$ and suppose

$$\int_T^{T+T^\alpha} \left| L\left(\frac{1}{2} + it, \pi\right) \right|^{2l} dt \ll_{\varepsilon, \pi} T^{\theta+\varepsilon}, \tag{3}$$

for certain $0 < \alpha \leq 1$ and $\theta \geq \alpha$, where $l \geq 1$ is an integer and $T \geq 3$. Ye and Zhang [24] established some bounds for $N_\pi(\sigma, T, T + T^\alpha)$ with $\frac{1}{2} \leq \sigma < 1$. Later, Dong, Liu and Zhang [25] obtained a sharper bound for $N_\pi(\sigma, T, T + T^\alpha)$ when σ is close to 1 and show a range of σ for which the density hypothesis holds. We shall keep on studying zero-density estimates for $L(s, \pi)$ in this strip and improve previous results when σ near $\frac{3}{4}$ and 1, respectively.

Theorem 2. *Let $L(s, \pi)$ be an automorphic L-function satisfying (3). Then for $\frac{3}{4} \leq \sigma \leq \frac{10}{13}$ and $2\sigma(2\alpha\theta - 16\theta + 3\alpha^2 l - 6\alpha^2) \geq 4\alpha\theta - 20\theta + 3\alpha^2 l - 12\alpha^2$ we have*

$$N_\pi(\sigma, T, T + T^\alpha) \ll T^{\frac{3\alpha^2(1-\sigma)}{\alpha(1-\sigma)-5+8\sigma}+\varepsilon},$$

and for $\frac{10}{13} < \sigma < 1$ and $2\sigma(6\theta\alpha - 22\theta + 9l\alpha^2 - 18\alpha^2) \geq 12\theta\alpha - 20\theta + 9l\alpha^2 - 36\alpha^2$, we have

$$N_\pi(\sigma, T, T + T^\alpha) \ll T^{\frac{9\alpha^2(1-\sigma)}{3\alpha(1-\sigma)+11\sigma-5}+\varepsilon}.$$

Theorem 3. *Let $L(s, \pi)$ be an automorphic L-function satisfying (3). Then for $\frac{3}{4} \leq \sigma \leq \frac{10}{13}$ and $2\sigma(\alpha\theta - 4\theta + 2\alpha^2 l - 2\alpha^2) \geq 2\alpha\theta - 5\theta + 2\alpha^2 l - 4\alpha^2$, we have*

$$N_\pi(\sigma, T, T + T^\alpha) \ll T^{\frac{4\alpha^2(1-\sigma)}{2\alpha(1-\sigma)-5+8\sigma}+\varepsilon},$$

and for $\frac{10}{13} < \sigma < 1$ and $\sigma(6\theta\alpha - 12\alpha^2 - 11\theta + 12l\alpha^2) \geq 6\theta\alpha - 12\alpha^2 - 5\theta + 6l\alpha^2$, we have

$$N_\pi(\sigma, T, T + T^\alpha) \ll T^{\frac{12\alpha^2(1-\sigma)}{6\alpha(1-\sigma)+11\sigma-5}+\varepsilon}.$$

Notation 1. *Throughout this paper, the letter ε represents a sufficiently small positive number, whose value may change from statement to statement. Constants, both explicit and implicit, in Vinogradov symbols $\ll$ may depend on ε and π.*

2. Some Lemmas

Lemma 1. *For $L(s, \pi)$ we have*

$$N_\pi(0, T, T+1) = \frac{m}{2\pi} \log T(1 + o(1)).$$

Proof. We can get this lemma by a standard winding number argument on (3) as in Davenport [26] and Rudnick and Sarnak [15]. □

Lemma 2 ([27], Lemma 1.7). *Let $\xi, \varphi_1, \ldots, \varphi_R$ be arbitrary vectors in an inner-product vector space over $\mathbb{C}$. If $a = \{a_n\}_{n=1}^\infty$ and $b = \{b_n\}_{n=1}^\infty$ are two vectors of $\mathbb{C}$, then the inner-product of a and b is defined as*

$$(a, b) = \sum_{n=1}^\infty a_n \bar{b}_n.$$

Then we have the inequality

$$\sum_{r \leq R} |(\xi, \varphi_r)| \leq \|\xi\| \left(\sum_{r,s \leq R} |(\varphi_r, \varphi_s)| \right)^{\frac{1}{2}}, \quad (4)$$

where $\|a\|^2 = (a, a)$.

Lemma 3 ([23], (4.60)). *Suppose that $Y, h > 0$ and $k \geq 1$ is an integer, we have*

$$\sum_{n=1}^\infty e^{-(\frac{n}{Y})^h} d_k(n) n^{-s} = (2\pi i)^{-1} \int_{2-i\infty}^{2+\infty} \zeta^k(s+w) Y^w \Gamma(1 + \frac{w}{h}) w^{-1} dw. \quad (5)$$

Lemma 4. *For a fixed θ satisfying $\frac{1}{2} < \theta < 1$, define*

$$S(\theta) = \sum_{r,s \leq R} |\zeta(\theta + it_r - it_s + iv')|^2,$$

where $T \leq t_r \leq T + T^\alpha$ ($1 \leq r \leq R$) and v' is defined by

$$|\zeta(\theta + it_r - it_s + iv')| = \max_{-\log^2 T \leq v \leq \log^2 T} |\zeta(\theta + it_r - it_s + iv)|.$$

Suppose that $|t_r - t_s| \geq 3\log^4 T$ for $r \neq s \leq R$, then we have

$$S\left(\frac{3}{4}\right) \ll T^\varepsilon \left(R^2 + R^{\frac{11}{8}} T^{\frac{\alpha}{4}}\right).$$

Proof. We can get this lemma by following the argument of ([23], Lemma 11.6). The main difference is that the interval of t_r now is $T \leq t_r \leq T + T^\alpha$. □

3. Proof of Theorem 1

We first consider the number of zeros $\rho = \beta + i\gamma$ of $L(s, \pi)$ in the rectangle

$$\sigma < \beta < 1, \quad T \leq \gamma \leq T + T^\alpha, \tag{6}$$

where $\sigma \geq \frac{1}{2}$, $T \geq 3$, and $0 < \alpha \leq 1$. We define $\mu_\pi(n)$ by

$$\frac{1}{L(s,\pi)} = \sum_{n=1}^{\infty} \frac{\mu_\pi(n)}{n^s}$$

for $\Re s > 1$. By the Euler product of $L(s, \pi)$ in (1), we have

$$\frac{1}{L(s,\pi)} = \prod_{p < \infty} \prod_{j=1}^{m} (1 - \alpha_\pi(p,j) p^{-s}).$$

Consequently $\mu_\pi(n)$ is a multiplicative function and

$$\mu_\pi(1) = 1,$$

$$\mu_\pi(p^k) = (-1)^k \sum_{1 \leq j_1 < \cdots < j_k \leq m} \prod_{v=1}^{k} \alpha_\pi(p, j_v)$$

for $k = 1, \ldots, m$ and $\mu_\pi(p^k) = 0$ for $k > m$. Then from $L(s, \pi) \cdot \frac{1}{L(s,\pi)} = 1$, we get

$$\sum_{d|n} \mu_\pi(d) A_\pi\left(\frac{n}{d}\right) = \begin{cases} 1, & n = 1, \\ 0, & n > 1. \end{cases}$$

Assume further that $s = \sigma + it$, $T \leq t \leq T + T^\alpha$, $1 \ll X \ll Y \leq T^A$ for some $A > 0$, and $X = X(T)$ and $Y = Y(T)$ are two parameters to be decided later. Let

$$M_X(s, \pi) = \sum_{n \leq X} \frac{\mu_\pi(n)}{n^s}.$$

Then we have

$$L(s, \pi) M_X(s, \pi) = \sum_{n=1}^{\infty} \frac{b_\pi(n)}{n^s}, \tag{7}$$

for $\Re s > 1$, where

$$b_\pi(n) = \begin{cases} 1, & \text{if } n = 1, \\ 0, & \text{if } 2 \leq n \leq X, \\ \sum_{\substack{d|n \\ d \leq X}} \mu_\pi(d) A_\pi\left(\frac{n}{d}\right), & \text{if } n > X. \end{cases}$$

In terms of (7), for $\sigma > 1$ and $\Re s > 0$, we obtain

$$\frac{1}{2\pi i}\int_\sigma L(s+\omega,\pi)M_X(s+\omega,\pi)\Gamma(\omega)Y^\omega d\omega = \frac{1}{2\pi i}\int_\sigma \sum_{n=1}^\infty \frac{b_\pi(n)}{n^{s+\omega}}\Gamma(\omega)Y^\omega d\omega.$$

From the inverse Mellin transform of $\Gamma(\omega)$, the right-hand side of the above formula can be written as

$$\frac{1}{2\pi i}\int_\sigma \Gamma(\omega)Y^\omega d\omega + \sum_{n>X}\frac{b_\pi(n)}{n^s}\frac{1}{2\pi i}\int_\sigma \Gamma(\omega)\left(\frac{Y}{n}\right)^\omega d\omega = e^{-\frac{1}{Y}} + \sum_{n>X}\frac{b_\pi(n)}{n^s}e^{-\frac{n}{Y}}.$$

Hence we have, for $\sigma > 1$ and $\Re s > 0$,

$$e^{-\frac{1}{Y}} + \sum_{n>X}\frac{b_\pi(n)}{n^s}e^{-\frac{n}{Y}} = \frac{1}{2\pi i}\int_\sigma L(s+\omega,\pi)M_X(s+\omega,\pi)\Gamma(\omega)Y^\omega d\omega. \quad (8)$$

Now we move the line of integration of (8) to $\Re\omega = u - \beta < 0$ for some suitable $\frac{1}{2} \leq u < 1$. Then integral on the right hand of (8) becomes

$$L(s,\pi)M_X(s,\pi) + \frac{1}{2\pi i}\int_{(u-\beta)} L(s+\omega,\pi)M_X(s+\omega,\pi)\Gamma(\omega)Y^\omega d\omega,$$

where $L(s,\pi)M_X(s,\pi)$ is the residue of the integrand at $\omega = 0$. Setting $\omega = u - \beta + iv$ and taking s equal to a non-trivial zero $\rho = \beta + i\gamma$, we have

$$\begin{aligned}&e^{-\frac{1}{Y}} + \sum_{n>X}\frac{b_\pi(n)}{n^\rho}e^{-\frac{n}{Y}}\\&= \frac{1}{2\pi}\int_{-\infty}^{+\infty} L(u+i\gamma+iv,\pi)M_X(u+i\gamma+iv,\pi)\Gamma(u-\beta+iv)Y^{u-\beta+iv}dv.\end{aligned} \quad (9)$$

Since $e^{-\frac{1}{Y}} \to 1$ and $\sum_{n>Y\log^2 Y}\frac{b_\pi(n)}{n^\rho}e^{-\frac{n}{Y}}$ contribute $o(1)$ as $Y \to \infty$, a non-trivial zero $\rho = \beta + i\gamma$ counted in $N_\pi(\sigma, T, T+T^\alpha)$ satisfies either

$$1 \ll \left|\sum_{X<n\leq Y\log^2 Y}\frac{b_\pi(n)}{n^\rho}e^{-\frac{n}{Y}}\right| \quad (10)$$

or

$$1 \ll \int_{-\infty}^{+\infty}\left|L(u+i\gamma+iv,\pi)M_X(u+i\gamma+iv,\pi)\Gamma(u-\beta+iv)Y^{u-\beta+iv}\right|dv. \quad (11)$$

For the integral in (11) we have

$$\int_{-\infty}^{-\log^2 T} + \int_{\log^2 T}^{+\infty} = o(1)$$

due to the fact that they are absolutely convergent. By Stirling's formula again, we can further remove the Γ function in (11) and get that a non-trivial zero $\rho = \beta + i\gamma$ counted in $N_\pi(\sigma, T, T+T^\alpha)$ satisfies either (10) or

$$1 \ll Y^{u-\beta}\int_{-\log^2 T}^{\log^2 T}|L(u+i\gamma+iv,\pi)M_X(u+i\gamma+iv,\pi)|dv. \quad (12)$$

We divide the elongated rectangle (6) into successive rectangles of length $3\log^4 T$ noting Lemma 1. These rectangles start at

$$\sigma < \beta < 1, \ T \leq \gamma \leq T + 3\log^4 T \tag{13}$$

and the last one may have a shorter length. Call these smaller rectangles as $I_1, I_2, \ldots$. The number of zeros are denoted by A_{ij} in all odd-numbered rectangles if $j = 1$ or in all even-numbered rectangles if $j = 2$, which satisfy (10) if $i = 1$, or (12) if $i = 2$. Then, we have

$$N_\pi(\sigma, T, T + T^\alpha) \leq A_{11} + A_{12} + A_{21} + A_{22}.$$

We can get a sequence of zeros $\rho_r^{(ij)} = \beta_r^{(ij)} + i\gamma_r^{(ij)}$ counted in A_{ij} for $r = 1, \ldots, R_{ij}$, if we choose a zero from each rectangle which contains at least one zero. Here, R_{ij} is the number of rectangles that contains at least one zero counted in A_{ij}. By Lemma 1, we note that each rectangle contains at most $\frac{3m}{2\pi} \log^5 T(1 + o(1))$ zeros. Consequently, we have

$$N_\pi(\sigma, T, T + T^\alpha) \leq (R_{11} + R_{12} + R_{21} + R_{22})\log^5 T. \tag{14}$$

Now we begin to estimate R_{1j}. By a dyadic subdivision on the sum in (10), we know that each $\rho_r^{(1j)} = \beta_r^{(1j)} + i\gamma_r^{(1j)}$ counted in R_{1j} satisfies

$$1 \ll \cdots + \left| \sum_{\frac{\sqrt{Y}}{2} < n < \sqrt{Y}} \frac{b_\pi(n)}{n^{\rho^{(1j)}}} e^{-\frac{n}{Y}} \right| + \left| \sum_{\sqrt{Y} < n < 2\sqrt{Y}} \frac{b_\pi(n)}{n^{\rho^{(1j)}}} e^{-\frac{n}{Y}} \right| + \cdots, \tag{15}$$

where there are $O(\log(Y \log^2 Y))$ terms. Then there exists $M_r = 2^{v^r}\sqrt{Y}$ for some $v^r \in \mathbb{Z}$ and $X \leq M_r \leq Y\log^2 Y$ such that

$$\sum_{M_r < n < 2M_r} \frac{b_\pi(n)}{n^{\rho^{(1j)}}} e^{-\frac{n}{Y}} \gg \frac{1}{\log Y}. \tag{16}$$

Raising (16) to kth power we get

$$\sum_{M_r^k < n \leq (2M_r)^k} \frac{c_\pi(n)}{n^{\rho^{(1j)}}} \gg \frac{1}{\log^k Y}, \tag{17}$$

with

$$c_\pi(n) = \sum_{\substack{n = n_1 n_2 \cdots n_k \\ M_r < n_i \leq 2M_r}} b_\pi(n_1) \cdots b_\pi(n_k) e^{-\frac{n_1 + n_2 + \cdots + n_k}{Y}}$$

and k is a natural number depending on M_r such that $M_r^k = N$, $(2M_r)^k = P \leq T^c$, from where $k \ll 1$ and $P \ll N$. We split the sum in (17) into subsums of length N and choose k so that $M_r^k \leq Y^r \log^{2r} Y < M_r^{k+1}$, where r is a fixed integer and $k \geq r \geq 1$ is satisfied. Then (17) can be written as

$$\sum_{N < n \leq 2N} \frac{c_\pi(n)}{n^{\rho^{(1j)}}} \gg \frac{1}{\log^D Y} \tag{18}$$

for some $D \asymp 1$ and

$$Y^{\frac{r}{r+1}} \log^{\frac{2r}{r+1}} Y \ll N \ll Y^r \log^{2r} Y. \tag{19}$$

By partial summation and (18), we have

$$R_{1j} \ll \log^D T \Bigg\{ \sum_{\rho^{(1j)}} \Bigg(\Bigg| \sum_{N < n \leq 2N} c_\pi(n) n^{-\sigma - i\gamma_r^{(1j)}} \Bigg| N^{\sigma - \beta_r^{(1j)}} \\ + \int_N^{2N} \Bigg| \sum_{N < n \leq u} c_\pi(n) n^{-\sigma - i\gamma_r^{(1j)}} \Bigg| N^{\sigma - \beta_r^{(1j)} - 1} du \Bigg) \Bigg\}. \tag{20}$$

We relabel $c_\pi(n)$ to satisfy $c_\pi(n) = 0$ for $n > u$. Then simplifying (20), we can get

$$R_{1j} \ll \log^D T \sum_{r=1}^{R_{1j}} \left| \sum_{N < n \leq 2N} c_\pi(n) n^{-\sigma - i\gamma_r^{(1j)}} \right|. \tag{21}$$

From now on, we let $\alpha = 1$ in (6). Now we apply Lemma 2 to (21) and take $\xi = \{\xi_n\}_{n=1}^\infty$ with $c_\pi(n) \ll n^\varepsilon$, where

$$\xi_n = \begin{cases} c_\pi(n)(e^{-\frac{n}{2N}} - e^{-\frac{n}{N}})^{-\frac{1}{2}} n^{-\sigma}, & N < n \leq 2N, \\ 0, & \text{otherwise}, \end{cases}$$

and $\varphi_r = \{\varphi_{r,n}\}_{n=1}^\infty$ with $\varphi_{r,n} = (e^{-\frac{n}{2N}} - e^{-\frac{n}{N}})^{\frac{1}{2}} n^{-i\gamma_r^{(1j)}}$ ($n = 1, 2, 3 \ldots$). Denoting the imaginary part of representative zeros of R_{1j} by $\gamma_1^{(1j)}, \ldots, \gamma_{R_{1j}}^{(1j)}$, we then have

$$R_{1j}^2 \ll \log^{2D} T \sum_{r \leq R_{1j}} \left| \sum_{N < n \leq 2N} \xi_n \varphi_{r,n} \right|^2 \ll \log^{2D} T \|\xi\|^2 \sum_{r,s \leq R_{1j}} |(\varphi_r, \varphi_s)|$$

$$\ll \log^{2D} T \left(\sum_{N < n \leq 2N} c_\pi^2(n) e^{-\frac{2n}{Y}} n^{-2\sigma} \right) \left(\sum_{r = s} |(\varphi_r, \varphi_s)| + \sum_{r \neq s} |(\varphi_r, \varphi_s)| \right)$$

$$\ll \log^{2D} T \left(\sum_{N < n \leq 2N} c_\pi^2(n) n^{-2\sigma} e^{-\frac{2n}{Y}} \right) \left(R_{1j} N + \sum_{r \neq s \leq R_{1j}} \left(H(i\gamma_r^{(1j)} - i\gamma_s^{(1j)}) \right) \right) \tag{22}$$

$$\ll T^\varepsilon \left(N^{2-2\sigma} R_{1j} + \sum_{r \neq s \leq R_{1j}} \left(H(i\gamma_r^{(1j)} - i\gamma_s^{(1j)}) \right) \right),$$

where

$$H(it) = \sum_{n=1}^\infty (e^{-\frac{n}{2N}} - e^{-\frac{n}{N}}) n^{-it}$$

$$= \frac{1}{2\pi i} \int_{2-i\infty}^{2+i\infty} \zeta(w + it)((2N)^w - N^w) \Gamma(w) dw, \tag{23}$$

since $1 \ll e^{-\frac{n}{2N}} - e^{-\frac{n}{N}} \ll 1$ for $N < n \leq 2N$, $\|\xi\|^2 \ll T^\varepsilon N^{1-2\sigma}$ and $H(0) \ll N$. Thus, we have

$$H(i\gamma_r^{(1j)} - i\gamma_s^{(1j)}) = \frac{1}{2\pi i} \int_{2-i\infty}^{2+i\infty} \zeta(w + i\gamma_r^{(1j)} - i\gamma_s^{(1j)})((2N)^w - N^w) \Gamma(w) dw. \tag{24}$$

Moving the line of integration in (24) to $\Re w = u < 1$, we encounter a simple pole at $w = 1 - i\gamma_r^{(1j)} + i\gamma_s^{(1j)}$ with residue $\ll N e^{-|\gamma_s^{(1j)} - \gamma_r^{(1j)}|}$, so that

$$H(i\gamma_r^{(1j)} - i\gamma_s^{(1j)})$$
$$= \frac{1}{2\pi i} \int_{u-i\infty}^{u+i\infty} \zeta(w + i\gamma_r^{(1j)} - i\gamma_s^{(1j)})((2N)^w - N^w) \Gamma(w) dw + O(N e^{-|\gamma_s^{(1j)} - \gamma_r^{(1j)}|}). \tag{25}$$

In view of $|\Gamma(s)| = (2\pi)^{\frac{1}{2}} |t|^{\sigma - \frac{1}{2}} e^{-\frac{\pi t}{2}} (1 + O(|t|^{-1}))$, the integral in (25) is $o(1)$ for $N \ll T^c$ if $|\Im w| \geq \log^2 T$, which gives

$$\sum_{r \neq s \leq R_{1j}} |H(i\gamma_r^{(1j)} - i\gamma_s^{(1j)})| \ll N \sum_{r \neq s \leq R_{1j}} e^{-|\gamma_s^{(1j)} - \gamma_r^{(1j)}|} + o(R_{1j}^2)$$

$$+ N^u \int_{-\log^2 T}^{\log^2 T} \sum_{r \neq s \leq R_{1j}} |\zeta(u + i\gamma_r^{(1j)} - i\gamma_s^{(1j)} + iv)| dv. \tag{26}$$

Since the $\gamma_r^{(1j)}$'s are at least $3\log^4 T$ apart, the first sum on the right side of (26) is $O(R_{1j})$. For the second sum on the right side of (26), we fix each s and let $\tau_r = \gamma_r^{(1j)} - \gamma_s^{(1j)} + v$. Then we have $|\tau_r| \leq 3T$ for $r = 1, 2, \ldots, R_{1j}$ and $|\tau_{r_1} - \tau_{r_2}| \geq 3\log^4 T$ for $r_1 \neq r_2$. Hence we get

$$\sum_{r \neq s \leq R_{1j}} \left(H(i\gamma_r^{(1j)} - i\gamma_s^{(1j)}) \right) \ll R_{1j}^2 N^u M_1(u, 3T) \log^2 T. \tag{27}$$

Inserting (27) into (22) we obtain

$$R_{1j}^2 \ll T^\varepsilon \left(R_{1j} N^{2-2\sigma} + R_{1j}^2 N^{1+u-2\sigma} M_1(u, 3T) \right).$$

Then we have for $\sigma \geq \frac{u+1}{2}$,

$$R_{1j} \ll \max_{X \leq N \leq Y \log^2 Y} N^{2-2\sigma} T^\varepsilon \ll Y^{2-2\sigma} T^\varepsilon, \tag{28}$$

if $X^{2\sigma-1-u} \gg M_1(u, 3T) T^\varepsilon$.

Now we turn to estimate R_{2j}. We may suppose first that $\sigma < 1 - \frac{C}{\log T}$ in view of the zero-free region. Note that in this case the zeros $\rho_r^{(2j)} = \beta_r^{(2j)} + i\gamma_r^{(2j)}$, $j = 1, 2$ satisfy

$$1 \ll Y^{u-\beta} \int_{-\log^2 T}^{\log^2 T} \left| L(u + i\gamma_r^{(2j)} + iv, \pi) M_X(u + i\gamma_r^{(2j)} + iv, \pi) \right| dv. \tag{29}$$

From the mean value theorem for integration, we can see that there exists $t_r^{(2j)} = \gamma_r^{(2j)} + v$, which makes (29) become

$$1 \ll Y^{u-\beta} \left| L(u + it_r^{(2j)}, \pi) M_X(u + it_r^{(2j)}, \pi) \right| \log^2 T. \tag{30}$$

Thus, from (30) we get

$$M_X(u + it_r^{(2j)}, \pi) \gg Y^{\sigma-u} (M_2(u, 4T) \log^2 T)^{-1}$$

for R_{2j} points $t_r^{(2j)}$ such that $|t_r^{(2j)}| \leq 4T$. Then there is a number N $(1 \ll N \leq X)$ such that

$$\sum_{N < n \leq 2N} \frac{\mu_\pi(n)}{n^{u+it_r^{(2j)}}} \gg Y^{\sigma-u} (M_2(u, 4T) \log^2 T)^{-1},$$

hence it is easy to get

$$1 \ll Y^{u-\sigma} M_2(u, 4T) \log^2 T \sum_{N < n \leq 2N} \frac{\mu_\pi(n)}{n^{u+it_r^{(2j)}}}.$$

We can apply Lemma 2 as in the previous case, but now the choice of ξ and φ_r are different. We shall take $\xi = \{\xi_n\}_{n=1}^\infty$ with $\xi_n = \mu_\pi(n)(e^{-\frac{n}{2N}} - e^{-\frac{n}{N}})^{-\frac{1}{2}} n^{-u}$ for $N < n \leq 2N$ and zero otherwise, $\varphi_r = \{\varphi_{r,n}\}_{n=1}^\infty$ with $\varphi_{r,n} = (e^{-\frac{n}{2N}} - e^{-\frac{n}{N}})^{\frac{1}{2}} n^{-it_r^{(2j)}}$ $(n = 1,2,3\ldots)$. Then

$$R_{2j}^2 \ll Y^{2u-2\sigma} M_2^{\ 2}(u,4T) \log^4 T \left(\sum_{r \leq R_{2j}} \Big| \sum_{N < n \leq 2N} \frac{\mu_\pi(n)}{n^{u+it_r^{(2j)}}} \Big| \right)^2$$

$$\ll Y^{2u-2\sigma} M_2^{\ 2}(u,4T) \log^4 T \|\xi\|^2 \sum_{r,s \leq R_{2j}} |(\varphi_r, \varphi_s)|$$

$$\ll Y^{2u-2\sigma} M_2^{\ 2}(u,4T) N^{1-2u+\varepsilon} \log^4 T \Big(R_{2j} N + \sum_{r \neq s \leq R_{2j}} H(it_r^{(2j)} - it_s^{(2j)}) \Big)$$

$$\ll Y^{2u-2\sigma} M_2^{\ 2}(u,4T) N^{2-2u} R_{2j} \log^5 T$$
$$+ Y^{2u-2\sigma} M_2^{\ 2}(u,4T) M_1(u,3T) N^{1-u} R_{2j}^2 \log^7 T,$$

Thus, we have
$$R_{2j} \ll X^{2-2u} Y^{2u-2\sigma} M_2^{\ 2}(u,4T) \log^5 T$$

if
$$Y^{2\sigma-2u} \gg M_1(u,3T) M_2^{\ 2}(u,4T) X^{1-u} \log^7 T.$$

Therefore X and Y can be chosen as
$$X = C_1 M_1(u,3T)^{\frac{1}{2\sigma-1-u}} T^\varepsilon,$$

$$Y = C_2 M_1(u,3T)^{\frac{1}{2\sigma-u-1}} M_2(u,4T)^{\frac{1}{\sigma-u}} T^\varepsilon.$$

We see that the bound for R_{2j} is smaller than the one for R_{1j}. Recalling (14) we have

$$N_\pi(\sigma, T, 2T) \ll Y^{2-2\sigma} T^\varepsilon$$
$$\ll \left(M_1(u,3T)^{\frac{1}{2\sigma-u-1}} M_2(u,4T)^{\frac{1}{\sigma-u}} \right)^{2-2\sigma} T^\varepsilon, \tag{31}$$

where $\frac{1}{2} \leq u \leq 1$, $\frac{u+1}{2} \leq \sigma < 1 - \frac{C}{\log T}$.

Let $u = k\sigma - (k-1)$ $(k > 2)$. Then in view of (31), we see that it is appropriate to take $k = 5$. Hence $u = 5\sigma - 4$, $\sigma \geq \frac{u+1}{2}$ is satisfied and $u \geq \frac{1}{2}$ for $\sigma \geq \frac{9}{10}$. Thus, Theorem 1 follows from (31) with $u = 5\sigma - 4$.

4. Proof of Theorem 2

Throughout the proof of Theorem 2, we restrict the range of zeros to (6). From the estimates of R_{1j}^2 in (22), we obtain now

$$R_{1j}^2 \ll T^\varepsilon \left(N^{2-2\sigma} R_{1j} + N^{1-2\sigma} \sum_{r \neq s \leq R_{1j}} |H(i\gamma_r^{(1j)} - i\gamma_s^{(1j)})| \right). \tag{32}$$

Recall the functional equation $\zeta(s) = \chi(s)\zeta(1-s)$ with

$$\chi(s) = \left(\frac{2\pi}{t} \right)^{\sigma+it-\frac{1}{2}} e^{i(t+\frac{\pi}{4})} (1 + O|t^{-1}|).$$

Moving the line of integration in $H(it)$ to $\Re w = \frac{1}{4}$ and applying the Cauchy–Schwarz inequality, we get

$$\sum_{r \neq s \leq R_{1j}} |H(i\gamma_r^{(1j)} - i\gamma_s^{(1j)})| \ll N \sum_{r \neq s \leq R_{1j}} e^{-|\gamma_r^{(1j)} - \gamma_s^{(1j)}|} + R_{1j}^2 + N^{\frac{1}{4}} T^{\frac{\alpha}{4}}$$

$$\times \int_{-\log^2 T}^{\log^2 T} \sum_{r \neq s \leq R_{1j}} |\zeta(\frac{3}{4} + i\gamma_r^{(1j)} - i\gamma_s^{(1j)} + iv)| dv \quad (33)$$

$$\ll R_{1j} N + R_{1j}^2 + T^{\varepsilon + \frac{\alpha}{4}} N^{\frac{1}{4}} R_{1j} \left(S(\frac{3}{4}) \right)^{\frac{1}{2}}$$

where the $S(\frac{3}{4})$ is from Lemma 4.

Substituting (33) into (32), we can get

$$R_{1j} \ll T^{\varepsilon} N^{2-2\sigma} + R_{1j} T^{\frac{\alpha}{4} + \varepsilon} N^{\frac{5-8\sigma}{4}} + T^{\frac{6\alpha}{5} + \varepsilon} N^{\frac{20-32\sigma}{5}}, \quad (34)$$

where we used Lemma 4 to $S(\frac{3}{4})$. For R_0 points lying in an interval of length $T = T_0 = N^{\frac{8\sigma-5}{\alpha} - \varepsilon}$ we have

$$R_0 \ll T^{\varepsilon}(N^{2-2\sigma} + T_0^{\frac{6\alpha}{5}} N^{\frac{20-32\sigma}{5}}) \ll T^{\varepsilon} N^{2-2\sigma} \text{ for } \frac{3}{4} \leq \sigma \leq \frac{10}{13}.$$

In (19), we take $r = 2$ to get $Y^{\frac{4}{3}} \log^{\frac{8}{3}} Y \ll N \ll Y^2 \log^4 Y$ and then

$$R_{1j} \ll R_0 \left(1 + \frac{T^{\alpha}}{T_0} \right) \ll T^{\varepsilon} N^{2-2\sigma} \left(1 + \frac{T^{\alpha}}{T_0} \right) \ll T^{\varepsilon} \left(Y^{4-4\sigma} + T^{\alpha} Y^{\frac{8\alpha(1-\sigma)+20-32\sigma}{3\alpha}} \right)$$

It follows from ([24], (5.21)) that

$$R_{2j} \ll T^{\theta + \varepsilon} Y^{l(1-2\sigma)}. \quad (35)$$

Consequently, we have

$$N_{\pi}(\sigma, T, T + T^{\alpha}) \ll T^{\varepsilon} \sum_{j=1}^{2} (R_{1j} + R_{2j}) \quad (36)$$

$$\ll T^{\varepsilon}(T^{\theta} Y^{l(1-2\sigma)} + Y^{4-4\sigma} + T^{\alpha} Y^{\frac{8\alpha(1-\sigma)+20-32\sigma}{3\alpha}}).$$

We set $Y^{4-4\sigma} = T^{\alpha} Y^{\frac{8\alpha(1-\sigma)+20-32\sigma}{3\alpha}}$, which is equivalent to $Y = T^{\frac{3\alpha^2}{4\alpha(1-\sigma)-20+32\sigma}}$. Thus, from (36) we get

$$N_{\pi}(\sigma, T, T + T^{\alpha}) \ll T^{\varepsilon}(Y^{4-4\sigma} + T^{\theta} Y^{l(1-2\sigma)})$$

$$= T^{\varepsilon}(T^{\frac{3\alpha^2(1-\sigma)}{\alpha(1-\sigma)-5+8\sigma}} + T^{\theta + \frac{3\alpha^2 l(1-\sigma)}{4\alpha(1-\sigma)-20+32\sigma}}). \quad (37)$$

Comparing the two terms in (37), we can get

$$N_{\pi}(\sigma, T, T + T^{\alpha}) \ll T^{\frac{3\alpha^2(1-\sigma)}{\alpha(1-\sigma)-5+8\sigma} + \varepsilon}$$

for $2\sigma(2\alpha\theta - 16\theta + 3\alpha^2 l - 6\alpha^2) \geq 4\alpha\theta - 20\theta + 3\alpha^2 l - 12\alpha^2$, from which we complete the proof of the first result of Theorem 2.

For R_0 points lying in an interval of length $T = T_0 = N^{\frac{11\sigma-5}{3\alpha}}$, we have

$$R_0 \ll T^{\varepsilon}(N^{2-2\sigma} + R_0 T_0^{\frac{\alpha}{4}} N^{\frac{5-8\sigma}{4}}) = T^{\varepsilon}(N^{2-2\sigma} + R_0 N^{\frac{10-13\sigma}{12}}),$$

which implies
$$R_0 \ll T^\varepsilon \frac{N^{2-2\sigma}}{1-N^{\frac{10-13\sigma}{12}}} \ll T^\varepsilon N^{2-2\sigma} \text{ for } \frac{10}{13} < \sigma < 1.$$

Then we have
$$R_{1j} \ll R_0(1+\frac{T^\alpha}{T_0}) \ll T^\varepsilon(N^{2-2\sigma} + T^\alpha N^{\frac{6\alpha(1-\sigma)-11\sigma+5}{3\alpha}}) \quad (38)$$
$$\ll T^\varepsilon(Y^{4-4\sigma} + T^\alpha Y^{\frac{24\alpha(1-\sigma)-44\sigma+20}{9\alpha}}).$$

Consequently, recalling (35) we have
$$N_\pi(\sigma, T, T+T^\alpha) \ll \sum_{j=1}^{2}(R_{1j}+R_{2j})\log^5 T \quad (39)$$
$$\ll T^\varepsilon(Y^{4-4\sigma} + T^\alpha Y^{\frac{24\alpha(1-\sigma)-44\sigma+20}{9\alpha}} + T^\theta Y^{l(1-2\sigma)}).$$

We choose $Y^{4-4\sigma} = T^\alpha Y^{\frac{24\alpha(1-\sigma)-44\sigma+20}{9\alpha}}$, which is equivalent to $Y = T^{\frac{9\alpha^2}{12\alpha(1-\sigma)+4(11\sigma-5)}}$. Thus, from (39) we have
$$N_\pi(\sigma, T, T+T^\alpha) \ll T^\varepsilon(Y^{4-4\sigma} + T^\theta Y^{l(1-2\sigma)}) \quad (40)$$
$$= T^\varepsilon(T^{\frac{9\alpha^2(1-\sigma)}{3\alpha(1-\sigma)+11\sigma-5}} + T^{\theta+\frac{9\alpha^2 l(1-2\sigma)}{12\alpha(1-\sigma)+4(11\sigma-5)}}).$$

Comparing the two terms in (40), we can get
$$N_\pi(\sigma, T, T+T^\alpha) \ll T^{\frac{9\alpha^2(1-\sigma)}{3\alpha(1-\sigma)+11\sigma-5}+\varepsilon}$$

for $2\sigma(18\alpha^2 - 6\theta\alpha + 22\theta - 9l\alpha^2) \le 36\alpha^2 - 12\theta\alpha + 20\theta - 9l\alpha^2$, from which we complete the proof of the second result of Theorem 2.

5. Proof of Theorem 3

The proofs of Theorems 2 and 3 are similar, and the main difference is the range of N. Here for completeness, we state some critical details. We let $r=1$ in (19) and get $Y^{\frac{1}{2}}\log Y \ll N \ll Y\log^2 Y$.

Unlike the previous (34), we now have
$$R_{1j} \ll T^\varepsilon N^{2-2\sigma} + R_{1j}T^{\frac{\alpha}{4}+\varepsilon}N^{\frac{5-8\sigma}{4}} + T^{\frac{6\alpha}{5}+\varepsilon}N^{\frac{20-32\sigma}{5}}.$$

For R_0 points lying in an interval of length $T=T_0=N^{\frac{8\sigma-5}{\alpha}-\varepsilon}$, we have
$$R_0 \ll T^\varepsilon(N^{2-2\sigma} + T_0^{\frac{6\alpha}{5}}N^{\frac{20-32\sigma}{5}}) \ll T^\varepsilon N^{2-2\sigma} \text{ for } \frac{3}{4} \le \sigma \le \frac{10}{13}.$$

Then
$$R_{1j} \ll R_0(1+\frac{T^\alpha}{T_0}) \ll T^\varepsilon N^{2-2\sigma}(1+\frac{T^\alpha}{T_0}) \ll T^\varepsilon(Y^{2-2\sigma}+T^\alpha Y^{\frac{2\alpha(1-\sigma)+5-8\sigma}{2\alpha}})$$

Consequently, recalling (35), we have
$$N_\pi(\sigma, T, T+T^\alpha) \ll T^\varepsilon \sum_{j=1}^{2}(R_{1j}+R_{2j}) \quad (41)$$
$$\ll T^\varepsilon(T^\theta Y^{l(1-2\sigma)} + Y^{2-2\sigma} + T^\alpha Y^{\frac{2\alpha(1-\sigma)+5-8\sigma}{2\alpha}}).$$

We set $Y^{2-2\sigma} = T^\alpha Y^{\frac{2\alpha(1-\sigma)+5-8\sigma}{2\alpha}}$ which is equivalent to $Y = T^{\frac{2\alpha^2}{2\alpha(1-\sigma)-5+8\sigma}}$. Thus, (41) becomes

$$N_\pi(\sigma, T, T+T^\alpha) \ll T^\varepsilon(Y^{2-2\sigma} + T^\theta Y^{l(1-2\sigma)})$$
$$= T^\varepsilon(T^{\frac{4\alpha^2(1-\sigma)}{2\alpha(1-\sigma)-5+8\sigma}} + T^{\theta + \frac{2\alpha^2 l(1-2\sigma)}{2\alpha(1-\sigma)-5+8\sigma}}). \tag{42}$$

Comparing the two terms in (42), we can get

$$N_\pi(\sigma, T, T+T^\alpha) \ll T^{\frac{4\alpha^2(1-\sigma)}{2\alpha(1-\sigma)-5+8\sigma}+\varepsilon}$$

for $2\sigma(\alpha\theta - 4\theta + 2\alpha^2 l - 2\alpha^2) \geq 2\alpha\theta - 5\theta + 2\alpha^2 l - 4\alpha^2$, from which we complete the proof of the first result of Theorem 3.

For R_0 points lying in an interval of length $T = T_0 = N^{\frac{11\sigma-5}{3\alpha}}$ we have

$$R_0 \ll T^\varepsilon(N^{2-2\sigma} + R_0 T_0^{\frac{\alpha}{4}} N^{\frac{5-8\sigma}{4}}) = T^\varepsilon(N^{2-2\sigma} + R_0 N^{\frac{10-13\sigma}{12}}),$$

which implies

$$R_0 \ll T^\varepsilon \frac{N^{2-2\sigma}}{1-N^{\frac{10-13\sigma}{12}}} \ll T^\varepsilon N^{2-2\sigma} \text{ for } \frac{10}{13} < \sigma \leq 1.$$

Then we have

$$R_{1j} \ll R_0(1+\frac{T^\alpha}{T_0}) \ll T^\varepsilon(N^{2-2\sigma} + T^\alpha N^{\frac{6\alpha(1-\sigma)-11\sigma+5}{3\alpha}})$$
$$\ll T^\varepsilon(Y^{2-2\sigma} + T^\alpha Y^{\frac{6\alpha(1-\sigma)-11\sigma+5}{6\alpha}}). \tag{43}$$

Consequently, recalling (35) we have

$$N_\pi(\sigma, T, T+T^\alpha) \ll \sum_{j=1}^{2}(R_{1j} + R_{2j})$$
$$\ll T^\varepsilon(Y^{2-2\sigma} + T^\alpha Y^{\frac{6\alpha(1-\sigma)-11\sigma+5}{6\alpha}} + T^\theta Y^{l(1-2\sigma)}). \tag{44}$$

We choose $Y^{2-2\sigma} = T^\alpha Y^{\frac{6\alpha(1-\sigma)-11\sigma+5}{6\alpha}}$ which is equivalent to $Y = T^{\frac{6\alpha^2}{6\alpha(1-\sigma)+11\sigma-5}}$. Thus, (44) becomes

$$N_\pi(\sigma, T, T+T^\alpha) \ll T^\varepsilon(Y^{2-2\sigma} + T^\theta Y^{l(1-2\sigma)})$$
$$= T^\varepsilon(T^{\frac{12\alpha^2(1-\sigma)}{6\alpha(1-\sigma)+11\sigma-5}} + T^{\theta + \frac{6\alpha^2 l(1-2\sigma)}{6\alpha(1-\sigma)+11\sigma-5}}). \tag{45}$$

Comparing the two terms in (45), we can get

$$N_\pi(\sigma, T, T+T^\alpha) \ll T^{\frac{12\alpha^2(1-\sigma)}{6\alpha(1-\sigma)+11\sigma-5}+\varepsilon},$$

for $\sigma(6\theta\alpha - 12\alpha^2 - 11\theta + 12\alpha^2 l) \geq 6\theta\alpha - 12\alpha^2 - 5\theta + 6\alpha^2 l$, from which we complete the proof of the second result of Theorem 3.

Author Contributions: Conceptualization, W.D. and H.L.; Methodology, D.Z.; Software, W.D.; Validation, W.D., H.L., and D.Z.; Formal Analysis, W.D.; Investigation, W.D.; Resources, H.L.; Data Curation, D.Z.; Writing—Original Draft Preparation, W.D.; Writing—Review and Editing, H.L.; Visualization, D.Z.; Supervision, D.Z.; Project Administration, D.Z.; Funding Acquisition, H.L. and D.Z. All authors have read and agreed to the published version of the manuscript.

Funding: This research was funded by National Natural Science Foundation of China (Grant Nos. 11771256 and 11801327.

Institutional Review Board Statement: Not applicable.

Informed Consent Statement: Not applicable.

Data Availability Statement: Data are contained within the article.

Conflicts of Interest: The authors declare no conflict of interest.

References

1. Huang, J.; Zhai, W.G.; Zhang, D.Y. Ω-result for the index of composition of an integral ideal. *AIMS Math.* **2021**, *6*, 4979–4988. [CrossRef]
2. Sui, Y.K.; Zhai, W.G.; Zhang, D.Y. Omega-Result for the index of composition of an integer. *Int. J. Number Theory* **2018**, *14*, 339–348. [CrossRef]
3. Zhang, D.Y.; Zhai, W.G. On the mean value of the index of composition of an integral ideal (II). *J. Number Theory* **2013**, *133*, 1086–1110. [CrossRef]
4. Zhang, D.Y.; Lü, M.M.; Zhai, W.G. On the mean value of the index of composition of an integer (II). *Int. J. Number Theory* **2013**, *9*, 431–445. [CrossRef]
5. Huang, J.; Liu, H.F. Divisor problems related to Hecke eigenvalues in three dimensions. *J. Math.* **2021**, *2021*, 9928233. [CrossRef]
6. Huang, J.; Liu, H.F.; Xu, F.X. Two-Dimension Divisor Problems Related to Symmetric L-function. *Symmetry* **2021**, *13*, 359. [CrossRef]
7. Liu, H.F.; Zhang, R. Some problems involving Hecke eigenvalues. *Acta Math. Hung.* **2019**, *159*, 287–298. [CrossRef]
8. Lü, G.S. On general divisor problems involving Hecke eigenvalues. *Acta Math. Hung.* **2012**, *135*, 148–159. [CrossRef]
9. Good, A. The square mean of Dirichlet series associated with cusp forms. *Mathematika* **1982**, *29*, 278–295. [CrossRef]
10. Jiang, Y.J.; Lü, G.S.; Yan, X.F. Mean value theorem connected with Fourier coefficients of Hecke-Maass forms for $SL(m, \mathbb{Z})$. *Math. Proc. Camb. Philos. Soc.* **2016**, *161*, 339–356. [CrossRef]
11. Lao, H.X. Mean value of Dirichlet series coefficients of Rankin-Selberg L-functions. *Lith. Math. J.* **2017**, *57*, 351–358. [CrossRef]
12. Zhang, D.Y.; Lau, Y.K.; Wang, Y.N. Remark on the paper "On products of Fourier coefficients of cusp forms". *Arch. Math.* **2017**, *108*, 263–269. [CrossRef]
13. Kowalski, E.; Michel, P. Zeros of families of Automorphic L-functions close to 1. *Pac. J. Math.* **2002**, *207*, 411–431. [CrossRef]
14. Liu, J.Y.; Ye, Y.B. Superposition of zeros of distinct L-functions. *Forum Math.* **2009**, *14*, 419–455. [CrossRef]
15. Rudnick, Z.; Sarnak, P. Zeros of principle L-functions and random matrix theory. *Duke Math. J.* **1996**, *81*, 269–322. [CrossRef]
16. Sankaranarayanan, A.; Sengupta, J. Zero density estimate of L-functions attached to Maass forms. *Acta Arith.* **2007**, *127*, 273–284. [CrossRef]
17. Xu, Z. A new zero density result of L-functions attached to Maass forms. *Acta Math. Sin.* **2011**, *27*, 1149–1162. [CrossRef]
18. Zhang, D.Y. Zero density Estimates for automorphic L-functions. *Acta Math. Sin.* **2009**, *25*, 945–960. [CrossRef]
19. Ingham, A.E. On the estimation of $N(\sigma, T)$. *Q. J. Math. Oxf. Ser.* **1940**, *11*, 291–292. [CrossRef]
20. Huxley, M.N. Large Values of Dirichlet Polynomials III. *Acta Arith.* **1975**, *27*, 434–444. [CrossRef]
21. Jutila, M. Zero-density estimates for L-functions. *Acta. Arith.* **1997**, *32*, 55–62. [CrossRef]
22. Bourgain, J. On large values estimates for Dirichlet polynomials and the density hypothesis for the Riemann zeta function. *Int. Math. Res. Not.* **2000**, *3*, 133–146. [CrossRef]
23. Ivić, A. *The Riemann Zeta Function: The Theory of the Riemann Zeta-Function with Applications*; John Wiley and Sons: New York, NY, USA, 1985.
24. Ye, Y.B.; Zhang, D.Y. Zero density for automorphic L-functions. *J. Number Theory* **2013**, *133*, 3877–3901. [CrossRef]
25. Dong, L.L.; Liu, H.F.; Zhang, D.Y. Zero density estimates for automorphic L-functions of GL_m. *Acta Math. Hung.* **2016**, *148*, 191–210. [CrossRef]
26. Davenport, H. *Multiplicatiive Number Theory*, 2nd ed.; Springer: New York, NY, USA, 1980.
27. Montgomery, H.L. *Topics in Multiplicative Number Theory*; Springer: Berlin, Germany, 1971.

Article

New Properties and Identities for Fibonacci Finite Operator Quaternions

Nazlıhan Terzioğlu [1], Can Kızılateş [1] and Wei-Shih Du [2,*]

[1] Department of Mathematics, Zonguldak Bülent Ecevit University, 67100 Zonguldak, Turkey; nazlihanterzioglu@gmail.com (N.T.); cankizilates@gmail.com (C.K.)
[2] Department of Mathematics, National Kaohsiung Normal University, Kaohsiung 82444, Taiwan
* Correspondence: wsdu@mail.nknu.edu.tw

Abstract: In this paper, with the help of the finite operators and Fibonacci numbers, we define a new family of quaternions whose components are the Fibonacci finite operator numbers. We also provide some properties of these types of quaternions. Moreover, we derive many identities related to Fibonacci finite operator quaternions by using the matrix representations.

Keywords: Fibonacci number; Fibonacci quaternion; finite operator; matrix representation

MSC: 11B39; 11R52; 05A15

1. Introduction

The quaternions can be viewed as a four-dimensional vector space defined over real numbers. A quaternion consists of four components, i.e., one real part and three imaginary parts. A quaternion is often represented in the following form:

$$q = q_0 + q_1 \mathbf{e}_1 + q_2 \mathbf{e}_2 + q_3 \mathbf{e}_3$$

where q_0, q_1, q_2, q_3 are all real numbers, and the elements $\{1, \mathbf{e}_1, \mathbf{e}_2, \mathbf{e}_3\}$ form the basis of the quaternion vector space. The $\{1, \mathbf{e}_1, \mathbf{e}_2, \mathbf{e}_3\}$ obeys, following multiplication rules:

$$\mathbf{e}_1^2 = \mathbf{e}_2^2 = \mathbf{e}_3^2 = \mathbf{e}_1 \mathbf{e}_2 \mathbf{e}_3 = -1,$$

and

$$\mathbf{e}_1 \mathbf{e}_2 = -\mathbf{e}_2 \mathbf{e}_1 = \mathbf{e}_3, \ \mathbf{e}_2 \mathbf{e}_3 = -\mathbf{e}_3 \mathbf{e}_2 = \mathbf{e}_1, \ \mathbf{e}_3 \mathbf{e}_1 = -\mathbf{e}_1 \mathbf{e}_3 = \mathbf{e}_2.$$

The conjugate of a quaternion is defined as:

$$q^* = q_0 - q_1 \mathbf{e}_1 - q_2 \mathbf{e}_2 - q_3 \mathbf{e}_3.$$

Quaternions have become increasingly useful for practitioners in research, both in theory and applications. For example, a considerable number—maybe even the majority—of research articles on quaternions frequently appear in journals of mathematical physics, and quantum mechanics based on quaternion analysis is considered mainstream physics. In engineering, quaternions are often used in control systems, and in computer science, they play a role in computer graphics. For implementers in these areas, the following books can serve as valuable reference tool [1–3].

One application of quaternions that has been taken up by mathematicians is to define quaternions whose coefficients are special integer sequences or special polynomials and then examine the algebraic features of these quaternion types. Horadam [4] defined the Fibonacci quaternions as

$$\mathbb{Q}F_n = F_n + F_{n+1}\mathbf{e}_1 + F_{n+2}\mathbf{e}_2 + F_{n+3}\mathbf{e}_3, \tag{1}$$

where F_n is the n-th Fibonacci number defined by

$$F_{n+2} = F_{n+1} + F_n, \qquad (2)$$

for $n \geq 2$, with the initial values $F_0 = 0$, $F_1 = 1$. Let us just say here that in recent years, some studies related to Fibonacci numbers have been carried out by researchers in connection with other fields of science as well as mathematics [5–7]. The Binet formula for the Fibonacci sequence is

$$F_n = \frac{\alpha^n - \beta^n}{\sqrt{5}},$$

where $\alpha = \frac{1+\sqrt{5}}{2}$ and $\beta = \frac{1-\sqrt{5}}{2}$. Additionally, the Binet-like formula of the $\mathbb{Q}F_n$ is as follows:

$$\mathbb{Q}F_n = \frac{\underline{\alpha}\alpha^n - \underline{\beta}\beta^n}{\sqrt{5}}, \qquad (3)$$

where

$$\begin{aligned}\underline{\alpha} &= 1 + \alpha \mathbf{e}_1 + \alpha^2 \mathbf{e}_2 + \alpha^3 \mathbf{e}_3,\\ \underline{\beta} &= 1 + \beta \mathbf{e}_1 + \beta^2 \mathbf{e}_2 + \beta^3 \mathbf{e}_3.\end{aligned}$$

This construction has previously been studied by many mathematicians; see, for example, refs. [8–21].

On the other hand, special numbers, special polynomials, and finite operators have been often employed in recent years by a large number of researchers in a variety of fields of science. In particular, special polynomials, combinatorial sums, and generating functions for special numbers and polynomials are the most essential tools for developing mathematical models and methods, computational algorithms, and the other practices. In [22] Simsek defined a nice operator, as follows:

$$\mathbb{Y}_{\lambda,\delta}[f;a,b](x) = \lambda E^a[f](x) + \delta E^b[f](x), \qquad (4)$$

where a, b are real parameters, λ, δ are complex parameters, and $E^a[f](x) = f(x+a)$. For any polynomial sequence $f_n(x)$ and $i \geq 1$, i-th finite operator $\mathbb{Y}_{\lambda,\delta}^{(i)}[f_n;a,b](x)$ (or shortly $f_n^{(i)}(x)$) is defined by the following relation:

$$\mathbb{Y}_{\lambda,\delta}^{(i)}[f_n;a,b](x) = f_n^{(i)}(x) = \mathbb{Y}_{\lambda,\delta}[f_n;a,b](x)\left(\mathbb{Y}_{\lambda,\delta}^{(i-1)}[f_n;a,b](x)\right) \qquad (5)$$

where $\mathbb{Y}_{\lambda,\delta}^{(1)}[f_n;a,b](x) = f_n^{(1)}(x) = \lambda f_n(x+a) + \delta f_n(x+b)$. Setting special values for a, b, λ, δ in Equation (4), Simsek derived the very essential operators used in the theory of finite difference methods for the numerical solution of differential equations, as in Table 1.

Table 1. Special cases of the new finite operator.

λ	δ	a	b	Operator
1	0	0	0	$I(f(x)) = f(x)$
1	-1	1	0	$\Delta(f(x)) = f(x+1) - f(x)$
1	-1	0	-1	$\nabla(f(x)) = f(x) - f(x-1)$
1/2	$-1/2$	1	0	$M(f(x)) = \frac{1}{2}(f(x+1) - f(x))$
1	-1	$a \to a+b$	$b \to a$	$G_{ab}(f(x)) = f(x+a+b) - f(x+a)$

These operators also have plenty of applications in mathematics, physics, and engineering. Utilizing this operator, Simsek defined two new classes of special polynomials and numbers. Moreover, he extensively examined several identities related to these new special polynomials and numbers, including other special polynomials. For more information related to special polynomials and special numbers, please see [22–29]. In [30] Kızılateş applied the finite operator to Horadam sequences, called Horadam finite operator sequences. Let a and b integer, λ and δ real parameters. The Horadam finite operator numbers are defined by

$$\Delta_{\lambda,\delta;a,b}^{(i)}(W_n) = \mathcal{W}_n^{(i)} = \lambda \Delta_{\lambda,\delta;a,b}^{(i-1)}(W_{n+a}) + \delta \Delta_{\lambda,\delta;a,b}^{(i-1)}(W_{n+b}),$$

or

$$\Delta_{\lambda,\delta;a,b}^{(i)}(W_n) = \mathcal{W}_n^{(i)} = \sum_{j=0}^{i} \binom{i}{j} \lambda^{i-j} \delta^j W_{n+jb+(i-j)a}, \qquad (6)$$

where

$$W_n = pW_{n-1} + qW_{n-2}, \quad n \geq 2 \qquad (7)$$

with the initial values $W_0 = r$, $W_1 = s$, and p, q are arbitrary integers. The author also examined some algebraic properties and matrix representations of these numbers. If we take $p = q = s = 1$ and $r = 0$ in Equation (6), we get the Fibonacci finite operator numbers as follows:

$$\Delta_{\lambda,\delta;a,b}^{(i)}(F_n) = \mathcal{F}_n^{(i)} = \lambda \Delta_{\lambda,\delta;a,b}^{(i-1)}(F_{n+a}) + \delta \Delta_{\lambda,\delta;a,b}^{(i-1)}(F_{n+b}). \qquad (8)$$

For $n, i \geq 1$, the Fibonacci finite operator sequence satisfies the recurrence relation as

$$\mathcal{F}_{n+1}^{(i)} = \mathcal{F}_n^{(i)} + \mathcal{F}_{n-1}^{(i)}. \qquad (9)$$

Additionally, the Binet-like formula for the Fibonacci finite operator sequence is given by

$$\mathcal{F}_n^{(i)} = \mathcal{F}_1^{(i)} F_n + \mathcal{F}_0^{(i)} F_{n-1}. \qquad (10)$$

The purpose of this research is to define a quaternion family using Fibonacci finite operators as its components. We also discuss some of the algebraic features of these quaternions. Next, we derive certain results by using the matrix representations of these quaternions. Numerous identities involving Fibonacci finite operator quaternions are established using these matrix representations.

2. Fibonacci Finite Operator Quaternions

In this part of the paper, we define the Fibonacci finite operator quaternions. We also studied some properties of these new types of quaternions.

Definition 1. *The Fibonacci finite operator quaternions, $\mathbb{Q}\mathcal{F}_n^{(i)}$, are defined by*

$$\mathbb{Q}\mathcal{F}_n^{(i)} = \mathcal{F}_n^{(i)} + \mathcal{F}_{n+1}^{(i)} \mathbf{e}_1 + \mathcal{F}_{n+2}^{(i)} \mathbf{e}_2 + \mathcal{F}_{n+3}^{(i)} \mathbf{e}_3. \qquad (11)$$

where $\mathcal{F}_n^{(i)}$ is the i-th finite operator numbers.

Note that Definition 1 is much more general to the Fibonacci quaternions defined in Equation (1). Only for $i = 1$, some special values of

$$\mathbb{Q}\mathcal{F}_n^{(1)} = \sum_{s=0}^{3} (\lambda F_{n+a+s} + \delta F_{n+b+s}) \mathbf{e}_s, \qquad (12)$$

as follows:

1. If we take $\lambda = 1$ and $\delta = a = b = 0$ in Equation (12), we get the identity operator for Fibonacci quaternion sequence $I(\mathbb{Q}\mathcal{F}_n^{(1)}) = \mathbb{Q}F_n$;
2. If we take $\lambda = 1$, $\delta = -1$, $a = 1$ and $b = 0$ in Equation (12), we obtain the forward difference operator for Fibonacci quaternion sequence $\Delta(\mathbb{Q}\mathcal{F}_n^{(1)}) = \mathbb{Q}F_{n+1} - \mathbb{Q}F_n$;

3. If we take $\lambda = 1, \delta = -1, a = 0$ and $b = -1$ in Equation (12), we obtain the backward difference operator for Fibonacci quaternion sequence $\nabla\left(\mathbb{Q}\mathcal{F}_n^{(1)}\right) = \mathbb{Q}F_n - \mathbb{Q}F_{n-1}$;
4. If we take $\lambda = \frac{1}{2}, \delta = \frac{-1}{2}, a = 1$ and $b = 0$ in Equation (12), we obtain the means operator for Fibonacci quaternion sequence $M\left(\mathbb{Q}\mathcal{F}_n^{(1)}\right) = \frac{1}{2}(\mathbb{Q}F_{n+1} - \mathbb{Q}F_n)$;
5. If we take $\lambda = 1, \delta = -1$, and substitute $a \to a+b, b \to a$ and $ab \neq 0$ in Equation (12), we obtain the Gould operator for Fibonacci quaternion sequence $G_{ab}\left(\mathbb{Q}\mathcal{F}_n^{(1)}\right) = \mathbb{Q}F_{n+a+b} - \mathbb{Q}F_{n+a}$.

From Equation (11), the Fibonacci finite operator quaternions can be written as

$$\mathbb{Q}\mathcal{F}_n^{(i)} = \mathcal{F}_n^{(i)} + u,$$

where $u = \mathcal{F}_{n+1}^{(i)}\mathbf{e}_1 + \mathcal{F}_{n+2}^{(i)}\mathbf{e}_2 + \mathcal{F}_{n+3}^{(i)}\mathbf{e}_3$.

The conjugate of the Fibonacci finite operator quaternions, $\mathbb{Q}\mathcal{F}_n^{(i)}$ is denoted by $\left(\mathbb{Q}\mathcal{F}_n^{(i)}\right)^*$ as

$$\left(\mathbb{Q}\mathcal{F}_n^{(i)}\right)^* = \mathcal{F}_n^{(i)} - u. \tag{13}$$

For the Fibonacci finite operator quaternions, we can easily obtain that

$$\mathbb{Q}\mathcal{F}_n^{(i)} + \left(\mathbb{Q}\mathcal{F}_n^{(i)}\right)^* = 2\mathcal{F}_n^{(i)}.$$

Theorem 1. *The recurrence relation for the Fibonacci finite operator quaternions; $\mathbb{Q}\mathcal{F}_n^{(i)}$ is*

$$\mathbb{Q}\mathcal{F}_n^{(i)} = \mathbb{Q}\mathcal{F}_{n-1}^{(i)} + \mathbb{Q}\mathcal{F}_{n-2}^{(i)}. \tag{14}$$

Proof. Using Equation (9), we find that

$$\mathbb{Q}\mathcal{F}_n^{(i)} = \mathcal{F}_n^{(i)} + \mathcal{F}_{n+1}^{(i)}\mathbf{e}_1 + \mathcal{F}_{n+2}^{(i)}\mathbf{e}_2 + \mathcal{F}_{n+3}^{(i)}\mathbf{e}_3$$
$$= \mathcal{F}_{n-1}^{(i)} + \mathcal{F}_{n-2}^{(i)} + \left(\mathcal{F}_n^{(i)} + \mathcal{F}_{n-1}^{(i)}\right)\mathbf{e}_1 + \left(\mathcal{F}_{n+1}^{(i)} + \mathcal{F}_n^{(i)}\right)\mathbf{e}_2 + \left(\mathcal{F}_{n+2}^{(i)} + \mathcal{F}_{n+1}^{(i)}\right)\mathbf{e}_3$$
$$= \left(\mathcal{F}_{n-1}^{(i)} + \mathcal{F}_n^{(i)}\mathbf{e}_1 + \mathcal{F}_{n+1}^{(i)}\mathbf{e}_2 + \mathcal{F}_{n+2}^{(i)}\mathbf{e}_3\right) + \left(\mathcal{F}_{n-2}^{(i)} + \mathcal{F}_{n-1}^{(i)}\mathbf{e}_1 + \mathcal{F}_n^{(i)}\mathbf{e}_2 + \mathcal{F}_{n+1}^{(i)}\mathbf{e}_3\right)$$
$$= \mathbb{Q}\mathcal{F}_{n-1}^{(i)} + \mathbb{Q}\mathcal{F}_{n-2}^{(i)}.$$

□

Theorem 2. *The Binet-like formula of the Fibonacci finite operator quaternions; $\mathbb{Q}\mathcal{F}_n^{(i)}$ is as follows:*

$$\mathbb{Q}\mathcal{F}_n^{(i)} = \frac{\underline{\alpha}\alpha^{n-1}\left(\alpha\mathcal{F}_1^{(i)} + \mathcal{F}_0^{(i)}\right) - \underline{\beta}\beta^{n-1}\left(\beta\mathcal{F}_1^{(i)} + \mathcal{F}_0^{(i)}\right)}{\sqrt{5}}. \tag{15}$$

Proof. Thanks to Equations (3) and (10), we have

$$\mathbb{Q}\mathcal{F}_n^{(i)} = \mathcal{F}_n^{(i)} + \mathcal{F}_{n+1}^{(i)}\mathbf{e}_1 + \mathcal{F}_{n+2}^{(i)}\mathbf{e}_2 + \mathcal{F}_{n+3}^{(i)}\mathbf{e}_3$$
$$= \mathcal{F}_1^{(i)}F_n + \mathcal{F}_0^{(i)}F_{n-1} + \left(\mathcal{F}_1^{(i)}F_{n+1} + \mathcal{F}_0^{(i)}F_n\right)\mathbf{e}_1$$
$$+ \left(\mathcal{F}_1^{(i)}F_{n+2} + \mathcal{F}_0^{(i)}F_{n+1}\right)\mathbf{e}_2 + \left(\mathcal{F}_1^{(i)}F_{n+3} + \mathcal{F}_0^{(i)}F_{n+2}\right)\mathbf{e}_3$$
$$= \mathcal{F}_1^{(i)}(F_n + F_{n+1}\mathbf{e}_1 + F_{n+2}\mathbf{e}_2 + F_{n+3}\mathbf{e}_3) + \mathcal{F}_0^{(i)}(F_{n-1} + F_n\mathbf{e}_1 + F_{n+1}\mathbf{e}_2 + F_{n+2}\mathbf{e}_3)$$
$$= \mathcal{F}_1^{(i)}\mathbb{Q}F_n + \mathcal{F}_0^{(i)}\mathbb{Q}F_{n-1}$$

$$= \mathcal{F}_1^{(i)} \frac{\underline{\alpha}\alpha^n - \underline{\beta}\beta^n}{\sqrt{5}} + \mathcal{F}_0^{(i)} \frac{\underline{\alpha}\alpha^{n-1} - \underline{\beta}\beta^{n-1}}{\sqrt{5}}$$

$$= \frac{\underline{\alpha}\alpha^{n-1}\left(\alpha\mathcal{F}_1^{(i)} + \mathcal{F}_0^{(i)}\right) - \underline{\beta}\beta^{n-1}\left(\beta\mathcal{F}_1^{(i)} + \mathcal{F}_0^{(i)}\right)}{\sqrt{5}}.$$

□

Theorem 3. *The generating function for the $\mathbb{Q}\mathcal{F}_n^{(i)}$ is as follows:*

$$\mathbb{Q}\mathcal{F}_n^{(i)}(x) = \frac{\mathbb{Q}\mathcal{F}_0^{(i)} + \left(\mathbb{Q}\mathcal{F}_1^{(i)} - \mathbb{Q}\mathcal{F}_0^{(i)}\right)x}{1 - x - x^2}.$$

Proof. Let $\mathbb{Q}\mathcal{F}_n^{(i)}(x)$ be the generating function of the Fibonacci finite operator quaternions. Namely,

$$\mathbb{Q}\mathcal{F}_n^{(i)}(x) = \sum_{n=0}^{\infty} \mathbb{Q}\mathcal{F}_n^{(i)} x^n.$$

Then, we have,

$$\mathbb{Q}\mathcal{F}_n^{(i)}(x) = \mathbb{Q}\mathcal{F}_0^{(i)} + \mathbb{Q}\mathcal{F}_1^{(i)} x + \mathbb{Q}\mathcal{F}_2^{(i)} x^2 + \cdots + \mathbb{Q}\mathcal{F}_n^{(i)} x^n + \cdots$$

$$-x\mathbb{Q}\mathcal{F}_n^{(i)}(x) = -\mathbb{Q}\mathcal{F}_0^{(i)} x - \mathbb{Q}\mathcal{F}_1^{(i)} x^2 - \mathbb{Q}\mathcal{F}_2^{(i)} x^3 - \cdots - \mathbb{Q}\mathcal{F}_n^{(i)} x^{n+1} - \cdots$$

$$-x^2\mathbb{Q}\mathcal{F}_n^{(i)}(x) = -\mathbb{Q}\mathcal{F}_0^{(i)} x^2 - \mathbb{Q}\mathcal{F}_1^{(i)} x^3 - \mathbb{Q}\mathcal{F}_2^{(i)} x^4 - \cdots - \mathbb{Q}\mathcal{F}_n^{(i)} x^{n+2} - \cdots$$

Using the above identities, we get

$$\left(1 - x - x^2\right)\mathbb{Q}\mathcal{F}_n^{(i)}(x) = \mathbb{Q}\mathcal{F}_0^{(i)} + \left(\mathbb{Q}\mathcal{F}_1^{(i)} - \mathbb{Q}\mathcal{F}_0^{(i)}\right)x + \sum_{n=2}^{\infty}\left(\mathbb{Q}\mathcal{F}_n^{(i)} - \mathbb{Q}\mathcal{F}_{n-1}^{(i)} - \mathbb{Q}\mathcal{F}_{n-2}^{(i)}\right)x^n$$

Following Equation (14), we have

$$\mathbb{Q}\mathcal{F}_n^{(i)}(x) = \frac{\mathbb{Q}\mathcal{F}_0^{(i)} + \left(\mathbb{Q}\mathcal{F}_1^{(i)} - \mathbb{Q}\mathcal{F}_0^{(i)}\right)x}{1 - x - x^2}.$$

□

Theorem 4. *The exponential generating function for the sequence $\mathbb{Q}\mathcal{F}_n^{(i)}$ is as follows:*

$$\sum_{n=0}^{\infty} \mathbb{Q}\mathcal{F}_n^{(i)} \frac{x^n}{n!} = \frac{\mathcal{F}_1^{(i)}\left(\underline{\alpha}e^{\alpha x} - \underline{\beta}e^{\beta x}\right) - \mathcal{F}_0^{(i)}\left(\underline{\alpha}\beta e^{\alpha x} - \underline{\beta}\alpha e^{\beta x}\right)}{\sqrt{5}}.$$

Proof. Using Equation (15), we get

$$\sum_{n=0}^{\infty} \mathbb{Q}\mathcal{F}_n^{(i)} \frac{x^n}{n!} = \sum_{n=0}^{\infty} \left(\frac{\underline{\alpha}\alpha^{n-1}\left(\alpha\mathcal{F}_1^{(i)} + \mathcal{F}_0^{(i)}\right) - \underline{\beta}\beta^{n-1}\left(\beta\mathcal{F}_1^{(i)} + \mathcal{F}_0^{(i)}\right)}{\sqrt{5}}\right) \frac{x^n}{n!}$$

$$= \frac{1}{\sqrt{5}} \left(\frac{\underline{\alpha}\left(\alpha\mathcal{F}_1^{(i)} + \mathcal{F}_0^{(i)}\right)}{\alpha} e^{\alpha x} - \frac{\underline{\beta}\left(\beta\mathcal{F}_1^{(i)} + \mathcal{F}_0^{(i)}\right)}{\beta} e^{\beta x}\right)$$

$$= \frac{\underline{\alpha}\beta e^{\alpha x}\left(\alpha\mathcal{F}_1^{(i)} + \mathcal{F}_0^{(i)}\right) - \underline{\beta}\alpha e^{\beta x}\left(\beta\mathcal{F}_1^{(i)} + \mathcal{F}_0^{(i)}\right)}{\sqrt{5}\alpha\beta}$$

$$= \frac{\mathcal{F}_1^{(i)}\left(\underline{\alpha}e^{\alpha x} - \underline{\beta}e^{\beta x}\right) - \mathcal{F}_0^{(i)}\left(\underline{\alpha}\beta e^{\alpha x} - \underline{\beta}\alpha e^{\beta x}\right)}{\sqrt{5}}.$$

□

Theorem 5. *For non-negative integer n, we have*

$$\sum_{t=0}^{n}(-1)^t\binom{n}{t}\mathbb{Q}\mathcal{F}_{2t+k}^{(i)} = (-1)^n\mathbb{Q}\mathcal{F}_{n+k}^{(i)}.$$

Proof. By virtue of Equation (15), we find that

$$\sum_{t=0}^{n}(-1)^t\binom{n}{t}\mathbb{Q}\mathcal{F}_{2t+k}^{(i)} = \sum_{t=0}^{n}\binom{n}{t}(-1)^t\left(\frac{\underline{\alpha}\alpha^{2t+k-1}\left(\alpha\mathcal{F}_1^{(i)} + \mathcal{F}_0^{(i)}\right) - \underline{\beta}\beta^{2t+k-1}\left(\beta\mathcal{F}_1^{(i)} + \mathcal{F}_0^{(i)}\right)}{\sqrt{5}}\right)$$

$$= \frac{\underline{\alpha}\alpha^{k-1}\left(\alpha\mathcal{F}_1^{(i)} + \mathcal{F}_0^{(i)}\right)}{\sqrt{5}}(1-\alpha^2)^n - \frac{\underline{\beta}\beta^{k-1}\left(\beta\mathcal{F}_1^{(i)} + \mathcal{F}_0^{(i)}\right)}{\sqrt{5}}(1-\beta^2)^n$$

$$= \frac{\underline{\alpha}\alpha^{k-1}\left(\alpha\mathcal{F}_1^{(i)} + \mathcal{F}_0^{(i)}\right)}{\sqrt{5}}(-\alpha)^n - \frac{\underline{\beta}\beta^{k-1}\left(\beta\mathcal{F}_1^{(i)} + \mathcal{F}_0^{(i)}\right)}{\sqrt{5}}(-\beta)^n$$

$$= (-1)^n \mathbb{Q}\mathcal{F}_{n+k}^{(i)}.$$

□

Theorem 6. *For non-negative integer n, we have*

$$\sum_{t=0}^{n}\binom{n}{t}\mathbb{Q}\mathcal{F}_{t}^{(i)} = \mathbb{Q}\mathcal{F}_{2n}^{(i)}.$$

Proof. From Equation (15), we have

$$\sum_{t=0}^{n}\binom{n}{t}\mathbb{Q}\mathcal{F}_{t}^{(i)} = \sum_{t=0}^{n}\binom{n}{t}\left(\frac{\underline{\alpha}\alpha^{t-1}\left(\alpha\mathcal{F}_1^{(i)} + \mathcal{F}_0^{(i)}\right) - \underline{\beta}\beta^{t-1}\left(\beta\mathcal{F}_1^{(i)} + \mathcal{F}_0^{(i)}\right)}{\sqrt{5}}\right)$$

$$= \frac{\underline{\alpha}\alpha^{-1}\left(\alpha\mathcal{F}_1^{(i)} + \mathcal{F}_0^{(i)}\right)}{\sqrt{5}}(1+\alpha)^n - \frac{\underline{\beta}\beta^{-1}\left(\beta\mathcal{F}_1^{(i)} + \mathcal{F}_0^{(i)}\right)}{\sqrt{5}}(1+\beta)^n$$

$$= \frac{\underline{\alpha}\alpha^{2n-1}\left(\alpha\mathcal{F}_1^{(i)} + \mathcal{F}_0^{(i)}\right)}{\sqrt{5}} - \frac{\underline{\beta}\beta^{2n-1}\left(\beta\mathcal{F}_1^{(i)} + \mathcal{F}_0^{(i)}\right)}{\sqrt{5}}$$

$$= \mathbb{Q}\mathcal{F}_{2n}^{(i)}.$$

□

Theorem 7. *For non-negative integer n, we have*

$$\sum_{t=0}^{n}\binom{n}{t}\left(\mathbb{Q}\mathcal{F}_t^{(i)}\right)^2 = 5^{\frac{n-2}{2}}\left((2\underline{\alpha}-12\alpha-9)\alpha^{n-2}\zeta + (-1)^n\left(2\underline{\beta}-12\beta-9\right)\beta^{n-2}\xi\right)$$

where $\zeta = \left(\alpha\mathcal{F}_1^{(i)} + \mathcal{F}_0^{(i)}\right)^2$ *and* $\xi = \left(\beta\mathcal{F}_1^{(i)} + \mathcal{F}_0^{(i)}\right)^2$.

Proof. The authors [16] proved that

$$(\underline{\alpha})^2 = (2\underline{\alpha} - (L_5+1)\alpha - L_4 - L_0) = (2\underline{\alpha} - 12\alpha - 9)$$

$$\left(\underline{\beta}\right)^2 = \left(2\underline{\beta} - (L_5+1)\beta - L_4 - L_0\right) = \left(2\underline{\beta} - 12\beta - 9\right),$$

where L_n is the n-th Lucas numbers defined by

$$L_n = L_{n-1} + L_{n-2},$$

for $n \geq 2$, with the initial values $L_0 = 2$ and $L_1 = 1$. Using (15), after some calculations, we have

$$\sum_{t=0}^{n} \binom{n}{t} \left(Q\mathcal{F}_t^{(i)}\right)^2 = \sum_{t=0}^{n} \binom{n}{t} \left(\frac{\underline{\alpha}\alpha^{t-1}\left(\alpha\mathcal{F}_1^{(i)} + \mathcal{F}_0^{(i)}\right) - \underline{\beta}\beta^{t-1}\left(\beta\mathcal{F}_1^{(i)} + \mathcal{F}_0^{(i)}\right)}{\sqrt{5}}\right)^2$$

$$= \frac{1}{5}\sum_{t=0}^{n}\binom{n}{t}\left(\underline{\alpha}\alpha^{t-1}\left(\alpha\mathcal{F}_1^{(i)} + \mathcal{F}_0^{(i)}\right) - \underline{\beta}\beta^{t-1}\left(\beta\mathcal{F}_1^{(i)} + \mathcal{F}_0^{(i)}\right)\right)^2$$

$$= \frac{1}{5}\left((\underline{\alpha})^2\left(\alpha\mathcal{F}_1^{(i)} + \mathcal{F}_0^{(i)}\right)^2 \sum_{t=0}^{n}\binom{n}{t}\alpha^{2t-2} + \left(\underline{\beta}\right)^2\left(\beta\mathcal{F}_1^{(i)} + \mathcal{F}_0^{(i)}\right)^2 \sum_{t=0}^{n}\binom{n}{t}\beta^{2t-2}\right)$$

$$= \frac{(\underline{\alpha})^2\alpha^{-2}\left(\alpha\mathcal{F}_1^{(i)} + \mathcal{F}_0^{(i)}\right)^2}{5}\left(1+\alpha^2\right)^n + \frac{\left(\underline{\beta}\right)^2\beta^{-2}\left(\beta\mathcal{F}_1^{(i)} + \mathcal{F}_0^{(i)}\right)^2}{5}\left(1+\beta^2\right)^n$$

$$= \frac{(\underline{\alpha})^2\alpha^{-2}\left(\alpha\mathcal{F}_1^{(i)} + \mathcal{F}_0^{(i)}\right)^2}{5}\left(\alpha\sqrt{5}\right)^n + \frac{\left(\underline{\beta}\right)^2\beta^{-2}\left(\beta\mathcal{F}_1^{(i)} + \mathcal{F}_0^{(i)}\right)^2}{5}\left(-\beta\sqrt{5}\right)^n$$

$$= 5^{\frac{n-2}{2}}\left((\underline{\alpha})^2\alpha^{n-2}\left(\alpha\mathcal{F}_1^{(i)} + \mathcal{F}_0^{(i)}\right)^2 + (-1)^n\left(\underline{\beta}\right)^2\beta^{n-2}\left(\beta\mathcal{F}_1^{(i)} + \mathcal{F}_0^{(i)}\right)^2\right)$$

$$= 5^{\frac{n-2}{2}}\left((2\underline{\alpha} - 12\alpha - 9)\alpha^{n-2}\zeta + (-1)^n\left(2\underline{\beta} - 12\beta - 9\right)\beta^{n-2}\bar{\zeta}\right).$$

□

3. Matrix Representations of Fibonacci Finite Operator Quaternions and Their New Properties

From past to present, matrix representations have been studied by many researchers for special integer sequences and various generalizations of these sequences. Halici [8] gave the following matrix representation to obtain the Cassini identity for Fibonacci quaternions defined by Horadam

$$\mathbf{M} = \begin{bmatrix} QF_2 & QF_1 \\ QF_1 & QF_0 \end{bmatrix}.$$

Similar to Fibonacci quaternion matrices, various matrix representations are given in different quaternion sequences and generalizations of these sequences. The best references here are [31–37]. Patel and Ray [33] defined the Fibonacci quaternion matrix as follows:

$$\mathbf{M} = \begin{bmatrix} QF_2 & QF_1 \\ QF_1 & QF_0 \end{bmatrix} \Longrightarrow \mathbf{MU}^{n-1} = \begin{bmatrix} QF_{n+1} & QF_n \\ QF_n & QF_{n-1} \end{bmatrix}, \quad (16)$$

where the matrix $\mathbf{U}$ satisfies the following matrix relation:

$$\mathbf{U} = \begin{bmatrix} 1 & 1 \\ 1 & 0 \end{bmatrix} \Longrightarrow \mathbf{U}^n = \begin{bmatrix} F_{n+1} & F_n \\ F_n & F_{n-1} \end{bmatrix}. \quad (17)$$

In the previous section, we have obtained some properties of Fibonacci finite operator quaternions by using the Binet-like formula. In this section of the our paper, based on Tan and Leung's paper [31] with a similar approach, we give matrix representations for these type of quaternions. Using these representation, we also derive several properties of

Fibonacci finite operator quaternions. From the recurrence relation of the Fibonacci finite operator numbers, we can easily see the matrix relation:

$$\mathbf{N} = \begin{bmatrix} \mathcal{F}_2^{(i)} & \mathcal{F}_1^{(i)} \\ \mathcal{F}_1^{(i)} & \mathcal{F}_0^{(i)} \end{bmatrix} \Longrightarrow \mathbf{N}\mathbf{U}^{n-1} = \begin{bmatrix} \mathcal{F}_{n+1}^{(i)} & \mathcal{F}_n^{(i)} \\ \mathcal{F}_n^{(i)} & \mathcal{F}_{n-1}^{(i)} \end{bmatrix}. \tag{18}$$

Considering the matrix equalities in Equations (16) and (18), we have a matrix representation of the Fibonacci finite operator quaternions as follows:

$$\left(\mathbf{N}\mathbf{U}^{n-1}\right)\mathbf{M} = \mathbf{M}\left(\mathbf{N}\mathbf{U}^{n-1}\right) = \begin{bmatrix} \mathbb{Q}\mathcal{F}_{n+2}^{(i)} & \mathbb{Q}\mathcal{F}_{n+1}^{(i)} \\ \mathbb{Q}\mathcal{F}_{n+1}^{(i)} & \mathbb{Q}\mathcal{F}_n^{(i)} \end{bmatrix}. \tag{19}$$

Let us point out here that although the matrix multiplication is not commutative, Equality Equation (19) is held. Namely,

$$\left(\mathbf{N}\mathbf{U}^{n-1}\right)\mathbf{M} = \begin{bmatrix} \mathcal{F}_{n+1}^{(i)} & \mathcal{F}_n^{(i)} \\ \mathcal{F}_n^{(i)} & \mathcal{F}_{n-1}^{(i)} \end{bmatrix} \begin{bmatrix} \mathbb{Q}F_2 & \mathbb{Q}F_1 \\ \mathbb{Q}F_1 & \mathbb{Q}F_0 \end{bmatrix}$$

$$= \begin{bmatrix} \mathcal{F}_{n+1}^{(i)}\mathbb{Q}F_2 + \mathcal{F}_n^{(i)}\mathbb{Q}F_1 & \mathcal{F}_{n+1}^{(i)}\mathbb{Q}F_1 + \mathcal{F}_n^{(i)}\mathbb{Q}F_0 \\ \mathcal{F}_n^{(i)}\mathbb{Q}F_2 + \mathcal{F}_{n-1}^{(i)}\mathbb{Q}F_1 & \mathcal{F}_n^{(i)}\mathbb{Q}F_1 + \mathcal{F}_{n-1}^{(i)}\mathbb{Q}F_0 \end{bmatrix}$$

$$= \begin{bmatrix} \mathbb{Q}F_2\mathcal{F}_{n+1}^{(i)} + \mathbb{Q}F_1\mathcal{F}_n^{(i)} & \mathbb{Q}F_1\mathcal{F}_{n+1}^{(i)} + \mathbb{Q}F_0\mathcal{F}_n^{(i)} \\ \mathbb{Q}F_2\mathcal{F}_n^{(i)} + \mathbb{Q}F_1\mathcal{F}_{n-1}^{(i)} & \mathbb{Q}F_1\mathcal{F}_n^{(i)} + \mathbb{Q}F_0\mathcal{F}_{n-1}^{(i)} \end{bmatrix}$$

$$= \begin{bmatrix} \mathbb{Q}F_2 & \mathbb{Q}F_1 \\ \mathbb{Q}F_1 & \mathbb{Q}F_0 \end{bmatrix} \begin{bmatrix} \mathcal{F}_{n+1}^{(i)} & \mathcal{F}_n^{(i)} \\ \mathcal{F}_n^{(i)} & \mathcal{F}_{n-1}^{(i)} \end{bmatrix}$$

$$= \mathbf{M}\left(\mathbf{N}\mathbf{U}^{n-1}\right).$$

We also have another matrix representation for the Fibonacci finite operator quaternions, as follows:

$$\mathbf{O} := \begin{bmatrix} \mathbb{Q}\mathcal{F}_2^{(i)} & \mathbb{Q}\mathcal{F}_1^{(i)} \\ \mathbb{Q}\mathcal{F}_1^{(i)} & \mathbb{Q}\mathcal{F}_0^{(i)} \end{bmatrix} \Longrightarrow \mathbf{U}^n\mathbf{O} = \mathbf{O}\mathbf{U}^n = \begin{bmatrix} \mathbb{Q}\mathcal{F}_{n+2}^{(i)} & \mathbb{Q}\mathcal{F}_{n+1}^{(i)} \\ \mathbb{Q}\mathcal{F}_{n+1}^{(i)} & \mathbb{Q}\mathcal{F}_n^{(i)} \end{bmatrix}. \tag{20}$$

Since the quaternion multiplication is non-commutative, the following theorem gives four Cassini's identities for Fibonacci finite operator quaternions.

Theorem 8. *For non-negative integer n, we find that*

$$\mathbb{Q}\mathcal{F}_{n+1}^{(i)}\mathbb{Q}\mathcal{F}_{n-1}^{(i)} - \left(\mathbb{Q}\mathcal{F}_n^{(i)}\right)^2 = (-1)^{n-1}\left(\mathbb{Q}\mathcal{F}_2^{(i)}\mathbb{Q}\mathcal{F}_0^{(i)} - \left(\mathbb{Q}\mathcal{F}_1^{(i)}\right)^2\right), \tag{21}$$

$$\mathbb{Q}\mathcal{F}_{n-1}^{(i)}\mathbb{Q}\mathcal{F}_{n+1}^{(i)} - \left(\mathbb{Q}\mathcal{F}_n^{(i)}\right)^2 = (-1)^{n-1}\left(\mathbb{Q}\mathcal{F}_0^{(i)}\mathbb{Q}\mathcal{F}_2^{(i)} - \left(\mathbb{Q}\mathcal{F}_1^{(i)}\right)^2\right), \tag{22}$$

$$\mathbb{Q}\mathcal{F}_{n+1}^{(i)}\mathbb{Q}\mathcal{F}_{n-1}^{(i)} - \left(\mathbb{Q}\mathcal{F}_n^{(i)}\right)^2 = (-1)^{n-1}\left(\mathbb{Q}F_2\mathbb{Q}F_0 - (\mathbb{Q}F_1)^2\right)\left(\left(\mathcal{F}_1^{(i)}\right)^2 - \mathcal{F}_1^{(i)}\mathcal{F}_0^{(i)} - \left(\mathcal{F}_0^{(i)}\right)^2\right), \tag{23}$$

$$\mathbb{Q}\mathcal{F}_{n-1}^{(i)}\mathbb{Q}\mathcal{F}_{n+1}^{(i)} - \left(\mathbb{Q}\mathcal{F}_n^{(i)}\right)^2 = (-1)^{n-1}\left(\mathbb{Q}F_0\mathbb{Q}F_2 - (\mathbb{Q}F_1)^2\right)\left(\left(\mathcal{F}_1^{(i)}\right)^2 - \mathcal{F}_1^{(i)}\mathcal{F}_0^{(i)} - \left(\mathcal{F}_0^{(i)}\right)^2\right). \tag{24}$$

Proof. For Equations (21) and (22), by using Equation (20), we get

$$\begin{vmatrix} \mathbb{Q}\mathcal{F}_{n+1}^{(i)} & \mathbb{Q}\mathcal{F}_n^{(i)} \\ \mathbb{Q}\mathcal{F}_n^{(i)} & \mathbb{Q}\mathcal{F}_{n-1}^{(i)} \end{vmatrix} = \left|\mathbf{U}^{n-1}\mathbf{O}\right| = |\mathbf{U}|^{n-1}|\mathbf{O}| = \begin{vmatrix} 1 & 1 \\ 1 & 0 \end{vmatrix}^{n-1} \begin{vmatrix} \mathbb{Q}\mathcal{F}_2^{(i)} & \mathbb{Q}\mathcal{F}_1^{(i)} \\ \mathbb{Q}\mathcal{F}_1^{(i)} & \mathbb{Q}\mathcal{F}_0^{(i)} \end{vmatrix}$$

$$\mathbb{Q}\mathcal{F}^{(i)}_{n+1}\mathbb{Q}\mathcal{F}^{(i)}_{n-1} - \left(\mathbb{Q}\mathcal{F}^{(i)}_n\right)^2 = (-1)^{n-1}\left(\mathbb{Q}\mathcal{F}^{(i)}_2 \mathbb{Q}\mathcal{F}^{(i)}_0 - \left(\mathbb{Q}\mathcal{F}^{(i)}_1\right)^2\right),$$

and

$$\mathbb{Q}\mathcal{F}^{(i)}_{n-1}\mathbb{Q}\mathcal{F}^{(i)}_{n+1} - \left(\mathbb{Q}\mathcal{F}^{(i)}_n\right)^2 = (-1)^{n-1}\left(\mathbb{Q}\mathcal{F}^{(i)}_0 \mathbb{Q}\mathcal{F}^{(i)}_2 - \left(\mathbb{Q}\mathcal{F}^{(i)}_1\right)^2\right).$$

Likewise, if we take the determinant on both sides of the matrix Equation (19), we obtain Equations (23) and (24), respectively. □

Theorem 9. *For integer $m, n \geq 1$, the following equalities hold:*

$$\mathcal{F}^{(i)}_n \mathbb{Q}F_{m+1} + \mathcal{F}^{(i)}_{n-1}\mathbb{Q}F_m = \mathbb{Q}\mathcal{F}^{(i)}_{m+n}, \tag{25}$$

$$F_n \mathbb{Q}\mathcal{F}^{(i)}_{m+1} + F_{n-1}\mathbb{Q}\mathcal{F}^{(i)}_m = \mathbb{Q}\mathcal{F}^{(i)}_{m+n}, \tag{26}$$

$$\mathbb{Q}\mathcal{F}^{(i)}_{m+1}\mathbb{Q}F_{n+1} + \mathbb{Q}\mathcal{F}^{(i)}_m \mathbb{Q}F_n = \mathbb{Q}F_2 \mathbb{Q}\mathcal{F}^{(i)}_{m+n} + \mathbb{Q}F_1 \mathbb{Q}\mathcal{F}^{(i)}_{m+n-1}, \tag{27}$$

$$\mathbb{Q}\mathcal{F}^{(i)}_{m+1}\mathbb{Q}\mathcal{F}^{(i)}_{n+1} + \mathbb{Q}\mathcal{F}^{(i)}_m \mathbb{Q}\mathcal{F}^{(i)}_n = \mathbb{Q}\mathcal{F}^{(i)}_2 \mathbb{Q}\mathcal{F}^{(i)}_{m+n} + \mathbb{Q}\mathcal{F}^{(i)}_1 \mathbb{Q}\mathcal{F}^{(i)}_{m+n-1}. \tag{28}$$

Proof. Substituting $n \to m+n-1$ into (19) and (20), we have

$$\begin{bmatrix} \mathbb{Q}\mathcal{F}^{(i)}_{m+n+1} & \mathbb{Q}\mathcal{F}^{(i)}_{m+n} \\ \mathbb{Q}\mathcal{F}^{(i)}_{m+n} & \mathbb{Q}\mathcal{F}^{(i)}_{m+n-1} \end{bmatrix} = \left(\mathbf{NU}^{m+n-2}\right)\mathbf{M} = \left(\mathbf{NU}^{n-1}\right)\left(\mathbf{U}^{m-1}\mathbf{M}\right)$$

$$\begin{bmatrix} \mathbb{Q}\mathcal{F}^{(i)}_{m+n+1} & \mathbb{Q}\mathcal{F}^{(i)}_{m+n} \\ \mathbb{Q}\mathcal{F}^{(i)}_{m+n} & \mathbb{Q}\mathcal{F}^{(i)}_{m+n-1} \end{bmatrix} = \begin{bmatrix} \mathcal{F}^{(i)}_{n+1} & \mathcal{F}^{(i)}_n \\ \mathcal{F}^{(i)}_n & \mathcal{F}^{(i)}_{n-1} \end{bmatrix} \begin{bmatrix} \mathbb{Q}F_{m+1} & \mathbb{Q}F_m \\ \mathbb{Q}F_m & \mathbb{Q}F_{m-1} \end{bmatrix}.$$

If we compare the corresponding entries of both matrix equations, we obtain the desired results of Equation (25).

From Equation (20) we see that

$$\begin{bmatrix} \mathbb{Q}\mathcal{F}^{(i)}_{m+n+1} & \mathbb{Q}\mathcal{F}^{(i)}_{m+n} \\ \mathbb{Q}\mathcal{F}^{(i)}_{m+n} & \mathbb{Q}\mathcal{F}^{(i)}_{m+n-1} \end{bmatrix} = \mathbf{U}^{m+n-1}\mathbf{O} = \mathbf{U}^{n-1}(\mathbf{U}^m \mathbf{O})$$

$$\begin{bmatrix} \mathbb{Q}\mathcal{F}^{(i)}_{m+n+1} & \mathbb{Q}\mathcal{F}^{(i)}_{m+n} \\ \mathbb{Q}\mathcal{F}^{(i)}_{m+n} & \mathbb{Q}\mathcal{F}^{(i)}_{m+n-1} \end{bmatrix} = \begin{bmatrix} F_n & F_{n-1} \\ F_{n-1} & F_{n-2} \end{bmatrix} \begin{bmatrix} \mathbb{Q}\mathcal{F}^{(i)}_{m+2} & \mathbb{Q}\mathcal{F}^{(i)}_{m+1} \\ \mathbb{Q}\mathcal{F}^{(i)}_{m+1} & \mathbb{Q}\mathcal{F}^{(i)}_m \end{bmatrix}.$$

If we compare the corresponding entries of both matrix equations, we obtain the desired result in Equation (26).

Likewise, substituting $n \to m+n-2$ into Equations (19) and (20), we have

$$\mathbf{M}\left(\mathbf{NU}^{m+n-3}\right)\mathbf{M} = \left(\mathbf{MNU}^{m-2}\right)\left(\mathbf{MU}^{n-1}\right),$$

$$\mathbf{O}\left(\mathbf{U}^{m+n-2}\right)\mathbf{O} = \left(\mathbf{OU}^{m-1}\right)\left(\mathbf{OU}^{n-1}\right).$$

If we equate the corresponding entries on both sides of the matrix equations, we obtain Equations (27) and (28), respectively. □

Corollary 1. *For $0 < n \in \mathbb{Z}$, the following equality holds:*

$$\left(\mathbb{Q}\mathcal{F}^{(i)}_{n+1}\right)^2 + \left(\mathbb{Q}\mathcal{F}^{(i)}_n\right)^2 = \mathbb{Q}\mathcal{F}^{(i)}_1 \mathbb{Q}\mathcal{F}^{(i)}_{2n+1} + \mathbb{Q}\mathcal{F}^{(i)}_0 \mathbb{Q}\mathcal{F}^{(i)}_{2n}.$$

Proof. Substituting $m \to n$ into Equation (28) and using Equation (14), we find that

$$\begin{aligned}
\left(\mathbb{Q}\mathcal{F}_{n+1}^{(i)}\right)^2 + \left(\mathbb{Q}\mathcal{F}_n^{(i)}\right)^2 &= \mathbb{Q}\mathcal{F}_2^{(i)}\mathbb{Q}\mathcal{F}_{2n}^{(i)} + \mathbb{Q}\mathcal{F}_1^{(i)}\mathbb{Q}\mathcal{F}_{2n-1}^{(i)} \\
&= \left(\mathbb{Q}\mathcal{F}_1^{(i)} + \mathbb{Q}\mathcal{F}_0^{(i)}\right)\mathbb{Q}\mathcal{F}_{2n}^{(i)} + \mathbb{Q}\mathcal{F}_1^{(i)}\mathbb{Q}\mathcal{F}_{2n-1}^{(i)} \\
&= \mathbb{Q}\mathcal{F}_1^{(i)}\left(\mathbb{Q}\mathcal{F}_{2n}^{(i)} + \mathcal{F}_{2n-1}^{(i)}\right) + \mathbb{Q}\mathcal{F}_0^{(i)}\mathbb{Q}\mathcal{F}_{2n}^{(i)} \\
&= \mathbb{Q}\mathcal{F}_1^{(i)}\mathbb{Q}\mathcal{F}_{2n+1}^{(i)} + \mathbb{Q}\mathcal{F}_0^{(i)}\mathbb{Q}\mathcal{F}_{2n}^{(i)}.
\end{aligned}$$

□

Corollary 2. *For $0 < n \in \mathbb{Z}$, the following equality holds:*

$$\left(\mathbb{Q}\mathcal{F}_{n+1}^{(i)}\right)^2 - \left(\mathbb{Q}\mathcal{F}_{n-1}^{(i)}\right)^2 = \mathbb{Q}\mathcal{F}_1^{(i)}\mathbb{Q}\mathcal{F}_{2n}^{(i)} + \mathbb{Q}\mathcal{F}_0^{(i)}\mathbb{Q}\mathcal{F}_{2n-1}^{(i)}.$$

Proof. Firstly, we get

$$\left(\mathbb{Q}\mathcal{F}_{n+1}^{(i)}\right)^2 - \left(\mathbb{Q}\mathcal{F}_{n-1}^{(i)}\right)^2 = \left(\left(\mathbb{Q}\mathcal{F}_{n+1}^{(i)}\right)^2 + \left(\mathbb{Q}\mathcal{F}_n^{(i)}\right)^2\right) - \left(\left(\mathbb{Q}\mathcal{F}_n^{(i)}\right)^2 + \left(\mathbb{Q}\mathcal{F}_{n-1}^{(i)}\right)^2\right). \tag{29}$$

After that, we perform the following computations

$$\begin{aligned}
\left(\mathbb{Q}\mathcal{F}_{n+1}^{(i)}\right)^2 + \left(\mathbb{Q}\mathcal{F}_n^{(i)}\right)^2 &= \begin{bmatrix} \mathbb{Q}\mathcal{F}_{n+1}^{(i)} & \mathbb{Q}\mathcal{F}_n^{(i)} \end{bmatrix} \begin{bmatrix} \mathbb{Q}\mathcal{F}_{n+1}^{(i)} \\ \mathbb{Q}\mathcal{F}_n^{(i)} \end{bmatrix} \\
&= \begin{bmatrix} \mathbb{Q}\mathcal{F}_1^{(i)} & \mathbb{Q}\mathcal{F}_0^{(i)} \end{bmatrix} \mathbf{U}^n \mathbf{U}^n \begin{bmatrix} \mathbb{Q}\mathcal{F}_1^{(i)} \\ \mathbb{Q}\mathcal{F}_0^{(i)} \end{bmatrix} \\
&= \begin{bmatrix} \mathbb{Q}\mathcal{F}_1^{(i)} & \mathbb{Q}\mathcal{F}_0^{(i)} \end{bmatrix} \mathbf{U}^{2n} \begin{bmatrix} \mathbb{Q}\mathcal{F}_1^{(i)} \\ \mathbb{Q}\mathcal{F}_0^{(i)} \end{bmatrix}.
\end{aligned} \tag{30}$$

Similarly, we also have

$$\begin{aligned}
\left(\mathbb{Q}\mathcal{F}_n^{(i)}\right)^2 + \left(\mathbb{Q}\mathcal{F}_{n-1}^{(i)}\right)^2 &= \begin{bmatrix} \mathbb{Q}\mathcal{F}_n^{(i)} & \mathbb{Q}\mathcal{F}_{n-1}^{(i)} \end{bmatrix} \begin{bmatrix} \mathbb{Q}\mathcal{F}_n^{(i)} \\ \mathbb{Q}\mathcal{F}_{n-1}^{(i)} \end{bmatrix} \\
&= \begin{bmatrix} \mathbb{Q}\mathcal{F}_1^{(i)} & \mathbb{Q}\mathcal{F}_0^{(i)} \end{bmatrix} \mathbf{U}^{n-1} \mathbf{U}^{n-1} \begin{bmatrix} \mathbb{Q}\mathcal{F}_1^{(i)} \\ \mathbb{Q}\mathcal{F}_0^{(i)} \end{bmatrix} \\
&= \begin{bmatrix} \mathbb{Q}\mathcal{F}_1^{(i)} & \mathbb{Q}\mathcal{F}_0^{(i)} \end{bmatrix} \mathbf{U}^{2n-2} \begin{bmatrix} \mathbb{Q}\mathcal{F}_1^{(i)} \\ \mathbb{Q}\mathcal{F}_0^{(i)} \end{bmatrix}.
\end{aligned} \tag{31}$$

By using Equations (29)–(31), we have

$$\begin{aligned}
\left(\mathbb{Q}\mathcal{F}_{n+1}^{(i)}\right)^2 - \left(\mathbb{Q}\mathcal{F}_{n-1}^{(i)}\right)^2 &= \left(\left(\mathbb{Q}\mathcal{F}_{n+1}^{(i)}\right)^2 + \left(\mathbb{Q}\mathcal{F}_n^{(i)}\right)^2\right) - \left(\left(\mathbb{Q}\mathcal{F}_n^{(i)}\right)^2 + \left(\mathbb{Q}\mathcal{F}_{n-1}^{(i)}\right)^2\right) \\
&= \begin{bmatrix} \mathbb{Q}\mathcal{F}_1^{(i)} & \mathbb{Q}\mathcal{F}_0^{(i)} \end{bmatrix} \mathbf{U}^{2n} \begin{bmatrix} \mathbb{Q}\mathcal{F}_1^{(i)} \\ \mathbb{Q}\mathcal{F}_0^{(i)} \end{bmatrix} - \begin{bmatrix} \mathbb{Q}\mathcal{F}_1^{(i)} & \mathbb{Q}\mathcal{F}_0^{(i)} \end{bmatrix} \mathbf{U}^{2n-2} \begin{bmatrix} \mathbb{Q}\mathcal{F}_1^{(i)} \\ \mathbb{Q}\mathcal{F}_0^{(i)} \end{bmatrix} \\
&= \begin{bmatrix} \mathbb{Q}\mathcal{F}_1^{(i)} & \mathbb{Q}\mathcal{F}_0^{(i)} \end{bmatrix} \left(\mathbf{U}^{2n} - \mathbf{U}^{2n-2}\right) \begin{bmatrix} \mathbb{Q}\mathcal{F}_1^{(i)} \\ \mathbb{Q}\mathcal{F}_0^{(i)} \end{bmatrix} \\
&= \begin{bmatrix} \mathbb{Q}\mathcal{F}_1^{(i)} & \mathbb{Q}\mathcal{F}_0^{(i)} \end{bmatrix} \mathbf{U}^{2n-2} \left(\mathbf{U}^2 - I\right) \begin{bmatrix} \mathbb{Q}\mathcal{F}_1^{(i)} \\ \mathbb{Q}\mathcal{F}_0^{(i)} \end{bmatrix}.
\end{aligned}$$

Following the Cayley–Hamilton theorem, we have

$$\mathbf{U}^2 - \mathbf{U} - I = [0]_{2\times 2}.$$

We also get

$$\left(\mathcal{QF}_{n+1}^{(i)}\right)^2 - \left(\mathcal{QF}_{n-1}^{(i)}\right)^2 = \begin{bmatrix} \mathcal{QF}_1^{(i)} & \mathcal{QF}_0^{(i)} \end{bmatrix} \mathbf{U}^{2n-2} \mathbf{U} \begin{bmatrix} \mathcal{QF}_1^{(i)} \\ \mathcal{QF}_0^{(i)} \end{bmatrix}$$

$$= \begin{bmatrix} \mathcal{QF}_1^{(i)} & \mathcal{QF}_0^{(i)} \end{bmatrix} \mathbf{U}^{2n-1} \begin{bmatrix} \mathcal{QF}_1^{(i)} \\ \mathcal{QF}_0^{(i)} \end{bmatrix}$$

$$= \begin{bmatrix} \mathcal{QF}_1^{(i)} & \mathcal{QF}_0^{(i)} \end{bmatrix} \begin{bmatrix} F_{2n} & F_{2n-1} \\ F_{2n-1} & F_{2n} \end{bmatrix} \begin{bmatrix} \mathcal{QF}_1^{(i)} \\ \mathcal{QF}_0^{(i)} \end{bmatrix}$$

$$= \begin{bmatrix} \mathcal{QF}_1^{(i)} & \mathcal{QF}_0^{(i)} \end{bmatrix} \begin{bmatrix} \mathcal{QF}_{2n}^{(i)} \\ \mathcal{QF}_{2n-1}^{(i)} \end{bmatrix}$$

$$= \mathcal{QF}_1^{(i)} \mathcal{QF}_{2n}^{(i)} + \mathcal{QF}_0^{(i)} \mathcal{QF}_{2n-1}^{(i)}.$$

So the proof is completed. □

Theorem 10. *For the Fibonacci finite operator quaternions, we have*

$$\mathcal{QF}_{n+r}^{(i)}\mathcal{QF}_{n+s}^{(i)} - \mathcal{QF}_n^{(i)}\mathcal{QF}_{n+r+s}^{(i)} = (-1)^n F_r \left(\left(\mathcal{F}_1^{(i)}\right)^2 - \mathcal{F}_0^{(i)}\mathcal{F}_2^{(i)} \right)(\mathcal{QF}_1\mathcal{QF}_s - \mathcal{QF}_0\mathcal{QF}_{s+1}).$$

Proof. Using Equations (25) and (26), we have the following computation:

$$\begin{bmatrix} \mathcal{QF}_{n+r}^{(i)} & \mathcal{QF}_n^{(i)} \end{bmatrix} = \begin{bmatrix} \mathcal{QF}_{n+1}^{(i)} & \mathcal{QF}_n^{(i)} \end{bmatrix} \begin{bmatrix} F_r & 0 \\ F_{r-1} & 1 \end{bmatrix}$$

$$= \begin{bmatrix} \mathcal{QF}_1 & \mathcal{QF}_0 \end{bmatrix} \begin{bmatrix} \mathcal{F}_{n+1}^{(i)} & \mathcal{F}_n^{(i)} \\ \mathcal{F}_n^{(i)} & \mathcal{F}_{n-1}^{(i)} \end{bmatrix} \begin{bmatrix} F_r & 0 \\ F_{r-1} & 1 \end{bmatrix},$$

and

$$\begin{bmatrix} \mathcal{QF}_{n+s}^{(i)} \\ -\mathcal{QF}_{n+r+s}^{(i)} \end{bmatrix} = \begin{bmatrix} 1 & 0 \\ -F_{r-1} & F_r \end{bmatrix} \begin{bmatrix} \mathcal{QF}_{n+s}^{(i)} \\ -\mathcal{QF}_{n+s+1}^{(i)} \end{bmatrix}$$

$$= \begin{bmatrix} 1 & 0 \\ -F_{r-1} & F_r \end{bmatrix} \begin{bmatrix} \mathcal{F}_{n-1}^{(i)} & -\mathcal{F}_n^{(i)} \\ -\mathcal{F}_n^{(i)} & \mathcal{F}_{n+1}^{(i)} \end{bmatrix} \begin{bmatrix} \mathcal{QF}_s \\ -\mathcal{QF}_{s+1} \end{bmatrix}.$$

We also have the following computation:

$$\begin{bmatrix} \mathcal{F}_{n+1}^{(i)} & \mathcal{F}_n^{(i)} \\ \mathcal{F}_n^{(i)} & \mathcal{F}_{n-1}^{(i)} \end{bmatrix} \begin{bmatrix} F_r & 0 \\ F_{r-1} & 1 \end{bmatrix} \begin{bmatrix} 1 & 0 \\ -F_{r-1} & F_r \end{bmatrix} \begin{bmatrix} \mathcal{F}_{n-1}^{(i)} & -\mathcal{F}_n^{(i)} \\ -\mathcal{F}_n^{(i)} & \mathcal{F}_{n+1}^{(i)} \end{bmatrix}$$

$$= \begin{bmatrix} \mathcal{F}_{n+1}^{(i)} & \mathcal{F}_n^{(i)} \\ \mathcal{F}_n^{(i)} & \mathcal{F}_{n-1}^{(i)} \end{bmatrix} (F_r I) \begin{bmatrix} \mathcal{F}_{n-1}^{(i)} & -\mathcal{F}_n^{(i)} \\ -\mathcal{F}_n^{(i)} & \mathcal{F}_{n+1}^{(i)} \end{bmatrix}$$

$$= F_r \begin{bmatrix} \mathcal{F}_{n+1}^{(i)} & \mathcal{F}_n^{(i)} \\ \mathcal{F}_n^{(i)} & \mathcal{F}_{n-1}^{(i)} \end{bmatrix} \begin{bmatrix} \mathcal{F}_{n-1}^{(i)} & -\mathcal{F}_n^{(i)} \\ -\mathcal{F}_n^{(i)} & \mathcal{F}_{n+1}^{(i)} \end{bmatrix}$$

$$= F_r \begin{bmatrix} \mathcal{F}_{n+1}^{(i)}\mathcal{F}_{n-1}^{(i)} - \left(\mathcal{F}_n^{(i)}\right)^2 & 0 \\ 0 & -\left(\mathcal{F}_n^{(i)}\right)^2 + \mathcal{F}_{n-1}^{(i)}\mathcal{F}_{n+1}^{(i)} \end{bmatrix}$$

$$\begin{aligned}
&= -F_r\left(\left(\mathcal{F}_n^{(i)}\right)^2 - \mathcal{F}_{n-1}^{(i)}\mathcal{F}_{n+1}^{(i)}\right)I \\
&= (-1)^n F_r\left(\left(\mathcal{F}_1^{(i)}\right)^2 - \mathcal{F}_0^{(i)}\mathcal{F}_2^{(i)}\right)I.
\end{aligned}$$

Then, we get

$$\begin{aligned}
\mathbb{Q}\mathcal{F}_{n+r}^{(i)}\mathbb{Q}\mathcal{F}_{n+s}^{(i)} - \mathbb{Q}\mathcal{F}_n^{(i)}\mathbb{Q}\mathcal{F}_{n+r+s}^{(i)} &= \begin{bmatrix} \mathbb{Q}\mathcal{F}_{n+r}^{(i)} & \mathbb{Q}\mathcal{F}_n^{(i)} \end{bmatrix} \begin{bmatrix} \mathbb{Q}\mathcal{F}_{n+s}^{(i)} \\ -\mathbb{Q}\mathcal{F}_{n+r+s}^{(i)} \end{bmatrix} \\
&= (-1)^n F_r\left(\left(\mathcal{F}_1^{(i)}\right)^2 - \mathcal{F}_0^{(i)}\mathcal{F}_2^{(i)}\right) \begin{bmatrix} \mathbb{Q}F_1 & \mathbb{Q}F_0 \end{bmatrix} \begin{bmatrix} \mathbb{Q}F_s \\ -\mathbb{Q}F_{s+1} \end{bmatrix} \\
&= (-1)^n F_r\left(\left(\mathcal{F}_1^{(i)}\right)^2 - \mathcal{F}_0^{(i)}\mathcal{F}_2^{(i)}\right)(\mathbb{Q}F_1\mathbb{Q}F_s - \mathbb{Q}F_0\mathbb{Q}F_{s+1}).
\end{aligned}$$

□

Corollary 3. *In the above theorem, substituting $n \to n-1$ and $r = s = 1$, we obtain Equations (23) and (24).*

4. Conclusions

In this paper, we introduced the Fibonacci finite operator quaternions by means of the finite operators and Fibonacci numbers. We also gave some properties of this new type of quaternions, such as recurrence relation, Binet-like formula, generating function, exponential generating function, and some sum formulas, including the Fibonacci finite operator quaternions. We obtained many identities related to Fibonacci finite operator quaternions by using the matrix representations. Indeed, for the interested readers of this work, the results presented here have the potential to motivate further research on the subject of the Fibonacci finite operator hyper complex numbers (Kızılateş and Kone [20]) or Fibonacci finite operator hybrid numbers (Szynal and Wloch [38]).

Author Contributions: Writing—original draft, N.T., C.K. and W.-S.D. All authors contributed equally to the manuscript. All authors have read and agreed to the published version of the manuscript.

Funding: The third author is partially supported by Grant No. MOST 110-2115-M-017-001 of the Ministry of Science and Technology of the Republic of China.

Institutional Review Board Statement: Not applicable.

Informed Consent Statement: Not applicable.

Data Availability Statement: Not applicable.

Acknowledgments: The authors wish to express their hearty thanks to the anonymous for their valuable suggestions and comments.

Conflicts of Interest: The authors declare no conflict of interest.

References

1. Hamilton, W.R. *Elements of Quaternions*; Longman, Green & Company: London, UK, 1866.
2. Rodman, L. *Topics in Quaternion Linear Algebra*; Princeton University Press: Princeton, NJ, USA, 2014.
3. Vince, J. *Quaternions for Computer Graphics*; Springer: London, UK, 2011.
4. Horadam, A.F. Complex Fibonacci numbers and Fibonacci quaternions. *Am. Math. Mon.* **1963**, *70*, 289–291. [CrossRef]
5. Caldarola, F.; d'Atri, G.; Maiolo, M.; Pirillo, G. New algebraic and geometric constructs arising from Fibonacci numbers. *Soft Comput.* **2020**, *24*, 17497–17508. [CrossRef]
6. Trojovskı, P. On Terms of Generalized Fibonacci Sequences which are Powers of their Indexes. *Mathematics* **2019**, *7*, 700. [CrossRef]
7. Battaloglu, R.; Simsek, Y. On New Formulas of Fibonacci and Lucas Numbers Involving Golden Ratio Associated with Atomic Structure in Chemistry. *Symmetry* **2021**, *13*, 1334. [CrossRef]
8. Halici, S. On Fibonacci quaternions. *Adv. Appl. Clifford Algebr.* **2012**, *22*, 321–327. [CrossRef]
9. Halici, S. On complex Fibonacci quaternions. *Adv. Appl. Clifford Algebr.* **2013**, *23*, 105–112. [CrossRef]

10. Horadam, A.F. Quaternion recurrence relations. *Ulam Q.* **1993**, *2*, 23–33.
11. Iyer, M.R. A note on Fibonacci quaternions. *Fibonacci Quart.* **1969**, *7*, 225–229.
12. Akyigit, M.; Koksal, H.H.; Tosun, M. Fibonacci generalized quaternions. *Adv. Appl. Clifford Algebr.* **2014**, *24*, 631–641. [CrossRef]
13. Tan, E.; Yilmaz, S.; Sahin, M. A note on bi-periodic Fibonacci and Lucas quaternions. *Chaos Solitons Fractals* **2016**, *85*, 138–142. [CrossRef]
14. Tan, E.; Yilmaz, S.; Sahin, M. On a new generalization of Fibonacci quaternions. *Chaos Solitons Fractals* **2016**, *82*, 1–4. [CrossRef]
15. Sahin, M.; Tan, E.; Yilmaz, S. The generalized bi-periodic Fibonacci quaternions and octonions. *Novi Sad J. Math.* **2019**, *49*, 67–79.
16. Polatli, E.; Kesim, S. On quaternions with generalized Fibonacci and Lucas number components. *Adv. Differ. Equ.* **2015**, *2015*, 169. [CrossRef]
17. Polatli, E. A generalization of Fibonacci and Lucas Quaternions. *Adv. Appl. Clifford Algebr.* **2016**, *26*, 719–730. [CrossRef]
18. Halici, S.; Karataş, A. On a generalization for quaternion sequences. *Chaos Solitons Fractals* **2017**, *98*, 178–182. [CrossRef]
19. Kızılateş, C.; Kone, T. On Fibonacci quaternions. *J. Anal.* **2021**, *29*, 1071–1082. [CrossRef]
20. Kızılateş, C.; Kone, T. On higher order Fibonacci hyper complex numbers. *Chaos Solitons Fractals* **2021**, *148*, 1–6. [CrossRef]
21. Kızılateş, C. On quaternions with incomplete Fibonacci and Lucas Components. *Util. Math.* **2019**, *110*, 263–269.
22. Simsek, Y. Some new families of special polynomials and numbers associated with Finite Operators. *Symmetry* **2020**, *12*, 237. [CrossRef]
23. Simsek, Y. Construction method for generating functions of special numbers and polynomials arising from analysis of new operators. *Math. Meth. Appl. Sci.* **2018**, *41*, 6934–6954. [CrossRef]
24. Ozdemir, G.; Simsek, Y. Generating functions for two-variable polynomials related to a family of Fibonacci type polynomials and numbers. *Filomat* **2016**, *30*, 969–975. [CrossRef]
25. Ozdemir, G.; Simsek, Y.; Milovanović, G.V. Generating functions for special polynomials and numbers including Apostol-type and Humbert-type polynomials. *Mediterr. J. Math.* **2017**, *14*, 1–17. [CrossRef]
26. Kilar, N.; Simsek, Y. Identities for special numbers and polynomials involving Fibonacci-type polynomials and Chebyshev polynomials. *Adv. Stud. Contemp. Math. Kyungshang* **2020**, *30*, 493–502.
27. Kilar, N.; Simsek, Y. A special approach to derive new formulas for some special numbers and polynomials. *Turk. J. Math.* **2020**, *44*, 2217–2240. [CrossRef]
28. Rayaguru, S.G.; Savin, D.; Panda, G.K. On some Horadam symbol elements. *Notes Number Theory Discret. Math.* **2019**, *25*, 91–112. [CrossRef]
29. Şentürk, G.Y.; Gürses, N.; Yüce, S. Fundamental properties of extended Horadam numbers. *Notes Number Theory Discret. Math.* **2021**, *27*, 219–235. [CrossRef]
30. Kızılateş, C. New families of Horadam numbers associated with finite operators and their applications. *Math. Meth. Appl. Sci.* **2021**, *44*, 14371–14381. [CrossRef]
31. Tan, E.; Leung, H.-H. Some results on Horadam quaternions. *Chaos Solitons Fractals* **2020**, *138*, 1–7. [CrossRef]
32. Bitim, B.D. Some identities of Fibonacci and Lucas quaternions by quaternion matrices. *Düzce Univ. J. SciTechnol.* **2019**, *7*, 606–615.
33. Patel, B.K.; Ray, P.K. On the properties of (p,q)-Fibonacci and (p,q)-Lucas quaternions. *Math. Rep.* **2019**, *21*, 15–25.
34. Cerda-Morales, G. On a generalization for tribonacci quaternions. *Mediterr. J. Math.* **2017**, *14*, 239. [CrossRef]
35. Cerda-Morales, G. Some properties of (p,q)-Fibonacci and Horadam quaternions. *Commun. Fac. Sci. Univ. Ank. Ser. A1* **2020**, *69*, 1104–1110.
36. Szynal-Liana, A.; Wloch, I. The Pell quaternions and the Pell octonions. *Adv. Appl. Clifford Algebr.* **2016**, *26*, 435–440. [CrossRef]
37. Szynal-Liana, A.; Wloch, I. A note on Jacobsthal quaternions. *Adv. Appl. Clifford Algebr.* **2016**, *26*, 441–447. [CrossRef]
38. Szynal-Liana, A.; Wloch, I. The Fibonacci hybrid numbers. *Utilitas Math.* **2019**, *110*, 3–10.

Article
Residuated Lattices with Noetherian Spectrum

Dana Piciu [1] and Diana Savin [2,*]

[1] Department of Mathematics, Faculty of Science, University of Craiova, A. I. Cuza Street 13, 200585 Craiova, Romania; dana.piciu@edu.ucv.ro
[2] Faculty of Mathematics and Computer Science, Transilvania University, Iuliu Maniu Street 50, 500091 Brașov, Romania
* Correspondence: diana.savin@unitbv.ro or dianet72@yahoo.com

Abstract: In this paper, we characterize residuated lattices for which the topological space of prime ideals is a Noetherian space. The notion of i-Noetherian residuated lattice is introduced and related properties are investigated. We proved that a residuated lattice is i-Noetherian iff every ideal is principal. Moreover, we show that a residuated lattice has the spectrum of a Noetherian space iff it is i-Noetherian.

Keywords: Noetherian residuated lattice; ideal; prime ideal; Noetherian spectrum; ring of algebraic integers; Bezout rings; Dedekind rings

MSC: 22A30; 03B50; 03G25; 06D35; 06B30; 11R04; 11R11; 12F05

Citation: Piciu, D.; Savin, D. Residuated Lattices with Noetherian Spectrum. *Mathematics* **2022**, *10*, 1831. https://doi.org/10.3390/math10111831

Academic Editor: Abdelmejid Bayad

Received: 19 April 2022
Accepted: 23 May 2022
Published: 26 May 2022

Copyright: © 2022 by the authors. Licensee MDPI, Basel, Switzerland. This article is an open access article distributed under the terms and conditions of the Creative Commons Attribution (CC BY) license (https://creativecommons.org/licenses/by/4.0/).

1. Introduction

Residuated lattices play the role of semantics for residuated logic. In 1939, Ward and Dilworth introduced commutative residuated lattices in [1]. Residuated lattices are known under many names: *BCK-lattices, full BCK-algebras, FL_{ew}-algebras,* or *integral residuated commutative l-monoids.*

These ordered structures have two historical sources: the study of residuation in the ideal lattices of rings and the algebrization of implication in intuitionistic logic.

The theory of residuated lattices was used to develop algebraic counterparts of fuzzy logics. Important examples of residuated lattices related to logic are Boolean algebras corresponding to basic logic, BL algebras corresponding to Hajek logic, and MV algebras corresponding to Łukasiewicz many-valued logic.

Complete studies on residuated lattices or their subvarieties were developed in [1–7].

Filters are important concepts in studying residuated lattices and the completeness of the corresponding logic, see [4,7,8].

Many authors [8–11] remarked that the notion of ideals is missing in residuated lattices and this lack is associated with the fact that there is no suitable algebraic addition in these structures. Refs. [9,10] introduced some types of ideals in residuated lattices. In MV algebras, by definition, ideals are kernels of homomorphisms, see [12]. In residuated lattices, ideals (in the sense of [10]) generalize the existing notion in *MV* algebras. However, ideals and the dual of filters are quite different in residuated lattices; the reason for this is the involution law.

The main scope of this paper is to characterize residuated lattices for which the topological space of prime ideals is a Noetherian space.

The paper is organized as follows:

In Section 2, we review some results that we use in the sequel.

Section 3 contains new results about ideals in residuated lattices. For a residuated lattice L, the lattice of ideals $(\mathbf{I}(\mathbf{L}), \subseteq)$ is a complete Brouwerian lattice. We show that in this lattice, every finite generated ideal is principal (Proposition 2). It is known that for a divisible residuated lattice, the quotient residuated lattice, via ideals, is an MV algebra, not just a divisible residuated lattice as in the case of filters (see [13]). Proposition 6 gives characterizations for ideals in this quotient MV algebra.

Using an interesting construction of Turunen and Mertanen (see [14]), which associates an MV algebra with any semidivisible residuated lattice, we prove the first theorem of isomorphism for residuated lattices via ideals (Theorem 1) and compare this result with the one obtained using filters.

In Section 4, using the model of MV algebras (see [15]), we introduce the concept of i-Noetherian residuated lattice as lattices in which $(\mathbf{I}(\mathbf{L}), \subseteq)$ is a Noetherian poset. We study this notion and show that a residuated lattice is i-Noetherian iff every ideal is principal (Theorem 2). Further, we establish some connections between i-Noetherian residuated lattices and residuated lattices for which $(\mathbf{F}(\mathbf{L}), \subseteq)$ is a Noetherian poset (Corollary 1).

We recall that a proper ideal of a residuated lattice L, is *prime* if it is a prime element in $(\mathbf{I}(\mathbf{L}), \subseteq)$. For a residuated lattice L, $Spec(L)$, the set of all prime ideals of L, can be endowed with the Zariski topology τ_L and $(Spec(L), \tau_L)$ becomes a compact topological space (see [16]).

A topological space is called *Noetherian* if it satisfies the descending chain condition on closed subsets (see [17]).

In Section 5, we prove that $Spec(L)$ is a Noetherian space iff L is an i-Noetherian residuated lattice (see Corollary 4).

In Section 6, we study certain connections between ideals in residuated lattices and ideals in certain types of unitary commutative rings, used in algebraic number theory.

2. Preliminaries

A *residuated lattice* ([1,3,5,6]) is an algebra $(L, \vee, \wedge, \odot, \rightarrow, 0, 1)$ satisfying the following axioms:

(RL_1) $(L, \vee, \wedge, 0, 1)$ is a bounded lattice;
(RL_2) $(L, \odot, 1)$ is a commutative monoid;
(RL_3) $x \odot z \leq y$ iff $z \leq x \rightarrow y$, for every $x, y, z \in L$.

The class $\mathcal{RL}$ of residuated lattices is equational; so, following Birkhoff's theorem (see [18]), $\mathcal{RL}$ is a *variety*.

Example 1 ([4,7]). *The real unit interval $I = [0,1]$ becomes a residuated lattice $(I, \max, \min, \odot, \rightarrow, 0, 1)$ called Gödel structure. The operations of multiplication and implication are given for $x, y \in [0,1]$ by $x \odot y = \min\{x, y\}$ and $x \rightarrow y = 1$ if $x \leq y$ and y otherwise.*

We recall three important subclasses of residuated lattices (see [4,7,19]):
A residuated lattice L is called the following:

(i) *divisible* if L verifies (DIV): $\quad x \odot (x \rightarrow y) = x \wedge y$;
(ii) *involutive* if L verifies (DN): $\quad x^{**} = x$;
(iii) *MV algebra* if L verifies (MV): $\quad (x \rightarrow y) \rightarrow y = (y \rightarrow x) \rightarrow x$.

We denote by $\mathcal{DIV}$ the class of divisible residuated lattices. Obviously, $\mathcal{DIV}$ is a subcategory of $\mathcal{RL}$.

Let L be a residuated lattice. For $x, y \in L$, we denote $x^* = x \rightarrow 0$ and $x \boxplus y = (x^* \odot y^*)^*$. For a natural number $n \geq 1$, we will use the notation $(n+1)x := nx \boxplus x$.

In a residuated lattice L, the following properties hold, for every $x, y, z \in L$ (see [1,5,7,10,13,16,20,21]):

(c_1) $x \leq y$ iff $x \rightarrow y = 1$;
(c_2) $x \rightarrow (y \rightarrow z) = (x \odot y) \rightarrow z = y \rightarrow (x \rightarrow z)$;
(c_3) $x \leq x^{**}$, $(x \odot y)^* = x \rightarrow y^* = y \rightarrow x^* = x^{**} \rightarrow y^*$;
(c_4) $x, y \leq x \boxplus y$, $x \boxplus y = y \boxplus x$, $(x \boxplus y) \boxplus z = x \boxplus (y \boxplus z)$;
(c_5) $(x \boxplus y)^{**} = x \boxplus y = x^{**} \boxplus y^{**}$;

126

(c_6) If L is divisible, $(x \to y)^{**} = x^{**} \to y^{**}$.

Definition 1 ([1,5,7]). *Let L_1 and L_2 be residuated lattices. A function $f : L_1 \to L_2$ is a morphism of residuated lattices iff f is a morphism of bounded lattices and $f(x \odot y) = f(x) \odot f(y)$, $f(x \to y) = f(x) \to f(y)$, for every $x, y \in L_1$.*

3. Filters and Ideals in Residuated Lattices

Definition 2 ([5,7]). *Let L be a residuated lattice. A filter of L is a subset $F \subseteq L$ such that*

(f_1) *If $x \in F$ and $x \leq y$, then $y \in F$;*
(f_2) *$x, y \in F$ implies $x \odot y \in F$.*

Filters *are also called* congruence filters *or* deductive systems, *see [7].*
We denote by $\mathbf{F}(\mathbf{L})$ the set of all filters of L.
In general, in residuated lattices, a dual operation to $\odot$ does not exist; so, a dual notion for filter does not exist either. Refs. [9,10] introduced some kind of ideal in residuated lattices, not dual to a filter. This concept generalizes the existing notion in MV algebras (see [2,12]).

Definition 3 ([13]). *A subset $I \subseteq L$ of a residuated lattice L is called an ideal of L if it satisfies*

(i_1) *If $y \in I$ and $x \leq y$, then $x \in I$;*
(i_2) *$x, y \in I$ implies $x \boxplus y \in I$.*

Trivial examples of ideals are $\{0\}$ and L.
We denote by $\mathbf{I}(\mathbf{L})$ the set of all ideals of L.
We recall that if $f : L_1 \to L_2$ is a morphism of residuated lattices, $i - Ker(f) = f^{-1}(0) = \{x \in L_1 : f(x) = 0\}$ is a proper ideal of L_1. Moreover, ideals are i-kernels of homomorphisms of residuated lattices (see [16]).
Obviously, if $I \in \mathbf{I}(\mathbf{L})$, then $0 \in I$ and $x \in I$ iff $x^{**} \in I$, (see [10]).
Ref. [13] gives an equivalent condition for ideals in residuated lattices: $I \in \mathbf{I}(\mathbf{L})$ iff [$0 \in I$ and $x, x^* \odot y \in I$ implies $y \in I$].

Example 2. *Let $L = \{0, a, b, c, 1\}$ be such that $0 < a, b < c < 1$, a, b are incomparable. Define $\to$ and $\odot$ as follows:*

$\to$	0	a	b	c	1
0	1	1	1	1	1
a	b	1	b	1	1
b	a	a	1	1	1
c	0	a	b	1	1
1	0	a	b	c	1

$\odot$	0	a	b	c	1
0	0	0	0	0	0
a	0	a	0	a	a
b	0	0	b	b	b
c	0	a	b	c	c
1	0	a	b	c	1

Then, $(L, \vee, \wedge, \odot, \to, 0, 1)$ becomes a residuated lattice (see [19]). We remark that $\mathbf{I}(\mathbf{L}) = \{\{0\}, \{0, a\}, \{0, b\}, L\}$ and $\mathbf{F}(\mathbf{L}) = \{\{1\}, \{1, c\}, \{1, a, c\}, \{1, b, c\}, L\}$.

Remark 1. *In a residuated lattice L, if $I \in \mathbf{I}(\mathbf{L})$ and $x \in I, y \in L$ such that $(x \boxplus y^*)^* \in I$, then $y \in I$. Indeed, since $I \in \mathbf{I}(\mathbf{L})$ and $(x \boxplus y^*)^* = (x^* \odot y^{**})^{**} \in I$, we deduce that $x^* \odot y^{**} \in I$. Then, from $x, x^* \odot y^{**} \in I$ we obtain $y^{**} \in I$, so $y \in I$.*

For a nonempty subset X of a residuated lattice L, we denote by $(X]$ the ideal of L generated by X and for $x \in L$ we denote $(\{x\}]$ by $(x]$, the *principal ideal* of L generated by x.

Proposition 1 ([10,16]). *Let L be a residuated lattice, $X \subseteq L$, and $x, y \in L$. Then,*

(i) $(X] = \{a \in L : a \leq x_1 \boxplus ... \boxplus x_n, \text{ for some } n \geq 1 \text{ and } x_1, ..., x_n \in X\}$;
(ii) $(x] = \{a \in L : a \leq nx, \text{ for some } n \geq 1\}$ and $(x] \cap (y] = (x^{**} \wedge y^{**}]$, $(x] \vee (y] = (x \boxplus y]$;

(iii) $(\mathbf{I}(\mathbf{L}), \subseteq)$ is a complete Brouwerian lattice in which for $I, J \in \mathbf{I}(\mathbf{L})$, $I \wedge J = I \cap J$ and $I \vee J = (I \cup J]$.

Proposition 2. *In a residuated lattice, every finitely generated ideal is principal.*

Proof. Let $I \in \mathbf{I}(\mathbf{L})$ be a finitely generated ideal. Then, there are $n \geq 1$ and $x_1, ..., x_n \in L$ such that $I = (\{x_1, ..., x_n\}]$. We show that $I = (x_1 \boxplus ... \boxplus x_n]$. By definition, $I = \cap \{J \in \mathbf{I}(\mathbf{L}) : \{x_1, ..., x_n\} \subseteq J\}$. Since, by (c_4), $x_i \leq x_1 \boxplus ... \boxplus x_n$ for every $i \in \{1, ..., n\}$ we deduce that $x_i \in (x_1 \boxplus ... \boxplus x_n]$; so, $\{x_1, ..., x_n\} \subseteq (x_1 \boxplus ... \boxplus x_n]$. Thus, $I \subseteq (x_1 \boxplus ... \boxplus x_n]$. Now, let $J \in \mathbf{I}(\mathbf{L})$ such that $\{x_1, ..., x_n\} \subseteq J$. Then, $x_1 \boxplus ... \boxplus x_n \in J$, so, $(x_1 \boxplus ... \boxplus x_n] \subseteq J$. Therefore, $(x_1 \boxplus ... \boxplus x_n] \subseteq I$. Hence, I is principal and $(\{x_1, ..., x_n\}] = (x_1 \boxplus ... \boxplus x_n]$. □

We recall some relationships between ideals and filters in residuated lattices proved in [13] using the set of complemented elements.

We denote a subset X of a residuated lattice L by

$$N(X) = \{x \in L : x^* \in X\}.$$

Proposition 3 ([13]). *Let L be a residuated lattice, $I \in \mathbf{I}(\mathbf{L})$, and $F \in \mathbf{F}(\mathbf{L})$. Then, $N(I) \in \mathbf{F}(\mathbf{L})$, $N(F) \in \mathbf{I}(\mathbf{L})$, $I = N(N(I))$, and $F \subseteq N(N(F))$.*

In the following, we establish other properties of this operator:

Lemma 1. *Let L be a residuated lattice; $X_1, X_2 \subseteq L$; and $I_1, I_2 \in \mathbf{I}(\mathbf{L})$. Then,*

(i) $X_1 \subseteq X_2$ implies $N(X_1) \subseteq N(X_2)$;
(ii) $I_1 \subseteq I_2$ iff $N(I_1) \subseteq N(I_2)$;
(iii) $I_1 = I_2$ iff $N(I_1) = N(I_2)$.

Proof.

(i) Suppose that $X_1 \subseteq X_2$ and let $x \in N(X_1)$. Then, $x^* \in X_1 \subseteq X_2$, so $x \in N(X_2)$ and $N(X_1) \subseteq N(X_2)$.
(ii) Suppose that $N(I_1) \subseteq N(I_2)$ and let $x \in I_1$. Then, $x^{**} \in I_1$, so $x^* \in N(I_1) \subseteq N(I_2)$. Then, $x^{**} \in I_2$; so, $x \in I_2$ and $I_1 \subseteq I_2$. Using (i), we deduce that $I_1 \subseteq I_2$ iff $N(I_1) \subseteq N(I_2)$.
(iii) Apply (ii).
□

In [10], a residuated lattice L and an ideal I of L a congruence relation $\approx_I$ on L is defined by $x \approx_I y$ iff $(x \to y)^*, (y \to x)^* \in I$. For $x \in L$, the congruence class of x is denoted by x/I and the quotient residuated lattice $L/\approx_I$ by L/I. Obviously, in L/I, $0 = 0/I = \{x \in L : x \in I\} = I$, $1 = 1/I = \{x \in L : x^* \in I\}$ and for $x, y \in L$, $x/I \leq y/I$ iff $(x \to y)^* \in I$.

We recall that (see [12]) for an MV algebra A and an ideal I of A, the binary relation $\sim_I$ on A defined by $x \sim_I y$ iff $x^* \odot y, x \odot y^* \in I$, for $x, y \in A$ is a congruence relation on A. Unlike in MV algebras, in a residuated lattice L, for $I \in \mathbf{I}(\mathbf{L})$, $\sim_I$ is only an equivalence relation on L (see [13]).

Proposition 4. *In a divisible residuated lattice L, the relations $\sim_I$ and $\approx_I$ coincide for every $I \in \mathbf{I}(\mathbf{L})$.*

Proof. In [13], it is proved that $\sim_I$ is a congruence relation on L, if L is divisible.

We have $x \sim_I y$ iff $x^* \odot y, x \odot y^* \in I$ iff $(x^* \odot y)^{**}, (x \odot y^*)^{**} \in I$ iff $(y \to x)^*$, $(x \to y)^* \in I$ iff $x \approx_I y$, since $(x^* \odot y)^{**} \stackrel{(c_3)}{=} (y^{**} \to x^{**})^* \stackrel{(c_6)}{=} (y \to x)^{***} = (y \to x)^*$, for every $x, y \in L$. □

It is known that, for a divisible residuated lattice, the quotient residuated lattice, via ideals, is an MV algebra:

Proposition 5 ([13]). *If L is a divisible residuated lattice and $I \in \mathbf{I}(\mathbf{L})$, $(L/\sim_I = L/\approx_I \stackrel{not}{=} L/I, \boxplus, ^*, I)$ is an MV algebra.*

Let L be a residuated lattice, $X \subseteq L$ be a nonempty subset, and $I \in \mathbf{I}(\mathbf{L})$. We denote

$$X/I = \{x/I : x \in X\}.$$

In the following, for a divisible residuated lattice L, we give a characterization for ideals in the quotient MV algebra L/I.

Proposition 6. *Let L be a divisible residuated lattice.*
(i) If $I, J \in \mathbf{I}(\mathbf{L})$ and $I \subseteq J$, then $J/I \in \mathbf{I}(L/I)$;
(ii) If $I \in \mathbf{I}(\mathbf{L})$ then in MV algebra L/I, the set of ideals is $\mathbf{I}(L/I) = \{J/I : J \in \mathbf{I}(\mathbf{L})$ and $I \subseteq J\}$;
(iii) If $I, I_1, I_2 \in \mathbf{I}(\mathbf{L})$ with $I \subseteq I_1, I_2$ and $I_1/I \subseteq I_2/I$, then $I_1 \subseteq I_2$.

Proof.
(i) Since L is divisible and $I \in \mathbf{I}(\mathbf{L})$, using Proposition 5, L/I is an MV algebra.
To prove that $J/I \in \mathbf{I}(L/I)$, first, let $x/I, y/I \in J/I$. Then, $x, y \in J$ and since $J \in \mathbf{I}(\mathbf{L})$, we deduce that $x \boxplus y \in J$; so, $(x \boxplus y)/I \in J/I$.
If $x/I \in L/I, y/I \in J/I$ and $x/I \leq y/I$, then $x \in L, y \in J$ and $(x/I)^* \boxplus (y/I) = 1/I$. We deduce that $(x^* \boxplus y)/I = 1/I$; so, $(x^* \boxplus y)^* \in I$. Since $I \subseteq J$, we have $(x^* \boxplus y)^* \in J$. Thus, $y, (x^* \boxplus y)^* \in J$ and since $J \in \mathbf{I}(\mathbf{L})$, using Remark 1, we conclude that $x \in J$; so, $x/I \in J/I$ and $J/I \in \mathbf{I}(L/I)$.

(ii) Using (i), $J/I \in \mathbf{I}(L/I)$, for every $J \in \mathbf{I}(\mathbf{L})$ with $I \subseteq J$.
Now, let $K/I \in \mathbf{I}(L/I)$. Since $I = 0/I \in K/I$, we deduce that $I \subseteq K$. To prove that $K \in \mathbf{I}(\mathbf{L})$, let $x, y \in K$. Then, $x/I, y/I \in K/I$, which is an ideal of L/I. We deduce that $(x/I) \boxplus (y/I) = (x \boxplus y)/I \in K/I$; so, $x \boxplus y \in K$. If $x \in L$ such that $x \leq y$ and $y \in K$, then $x \to y = 1$; so, $(x \to y)^* = 0 \in K$.
Since L is divisible, using (c_6), we deduce that $(x \to y)^* = (x \to y)^{***} = (x^{**} \to y^{**})^* = (x^{**} \odot y^*)^{**} = (x^* \boxplus y)^*$. Since $y, (x^* \boxplus y)^* \in K$, using Remark 1, we obtain $x \in K$; thus, $K \in \mathbf{I}(\mathbf{L})$.

(iii) Using (i), $I_1/I, I_2/I \in \mathbf{I}(L/I)$. Now, let $x \in I_1$. Then, $x/I \in I_2/I$, so $x/I = y/I$, for some $y \in I_2$. Thus, $(x \to y)^*, (y \to x)^* \in I$. Since $I \subseteq I_2$ and $(x \to y)^* = [x^* \boxplus y]^*$ we deduce that $x \in I_2$—that is, $I_1 \subseteq I_2$.
□

In [14], Turunen and Mertanen defined the MV center of a divisible residuated lattice L,

$$MV(L) = \{x^* : x \in L\} = \{x \in L : x^{**} = x\},$$

and proved that, in this case, $(MV(L), \boxplus, ^*, 0)$ is an MV algebra. Using this construction, which associates an MV algebra to any divisible residuated lattice, in the following we prove the first theorem of isomorphism for residuated lattices via ideals:

Theorem 1. *Let L_1 and L_2 be residuated lattices such that L_1 is divisible. If $f : L_1 \to L_2$ is a morphism of residuated lattices, $L_1/i - Ker(f) \approx MV(Imf)$ (as MV algebras).*

Proof. Since $\mathcal{DIV}$ is a subvariety of $\mathcal{RL}$ and i-$Ker(f) \in \mathbf{I}(\mathbf{L})$, $L_1/i - Ker(f)$ and Imf are divisible residuated lattices.
Moreover, L_1/i-$Ker(f)$ and $MV(Imf)$ are MV algebras.

Now, we define $\phi : L_1/i\text{-}Ker(f) \to MV(Imf)$ by $\phi(x/i - Ker(f)) = f(x)^{**}$, for every $x \in L_1$.

Obviously, ϕ is well-defined and a one-to-one map since for every $x, y \in L_1$ we have $x/i - Ker(f) = y/i - Ker(f)$ iff $x^{**}/i - Ker(f) = y^{**} / i - Ker(f)$ iff $x^* \odot y^{**}, x^{**} \odot y^* \in i - Ker(f)$ iff $f(x^* \odot y^{**}) = f(x^{**} \odot y^*) = 0$ iff $f(x)^* \odot f(y)^{**} = f(x)^{**} \odot f(y)^* = 0$ iff $f(y)^{**} \leq_{MV} f(x)^{**}, f(x)^{**} \leq_{MV} f(y)^{**}$ iff $f(x)^{**} = f(y)^{**}$ iff $\phi(x/i - Ker(f)) = \phi(y/i - Ker(f))$.

By definition, ϕ is onto and clearly a morphism of MV algebra since f is a morphism of residuated lattices:

$$\phi((x/i - Ker(f) \boxplus (y/i - Ker(f))) = \phi((x \boxplus y)/i - Ker(f)) = f(x \boxplus y)^{**} =$$

$$= [f(x) \boxplus f(y)]^{**} \stackrel{(c_5)}{=} [f(x)]^{**} \boxplus [f(y)]^{**} = \phi((x/i - Ker(f)) \boxplus \phi(y/i - Ker(f)),$$

$$\phi((x/i - Ker(f))^*) = \phi(x^*/i - Ker(f)) = [f(x^*)]^{**} = [f(x)^{**}]^* = [\phi(x/i - Ker(f))]^*$$

and $\phi(0/i - Ker(f)) = [f(0)]^{**} = 0^{**} = 0$, for every $x, y \in L_1$.

We conclude that f is an isomorphism of MV algebras. □

Remark 2. *Unlike in MV algebras, we remark that ideals and filters behave quite differently in residuated lattices and generate different constructions.*

4. i-Noetherian Residuated Lattices

In the following, using the model of MV algebras, see [15], we introduce and characterize the concept of i-Noetherian residuated lattice.

We recall that a poset $(A, \leq)$ is Noetherian if every increasing chain $a_1 \leq a_2 \leq \ldots$ of elements of A is stationary, i.e., there is a natural number $n \geq 1$ such that $a_i = a_n$, for every $i \geq n$ (see [22]).

Definition 4. *A residuated lattice L is called i-Noetherian if the poset $(\mathbf{I}(\mathbf{L}), \subseteq)$ is Noetherian.*

Example 3. *Let L be the Gődel structure, see Example 1. Then, for every $x \neq 0$, $x^* = 0$; so, $x^{**} = 1$. We deduce that Gődel structure is an i-Noetherian residuated lattice since $\mathbf{I}(\mathbf{L}) = \{\{0\}, L\}$.*

We recall that [23] introduced the notion of *Noetherian BL algebra*, Ref. [20] generalized these results and studied the concept of *Noetherian residuated lattice* as a lattice with the property that every increasing chain of filters is stationary.

In this paper, we study some connections between i-Noetherian and Noetherian residuated lattices.

Proposition 7. *If L is a Noetherian residuated lattice (in the sense of [20]), the poset $(\mathbf{I}(\mathbf{L}), \subseteq)$ is Noetherian.*

Proof. Let $I_1 \subseteq I_2 \subseteq \ldots$ be an increasing chain of ideals of L. Using Proposition 3 and Lemma 1 (ii), $N(I_1) \subseteq N(I_2) \subseteq \ldots$ is an increasing chain of filters of L. Since L is Noetherian, there is a natural number $n \geq 1$ such that $N(I_i) = N(I_n)$, for every $i \geq n$. Using Lemma 1 (iii), $I_i = I_n$, for every $i \geq n$. □

Remark 3. *The converse implication in Proposition 7 is not true. For example, let L be the Gődel structure, which is i-Noetherian, see Example 3. Then, for every $n \geq 1$, $F_n = [\frac{1}{n}, 1]$ is a filter of L and $F_1 \subseteq F_2 \subseteq \ldots$ is an increasing chain in $(\mathbf{F}(\mathbf{L}), \subseteq)$ that is not stationary; so, L is not Noetherian.*

The next result is a consequence of Proposition 7 and Remark 3:

Corollary 1. *Every Noetherian residuated lattice is i-Noetherian.*

We conclude that for a residuated lattice

$$Noetherian \Rightarrow i-Noetherian$$

$$i-Noetherian \not\Rightarrow Noetherian.$$

Corollary 2. *If L is an involutive residuated lattice, the notions of Noetherian and i-Noetherian coincide.*

Proof. Suppose that L is i-Noetherian.

First, we prove that for $F_1, F_2 \in \mathbf{F}(\mathbf{L})$, $N(F_1) \subseteq N(F_2)$ implies $F_1 \subseteq F_2$. Let $x \in F_1$. Since $F_1 \in \mathbf{F}(\mathbf{L})$ and $x \leq x^{**}$, we have $x^{**} \in F_1$. Then, $x^* \in N(F_1) \subseteq N(F_2)$; so, $x^{**} \in F_2$. Since L is involutive, $x = x^{**} \in F_2$ and $F_1 \subseteq F_2$.

Using Lemma 1 (i), we deduce that $F_1 = F_2$ iff $N(F_1) = N(F_2)$.

Now, let $F_1 \subseteq F_2 \subseteq ...$ be an increasing chain in $\mathbf{F}(\mathbf{L})$. Using Proposition 3 and Lemma 1, $N(F_1) \subseteq N(F_2) \subseteq ...$ is an increasing chain in $\mathbf{I}(\mathbf{L})$. Since L is i-Noetherian, there exists a natural number $n \geq 1$ such that $N(F_i) = N(F_n)$, for every $i \geq n$. Thus, $F_i = F_n$, for every $i \geq n$. We deduce that L is Noetherian.

Using Corollary 1, we conclude that the notions of Noetherian and i-Noetherian coincide if L is involutive. □

Remark 4. *For MV algebras, the notions of Noetherian and i-Noetherian coincide since MV algebras are involutive residuated lattices and the notions of ideal and filter are dual.*

We recall that a poset $(A, \leq)$ is Noetherian iff every nonempty subset of A has a maximal element, see [22]. Using this result, we give a characterization for i-Noetherian residuated lattices:

Theorem 2. *A residuated lattice L is i-Noetherian iff every ideal of L is principal.*

Proof. First, suppose that every ideal of L is principal and let $I_1 \subseteq I_2 \subseteq ...$ be an increasing chain in $\mathbf{I}(\mathbf{L})$.

Since $I = \bigcup_{i \geq 1} I_i \in \mathbf{I}(\mathbf{L})$, there exists $x \in L$ such that $I = (x]$. Then, there is a natural number $n \geq 1$ such that $x \in I_n$. Thus, $I = (x] \subseteq I_n \subseteq I$. Hence, $I_i = I_n$, for every $i \geq n$ and L is i-Noetherian.

Conversely, suppose that L is i-Noetherian and let $I \in \mathbf{I}(\mathbf{L})$ such that I is not principal. If we denote that $\mathcal{S}_I = \{K \in \mathbf{I}(\mathbf{L}) : K$ is principal and $K \subseteq I\}$, then we remark that $<0> = \{0\} \subseteq I$; so, $\mathcal{S}_I \neq \emptyset$.

Since L is i-Noetherian, $(\mathbf{I}(\mathbf{L}), \subseteq)$ is a Noetherian poset and $\mathcal{S}_I \subseteq \mathbf{I}(\mathbf{L})$ has a maximal element J. Thus, $J \subseteq I$ and J is principal—that is, $J = (j]$, for some $j \in L$. Since I is not principal, $J \neq I$; so, there is $i \in I \setminus J$. Hence, $J \subset (i \boxplus j] \in \mathcal{S}_I$ is a contradiction, since J is the maximal element of $\mathcal{S}_I$. □

Example 4. *Let L be the residuated lattice $L = \{0, a, b, c, 1\}$ from Example 2. Then, $\mathbf{I}(\mathbf{L}) = \{\{0\}, \{0, a\}, \{0, b\}, L\}$ and every ideal is principal $\{0\} = (0]$, $\{0, a\} = (a]$, $\{0, b\} = (b]$, $L = (1]$. By Theorem 2, L is i-Noetherian.*

Proposition 8. *Every subalgebra of an i-Noetherian residuated lattice is i-Noetherian.*

Proof. Let L be an i-Noetherian residuated lattice and $L' \subseteq L$ be a subalgebra of L. Obviously, $\mathbf{I}(\mathbf{L'}) = \{I \cap L' : I \in \mathbf{I}(\mathbf{L})\}$. We deduce that L' is also i-Noetherian. □

Proposition 9. *Let L be a divisible residuated lattice and $I \in \mathbf{I}(\mathbf{L})$. If L is i-Noetherian, L/I is an i-Noetherian MV algebra.*

Proof. Let $I_1/I \subseteq I_2/I \subseteq ...$ be an increasing chain of ideals in L/I, see Proposition 6 (*ii*). Using Proposition 6 (*iii*), we obtain an increasing chain of ideals in $L : I \subseteq I_1 \subseteq I_2 \subseteq ...$. Since L is i-Noetherian, there is $n \geq 1$ such that $I_i = I_n$, for every $i \geq n$. Thus, $I_i/I = I_n/I$, for every $i \geq n$; so, L/I is i-Noetherian. □

Theorem 3. *The MV center of any homomorphic image of a divisible and i-Noetherian residuated lattice is i-Noetherian.*

Proof. Let L_1 be a divisible residuated lattice that is i-Noetherian, L_2 be a residuated lattice, and $f : L_1 \to L_2$ be a morphism of residuated lattices. Since $\mathcal{DIV}$ is a subvariety of $\mathcal{RL}$, $f(L_1)$ is a divisible residuated lattice. Using Turunen and Mertanen's result (see [14]), $MV(f(L_1))$ is an MV algebra. Since $i - Ker(f) \in \mathbf{I}(\mathbf{L}_1)$ using Isomorphism Theorem 1, L_1 / i-$Ker(f) \approx MV(Imf)$, as MV algebras. From Proposition 9, we deduce that L_1 / i-$Ker(f)$ is an i-Noetherian MV algebra; so, $MV(Imf)$ is i-Noetherian. □

Remark 5. *Theorem 3 generalizes Dymek's result ([15]): Any homomorphic image of an i-Noetherian (= Noetherian) MV algebra is Noetherian.*

Using Theorem 3, we deduce the following:

Corollary 3. *Let L_1, L_2 be residuated lattices and $f : L_1 \to L_2$ be an onto morphism of residuated lattices. If L_1 is divisible and i-Noetherian, L_2 is divisible and $MV(L_2)$ is i-Noetherian.*

5. Noetherian Spectrum in Residuated Lattices

In the following, we establish connections between i-Noetherian residuated lattices and those residuated lattices for which their spectrum is a Noetherian space.

In this way, we translated some important results from theory of rings to the case of residuated lattices.

We recall that an ideal P of a residuated lattice L is called *prime* if $P \neq L$ and P is a prime element in $(\mathbf{I}(\mathbf{L}), \subseteq)$, see [13].

For a residuated lattice L, we denote by $Spec(L)$ the set of prime ideals. It is known that $Spec(L)$ can be endowed with the Zariski topology τ_L :

$\{V(I)\}_{I \in \mathbf{I}(\mathbf{L})}$ is the family of closed subsets of $Spec(L)$ and $\{D(I)\}_{I \in \mathbf{I}(\mathbf{L})}$ is the family of open subsets of $Spec(L)$, where for $I \in I(L)$ and $x \in L$,

$$V(I) = \{P \in Spec(L) : I \subseteq P\}, D(I) = \{P \in Spec(L) : I \nsubseteq P\}$$

and $D(x) = D((x]) = \{P \in Spec(L) : x \notin P\}.$

Thus, $\tau_L = \{D(I)\}_{I \in \mathbf{I}(\mathbf{L})}$ is a topology on $Spec(L)$ and the topological space $(Spec(L), \tau_L)$ is called the *prime spectrum* of L. Moreover, the family $\{D(x)\}_{x \in L}$ is a basis for the topology τ_L on $Spec(L)$, see [16].

Proposition 10 ([16]). *Let L be a residuated lattice. Then,*

(*i*) $D(\{1\}) = D(L) = \mathcal{P}(L)$ and $D(\{0\}) = D(\varnothing) = \varnothing$;
(*ii*) For every family $\{I_k\}_{k \in K} \in \mathbf{I}(\mathbf{L})$, $\bigcup_{k \in K} D(I_k) = D(\bigvee_{k \in K} I_k)$;
(*iii*) For every $I, J \in \mathbf{I}(\mathbf{L})$, $D(I) \cap D(J) = D(I \cap J)$ and $[D(I) = D(J)$ iff $I = J]$;
(*iv*) $D(x^{**} \wedge y^{**}) = D(x) \cap D(y)$ and $D(x) \cup D(y) = D(x \boxplus y)$, for every $x, y \in L$.

Lemma 2. *If L is a residuated lattice and $I \in \mathbf{I}(\mathbf{L})$, then $D(I) = \bigcup_{x \in I} D(x)$.*

Proof. Using Proposition 10, $D(x) \subseteq D(I)$, for every $x \in I$, so $\bigcup_{x \in I} D(x) \subseteq D(I)$.

Now, let $P \in D(I)$. Then, $I \nsubseteq P$. Thus, there is $x_0 \in I$ such that $x_0 \notin P$. We deduce that $P \in D(x_0)$; so, $P \in \bigcup_{x \in I} D(x)$. Then, $D(I) \subseteq \bigcup_{x \in I} D(x)$. □

We give a characterization for compact open subsets of $Spec(L)$:

Theorem 4. *The compact open subsets of $Spec(L)$ are $D(x)$ with $x \in L$.*

Proof. Obviously, for every $x \in L$, $D(x)$ is an open subset of $Spec(L)$.

To prove that $D(x)$ is compact, let $D(x) = \underset{k \in K}{\cup} D(x_k)$.

From Proposition 10, we deduce that $D(x) = D(\underset{k \in K}{\cup} \{x_k\})$; so, $(x] = (\underset{k \in K}{\cup} \{x_k\}]$. Then, $x \in (\underset{k \in K}{\cup} \{x_k\}]$; so, there are $m \geq 1$, $k_1, ..., k_m \in K$, such that $x \leq x_{k_1} \boxplus ... \boxplus x_{k_m}$.

It follows that $D(x) \subseteq D(x_{k_1} \boxplus ... \boxplus x_{k_m}) = D(x_{k_1}) \cup ... \cup D(x_{k_m})$. Since $D(x_{k_1}) \cup ... \cup D(x_{k_m}) \subseteq D(x)$, we deduce that $D(x) = D(x_{k_1}) \cup ... \cup D(x_{k_m})$—that is, $D(x)$ is compact.

Conversely, we will prove that for any open compact subset $D(I)$ of $Spec(L)$, with $I \in \mathbf{I}(\mathbf{L})$, there is some $x \in L$ such that $D(I) = D(x)$.

By Lemma 2, $D(I) = \underset{x \in I}{\cup} D(x)$. Since $D(I)$ is compact, there are $n \geq 1$ and $x_1, ..., x_n \in I$ such that $D(x) = D(x_1) \cup ... \cup D(x_n) = D(x_1 \boxplus ... \boxplus x_n)$, by Proposition 10. □

Example 5. *Let $L = \{0, a, b, c, 1\}$ be the residuated lattice from Example 2. We remark that*

$$\mathbf{I}(\mathbf{L}) = \{\{0\}, \{0, a\}, \{0, b\}, L\} \text{ and } Spec(L) = \{\{0, a\}, \{0, b\}\}$$

$$D(\{0\}) = \varnothing, D(L) = Spec(L), D(\{0, a\}) = \{0, b\}, D(\{0, b\}) = \{0, a\},$$

$$D(0) = \varnothing, D(a) = \{0, b\}, D(b) = \{0, a\}, D(c) = D(1) = Spec(L)$$

so, $\tau_L = \mathcal{P}(Spec(L))$.

We recall that a topological space is called *Noetherian* [17] if it satisfies the descending chain condition on closed subsets (that is, every decreasing chain of closed subsets is stationary).

Remark 6. *If L is a residuated lattice with $Spec(L)$ finite, $Spec(L)$ is a Noetherian space.*

Example 6. *If L is the residuated lattice $L = \{0, a, b, c, 1\}$ from Example 2, $Spec(L)$ is finite; so, $Spec(L)$ is a Noetherian space.*

Another characterization for Noetherian spaces is the following:

Proposition 11 ([17]). *A topological space is Noetherian iff every open set is compact.*

Using this result, we deduce the following:

Theorem 5. *Let L be a residuated lattice. Then, the following are equivalent:*

(i) $Spec(L)$ is Noetherian;
(ii) Every ideal of L is principal.

Proof. Using Proposition 11 and Theorem 4, $Spec(L)$ is *Noetherian* iff for every $I \in \mathbf{I}(\mathbf{L})$ there is $x \in L$ such that $D(I) = D(x)$. Since $D(x) = D((x])$, by Proposition 10, $D(I) = D((x])$ iff $I = (x]$. We conclude that $Spec(L)$ is *Noetherian* iff for every $I \in \mathbf{I}(\mathbf{L})$ there is $x \in L$ such that $I = (x]$. □

By Theorems 2 and 5, we obtain the relationship between i-Noetherian residuated lattices and residuated lattices with Noetherian spectrum:

Corollary 4. *A residuated lattice L is i-Noetherian iff $Spec(L)$ is a Noetherian space.*

6. Ideals in Residuated Lattices and Ideals in Unitary Commutative Rings (Similarities and Differences)

6.1. Differences

If in any residuated lattice, every finitely generated ideal is principal (according to Proposition 2), there are unitary commutative rings in which there are finitely generated ideals that are not principal. We give an example in this regard by considering the quadratic field $\mathbb{Q}\left(\sqrt{26}\right)$. Since $26 \equiv 2 \pmod{4}$, the ring of algebraic integers of this quadratic field is $\mathbb{Z}\left[\sqrt{26}\right] = \left\{a + b\sqrt{26} \mid a, b \in \mathbb{Z}\right\}$.

In the proof of Proposition 2, we used the fact that if $x, y \in I$ (where I is an ideal in a residuated lattice L), $x \leq x \boxplus y$ and $y \leq x \boxplus y$. However, this thinking is generally not true in an ideal of unitary commutative ring. For example, in the ring $\left(\mathbb{Z}\left[\sqrt{26}\right], +, \cdot\right)$, if we take the ideal $I = \mathbb{Z}\left[\sqrt{26}\right]$ and $x, y \in \mathbb{Z}\left[\sqrt{26}\right]$, $x = 1 + \sqrt{26}$, $y = -3 - 2\sqrt{26}$, it results $x + y = -2 - \sqrt{26}$ and $x \not\leq x + y$; therefore, for ideals in unitary rings, a proof similar to that in Proposition 2 does not work.

We recall the following results.

Proposition 12 ([24]). *For any algebraic number field K, the ring of algebraic integers of K is a Dedeking ring.*

Proposition 13 ([24,25]). *In a Dedekind ring, any ideal is finitely generated, with a maximum of 2 generators.*

So, in the ring $\mathbb{Z}\left[\sqrt{26}\right]$, any ideal is finitely generated, with a maximum of 2 generators. However, we are showing that $\mathbb{Z}\left[\sqrt{26}\right]$ is not a principal ring.

It is easy to prove that $2, 13, \sqrt{26}$ are irreducible elements of this ring; so, $26 = 2 \cdot 13 = \sqrt{26} \cdot \sqrt{26}$ are two decompositions into irreducible elements of 26 in the ring $\mathbb{Z}\left[\sqrt{26}\right]$. It results that $\mathbb{Z}\left[\sqrt{26}\right]$ is not a factorial ring; so, it is not a principal ring.

In conclusion, $\mathbb{Z}\left[\sqrt{26}\right]$ is a Dedekind ring (so, it is a Noetherian ring), but it is not a principal ring.

6.2. Similarities

If $(R, +, \cdot)$ is a unitary commutative ring and $x \in R$, we denote by (x) the principal ideal generated by x, of the ring R.

We asked ourselves if there are unitary commutative rings in which every finitely generated ideal is principal and also if these rings can be endowed similar to a residuated lattices. The answer is yes:

Example 7. *Let M be a nonempty set and let $P(M)$ be the set of all subsets of the set M. If we consider the composition laws "+", "$\cap$": $P(M) \times P(M) \to P(M)$, $A + B = (A \setminus B) \cup (B \setminus A) = A \Delta B$, $(\forall)$ $A, B \in P(M)$, $A \odot B = A \cap B$, $(\forall)$ $A, B \in P(M)$, it is easy to remark that $(P(M), +, \odot)$ is a unitary commutative boolean ring, with identity elements: $\emptyset$ for "+", M for "$\cap$". So, $A^2 = A$ and $A + A = \emptyset$, $(\forall)$ $A \in P(M)$.*

Moreover, $(P(M), \subseteq, \vee, \wedge, \odot, \to, \emptyset, M)$ is a residuated lattice, in which $A \vee B = A \cup B$, $A \wedge B = A \cap B$, and $A \to B = C_M A \cup B$, $(\forall)$ $A, B \in P(M)$. We remark that, in this residuated lattice, for $A, B \in P(M)$, we have

$$A \boxplus B = (A^* \odot B^*)^* = C_M\left((C_M A) \cap (C_M B)\right) =$$

$$= (C_M(C_M A)) \cup (C_M(C_M B)) = A \cup B.$$

We consider the case when M is a finite set, so all ideals of the ring $(P(M), +, \odot)$ are finite generated.

For example, if we take Card $M = 3$, let us to look at the ideals in the unitary commutative boolean ring $(P(M), +, \odot)$ and at the ideals in the residuated lattice $(P(M), \subseteq, \vee, \wedge, \odot, \rightarrow, \emptyset, M)$.

We denote $M = \{1, 2, 3\}$. Let I be an ideal of the ring $(P(M), +, \odot)$. Since $Card(P(M)) = 8$ and applying Lagrange's theorem, it results that Card $I \in \{1, 2, 4, 8\}$. Knowing that the ring $(P(M), +, \odot)$ is boolean, we obtain that the ideals of the ring $(P(M), +, \odot)$ are as follows:

$$I_1 = \{\emptyset\} = (\emptyset), I_2 = \{\emptyset, \{1\}\} = (\{1\}),$$

$$I_3 = \{\emptyset, \{2\}\} = (\{2\}), I_4 = \{\emptyset, \{3\}\} = (\{3\}),$$

$$I_5 = \{\emptyset, \{1\}, \{2\}, \{1,2\}\} = \left\{ \{1,2\} \bigcap X | X \in P(M) \right\} = (\{1,2\}),$$

$$I_6 = \{\emptyset, \{1\}, \{3\}, \{1,3\}\} = \left\{ \{1,3\} \bigcap X | X \in P(M) \right\} = (\{1,3\}),$$

$$I_7 = \{\emptyset, \{2\}, \{3\}, \{2,3\}\} = \left\{ \{2,3\} \bigcap X | X \in P(M) \right\} = (\{2,3\}),$$

$$I_8 = P(M) = (\{1,2,3\}).$$

So, all the ideals of the ring $(P(M), +, \odot)$ are principal ideals.

We are finding all the ideals of the residuated lattice $(P(M), \subseteq, \vee, \wedge, \odot, \rightarrow, \emptyset, M)$, which is a Boolean algebra. According to Proposition 1, if $X \subseteq P(M)$, then, the ideal generated by X in the residuated lattice $(P(M), \subseteq, \vee, \wedge, \odot, \rightarrow, \emptyset, M)$ is $(X] = \{A \in P(M) : A \subseteq X_1 \boxplus \ldots \boxplus X_n,$ for some $n \geq 1$ and $X_1, \ldots, X_n \in X\}$. It results that the ideals of the residuated lattice $(P(M), \subseteq, \vee, \wedge, \odot, \rightarrow, \emptyset, M)$ are as follows:

$$J_1 = \{\emptyset\} = (\emptyset], J_2 = \{\emptyset, \{1\}\} = (\{1\}],$$

$$J_3 = \{\emptyset, \{2\}\} = (\{2\}], J_4 = \{\emptyset, \{3\}\} = (\{3\}],$$

$$J_5 = (\{1\} \boxplus \{2\}] = (\{1,2\}] = \{\emptyset, \{1\}, \{2\}, \{1,2\}\},$$

$$J_6 = (\{1\} \boxplus \{3\}] = (\{1,3\}] = \{\emptyset, \{1\}, \{3\}, \{1,3\}\},$$

$$J_7 = (\{2\} \boxplus \{3\}] = (\{2,3\}] = \{\emptyset, \{2\}, \{3\}, \{2,3\}\},$$

$$J_8 = (\{1\} \boxplus \{2\} \boxplus \{3\}] = (\{1,2,3\}] = P(M).$$

So, we obtain that all ideals of the residuated lattice $(P(M), \subseteq, \vee, \wedge, \odot, \rightarrow, \emptyset, M)$ are principal ideals and $I_l = J_l$, for $(\forall)$ $l = \overline{1,8}$—that is, the ideals of the boolean ring $(P(M), +, \odot)$ coincide with the ideals of the residuated lattice $(P(M), \subseteq, \vee, \wedge, \odot, \rightarrow, \emptyset, M)$. Further, according to Theorem 2, it results that the lattice $(P(M), \subseteq, \vee, \wedge, \odot, \rightarrow, \emptyset, M)$ is an i-Notherian residuated lattice. Moreover $(P(M), +, \odot)$ is a Notherian ring (in the sense of [24,25]).

We asked ourselves if this analogy between the ideals of the boolean ring $(P(M), +, \odot)$ and the ideals of the residuated lattice $(P(M), \subseteq, \vee, \wedge, \odot, \rightarrow, \emptyset, M)$ is preserved for any finite set M. The answer is affirmative. To obtain this, we need some results.

Proposition 14 ([25]). *Let R be a unitary commutative ring and let I be an idempotent ideal of the ring R. If I is finitely generated, there is an idempotent element $e \in I$ such that $I = eR$.*

Definition 5 ([24]). *A Bezout domain is an integral domain in which every finitely generated ideal is principal.*

There are rings in which every finitely generated ideal is principal, but they have divisors of zero.

We introduce the following definition.

Definition 6. *A unitary commutative ring with zero divisors, in which every finitely generated ideal is principal, is called a Bezout ring with zero divisors.*

We obtain the following results.

Proposition 15. *If $(R, +, \cdot)$ is a Boolean ring, any ideal of R is idempotent.*

Proof. Let I be an ideal of R.
$I^2 = \{x_1 \cdot y_1 + x_2 \cdot y_2 + \ldots + x_n \cdot y_n \mid n \in \mathbb{N}^*, x_i, y_i \in I, i = \overline{1,n}\}$. It is clear that $I^2 \subseteq I$. We prove that $I \subseteq I^2$. Let $x \in I$. Since $x = x^2$, it results that $x \in I^2$, so $I \subseteq I^2$. We obtain that $I^2 = I$. □

Proposition 16. *Any Boolean ring is a Bezout ring with zero divisors.*

Proof. It results immediately, using Proposition 15, Proposition 14, and Definition 6. □

Taking into account the results obtained, we deduce the following:

Corollary 5. *Let M be a nonempty set. Then,*

(i) *In the residuated lattice $(P(M), \subseteq, \vee, \wedge, \odot, \rightarrow, \emptyset, M)$ all finitely generated ideals are principal;*

(ii) *The ring $(P(M), +, \odot)$ is a Bezout ring with zero divisors;*

(iii) *If M is finite, the ideals of the boolean ring $(P(M), +, \odot)$ are principal and these ideals coincide with the ideals of the residuated lattice $(P(M), \subseteq, \vee, \wedge, \odot, \rightarrow, \emptyset, M)$. Further, the lattice $(P(M), \subseteq, \vee, \wedge, \odot, \rightarrow, \emptyset, M)$ is an i-Notherian residuated lattice and the ring $(P(M), +, \odot)$ is a Notherian ring.*

Author Contributions: The work presented here was carried out in collaboration between both authors. Both authors have contributed to the manuscript. All authors have read and agreed to the published version of the manuscript.

Funding: The financial support from Transilvania University of Braşov.

Institutional Review Board Statement: Not applicable

Informed Consent Statement: Not applicable

Data Availability Statement: Not applicable.

Acknowledgments: The authors express their gratitude to the anonymous reviewers and editor for their careful reading of the manuscript and for many valuable remarks and suggestions. The second author acknowledges the financial support from Transilvania University of Braşov.

Conflicts of Interest: The authors declare no conflict of interest.

References

1. Ward, M.; Dilworth, R.P. Residuated lattices. *Trans. Am. Math. Soc.* **1939**, *45*, 335–354. [CrossRef]
2. Chang, C.C. Algebraic analysis of many-valued logic. *Trans. Am. Math. Soc.* **1958**, *88*, 467–490 [CrossRef]
3. Dilworth, R.P. Non-commutative residuated lattices. *Trans. Am. Math. Soc.* **1939**, *46*, 426–444 [CrossRef]
4. Hájek, P. *Metamathematics of Fuzzy Logic*; Kluwer Academic Publication: Dordrecht, The Netherlands, 1998.
5. Jipsen, P.; Tsinakis, C. A survey of residuated lattices. In *Ordered Algebraic Structures*; Martinez, J., Ed.; Kluwer Academic Publication: Dordrecht, The Netherlands, 2002; pp. 19–56.
6. Krull, W. Axiomatische Begründung der allgemeinen Ideal theorie. *Sitzungsberichte Phys. Med. Soc. Erlangen.* **1924**, *56*, 47–63.
7. Turunen, E. *Mathematics Behind Fuzzy Logic*; Physica-Verlag: Heidelberg, Germany, 1999.
8. Di Nola, A.; Sessa, S.; Esteva, F.; Godo, L.; Garcia, P. The variety generated by perfect BL-algebras: An algebraic approach in fuzzy logic setting. *Ann. Math. Artif. Intell.* **2002**, *35*, 197–214. [CrossRef]
9. Lele, C.; Nganou, J.B. MV-algebras derived from ideals in BL-algebras. *Fuzzy Sets Syst.* **2013**, *218*, 103–113. [CrossRef]
10. Liu, Y.; Qin, Y.; Qin, X.; Xu, Y. Ideals and fuzzy ideals in residuated lattices. *Int. J. Math. Learn Cyber.* **2017**, *8*, 239–253. [CrossRef]
11. Rachůnek, J.; Šalounová, D. *Ideals and Involutive Filters in Residuated Lattices*; SSAOS: London, UK, 2014.

12. Cignoli, R.; D'Ottaviano, I.M.L.; Mundici, D. *Algebraic Foundations of Many-Valued Reasoning*; Trends in Logic-Studia Logica Library 7; Kluwer Acadademic Publication: Dordrecht, The Netherlands, 2000.
13. Buşneag, D.; Piciu, D.; Dina, A. Ideals in residuated lattices. *Carpathian J. Math.* **2021**, *37*, 53–63. [CrossRef]
14. Turunen, E.; Mertanen, J. States on semi-divisible residuated lattices. *Soft Comput.* **2008**, *12*, 353–357. [CrossRef]
15. Dimek, G. Noetherian and Artinian pseudo MV algebras. *Discuss. Math. Gen. Algebra Appl.* **2008**, *28*, 209–225 [CrossRef]
16. Piciu, D. Prime, minimal prime and maximal ideals spaces in residuated lattices. *Fuzzy Sets Syst.* **2021**, *405*, 47–64. [CrossRef]
17. Hartshorne, R. *Algebraic Geometry*; Springer: Berlin/Heidelberg, Germany, 1977.
18. Birkhoff, G. *Lattice Theory*, 3rd ed.; American Mathematical Society Colloquim Publications: Ann Arbor, MI, USA, 1967; Volume 25.
19. Iorgulescu, A. *Algebras of Logic as BCK Algebras*; A.S.E.: Bucharest, Romania, 2009.
20. Buşneag, D.; Piciu, D.; Holdon, L.; Dobre, L. Noetherian and Artinian algebras in the general case of residuated lattices. *Bull. Math. Soc. Sci. Math. Roum.* **2019**, *3*, 229–238.
21. Golzarpoor, J.; Mehrpooya, M.; Mehrshad, S. Pseudo-valuations on commutative BE-algebras. *Bull. Transilv. Univ. Bras. Ser. III* **2021**, *1*, 129–142. [CrossRef]
22. Năstăsescu, C. *Theory of Dimension in Noncommutative Algebras*; Ed. Academiei: Bucureşti, Romania, 1983.
23. Motamed, S.; Moghaderi, J. Noetherian and artinian BL algebras. *Soft Comput.* **2012**, *18*, 419–429. [CrossRef]
24. Albu, T.; Ion, I.D. *Chapters of the Algebraic Number Theory*; Academy Publishing House: Bucharest, Romania, 1984. (In Romanian)
25. Savin, D.; Ştefănescu, M. *Lessons of Arithmetics and Number Theory*; Matrix Rom Publishing House: Bucharest, Romania, 2008. (In Romanian)

Article

A Generalized Bohr–Jessen Type Theorem for the Epstein Zeta-Function

Antanas Laurinčikas [1,†] and Renata Macaitienė [2,*,†]

1. Institute of Mathematics, Faculty of Mathematics and Informatics, Vilnius University, Naugarduko Str. 24, LT-03225 Vilnius, Lithuania; antanas.laurincikas@mif.vu.lt
2. Institute of Regional Development, Šiauliai Academy, Vilnius University, Vytauto Str. 84, LT-76352 Šiauliai, Lithuania
* Correspondence: renata.macaitiene@sa.vu.lt; Tel.: +370-699-66-080
† These authors contributed equally to this work.

Abstract: Let Q be a positive defined $n \times n$ matrix and $Q[\underline{x}] = \underline{x}^T Q \underline{x}$. The Epstein zeta-function $\zeta(s; Q)$, $s = \sigma + it$, is defined, for $\sigma > \frac{n}{2}$, by the series $\zeta(s; Q) = \sum_{\underline{x} \in \mathbb{Z}^n \setminus \{\underline{0}\}} (Q[\underline{x}])^{-s}$, and is meromorphically continued on the whole complex plane. Suppose that $n \geqslant 4$ is even and $\varphi(t)$ is a differentiable function with a monotonic derivative. In the paper, it is proved that $\frac{1}{T} \operatorname{meas}\{t \in [0, T] : \zeta(\sigma + i\varphi(t); Q) \in A\}$, $A \in \mathcal{B}(\mathbb{C})$, converges weakly to an explicitly given probability measure on $(\mathbb{C}, \mathcal{B}(\mathbb{C}))$ as $T \to \infty$.

Keywords: Epstein zeta-function; limit theorem; weak convergence; Haar measure

MSC: 11M46; 11M06

1. Introduction

It is well known that the Riemann zeta-function

$$\zeta(s) = \sum_{m=1}^{\infty} \frac{1}{m^s}, \quad s = \sigma + it, \quad \sigma > 1,$$

shows analytic continuation to the whole complex plane, except for a simple pole at the point $s = 1$, and satisfies functional equation

$$\pi^{-\frac{s}{2}} \Gamma\left(\frac{s}{2}\right) \zeta(s) = \pi^{-\frac{1-s}{2}} \Gamma\left(\frac{1-s}{2}\right) \zeta(1-s),$$

where $\Gamma(s)$ denotes the Euler gamma-function. The majority of other zeta-functions also have similar equations, which are referred to as the Riemann type. Epstein in [1] raised a question to find the most general zeta-function with a functional equation of the Riemann type and introduced the following zeta-function. Let Q be a positive defined quadratic $n \times n$ matrix, and $Q[\underline{x}] = \underline{x}^T Q \underline{x}$ for $\underline{x} \in \mathbb{Z}^n$. Epstein defined, for $\sigma > \frac{n}{2}$, the function

$$\zeta(s; Q) = \sum_{\underline{x} \in \mathbb{Z}^n \setminus \{\underline{0}\}} (Q[\underline{x}])^{-s},$$

continued analytically it to the whole complex plane, except for a simple pole at the point $s = \frac{n}{2}$ with residue $\frac{\pi^{\frac{n}{2}}}{\Gamma(\frac{n}{2})\sqrt{\det Q}}$, and proved the functional equation

$$\pi^{-s} \Gamma(s) \zeta(s; Q) = (\det Q)^{-\frac{1}{2}} \pi^{s - \frac{n}{2}} \Gamma\left(\frac{n}{2} - s\right) \zeta\left(\frac{n}{2} - s; Q^{-1}\right).$$

In [2], Bohr and Jessen proved a probabilistic limit theorem for the function $\zeta(s)$. We recall its modern version. Denote by $\mathcal{B}(\mathbb{X})$ the Borel σ-field of the topological space $\mathbb{X}$, and

by meas$A$ the Lebesgue measure of a measurable set $A \subset \mathbb{R}$. Then, on $(\mathbb{C}, \mathcal{B}(\mathbb{C}))$, there exists a probability measure P_σ such that, for $\sigma > \frac{1}{2}$,

$$\frac{1}{T}\text{meas}\{t \in [0, T] : \zeta(\sigma + it) \in A\}, \quad A \in \mathcal{B}(\mathbb{C}), \tag{1}$$

converges weakly to P_σ as $T \to \infty$ (see, for example, [3] (Theorem 1.1, p. 149). In [4], the latter limit theorem was generalized for the Epstein zeta-function $\zeta(s; Q)$ with even $n \geq 4$ and integers $Q[\underline{x}]$. Namely, on $(\mathbb{C}, \mathcal{B}(\mathbb{C}))$, there exists an explicitly given probability measure $P_{Q,\sigma}$ such that, for $\sigma > \frac{n-1}{2}$,

$$\frac{1}{T}\text{meas}\{t \in [0, T] : \zeta(\sigma + it; Q) \in A\}, \quad A \in \mathcal{B}(\mathbb{C}),$$

converges weakly to $P_{Q,\sigma}$ as $T \to \infty$.

For the function $\zeta(s)$, more general limit theorems are also considered. In place of (1), the weak convergence for

$$\frac{1}{T}\text{meas}\{t \in [0, T] : \zeta(\sigma + i\varphi(t)) \in A\}, \quad A \in \mathcal{B}(\mathbb{C}),$$

with certain measurable function $\varphi(t)$ is studied. For example, theorems of such a kind follow from limit theorems in the space of analytic functions proved in [5].

Suppose that the function $\varphi(t)$ is defined for $t \geq T_0 > 0$, is increasing to $+\infty$, and has a monotonic derivative $\varphi'(t)$ satisfying the estimate

$$\varphi(2t)\frac{1}{\varphi'(t)} \ll t, \quad t \to \infty.$$

Denote the class of the above functions by $W(T_0)$.

The aim of this paper is to prove a limit theorem for

$$\hat{P}_{T,Q,\sigma}(A) \stackrel{def}{=} \frac{1}{T}\text{meas}\{t \in [0, T] : \zeta(\sigma + i\varphi(t); Q) \in A\}, \quad A \in \mathcal{B}(\mathbb{C}),$$

when $\varphi(t) \in W(T_0)$. In place of $\hat{P}_{T,Q,\sigma}$ one can consider

$$P_{T,Q,\sigma}(A) \stackrel{def}{=} \frac{1}{T}\text{meas}\{t \in [T, 2T] : \zeta(\sigma + i\varphi(t); Q) \in A\}, \quad A \in \mathcal{B}(\mathbb{C}).$$

It is easily seen that the weak convergence of $\hat{P}_{T,Q,\sigma}$ to $P_{Q,\sigma}$ as $T \to \infty$ is equivalent to that of $P_{T,Q,\sigma}$. Actually, if $\hat{P}_{T,Q,\sigma}$ converges weakly to $P_{Q,\sigma}$ as $T \to \infty$, then

$$\lim_{T \to \infty} \hat{P}_{T,Q,\sigma}(A) = P_{Q,\sigma}(A)$$

for every continuity set A of the measure $P_{Q,\sigma}$. Since

$$P_{T,Q,\sigma}(A) = 2\hat{P}_{2T,Q,\sigma}(A) - \hat{P}_{T,Q,\sigma}(A),$$

we obtain that

$$\lim_{T \to \infty} P_{T,Q,\sigma}(A) = P_{Q,\sigma}(A), \tag{2}$$

i.e., $P_{T,Q,\sigma}$ converges weakly to $P_{Q,\sigma}$ as $T \to \infty$.

Now, suppose that (2) is true. Then

$$XP_{X,Q,\sigma}(A) = XP_{Q,\sigma}(A) + g_A(X)X,$$

where $g_A(X) \to 0$ as $X \to \infty$. Taking $X = T2^{-j}$ and summing the above equality over $j \in \mathbb{N}$, we obtain, ue of σ-additivity of the Lebesgue measure,

$$\hat{P}_{T,Q,\sigma}(A) = P_{Q,\sigma}(A) + \sum_{j=1}^{\infty} g_A(T2^{-j})2^{-j}. \tag{3}$$

Let $\epsilon > 0$. We fix j_0 such that

$$\sum_{j>j_0} 2^{-j} < \epsilon.$$

Then

$$\sum_{j=1}^{\infty} g_A(T2^{-j})2^{-j} \ll_A \sum_{j \leq j_0} g_A(T2^{-j}) + \epsilon.$$

Thus, taking $T \to \infty$ and then $\epsilon \to 0$, we find

$$\lim_{T \to \infty} \sum_{j=1}^{\infty} g_A(T2^{-j})2^{-j} = 0.$$

This together with (3) shows that

$$\hat{P}_{T,Q,\sigma}(A) = P_{Q,\sigma}(A) + o(1), \quad T \to \infty,$$

i.e., $\hat{P}_{T,Q,\sigma}$ converges weakly to $P_{Q,\sigma}$ as $T \to \infty$.

Since, in the case of $P_{T,Q,\sigma}$ the function $\varphi(t)$ occurs for large values of t, the study of $P_{T,Q,\sigma}$ sometimes is more convenient than that of $\hat{P}_{T,Q,\sigma}$. Therefore, we will prove a limit theorem for $P_{T,Q,\sigma}$.

As in [3], we use the decomposition [6]

$$\zeta(s;Q) = \zeta(s;E_Q) + \zeta(s;F_Q),$$

where $\zeta(s;E_Q)$ and $\zeta(s;F_Q)$ are zeta-functions of certain Eisenstein series and of a certain cusp form, respectively. The latter decomposition and the results of [7], [8]—see also [9]—imply that, for $\sigma > \frac{n-1}{2}$,

$$\zeta(s;Q) = \sum_{k=1}^{K} \sum_{l=1}^{L} \frac{a_{kl}}{k^s l^s} L(s, \chi_k) L\left(s - \frac{n}{2} + 1, \psi_l\right) + \sum_{m=1}^{\infty} \frac{f_Q(m)}{m^s}, \tag{4}$$

where $a_{kl} \in \mathbb{C}$, $K, L \in \mathbb{N}$, $L(s, \chi_k)$ and $L(s, \psi_l)$ are Dirichlet L-functions, and the series is absolutely convergent for $\sigma > \frac{n-1}{2}$. Equality (4) is the main relation for investigation of the function $\zeta(s;Q)$. Before the statement of a limit theorem, we construct a $\mathbb{C}$-valued random element connected to $\zeta(s;Q)$.

Let $\mathbb{P}$ is the set of all prime numbers, $\gamma = \{s \in \mathbb{C} : |s| = 1\}$, and

$$\Omega = \prod_{p \in \mathbb{P}} \gamma_p,$$

where $\gamma_p = \gamma$ for all $p \in \mathbb{P}$. The infinite-dimensional torus Ω is a compact topological Abelian group; therefore, the probability Haar measure can be defined on $(\Omega, \mathcal{B}(\Omega))$. This gives the probability space $(\Omega, \mathcal{B}(\Omega), m_H)$. Denote by $\omega(p)$ the pth, $p \in \mathbb{P}$, component of an element $\omega \in \Omega$, and extend the function $\omega(p)$ to the whole set $\mathbb{N}$ by the formula

$$\omega(m) = \prod_{\substack{p^l \mid m \\ p^{l+1} \nmid m}} \omega^l(p), \quad m \in \mathbb{N}.$$

On the probability space $(\Omega, \mathcal{B}(\Omega), m_H)$, for $\sigma > \frac{n-1}{2}$, define the $\mathbb{C}$-valued random element by

$$\zeta(\sigma, \omega; Q) = \sum_{k=1}^{K} \sum_{l=1}^{L} \frac{a_{kl}\omega(k)\omega(l)}{k^\sigma l^\sigma} L(\sigma, \omega, \chi_k) L\left(\sigma - \frac{n}{2} + 1, \omega, \psi_l\right)$$
$$+ \sum_{m=1}^{\infty} \frac{f_Q(m)\omega(m)}{m^\sigma},$$

where

$$L(\sigma, \omega, \chi_k) = \prod_{p \in \mathbb{P}} \left(1 - \frac{\chi_k(p)\omega(p)}{p^\sigma}\right)^{-1},$$

and

$$L\left(\sigma - \frac{n}{2} + 1, \omega, \psi_l\right) = \prod_{p \in \mathbb{P}} \left(1 - \frac{\psi_l(p)\omega(p)}{p^{\sigma - \frac{n}{2} + 1}}\right)^{-1}.$$

Now, denote by $P_{\zeta, Q, \sigma}$ the distribution of $\zeta(\sigma, \omega; Q)$, i.e.,

$$P_{\zeta, Q, \sigma}(A) = m_H\{\omega \in \Omega : \zeta(\sigma, \omega; Q) \in A\}, \quad A \in \mathcal{B}(\mathbb{C}).$$

Because $n \geq 4$, $\sigma - \frac{n}{2} + 1 > \frac{1}{2}$ for $\sigma > \frac{n-1}{2}$. Therefore, the second Euler product for Dirichlet L-function is convergent for almost all ω and defines a random variable.

The main the result of the paper is the following theorem.

Theorem 1. *Suppose that $\varphi(t) \in W(T_0)$, $n \geq 4$ and $\sigma > \frac{n-1}{2}$ is fixed. Then $P_{T, Q, \sigma}$ converges weakly to the measure $P_{\zeta, Q, \sigma}$ as $T \to \infty$.*

Since the representation (4) depends on Q, the random element $\zeta(\sigma, \omega; Q)$ depends on Q. Thus, the limit measure $P_{\zeta, Q, \sigma}$ also depends on Q.

2. Some Estimates

We will consider the measure $P_{T, Q, \sigma}$; therefore, we suppose that $t \in [T, 2T]$ with large T. Let χ be a Dirichlet character modulo q, and $L(s, \chi)$ be a corresponding Dirichlet L-function.

Lemma 1. *Suppose that $\varphi(t) \in W(T_0)$ and $\sigma > \frac{1}{2}$ is fixed. Then, for $\tau \in \mathbb{R}$,*

$$\int_T^{2T} |L(\sigma + i\varphi(t) + i\tau, \chi)|^2 d\tau \ll_{\sigma, \chi, \varphi} T(1 + |\tau|).$$

Proof. It is well known that, for fixed $\sigma > \frac{n-1}{2}$,

$$\int_{-T}^{T} |L(\sigma + it, \chi)|^2 dt \ll_{\sigma, \chi} T. \tag{5}$$

An application of the mean value theorem, in view of (5), gives

$$I(T,\chi,\sigma) \stackrel{def}{=} \int_T^{2T} |L(\sigma+i\varphi(t)+i\tau,\chi)|^2 dt = \int_T^{2T} \frac{1}{\varphi'(t)} |L(\sigma+i\varphi(t)+i\tau,\chi)|^2 d\varphi(t)$$

$$= \int_T^{2T} \frac{1}{\varphi'(t)} d\left(\int_T^{\varphi(t)+\tau} |L(\sigma+iu,\chi)|^2 du\right) = \frac{1}{\varphi'(T)} \int_T^{\xi} d\left(\int_T^{\varphi(t)+\tau} |L(\sigma+iu,\chi)|^2 du\right)$$

$$= \frac{1}{\varphi'(T)} \int_{\varphi(T)+\tau}^{\varphi(\xi)+\tau} |L(\sigma+iu,\chi)|^2 du \leq \frac{1}{\varphi'(T)} \int_{\varphi(T)-|\tau|}^{\varphi(2T)+|\tau|} |L(\sigma+iu,\chi)|^2 du$$

$$\leq \frac{1}{\varphi'(T)} \int_{-\varphi(2T)-|\tau|}^{\varphi(2T)+|\tau|} |L(\sigma+iu,\chi)|^2 du \ll_{\sigma,\chi} \frac{1}{\varphi'(T)}(\varphi(2T)+|\tau|),$$

where $T \leq \xi \leq 2T$ and $\varphi'(t)$ is increasing. Thus, by the definition of the class $W(T_0)$,

$$I(T,\chi,\sigma) \ll_{\sigma,\chi} \frac{\varphi(2T)}{\varphi'(T)}\left(1+\frac{|\tau|}{\varphi(2T)}\right) \ll_{\sigma,\chi,\varphi} T(1+|\tau|).$$

If $\varphi'(t)$ is decreasing, then similarly we have

$$I(T,\chi,\sigma) = \frac{1}{\varphi'(2T)} \int_{\xi}^{2T} d\left(\int_T^{\varphi(t)+\tau} |L(\sigma+iu,\chi)|^2 du\right) = \frac{1}{\varphi'(2T)} \int_{\varphi(\xi)+\tau}^{\varphi(2T)+\tau} |L(\sigma+iu,\chi)|^2 du$$

$$\leq \frac{1}{\varphi'(2T)} \int_{\varphi(2T)+\tau}^{\varphi(2T)+\tau} |L(\sigma+iu,\chi)|^2 du \ll_{\sigma,\chi} \frac{1}{\varphi'(2T)}(\varphi(2T)+|\tau|)$$

$$\ll_{\sigma,\chi} \frac{\varphi(4T)}{\varphi'(2T)}(1+|\tau|) \ll_{\sigma,\chi,\varphi} T(1+|\tau|).$$

□

Let $\theta > 0$ be a fixed number, and

$$v_N(m) = \exp\left\{-\left(\frac{m}{N}\right)^\theta\right\}, \quad m, N \in \mathbb{N},$$

where $\exp\{a\} = e^a$. Put

$$L_N(s,\chi) = \sum_{m=1}^{\infty} \frac{\chi(m)v_N(m)}{m^s}.$$

Then, by the exponential decreasing of $v_N(m)$, the latter series is absolutely convergent for $\sigma > \sigma_0$ with arbitrary finite σ_0. Define

$$\zeta_N(s;Q) = \sum_{k=1}^{K}\sum_{l=1}^{L} \frac{a_{kl}}{k^s l^s} L(s,\chi_k) L_N\left(s-\frac{n}{2}+1,\psi_l\right) + \sum_{m=1}^{\infty} \frac{f_Q(m)}{m^s}.$$

Then the series for $\zeta_N(s;Q)$ is absolutely convergent for $\sigma > \frac{n-1}{2}$. It turns out that $\zeta_N(s;Q)$ approximates well in the mean the function $\zeta(s;Q)$. More precisely, we have the following result.

Lemma 2. *Suppose that $\varphi(t) \in W(T_0)$ and $\sigma > \frac{n-1}{2}$ is fixed. Then*

$$\lim_{N \to \infty} \limsup_{T \to \infty} \frac{1}{T} \int_T^{2T} |\zeta(\sigma + i\varphi(t); Q) - \zeta_N(\sigma + i\varphi(t); Q)| \, dt = 0.$$

Proof. Let θ be from the definition of $v_N(m)$; $\Gamma(s)$ denotes the Euler gamma-function, and

$$l_N(s) = \frac{s}{\theta} \Gamma\left(\frac{s}{\theta}\right) N^s.$$

Then, the Mellin formula

$$\frac{1}{2\pi i} \int_{b-i\infty}^{b+i\infty} \Gamma(s) a^{-s} \, ds = e^{-a}, \quad a, b > 0,$$

leads, for $\theta_1 > \frac{1}{2}$, to

$$L_N(s, \chi) = \frac{1}{2\pi i} \int_{\theta_1 - i\infty}^{\theta_1 + i\infty} L(s + z, \chi) l_N(z) \frac{dz}{z}. \tag{6}$$

Denote by χ_0 the principal Dirichlet character modulo q. Since the function $L(s, \chi)$ is entire for $\chi \neq \chi_0$, and $L(s, \chi_0)$ has a simple pole at the point $s = 1$ with residue

$$a_q \stackrel{def}{=} \prod_{p|q} \left(1 - \frac{1}{p}\right),$$

the residue theorem and (6) give

$$L_N(s, \chi) - L(s, \chi) = \frac{1}{2\pi i} \int_{-\theta_2 - i\infty}^{-\theta_2 + i\infty} L(s + z, \chi) l_N(z) \frac{dz}{z} + R_N(s, \chi),$$

where $0 < \theta_2 < 1$ and

$$R_N(s, \chi) = \begin{cases} 0 & \text{if } \chi \neq \chi_0, \\ a_q \frac{l_N(1-s)}{1-s} & \text{if } \chi = \chi_0. \end{cases}$$

Therefore,

$$|L(\sigma + i\varphi(t), \chi) - L_N(\sigma + i\varphi(t), \chi)|$$
$$\ll \int_{-\infty}^{\infty} |L(\sigma - \theta_2 + i\varphi(t) + i\tau, \chi)| \frac{|l_N(-\theta_2 + i\tau)|}{|-\theta_2 + i\tau|} \, d\tau + |R_N(\sigma + i\varphi(t), \chi)|.$$

Hence, we have that

$$\frac{1}{T} \int_T^{2T} |L(\sigma + i\varphi(t), \chi) - L_N(\sigma + i\varphi(t), \chi)| \, dt \ll I_1 + I_2, \tag{7}$$

where

$$I_1 = \int_{-\infty}^{\infty} \left(\left(\frac{1}{T} \int_T^{2T} |L(\sigma - \theta_2 + i\varphi(t) + i\tau, \chi)| dt\right) \frac{l_N(-\theta_2 + i\tau)}{|-\theta_2 + i\tau|}\right) d\tau$$

and
$$I_2 = \frac{1}{T}\int_T^{2T} |R_N(\sigma + i\varphi(t), \chi)|\, dt.$$

It is well known that, uniformly in $\sigma_1 \leq \sigma \leq \sigma_2$ with arbitrary $\sigma_1 < \sigma_2$,

$$\Gamma(\sigma + it) \ll \exp\{-c|t|\}, \quad |t| \geq t_0 > 0, \quad c > 0. \tag{8}$$

Therefore,
$$\frac{l_N(1 - \sigma - i\varphi(t))}{1 - \sigma - i\varphi(t)} \ll_\theta N^{1-\sigma} \exp\left\{-\frac{c}{\theta}\varphi(t)\right\},$$

and
$$I_2 \ll_{\theta,q} N^{1-\sigma}\frac{1}{T}\int_T^{2T} \exp\left\{-\frac{c}{\theta}\varphi(t)\right\} dt \ll_{\theta,q} N^{1-\sigma}\exp\left\{-\frac{c}{\theta}\varphi(T)\right\}. \tag{9}$$

Suppose that $\sigma > \frac{1}{2}$ and θ_2 is such that $\sigma - \theta_2 > \frac{1}{2}$. Then, in view of (8) again,

$$\frac{l_N(-\theta_2 + i\tau)}{-\theta_2 + i\tau} \ll_\theta N^{-\theta_2}\exp\left\{-\frac{c}{\theta}|\tau|\right\},$$

Therefore, Lemma 1 implies

$$I_1 \ll_{\theta,\sigma,\theta_2,\chi} N^{-\theta_2}\int_{-\infty}^{\infty}(1+|\tau|)\exp\left\{-\frac{c}{\theta}|\tau|\right\} d\tau \ll_{\theta,\sigma,\theta_2,\chi} N^{-\theta_2}.$$

This, (9) and (7) show that, for fixed $\sigma > \frac{1}{2}$,

$$\lim_{N\to\infty}\limsup_{T\to\infty}\frac{1}{T}\int_T^{2T}|L(\sigma + i\varphi(t),\chi) - L_N(\sigma + i\varphi(t),\chi)|\, dt = 0.$$

Since $\sigma > \frac{n-1}{2}$, we have $\sigma - \frac{n}{2} + 1 > \frac{1}{2}$. Therefore, for $\sigma > \frac{n-1}{2}$,

$$\lim_{N\to\infty}\limsup_{T\to\infty}\frac{1}{T}\int_T^{2T}\left|L\left(\sigma - \frac{n}{2} + 1 + i\varphi(t),\psi_l\right) - L_N\left(\sigma - \frac{n}{2} + 1 + i\varphi(t),\psi_l\right)\right| dt = 0.$$

Hence,
$$\lim_{N\to\infty}\limsup_{T\to\infty}\frac{1}{T}\int_T^{2T}|\zeta(\sigma + i\varphi(t);Q) - \zeta_N(\sigma + i\varphi(t);Q)|\, dt$$

$$\ll_Q \lim_{N\to\infty}\limsup_{T\to\infty}\frac{1}{T}\sum_{l=1}^{L}\int_T^{2T}\left|L\left(\sigma - \frac{n}{2} + 1 + i\varphi(t),\psi_l\right) - L_N\left(\sigma - \frac{n}{2} + 1 + i\varphi(t),\psi_l\right)\right| dt = 0.$$

□

3. Limit Theorems

We divide the proof of Theorem 1 into lemmas that are limit theorems in some spaces. We start with a lemma on the torus Ω. For $A \in \mathcal{B}(\Omega)$, define

$$Q_T(A) = \frac{1}{T}\mathrm{meas}\left\{t \in [T, 2T] : \left(p^{-i\varphi(t)} : p \in \mathbb{P}\right) \in A\right\}.$$

Lemma 3. *Suppose that $\varphi(t) \in W(T_0)$. Then Q_T converges weakly to the Haar measure m_H as $T \to \infty$.*

Proof. We will apply the Fourier transform method. Let $g_T(\underline{k})$, $\underline{k} = (k_p : k_p \in \mathbb{Z}, p \in \mathbb{P})$ be the Fourier transform of Q_T, i.e.,

$$g_T(\underline{k}) = \int_\Omega \left(\prod_{p \in \mathbb{P}}^* \omega^{k_p}(p) \right) dQ_T,$$

where "*" indicates that only a finite number of integers k_p are distinct from zero. Thus, by the definition of Q_T,

$$g_T(\underline{k}) = \frac{1}{T} \int_T^{2T} \prod_{p \in \mathbb{P}}^* \left(p^{-ik_p \varphi(t)} \right) dt = \frac{1}{T} \int_T^{2T} \exp\left\{ -i\varphi(t) \sum_{p \in \mathbb{P}}^* k_p \log p \right\} dt. \tag{10}$$

Obviously,

$$g_T(\underline{0}) = 1. \tag{11}$$

Now, suppose that $\underline{k} \neq \underline{0}$. Since the set $\{\log p : p \in \mathbb{P}\}$ is linearly independent over the field of rational numbers, we have

$$A_{\underline{k}} \stackrel{def}{=} \sum_{p \in \mathbb{P}}^* k_p \log p \neq 0.$$

Then

$$\int_T^{2T} \cos(A_{\underline{k}} \varphi(t)) dt = \frac{1}{A_{\underline{k}}} \int_T^{2T} \frac{1}{\varphi'(t)} d\sin(A_{\underline{k}} \varphi(t))$$

$$= \frac{1}{A_{\underline{k}}} \begin{cases} (\varphi'(T))^{-1} \int_T^\zeta d\sin(A_{\underline{k}} \varphi(t)) & \text{if } \varphi'(t) \text{ is increasing,} \\ (\varphi'(2T))^{-1} \int_\zeta^{2T} d\sin(A_{\underline{k}} \varphi(t)) & \text{if } \varphi'(t) \text{ is decreasing} \end{cases}$$

$$\ll \frac{1}{|A_{\underline{k}}|} \begin{cases} (\varphi'(T))^{-1} & \text{if } \varphi'(t) \text{ is increasing,} \\ (\varphi'(2T))^{-1} & \text{if } \varphi'(t) \text{ is decreasing,} \end{cases}$$

where $T \leq \zeta \leq 2T$. Since $\varphi(t) \in W(T_0)$,

$$\begin{cases} (\varphi'(T))^{-1} & \text{if } \varphi'(t) \text{ is increasing,} \\ (\varphi'(2T))^{-1} & \text{if } \varphi'(t) \text{ is decreasing} \end{cases} = o(T)$$

as $T \to \infty$. Therefore,

$$\int_T^{2T} \cos(A_{\underline{k}} \varphi(t)) dt = o(T), \quad T \to \infty. \tag{12}$$

Similarly, we find that

$$\int_T^{2T} \sin(A_{\underline{k}} \varphi(t)) dt = o(T), \quad T \to \infty.$$

Thus, (10)–(12) show that

$$\lim_{T \to \infty} g_T(\underline{k}) = \begin{cases} 1 & \text{if } \underline{k} = \underline{0}, \\ 0 & \text{if } \underline{k} \neq \underline{0}. \end{cases}$$

Since the right-hand side of the latter equality is the Fourier transform of the Haar measure m_H, the lemma is proved. □

For $A \in \mathcal{B}(\mathbb{C})$, define

$$P_{T,N,Q,\sigma}(A) = \frac{1}{T}\text{meas}\{t \in [T, 2T] : \zeta_N(\sigma + i\varphi(t); Q) \in A\}.$$

To prove the weak convergence for $P_{T,N,Q,\sigma}$ as $T \to \infty$, consider the function $u_{N,\sigma} : \Omega \to \mathbb{C}$ given by the formula

$$u_{N,\sigma}(\omega) = \zeta_N(\sigma, \omega; Q),$$

where

$$\zeta_N(\sigma, \omega; Q) = \sum_{m=1}^{\infty} \frac{w_N(m)\omega(m)}{m^\sigma},$$

and

$$\sum_{m=1}^{\infty} \frac{w_N(m)}{m^s}$$

is the Dirichlet series for $\zeta_N(s; Q)$. Clearly, the above series are absolutely convergent for $\sigma > \frac{n-1}{2}$. The absolute convergence of the series for $\zeta_N(s, \omega; Q)$ implies the continuity for the function u_N. Therefore, the function u_N is $(\mathcal{B}(\Omega), \mathcal{B}(\mathbb{C}))$-measurable, and we can define the probability measure $V_{N,\sigma} = m_H u_{N,\sigma}^{-1}$, where

$$m_H u_{N,\sigma}^{-1}(A) = m_H\left(u_{N,\sigma}^{-1} A\right), \quad A \in \mathcal{B}(\mathbb{C}).$$

Lemma 4. *Suppose that $\varphi(t) \in W(T_0)$ and $\sigma > \frac{n-1}{2}$ is fixed. Then, $P_{T,N,Q,\sigma}$ converges weakly to $V_{N,\sigma}$ as $T \to \infty$.*

Proof. By the definitions of $P_{T,N,Q,\sigma}$, Q_T and $u_{N,\sigma}$, for all $A \in \mathcal{B}(\mathbb{C})$,

$$P_{T,N,Q,\sigma}(A) = \frac{1}{T}\text{meas}\left\{\tau \in [T, 2T] : \left(p^{-i\varphi(t)} : p \in \mathbb{P}\right) \in u_{N,\sigma}^{-1}\right\} = Q_T\left(u_{N,\sigma}^{-1}\right).$$

Thus, $P_{T,N,Q,\sigma} = Q_T u_{N,\sigma}^{-1}$. Therefore, the lemma is a consequence of Theorem 5.1 from [10], continuity of $u_{N,\sigma}$ and Lemma 3. □

The measure $V_{N,\sigma}$ is very important for the proof of Theorem 1. Since $V_{N,\sigma}$ is independent of the function $\varphi(t)$, the following limit relation is true.

Lemma 5. *Suppose that $\sigma > \frac{n-1}{2}$ is fixed. Then $V_{N,\sigma}$ converges weakly to $P_{\zeta,Q,\sigma}$ as $N \to \infty$.*

Proof. In the proof of Theorem 2 from [4], it is obtained (relation (12)) that $V_{N,\sigma}$ converges weakly to a certain measure P_σ, and, at the end of the proof, the measure P_σ is identified by showing that $P_\sigma = P_{\zeta,Q,\sigma}$. □

For convenience, we recall Theorem 4.2 of [10]. Denote by $\xrightarrow{\mathcal{D}}$ the convergence in distribution.

Lemma 6. *Suppose that the space $(\mathbb{X}, \rho)$ is separable, and $\mathbb{X}$-valued random elements $Y_n, X_{1N}, X_{2N}, \ldots$ are defined on the same probability space with measure P. Let, for every k,*

$$X_{kN} \xrightarrow[N \to \infty]{\mathcal{D}} X_k,$$

and

$$X_k \xrightarrow[k \to \infty]{\mathcal{D}} X.$$

If, for every $\varepsilon > 0$,

$$\lim_{k \to \infty} \limsup_{N \to \infty} P(\rho(X_{kN}, Y_N) \geq \varepsilon) = 0,$$

then $Y_N \xrightarrow[N \to \infty]{\mathcal{D}} X$.

Proof of Theorem 1. Suppose that ξ_T is a random variable defined on a certain probability space $(\hat{\Omega}, \mathcal{B}(\hat{\Omega}), P)$ and distributed uniformly in $[T, 2T]$. Since the function $\varphi(t)$ is continuous, it is thus measurable, and $\varphi(\xi_T)$ is a random variable as well. Denote by $X_{N,\sigma}$ the complex valued random element having the distribution $V_{N,\sigma}$, and, on the probability space $(\hat{\Omega}, \mathcal{B}(\hat{\Omega}), P)$, define the random element

$$X_{T,N,\sigma} = \zeta_N(\sigma + i\varphi(\xi_T); Q).$$

Then, in view of Lemma 4,

$$X_{T,N,\sigma} \xrightarrow[T \to \infty]{\mathcal{D}} X_{N,\sigma}, \tag{13}$$

and, by Lemma 5,

$$X_{N,\sigma} \xrightarrow[N \to \infty]{\mathcal{D}} P_{\zeta,Q,\sigma}. \tag{14}$$

Define one more complex-valued random element

$$Y_{T,\sigma} = \zeta(\sigma + i\varphi(\xi_T); Q).$$

Then, an application of Lemma 2 gives, for $\varepsilon > 0$,

$$\lim_{N \to \infty} \limsup_{T \to \infty} P\{|X_{T,N,\sigma} - Y_{T,\sigma}| \geq \varepsilon\}$$

$$\leq \frac{1}{\varepsilon T} \int_T^{2T} |\zeta(s + i\varphi(t); Q) - \zeta_N(s + i\varphi(t); Q)| dt = 0.$$

This, relations (13) and (14) show that all hypotheses of Lemma 6 are satisfied. Therefore,

$$Y_{T,\sigma} \xrightarrow[T \to \infty]{\mathcal{D}} P_{\zeta,Q,\sigma},$$

and this is equivalent to the assertion of the theorem. □

4. Concluding Remarks

By Bohr and Jessen's works, it is known that the asymptotic behavior of the Dirichlet series can be characterized by probabilistic limit theorems. It turns out that Bohr–Jessen's ideas can also be applied for the Epstein zeta-function $\zeta(s; Q)$ whose definition involves a positive defined $n \times n$ matric Q. We prove that, for any fixed $\sigma > \frac{n-1}{2}$,

$$\frac{1}{T} \text{meas}\{t \in [T, 2T] : \zeta(\sigma + i\varphi(t); Q) \in A\}, \quad A \in \mathcal{B}(\mathbb{C}),$$

converges weakly to an explicitly given probability measure on $(\mathbb{C}, \mathcal{B}(\mathbb{C}))$ as $T \to \infty$. Here $\varphi(t)$ is an increasing differentiable function such that

$$\frac{\varphi(2t)}{\varphi'(t)} \ll t, \quad t \to \infty.$$

For example, $\varphi(t)$ can be a polynomials or the Gram function. We recall that the Gram function $g(t)$ is the solution of the equation

$$\theta(\tau) = (t-1)\pi, \quad t \geq 0,$$

where $\theta(\tau)$ is the increment of the argument of the function $\pi^{-\frac{s}{2}}\Gamma(\frac{s}{2})$ along the segment connecting the points $s = \frac{1}{2}$ and $s = \frac{1}{2} + i\tau$. It is known [11] that

$$g(t) = \frac{2\pi t}{\log t}(1 + o(1))$$

and

$$g'(t) = \frac{2\pi}{\log t}(1 + o(1))$$

as $t \to \infty$.

Author Contributions: Investigation, A.L. and R.M.; writing—original draft preparation, A.L. and R.M.; writing—review and editing, A.L. and R.M. All authors have read and agreed to the published version of the manuscript.

Funding: Renata Macaitienė is funded by the Research Council of Lithuania (LMTLT), agreement No. S-MIP-22-81.

Conflicts of Interest: The authors declare no conflict of interest.

References

1. Epstein, P. Zur Theorie allgemeiner Zetafunktionen. *Math. Ann.* **1903**, *56*, 615–644. [CrossRef]
2. Bohr, H.; Jessen, B. Über die Wertverteilung der Riemanschen Zetafunktion, Zweite Mitteilung. *Acta Math.* **1932**, *58*, 1–55. [CrossRef]
3. Laurinčikas, A. *Limit Theorems for the Riemann Zeta-Function*; Kluwer Academic Publishers: Dordrecht, The Netherlands; Boston, MA, USA; London, UK, 1996.
4. Laurinčikas, A.; Macaitienė, R. A Bohr-Jessen type theorem for the Epstein zeta-function. *Results Math.* **2018**, *73*, 147–163. [CrossRef]
5. Laurinčikas, A.; Macaitienė, R.; Šiaučiūnas, D. Generalization of the Voronin Theorem. *Lith. Math. J.* **2019**, *59*, 156–168. [CrossRef]
6. Fomenko, O.M. Order of the Epstein zeta-function in the critical strip. *J. Math. Sci.* **2002**, *110*, 3150–3163. [CrossRef]
7. Hecke, E. Über Modulfunktionen und die Dirichletchen Reihen mit Eulerscher Produktentwicklung. I, II. *Math. Ann.* **1937**, *114*, 1–28. 316–351. [CrossRef]
8. Iwaniec H. *Topics in Classical Automorphic Forms, Graduate Studies in Mathematics*; American Mathematical Society: Providence, RI, USA, 1997; Volume 17.
9. Nakamura, T.; Pańkowski, Ł. On zeros and c-values of Epstein zeta-functions. *Šiauliai Math. Semin.* **2013**, *8*, 181–195.
10. Billingsley, P. *Convergence of Probability Measures*; Willey: New York, NY, USA, 1968.
11. Korolev, M.A. Gram's law in the theory of the Riemann zeta-function. Part 1. *Proc. Steklov Inst. Math.* **2016**, *292*, 1–146. [CrossRef]

 *mathematics*

Article

Some Remarks on the Divisibility of the Class Numbers of Imaginary Quadratic Fields

Kwang-Seob Kim

Department of Mathematics, Chosun University, 309 Pilmundaero, Gwangju 61452, Korea; kwang12@chosun.ac.kr

Abstract: For a given integer n, we provide some families of imaginary quadratic number fields of the form $\mathbb{Q}(\sqrt{4q^2 - p^n})$, whose ideal class group has a subgroup isomorphic to $\mathbb{Z}/n\mathbb{Z}$.

Keywords: class number; imaginary quadratic fields; divisibility of class number

MSC: 11R29; 11R11

Citation: Kim, K.-S. Some Remarks on the Divisibility of the Class Numbers of Imaginary Quadratic Fields. *Mathematics* **2022**, *10*, 2488. https://doi.org/10.3390/math10142488

Academic Editors: Diana Savin, Nicusor Minculete and Vincenzo Acciaro

Received: 8 June 2022
Accepted: 10 July 2022
Published: 17 July 2022

Copyright: © 2022 by the authors. Licensee MDPI, Basel, Switzerland. This article is an open access article distributed under the terms and conditions of the Creative Commons Attribution (CC BY) license (https://creativecommons.org/licenses/by/4.0/).

1. Introduction

The class number of a number field is by definition the order of the ideal class group of its ring of integers. Thus, a number field has class number one if and only if its ring of integers is a principal ideal domain. In this sense, the ideal class group measures how far R is from being a principal ideal domain, and hence from satisfying unique prime factorization. The divisibility properties of class numbers are very important to know the structure of ideal class groups of number fields. Numerous results about the divisibility of the class numbers of quadratic fields have been introduced by many authors ([1–15]). By their works, it was shown that there exist infinitely many imaginary quadratic number fields whose ideal class numbers are multiples of n. They proved that there exist infinitely many imaginary quadratic number fields such that the ideal class group has a cyclic subgroup of order n. Most of such families are of the type $\mathbb{Q}(\sqrt{x^2 - t^n})$ or of the type $\mathbb{Q}(\sqrt{x^2 - 4t^n})$, where x and t are positive integers with some restrictions. (For the case of $\mathbb{Q}(\sqrt{x^2 - t^n})$, see [1,2,6,7,9,11–13,15] and for the case of $\mathbb{Q}(\sqrt{x^2 - 4t^n})$ see [3–5,8,10,14]).

Recently, K. Chakraborty, A. Hoque, Y. Kishi and P.P. Pandey considered the family $K_{p,q} = \mathbb{Q}(\sqrt{q^2 - p^n})$ when p and q were distinct odd prime numbers and $n \geq 3$ was an odd integer (see Theorem 1.2 of [2]). However, they just dealt with the case when n was an odd integer. We want to deal with the case when n is an even integer. In this article, we treat the family $K_{p,2q} = \mathbb{Q}(\sqrt{4q^2 - p^n})$ when p and q are distinct odd prime numbers.

2. Preliminaries

In this section, we review some previous results which we will use.

2.1. Being a pth Power

Proposition 1. *(Proposition 2.2 in [2]). Let $d \equiv 5 \pmod{8}$ be an integer and ℓ be a prime. For odd integers a, b, we have*

$$\left(\frac{a + b\sqrt{d}}{2}\right)^\ell \in \mathbb{Z}[d] \text{ if and only if } \ell = 3.$$

Definition 1. *If L/K is a Galois extension and α is in L, then the trace of α is the sum of all the Galois conjugates of α, i.e.,*

$$Tr(\alpha) = \sum_{\sigma \in \mathrm{Gal}(L/K)} \sigma(\alpha),$$

where $\text{Gal}(L/K)$ denotes the Galois group of L/K.

Lemma 1. *(Lemma 4 in [10]). Let K be a quadratic number field and O_K be its ring of algebraic integers. If $\alpha \in O_K$, then α is a square in O_K if and only if there exists $A \in \mathbb{Z}$ such that $N(\alpha) = A^2$ and such that $Tr(\alpha) + 2A$ is a square in $\mathbb{Z}$. If K is imaginary, we may assume that $A \geq 0$.*

2.2. Result of Y. Bugeaud and T. N. Shorey

In this section, we review a result of Y. Bugeaud and T.N. Shorey (see [16]). Let F_n be the nth Fibonacci sequence and L_n be the nth Lucas sequence. Let us define the sets $\mathcal{F}$ and $\mathcal{G} \subset \mathbb{N} \times \mathbb{N} \times \mathbb{N}$ by

$$\mathcal{F} := \{(F_{h_1 - 2\epsilon}, L_{h_1 + \epsilon}, F_{h_1}) | h_1 \in \mathbb{N} \text{ s.t. } h_1 \geq 2 \text{ and } \epsilon \in \{\pm 1\}\}$$

and

$$\mathcal{G} := \{(1, 4p_1^{h_2} - 1, p_1) | p_1 \text{ is a prime number and } h_2 \in \mathbb{N}\}.$$

For $\lambda \in \{1, \sqrt{2}, 2\}$, we define the set $\mathcal{H}_\lambda \subset \mathbb{N} \times \mathbb{N} \times \mathbb{N}$ by

$$\mathcal{H}_\lambda := \left\{ (D_1, D_2, p) \,\middle|\, \begin{array}{l} D_1, D_2 \text{ and } p \text{ are mutually coprime positive integers with} \\ p \text{ an odd prime and there exist positive integers } r, s \text{ such} \\ \text{that } D_1 s^2 + D_2 = \lambda^2 p^r \text{ and } 3D_1 s^2 - D_2 = \pm \lambda^2 \end{array} \right\}$$

Theorem 1. *(Theorem 1 in [16]). Let D_1, D_2 and p be mutually coprime positive integers with p a prime number. Let $\lambda \in \{1, \sqrt{2}, 2\}$ be such that $\lambda = 2$ if $p = 2$. We assume that D_2 is odd if $\lambda \in \{\sqrt{2}, 2\}$. Then, the number of positive integer solutions (x, y) of the equation*

$$D_1 x^2 + D_2 = \lambda^2 p^y \tag{1}$$

is at most one except for

$$(\lambda, D_1, D_2, p) \in \mathcal{E} := \left\{ \begin{array}{l} (2, 13, 3, 2), (\sqrt{2}, 7, 11, 3), (1, 2, 1, 3), (2, 7, 1, 2), \\ (\sqrt{2}, 1, 1, 5), (\sqrt{2}, 1, 1, 13), (2, 1, 3, 7). \end{array} \right\}$$

or

$$(D_1, D_2, p) \in \mathcal{F} \cup \mathcal{G} \cup \mathcal{H}_\lambda.$$

We recall the result of J.H.E Cohn [17] about the appearance of squares in the Lucas sequence.

Theorem 2. *Let L_n be the nth Lucas sequence. Then, the only perfect square appearing in the Lucas sequences are $L_1 = 1$ and $L_3 = 4$.*

3. Main Result

In this section, we will describe the main result. Here is the crucial theorem.

Theorem 3. *Suppose that $n \geq 3$ is an integer and q is an odd prime number such that $(q, n) = 1$ and $q \not\equiv \pm 1 \pmod{\ell}$ for all odd prime number $\ell \neq 3$ dividing n. Let p be an odd prime number with $4q^2 < p^n$ and $(q, p) = 1$. Let d be the square-free part of $4q^2 - p^n$, i.e., $4q^2 - p^n = m^2 d$ for some positive integer m. Assume that $2q \not\equiv \pm 1 \pmod{|d|}$. Moreover, we assume $q \not\equiv 2 \pmod 3$ when $3 | n$. Then, we have the following:*

(i) Assume that n is an even integer or $p \equiv 1 \pmod 4$. Then, the class number of $K_{p,2q} = \mathbb{Q}(\sqrt{d})$ is divisible by n.

(ii) Assume that n is an odd integer and $p \equiv 3 \pmod 4$. Moreover, we assume $p^{n/3} \neq (4q+1)/3$ when $3|n$. Then, the class number of $K_{p,2q} = \mathbb{Q}(\sqrt{d})$ is divisible by n.

Remark 1. *By Dirichlet's theorem on arithmetic progressions, we know that there exist infinitely many q such that $q \not\equiv \pm 1 \pmod{\ell}$ for all odd prime number $\ell \neq 3$ dividing n.*

Theorem 4. *Let n, q be as in Theorem 3. For each q, the class number of $K_{p,2q}$ is divisible by n for all but finitely many p's. Furthermore, for each q there are infinitely many fields $K_{p,2q}$.*

4. Proof of Main Theorem

4.1. Crucial Proposition

Lemma 2. *Let p, d and m be as in Theorem 3 (i) or (ii). Let ℓ be an odd prime such that*

$$\alpha = 2q + m\sqrt{d} = (a + b\sqrt{d})^\ell$$

for some integer a and b. Then, $a | 2q$ if and only if $-a | 2q$.

Proof. Suppose that

$$\alpha = 2q + m\sqrt{d} = (a + b\sqrt{d})^\ell.$$

If we compare the real parts, we know that

$$2q = a^\ell + \sum_{i=1}^{(\ell-1)/2} \binom{\ell}{2i} a^{\ell-2i} b^{2i} d^i.$$

This implies that $a | 2q$. Since $a | 2q$, we also know that $-a | 2q$. Similarly, $-a | 2q$ implies that $a | 2q$. □

Proposition 2. *Let n, q, p, d and m be as in Theorem 3 (i) or (ii). Then, the element $\alpha = 2q + m\sqrt{d}$ is not an ℓth power of an element in the ring of integers of $K_{p,2q}$ for any odd prime divisor ℓ of n. In addition, α and $-\alpha$ are not a square in $\mathcal{O}_{K_{p,2q}}$.*

Proof. (i) Assume that n is an even integer or $p \equiv 1 \pmod{4}$. Moreover, we assume $p^{n/3} \neq (q+16)/3$ when $3 | n$. Since n is an even integer or $p \equiv 1 \pmod{4}$, we know that $d \equiv 3 \pmod{4}$. Let ℓ be an odd prime divisor of n. If $\alpha = 2q + m\sqrt{d}$ is an ℓth power, then

$$\alpha = 2q + m\sqrt{d} = (a + b\sqrt{d})^\ell$$

for some integer a and b. If we compare the real parts, we know that

$$2q = a^\ell + \sum_{i=1}^{(\ell-1)/2} \binom{\ell}{2i} a^{\ell-2i} b^{2i} d^i.$$

This implies that $a | 2q$. By Lemma 2, we can assume that $a = 2q, a = q, a = 2$ or $a = 1$.

Case (i-A1): $a = 2, \ell \neq 3$
Comparing the real parts, we have

$$2q = (\pm 2)^\ell + \sum_{i=1}^{(\ell-1)/2} \binom{\ell}{2i} (\pm 2)^{\ell-2i} b^{2i} d^i \equiv \pm 2 \pmod{\ell}.$$

From these, we have $q \equiv \pm 1 \pmod{\ell}$, which violates our assumption.

Case (i-A2): $a = 2, \ell = 3$
Suppose that

$$\alpha = 2q + m\sqrt{d} = (2 + b\sqrt{d})^3.$$

Comparing the real parts, we have

$$2q = 8 + 6b^2 d. \tag{2}$$

Since $d < 0$, we have $q = 4 + 3b^2 d < 0$. This is impossible.

Case (i-B1): $a = q$, $\ell \neq 3$
Comparing the real parts, we have

$$2q = (\pm q)^\ell + \sum_{i=1}^{(\ell-1)/2} \binom{\ell}{2i} (\pm q)^{\ell-2i} b^{2i} d^i \equiv \pm q \pmod{\ell}.$$

Thus, we get $3q \equiv 0 \pmod{\ell}$ or $q \equiv 0 \pmod{\ell}$, which contradicts the assumption "$(q, n) = 1$" and "$\ell \neq 3$".

Case (i-B2): $a = q$, $\ell = 3$
Suppose that

$$\alpha = 2q + m\sqrt{d} = (q + b\sqrt{d})^3.$$

Comparing the real parts, we have

$$2q = q^3 + 3qb^2 d. \tag{3}$$

By (3), we have $2 = q^2 + 3b^2 d$, and hence $2 \equiv q^2 \pmod{3}$. This is impossible.

Case (i-C): $a = 2q$
We have $2q + m\sqrt{d} = (2q + b\sqrt{d})^\ell$. Taking the norm on both sides, we obtain

$$p^n = (4q^2 - b^2 d)^\ell.$$

If we write $D_1 = -d > 0$, we have

$$D_1 b^2 + 4q^2 = p^{n/\ell}.$$

We also obtain

$$D_1 m^2 + 4q^2 = p^n.$$

Then, we easily know that $(|b|, n/\ell)$ and (m, n) are distinct solutions of (1) for $D_1 = -d > 0$, $D_2 = 4q^2$, $\lambda = 1$. The next thing we have to do is to show that $(1, D_1, D_2, p) \notin \mathcal{E}$ and $(D_1, D_2, p) \notin \mathcal{F} \cup \mathcal{G} \cup \mathcal{H}_\lambda$. Clearly, $(1, D_1, D_2, p) \notin \mathcal{E}$ and $(D_1, D_2, p) \notin \mathcal{G}$. By Theorem 2, we know that $(D_1, D_2, p) \notin \mathcal{F}$. Finally suppose that $(D_1, D_2, p) \in \mathcal{H}_\lambda$. Then, there exist positive integers r, s such that

$$3D_1 s^2 - 4q^2 = \pm 1 \tag{4}$$

and

$$D_1 s^2 + 4q^2 = p^r. \tag{5}$$

By (4), we have $q \neq 3$, and hence we have $3D_1 s^2 - 4q^2 = -1$. From this together with (5), we obtain

$$16q^2 = 3p^r + 1,$$

that is,

$$(4q - 1)(4q + 1) = 3p^r.$$

This implies that $4q - 1 = 1$ or $4q - 1 = 3$. It contradicts the fact that q is an odd prime number. Hence, $(D_1.D_2, p) \notin \mathcal{H}_1$. By Theorem 1, the equation

$$-dx^2 + 4q^2 = p^y$$

has at most one integer solutions (x, y). Thus, $a \neq 2q$.

Case (i-D) : $a = 1$
Comparing the real parts, we have

$$2q = (1)^\ell + \sum_{i=1}^{(\ell-1)/2} \binom{\ell}{2i} (1)^{\ell-2i} b^{2i} d^i \equiv 1 \pmod{|d|}.$$

It contradicts our assumption "$2q \equiv 1 \pmod{|d|}$".

(ii) Assume that n is an odd integer and $p \equiv 3 \pmod 4$. Then, we know that $d \equiv 1 \pmod 4$. Moreover, we assume $p^{n/3} \neq (4q+1)/3$ when $3 | n$. Let ℓ be an odd prime divisor of n. If $\alpha = 2q + m\sqrt{d}$ is an ℓth power, then

$$\alpha = 2q + m\sqrt{d} = \left(\frac{a + b\sqrt{d}}{2} \right)^\ell, \ a \equiv b \pmod 2.$$

for some integer a and b. In case both a and b are even, then we can proceed as in the above and obtain a contradiction. Thus, we can assume that both a and b are odd. If we take the norm on both sides we obtain

$$4p^{n/\ell} = a^2 - b^2 d. \tag{6}$$

Since a and b are odd integers and $p \neq 2$, we can get $d \equiv 5 \pmod 8$. By Proposition 1, we know that $\ell = 3$. Thus, we have

$$\alpha = 2q + m\sqrt{d} = \left(\frac{a + b\sqrt{d}}{2} \right)^3.$$

Comparing the real parts, we have

$$16q = a(a^2 + 3b^2 d). \tag{7}$$

Since a is an odd integer, we have $a = 1$ or $a = q$.

Case (ii-A) : $a = 1$
By (7) and $d < 0$, we have $16q = 1 + 3b^2 d < 0$. This is not possible.

Case (ii-B) : $a = q$
By (6) and (7), we have

$$4p^{n/3} = q^2 - b^2 d \text{ and } 16 = q^2 + 3b^2 d.$$

From these, we have $3p^{n/3} = q^2 - 4 = (q-2)(q+2)$. This implies that $q - 2 = 3$ or $q + 2 = 3$. Since q is a prime, we have $q - 2 = 3$ and $p^{n/3} = q + 2 = 7$. These violate our assumption $p^{n/3} \neq (4q+1)/3$.
□

4.2. Proof of Theorem 3

Next, we prove Theorem 3.

Proof of Theorem 3. Let n, q, p, d and m be as in Theorem 3 (i) or (ii). Set $\alpha = 2q + m\sqrt{d}$. We can easily check that α and $\bar{\alpha}$ are coprime and $N(\alpha) = \alpha\bar{\alpha} = p^n$. This implies that $(\alpha) = \mathfrak{a}^n$ for some integral ideal $\mathfrak{a}$ of $K_{p,2q}$. It suffices to show that the order of $[\mathfrak{a}]$ in the ideal class group of $K_{p,2q}$ is n. If this is not the case, we have $(\alpha) = (\beta)^\ell$ for some integer β in $\mathcal{O}_{K_{p,2q}}$ and some prime divisor ℓ of n. Since $K_{p,2q}$ is an imaginary quadratic field, the only units of $\mathcal{O}_{K_{p,2q}}$ are ± 1. Thus, we have $\alpha = \pm \beta^\ell$. If ℓ is an odd prime, we have $\alpha = \gamma^\ell$ where $\gamma = \pm \beta$. This contradicts Proposition 2. Next, let us consider the case of $\ell = 2$. Then, we have $\alpha = \pm \beta^2$. It means that α or $-\alpha$ is a square in $\mathcal{O}_{K_{p,2q}}$, which contradicts Proposition 2. Hence, the order of $[\mathfrak{a}]$ in the ideal class group of $K_{p,2q}$ is n. □

4.3. Proof of Theorem 4

We are now in a position to prove the main theorem

Proof. Let n and q be as in Theorem 3. For any positive integer D, the curve

$$DX^2 + 4q^2 = Y^n \tag{8}$$

is an irreducible algebraic curve of genus > 0 (see [18]). By Siegel's theorem (see [19]), there are only finitely many integral points (X, Y) on the curve (8). Thus, for each $d < 0$, there are at most finitely many primes p such that

$$-dx^2 + 4q^2 = p^n.$$

It means that there are infinitely many fields $K_{p,2q}$ for the fixed prime q. In addition, we have $|d| > 2q + 1$ for sufficiently large p, so $2q \not\equiv \pm 1 \pmod{|d|}$. Further, if p is large enough, then $p^{n/3} \neq (q+16)/3$ and $p^{n/3} \neq (4q+1)/3$. Hence, the class number of $K_{p,2q}$ is divisible by n for a sufficiently large p. □

5. Numerical Examples

In this section, we give several examples. All computations in this section are based on the Magma program. For example, Table 1 is the list of imaginary quadratic fields $K_{p,2q}$ corresponding to $n = 3$ and $p \leq 19$. In the below Tables 2–8, we use * in the column for class number to indicate the failure of condition "$p^{n/3} \neq (q+16)/3$" or "$p^{n/3} \neq (4q+1)/3$". Furthermore, the appearance of ** in the column for a class number indicates the failure of condition "$2q \not\equiv \pm 1 \pmod{|d|}$". Finally, the appearance of *** in the column for a class number indicates the failure of condition "$q \not\equiv \pm 1 \pmod{\ell}$" for an odd prime divisor $\ell \neq 3$ of n.

Table 1. Numerical examples for $n = 3$.

p	q	$4q^2 - p^3$	d	$h(d)$	p	q	$4q^2 - p^3$	d	$h(d)$
7	5	-243	-3	1 *	11	5	-1231	-1231	27
11	7	-1135	-1135	18	11	13	-655	-655	12
11	17	-175	-7	1 *	13	5	-2097	-233	12
13	7	-2001	-2001	48	13	11	-1713	-1713	36
13	17	-1041	-1041	36	13	19	-753	-753	12
17	5	-4813	-4813	30	17	7	-4717	-4717	24
17	11	-4429	-4429	60	17	13	-4237	-4237	24
17	19	-3469	-3469	30	17	23	-2797	-2797	18
17	29	-1549	-1549	18	17	31	-1069	-1069	30
19	5	-6759	-751	15	19	7	-6663	-6663	60
19	11	-6375	-255	12	19	13	-6183	-687	12
19	17	-5703	-5703	54	19	23	-4743	-527	18
19	29	-3495	-3495	36	19	31	-3015	-335	18
19	37	-1383	-1383	18	19	41	-135	-15	2 *

Table 2. Numerical examples for $n = 4$.

p	q	$4q^2 - p^4$	d	$h(d)$	p	q	$4q^2 - p^4$	d	$h(d)$
5	3	−589	−589	16	5	7	−429	−429	16
5	11	−141	−141	8	7	3	−2365	−2365	32
7	5	−2301	−2301	48	7	11	−1917	−213	8
7	13	−1725	−69	8	7	17	−1245	−1245	32
7	19	−957	−957	16	7	23	−285	−285	16
11	3	−14,605	14,605	80	11	5	−14,541	−14,541	64
11	7	−14,445	1605	16	11	13	−13,965	−285	16
11	17	−13,485	−13,485	128	11	19	−13,197	−13,197	48
11	23	−12,525	−501	16	11	29	−11,277	−11,277	32
11	31	−10,797	−10,797	64	11	37	−9165	−9165	64
11	41	−7917	−7917	32	11	43	−7245	−805	16
11	47	−5805	−645	16	11	53	−3405	−3405	48
11	59	−717	−717	16					

Table 3. Numerical examples for $n = 5$.

p	q	$4q^2 - p^5$	d	$h(d)$	p	q	$4q^2 - p^5$	d	$h(d)$
3	7	−47	−47	5	5	3	−3089	−3089	40
5	7	−2929	−2929	40	5	11	−2641	−2641	20
5	13	−2449	−2449	40	5	17	−1969	−1969	20
5	19	−1681	−1	1 **	5	23	−1009	−1009	20
7	3	−16,771	−16,771	40	7	5	−16,707	−16,707	20
7	11	−16,323	−16,323	30	7	13	−16,131	−16,131	40
7	17	−15,651	−1739	20	7	19	−15,363	−1707	10
7	23	−14,691	−14,691	40	7	29	−13,443	−13,443	30
7	31	−12,963	−12,963	20	7	37	−11,331	−1259	15
7	41	−10,083	−10,083	20	7	43	−9411	−9411	30
7	47	−7971	−7971	30	7	53	−5571	−619	5
7	59	−2883	−3	1 **	7	61	−1923	−1923	10

Table 4. Numerical examples for $n = 6$.

p	q	$4q^2 - p^6$	d	$h(d)$	p	q	$4q^2 - p^6$	d	$h(d)$
3	5	−629	−629	36	3	7	−533	−533	12
3	11	−245	−5	2 *	3	13	−53	−53	6
5	3	−15,589	−15,589	72	5	7	−15,429	−15,429	96
5	11	−15,141	−309	12	5	13	−14,949	−1661	48
5	17	−14,469	−14,469	96	5	19	−14,181	−14,181	96
5	23	−13,509	−1501	24	5	29	−12,261	−12,261	72
5	31	−11,781	−1309	24	5	37	−10,149	−10,149	120
5	41	−8901	−989	36	5	43	−8229	−8229	48
5	47	−6789	−6789	72	5	53	−4389	−4389	48
5	59	−1701	−21	4 *	5	61	−741	−741	24
7	3	−117,613	−117,613	168	7	5	−117,549	−13,061	156
7	11	−117,165	−117,165	240	7	13	−116,973	−12,997	60
7	17	−116,493	−116,493	192	7	19	−116,205	−116,205	192
7	23	−115,533	−12,837	72	7	29	−114,285	−114,285	240
7	31	−113,805	−1405	24	7	37	−112,173	−112,173	240
7	41	−110,925	−493	12	7	43	−110,253	−110,253	288

Table 4. *Cont.*

p	q	$4q^2 - p^6$	d	$h(d)$	p	q	$4q^2 - p^6$	d	$h(d)$
7	47	−108,813	−108,813	240	7	53	−106,413	−106,413	216
7	59	−103,725	−461	30	7	61	−102,765	−102,765	192
7	67	−99,693	−11,077	48	7	71	−97,485	−97,485	192
7	73	−96,333	−96,333	192	7	79	−92,685	−92,685	288
7	83	−90,093	−90,093	192	7	89	−85,965	−85,965	240
7	97	−80,013	−80,013	192	7	101	−76,845	−76,845	192
7	103	−75,213	−8357	72	7	107	−71,853	−71,853	144
7	109	−70,125	−2805	48	7	113	−66,573	−7397	72
7	127	−53,133	−53,133	120	7	131	−49,005	−5	2 *
7	137	−42,573	−42,573	120	7	139	−40,365	−4485	48
7	149	−28,845	−3205	24	7	151	−26,445	−26,445	96
7	157	−19,053	−2117	36	7	163	−11,373	−11,373	72
7	167	−6093	−677	30					

Table 5. Numerical examples for $n = 7$.

p	q	$4q^2 - p^7$	d	$h(d)$	p	q	$4q^2 - p^7$	d	$h(d)$
3	5	−2087	−2087	35	3	11	−1703	−1703	28
3	13	−1511	−1511	49	3	17	−1031	−1031	35
3	19	−743	−743	21	3	23	−71	−71	7
5	3	−78,089	−78,089	280	5	11	−77,641	−77,641	112
5	13	−77,449	−77,449	112	5	17	−76,969	−76,969	196
5	19	−76,681	−76,681	140	5	23	−76,009	−76,009	224
5	29	−74,761	−74,761	140	5	31	−74,281	−74,281	140
5	37	−72,649	−72,649	168	5	41	−71,401	−71,401	140
5	43	−70,729	−70,729	140	5	47	−69,289	−69,289	196
5	53	−66,889	−66,889	112	5	59	−64,201	−64,201	112
5	61	−63,241	−63,241	196	5	67	−60,169	−60,169	112
5	71	−57,961	−57,961	112	5	73	−56,809	−56,809	112
5	79	−53,161	−53,161	168	5	83	−50,569	−50,569	168
5	89	−46,441	−46,441	140	5	97	−40,489	−40,489	140
5	101	−37,321	−37,321	84	5	103	−35,689	−35,689	112
5	107	−32,329	−32,329	140	5	109	−30,601	−30,601	112
5	113	−27,049	−27,049	84	5	127	−13,609	−13,609	56
5	131	−9481	−9481	84	5	137	−3049	−3049	28
5	139	−841	−1	1 **					

Table 6. Numerical examples for $n = 8$.

p	q	$4q^2 - p^8$	d	$h(d)$	p	q	$4q^2 - p^8$	d	$h(d)$
3	5	−6461	−6461	96	3	7	−6365	−6365	64
3	11	−6077	−6077	48	3	13	−5885	−5885	96
3	17	−5405	−5405	64	3	19	−5117	−5117	64
3	23	−4445	−4445	64	3	29	−3197	−3197	64
3	31	−2717	−2717	32	3	37	−1085	−1085	32

158

Table 7. Numerical examples for $n = 9$.

p	q	$4q^2 - p^9$	d	$h(d)$	p	q	$4q^2 - p^9$	d	$h(d)$
3	5	−19,583	−19,583	99	3	7	−19,487	−19,487	144
3	11	−19,199	−19,199	162	3	13	−19,007	−19,007	108
3	17	−18,527	−18,527	108	3	19	−18,239	−18,239	144
3	23	−17,567	−17,567	90	3	29	−16,319	−16,319	153
3	31	−15,839	−15,839	180	3	37	−14,207	−14,207	81
3	41	−12,959	−12,959	99	3	43	−12,287	−12,287	90
3	47	−10,847	−10,847	63	3	53	−8447	−8447	99
3	59	−5759	−5759	108	3	61	−4799	−4799	63
3	67	−1727	−1727	36					

Table 8. Numerical examples for $n = 10$.

p	q	$4q^2 - p^{10}$	d	$h(d)$	p	q	$4q^2 - p^{10}$	d	$h(d)$
3	7	−58,853	−58,853	180	3	11	−58,565	−58,565	240
3	13	−58,373	−58,373	240	3	17	−57,893	−57,893	280
3	23	−56,933	−197	10	3	29	−55,685	−55,685	160
3	31	−55,205	−55,205	240	3	37	−53,573	−317	10
3	41	−52,325	−2093	40	3	43	−51,653	−51,653	160
3	47	−50,213	−50,213	120	3	53	−47,813	−47,813	260
3	59	−45,125	−5	2 ***	3	61	−44,165	−365	20
3	67	−41,093	−41,093	240	3	71	−38,885	−38,885	160
3	73	−37,733	−37,733	160	3	79	−34,085	−34,085	200
3	83	−31,493	−31,493	120	3	89	−27,365	−27,365	120
3	97	−21,413	−437	20	3	101	−18,245	−18,245	160
3	103	−16,613	−16,613	100	3	107	−13,253	−13,253	80
3	109	−11,525	−461	30	3	113	−7973	−7973	80

Funding: This study was supported by research funds from Chosun University 2022.

Conflicts of Interest: The author declares no conflict of interest.

References

1. Ankeny, N.; Chowla, S. On the divisibility of the class numbers of quad-ratic fields. *Pac. J. Math.* **1955**, *5*, 321–324. [CrossRef]
2. Chakraborty, K.; Hoque, A.; Kishi, Y.; Pandey, P.P. Divisibility of the class numbers of imaginary quadratic fields. *J. Number Theory* **2018**, *185*, 339–348. [CrossRef]
3. Cohn, J.H.E. On the class number of certain imaginary quadratic fields. *Proc. Am. Math. Soc.* **2002**, *130*, 1275–1277. [CrossRef]
4. Gross, B.H.; Rohrlich, D.E. Some results on the Mordell–Weil group of the Jacobian of the Fermat curve. *Invent. Math.* **1978**, *44*, 201–224. [CrossRef]
5. Ishii, K. On the divisibility of the class number of imaginary quadratic fields. *Proc. Jpn. Acad. Ser. A* **2011**, *87*, 142–143. [CrossRef]
6. Ito, A. A note on the divisibility of class numbers of imaginary quadratic fields $\mathbb{Q}(\sqrt{a^2 - k^n})$. *Proc. Jpn. Acad. Ser. A* **2011**, *87*, 151–155. [CrossRef]
7. Ito, A. Remarks on the divisibility of the class numbers of imaginary quad-ratic fields $\mathbb{Q}(\sqrt{2^{2k} - q^n})$. *Glasg. Math. J.* **2011**, *53*, 379–389. [CrossRef]
8. Ito, A. Notes on the divisibility of the class numbers of imaginary quadratic fields $\mathbb{Q}(\sqrt{3^{2e} - 4k^n})$. *Abh. Math. Semin. Univ. Hambg.* **2015**, *85*, 1–21. [CrossRef]
9. Kishi, Y. Note on the divisibility of the class number of certain imaginary quadratic fields. *Glasg. Math. J.* **2009**, *51*, 187–191. [CrossRef]
10. Louboutin, S.R. On the divisibility of the class number of imaginary quadratic number fields. *Proc. Am. Math. Soc.* **2009**, *137*, 4025–4028. [CrossRef]
11. Murty, M.R. The ABC conjecture and exponents of class groups of quadrat-ic fields. *Contemp. Math.* **1998**, *210*, 85–95.
12. Murty, M.R. Exponents of class groups of quadratic fields. In *Topics in Number Theory*; Mathematics and Its Applications; Kluwer Academic Publishers: University Park, PA, USA; Dordrecht, The Netherlands, 1999; Volume 467, pp. 229–239.
13. Soundararajan, K. Divisibility of class numbers of imaginary quad-ratic fields. *J. Lond. Math. Soc.* **2000**, *61*, 681–690. [CrossRef]
14. Yamamoto, Y. On unramified Galois extensions of quadratic number fields. *Osaka J. Math.* **1970**, *7*, 57–76.

15. Zhu, M.; Wang, T. The divisibility of the class number of the imaginary quadratic field $\mathbb{Q}(\sqrt{2^{2m}-k^n})$. *Glasg. Math. J.* **2012**, *54*, 149–154.
16. Bugeaud, Y.; Shorey, T.N. On the number of solutions of the generalized Ra-manujan–Nagell equation. *J. Reine Angew. Math.* **2001**, *539*, 55–74.
17. Cohn, J.H.E. Square Fibonacci numbers, etc. *Fibonacci Quart.* **1964**, *2*, 109–113.
18. Schmidt, W.M. *Equations over Finite Fields, an Elementary Approach*; Lecture Notes in Math.; Springer: Berlin, Germany; New York, NY, USA, 1976; Volume 536.
19. Evertse, J.-H.; Silverman, J.H. Uniform bounds for the number of solutions to $Y^n = f(X)$. *Math. Proc. Cambridge Philos. Soc.* **1986**, *100*, 237–248. [CrossRef]

Article

Novel Authentication Protocols Based on Quadratic Diophantine Equations

Avinash Vijayarangan [1,†], Veena Narayanan [2,*,†], Vijayarangan Natarajan [3,†] and Srikanth Raghavendran [2,†]

1. School of Computing, SASTRA Deemed University, Thanjavur 613401, India
2. School of Arts, Science, Humanities and Education, SASTRA Deemed University, Thanjavur 613401, India
3. Travel and Hospitality-Strategic Initiative Group, TCS Ltd., Chennai 600113, India
* Correspondence: veenanarayanan@maths.sastra.ac.in
† These authors contributed equally to this work.

Abstract: The Diophantine equation is a strong research domain in number theory with extensive cryptography applications. The goal of this paper is to describe certain geometric properties of positive integral solutions of the quadratic Diophantine equation $x_1^2 + x_2^2 = y_1^2 + y_2^2$ ($x_1, x_2, y_1, y_2 > 0$), as well as their use in communication protocols. Given one pair (x_1, y_1), finding another pair (x_2, y_2) satisfying $x_1^2 + x_2^2 = y_1^2 + y_2^2$ is a challenge. A novel secure authentication mechanism based on the positive integral solutions of the quadratic Diophantine which can be employed in the generation of one-time passwords or e-tokens for cryptography applications is presented. Further, the constructive cost models are applied to predict the initial effort and cost of the proposed authentication schemes.

Keywords: Diophanitne equation; trapdoor functions; authentication communication protocols

MSC: 11D09; 11T71

Citation: Vijayarangan, A.; Narayanan, V.; Natarajan, V.; Raghavendran, S. Novel Authentication Protocols Based on Quadratic Diophantine Equations. *Mathematics* 2022, 10, 3136. https://doi.org/10.3390/math10173136

Academic Editors: Diana Savin, Nicusor Minculete and Vincenzo Acciaro

Received: 10 August 2022
Accepted: 29 August 2022
Published: 1 September 2022

Copyright: © 2022 by the authors. Licensee MDPI, Basel, Switzerland. This article is an open access article distributed under the terms and conditions of the Creative Commons Attribution (CC BY) license (https://creativecommons.org/licenses/by/4.0/).

1. Introduction

Number theory is the branch of mathematics that focuses on the appealing qualities of integers. Number theory is known as the Queen of Mathematics because of many unanswered problems it contains. With the advancement of supercomputers, number theory is now used in various engineering domains, particularly in cryptography. Everybody relies on online exchanges in the current advanced period, where security plays an enormous role. To ensure online safety, cryptographic algorithms that are developed using number theoretic ideas play a significant task. Cryptography is typically defined as the study of mathematical approaches for achieving various information security goals such as secrecy, authenticity, integrity, non-repudiation, and so on. The term refers to a subset of strategies rather than the mechanism of delivering data security. In most cryptographic algorithms, the generation of large prime numbers is required to encrypt and decrypt the messages passed through the online channel.

The reasoning of Diophantine equations and their applications is a growing field in number theory. The Diophantine equation is a multivariate polynomial equation with integer coefficients which seeks only integral solutions. Subsequently, the Diophantine problem is notable to be a difficult problem and is relied upon to be utilized in cryptography applications. In general, Diophantine equations have been solved by considering the ring of integers, Z. But, because of its arising applications, presently the specialists are begun to think about the problem over arbitrary rings. The linear Diophantine equation $ax + by = c$ is the simplest form of the Diophantine equation, where a, b, c are integers and x, y are unknown integers. Another important class of Diophantine equation is the Pell's equation. The Indian mathematicians Brahmagupta and Bhaskara were the first to explore the Pell's equation. Since ancient times, Pell's Equation, which pertains to the cyclic group and has several solutions, has been used in the domain of number theory for a wide range of applications. Numerous disciplines are now addressing the binary quadratic Diophantine equations, both homogeneous and non-homogeneous. Since various Diophantine problems are evolving day by day, various mathematicians across the globe study these problems. Many cryptography methods have been developed based on these characteristics [1–8]. Thirumala et al. [9] recently devised an efficient technique based on Pell's equation that provides good reliability in opposition to side-channel exploits such as timing attacks. RSA (Rivest–Shamir–Adleman) is a widely used public key cryptographic method in security systems. Raghunandan et al. [10] used the generalized Pell's equation for compelling the safety of RSA.

A trapdoor function is one that is computationally simple in one direction but hard to determine in the reverse directions (identifying its inverse) without particular information. In cryptography, trapdoor functions are usually applied. Mathematically, if f is a trapdoor function, then there exists a secret information t, such that given $f(x)$ and t, it is straightforward to compute x. Making trapdoors is regarded as the core of the process of developing public key cryptosystems. Bijective trapdoor functions are universally recognized as adequate for public key cryptography [11,12]. The recent developments in the theory of trapdoor functions can be seen in [13,14]. An authentication protocol is a kind of protocol that is intended to secure the exchange of authentication data between two or more clients. The factors to be taken into account in the authentication process are

- A protocol must constitute at least two clients, and everyone associated must be aware of the protocol ahead of time.
- The protocol must be followed by all the concerned clients.
- The steps involved in the protocol must be well defined.
- A protocol must be comprehensive, containing instructions for every possible scenario.

"Smart" devices and technologies have enabled substantial advancements in industry revenue and safety in recent decades. Hernández-Álvarez et al. [15] developed a new device to avail estimates of the temperature of diabetic foot where cryptographic protocols are present to ensure data security. Bullón Pérez et al. [16] performed another interesting research on Blockchain systems in the retail sector. In 2017, Rey and Dios [17] carried out a critical review on cryptographic protocols on wireless sensor networks concentrating on secret key cryptosystems. Malware has now emerged as a possible threat to the IoT, and hence to Wireless Sensor Networks. Batista et al. [18] presented an Agent-Based design for assessing trojan transmission on these networks. Recently, Martinez et al. [19] performed a critical review on the cryptographic techniques associated with block chain and bitcoin. Okumura [20] developed a new public key cryptosystem based on Diophantine equations of degree increasing type. He used those type of Diophantine equations to recover the plaintext. Murthy and Swamy [21] derived a new authentication protocol as well as a new encryption-decryption algorithm based on the Pell's equation. Later, Alvarez et al. [22] and Youssef [23] modified the algorithm developed by [21]. Recently, Alecci and Dutto [24] studied the use of Pell hyperbolas in cryptosystems with security based on the discrete logarithm problem.

In the present work, the authors aim to develop a new authentication protocol based on the geometric properties of solutions of the second degree Diophantine equation $u_1^2 + u_2^2 = v_1^2 + v_2^2$ and also analysed the initial cost and effort required to develop a new software for this protocol using the basic constructive cost models (COCOMO).

2. Mathematical Properties of the Equation $u_1^2 + u_2^2 = v_1^2 + v_2^2$

This section deals with the study on mathematical properties of the equation $u_1^2 + u_2^2 = v_1^2 + v_2^2$.

Theorem 1. *The positive integral solutions of the Diophantine equation $u_1^2 + u_2^2 = v_1^2 + v_2^2$ do not lie on a straight line with slope $m = -\left[\frac{u_1 + v_1}{u_2 + v_2}\right]$.*

Proof. The Diophantine equation $u_1^2 + u_2^2 = v_1^2 + v_2^2$ can be written as

$$u_1^2 - v_1^2 = v_2^2 - u_2^2 \tag{1}$$

$$(u_1 - v_1)(u_1 + v_1) = (v_2 - u_2)(v_2 + u_2) \tag{2}$$

$$\frac{v_2 - u_2}{u_1 - v_1} = \frac{u_1 + v_1}{u_2 + v_2} \tag{3}$$

$$\frac{v_2 - u_2}{v_1 - u_1} = -\left[\frac{u_1 + v_1}{u_2 + v_2}\right] \tag{4}$$

Let $m = \frac{v_2 - u_2}{v_1 - u_1} = 1$ which is the slope of the straight line joining (u_1, u_2) and (v_1, v_2). It follows that the relationship (4) gives $u_1 + u_2 + v_1 + v_2 = 0$. It is not true due to positive integral solutions of the Diophantine equation. Hence the positive integral solutions do not lie on a straight line when $m = 1$. Also, (4) does not hold when $m > 1$ or $m < 1$. □

Note 1. *In general, a slope of the straight line joining (u_1, v_1) and (u_2, v_2) is $m = \frac{v_2 - v_1}{u_2 - u_1}$. The relationship (4) does not hold when $m > 1$ or $m < 1$. If $m < 1$, consider the case when $m = 0$. Then $\left[\frac{u_1 + v_1}{u_2 + v_2}\right] = 0$ implies that $u_1 = -v_1$. Also from (4), it is clear that $u_2 = v_2$ when $m = 0$. Hence, we obtain the solution of $u_1^2 + u_2^2 = v_1^2 + v_2^2$ as $\{u_1, u_2\}, \{-u_1, u_2\}$ which is considered as the equivalent solution but not distinct.*

Theorem 2. *Let one pair (u_1, v_1) of the Diophantine equation $u_1^2 + u_2^2 = v_1^2 + v_2^2$ be known. Then the distance δ between the constructed points (u_1, u_2) and (v_1, v_2) satisfies the condition $\frac{\delta^2}{2} > k$ where $k = u_1(u_1 - v_1)$ provided $u_2 > v_2$.*

Proof. Given one pair (u_1, v_1), finding out another pair (u_2, v_2) satisfying $u_1^2 + u_2^2 = v_1^2 + v_2^2$ is a challenge. Let δ be the distance between the constructed points (u_1, u_2) and (v_1, v_2), where u_2 and v_2 are unknown. Then $\delta = \sqrt{(v_1 - u_1)^2 + (v_2 - u_2)^2}$. This implies $\delta^2 = (v_1 - u_1)^2 + (v_2 - u_2)^2 = v_1^2 + u_1^2 - 2u_1v_1 + v_2^2 + u_2^2 - 2u_2v_2$. Since $u_1^2 + u_2^2 = v_1^2 + v_2^2$, $\delta^2 = 2(u_1^2 + u_2^2) - 2u_1v_1 - 2u_2v_2$. So $\frac{\delta^2}{2} = u_1(u_1 - v_1) + u_2(u_2 - v_2)$. Given (u_1, v_1), $u_1(u_1 - v_1)$ becomes a constant and let it be k. Then $\frac{\delta^2}{2} - k = u_2(u_2 - v_2) > 0$, provided $u_2 > v_2$. This implies that $\frac{\delta^2}{2} > k$. □

Theorem 3. *If one pair (u_1, v_1) is known, then the other point (u_2, v_2) of the Diophantine equation $u_1^2 + u_2^2 = v_1^2 + v_2^2$ satisfies $u_2 < v_2$ or $u_2 > v_2$.*

Proof. Consider $u_1^2 + u_2^2 = v_1^2 + v_2^2$. This can be written as $u_1^2 - v_1^2 = v_2^2 - u_2^2$ which implies $(u_1 - v_1)(u_1 + v_1) = (v_2 - u_2)(v_2 + u_2)$. Since all $u_i's$ and $v_i's$ are positive, $\frac{(u_1 - v_1)}{(v_2 - u_2)} > 0$. Thus $(u_1 - v_1) = k(v_2 - u_2); k > 0$. For the given (u_1, v_1), $(u_1 - v_1)$ is a constant. Let us assume that $(u_1 - v_1) < 0$. Then $(v_2 - u_2) < 0$ which implies $u_2 > v_2$. Similarly, if $(u_1 - v_1) > 0$, then $(v_2 - u_2) > 0$ which implies $u_2 < v_2$. □

Theorem 4. *If (u_1, v_1) is known and u_2 is chosen as $u_2 > u_1$ and $u_2 > v_1, v_2$ then the upper bound for the distance d between the points (u_1, v_1) and (u_2, v_2) which satisfies the relation $u_1^2 + u_2^2 = v_1^2 + v_2^2$ is given by $d^2 < 2\lambda^2(u_1 + v_1)^2$ where $\lambda > 0.5$.*

Proof. Let d be the distance between (u_1, v_1) and (u_2, v_2). Then, we have $d^2 = (v_2 - v_1)^2 + (u_2 - u_1)^2$. Since $u_2 > v_2$,

$$\begin{aligned} d^2 &< (u_2 - v_1)^2 + (u_2 - u_1)^2 \\ &= u_2^2 + v_1^2 - 2u_2v_1 + u_2^2 + u_1^2 - 2u_1u_2 \\ &= u_1^2 + 2u_2^2 + v_1^2 - 2u_1u_2 - 2u_2v_2 \end{aligned}$$

Since $u_2 > v_2$, $(v_2 - v_1) < u_2$ and $(u_2 - u_1) < u_2$. Thus $d^2 < 2u_2^2$. Since $u_2 > u_1, v_1$ we have $u_2 > \left(\frac{u_1 + v_1}{2}\right)$ or $u_2 = \lambda(u_1 + v_1)$, where $\lambda > 0.5$. Hence $\frac{d^2}{2} < \lambda^2(u_1 + v_1)^2$ follows. $\square$

Note 2. *Let one positive integral pair (u_1, v_1) of the Diophantine equation $u_1^2 + u_2^2 = v_1^2 + v_2^2$ be known. Then we are finding out the relationship between δ and d (from Theorems 2 and 4) given as*

$$\begin{aligned}
\delta^2 &= (v_1 - u_1)^2 + (v_2 - u_2)^2 = 2(u_1^2 + u_2^2) - 2u_1v_1 - 2u_2v_2 \\
d^2 &= (u_2 - u_1)^2 + (v_2 - v_1)^2 = 2(u_1^2 + u_2^2) - 2u_1u_2 - 2v_1v_2 \\
\delta^2 - d^2 &= 2(u_1u_2 + v_1v_2) - 2(u_1v_1 + u_2v_2) \\
\frac{\delta^2 - d^2}{2} &= u_1u_2 + v_1v_2 - t - u_2v_2, \text{ where } t = u_1v_1 \\
&< (u_1 + v_1)u_2 - u_2^2 - t, \text{ where } v_2 < u_2 \\
&= \alpha u_2 - u_2^2 - t, \text{ where } \alpha = u_1 + u_2
\end{aligned}$$

Example 1. *Let $u_1 = 1$ and $v_1 = 5$. Given $u_1 < v_1$. Then $\delta^2 = (5 - 1)^2 + (v_2 - u_2)^2 = 16 + (v_2 - u_2)^2$. It follows $\delta^2 > 17$ as $(v_2 - u_2)^2 \geq 1$. Now $d^2 < 1 + 25 + 2u_2^2 - 12u_2$ which implies $d^2 < 26 + 2u_2(u_2 - 6)$. But $u_2 = \lambda(u_1 + v_1)$, where $\lambda > 0.5$. Let us choose $\lambda = 7/6$. Then $u_2 = 7$ and $d^2 < 26 + 14(7 - 6) = 40$. Hence $\delta^2 - d^2 < 4$.*

Example 2. *Let $u_1 = 2$ and $v_1 = 5$. Then $\delta^2 = (5 - 2)^2 + (v_2 - u_2)^2$. Thus, $\delta^2 > 10$. Now, $d^2 < 25 + 4 + 2u_2^2 - 14u_2$. But, $u_2 = \lambda(u_1 + v_1)$, where $\lambda > 0.5$. By taking $\lambda = 11/7$, we get $u_2 = 11$ and $d^2 < 117$. Hence $\delta^2 - d^2 < 24$.*

Example 3. *Let us have $(u_1, v_1) = (5, 2)$ and $(u_2, v_2) = (10, 11)$ satisfying the Diophantine equation $u_1^2 + u_2^2 = v_1^2 + v_2^2$ where $u_2 > u_1, v_1$ and $u_2 < v_2$. The slope of the line between (u_1, v_1) and (u_2, v_2) is $m = \frac{\Delta y}{\Delta x} = \frac{v_2 - v_1}{u_2 - u_1} = \frac{9}{5} = 1.8$. Let θ be the angle of inclination. Then $\theta = \tan^{-1}(\frac{\Delta y}{\Delta x}) = 60.9454°$. Further, distance $d = \sqrt{(\Delta x)^2 + (\Delta y)^2} = \sqrt{106} = 10.29563$ units. Therefore, the equation of the line is $y = 1.8x - 7$. Now we can construct a right-angled triangle with vertices $(u_1, v_1), (u_2, v_2)$ and $(u_1 + \Delta x, y_1)$ as in Figure 1.*

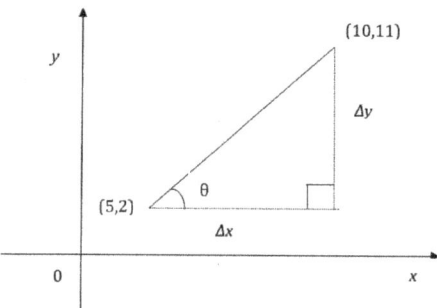

Figure 1. Construction of a right angled triangle using Δx.

Example 4. *Let us have $(u_1, v_1) = (10, 2)$ and $(u_2, v_2) = (5, 11)$ satisfying the Diophantine equation $u_1^2 + u_2^2 = v_1^2 + v_2^2$ where $u_1 > u_2$ and $v_2 > v_1$. The slope of the line between (u_1, v_1) and (u_2, v_2) is $m = \frac{\Delta y}{\Delta x} = \frac{v_2 - v_1}{u_2 - u_1} = \frac{9}{(-5)} = -1.8$. Let θ be the angle of inclination. Then $\theta = \tan^{-1}(\frac{\Delta y}{\Delta x} + 180°) = 119.05460°$. Further, distance $d = \sqrt{(\Delta x)^2 + (\Delta y)^2} = \sqrt{106} = 10.29563$ units. Therefore the equation of the line is $y = -1.8x + 20$. Now we can construct another right angled triangle with vertices $(u_1, v_1), (u_2, v_2)$ and $(u_2, v_2 - \Delta y)$ as in Figure 2.*

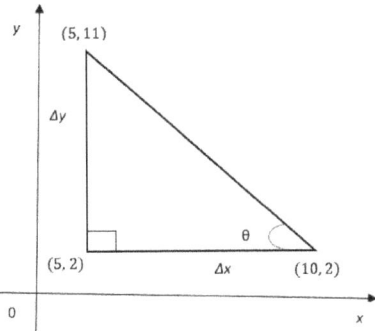

Figure 2. Construction of a right angled triangle using Δy.

Theorem 5. *If the two points (u_1, v_1) and (u_2, v_2) are the solutions of the quadratic Diophantine equation $u_1^2 + u_2^2 = v_1^2 + v_2^2$ where $u_2 > u_1$ and $v_2 > v_1$, then the four points (u_1, v_1), $(u_1 + \Delta x, v_1)$, (u_2, v_2) and $(u_1, v_1 + \Delta y)$ constitute a rectangle where $\Delta x = u_2 - u_1 > 0$ and $\Delta y = v_2 - v_1 > 0$.*

Proof. Given that $\Delta x = u_2 - u_1 > 0$ and $\Delta y = v_2 - v_1 > 0$. Let the given points $A(u_1, v_1)$, $B(u_1 + \Delta x, v_1)$, $C(u_2, v_2)$ and $D(u_1, v_1 + \Delta y)$ be the four vertices of a four-sided polygon. By two-dimensional geometry, either Δx and Δy denote the length and width of the polygon ($\Delta x > \Delta y$) or Δx and Δy be the width and length ($\Delta y > \Delta x$). The distance d between the points (u_1, v_1) and (u_2, v_2) acts as a diagonal of the polygon as in Figure 3.

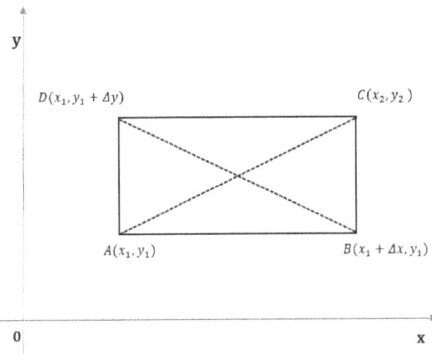

Figure 3. Construction of a rectangle.

Thus, we obtain two right-angled triangle, say $\triangle ABC$ and $\triangle ADC$ having the same hypotenuse d. Similarly, the right-angled triangles $\triangle BAD$ and $\triangle BCD$ have the hypotenuse as $d' = \sqrt{(\Delta y)^2 + (\Delta x)^2}$. Note that $d = d'$. Thus, the two diagonals of the polygon ABCD are equal and with the choice of u_1, u_2, v_1, v_2 it is clear that ABCD is a rectangle. □

3. Existence of Trapdoor Function in Diophantine Cryptography

Everybody depends on the secret key to guarantee the security of data. So, it must be assured that the secret key is extremely difficult to crack. Note that cryptanalysis is the field of attacking cryptosystems. One method of cryptanalysis involves the attacker possessing both the message's plaintext and ciphertext and attempting to decipher the key that converts the plaintext to the ciphertext. Using a brute-force attack, or checking all potential keys, is one way they can achieve this. The key space, or range of potential keys, should be very large in order to protect against a brute-force attack. A secret key shared by two users is used in symmetric-key cryptography. Party A can encrypt data with the secret key and transfer the output to Party B, who can decrypt and interpret data with the same key. Key management, or the secure exchange of secret keys between users, is the secure framework for symmetric cryptography. The drawback of the symmetric key cryptography is Key distribution and management is a serious problem—for N users $O(N^2)$ keys are needed. In this section, we have invented a secure authentication communication protocol between client and server using Diophantine equation $x_1^2 + x_2^2 = y_1^2 + y_2^2$ as in Figure 4.

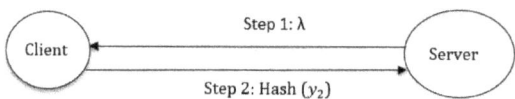

Figure 4. Diophantine authentication protocol.

In the step 1, Server sends a trapdoor information (message) λ to Client. The server keeps a distinct pair of 128/256-bit session key (x_1, y_1) to each client. During every transaction, the server generates a trapdoor information in accordance with session key to each client. Each client receives a distinct trapdoor information λ computed by server. In the step 2, the client computes $x_2 = \lambda(x_1 + y_1)$ and $y_2^2 = x_1^2 + x_2^2 - y_1^2$. Then the client sends Hash(y_2) to server which verifies the result. Then the authentication mechanism has been established between both parties. In this protocol, when λ and y_2 are hacked by an attacker, it is computationally challenge to retrieve the values x_1, y_1 and x_2 due to Diophantine equation. It is observed that the client uses the x_2 as one time password (OTP)/E-token for any network transactions. Similar to the above protocol, we can send y_2 instead of Hash(y_2) to server as a plaintext. It is termed as transparent (naked) Diophantine authentication protocol. Along with big data tools, the proposed protocol helps to generate, distribute, store and revoke a large volume of E-tokens and keeps an eye on cryptographic attacks.

The ElGamal cryptosystem, a subset of public key cryptography, is based on the Discrete Logarithm Problem (DLP). It is vulnerable to the man-in-the-middle attack, chosen-plaintext attacks and not useful for one way communication. The computational complexity of DLP has come around $O(n \log n)$ where n is the amount of resources or operations required to execute the discrete logarithm. In the present study, the authors described Diophantine cryptography that could be solved in $O(n^2)$. It is useful to one-way communication system. Due to high computational complexity to crack or identify an exact integral solution to a given Diophantine equation, it is a real challenge to perform rudimentary cryptographic attacks.

Given a point (x_1, y_1), estimating another point (x_2, y_2) satisfying $x_1^2 + x_2^2 = y_1^2 + y_2^2$ is computationally difficult for higher integral values. But for smaller integral values this process is not so hard. For the given point (x_1, y_1), an attacker can try to form a rectangle in which a right angled triangle with angles $\theta_1, \theta_2, 90°$ where $\theta_1 + \theta_2 = 90°$. The attacker requires to vary θ_1 and θ_2 and verify the Diophantine relationship. It needs $O(n^2)$ computations. Subsequently, the attacker tries to make two right angled triangles comprised into a rectangle which inscribed in a circle must have its diagonal as the diameter of the circle. The attacker computes the perimeter of the rectangle and verifies whether perimeter is equal to $2(\Delta x + \Delta y)$. Gradually, the attacker increases the perimeter of the rectangle and the corresponding area of the circle in order to find a suitable point (x_2, y_2). This ensures the existence of trapdoor function in Diophantine and very hard to crack this challenge. Algorithm 1 describes the pseudocode for the authentication protocol based on the equation $x_1^2 + x_2^2 = y_1^2 + y_2^2$.

Algorithm 1 Pseudocode for the authentication protocol

Input: B, the trapdoor message in a binary form.
Input: $x_1, y_1 > 0$.
Output: decimal $= 0$, base $= 1$
  while $B \neq 0$ **do**
  remainder = B% 10
  decimal = decimal + remainder * base
  B = B / 10
  base = base * 2
  end while
Output: n = decimal
  $x_2 \leftarrow n * (x_1 + y_1)$;
  $y_2 \leftarrow sqrt\{x_1^2 + x_2^2 - y_1^2\}$;
  $sum1 \leftarrow x_1^2 + x_2^2$;
  $sum2 \leftarrow y_1^2 + y_2^2$;
  if $sum1 == sum2$ **then**
    Trapdoor is possible using Diophantine equation;
  else
    No solution
  end if

It is to be noted that the 128/256-bit session key (x_1, y_1) and the trapdoor message λ act as the secret keys and it should be known to the server as well as clients to do the authentication. As a result, any safe key exchange mechanism should be used to exchange the keys. The symmetric cryptography is exposed in two ways: the requirement to communicate the key raises the risk of it being intercepted in transit, and quantum computers can employ Grover's algorithm to enhance the accuracy of a brute-force attack. Since quantum algorithms do not completely break Hash-based digital signatures, the newly discovered authentication systems enable a secure digital data transmission.

In the symmetric key cryptography, a private key of a specific size is developed using a source of randomness. There is no mathematical proof (or analysis) to crack a private key because of the random creation process and the non-availability of patterns. Eventhough, brute-force attacks are included in cryptanalysis, a brute-force attack entails attempting to decipher the ciphertext and retrieve the plaintext using every feasible key. In order to find the correct key, an attacker would have to test 50% of all possible keys. As a result, a secret (or private key) with suitable entropy and length could adequately safeguard encrypted data. Grover's approach, on the other hand, can leverage qubit superposition to expedite the brute-force attack by a quadratic factor. Also, when a cryptographic algorithm permits to use, doubling the symmetric key sizes keeps this type of encryption safe. However, doubling the key size is not a simple operation. When a cryptographic algorithm is deployed by a software under the environment of Cloud setup, it is quite simple since an update may provide for an efficient key-size change.

4. Cost and Effort Evaluation Using COCOMO Equations

One of the most widely used software prediction models is the constructive cost model (COCOMO). The two key factors that determine the integrity of any software development project are effort and schedule, both of which are consequences of COCOMO. One can choose a model of COCOMO based on the requirements on accuracy and correctness. There are three COCOMO models: Basic, Intermediate and Complex. Basic COCOMOs are developed for a rapid and fuzzy analysis of software estimation. Intermediate models consider cost drivers into account, while complex models take the influence of individual project phases. All these models can be used for various software developments under the Cloud based on the characteristics of the different system types: organic, semi-detached, and embedded.

This section explains how to create software utilising organic COCOMO equations to implement the new authentication protocol that is discussed in Section 3. For organic model software projects, the fundamental COCOMO equations are

$$X = \alpha \times (l)^\beta \qquad (5)$$
$$R = \gamma \times (X)^\delta \qquad (6)$$
$$P = X/R \qquad (7)$$

where X is the effort applied in persons-months, R is the build-up time in chronological months, l is the calculated number of lines of code for the project (expressed in thousands) and P is the number of persons. Table 1 represents the values of the coefficients and exponents in COCOMO equations for different project types as in [25].

Table 1. Coefficients and exponent values as in [25].

Software Project	α	β	γ	δ
Organic	2.4	1.05	2.5	0.38
Semi-detached	3.0	1.12	2.5	0.35
Embedded	3.6	1.20	2.5	0.32

The COCOMO parameter is used to quantify the workload of software and runtime after l has been evaluated. The COCOMO equation shows that as l increases, the workload and duration increase as well. Table 2 represent the estimated work, time, and labor involved in creating each line of code in the program using basic COCOMO equations.

Table 2. Approximated values of COCOMO attributes.

Code Length (Lines in Thousands)	Effort	Time Period	Manpower
50	0.10	1.04	0.09
150	0.33	1.64	0.20
550	1.28	2.75	0.47
1200	2.91	3.75	0.78
1400	3.42	3.99	0.86
2000	4.96	4.59	1.08
5000	13.00	6.62	1.96

The number of lines of code for C++ program developed for the protocol is 42. Thus for authentication protocol, the effort $X = 0.086$ persons-months, time $R = 0.9841$ months and the manpower $P = 0.874$ persons. Hence, using the basic COCOMO equations, the initial cost, effort and manpower can be derived for developing a new software in order to implement the authentication protocol.

5. Conclusions

In the present work, some geometric properties of quadratic Diophantine equations are derived and explained their uses in the communication protocols. Also, a new secure authentication mechanism based on the positive integral solutions of the quadratic Diophantine is presented which can be employed in the generation of one-time passwords or E-tokens for cryptography applications. Further, the existence of trapdoor functions in Diophantine equation is well analysed. It is noted that the proposed authentication protocol is secure either performing Hashing method or without Hashing. Also, the initial cost and effort of a new software library under the environment of Cloud are determined for implementing the authentication protocols using basic COCOMO equations.

Author Contributions: Conceptualization, V.N. (Vijayarangan Natarajan) and V.N. (Veena Narayanan); software, A.V.; writing—original draft preparation, V.N. (Veena Narayanan); writing—review and editing, V.N. (Veena Narayanan); supervision, S.R.; project administration, S.R. All authors have read and agreed to the published version of the manuscript.

Funding: This research received no external funding.

Institutional Review Board Statement: Not applicable.

Informed Consent Statement: Not applicable.

Data Availability Statement: Not applicable.

Acknowledgments: The authors gratefully acknowledge TATA Realty-SASTRA Srinivasa Ramanujan research chair for supporting this research.

Conflicts of Interest: The authors declare no conflict of interest.

References

1. Barbeau, E.J. *Pell's Equation Problem Books in Mathematics*; Springer: New York, NY, USA, 2003; Volume XII, p. 212. ISBN 0-387-95529-1.
2. Burton, D.M. *Elementary Number Theory*, 6th ed.; International Series in Pure and Applied Mathematics; McGraw-Hill Higher Education: New York, NY, USA, 2007.
3. Chen, C.Y.; Chang, C.C.; Yang, W.P. Fast RSA Type Cryptosystem Based on Pell Equation. In Proceedings of the International Conference on Cryptology and Information Security, Kyongju, Korea, 3–7 November 1996; pp. 1–5.
4. Gysin, M.; Sebery, J. How to use Pell's equation in cryptography. *Preprint.* 1999. Available online: https://scholar.google.com.hk/scholar?hl=en&as_sdt=0%2C5&q=How+to+use+Pell%E2%80%99s+equation+in+cryptography&btnG= (accessed on 20 July 2022).
5. Padhye, S. A Public Key Cryptosystem Based on Pell Equation. *Cryptology ePrint Archive.* 2006. Available online: https://eprint.iacr.org/2006/191 (accessed on 20 July 2022).
6. Raghunan, K.R.; Dsouza, R.R.; Rakshith, N.; Shetty, S.; Aithal, G. Analysis of an Enhanced Dual RSA Algorithm Using Pell's Equation to Hide Public Key Exponent and a Fake Modulus to Avoid Factorization Attack. In *Advances in Artificial Intelligence and Data Engineering. Advances in Intelligent Systems and Computing*; Chiplunkar, N., Fukao, T., Eds.; Springer: Singapore, 2021; Volume 1133, pp. 809–823.
7. Raghunan, K.R.; Nireshwalya, S.N.; Sudhir, S.; Bhat, M.S.; Tanvi, H.M. Securing Media Information Using Hybrid Transposition Using Fisher Yates Algorithm and RSA Public Key Algorithm Using Pell's Cubic Equation. In *Advances in Artificial Intelligence and Data Engineering. Advances in Intelligent Systems and Computing*; Chiplunkar, N., Fukao, T., Eds.; Springer: Singapore, 2021; Volume 1133, pp. 975–993.
8. Rao, K.M.; Avadhani, P.S.; Bhaskari, D.L.; Sarma, K.S. An Identity Based Encryption Scheme based on Pell's Equation With Jacobi Symbol. *Int. J. Res. Eng. Sci.* **2013**, *1*, 17–20.
9. Thirumala, C.; Mohan, S.; Srivatsava, G. An efficient public key secure scheme for cloud and IoT security. *Comput. Commun.* **2020**, *150*, 634–643.
10. Raghunandan, K.R.; Aithal, G.; Shetty, S.; Bhavya, K. Key Generation Using Generalized Pell's Equation in Public Key Cryptography Based on the Prime Fake Modulus Principle to Image Encryption and Its Security Analysis. *Cybern. Inf. Technol.* **2020**, *20*, 86–101. [CrossRef]
11. Goldwasser, S.; Micali, S. Probabilistic Encryption. *J. Comput. Syst. Sci.* **1984**, *28*, 270–299. [CrossRef]
12. Yao, A. Theory and applications of trapdoor functions. In Proceedings of the 23rd Symposium on Foundations of Computer Science, Washington, DC, USA, 3–5 November 1982; [CrossRef]
13. Baodong, Q. Tightly Secure Lossy Trapdoor Functions: Constructions and Applications. *Secur. Commun. Netw.* **2019**, *2019*, 1–13.
14. Kiltz, E.; Mohassel, P.; Neill, A. Adaptive Trapdoor Functions and Chosen-Ciphertext Security. In *Advances in Cryptology EURO-CRYPT 2010*; Gilbert, H., Ed.; Lecture Notes in Computer Science; Springer: Berlin/Heidelberg, Germany, 2010; Volume 6110. [CrossRef]
15. Hernández-Álvarez, L.; Bullón Pérez, J.J.; Batista, F.K.; Queiruga-Dios, A. Security Threats and Cryptographic Protocols for Medical Wearables. *Mathematics* **2022**, *10*, 886.
16. Bullón Pérez, J.J.; Queiruga-Dios, A.; Gayoso Martínez, V.; Martín del Rey, Á. Traceability of Ready-to-Wear Clothing through Blockchain Technology. *Sustainability* **2020**, *12*, 7491. [CrossRef]
17. Rey, A.M.d.; Dios, A.Q. Cryptographic Protocols in Wireless Sensor Networks: A Critical Review. *Proceedings* **2017** *1*, 748. [CrossRef]
18. Batista, F.K.; Martín del Rey, A.; Queiruga-Dios, A. A New Individual-Based Model to Simulate Malware Propagation in Wireless Sensor Networks. *Mathematics* **2020**, *8*, 410. [CrossRef]
19. Martínez, V.G.; Hernández-Álvarez, L.; Encinas, L.H. Analysis of the Cryptographic Tools for Blockchain and Bitcoin. *Mathematics* **2020**, *8*, 131. [CrossRef]

20. Okumura, S. A public key cryptosystem based on Diophantine equations of degree increasing type. *Pac. J. Math. Ind.* **2015**, *7*, 1–13. [CrossRef]
21. Murthy, N.; Swamy, M.N.S. Cryptographic applications of Brahmagupta-Bhāskara equation. *Regul. Pap. IEEE Trans. Circuits Syst.* **2006**, *53*, 1565–1571. [CrossRef]
22. Alvarez, G.; Hernández Encinas, L.; Munoz Masqué, J. Known-Plaintext Attack to Two Cryptosystems Based on the BB Equation. *IEEE Trans. Circuits Syst. II Express Briefs* **2008**, *55*, 423–426. [CrossRef]
23. Youssef, A.M. A Comment on Cryptographic Applications of Brahmagupta Bhaskara Equation. *IEEE Trans. Circuits Syst. Regul. Pap.* **2007**, *54*, 927–928. [CrossRef]
24. Alecci, G.; Dutto, S. Pell hyperbolas in DLP based cryptosystems. *arXiv* **2021**, arXiv:2111.09632. [CrossRef]
25. Mahmood, Y.; Abdulqader, A. A platform for porting IPv4 applications to IPv6. *Int. J. Comput. Digit. Syst.* **2021**, *10*, 501–509.

Article

On the Classification of Telescopic Numerical Semigroups of Some Fixed Multiplicity

Ying Wang [1,2], Muhammad Ahsan Binyamin [3,*], Iqra Amin [3], Adnan Aslam [4,*] and Yongsheng Rao [2]

1. Department of Network, Software Engineering Institute of Guangzhou, Guangzhou 510980, China
2. Institute of Computing Science and Technology, Guangzhou University, Guangzhou 510006, China
3. Department of Mathematics, Government College University, Faisalabad 38000, Pakistan
4. Department of Natural Sciences and Humanities, University of Engineering and Technology, Lahore 54000, Pakistan
* Correspondence: ahsanbanyamin@gmail.com (M.A.B.); adnanaslam15@yahoo.com (A.A.)

Abstract: The telescopic numerical semigroups are a subclass of symmetric numerical semigroups widely used in algebraic geometric codes. Suer and Ilhan gave the classification of triply generated telescopic numerical semigroups up to multiplicity 10 and by using this classification they computed some important invariants in terms of the minimal system of generators. In this article, we extend the results of Suer and Ilhan for telescopic numerical semigroups of multiplicities 8 and 12 with embedding dimension four. Furthermore, we compute two important invariants namely the Frobenius number and genus for these classes in terms of the minimal system of generators.

Keywords: telescopic numerical semigroup; embedding dimension; multiplicity; genus; Frobenius number

MSC: 20M14; 20M30

1. Introduction

In the beginning, the numerical semigroup theory was utilized in elementary number theory. Currently, it interacts in many fields such as commutative algebra, graph theory, algebraic geometry, combinatorics, coding theory, etc. The numerical semigroup is related to the problem of determining nonnegative integers $\mathbb{N}$ that can be expressed in the form $x_1 a_1 + x_2 a_2 + \ldots + x_r a_r$ for a given set $\{a_1, a_2, \ldots, a_r\}$ of positive integers and for arbitrary nonnegative integers $x_1, x_2, \ldots, x_r$. This problem was studied by many mathematicians such as Frobenius and Sylvester [1] at the end of the 19th century. Modern studies on the Frobenius problem started with Brauers and continues until today. During the second half of the twentieth century, interest in the study of numerical semigroups resurfaced because of their applications in algebraic geometry.

Assi et al. [2] discussed some important applications of a numerical semigroup in the solution of linear Diophantine equations, algebraic geometry, and the factorization of monoids. Bras-Amoros [3] presented some results on one-point codes related to numerical semigroups. In [4], Bras-Amoros proved that the sequence (v_i) and the binary operation $\oplus$ uniquely determined the corresponding numerical semigroup. He used the concept of the (v_i) sequence to improve the dimension of existing codes and drive bounds on the minimum distance. Bras-Amoros [5] proved that the $\oplus$ operation of the semigroups was important to define other classes of improved codes. Delgado et al. [6] introduced a GAP package for computations related to the numerical semigroup theory. In [7], Feng et al. presented a simple approach to constructing codes. Hoholdt et al. [8] provided a survey of the existing literature on the decoding of algebraic geometric codes. To study different concepts related to numerical semigroups and their applications in coding theory, the readers can see [9].

Let $\mathbb{N}$ be a set of nonnegative integers. A set $Y \subset \mathbb{N}$ is said to be a numerical semigroup if it is closed under addition, $0 \in \mathbb{N}$, and $\mathbb{N} \setminus Y$ is finite. The smallest positive integer that belongs to the set Y denoted by $m(Y)$ is called the multiplicity of Y. The elements of the set $\mathbb{N} \setminus Y$ are called gaps. We denote the set $\mathbb{N} \setminus Y$ by $G(Y)$ and call it a gap set of Y. The largest integer that belongs to $G(Y)$ is called the Frobenius number of Y and it is denoted by $\mathfrak{F}(Y)$. Frobenius asked how to find the largest b such that the Diophantine equation $a_1 x_1 + a_2 x_2 + \cdots + a_n x_n = b$, where $a_1, a_2, \ldots, a_n, b \in \mathbb{N}$ has no solution over nonnegative integers. Since then, this problem is known as the Frobenius problem. More explicitly Frobenius's problem asks for a formula in terms of the minimal generating set for the largest element of the complement $\mathbb{N} \setminus Y$. It is well-known that every numerical semigroup is finitely generated. We say that Y is generated by a set $S = \{s_1, s_2, \ldots, s_n\}$ if every $a \in Y$ can be written as a linear combination of elements of S. In other words $a = a_1 s_1 + a_2 s_2 + \cdots + a_n s_n$, where $a_1, a_2, \ldots, a_n$ are nonnegative integers. We use the notation $Y = \langle S \rangle = \langle s_1, s_2, \ldots, s_n \rangle$ if Y is generated by $s_1, s_2, \ldots, s_n$. If no proper subset of S generates Y, then we say that S is the minimal system of the generator of Y. Since the cancellation law holds in S, there always exists a unique minimal system of generators of Y. If S is the minimal system of the generator of Y, then the number of elements in set S denoted by $e(Y)$ is called the embedding dimension of Y. It is an easy observation that $e(Y) \leq m(Y)$. For more details related to numerical semigroup, the readers can see the book by [10]. Let $s_1 < s_2 < \ldots < s_l$ be a sequence of positive integers such that $\gcd(s_1, s_2, \ldots, s_l) = 1$. Let $d_j = \gcd(s_1, s_2, \ldots, s_j)$ and $S_j = \{\frac{s_1}{d_j}, \frac{s_2}{d_j}, \ldots, \frac{s_j}{d_j}\}$ for $j = 1, 2, \ldots, l$. Assume that $d_0 = 0$ and Y_i is a semigroup generated by S_i. If $\frac{s_j}{d_j} \in S_{j-1}$ for $j = 1, 2, \ldots, l$, then the sequence $(s_1, s_2, \ldots, s_l)$ is called telescopic. The semigroup generated by a telescopic sequence is called the telescopic semigroup [11]. Let $Y = \langle s_1, s_2, s_3 \rangle$ with $\gcd(s_1, s_2, s_3) = 1$. Then, Y is a triply generated telescopic semigroup if $s_3 \in \langle \frac{s_1}{d}, \frac{s_2}{d} \rangle$ where $d = \gcd(s_1, s_2)$ [12].

Kirfel and Pellikaan [11] showed that a proper subclass of a symmetric numerical semigroup was a class of telescopic numerical semigroup and they worked on the Feng–Rao distance. Garcia-Sanchez et al. [13] established a relationship between the second Feng–Rao number and the multiplicity of the telescopic numerical semigroup. Currently, telescopic numerical semigroups continue to be updated with applications in algebraic error-correcting codes. Sedat Ilhan [14] showed that a triply generated numerical semigroup $A = \langle a, a+2, 2a+1 \rangle$ with $a > 2$ an even integer was a telescopic numerical semigroup. In [15–17], Suer and Ilhan provided some classes of telescopic numerical semigroups with embedding dimension three and multiplicities 4, 6, 8, 9, and 10. They also calculated the Genus, Frobenius number, and Sylvester number in these cases. In this work, we characterize all numerical semigroups of embedding dimension four with multiplicities 8 and 12. Furthermore, explicit expressions are obtained to compute the Genus and Frobenius number by using the following Lemma.

Lemma 1. *Let $Y = \langle s_1, s_2, \ldots, s_n \rangle$ be a numerical semigroup and $d = \gcd(s_1, s_2, \ldots, s_{n-1})$. Let $S = \langle \frac{s_1}{d}, \frac{s_2}{d}, \ldots, \frac{s_{n-1}}{d}, s_n \rangle$, then*
1. $\mathfrak{F}(Y) = d\mathfrak{F}(S) + s_n(d-1)$.
2. $\mathfrak{g}(Y) = s\mathfrak{F}(S) + \frac{(d-1)(s_n - 1)}{2}$.

The paper is organized as follows: In the second section, we prove that if a telescopic numerical semigroup has embedding dimension four, then its multiplicity is at least the product of three primes. In light of this result, we give a complete characterization of telescopic numerical semigroups having embedding dimension four and multiplicity eight. Section 3 deals with the classification of telescopic numerical semigroups having embedding dimension four and multiplicity 12. In both cases, we give explicit expressions for the Frobenius number and Genus. In the end, the conclusion contains some open problems related to the study.

2. Telescopic Numerical Semigroup with Multiplicity Eight and Embedding Dimension Four

In this section, we give a characterization of numerical semigroups with embedding dimension four and multiplicity eight. In the following lemma, we give a condition on the multiplicity of a telescopic numerical semigroup with embedding dimension four.

Lemma 2. *Let Y be a telescopic numerical semigroup with embedding dimension four. Then, following conditions hold:*

1. $1 < d_2, d_3 < m(Y)$.
2. $d_2 > d_3$.
3. *The multiplicity of Y is the product of at least three prime numbers.*

Proof. We may assume that $Y = \langle s_1, s_2, s_3, s_4 \rangle$. To prove (1), we need to show that $d_2, d_3 \notin \{1, m(Y)\}$. If $d_2 = 1$, then by the definition of a telescopic numerical semigroup $d_3 = 1$ and therefore $s_3 \in S_2 = \langle s_1, s_2 \rangle$. This implies an embedding dimension of Y is less than four, a contradiction. This gives $d_2 > 1$. Similar arguments give $d_3 > 1$. Now, if $d_2 = m(Y)$ (or $d_3 = m(Y)$) then s_2 is a multiple of s_1 (or s_3 is a multiple of s_1). This implies the embedding dimension of Y is less than four, which is again not possible.

To prove (2), we only need to show that $d_2 \neq d_3$, then, from definition of telescopic numerical semigroups, it follows that $d_2 > d_3$. Thus, if $d_2 = d_3$, then

$$\frac{s_3}{d_3} \in \langle \frac{s_1}{d_2}, \frac{s_2}{d_2} \rangle,$$

that is

$$\frac{s_3}{d_2} \in \langle \frac{s_1}{d_2}, \frac{s_2}{d_2} \rangle.$$

This implies $s_3 \in \langle s_1, s_2 \rangle$, which is not possible as the embedding dimension of Y is four.

To prove (3), we need to show that s_1 is neither a prime nor a product of two primes. If s_1 is prime, then clearly the embedding dimension of Y cannot be four. So let $s_1 = p_1 p_2$, where p_1 and p_2 are two prime numbers. From (1), we have $d_2 = p_1$ or $d_2 = p_2$. In both cases, we get $d_3 = 1$, which is a contradiction as $d_3 > 1$ (see (1)). Hence, s_1 must be the product of at least three prime numbers. □

Now, we give a classification of telescopic numerical semigroups with embedding dimension four and multiplicity eight. Furthermore, we compute the genus and the Frobenius number in terms of minimal set of generators.

Theorem 1. *Let Y be a numerical semigroup with embedding dimension four and multiplicity eight. Then, Y is telescopic if and only if Y is a member of one of the following families:*

1. $\alpha = \{\langle 8, 8e_1 + 4, 8e_2 + 2, 8e_2 + 2 + j \rangle : e_1, e_2 \in \mathbb{Z}^+, e_1 < e_2\}$, *where j is an odd integer.*
2. $\beta = \{\langle 8, 8e_1 + 4, 8e_2 + 6, 8e_2 + 6 + j \rangle : e_1, e_2 \in \mathbb{Z}^+, e_1 \leq e_2\}$, *where j is an odd integer.*

Proof. ($\Rightarrow$) Let $Y = \langle 8, A, B, C \rangle$ be a telescopic numerical semigroup of embedding dimension four, then $d_2 = \gcd(8, A)$, $d_3 = \gcd(8, A, B)$. From (1) of Lemma 2, we have $d_2, d_3 \in \{2, 4\}$. Moreover, (2) of Lemma 2 gives $d_2 = 4$ and $d_3 = 2$. This implies $A = 8e_1 + 4$ and $B = 8e_2 + 2$ or $8e_2 + 6$, where $e_1, e_2 \in \mathbb{Z}^+$. If $A = 8e_1 + 4$ and $B = 8e_2 + 2$, then we may assume that $Y = \langle 8, 8e_1 + 4, 8e_2 + 2, 8e_2 + 2 + j \rangle$ with $e_1 < e_2$. Since $\gcd(8, A, B, C) = 1$, $2 \nmid j$. As Y is telescopic and

$$\mathfrak{F}(\langle 4, 4e_1 + 2, 4e_2 + 1 \rangle) = 4e_1 + 4e_2 - 1 < 8e_2 + 2 + j,$$

this implies $8e_2 + 2 + j \in \langle 4, 4e_1 + 2, 4e_2 + 1 \rangle$ for all odd values of j and therefore, $Y \in \alpha$. Now, if $A = 8e_1 + 4$ and $B = 8e_2 + 6$, then similar arguments imply $Y \in \beta$.

($\Leftarrow$) Let $Y \in \alpha$, then $\gcd(8, 8e_1 + 4) = 4$ and $\gcd(8, 8e_1 + 4, 8e_2 + 2) = 2$. Note that

$$\langle \frac{8}{4}, \frac{8e_1 + 4}{4} \rangle = \langle 2, 2e_1 + 1 \rangle.$$

Since $\mathfrak{F}(\langle 2, 2e_1 + 1 \rangle) = 2e_1 - 1 < 4e_2 + 1$ for some $e_1 < e_2$,

$$4e_2 + 1 \in \langle 2, 2e_1 + 1 \rangle.$$

Furthermore, $\langle \frac{8}{2}, \frac{8e_1+4}{2}, \frac{8e_2+2}{2} \rangle = \langle 4, 4e_1 + 2, 4e_2 + 1 \rangle$. Then, $\mathfrak{F}(\langle 4, 4e_1 + 2, 4e_2 + 1 \rangle) = 4e_2 + 4e_1 - 1 < 8e_2 + 2 + j$. This implies

$$8e_2 + 2 + j \in \langle 4, 4e_1 + 2, 4e_2 + 1 \rangle.$$

Hence, Y is telescopic.

Now, if $Y \in \beta$ then $\gcd(8, 8e_1 + 4) = 4$ and $\gcd(8, 8e_1 + 4, 8e_2 + 6) = 2$. Since

$$\langle \frac{8}{4}, \frac{8e_1 + 4}{4} \rangle = \langle 2, 2e_1 + 1 \rangle,$$

$\mathfrak{F}(\langle 2, 2e_1 + 1 \rangle) = 2e_1 - 1 < 4e_2 + 3$ for some $e_1 \leq e_2$. This implies

$$4e_2 + 3 \in \langle 2, 2e_1 + 1 \rangle.$$

Furthermore, $\langle \frac{8}{2}, \frac{8e_1+4}{2}, \frac{8e_2+6}{2} \rangle = \langle 4, 4e_1 + 2, 4e_2 + 3 \rangle$. Then, $\mathfrak{F}(\langle 4, 4e_1 + 2, 4e_2 + 3 \rangle) = 4e_1 + 4e_2 + 1 < 8e_2 + 6 + j$. This implies

$$8e_2 + 6 + j \in \langle 4, 4e_1 + 2, 4e_2 + 3 \rangle.$$

Hence, Y is telescopic. □

Corollary 1. *Let Y be a telescopic numerical semigroup of multiplicity eight.*
1. *If $Y \in \alpha$, then $\mathfrak{F}(Y) = 8e_1 + 8e_2 - 2 + x$ and $\mathfrak{g}(Y) = 4e_1 + 8e_2 + \frac{i+1}{2}$.*
2. *If $Y \in \beta$, then $\mathfrak{F}(Y) = 8e_1 + 8e_3 + 2 + y$ and $\mathfrak{g}(Y) = 4e_1 + 8e_2 + \frac{i+9}{2}$.*

Proof. Let $Y \in \alpha$, then $\gcd(8, 8e_1 + 4, 8e_2 + 2) = 2$ for $e_1 < e_2$. Consider

$$T = \langle \frac{8}{2}, \frac{8e_1+4}{2}, \frac{8e_2+2}{2} \rangle = \langle 4, 4e_1 + 2, 4e_2 + 1 \rangle.$$

By using Lemma 1, we get

$$\mathfrak{F}(T) = 2(2e_1 - 1) + (2 - 1)(4e_2 + 1) = 4e_1 + 4e_2 - 1.$$

This implies

$$\mathfrak{F}(Y) = 2(4e_1 + 4e_2 - 1) + (2 - 1)(8e_2 + 2 + j) = 8(e_1 + 2e_2) + j.$$

Since $\mathfrak{g}(Y) = \frac{\mathfrak{F}(Y)+1}{2}$, $\mathfrak{g}(Y) = 4(e_1 + 2e_2) + \frac{j+1}{2}$. The remaining cases can be proved in a similar way. □

3. Telescopic Numerical Semigroup with Multiplicity 12 and Embedding Dimension Four

In this section, we classify all telescopic numerical semigroups with embedding dimension four and multiplicity 12. Furthermore, we compute the genus and Frobenius number for these classes in terms of the minimal set of generators.

Theorem 2. *Let* Y *be a numerical semigroup with embedding dimension four and multiplicity 12. Then, Y is telescopic if and only if Y is a member of one of the following families:*

1. $\alpha_1 = \{\langle 12, 12e_1 + 4, 12e_2 + 2, 12e_2 + 2 + j\rangle : e_1, e_2 \in \mathbb{Z}^+, e_1 < e_2, j \text{ is a positive odd integer and } j \neq 3, 9, 15, \ldots, 12e_1 - 6e_2 - 3\}$.
2. $\alpha_2 = \{\langle 12, 12e_1 + 4, 12e_2 + 6, 12e_2 + 6 + j\rangle : e_1, e_2 \in \mathbb{Z}^+, e_1 \leq e_2, j \text{ is a positive odd integer and } j \neq 1, 7, 13, \ldots, 12e_1 - 6e_2 - 5\}$.
3. $\alpha_3 = \{\langle 12, 12e_1 + 4, 12e_2 + 10, 12e_2 + 10 + j\rangle : e_1, e_2 \in \mathbb{Z}^+, e_1 \leq e_2, j \text{ is a positive odd integer and } j \neq 5, 11, 17, \ldots, 12e_1 - 6e_2 - 7\}$.
4. $\alpha_4 = \{\langle 12, 12e_1 + 8, 12e_2 + 2, 12e_2 + 2 + j\rangle : e_1, e_2 \in \mathbb{Z}^+, e_1 < e_2, j \text{ is a positive odd integer and } j \neq 1, 7, 13, \ldots, 12e_1 - 6e_2 - 5\}$.
5. $\alpha_5 = \{\langle 12, 12e_1 + 8, 12e_2 + 6, 12e_2 + 6 + j\rangle : e_1, e_2 \in \mathbb{Z}^+, e_1 < e_2, j \text{ is a positive odd integer and } j \neq 5, 11, 17, \ldots, 12e_1 - 6e_2 - 1\}$.
6. $\alpha_6 = \{\langle 12, 12e_1 + 8, 12e_3 + 10, 12e_3 + 10 + j\rangle : e_1, e_2 \in \mathbb{Z}^+, e_1 \leq e_2, j \text{ is a positive odd integer and } j \neq 3, 9, 15, \ldots, 12e_1 - 6e_2 - 3\}$.
7. $\alpha_7 = \{\langle 12, 12e_1 + 6, 12e_2 + 2, 12e_2 + 2 + j\rangle : e_1, e_2 \in \mathbb{Z}^+, e_1 < e_2, j \text{ is a positive odd integer and } j \neq 3, 9, 15, \ldots, 6e_1 - 3\}$.
8. $\alpha_8 = \{\langle 12, 12e_1 + 6, 12e_2 + 3, 12e_2 + 3 + j\rangle : e_1, e_2 \in \mathbb{Z}^+, e_1 < e_2, j \text{ is a positive odd integer and } 3 \nmid j\}$.
9. $\alpha_9 = \{\langle 12, 12e_1 + 6, 12e_2 + 4, 12e_2 + 4 + j\rangle : e_1, e_2 \in \mathbb{Z}^+, e_1 < e_2, j \text{ is a positive odd integer and } j \neq 3, 9, 12, \ldots, 6e_1 - 3\}$.
10. $\alpha_{10} = \{\langle 12, 12e_1 + 6, 12e_3 + 8, 12e_3 + 8 + j\rangle : e_1, e_2 \in \mathbb{Z}^+, e_1 \leq e_2, j \text{ is a positive odd integer and } j \neq 3, 9, 12, \ldots, 6e_1 - 3\}$.
11. $\alpha_{11} = \{\langle 12, 12e_1 + 6, 12e_3 + 9, 12e_3 + 9 + j\rangle : e_1, e_2 \in \mathbb{Z}^+, e_1 \leq e_2, j \text{ is a positive odd integer and } 3 \nmid j\}$.
12. $\alpha_{12} = \{\langle 12, 12e_1 + 6, 12e_2 + 10, 12e_2 + 10 + j\rangle : e_1, e_2 \in \mathbb{Z}^+, e_1 \leq e_2, j \text{ is a positive odd integer and } j \neq 3, 9, 12, \ldots, 6e_1 - 3\}$.

Proof. ($\Rightarrow$) Let $Y = \langle 12, A, B, C\rangle$ be a telescopic numerical semigroup of embedding dimension four, then $d_2 = \gcd(12, A)$, $d_3 = \gcd(12, A, B)$. From (1) of Lemma 2, we have $d_2, d_3 \in \{2, 3, 4, 6\}$. Moreover, (2) of Lemma 2 gives the following possibilities:

- $d_2 = 4$ and $d_3 = 2$.
- $d_2 = 6$ and $d_3 = 2$.
- $d_2 = 6$ and $d_3 = 3$.

If $d_2 = 4$ and $d_3 = 2$, then $A \in \{12e_1 + 4, 12e_1 + 8\}$ and $B \in \{12e_2 + 2, 12e_2 + 6, 12e_2 + 10\}$. Now, if $A = 12e_1 + 4$ and $B = 12e_2 + 2$, then we may assume that $Y = \{\langle 12, 12e_1 + 4, 12e_2 + 2, 12e_2 + 2 + j\rangle\}$ with $e_1 < e_2$. Since $\gcd(12, A, B, C) = 1$, j must be an odd integer. Note that

$$\mathfrak{F}(\langle 6, 6e_1 + 2, 6e_2 + 1\rangle) = 12e_1 + 6e_2 - 1.$$

If $j > 12e_1 - 6e_2 - 3$, then $12e_2 + 2 + j > \mathfrak{F}(\langle 6, 6e_1 + 2, 6e_2 + 1\rangle)$. This implies $12e_2 + 2 + j \in \langle 6, 6e_1 + 2, 6e_2 + 1\rangle$ for all odd values of j. Now, if $j < 12e_1 - 6e_2 - 3$, then $12e_2 + 2 + j < \mathfrak{F}(\langle 6, 6e_1 + 2, 6e_2 + 1\rangle)$. Since Y is telescopic, we can write

$$12e_2 + 2 + j = 6a + (6e_1 + 2)b + (6e_1 + 1)c,$$

where $a, b, c \geq 0$. Since j is odd, c is also odd. We have the following possible solutions:

(i) $e_2 < a \leq 2e_1 - 1$, $b = 0$, and $c = 1$.
(ii) $2e_2 - 2e_1 \leq a \leq e_1 - 1$, $b = 1$, and $c = 1$.

If $e_2 < a \leq 2e_1 - 1$, $b = 0$, and $c = 1$, then $j = 6(a - e_2) - 1$, and if $2e_2 - 2e_1 \leq a \leq e_1 - 1$, $b = 1$, and $c = 1$, then $j = 6(a + e_1 - e_2) + 1$. Both solutions give j as an odd integer that cannot be the multiple of three, i.e., if $12e_2 + 2 + j < \mathfrak{F}(\langle 6, 6e_1 + 2, 6e_2 + 1\rangle)$, then $12e_2 + 2 + j \in \langle 6, 6e_1 + 2, 6e_2 + 1\rangle$, when $j \neq 3, 6, 9, 12, 15, \ldots, 12e_1 - 6e_2 - 3$. This implies $Y \in \alpha_1$. In a similar way, we can show that $Y \in \{\alpha_2, \alpha_3, \alpha_4, \alpha_5, \alpha_6\}$ for the remaining possibilities of this case.

If $d_2 = 6$ and $d_3 = 2$, then $A = 12e_1 + 6$ and $B \in \{12e_2 + 2, 12e_2 + 4, 12e_2 + 8, 12e_2 + 10\}$. Now, if $A = 12e_1 + 6$ and $B = 12e_2 + 2$, then we may assume that $Y = \langle 12, 12e_1 + 6, 12e_2 + 2, 12e_2 + 2 + j \rangle$ with $e_1 < e_2$. Since $\gcd(12, A, B, C) = 1$, $2 \nmid j$. If $j > 6e_1 - 3$, then $12e_2 + 2 + j > \mathfrak{F}(\langle 6, 6e_1 + 3, 6e_2 + 1 \rangle)$ and for $j < 6e_1 - 3$, we have $12e_2 + 2 + j < \mathfrak{F}(\langle 6, 6e_1 + 3, 6e_2 + 1 \rangle)$. Since Y is telescopic, we can assume that

$$12e_2 + 2 + j = 6a + (6e_1 + 3)b + (6e_2 + 1)c,$$

and both b and c cannot be even or odd at the same time. As $12e_2 + 2 + j < \mathfrak{F}(\langle 6, 6e_1 + 3, 6e_2 + 1 \rangle)$, we have the following:

(i) $a \leq e_1 + e_2 - 1, b = 0$, and $c = 1$.
(ii) $a \leq 2e_2 - 1, b = 1$, and $c = 0$.
(iii) $a \leq 2(e_2 - e_1 - 1), b = 3$, and $c = 0$.

All three solutions above imply $j \neq 3, 9, \ldots, 6e_1 - 3$ and therefore $Y \in \alpha_7$. The remaining possibilities give $Y \in \alpha_9$ or $Y \in \alpha_{10}$ or $Y \in \alpha_{12}$.

Now if $d_2 = 6$ and $d_3 = 3$, then $A = 12e_1 + 6$ and $B = 12e_2 + 3$ or $B = 12e_2 + 9$. If $A = 12e_1 + 6$ and $B = 12e_2 + 3$, then we may assume that $Y = \langle 12, 12e_1 + 6, 12e_2 + 3, 12e_2 + 3 + j \rangle$ with $e_1 < e_2$. Since $\gcd(12, A, B, C) = 1$, $3 \nmid j$. Note that

$$\mathfrak{F}(\langle 4, 4e_1 + 2, 4e_2 + 1 \rangle) = 4e_1 + 4e_2 - 1 < 12e_2 + 3 + j.$$

Since Y is telescopic, $12e_2 + 3 + j \in \langle 4, 4e_1 + 2, 4e_2 + 1 \rangle$ for all values of j except when $3 \nmid j$, therefore $Y \in \alpha_8$. Similarly if $A = 12e_1 + 6$ and $B = 12e_2 + 9$, then $Y \in \alpha_{11}$.

($\Leftarrow$) Let $Y \in \alpha_1$, then $\gcd(12, 12e_1 + 4) = 4$ and $\gcd(12, 12e_1 + 4, 12e_2 + 2) = 2$. Note that

$$\langle \frac{12}{4}, \frac{12e_1 + 4}{4} \rangle = \langle 3, 3e_1 + 1 \rangle.$$

Since $\mathfrak{F}(\langle 3, 3e_1 + 1 \rangle) = 6e_1 - 1 < 6e_2 + 1$ for some $e_1 < e_2$, therefore

$$6e_2 + 1 \in \langle 3, 3e_1 + 1 \rangle.$$

Let $x = 12e_2 + 2 + j$, where j is an odd integer and $j \neq 3, 9, 12, \ldots, 12e_1 - 6e_2 - 3$. If $j > 12e_1 - 6e_2 - 3$ then we can write $j = 12e_1 - 6e_2 - 3 + 2k$ for $k \geq 1$. This gives

$$x = 12e_2 + 2 + 12e_1 - 6e_2 - 3 + 2k = 12e_1 + 6e_2 - 1 + 2k > \mathfrak{F}(\langle 6, 6e_1 + 3, 6e_2 + 1 \rangle),$$

therefore $x \in \langle 6, 6e_1 + 3, 6e_2 + 1 \rangle$. Now, if $j < 12e_1 - 6e_2 - 3$ then we can write $j = 12e_2 + 2 + 12e_1 - 3 - 2k$, where $k = 1 + 3q_1$ or $k = 2 + 3q_2$ for some integers q_1, q_2. If $k = 1 + 3q_1$, then $j = 6(2e_1 - e_2 - q_1 - 1) + 1$. Since $j > 0$, $2e_1 - e_2 - q_1 - 1 \geq 0$. This implies $2e_1 \geq e_2 + q_1 + 1$. As $e_2 > e_1$, $e_1 > q_1 + 1$. Therefore, $x = 6(e_1 - q_1 - 1) + (6e_1 + 2) + (6e_2 + 1)$. Since $e_1 > q_1 + 1, e_1 - q_1 - 1 > 0$. This gives $x \in \langle 6, 6e_1 + 2, 6e_2 + 1 \rangle$. Now, if $k = 2 + 3q_2$, then $j = 6(2e_1 - e_2 - q_2 - 1) - 1$. Since $j > 0$, $2e_1 - e_2 - q_2 - 1 > 0$. So $x = 6(2e_1 - q_2 - 1) + (6e_2 + 1)$. Since $2e_1 - e_2 - q_2 - 1 > 0$, $2e_1 - q_2 - 1 > 0$. This gives $x \in \langle 6, 6e_1 + 2, 6e_2 + 1 \rangle$. Consequently Y is telescopic. Cases (2) to (6) can be proved in a similar way.

Now, let $Y \in \alpha_7$; then, $\gcd(12, 12e_1 + 6) = 6$ and $\gcd(12, 12e_1 + 6, 12e_2 + 2) = 2$. Note that

$$\langle \frac{12}{6}, \frac{12e_1 + 6}{6} \rangle = \langle 2, 2e_1 + 1 \rangle.$$

Since $\mathfrak{F}(\langle 2, 2e_1 + 1 \rangle) = 2e_1 - 1 < 6e_2 + 1$ for some $e_1 < e_2$,

$$6e_2 + 1 \in \langle 2, 2e_1 + 1 \rangle.$$

Let $x = 12e_2 + 2 + j$, where j is an odd integer and $j \neq 3, 9, 12, \ldots, 6e_1 - 3$. If $j > 6e_1 - 3$, then we can write $j = 6e_1 - 3 + 2k$ for $k \geq 1$. This gives

$$x = 12e_2 + 2 + 6e_1 - 3 + 2k = 12e_2 + 6e_1 - 1 + 2k > \mathfrak{F}(\langle 6, 6e_1 + 3, 6e_2 + 1 \rangle),$$

therefore $x \in \langle 6, 6e_1 + 3, 6e_2 + 1 \rangle$. Now, if $j < 6e_1 - 3$, then we can write $j = 6e_1 - 3 - 2k$, where either $k = 1 + 3q_1$ or $k = 2 + 3q_2$ for some integers q_1, q_2. If $k = 1 + 3q_1$, then $j = 6e_1 - 6q_1 - 6 + 1$. Since $j > 0$, $6e_1 - 6q_1 - 6 \geq 0$. This implies $e_1 \geq q_1 + 1$. As $e_2 > e_1$, $e_2 > q_1 + 1$. Now, $x = 12e_2 + 2 + 6e_1 - 6q_1 - 5 = 6(2e_2 - q_1 - 1) + (6e_1 + 3)$. Since $e_2 > q_1 + 1$, $2e_2 - q_1 - 1 > 0$. This gives $x \in \langle 6, 6e_1 + 3, 6e_2 + 1 \rangle$. Now, if $k = 2 + 3q_2$, then $j = 6(e_1 - q_2 - 1) - 1$. Since $j > 0$, $e_1 - q_2 - 1 > 0$. This implies $e_1 + e_2 - q_2 - 1 > 0$. Now, we can write $x = 6(e_1 + e_2 - q_2 - 1) + (6e_2 + 1)$. This gives $x \in \langle 6, 6e_1 + 3, 6e_2 + 1 \rangle$. Consequently Y is telescopic. Cases $(9), (10)$, and (12) can be proved in a similar way.

Let $Y \in \alpha_8$; then, $\gcd(12, 12e_1 + 6) = 6$ and $\gcd(12, 12e_1 + 6, 12e_2 + 3) = 3$. Note that

$$\langle \frac{12}{6}, \frac{12e_1 + 6}{6} \rangle = \langle 2, 2e_1 + 1 \rangle.$$

Since $\mathfrak{F}(\langle 2, 2e_1 + 1 \rangle) = 2e_1 - 1 < 4e_2 + 1$ for some $e_1 < e_2$,

$$4e_2 + 1 \in \langle 2, 2e_1 + 1 \rangle.$$

Furthermore, $\langle \frac{12}{3}, \frac{12e_1 + 6}{3}, \frac{12e_2 + 3}{3} \rangle = \langle 4, 4e_1 + 2, 4e_2 + 1 \rangle$. Then, $\mathfrak{F}(\langle 4, 4e_1 + 2, 4e_2 + 1 \rangle) = 4e_1 + 4e_2 - 1 < 12e_2 + 3 + j$. This implies

$$12e_2 + 2 + j \in \langle 4, 4e_1 + 2, 4e_2 + 1 \rangle.$$

Hence, Y is telescopic. (11) can be proved in a similar way as we proved (8). □

Corollary 2. *Let Y be a telescopic numerical semigroup of multiplicity eight.*

1. *If $Y \in \alpha_1$, then $\mathfrak{F}(Y) = 24(e_1 + e_2) + j$ and $\mathfrak{g}(Y) = 12(e_1 + e_2) + \frac{j+1}{2}$.*
2. *If $Y \in \alpha_2$, then $\mathfrak{F}(Y) = 24(e_1 + e_2) + j + 8$ and $\mathfrak{g}(Y) = 12(e_1 + e_2) + \frac{j+9}{2}$.*
3. *If $Y \in \alpha_3$, then $\mathfrak{F}(Y) = 24(e_1 + e_2) + j + 16$ and $\mathfrak{g}(Y) = 12(e_1 + e_2) + \frac{j+17}{2}$.*
4. *If $Y \in \alpha_4$, then $\mathfrak{F}(Y) = 24(e_1 + e_2) + j + 8$ and $\mathfrak{g}(Y) = 12(e_1 + e_2) + \frac{j+9}{2}$.*
5. *If $Y \in \alpha_5$, then $\mathfrak{F}(Y) = 24(e_1 + e_2) + j + 16$ and $\mathfrak{g}(Y) = 12(e_1 + e_2) + \frac{j+17}{2}$.*
6. *If $Y \in \alpha_6$, then $\mathfrak{F}(Y) = 24(e_1 + e_2) + j + 24$ and $\mathfrak{g}(Y) = 12(e_1 + e_2) + \frac{j+25}{2}$.*
7. *If $Y \in \alpha_7$, then $\mathfrak{F}(Y) = 12(e_1 + 3e_2) + j$ and $\mathfrak{g}(Y) = 6(e_1 + 3e_2) + \frac{j+1}{2}$.*
8. *If $Y \in \alpha_8$, then $\mathfrak{F}(Y) = 12e_1 + 18e_2 + j + 1$ and $\mathfrak{g}(Y) = 6e_1 + 9e_2 + \frac{j+1}{2}$.*
9. *If $Y \in \alpha_9$, then $\mathfrak{F}(Y) = 12(e_1 + 3e_2) + j + 8$ and $\mathfrak{g}(Y) = 6(e_1 + 3e_2) + \frac{j+9}{2}$.*
10. *If $Y \in \alpha_{10}$, then $\mathfrak{F}(Y) = 12(e_1 + 3e_2) + j + 18$ and $\mathfrak{g}(Y) = 6(e_1 + 3e_2) + \frac{j+19}{2}$.*
11. *If $Y \in \alpha_{11}$, then $\mathfrak{F}(Y) = 8e_1 + 20e_2 + j + 11$ and $\mathfrak{g}(Y) = 4e_1 + 10e_2 + \frac{j+12}{2}$.*
12. *If $Y \in \alpha_{12}$, then $\mathfrak{F}(Y) = 12(e_1 + 3e_2) + j + 24$ and $\mathfrak{g}(Y) = 6(e_1 + 3e_2) + \frac{j+25}{2}$.*

Proof. Let $Y \in \alpha_1$; then, $\gcd(12, 12e_1 + 4, 12e_2 + 2) = 2$ for $e_1 < e_2$. Consider

$$T = \langle \frac{12}{2}, \frac{12e_1 + 4}{2}, \frac{12e_2 + 2}{2} \rangle = \langle 6, 6e_1 + 2, 6e_2 + 1 \rangle.$$

By using Lemma 1, we get

$$\mathfrak{F}(T) = 2(6e_1 - 1) + (2 - 1)(6e_2 + 1) = 12e_1 + 6e_2 - 1.$$

This implies

$$\mathfrak{F}(Y) = 2(12e_1 + 6e_2 - 1) + (2 - 1)(12e_2 + 2 + j) = 24(e_1 + e_2) + j.$$

Since $\mathfrak{g}(Y) = \frac{\mathfrak{F}(Y)+1}{2}$, $\mathfrak{g}(Y) = 12(e_1 + e_2) + \frac{j+1}{2}$. The remaining cases can be proved in a similar way. □

Example 1. Let $Y = \langle 12, 40, 46, 46 + j \rangle$. We want to find the values of j for which this numerical semigroup is telescopic. Since $\gcd(12, 40) = 4$ and $\mathfrak{F}(\langle \frac{12}{4}, \frac{40}{4} \rangle) = 17 < \frac{46}{2} = 23$, it follows that $23 \in \langle 3, 10 \rangle$. Furthermore, $\mathfrak{F}(\langle \frac{12}{2}, \frac{40}{2}, \frac{46}{2} \rangle) = 57$. Now, we need to check for which values of j, the expression $46 + j \in \langle \frac{12}{2}, \frac{40}{2}, \frac{46}{2} \rangle$ holds. By definition of a numerical semigroup, $\gcd(12, 40, 46, 46 + j) = 1$, therefore j must be a positive odd integer. Note that $46 + j \in \langle 6, 20, 23 \rangle$ for all $j > 11$. For $j = 1$, $47 \in \langle 6, 20, 23 \rangle$. For $j = 3$, $49 \in \langle 6, 20, 23 \rangle$. For $j = 5$, $51 \notin \langle 6, 20, 23 \rangle$. For $j = 7$, $53 \in \langle 6, 20, 23 \rangle$. For $j = 9$, $55 \in \langle 6, 20, 23 \rangle$. For $j = 11$, $57 \notin \langle 6, 20, 23 \rangle$. This shows that Y is a telescopic numerical semigroup for all positive odd values of j except $j = 5, 11$. Moreover, $\mathfrak{F}(Y) = 160 + j$ and $\mathfrak{g}(Y) = 72 + \frac{j+17}{2}$.

4. Conclusions

Numerical semigroups are among the simplest objects to study, but they are involved in very hard problems. They have applications in many applied fields including cryptography, error-correcting codes, and combinatorial structures for privacy applications. In this work, we studied a couple of classes of the telescopic numerical semigroup of embedding dimension four. We proved that if a telescopic numerical semigroup had embedding dimension four, then its multiplicity was at least a multiple of three primes. The first two classes among them were the telescopic numerical semigroups with embedding dimension four and multiplicities 8 and 12. We gave a complete classification of telescopic numerical semigroups for these two classes. In the future, one can characterize the numerical semigroups of embedding dimension four and multiplicities 16 and 18.

Author Contributions: Formal analysis, Y.W. and I.A.; Investigation, M.A.B., I.A., A.A. and Y.R.; Methodology, Y.W., M.A.B., A.A. and Y.R.; Validation, Y.W. and Y.R.; Writing—original draft, I.A.; Writing—review & editing, M.A.B. and A.A. All authors have read and agreed to the published version of the manuscript.

Funding: This work was supported by the National Natural Science Foundation of China (No. 62172116, 61972109) and the Guangzhou Academician and Expert Workstation (No. 20200115-9).

Data Availability Statement: Not applicable

Conflicts of Interest: The authors declare no conflict of interest.

References

1. Sylvester, J.J. Mathematichal questions with their solutions. *Educ. Times* **1884**, *41*, 171–178.
2. Assi, A.; Garcia-Sanchez, P.A. Constructing the set of complete intersection numerical semigroups with a given Frobenius number. *Appl. Algebra Eng. Commun. Comput.* **2013**, *24*, 133–148. [CrossRef]
3. Bras-Amoros, M. Acute semigroups, the order bound on the minimum distance, and the Feng-Rao improvements. *IEEE Trans. Inform. Theory* **2004**, *50*, 1282–1289. [CrossRef]
4. Bras-Amoros, M. Addition Behavior of a Numerical Semigroup. *Semin. Congr.* **2005**, *11*, 21–28.
5. Bras-Amoros, M. A note on numerical semigroups. *IEEE Trans. Inf. Theory* **2007**, *53*, 821–823. [CrossRef]
6. Delgado, M.; Garcia-Sanchez, P.A. Numericalsgps, a GAP package for numerical semigroups. *Acm Commun. Comput. Algebra* **2016**, *50*, 12–24. [CrossRef]
7. Feng, G.L.; Rao, T.R. A simple approach for construction of algebraic geometric codes from affine plane curves. *IEEE Trans. Inf. Theory* **1994**, *40*, 1003–1012. [CrossRef]
8. Hoholdt, T.; Pellikaan, R. On the decoding of algebraic-geometric codes. *IEEE Trans. Inf. Theory* **1995**, *41*, 1589–1614. [CrossRef]
9. Bras-Amors, M. Numerical semigroups and codes. *Algebr. Geom. Model. Inf. Theory* **2013**, *1*, 167–218.
10. Rosales, J.C.; Garcia-Sanchez, P.A. Numerical Semigroups. In *Developments in Mathematics*; Springer: New York, NY, USA, 2009; Volume 20. [CrossRef]
11. Kirfel, C.; Pellikaan, R. The minimum distance of codes in an array coming from telescopic semigroups. *IEEE Trans. Inf. Theory* **1995**, *41*, 1720–1732. [CrossRef]
12. Matthews, G.L. On Triply-Generated telescopic semigroups and chains of semigroups. *Congr. Numer.* **2001**, *154*, 117–123.
13. Garcia-Sanchez, P.A.; Heredia, B.A.; Leamer, M.J. Apery Sets and Feng-Rao numbers over telescopic numerical semigroups. *arXiv* **2016**, arXiv:1603.09301.

14. Ilhan, S. On a class of telescopic numerical semigroups. *Int. J. Contemp. Math. Sci.* **2006**, *1*, 81–83. [CrossRef]
15. Suer, M.; Ilhan, S. On telescopic numerical semigroup families with embedding dimension 3. *J. Sci. Technol.* **2019**, *12*, 457–462.
16. Suer, M.; lhan, S. On triply generated telescopic semigroups with multiplicity 8 and 9. *Bulg. Acad. Sci.* **2020**, *72*, 315–319.
17. Suer, M.; lhan, S. Telescopic numerical semigroups with multiplicity Ten and embedding dimension three. *J. Univers. Math.* **2022**, *5*, 139–148. [CrossRef]

Article

Pauli Gaussian Fibonacci and Pauli Gaussian Lucas Quaternions

Ayşe Zeynep Azak

Faculty of Education, Mathematics and Science Education Department, Sakarya University, Sakarya 54300, Turkey; apirdal@sakarya.edu.tr; Tel.: +90-0264-295-7165

Abstract: We have investigated new Pauli Fibonacci and Pauli Lucas quaternions by taking the components of these quaternions as Gaussian Fibonacci and Gaussian Lucas numbers, respectively. We have calculated some basic identities for these quaternions. Later, the generating functions and Binet formulas are obtained for Pauli Gaussian Fibonacci and Pauli Gaussian Lucas quaternions. Furthermore, Honsberger's identity, Catalan's and Cassini's identities have been given for Pauli Gaussian Fibonacci quaternions.

Keywords: Pauli matrix; Pauli quaternion; Fibonacci quaternion; Pauli Gaussian Fibonacci quaternion; Pauli Gaussian Lucas quaternion

MSC: 11B37; 11B39; 20G20

Citation: Azak, A.Z. Pauli Gaussian Fibonacci and Pauli Gaussian Lucas Quaternions. *Mathematics* **2022**, *10*, 4655. https://doi.org/10.3390/math10244655

Academic Editors: Diana Savin, Nicusor Minculete and Vincenzo Acciaro

Received: 10 November 2022
Accepted: 5 December 2022
Published: 8 December 2022

Copyright: © 2022 by the authors. Licensee MDPI, Basel, Switzerland. This article is an open access article distributed under the terms and conditions of the Creative Commons Attribution (CC BY) license (https:// creativecommons.org/licenses/by/ 4.0/).

1. Introduction

The set of complex numbers with integer coefficients was first described by Carl Friedrich Gauss, and these numbers were called Gaussian numbers [1]. Then, Horadam gave the definition of the n-th generalized complex Fibonacci quaternion and provided some identities regarding these numbers. Furthermore, he defined Fibonacci quaternions [2]. Gaussian Fibonacci and Gaussian Lucas sequences were introduced by Jordan. Moreover, some basic identities and summation formulas were obtained [3]. The recurrence relation of the Gaussian Fibonacci numbers GF_n for $n > 1$ is defined by

$$GF_n = GF_{n-1} + GF_{n-2}$$

where $GF_0 = i$, $GF_1 = 1$. These recurrence relations also satisfy the following equality $GF_n = F_n + iF_{n-1}$ where F_n is the n-th Fibonacci number [3,4]. In the same manner, the recurrence relation of the Gaussian Lucas numbers GL_n for $n > 2$ is defined by

$$GL_n = GL_{n-1} + GL_{n-2}$$

where $GL_0 = 2 - i$, $GL_1 = 1 + 2i$. Again, the following equality can be observed

$$GL_n = L_n + iL_{n-1}$$

where L_n is the n-th Lucas number [3,4].

An extension of the Fibonacci numbers to the complex plane was discussed by Berzsenyi [5].

The algebras of the complex numbers, quaternions, octonions, and sedenions are found by using a doubling procedure. This procedure is called as Cayley–Dickson process. In this regard, we extend the field of real numbers to complex numbers via this process. The complex number system is both commutative and associative. However, the quaternions are not commutative, although they are associative. On the other hand, octonions and sedenions are both non-commutative and non-associative. The main question is, why do we need these expanding number systems? It is because quaternions have applications in quantum mechanics, computer graphics, and vision [6–8]. Octonions are used in quantum information theory and robotics [9,10]. Sedenions are used in neural networks, time series, and traffic forecasting problems [11,12].

The sequences in finite fields whose terms depend in a simple manner on their predecessors are of importance for a variety of applications. Because it is easy to generate by recursive procedures, and these sequences have advantageous features from the computational viewpoint [13]. Thus, mathematicians increased the number of terms to be added at the beginning and turned to studies on number sequences similar to Fibonacci numbers, such as tribonacci, tetranacci, pentanacci, etc. Later, these studies were carried over to Cayley algebras, see [14–32]. Thus, one of the most active research areas of recent years has come to the fore, and studies on Cayley algebras have attracted researchers in various ways.

Complex Fibonacci quaternions have been defined by Halici [33]. Then, Binet's formula, generating functions and the matrix representation of these quaternions have been proven. Recently, n-th quaternion Gaussian Lucas numbers have been introduced to the literature. The Binet formula, some summation formulas, and the Cassini identity have been given by using the matrix representation of Gaussian Lucas numbers [34]. This time, they have expressed the quaternions instead of the Gaussian Lucas numbers by taking the Gaussian Fibonacci coefficients. In this way, the Binet formula, generating function ve some identities regarding the norm of these quaternions have been derived [35].

The Binet formula of the Gaussian Fibonacci sequence and Gaussian Lucas sequence are

$$GF_n = \frac{1}{\alpha - \beta}\{(1 - i\beta)\alpha^n - (1 - i\alpha)\beta^n\}$$

and

$$GL_n = \frac{\alpha^n - \beta^n}{\alpha - \beta}GL_1 + \frac{\alpha^{n-1} - \beta^{n-1}}{\alpha - \beta}GL_0$$

respectively, where α and β denote the roots of the characteristic equation for Gaussian Fibonacci sequence and GL_0, GL_1 denote the initial values for the Gaussian Lucas numbers [34,35].

The Pauli matrices that have been introduced by Wolfgang Pauli form a set of 2×2 complex matrices as follows:

$$1 = \begin{bmatrix} 1 & 0 \\ 0 & 1 \end{bmatrix}, \quad \sigma_1 = \begin{bmatrix} 0 & 1 \\ 1 & 0 \end{bmatrix}, \quad \sigma_2 = \begin{bmatrix} 0 & -i \\ i & 0 \end{bmatrix}, \quad \sigma_3 = \begin{bmatrix} 1 & 0 \\ 0 & -1 \end{bmatrix}$$

The multiplication rules are given by

$$\sigma_1^2 = \sigma_2^2 = \sigma_3^2 = 1, \quad \sigma_1\sigma_2 = -\sigma_2\sigma_1 = i\sigma_3$$
$$\sigma_2\sigma_3 = -\sigma_3\sigma_2 = i\sigma_1, \quad \sigma_3\sigma_1 = -\sigma_1\sigma_3 = i\sigma_2$$

Further, these matrices are Hermitian and unitary. These 2×2 types of Hermitian matrices form a basis for the real vector space and the span of $\{I, i\sigma_1, i\sigma_2, i\sigma_3\}$ is isomorphic to the real algebra of quaternions [36,37].

The Pauli quaternions are defined by Kim as follows:

$$q = a_0 1 + a_1 \sigma_1 + a_2 \sigma_2 + a_3 \sigma_3,$$

where $1, \sigma_1, \sigma_2$ and σ_3 represent the Pauli matrices.

Let $q = a_0 1 + a_1 \sigma_1 + a_2 \sigma_2 + a_3 \sigma_3$ and $p = b_0 1 + b_1 \sigma_1 + b_2 \sigma_2 + b_3 \sigma_3$ be Pauli quaternions, then the product of these quaternions are given by [37]

$$q.p = (a_0 b_0 + a_1 b_1 + a_2 b_2 + a_3 b_3)1 + \{(a_0 b_1 + a_1 b_0) + i(a_2 b_3 - a_3 b_2)\}\sigma_1 \\ + \{(a_0 b_2 + a_2 b_0) + i(a_3 b_1 - a_1 b_3)\}\sigma_2 \\ + \{(a_0 b_3 + a_3 b_0) + i(a_1 b_2 - a_2 b_1)\}\sigma_3.$$

The conjugate and the norm of Pauli quaternions are

$$q^* = a_0 1 - a_1 \sigma_1 - a_2 \sigma_2 - a_3 \sigma_3$$

and

$$N(q) = \sqrt{|q.q^*|} = \sqrt{|a_0^2 - a_1^2 - a_2^2 - a_3^2|},$$

respectively [37].

Torunbalcı has presented Pauli Fibonacci and Pauli Lucas quaternions by taking the real coefficients of Pauli quaternion as the Fibonacci number sequence. Honsberger's, d'Ocagne's, Catalan, Cassini identities, generating function and Binet formula and the matrix representation have been given for the Pauli Fibonacci quaternions [38].

In a recent paper [39] on a base of quaternions, the families of associated sequences of real polynomials and numbers were defined. Quaternion equivalents for quasi-Fibonacci numbers (shortly quaternaccis) were introduced. In OEIS, there is a number of quaternacci sequences connected with generalized Gaussian Fibonacci integers. We are also interested in quaternions with coefficients of Gaussian Fibonacci numbers.

Especially, in this work, our aim is to introduce Pauli Gaussian Fibonacci quaternions and Pauli Lucas quaternions whose coefficients consist of Gaussian Fibonacci numbers and Gaussian Lucas numbers, respectively. We called these numbers the Pauli Gaussian Fibonacci and Pauli Gaussian Lucas numbers, respectively. Then, some algebraic properties of these quaternions have been shown. Moreover, some identities and formulas for these quaternions have been obtained.

2. The Pauli Gaussian Fibonacci Quaternions

In this section, the definition of Pauli Gaussian Fibonacci and Pauli Gaussian Lucas quaternions will be given. Then, some algebraic properties, identities and theorems are given for Pauli Gaussian Fibonacci and Pauli Gaussian Lucas quaternions.

Definition 1. *The Pauli Gaussian Fibonacci and Pauli Gaussian Lucas quaternions are defined by*

$$Q_p GF_n = GF_n 1 + GF_{n+1} \sigma_1 + GF_{n+2} \sigma_2 + GF_{n+3} \sigma_3$$

and

$$Q_p GL_n = GL_n 1 + GL_{n+1} \sigma_1 + GL_{n+2} \sigma_2 + GL_{n+3} \sigma_3$$

respectively, where GF_n and GL_n are the n-th Gaussian Fibonacci and Gaussian Lucas numbers.

Furthermore, these numbers are related to Pauli Fibonacci and Pauli Lucas quaternions as follows

$$Q_p GF_n = Q_p F_n + i Q_p F_{n-1}$$

and

$$Q_p GL_n = Q_p L_n + i Q_p L_{n-1}$$

respectively.

In order to obtain the recursive relations for Pauli Gaussian Fibonacci and Pauli Gaussian Lucas quaternions, we will consider the relations $GF_{n+2} = GF_n + GF_{n+1}$ and $GL_{n+2} = GL_n + GL_{n+1}$ for Gaussian Fibonacci and Gaussian Lucas numbers, respectively.

Hence, for $n \geq 0$

$$Q_pGF_{n+2} = Q_pGF_n + Q_pGF_{n+1}$$

and

$$Q_pGL_{n+2} = Q_pGL_n + Q_pGL_{n+1}$$

respectively.

Definition 2. *The conjugates of the Pauli Gaussian Fibonacci quaternion Q_pGF_n and the Pauli Gaussian Lucas quaternion Q_pGL_n are defined by*

$$\overline{Q_pGF_n} = GF_n 1 - GF_{n+1}\sigma_1 - GF_{n+2}\sigma_2 - GF_{n+3}\sigma_3$$

and

$$\overline{Q_pGL_n} = GL_n 1 - GL_{n+1}\sigma_1 - GL_{n+2}\sigma_2 - GL_{n+3}\sigma_3$$

respectively.

The addition, subtraction and multiplication of two Pauli Gaussian Fibonacci quaternions Q_pGF_n and Q_pGF_m aregiven by

$$Q_pGF_n \pm Q_pGF_m = (GF_n \pm GF_m).1 + (GF_{n+1} \pm GF_{m+1})\sigma_1 \\ + (GF_{n+2} \pm GF_{m+2})\sigma_2 + (GF_{n+3} \pm GF_{m+3})\sigma_3 \quad (1)$$

and

$$Q_pGF_n \times Q_pGF_m = (GF_n.GF_m + GF_{n+1}.GF_{m+1} + GF_{n+2}.GF_{m+2} + GF_{n+3}.GF_{m+3}).1 \\ + (GF_{n+1}.GF_m + GF_n.GF_{m+1} - iGF_{n+3}.GF_{m+2} + iGF_{n+2}.GF_{m+3})\sigma_1 \\ + (GF_{n+2}.GF_m + iGF_{n+3}.GF_{m+1} + GF_n.GF_{m+2} - iGF_{n+1}.GF_{m+3})\sigma_2 \\ + (GF_{n+3}.GF_m - iGF_{n+2}.GF_{m+1} + iGF_{n+1}.GF_{m+2} + GF_n.GF_{m+3})\sigma_3 \quad (2)$$

respectively.

Note that $Q_pGF_n \times Q_pGF_m \neq Q_pGF_m \times Q_pGF_n$.

In this case, the norm of any Pauli Gaussian Fibonacci quaternion can be written as

$$N^2_{Q_pGF_n} = Q_pGF_n \times \overline{Q_pGF_n} = \left| GF_n^2 - GF_{n+1}^2 - GF_{n+2}^2 - GF_{n+3}^2 \right|.$$

So, the scalar and vectorial part of any Pauli Gaussian Fibonacci quaternion is represented by

$$S_{Q_pGF_n} = GF_n, \quad V_{Q_pGF_n} = GF_{n+1}\sigma_1 + GF_{n+2}\sigma_2 + GF_{n+3}\sigma_3.$$

In addition, Equation (2) can be rewritten in terms of the scalar and vector parts of the Pauli Gaussian Fibonacci quaternion as follows.

$$Q_pGF_n \times Q_pGF_m = S_{Q_pGF_n} S_{Q_pGF_m} + \left\langle V_{Q_pGF_n}, V_{Q_pGF_m} \right\rangle + S_{Q_pGF_n} V_{Q_pGF_m} \\ + S_{Q_pGF_m} V_{Q_pGF_n} + V_{Q_pGF_n} \wedge V_{Q_pGF_m}.$$

With the aid of Equation (2), the following Pauli Gaussian Fibonacci quaternion can be expressed as a matrix form

$$Q_pGF_n \times Q_pGF_m = \begin{bmatrix} GF_n & GF_{n+1} & GF_{n+2} & GF_{n+3} \\ GF_{n+1} & GF_n & -iGF_{n+3} & iGF_{n+2} \\ GF_{n+2} & iGF_{n+3} & GF_n & -iGF_{n+1} \\ GF_{n+3} & -iGF_{n+2} & iGF_{n+1} & GF_n \end{bmatrix} \begin{bmatrix} GF_m \\ GF_{m+1} \\ GF_{m+2} \\ GF_{m+3} \end{bmatrix}.$$

Theorem 1. *Let Q_pGF_n, Q_pGL_n and GF_n denote the Gaussian Fibonacci number, Gaussian Lucas number and the Gaussian Fibonacci number, respectively. For $n \geq 1$, we get the following relations*

(i)
$$Q_pGF_{n+1} + Q_pGF_{n-1} = Q_pGL_n$$

(ii)
$$Q_pGF_n + Q_pGF_{n-1} = Q_pGF_{n+1}$$

(iii)
$$Q_pGF_{n+2} - Q_pGF_{n-2} = Q_pGL_n$$

(iv)
$$Q_pGF_n - Q_pGF_{n+1}\sigma_1 - Q_pGF_{n+2}\sigma_2 - Q_pGF_{n+3}\sigma_3 = GF_n - GF_{n+2} - GF_{n+4} - GF_{n+6}$$

Proof. (i) Considering Equation (1) and using the identity $GF_{n+1} + GF_{n-1} = GL_n$ [3], we have the proof as follows

$$\begin{aligned} Q_pGF_{n+1} + Q_pGF_{n-1} &= (GF_{n+1} + GF_{n-1}).1 + (GF_{n+2} + GF_n)\sigma_1 \\ &\quad + (GF_{n+3} + GF_{n+1})\sigma_2 + (GF_{n+4} + GF_{n+2})\sigma_3 \\ &= GL_n 1 + GL_{n+1}\sigma_1 + GL_{n+2}\sigma_2 + GL_{n+3}\sigma_3 \\ &= Q_pGL_n. \end{aligned}$$

(ii) If we use Equation (1) and the recurrence relation of the Gaussian Fibonacci numbers, the proof can be easily seen.

(iii) Using Equation (1) and the recurrence relation of the Gaussian Fibonacci numbers, we obtain

$$\begin{aligned} Q_pGF_{n+2} - Q_pGF_{n-2} &= (GF_{n+1} + GF_{n-1}).1 + (GF_{n+2} + GF_n)\sigma_1 \\ &\quad + (GF_{n+3} + GF_{n+1})\sigma_2 + (GF_{n+4} + GF_{n+2})\sigma_3. \end{aligned}$$

By substituting the identity $GF_{n+1} + GF_{n-1} = GL_n$ [3] into the previous equation we get

$$Q_pGF_{n+2} - Q_pGF_{n-2} = Q_pGL_n.$$

(iv) Multiplying both sides of the Pauli Gaussian Fibonacci quaternions Q_pGF_{n+1}, Q_pGF_{n+2}, Q_pGF_{n+3} by $-\sigma_1$, $-\sigma_2$ and $-\sigma_3$ respectively gives

$$\begin{aligned} -Q_pGF_{n+1}\sigma_1 - Q_pGF_{n+2}\sigma_2 - Q_pGF_{n+3}\sigma_3 &= -GF_{n+1}\sigma_1 - GF_{n+2}1 + iGF_{n+3}\sigma_3 - iGF_{n+4}\sigma_2 \\ &\quad - GF_{n+2}\sigma_2 - iGF_{n+3}\sigma_3 - GF_{n+4}1 + iGF_{n+5}\sigma_1 \\ &\quad - GF_{n+3}\sigma_3 + iGF_{n+4}\sigma_2 - iGF_{n+5}\sigma_1 - GF_{n+6}1 \\ &= -GF_{n+1}\sigma_1 - GF_{n+2}\sigma_2 - GF_{n+3}\sigma_3 \\ &\quad - (GF_{n+2} + GF_{n+4} + GF_{n+6})1. \end{aligned}$$

Then, adding the above equation with Q_pGF_n yields

$$\begin{aligned} &Q_pGF_n - Q_pGF_{n+1}\sigma_1 - Q_pGF_{n+2}\sigma_2 - Q_pGF_{n+3}\sigma_3 \\ &= GF_n 1 + GF_{n+1}\sigma_1 + GF_{n+2}\sigma_2 + GF_{n+3}\sigma_3 - GF_{n+1}\sigma_1 - GF_{n+2}\sigma_2 - GF_{n+3}\sigma_3 \\ &\quad -(GF_{n+2} + GF_{n+4} + GF_{n+6})1 \\ &= (GF_n - GF_{n+2} - GF_{n+4} - GF_{n+6})1. \end{aligned}$$

□

Theorem 2 (Honsberger's Identity). *For $n, m \geq 0$ and GF_n, the Honsberger identity for the Pauli Gaussian Fibonacci quaternions is given by*

$$Q_pGF_n \times Q_pGF_m + Q_pGF_{n+1} \times Q_pGF_{m+1} = (2Q_pGF_{n+m} + 9F_{n+m+1} + 5F_{n+m+2})(1+2i).$$

Proof. By the Equations (1) and (2), we get

$$Q_pGF_n \times Q_pGF_m + Q_pGF_{n+1} \times Q_pGF_{m+1}$$
$$= [(GF_n.GF_m + GF_{n+1}.GF_{m+1}) + (GF_{n+2}.GF_{m+2} + GF_{n+3}.GF_{m+3})$$
$$+ (GF_{n+1}.GF_{m+1} + GF_{n+2}.GF_{m+2}) + (GF_{n+3}.GF_{m+3} + GF_{n+4}.GF_{m+4})]1$$
$$+ [(GF_{n+1}.GF_m + GF_{n+2}.GF_{m+1}) + (GF_n.GF_{m+1} + GF_{n+1}.GF_{m+2})$$
$$+ i(GF_{n+2}.GF_{m+3} + GF_{n+3}.GF_{m+4}) - i(GF_{n+3}.GF_{m+2} + GF_{n+4}.GF_{m+3})]\sigma_1$$
$$+ [(GF_{n+2}.GF_m + GF_{n+3}.GF_{m+1}) + (GF_n.GF_{m+2} + GF_{n+1}.GF_{m+3})$$
$$+ i(GF_{n+3}.GF_{m+1} + GF_{n+4}.GF_{m+2}) - i(GF_{n+1}.GF_{m+3} + GF_{n+2}.GF_{m+4})]\sigma_2$$
$$+ [(GF_{n+3}.GF_m + GF_{n+4}.GF_{m+1}) + (GF_n.GF_{m+3} + GF_{n+1}.GF_{m+4})$$
$$+ i(GF_{n+1}.GF_{m+2} + GF_{n+2}.GF_{m+3}) - i(GF_{n+2}.GF_{m+1} + GF_{n+3}.GF_{m+2})]\sigma_3.$$

Using the identity $GF_n GF_m + GF_{n+1} GF_{m+1} = F_{n+m}(1+2i)$ [3], we obtain

$$Q_pGF_n \times Q_pGF_m + Q_pGF_{n+1} \times Q_pGF_{m+1}$$
$$= ((F_{n+m} + F_{n+m+2} + F_{n+m+4} + F_{n+m+6}).1$$
$$+ 2(F_{n+m+1}\sigma_1 + F_{n+m+2}\sigma_2 + F_{n+m+3}\sigma_3))(1+2i).$$

If the necessary arrangements are made in the last equation, we have

$$Q_pGF_n \times Q_pGF_m + Q_pGF_{n+1} \times Q_pGF_{m+1} = (2Q_pGF_{n+m} + 9F_{n+m+1}1 + 5F_{n+m+2}1)(1+2i).$$

Thus, the claim is verified. □

Theorem 3 (Generating Function). *The generating functions of the Pauli Gaussian Fibonacci quaternions and Pauli Gaussian Lucas quaternions are as follows:*

$$g(x) = \sum_{n=0}^{\infty} Q_pGF_n.x^n = \frac{Q_pGF_0 + (Q_pGF_1 - Q_pGF_0)x}{1-x-x^2}$$

and

$$h(x) = \sum_{n=0}^{\infty} Q_pGL_n.x^n = \frac{Q_pGL_0 + (Q_pGL_1 - Q_pGL_0)x}{1-x-x^2}$$

respectively.

Proof. Let us use the definition of a generating function of Q_pGF_n as follows

$$g(x) = Q_pGF_0 + Q_pGF_1.x + Q_pGF_2.x^2 + \cdots + Q_pGF_n.x^n + \ldots \quad (3)$$

Multiplying both sides of the Equation (3) by $-x$ and $-x^2$ gives

$$-xg(x) = -Q_pGF_0.x - Q_pGF_1.x^2 - Q_pGF_2.x^3 - \cdots + Q_pGF_n.x^{n+1} - \ldots \quad (4)$$

and

$$-x^2g(x) = -Q_pGF_0.x^2 - Q_pGF_1.x^3 - Q_pGF_2.x^4 - \cdots + Q_pGF_n.x^{n+2} - \ldots \quad (5)$$

If we add the Equations (3)–(5) and use Theorem 1, we conclude that

$$\left(1 - x - x^2\right)g(x) = Q_pGF_0 + (Q_pGF_1 - Q_pGF_0)x$$

Then, we write

$$g(x) = \sum_{n=0}^{\infty} Q_pGF_n.x^n = \frac{Q_pGF_0 + (Q_pGF_1 - Q_pGF_0)x}{1-x-x^2}.$$

Let us write the generating function of Q_pGL_n as follows

$$h(x) = Q_pGL_0 + Q_pGL_1.x + Q_pGL_2.x^2 + \cdots + Q_pGL_n.x^n + \ldots \qquad (6)$$

The proof can be easily seen if we apply a similar method used to prove the generating function for the Pauli Gaussian Fibonacci quaternions to the Equation (6). □

Now, we will obtain the Binet formulas, which give us the n-th Pauli Gaussian Fibonacci and Pauli Gaussian Lucas quaternions, respectively.

Theorem 4 (Binet's Formula). *(i) For $n \geq 1$, Binet formula of the Pauli Gaussian Fibonacci quaternions is given by*

$$Q_pGF_n = c\alpha^n\hat{\alpha} + d\beta^n\hat{\beta}$$

where $c = \frac{1-\beta i}{\alpha - \beta}$, $d = \frac{-1+\alpha i}{\alpha - \beta}$, $\alpha = \frac{1+\sqrt{5}}{2}$ and $\beta = \frac{1-\sqrt{5}}{2}$.
(ii) For $n \in \mathbb{N}$, the Binet formula of the Pauli Gaussian Lucas quaternions is given by

$$Q_pGL_n = Q_pF_nGL_1 + Q_pF_{n-1}GL_0.$$

This last formula gives us the relationship between Pauli Fibonacci quaternions and Gaussian Lucas numbers.

Proof. (i) Applying the Binet's formula of the Gaussian Fibonacci to Q_pGF_n, we get

$$\begin{aligned}Q_pGF_n = (c\alpha^n\hat{\alpha} + d\beta^n\hat{\beta})1 + (c\alpha^{n+1}\hat{\alpha} + d\beta^{n+1}\hat{\beta})\sigma_1 \\ + (c\alpha^{n+2}\hat{\alpha} + d\beta^{n+2}\hat{\beta})\sigma_2 + (c\alpha^{n+3}\hat{\alpha} + d\beta^{n+3}\hat{\beta})\sigma_3.\end{aligned} \qquad (7)$$

If Equation (7) is arranged, we have

$$Q_pGF_n = c\alpha^n(1 + \alpha\sigma_1 + \alpha^2\sigma_2 + \alpha^3\sigma_3) + d\beta^n(1 + \beta\sigma_1 + \beta^2\sigma_2 + \beta^3\sigma_3)$$
$$Q_pGF_n = c\alpha^n\hat{\alpha} + d\beta^n\hat{\beta}.$$

such that

$$\hat{\alpha} = 1 + \alpha\sigma_1 + \alpha^2\sigma_2 + \alpha^3\sigma_3$$

and

$$\hat{\beta} = 1 + \beta\sigma_1 + \beta^2\sigma_2 + \beta^3\sigma_3.$$

(ii) Applying Binet's formula of the Gaussian Lucas to Q_pGL_n, we get

$$\begin{aligned}Q_pGL_n = \left(\frac{\alpha^n - \beta^n}{\alpha - \beta}GL_1 + \frac{\alpha^{n-1} - \beta^{n-1}}{\alpha - \beta}GL_0\right)1 \\ + \left(\frac{\alpha^{n+1} - \beta^{n+1}}{\alpha - \beta}GL_1 + \frac{\alpha^n - \beta^n}{\alpha - \beta}GL_0\right)\sigma_1 \\ + \left(\frac{\alpha^{n+2} - \beta^{n+2}}{\alpha - \beta}GL_1 + \frac{\alpha^{n+1} - \beta^{n+1}}{\alpha - \beta}GL_0\right)\sigma_2 \\ + \left(\frac{\alpha^{n+3} - \beta^{n+3}}{\alpha - \beta}GL_1 + \frac{\alpha^{n+2} - \beta^{n+2}}{\alpha - \beta}GL_0\right)\sigma_3.\end{aligned} \qquad (8)$$

Equation (8) can be stated in terms of Fibonacci numbers as follows:

$$\begin{aligned}Q_pGL_n &= (F_n 1 + F_{n+1}\sigma_1 + F_{n+2}\sigma_2 + F_{n+3}\sigma_3)GL_1 \\ &\quad + (F_{n-1}1 + F_n\sigma_1 + F_{n+1}\sigma_2 + F_{n+2}\sigma_3)GL_0 \\ &= Q_pF_nGL_1 + Q_pF_{n-1}GL_0.\end{aligned}$$

□

Example 1. *Let Q_pGF_2 be Pauli Gaussian Fibonacci quaternion. Applying Theorem 4 for $n = 2$, we get*

$$Q_pGF_2 = \frac{(1-\beta i)\alpha^2(1+\alpha\sigma_1+\alpha^2\sigma_2+\alpha^3\sigma_3)+(-1+\alpha i)\beta^2(1+\beta\sigma_1+\beta^2\sigma_2+\beta^3\sigma_3)}{\sqrt{5}}$$
$$= (1+i)1 + (2+i)\sigma_1 + (3+2i)\sigma_2 + (5+3i)\sigma_3.$$

Furthermore, the above Pauli Gaussian Fibonacci quaternion is written by

$$Q_pGF_2 = (11 + 2\sigma_1 + 3\sigma_2 + 5\sigma_3) + i(11 + 1\sigma_1 + 2\sigma_2 + 3\sigma_3)$$
$$Q_pGF_2 = Q_pF_2 + iQ_pF_1.$$

Notice that the real and the imaginary parts of the Pauli Gaussian Fibonacci quaternion correspond Pauli Fibonacci quaternions for $n = 2$ and $n = 1$.

Theorem 5 (d'Ocagne's Identity). *For $n, m \geq 0$, the following identity holds*

$$Q_pGF_m \times Q_pGF_{n+1} - Q_pGF_{m+1} \times Q_pGF_n = \left(\frac{i-2}{\sqrt{5}}\right)[\beta^m\alpha^n\hat{\beta}\hat{\alpha} - \beta^m\alpha^n\hat{\alpha}\hat{\beta}].$$

Proof. Considering the Binet formula in Theorem 4 and making some necessary calculations, the following expression is obtained.

$$Q_pGF_m \times Q_pGF_{n+1} - Q_pGF_{m+1} \times Q_pGF_n$$
$$= (cd)\left[(\beta^m\alpha^{n+1} - \beta^{m+1}\alpha^n)\hat{\beta}\hat{\alpha} + (\alpha^m\beta^{n+1} - \alpha^{m+1}\beta^n)\hat{\alpha}\hat{\beta}\right]$$
$$= (cd)\left[\beta^m\alpha^n(\alpha-\beta)\hat{\beta}\hat{\alpha} - \beta^m\alpha^n(\alpha-\beta)\hat{\alpha}\hat{\beta}\right].$$

To achieve our purpose, we now put the values $cd = dc = \frac{i-2}{5}$, $\alpha - \beta = \sqrt{5}$ in the above equality. Thus, the proof is completed. □

Theorem 6. *(Catalan's Identity) For $n \geq 1$, the Catalan identity for the Pauli Gaussian Fibonacci quaternions is*

$$Q_pGF_n^2 - Q_pGF_{n+r} \times Q_pGF_{n-r}$$
$$= (-1)^{n+1}\frac{(2-i)}{5}\left[\left(1 - \left(\frac{-3+\sqrt{5}}{2}\right)^r\right)\hat{\beta}\hat{\alpha} + \left(1 - \left(\frac{-3-\sqrt{5}}{2}\right)^r\right)\hat{\alpha}\hat{\beta}\right].$$

Proof. Using the Binet formula for Pauli Gaussian Fibonacci quaternions, we have

$$Q_pGF_n^2 - Q_pGF_{n+r} \times Q_pGF_{n-r}$$
$$= (c\alpha^n\hat{\alpha} + d\beta^n\hat{\beta})(c\alpha^n\hat{\alpha} + d\beta^n\hat{\beta}) - (c\alpha^{n+r}\hat{\alpha} + d\beta^{n+r}\hat{\beta})(c\alpha^{n-r}\hat{\alpha} + d\beta^{n-r}\hat{\beta})$$
$$= dc((\beta\alpha)^n - \beta^{n+r}\alpha^{n-r})\hat{\beta}\hat{\alpha} + cd((\alpha\beta)^n - \alpha^{n+r}\beta^{n-r})\hat{\alpha}\hat{\beta}.$$

Note that we have the following identities

$$\hat{\alpha} = 1 + \left(\frac{1+\sqrt{5}}{2}\right)\sigma_1 + \left(\frac{3+\sqrt{5}}{2}\right)\sigma_2 + \left(2+\sqrt{5}\right)\sigma_3,$$
$$\hat{\beta} = 1 + \left(\frac{1-\sqrt{5}}{2}\right)\sigma_1 + \left(\frac{3-\sqrt{5}}{2}\right)\sigma_2 + \left(2-\sqrt{5}\right)\sigma_3,$$
$$\hat{\alpha}\hat{\beta} = \left(1 - \sqrt{5}i\right)\sigma_1 + \left(3 - \sqrt{5}i\right)\sigma_2 + \left(4 + \sqrt{5}i\right)\sigma_3,$$
$$\hat{\beta}\hat{\alpha} = \left(1 + \sqrt{5}i\right)\sigma_1 + \left(3 + \sqrt{5}i\right)\sigma_2 + \left(4 - \sqrt{5}i\right)\sigma_3.$$

□

It is well-known that if $r = 1$ the Cassini identity corresponds to the Cassini identity. Thus, the following corollary can be given.

Corollary 1. *For $n \geq 1$, the Cassini identity for the Pauli Gaussian Fibonacci quaternions is*

$$Q_pGF_n^2 - Q_pGF_{n+1} \times Q_pGF_{n-1} = (-1)^{n+1}\frac{(2-i)}{5}\left[\left(\frac{5-\sqrt{5}}{2}\right)\hat{\beta}\hat{\alpha} + \left(\frac{5+\sqrt{5}}{2}\right)\hat{\alpha}\hat{\beta}\right].$$

Example 2. *Let Q_pGF_5, Q_pGF_3 and Q_pGF_1 be Pauli Gaussian Fibonacci quaternions. If we consider Theorem 6 for $n = 3$ and $r = 2$, the calculations give the following equality*

$$\begin{aligned}
Q_pGF_3^2 &- Q_pGF_5 \times Q_pGF_1 \\
&= (-1)^4 \tfrac{(2-i)}{5} \Big[\Big(\tfrac{-5+3\sqrt{5}}{2}\Big)\Big(\big(1+\sqrt{5}i\big)\sigma_1 + \big(3+\sqrt{5}i\big)\sigma_2 + \big(4-\sqrt{5}i\big)\sigma_3\Big) \\
&\quad + \Big(\tfrac{-5-3\sqrt{5}}{2}\Big)\Big(\big(1-\sqrt{5}i\big)\sigma_1 + \big(3-\sqrt{5}i\big)\sigma_2 + \big(4+\sqrt{5}i\big)\sigma_3\Big) \Big] \\
&= \tfrac{(2-i)}{5}[(-5+15i)\sigma_1 + (-15+15i)\sigma_2 + (-20-15i)\sigma_3] \\
&= (2-i)[(-1+3i)\sigma_1 + (-3+3i)\sigma_2 + (-4-3i)\sigma_3].
\end{aligned}$$

Catalan identity for $n = 3$ and $r = 2$ obtained from Aydın (see [38]), we found

$$\begin{aligned}
Q_pF_3^2 - Q_pF_5 \times Q_pF_1 &= (-1)^1 F_2[(1-i)\sigma_1 + (3-i)\sigma_2 + (4+i)\sigma_3] \\
Q_pF_3^2 - Q_pF_5 \times Q_pF_1 &= -[(1-i)\sigma_1 + (3-i)\sigma_2 + (4+i)\sigma_3].
\end{aligned}$$

where Q_pF_1, Q_pF_3 and Q_pF_5 are Pauli Fibonacci quaternions.

Example 3. *Let Q_pGF_3, Q_pGF_2 and Q_pGF_1 be Pauli Gaussian Fibonacci quaternions. If we consider Corollary for $n = 3$ and $r = 1$, the calculations give the following equality*

$$\begin{aligned}
Q_pGF_3^2 &- Q_pGF_4 \times Q_pGF_2 \\
&= (-1)^4 \tfrac{(2-i)}{5} \Big[\Big(\tfrac{5-\sqrt{5}}{2}\Big)\Big(\big(1+\sqrt{5}i\big)\sigma_1 + \big(3+\sqrt{5}i\big)\sigma_2 + \big(4-\sqrt{5}i\big)\sigma_3\Big) \\
&\quad + \Big(\tfrac{5+\sqrt{5}}{2}\Big)\Big(\big(1-\sqrt{5}i\big)\sigma_1 + \big(3-\sqrt{5}i\big)\sigma_2 + \big(4+\sqrt{5}i\big)\sigma_3\Big) \Big] \\
&= \tfrac{(2-i)}{5}[(5-5i)\sigma_1 + (15-5i)\sigma_2 + (20+5i)\sigma_3] \\
&= (2-i)[(1-i)\sigma_1 + (3-i)\sigma_2 + (4+i)\sigma_3].
\end{aligned}$$

On the other hand, if we consider the Cassini identity for $n = 3$ and $r = 1$ obtained from Aydın (see [38]), we found

$$\begin{aligned}
Q_pF_3^2 - Q_pF_4 \times Q_pF_2 &= (-1)^2 F_1[(1-i)\sigma_1 + (3-i)\sigma_2 + (4+i)\sigma_3] \\
Q_pF_3^2 - Q_pF_4 \times Q_pF_2 &= (1-i)\sigma_1 + (3-i)\sigma_2 + (4+i)\sigma_3.
\end{aligned}$$

where Q_pF_1, Q_pF_2 and Q_pF_3 are Pauli Fibonacci quaternions.

3. Conclusions

In this research, we have extended the quaternions in [38] to the complex case by taking the components of Gaussian Fibonacci and Gaussian Lucas numbers. We have obtained some identities and formulas for these special quaternions, which are specific to Fibonacci quaternions. On the other hand, Pauli matrices and Pauli quaternions have applications in many areas, including quantum mechanics and quantum field theory. We believe that it will be a resource for researchers working in these fields.

Funding: This research received no external funding.

Data Availability Statement: Not applicable.

Conflicts of Interest: The author declares no conflict of interest.

References

1. Gauss, C.F. *Theoria Residuorum Biquadraticorum*; Commentatio Prima Sumtibus Dieterichtianis, Gottingae; Cambridge University Press: Cambridge, UK, 1832.
2. Horadam, A.F. Complex Fibonacci Numbers and Fibonacci Quaternions. *Am. Math. Mon.* **1963**, *70*, 289–291. [CrossRef]
3. Jordan, J.H. Gaussian Fibonacci and Lucas Numbers. *Fibonacci Quart.* **1965**, *3*, 315–318.
4. Koshy, T. *Fibonacci and Lucas Numbers with Applications*; Wiley-Interscience Publication: New York, NY, USA, 2001.
5. Berzsenyi, G. Gaussian Fibonacci Numbers. *Fibonacci Quart.* **1977**, *15*, 233–236.

6. Mc Carthy, J.M. *Introduction to Theoretical Kinematics*; MIT Press: Cambridge, MA, USA, 1990.
7. Shoemake, K. Animation Rotation with Quaternion Curves. In Proceedings of the SIGGRAPH '85: 12th Annual Conference on Computer Graphics and Interactive Techniques, San Francisco, CA, USA, 22–26 July 1985; Volume 19, pp. 245–254.
8. Silberstein, L. LXXVI. Quaternionic Form of Relativity. *Lond. Edinb. Dubl. Phil. Mag.* **1912**, *23*, 790–809. [CrossRef]
9. Blake, C.S. Sporadic SICs and the Normed Division Algebras. *Found. Phys.* **2017**, *47*, 1060–1064.
10. Wu, J.; Sun, Y.; Wang, M.; Liu, M. Hand-eye Calibration: 4-D procrustes Analysis Approach. *IEEE Trans. Instrum. Meas.* **2019**, *69*, 2966–2981. [CrossRef]
11. Kopp, M.; Kreil, D.; Neun, M.; Jonietz, D.; Martin, H.; Herruzo, P.; Gruca, A.; Soleymani, A.; Wu, F.; Liu, Y.; et al. Traffic4cast at Neurips 2020—Yet More on the Unreasonable Effectiveness of Gridded Geo-spatial Processes. In Proceedings of the NeurIPS 2020 Competition and Demonstration Track, Virtual Event, 6–12 December 2021; Escalante, H.J., Hofmann, K., Eds.; Volume 133, pp. 325–343.
12. Saoud, L.S.; Al-Marzouqi, H. Metacognitive Sedenion-Valued Neural Network and Its Learning Algorithm. *IEEE Access* **2020**, *8*, 144823–144838. [CrossRef]
13. Lidl, R.; Niederreiter, H. *Introduction to Finite Fields and Their Applications*; Cambridge University Press: Cambridge, UK, 1994.
14. Akkus, I.; Kızılaslan, G. On Some Properties of Tribonacci Quaternions. *An. Şiinţ. Univ. Ovidius Constanta* **2018**, *26*, 5–20. [CrossRef]
15. Akyiğit, M.; Hidayet, H.K.; Tosun, M. Fibonacci Generalized Quaternions. *Adv. Appl. Clifford Algebr.* **2014**, *24*, 631–641. [CrossRef]
16. Bilgici, G.; Tokeşer, Ü.; Ünal, Z. Fibonacci and Lucas Sedenions. *J. Integer Seq.* **2017**, *20*, 1–11.
17. Catarino, P.; Campos, H. From Fibonacci Sequence to More Recent Generalisations. In *Mathematics and Its Applications in Science and Engineering*; Springer: Cham, Swiztherland, 2022.
18. Cerda-Morales, G. On a Generalization for Tribonacci Quaternions. *Mediterr. J. Math.* **2017**, *14*, 239. [CrossRef]
19. Cerda-Morales, G. The Unifying Formula for All Tribonacci-type Octonions Sequences and Their Properties. *Konuralp J. Math.* **2019**, *7*, 292–299.
20. Cereceda, J.L. Binet's formula for generalized tribonacci numbers. *Int. J. Math. Edu. Sci. Technol.* **2015**, *46*, 1235–1243. [CrossRef]
21. Flaut, C.; Shpakivskyi, V. On Generalized Fibonacci Quaternions and Fibonacci-Narayana Quaternions. *Adv. Appl. Clifford Algebr.* **2013**, *23*, 673–688. [CrossRef]
22. Halici, S.; Karatas, A. On a Generalizaton for Fibonacci Quaternions. *Chaos Solitons Fractals* **2017**, *98*, 178–182. [CrossRef]
23. Halici, S. On Fibonacci Quaternions. *Adv. Appl. Clifford Algebr.* **2017**, *22*, 321–327. [CrossRef]
24. Iyer, M.R. Some Results on Fibonacci Quaternions. *Fibonacci Quart.* **1969**, *7*, 201–210.
25. Karataş, A.; Halıcı, S. Horadam Octonions. *An. Şiinţ. Univ. Ovidius Constanta* **2017**, *25*, 97–106. [CrossRef]
26. Kızılateş, C.; Kirlak, S. A New Generalization of Fibonacci and Lucas Type Sedenions. *J. Discret. Math. Sci. Cryptogr.* **2022**, 1–12. [CrossRef]
27. Savin, D. Some Properties of Fibonacci Numbers, Fibonacci Octonions, and Generalized Fibonacci-Lucas Octonions. *Adv. Differ. Equ.* **2015**, *2015*, 298. [CrossRef]
28. Soykan, Y. Tribonacci and Tribonacci-Lucas Sedenions. *Mathematics* **2019**, *7*, 74. [CrossRef]
29. Soykan, Y. Tetranacci and Tetranacci-Lucas Quaternions. *Asian Res. J. Math.* **2019**, *15*, 1–24. [CrossRef]
30. Soykan, Y.; Okumuş, İ.; Taşdemir, E. On Generalized Tribonacci Sedenions. *Sarajevo J. Math.* **2020**, *16*, 103–122.
31. Soykan, Y.; Özmen, N.; Göcen, M. On Generalized Pentanacci Quaternions. *Tbil. Math. J.* **2020**, *13*, 169–181. [CrossRef]
32. Spickerman, W.R. Binet's Formula for the Tribonacci Sequence. *Fibonacci Quart.* **1982**, *20*, 118–120.
33. Halici, S. On Complex Fibonacci Quaternions. *Am. Math. Mon.* **2013**, *23*, 105–112. [CrossRef]
34. Halici, S. On Quaternion-Gaussian Lucas Numbers. *Math. Meth. Appl. Sci.* **2021**, *44*, 7601–7606. [CrossRef]
35. Halici, S.; Cerda-Morales, G. On Quaternion-Gaussian Fibonacci Numbers and Their Properties. *An. Şiinţ. Univ. Ovidius Constanta* **2021**, *29*, 71–82. [CrossRef]
36. Condon, E.U.; Morse, P.M. *Quantum Mechanics*; McGraw-Hill: New York, NY, USA, 1929.
37. Kim, J.E. A Representation of de Moivre's Formula Over Pauli Quaternions. *Ann. Acad. Rom. Sci. Ser. Math. Appl.* **2017**, *9*, 145–151.
38. Aydın, F.T. Pauli-Fibonacci Quaternions. *Notes Number Theory Discret. Math.* **2021**, *27*, 184–193. [CrossRef]
39. Bajorska-Harapińska, B.; Smoleń, B.; Wituła, R. On Quaternion Equivalents for Quasi-Fibonacci Numbers, Shortly Quaternaccis. *Adv. Appl. Clifford Algebr.* **2019**, *29*, 54. [CrossRef]

Article

Almost Repdigit k-Fibonacci Numbers with an Application of k-Generalized Fibonacci Sequences

Alaa Altassan [1] and Murat Alan [2,*]

[1] Department of Mathematics, King Abdulaziz University, Jeddah 21589, Saudi Arabia
[2] Department of Mathematics, Yildiz Technical University, Istanbul 34210, Turkey
* Correspondence: alan@yildiz.edu.tr; Tel.: +90-212-383-4335

Abstract: In this paper, we define the notion of almost repdigit as a positive integer whose digits are all equal except for at most one digit, and we search all terms of the k-generalized Fibonacci sequence which are almost repdigits. In particular, we find all k-generalized Fibonacci numbers which are powers of 10 as a special case of almost repdigits. In the second part of the paper, by using the roots of the characteristic polynomial of the k-generalized Fibonacci sequence, we introduce k-generalized tiny golden angles and show the feasibility of this new type of angles in application to magnetic resonance imaging.

Keywords: k-Fibonacci numbers; repdigits; almost repdigits; linear forms in logarithms; MR imaging; tiny golden angles; k-generalized tiny golden angles

MSC: 11B37; 11B39; 11J86

Citation: Altassan, A.; Alan, M. Almost Repdigit k-Fibonacci Numbers with an Application of k-Generalized Fibonacci Sequence. *Mathematics* 2023, 11, 455. https://doi.org/10.3390/math11020455

Academic Editors: Diana Savin, Nicusor Minculete and Vincenzo Acciaro

Received: 2 December 2022
Revised: 8 January 2023
Accepted: 10 January 2023
Published: 14 January 2023

Copyright: © 2023 by the authors. Licensee MDPI, Basel, Switzerland. This article is an open access article distributed under the terms and conditions of the Creative Commons Attribution (CC BY) license (https:// creativecommons.org/licenses/by/ 4.0/).

1. Introduction

Let $k \geq 2$ be an integer. The k-generalized Fibonacci sequence or, for simplicity, the k-Fibonacci sequence is a sequence given by the recurrence relation

$$F_n^{(k)} = F_{n-1}^{(k)} + \cdots + F_{n-k}^{(k)} \quad \text{for all} \quad n \geq 2,$$

with the initial values $F_i^{(k)} = 0$ for $i = 2-k, \ldots, 0$ and $F_1^{(k)} = 1$. For $k = 2$, this sequence is the well-known Fibonacci sequence and, in this case, we may omit the superscript (k) in the notation.

Recall that, a positive integer whose all digits are equal is called a repdigit. In many cases, the relations between repdigits and k-Fibonacci numbers have already been settled by a number of authors in many papers, see for example [1–12]. In this study, we shall consider the numbers similar to the repdigits. Our motivation to study this kind of numbers comes from the terms of classical Fibonacci sequences.

Three consecutive Fibonacci numbers $F_{12} = 144$, $F_{13} = 233$ and $F_{14} = 377$ have a similar property that all digits are equal except only one digit. Thus, we call a positive integer whose digits are all equal except for at most one digit is an *almost repdigit*. These are the numbers of the form

$$a\left(\frac{10^{d_1}-1}{9}\right) + (b-a)10^{d_2}, \quad 0 \leq d_2 < d_1 \quad \text{and} \quad 0 \leq a, b \leq 9$$

The square and perfect power almost repdigits were examined in [13,14], without being attributed a specific name. In this paper, we search all almost repdigits in k-Fibonacci numbers for all $k \geq 2$. In particular, as a special case of almost repdigits, we search all

k-Fibonacci numbers that are powers of 10. In other words, we consider the Diophantine equation

$$F_n^{(k)} = a\left(\frac{10^{d_1}-1}{9}\right) + (b-a)10^{d_2}, \quad 0 \le d_2 < d_1 \quad \text{and} \quad 0 \le a, b \le 9 \tag{1}$$

in non-negative integers d_1, d_2, a and b. We state the main results of this paper as follows.

Theorem 1. *The Diophantine Equation* (1) *has solutions only in the cases* $F_{12}^{(2)} = 144$, $F_{13}^{(2)} = 233$, $F_{14}^{(2)} = 377$, $F_{12}^{(4)} = 773$, $F_{11}^{(5)} = 464$, $F_{13}^{(7)} = 2000$, $F_{10}^{(8)} = 255$ *and* $F_{11}^{(9)} = 511$ *when* $F_n^{(k)}$ *has at least three digits.*

To eliminate the trivial cases, the above theorem is stated for numbers with at least three digits, since all integers having one or two digits are trivially almost repdigits. Thus, we also take $d_1 \ge 3$ and $n > 5$.

The proofs of the above theorems come from two effective methods for Diophantine equations. One of them is linear forms in logarithms of algebraic numbers due to Matveev [15], whereas the other one is a version of the reduction algorithm due to Dujella and Pethő [16], which was in fact originally introduced by Baker and Davenport in [17]. In the application of these methods, we frequently need some calculations and computations. For all computations, we use the software Mathematica. Some details of the tools used in this study will be given in the next section.

In addition to all theoretical calculations, in the last section, we give some results which invite the researchers to use the roots of the characteristic polynomial of the k-generalized Fibonacci sequences in application, especially for magnetic resonance imaging. It is well known that, when $k = 2$, the positive root of the characteristic polynomial of the sequence $F_n^{(k)}$ is $\phi = \dfrac{1+\sqrt{5}}{2}$, that is the famous golden ratio. The golden angle is defined by $\psi_{\text{gold}} = \pi/\phi$, which is an angle that is calculated by dividing the semicircle by the golden ratio. Among other things, in [18], tiny golden angles are introduced and the authors showed the advantages of these angles for dynamic magnetic resonance imaging. In the last section of this paper, we introduce the k-generalized tiny golden angles which are based on k-generalized Fibonacci sequences and remark that these newly introduced angles are closely correlated with tiny golden angles. Thus, these new angles are also potentially applicable for magnetic resonance imaging. As a result, we open a new approach for researchers who are working in the healthcare field to apply this in MRI for diagnosing heart diseases, cancer, etc.

2. The Tools

Let θ be an algebraic number, and let

$$c_0 x^d + c_1 x^{d-1} + \cdots + c_d = c_0 \prod_{i=1}^{d}(x - \theta^{(i)})$$

be its minimal polynomial over $\mathbb{Z}$, with degree d, where the c_i's are relatively prime integers with $c_0 > 0$, and the $\theta^{(i)}$'s are conjugates of θ.

The logarithmic height of θ is defined by

$$h(\theta) = \frac{1}{d}\left(\log c_0 + \sum_{i=1}^{d} \log\left(\max\{|\theta^{(i)}|, 1\}\right)\right).$$

If $\theta = r/s$ is a rational number with relatively prime integers r and s and $s > 0$, then $h(r/s) = \log \max\{|r|, s\}$. The following properties are very useful in calculating a logarithmic height :

- $h(\theta_1 \pm \theta_2) \leq h(\theta_1) + h(\theta_2) + \log 2$.
- $h(\theta_1 \theta_2^{\pm 1}) \leq h(\theta_1) + h(\theta_2)$.
- $h(\theta^s) = |s|h(\theta), s \in \mathbb{Z}$.

Theorem 2 (Matveev's Theorem). *Assume that $\alpha_1, \ldots, \alpha_t$ are positive real algebraic numbers in a real algebraic number field $\mathbb{K}$ of degree $d_\mathbb{K}$ and let $b_1, \ldots, b_t$ be rational integers, such that*

$$\Lambda := \alpha_1^{b_1} \cdots \alpha_t^{b_t} - 1,$$

is not zero. Then

$$|\Lambda| > \exp\left(K(t) d_\mathbb{K}^2 (1 + \log d_\mathbb{K})(1 + \log B) A_1 \cdots A_t\right),$$

where

$$K(t) := -1.4 \times 30^{t+3} \times t^{4.5} \quad \text{and} \quad B \geq \max\{|b_1|, \ldots, |b_t|\},$$

and

$$A_i \geq \max\{d_\mathbb{K} h(\alpha_i), |\log \alpha_i|, 0.16\}, \quad \text{for all} \quad i = 1, \ldots, t.$$

For a real number θ, we put $||\theta|| = \min\{|\theta - n| : n \in \mathbb{Z}\}$, which represents the distance from θ to the nearest integer. Now, we cite the following lemma which we will use to reduce some upper bounds on the variables.

Lemma 1 ([19] (Lemma 1)). *Let M be a positive integer, and let p/q be a convergent of the continued fraction of the irrational τ such that $q > 6M$. Let A, B, μ be some real numbers with $A > 0$ and $B > 1$. If $\epsilon := ||\mu q|| - M||\tau q|| > 0$, then there is no solution to the inequality*

$$0 < |u\tau - v + \mu| < AB^{-w},$$

in positive integers u, v and w with

$$u \leq M \quad \text{and} \quad w \geq \frac{\log(Aq/\epsilon)}{\log B}.$$

3. Properties of k-Fibonacci Numbers

From its defining recurrence relation, the characteristic polynomial of k-Fibonacci sequence is

$$\Psi_k(x) = x^k - x^{k-1} - \cdots - x - 1,$$

which is an irreducible polynomial over $\mathbb{Q}[x]$. The polynomial $\Psi_k(x)$ has exactly one real distinguished root $\alpha(k)$ outside the unit circle [20–22]. The other roots of $\Psi_k(x)$ are strictly inside the unit circle [21]. This root $\alpha(k)$, say for simplicity α, is located in the interval

$$2(1 - 2^{-k}) < \alpha < 2 \quad \text{for all} \quad k \geq 2.$$

Let

$$f_k(x) = \frac{x - 1}{2 + (k+1)(x - 2)}.$$

It is known that the inequalities

$$1/2 < f_k(\alpha) < 3/4 \quad \text{and} \quad |f_k(\alpha_i)| < 1, \quad 2 \leq i \leq k, \tag{2}$$

hold, where $\alpha := \alpha_1, \cdots, \alpha_k$ are all the roots of $\Psi_k(x)$ [19] (Lemma 2). In particular, we deduce that $f_k(\alpha)$ is not an algebraic integer. In the same lemma, it is also proven that

$$h(f_k(\alpha)) < 3 \log k \quad \text{holds} \quad \forall k \geq 2, \tag{3}$$

which will be useful in our study.

In [23], Dresden and Du showed that

$$F_n^{(k)} = \sum_{i=1}^{k} f_k(\alpha_i)(\alpha_i)^{n-1} \quad \text{and} \quad \left| F_n^{(k)} - f_k(\alpha)\alpha^{n-1} \right| < 1/2 \tag{4}$$

for all $k \geq 2$. In this section, we finally note that, as in the classical $k = 2$ case, we have the similar bounds as

$$\alpha^{n-2} \leq F_n^{(k)} \leq \alpha^{n-1} \tag{5}$$

for all $n \geq 1$ and $k \geq 2$ [24].

4. Proof of Theorem 1

First, we may directly derive some relations between the variables that will be useful in our subsequent study. From (1) and (5), we obtain

$$10^{d_1 - 2} < a \left(\frac{10^{d_1} - 1}{9} \right) + (b - a)10^{d_2} = F_n^{(k)} \leq \alpha^{n-1} < 2^{n-1},$$

and

$$((1 + \sqrt{5})/2)^{n-2} \leq \alpha^{n-2} \leq F_n^{(k)} = a \left(\frac{10^{d_1} - 1}{9} \right) + (b - a)10^{d_2} \leq 2 \times 10^{d_1},$$

which implies that

$$d_1 < \frac{\log 2}{\log 10}(n - 1) + 2 < 0.31n + 1.8 < n - 1 \tag{6}$$

and

$$0.2n - 0.8 < \frac{\log((1 + \sqrt{5})/2)}{\log 10}(n - 2) - \frac{\log 2}{\log 10} < d_1 \tag{7}$$

for all $n > 5$.

We will treat the case $a = 0$ separately in the last part of this section, in which case Equation (1) turns into $F_n^{(k)} = b10^{d_2}$.

4.1. The Case $n \leq k + 1$ and Almost Repdigits of the Form 2^n

Assume that $n \leq k + 1$. Then, $F_n^{(k)} = 2^{n-2}$, and hence Equation (1) can be written as

$$9 \times 2^{n-2} = a\left(10^{d_1} - 1\right) + 9(b - a)10^{d_2}.$$

From (6),

$$0 \equiv -a \pmod{2^{d_2}}.$$

Thus, $d_2 \leq 3$. By modulo 2^{d_1}, we find

$$0 \equiv -a + (b - a)10^{d_2} \pmod{2^{d_1}},$$

which means $2^{d_1} < 10^4$, that is $d_1 \leq 13$. Hence, from (7), we see that $n < 70$. Computations with Mathematica show that, when $n < 70$, there is no almost repdigit of the form 2^{n-2} with at least three digits.

Thus, from now on, we take $n \geq k + 2$.

4.2. A Bound for n Depending on k

Now, assume that $n \geq k+2$. First, we rewrite (1) as

$$F_n^{(k)} + a/9 - (b-a)10^{d_2} = a10^{d_1}/9,$$

and, by using (4), we obtain

$$\left|f_k(\alpha)\alpha^{n-1} - a10^{d_1}/9\right| = \left|F_n^{(k)} - f_k(\alpha)\alpha^{n-1} + a/9 - (b-a)10^{d_2}\right|$$
$$\leq (1/2) + \left|a/9 - (b-a)10^{d_2}\right|.$$

By dividing both sides by $a10^{d_1}/9$, we obtain

$$|\Lambda_1| \leq \frac{9/2}{10^{d_1}} + \frac{1}{10^{d_1}} + \frac{|b-a|(9/a)}{10^{d_1-d_2}} \leq \frac{78}{10^{d_1-d_2}}, \tag{8}$$

where

$$\Lambda_1 := \alpha^{n-1}10^{-d_1}f_k(\alpha)9/a - 1.$$

Let $\eta_1 := \alpha$, $\eta_2 := 10$, $\eta_3 := f_k(\alpha)9/a$ and $b_1 := n-1$, $b_2 := -d_1$, $b_3 := 1$ where η_1, η_2 and η_3 belong to the real number field $\mathbb{K} = \mathbb{Q}(\alpha)$ with degree $d_\mathbb{K} = k$. By (6), we take $B := n-1 > d_1$.

Since $h(\eta_1) = (1/k)\log(\alpha)$ and $h(\eta_2) = \log 10$, we take $A_1 = \log \alpha$ and $A_2 = k\log(10)$. Furthermore, from (3), $h(\eta_3) \leq h(9/a) + h(f_k(\alpha)) \leq \log(9) + 3\log k < 7\log k$ holds for all $k \geq 2$. Thus, we take $A_3 = 7k\log k$.

We also have $\Lambda_1 \neq 0$. Indeed, if $\Lambda_1 = 0$, then we obtain

$$a10^{d_1}/9 = f_k(\alpha)\alpha^{n-1}.$$

Conjugating both sides of this relation by any one of the automorphisms $\sigma_i : \alpha \to \alpha_i$ for any $i \geq 2$ and by taking the absolute values, by (2), we find that

$$100 < 10^3/9 \leq |a10^{d_1}/9| = |f_k(\alpha_i)||\alpha_i|^{n-1} < 1,$$

which is clearly false. Thus, $\Lambda_1 \neq 0$. With these notations, by Theorem 2, we obtain that

$$\log|\Lambda_1| > -1.4 \times 30^6 \times 3^{4.5} \times k^2(1+\log k)(1+\log(n-1))\log \alpha \times k\log 10 \times 7k\log k.$$

On the other hand, from (8), we have that $\log|\Lambda_1| < \log 78 - (d_1-d_2)\log 10$. From the last two inequalities, we obtain

$$d_1 - d_2 < 4.2 \times 10^{12} \times k^4(\log k)^2 \log(n-1), \tag{9}$$

where we used the facts that $\log(\alpha) \leq \log(2)$, $1 + \log k < 3\log k$ and $(1+\log(n-1)) < 2\log(n-1)$ hold for all $k \geq 2$ and $n \geq 5$.

Now, we turn back to Equation (1) and rewrite it as follows

$$F_n^{(k)} + a/9 = a10^{d_1}/9 + (b-a)10^{d_2}.$$

Again, from (4), we write

$$\left|f_k(\alpha)\alpha^{n-1} - 10^{d_1}((a/9) + (b-a)10^{d_2-d_1})\right| \leq \left|F_n^{(k)} - f_k(\alpha)\alpha^{n-1} + a/9\right|$$
$$\leq (1/2) + (a/9) \leq 3/2.$$

This time, we divide both sides by $f_k(\alpha)\alpha^{n-1}$ to obtain

$$|\Lambda_2| \leq \frac{3}{2}\frac{1}{f_k(\alpha)\alpha^{n-1}} \leq \frac{3}{\alpha^{n-1}}, \quad (10)$$

where

$$\Lambda_2 := \alpha^{-(n-1)}10^{d_1}f_k(\alpha)^{-1}((a/9)+(b-a)10^{d_2-d_1})-1.$$

Since

$$\frac{1}{90} \leq \frac{1}{9}-\frac{1}{10} \leq \frac{a}{9}-\frac{a}{10^{d_1-d_2}}+\frac{b}{10^{d_1-d_2}} \leq (a/9)+(b-a)10^{d_2-d_1},$$

we have that

$$11 < 10^3\frac{1}{90} \leq 10^{d_1}((a/9)+(b-a)10^{d_2-d_1}).$$

Thus, the similar argument that has been used before for Λ_1, shows that Λ_2 is not zero too.

Let $\eta_1 := \alpha$, $\eta_2 := 10$ and $\eta_3 := f_k(\alpha)^{-1}((a/9)+(b-a)10^{d_2-d_1})$ with $b_1 := -(n-1)$, $b_2 := d_1$, $b_3 := 1$. All η_1, η_2 and η_3 belong to the real number field $\mathbb{K} = \mathbb{Q}(\alpha)$, and therefore we take $d_\mathbb{K} = 2$, to be the degree of the number field $\mathbb{K}$.

Since $h(\eta_1) = (1/k)\log(\alpha)$ and $h(\eta_2) = \log 10$ we take $A_1 = \log(\alpha)$ and $A_2 = k\log(10)$. Using the properties of logarithmic height, we obtain:

$$h(\eta_3) \leq h(f_k(\alpha)^{-1}) + h((a/9)+(b-a)10^{d_2-d_1})$$
$$\leq 3\log k + h(a/9) + h(b-a) + h(10^{d_2-d_1}) + \log(2)$$
$$\leq 3\log k + \log(144) + |d_2-d_1|\log(10)$$
$$< 11\log k + |d_2-d_1|\log(10).$$

By applying Theorem 2, we get a bound for $\log|\Lambda_2|$. Then by combining this bound with the one comes from (10), we get

$$n-1 < 2\times 10^{12}k^4 \log k \log(n-1)(11\log k + |d_1-d_2|\log(10)).$$

From (9), we may write

$$11\log k + (d_1-d_2)\log(10 < 4.2\times 10^{12}\times k^4(\log k)^2\log(n-1)\log(10) + 11\log k$$
$$< 10^{13}\times k^4(\log k)^2\log(n-1).$$

Now, by substituting this estimate into the above equation, we obtain

$$n-1 < 2\times 10^{12}k^4\log k\log(n-1)10^{13}\times k^4(\log k)^2\log(n-1)$$
$$< 2\times 10^{25}k^8(\log k)^3(\log(n-1))^2.$$

From this relation, we may obtain a bound on n, depending on k. To do this, we need the following lemma from ([25] Lemma 7).

Lemma 2. *Let $m \geq 1$ and $T > (4m^2)^m$. Then, we have*

$$\frac{x}{(\log x)^m} < T \Rightarrow x < 2^m T(\log(T))^m.$$

We take $T := 2\times 10^{25}k^8(\log k)^3$, so that

$$(\log(T))^2 < (\log(2) + 25\log(10) + 8\log k + 3\log(\log k))^2$$
$$< (\log k + 100\log k + 11\log k)^2 < 112^2(\log k)^2.$$

Thus, from Lemma 2, we may end this subsection with the following bound of n, which is the aim of this part.

$$n < 1.1 \times 10^{30} k^8 (\log k)^5. \tag{11}$$

Now, we treat the cases $k \leq 470$ and $k > 470$ separately.

4.3. The Case $k \leq 470$

Let $2 \leq k \leq 470$. Then, from (11), n is also bounded above. Let

$$\Gamma_1 := (n-1)\log \alpha - d_1 \log 10 + \log(f_k(\alpha) \times 9/a).$$

Then

$$|\Lambda_1| := |\exp(\Gamma_1) - 1| < 78/10^{d_1-d_2}.$$

We claim that $d_1 - d_2 < 145$. Suppose that $d_1 - d_2 > 3$. Then, $78/10^{d_1-d_2} < 1/2$ and therefore $|\Gamma_1| < \dfrac{156}{10^{d_1-d_2}}$. Thus, we have

$$0 < \left| (n-1)\frac{\log \alpha}{\log 10} - d_1 + \frac{\log(f_k(\alpha) \times 9/a)}{\log 10} \right| < 156/10^{d_1-d_2} \log 10. \tag{12}$$

For all $2 \leq k \leq 470$, we take $M_k := 1.1 \times 10^{30} k^8 (\log k)^5 > n$ and $\tau_k = \dfrac{\log \alpha}{\log 10}$. For each k, we find a convergent p_i/q_i of the continued fraction of irrational τ_k, such that $q_i > 6M_k$. Then, we calculate $\epsilon_{(k,a)} := ||\mu_{(k,a)} q_i|| - M_k ||\tau_k q_i||$ for each $a \in \{1, 2, \ldots, 9\}$, where

$$\mu_{(k,a)} := \frac{\log(f_k(\alpha) \times 9/a)}{\log 10}.$$

If $\epsilon_{(k,a)} < 0$, then we repeat the same calculation for q_{i+1}. For each k, we found such a denominator of τ_k, such that $\epsilon_{(k,a)} > 0$, in particular, which also implies that $\mu_{(k,a)} \notin \mathbb{Z}$. In fact, we have $0.7 \times 10^{-42} < \epsilon_{(k,a)}$. Thus, from Lemma 1, we find an upper bound on $d_1 - d_2$ for each $2 \leq k \leq 470$ and none of these bounds are greater than 142. Thus, we conclude that $d_1 - d_2 < 145$, as we claimed previously.

Let

$$\Gamma_2 := -(n-1)\log \alpha + d_1 \log 10 + \log(f_k(\alpha)^{-1} \times ((a/9) + (b-a)10^{d_2-d_1})),$$

so that

$$|\Lambda_2| := |\exp(\Gamma_2) - 1| < 3/\alpha^{n-1} < 1/2.$$

$\Gamma_2 \neq 0$, since Λ_2. Hence, we obtain

$$\left| (n-1)\frac{\log \alpha}{\log 10} - d_1 - \frac{\log(f_k(\alpha)^{-1}(\frac{a}{9} + \frac{b-a}{10^{d_1-d_2}}))}{\log 10} \right| < \frac{6}{\alpha^{n-1} \log 10}. \tag{13}$$

This time, we calculate $\epsilon_{(k,d_1-d_2,a,b)} := ||\mu_{(k,d_1-d_2,a,b)} q_i|| - M_k ||\tau_k q_i||$ for each $d_1 - d_2 \in \{1, 2, \ldots, 145\}$, $a \in \{1, 2, \ldots, 9\}$ and $b \in \{0, 1, \ldots, 9\}$, where

$$\mu_{(k,d_1-d_2,a,b)} := -\frac{\log(f_k(\alpha)^{-1} \times ((a/9) + (b-a)10^{d_2-d_1}))}{\log 10}.$$

If we encounter $\epsilon_{(k,d_1-d_2,a,b)} < 0$, for any values of $d_1 - d_2$, a or b, then, we take the denominator q_{i+1} instead of q_i, as we did previously. For each k, we find such a denominator of τ_k such that $\epsilon_{(k,d_1-d_2,a,b)} > 0$. Thus, applying Lemma 1 to Equation (13), we obtain an upper bound on $n-1$ for each $2 \leq k \leq 470$. Let us denote this upper bound by $n(k)$. Some of these bounds are $n(2) < 176$, $n(3) < 149$, $n(10) < 151$, $n(100) < 180$, $n(200) < 197$, $n(300) < 296$, $n(400) < 396$ and $n(470) < 465$, which show that, for some values of k, there is only a few values of n satisfying $n \geq k+2$. We use this estimate to shorten the runtime in the following computer search.

With the help of a computer program in Mathematica, and by using the bounds given in (6), we search all the variables in the range $2 \leq k \leq 470$, $k+2 \leq n \leq n(k)$, $0 \leq d_2 < d_1 < 0.31n + 1.8$, $1 \leq a \leq 9$ and $0 \leq b \leq 9$ satisfying (1). We find that $F_{12}^{(2)} = 144$, $F_{13}^{(2)} = 233$, $F_{14}^{(2)} = 377$, $F_{12}^{(4)} = 773$, $F_{11}^{(5)} = 464$, $F_{10}^{(8)} = 255$ and $F_{11}^{(9)} = 511$ are the only solutions of (1) when $k \leq 470$ and $a \neq 0$, with at least three digits, as we claimed in Theorem 1, see also Table A1 in the Appendix A. Now, we turn our focus to the case $k > 470$.

4.4. The Case $k > 470$

We use the following lemma.

Lemma 3 ([3] (Lemma 3)). *If $n < 2^{k/2}$, then the following estimates hold:*

$$F_n^{(k)} = 2^{n-2}(1 + \zeta(n,k)), \quad \text{where} \quad |\zeta(n,k)| < \frac{2}{2^{k/2}}.$$

For $k > 470$, the inequality $n < 1.1 \times 10^{30} k^8 (\log k)^5 < 2^{k/2}$, holds and hence from Lemma 3, we have

$$\left| 2^{n-2} - F_n^{(k)} \right| < \frac{2^{n-1}}{2^{k/2}}. \tag{14}$$

Now, we turn back to (1), one more time to rewrite it as

$$\left| F_n^{(k)} - (a/9)10^{d_1} \right| < (a/9) + |b-a|10^{d_2}. \tag{15}$$

Thus, combining (14) and (15), we obtain

$$\left| 2^{n-2} - (a/9)10^{d_1} \right| < \frac{2^{n-1}}{2^{k/2}} + (a/9) + |b-a|10^{d_2}.$$

By multiplying both sides by $(9/a)10^{-d_1}$, we find

$$\left| 2^{n-2} 10^{-d_1} 9/a - 1 \right| < \frac{2^{n-1}}{2^{k/2}} \frac{9}{10^{d_1} a} + \frac{1}{10^{d_1}} + \frac{72}{10^{d_1 - d_2}}.$$

Note that, the estimates

$$\frac{9 \times 2^{n-1}}{a 10^{d_1}} < \frac{2}{(1+\zeta)} \frac{9 \times F_n^{(k)}}{a 10^{d_1}} < \frac{2}{0.999}\left(1 + \frac{1}{10^{d_1}} + \frac{72}{10^{d_1-d_2}}\right)$$

$$< \frac{2}{0.999}\left(1 + \frac{1}{10^3} + \frac{72}{10}\right) < 17$$

hold for all $k > 470$. Therefore, we have

$$|\Lambda_3| := \left| 2^{n-2} 10^{-d_1} 9/a - 1 \right| < \frac{1}{2^\lambda}, \tag{16}$$

where $\lambda := \min\{(k/2) - 6, (d_1 - d_2)\frac{\log(10)}{\log(2)} - 8\}$.

Let $\eta_1 := 2$, $\eta_2 := 10$, $\eta_3 := 9/a$ and $b_1 := n-2$, $b_2 := -d_1$, $b_3 := 1$. We take $t = 3$ if $a \neq 9$ and $t = 2$ if $a = 9$. We take $\mathbb{K} = \mathbb{Q}$, $d_\mathbb{K} = 1$ and $B := n$. Clearly, $\Lambda_3 \neq 0$. Thus, from Theorem 2, we obtain

$$\log|\Lambda_3| > -1.4 \times 30^6 \times 3^{4.5}(1 + \log n)\log 2 \times \log 9 \times \log 10,$$

if $a \neq 9$, and

$$\log|\Lambda_3| > -1.4 \times 30^5 \times 2^{4.5}(1 + \log n)\log 2 \times \log 10,$$

if $a = 9$. Then, in either case, by using the fact $\log(\Lambda_3) < -\lambda \log 2$ from (16), we find

$$\lambda < 1.5 \times 10^{12} \log n$$
$$< 1.5 \times 10^{12} \times 45 \log k < 6.8 \times 10^{13} \log k.$$

In the above, we used the fact that

$$\log n < \log(1.1 \times 10^{30} k^8 (\log k)^5)$$
$$< \log(1.1) + 30\log(10) + 8\log k + 5\log\log k$$
$$< 45 \log k.$$

Thus, if $\lambda := (k/2) - 6$, then we obtain a bound $k < 5 \times 10^{15}$.
If $\lambda := (d_1 - d_2)\dfrac{\log(10)}{\log(2)} - 8$, then we obtain

$$d_1 - d_2 < 2.1 \times 10^{13} \log k. \tag{17}$$

Even in this case, we may obtain a bound for k with a little bit more effort. For this purpose, we rewrite (1) as follows

$$\left| F_n^{(k)} - (a/9)10^{d_1} - (b-a)10^{d_2} \right| \leq (a/9) \leq 1. \tag{18}$$

Combining (18) and (14), we have

$$\left| 2^{n-2} - 10^{d_1}((a/9) + (b-a)10^{d_2-d_1}) \right| < 1 + \frac{2^{n-1}}{2^{k/2}},$$

and from this relation, we obtain

$$|\Lambda_4| := \left| 2^{-(n-2)}10^{d_1}((a/9) + (b-a)10^{d_2-d_1}) - 1 \right| < \frac{2}{2^{k/2}} + \frac{1}{2^{n-2}} \leq \frac{3}{2^{k/2}}. \tag{19}$$

Let $\eta_1 := 2$, $\eta_2 := 10$, $\eta_3 := (a/9) + (b-a)10^{d_2-d_1}$ and $b_1 := -(n-2)$, $b_2 := -d_1$, $b_3 := 1$. Then, we take $\mathbb{K} = \mathbb{Q}$, $d_\mathbb{K} = 1$, $B := n > n - 2$. $h(\eta_1) = \log 2$, $h(\eta_2) = \log 10$ and

$$h(\eta_3) = h(a/9) + h(b-a) + |d_2 - d_1|\log 10 + \log 2 < \log 144 + (d_1 - d_2)\log 10.$$

Moreover, $\Lambda_4 \neq 0$. Indeed, $2^{n-2} = 10^{d_1}(a/9) + (b-a)10^{d_2}$ implies that $a = 9$ and $d_2 = 0$. For $d_1 = 3$, the equation $2^{n-2} = 10^{d_1} + b - 9$ clearly has no solution in integers. Therefore, $d_1 > 3$, and the congruence consideration modulo 2^4, shows that this equation has no integer solutions for $0 \leq b \leq 9$. Thus, $\Lambda_4 \neq 0$.

Moreover, applying Theorem 2 to Λ_4, together with (19) gives that

$$\log 3 - (k/2)\log 2 < -1.4 \times 30^6 \times 3^{4.5}(1 + \log n)\log 2 \times \log 10 \times (\log 144 + (d_1 - d_2)\log 10).$$

By substituting the upper bound of $d_1 - d_2$ given in (17) into the above inequality and using the estimate $\log 144 < \log k$ and $\log n < 45\log k$, we obtain an upper bound for k as follows

$$k < 2 \times 10^{31}.$$

Thus, by (11), we have also a bound for n as

$$n < 5.5 \times 10^{289}.$$

4.5. Reducing the Bound on k

The above upper bounds are far from being able to directly search for the solutions. Thus, this subsection is devoted to reducing these bounds. Let

$$|\Gamma_3| := (n-2)\log 2 - d_1 \log 10 + \log(9/a). \tag{20}$$

Then, $\Lambda_3 := |\exp(\Gamma_3) - 1| < \frac{1}{2^\lambda}$. Suppose that $\lambda > 2$. Then, $\frac{1}{2^\lambda} < \frac{1}{2}$ and hence we obtain $|\Gamma_3| < \frac{2}{2^\lambda}$. Now, we work on the Γ_3 according to the case $a = 9$ and $a \neq 9$, separately. Assume that $a = 9$. Then, from (20)

$$\left| \frac{\log 2}{\log 10} - \frac{d_1}{n-2} \right| < \frac{2}{2^\lambda (n-2) \log 10}. \tag{21}$$

If $\frac{2}{2^\lambda(n-2)\log 10} < \frac{1}{2(n-2)^2}$, then $\frac{d_1}{n-2}$ is a convergent of continued fraction expansion of irrational $\log 2/\log 10$, say $\frac{p_i}{q_i}$. Since p_i and q_i are relatively prime, we deduce that $q_i \leq n-2 < 5.5 \times 10^{289}$. A quick search with Mathematica shows that $i < 585$. Let $[a_0, a_1, a_2, a_3, a_4, \ldots] = [0, 3, 3, 9, 2, 2, \ldots]$ be the continued fraction expansion of $\log 2/\log 10$. Then, $\max\{a_i\} = 5393$ for $i = 0, 1, 2, \ldots, 589$. Thus, from the well-known property of continued fractions, see for example ([26] Theorem 1.1.(iv)), we write

$$\frac{1}{5395 \times (n-2)^2} \leq \frac{1}{(a_i + 2)(n-2)^2} < \left| \frac{\log 2}{\log 10} - \frac{d_1}{n-2} \right| < \frac{2}{2^\lambda (n-2) \log 10}.$$

Thus, from the inequality

$$2^\lambda < \frac{2 \times 5395 \times 5.5 \times 10^{289}}{\log 10} < 2.58 \times 10^{293} < 2^{975},$$

we find $\lambda < 975$. If

$$\frac{2}{2^\lambda (n-2)\log 10} > \frac{1}{2(n-2)^2},$$

then this bound clearly holds.

Assume that $a \neq 9$. Then, from (20), we write

$$0 < \left| (n-2)\frac{\log 2}{\log 10} - d_1 + \frac{\log(9/a)}{\log 10} \right| < \frac{2}{2^\lambda \log 10}.$$

Let $M := 5.5 \times 10^{289} > n$, $\tau = \frac{\log 2}{\log 10}$, and $\mu_a := \log(9/a)/\log 10$. By letting the parameters $A := \frac{2}{\log 10}$, $B := 2$ and

$$\epsilon := 0.159626 \leq \epsilon_a := ||\mu_a q_{587}|| - M||\tau q_{587}||$$

for all $a \in \{1, 2, \ldots, 8\}$, from Lemma 1, we find that $\lambda < 970$. Thus, regardless of whether $a = 9$, we have that $\lambda < 975$.

If $\lambda = k/2 - 6$, then $k < 1962$. If $\lambda = (d_1 - d_2)\frac{\log(10)}{\log(2)} - 8$, then

$$d_1 - d_2 < 295.92 < 300.$$

We show that this case also leads to an upper bound for k as $k < 1985$. Let

$$\Gamma_4 = \left|(n-2)\log 2 - d_1 \log 10 - \log((a/9) + (b-a)10^{d_2-d_1})\right|.$$

Then

$$|\Lambda_4| := |\exp(\Gamma_4) - 1| < \frac{6}{2^{k/2}} < \frac{1}{2}.$$

So

$$0 < \left|\frac{\Gamma_4}{\log 10}\right| < \frac{3}{2^{k/2}\log 10}. \tag{22}$$

Let M and τ be as above and $\mu_{(a,b,d_1-d_2)} := -\dfrac{\log(a/9) + (b-a)10^{d_2-d_1}}{\log 10}$. We apply Lemma 1 to (22) with the parameters

$A := \dfrac{6}{\log 10}$, $B := 2$, $\omega := k/2$ and $\epsilon_{(a,b,d_1-d_2)} := ||\mu_{(a,b,d_1-d_2)}q_{593}|| - M||\tau q_{593}||$.

By calculation with Mathematica, we find that

$$0.000059 < \epsilon_{(6,7,59)} \leq \epsilon_{(a,b,d_1-d_2)}$$

holds for all $a \in \{1, 2, \ldots, 8\}$, $b \in \{1, 2, \ldots, 9\}$ and $d_1 - d_2 \in \{1, 2, \ldots, 300\}$. Thus, by Lemma 1, we deduce that $k < 1985$. Hence, from (11), $n < 6.7 \times 10^{60}$.

With this new and better bound on k, we repeat the same steps starting from the beginning of this subsection, but we take $M := 6.7 \times 10^{60}$. Regardless of whether $a = 9$, similar calculations on Γ_3 show that $\lambda < 215$. Thus, if $\lambda = (k/2) - 6$, then $k < 443$, whereas $\lambda = (d_1 - d_2)\dfrac{\log(10)}{\log(2)} - 8$ gives

$$d_1 - d_2 < 68.$$

We work on Γ_4 as we did before but with q_{135}. Thus, we find that

$$0.000072 < \epsilon_{(5,6,2)} \leq \epsilon_{(a,b,d_1-d_2)},$$

for all $a, b, d_1 - d_2$. With these parameters, by Lemma 1, we find $k/2 < 228.93$, which means that $k < 458$, which contradicts our assumption that $k > 470$. This completes the proof for $a \neq 0$.

4.6. The Case $a = 0$ and k-Fibonacci Numbers as Powers of 10

Let $a = 0$. Then, Equation (1) is of the form

$$F_n^{(k)} = b 10^{d_2}. \tag{23}$$

Clearly, we take $b \neq 0$. In fact, our previous work contains most of the material to solve this equation, with some small manipulation on the variables. So, in any applicable case, we follow the previous notation to prevent the recalculation.

By (23), Λ_2 which was given in (10) is valid as

$$|\Lambda_2| := |\alpha^{-(n-1)} 10^{d_2} b f_k(\alpha)^{-1} - 1| \leq \frac{1}{\alpha^{n-1}},$$

and $\Lambda_2 \neq 0$. This time, we set $\eta_1 := \alpha$, $\eta_2 := 10$, $\eta_3 := b f_k(\alpha)^{-1}$ with $b_1 := -(n-1)$, $b_2 := d_2$, $b_3 := 1$. Therefore,

$$h(\eta_3) \leq h(b) + h(f_k(\alpha)^{-1}) \leq \log 9 + 3\log k < 7\log k.$$

Using the bound given in (5) together with (23), we see that $d_2 \log 10 < (n-1) \log \alpha$, which means $d_2 < n - 1$. Thus, $B := n - 1$. Applying Theorem 2, as we did before for Λ_2, we obtain that
$$n - 1 < 1.4 \times 10^{13} k^4 \log^2 k \log(n-1).$$

We take $T := 1.4 \times 10^{13} k^4 \log^2 k$. Then $\log T < 60 \log k$ for all $k \geq 2$. Thus, from Lemma 2, we find
$$n < 2.1 \times 10^{17} k^4 \log^4 k. \tag{24}$$

If $k \leq 470$, then $n < 3 \times 10^{29}$. By performing the previous calculations, as we did before for (13) to the inequality,
$$0 < \left| (n-1) \frac{\log \alpha}{\log 10} - d_2 - \frac{\log(b f_k(\alpha)^{-1})}{\log 10} \right| < \frac{6}{\alpha^{n-1} \log 10},$$

we see that the same bounds strictly hold for the case $a = 0$. Hence, a computer search shows that we have only one solution of (23) which is $F_{13}^{(7)} = 2000$.

For $k > 470$, from (14), we write
$$0 \neq \Lambda_4' := \left| 2^{-(n-2)} 10^{d_2} b - 1 \right| \leq \frac{2}{2^{k/2}}.$$

By taking $(\eta_1, |b_1|) := (2, n-2)$, $(\eta_2, |b_2|) := (10, d_2)$ and $(\eta_3, |b_3|) := (b, 1)$, from Theorem 2 together with (24), we find $k < 4 \times 10^{14}$ and hence, from (24), $n < 6.9 \times 10^{81}$. To reduce these bounds, we write
$$\Gamma_4' := |(n-2) \log 2 - d_2 \log 10 - \log b|,$$

so that, as we did before, we obtain
$$0 < \left| (n-2) \frac{\log 2}{\log 10} - d_2 - \frac{\log b}{\log 10} \right| < \frac{4}{2^{k/2} \log 10}. \tag{25}$$

Assume that $b \notin \{1, 2, 4, 5, 8\}$. Then, applying Lemma 1 by choosing the parameters as $M := 6.9 \times 10^{81}$, $\mu_b := -\log b / \log 10$, $\epsilon_b := ||\mu_b q_{170}|| - M ||\tau q_{170}||$ and the others as in the previous section, we find that $k < 564$. If b is 1,2,4,5 or 8 then, from Γ_4', we have that
$$\left| \frac{\log 2}{\log 10} - \frac{u}{v} \right| < \frac{4}{2^{k/2} vs. \log 10},$$

where $\frac{u}{v}$ is $\frac{d_2}{n-2}, \frac{d_2}{n-3}, \frac{d_2}{n-4}, \frac{d_2+1}{n-1}$ and $\frac{d_2}{n-5}$, respectively. We use the theory of continued fractions as we did before for (21), to obtain that $k < 572$. Thus, from (24), we obtain a reduced bound as $n < 4 \times 10^{31}$. We repeat the same reduction algorithm with $M := 4 \times 10^{31}$ and as a result we obtain that $k < 440$, a contradiction. This completes the proof.

5. An Application of k-Generalized Tiny Golden Angles to MR Imaging

Studying the Fibonacci sequence and its properties has been an interesting point of research for many years. Indeed, the Fibonacci sequence which is associated with the golden ratio exists naturally in biological settings. This sequence appears in tree's branches, phyllotaxis, flowers, and the human body. Therefore, it has applications in the growth of living things [27]. Moreover, recent applications were introduced in several areas of research including healthcare and medical fields.

In [28], Jiancheng Zou et al. introduced a novel family of image scrambling transforms, which can be applied in medical imaging, based on the distinguished generalized Fibonacci sequence, and the experiments showed that the proposed methods have many advantages.

Carlos Davrieux and Juan Davrieux associated the anatomical distribution of the human biliary tree with the Fibonacci sequence. Furthermore, they carried out a bibliographic analysis of the relation of this sequence to medicine [29].

In [30], the multidimensional golden means were derived from modified Fibonacci sequences and used to introduce a tool that is useful for 3D adaptive imaging which leads to improve specificity in breast MRI. During the year 2021, a new diagnostic technique for breast cancer detection was introduced by applying Fibonacci sequence, golden ratio and predictive algorithm to mammography and ultrasonography [31].

In [18], the authors introduced a new sequence of angles (tiny golden angels) which is based on a generalized Fibonacci sequence [32]. They showed that the tiny golden angles exhibit properties that are very similar to the original golden angle, and the advantages of the new angles for MRI in combination with fully balanced steady-state free precession sequences. These were applied for dynamic imaging of the temporomandibular joint and the heart. In 2021, Alexander Fyrdahl et al. proposed a novel generalization which allows for whole-heart volumetric imaging with retrospective binning and reduced eddy current artifacts. They showed that the tiny golden angle scheme was successful in reducing the angular step in cardio-respiratory-binned golden-angle imaging [33]. In what follows, by using the roots of characteristic polynomial of k-generalized Fibonacci sequences, we give a generalization of the notion of tiny golden angle.

Let $\phi = \dfrac{1+\sqrt{5}}{2}$ be the golden ratio. The golden angle is defined as the angle that is resulted from dividing the semicircle by the golden ratio, that is the angle $\psi_{\text{gold}} = \pi/\phi$. In [18], a new sequence of angles are constructed by the relation

$$\frac{\psi_N}{\pi - N\psi_N} = \phi.$$

Solving the above equation for ψ_N leads to the sequence of angles

$$\psi_N = \frac{\pi}{\phi + N - 1}.$$

For $N = 1$ and $N = 2$, these angles are golden angle and complementary small golden angles as $\psi_1 = \pi/\phi$ and $\psi_2 = \dfrac{\pi}{\phi + 1} = \pi - \psi_1$. The tiny golden angles are defined to be the angles ψ_N, for $N > 2$. In [18], the advantages of using tiny golden angles instead of using the usual golden angle are examined by giving many experimental data including the real-time cardiac imaging ([18] Figure 7). In this paper, we define the k-generalized tiny golden angles $\psi_N^{(k)}$ as follows

$$\frac{\psi_N^{(k)}}{\pi - N\psi_N^{(k)}} = \alpha(k), \quad k \geq 2,$$

where $\alpha(k)$ is the unique root of the characteristic polynomial of $F_n^{(k)}$ which is placed outside the unit circle. Solving this equation for $\psi_N^{(k)}$, and using the fact that $\dfrac{1}{\alpha(k)} = \alpha(k)^{k-1} - \sum_{i=0}^{k-2} \alpha(k)^i$, we find that

$$\psi_N^{(k)} = \frac{\pi}{\alpha(k)^{k-1} - \sum_{i=0}^{k-2} \alpha(k)^i + N}.$$

If $k = 2$, then $\psi_N^{(2)}$ is just tiny golden angles ψ_N. Thus, we call all $\psi_N^{(k)}$ for $N > 2$ k-generalized tiny golden angles. In Table 1, we give some numerical values of $\psi_N^{(k)}$ for some distinct values of k to compare the results with tiny golden angles when $k = 2$. Table 1 shows that the values of tiny golden angles and k-generalized tiny golden angles are very close.

Thus, we believe that, because of this correlation, a more detailed study with experimental data will reveal the practical efficiency of this k-generalized tiny golden angles.

Table 1. The First Ten Elements of the Sequence $\psi_N^{(k)}$ for $k = 2, 3, 4, 7$ and 10 as degree.

N	$\psi_N^{(2)}$	$\psi_N^{(3)}$	$\psi_N^{(4)}$	$\psi_N^{(7)}$	$\psi_N^{(10)}$
1	111.24611...°	116.60379...°	118.51539...°	119.83884...°	119.98031...°
2	68.75388...°	70.76336...°	71.46288...°	71.94195...°	71.99291...°
3	49.75077...°	50.79452...°	51.15394...°	51.39894...°	51.42495...°
4	38.97762...°	39.61538...°	39.83367...°	39.98207...°	39.99781...°
5	32.03967...°	32.46935...°	32.61584...°	32.71527...°	32.72580...°
6	27.19840...°	27.50741...°	27.61248...°	27.68371...°	27.69125...°
7	23.62814...°	23.86100...°	23.94002...°	23.99354...°	23.99921...°
8	20.88643...°	21.06818...°	21.12976...°	21.17144...°	21.17585...°
9	18.71484...°	18.86063...°	18.90996...°	18.94334...°	18.94687...°
10	16.95229...°	17.07182...°	17.11223...°	17.13956...°	17.14245...°

6. Discussion

It is known that the largest repdigit in the Fibonacci sequence is 55 [34]. When we look at the subsequent terms of this sequence, one can see that the consecutive three terms $F_{12} = 144$, $F_{13} = 233$ and $F_{14} = 377$ of this sequence have the property that all digits are equal except for at most one digit, which we have called almost repdigits. Thus, it is natural to ask whether there are any other almost repdigits in the Fibonacci sequence? In this paper, we give an answer to this question not only for classical Fibonacci numbers but also for the order $k \geq 2$ generalization of this sequence. In particular, we show that $F_{13}^{(7)} = 2000$ is the largest almost repdigit in the k-Fibonacci sequences.

At the end of the paper, we also open the door for an application of k-generalized Fibonacci sequences for interested readers.

7. Recommendations

Recently, specific Fibonacci numbers with some special properties were calculated. Among the most popular numbers were Fibonacci numbers which were concatenations of two or three repdigits. These calculations and more were also performed on generalized Fibonacci sequence and other sequences [1,2,5,12,35,36]. In our paper, we defined almost repdigit Fibonacci numbers and found them in the generalized case. Since repdigit and almost repdigit numbers seem special, we recommend researchers who are interested in applications of Fibonacci numbers to take a closer look at these specific numbers and consider them in their studies.

Author Contributions: Conceptualization, A.A. and M.A.; Methodology, A.A. and M.A.; Software, M.A.; Validation, A.A.; Formal analysis, A.A. and M.A.; Investigation, A.A. and M.A.; Resources, A.A.; Data curation, A.A.; Writing—original draft, A.A. and M.A.; Writing—review & editing, A.A. and M.A.; Visualization, A.A.; Supervision, A.A.; Project administration, A.A.; Funding acquisition, A.A. All authors contributed equally to the manuscript. All authors have read and agreed to the published version of the manuscript.

Funding: This research work was funded by Institutional Fund Projects under grant no. (IFPIP: 516-247-1443). The authors gratefully acknowledge technical and financial support provided by the Ministry of Education and King Abdulaziz University, DSR, Jeddah, Saudi Arabia.

Institutional Review Board Statement: Not applicable.

Informed Consent Statement: Not applicable.

Data Availability Statement: Not applicable.

Conflicts of Interest: The authors declare no conflict of interest.

Appendix A

Table A1. The First 15 Elements of the Sequence $F_n^{(k)}$: for $2 \leq k \leq 9$ and $1 \leq n \leq 15$. The circled numbers are all almost repdigits given in Theorem 1.

k = 2	$F_n^{(2)}$:	1,	1,	2,	3,	5,	8,	13,	21,	34,	55,	89,	(144),	(233),	(377), 610
k = 3	$F_n^{(3)}$:	1,	1,	2,	4,	7,	13,	24,	44,	81,	149,	274,	504,	927,	1705, 3136
k = 4	$F_n^{(4)}$:	1,	1,	2,	4,	8,	15,	29,	56,	108,	208,	401,	(773),	1490,	2872, 5536
k = 5	$F_n^{(5)}$:	1,	1,	2,	4,	8,	16,	31,	61,	120,	236,	(464),	912,	1793,	3525, 6930
k = 6	$F_n^{(6)}$:	1,	1,	2,	4,	8,	16,	32,	63,	125,	248,	492,	976,	1936,	3840, 7617
k = 7	$F_n^{(7)}$:	1,	1,	2,	4,	8,	16,	32,	64,	127,	253,	504,	1004,	(2000),	3984, 7936
k = 8	$F_n^{(8)}$:	1,	1,	2,	4,	8,	16,	32,	64,	128,	(255),	509,	1016,	2028,	4048, 8080
k = 9	$F_n^{(9)}$:	1,	1,	2,	4,	8,	16,	32,	64,	128,	256,	(511),	1021,	2040,	4076, 8144

References

1. Alahmadi, A.; Altassan, A.; Luca, F.; Shoaib, H. k-generalized Fibonacci numbers which are concatenations of two repdigits. *Glasnik Matematički* **2021**, *56*, 29–46. [CrossRef]
2. Bravo, E.F.; Bravo, J.J.; Gómez, C.A. Generalized Lucas Numbers Which are Concatenations of Two Repdigits. *Results Math.* **2021** *76*, 1–16. [CrossRef]
3. Bravo, J.J.; Gómez, C.A.; Luca, F. A Diophantine equation in k-Fibonacci numbers and repdigits. *Colloq. Math.* **2018**, *152*, 299–315. [CrossRef]
4. Bravo, J.J.; Luca, F. Repdigits in k-Lucas sequences. *Proc. Indian Acad. Sci. Math. Sci.* **2014**, *124*, 141–154. [CrossRef]
5. Bravo, J.J.; Luca F. On a conjecture about repdigits in k-generalized Fibonacci sequences. *Publ. Math. Debr.* **2013**, *82*, 623–639. [CrossRef]
6. Bravo, J.J.; Luca, F. Repdigits as sums of two k-Fibonacci numbers. *Monatshefte Math.* **2015**, *176*, 31–51. [CrossRef]
7. Coufal, P.; Trojovský, P. Repdigits as Product of Terms of k-Bonacci Sequences. *Mathematics* **2021**, *9*, 682. [CrossRef]
8. Herrera, J.L.; Bravo, J.J.; Gómez, C.A. Curious Generalized Fibonacci Numbers. *Mathematics* **2021**, *9*, 2588. [CrossRef]
9. Marques, D. On k-generalized Fibonacci numbers with only one distinct digit. *Util. Math.* **2015**, *98*, 23–31.
10. Rihane, S.E.; Togbé, A. On the intersection between k-Lucas sequences and some binary sequences. *Period. Math. Hung.* **2022**, *84*, 125–145. [CrossRef]
11. Rihane, S.E. k-Fibonacci and k-Lucas Numbers as Product of Two Repdigits. *Results Math.* **2021**, *76*, 1–20. [CrossRef]
12. Şiar, Z.; Keskin, R. k-Generalized Pell Numbers Which are Concatenation of Two Repdigits. *Mediterr. J. Math.* **2022**, *19*, 1–17. [CrossRef]
13. Gica, A.; Panaitopol, L. On Obláth's problem. *J. Integer Seq.* **2003**, *6*, 3.
14. Kihel, O.; Luca, F.; Morelia, M. Perfect powers with all equal digits but one. *J. Integer Seq.* **2005**, *8*, 3.
15. Matveev, E.M. An explicit lower bound for a homogeneous rational linear form in the logarithms of algebraic numbers, II. *Izv. Ross. Akad. Nauk Ser. Mat.* **2000**, *64*, 125–180. Translation in *Izv. Math.* **2000**, *64*, 1217–1269. [CrossRef]
16. Dujella, A.; Pethő, A. A generalization of a theorem of Baker and Davenport. *Quart. J. Math. Oxford Ser.* **1998**, *49*, 291–306. [CrossRef]
17. Baker, A.; Davenport, H. The equations $3x^2 - 2 = y^2$ and $8x^2 - 7 = z^2$. *Quart. J. Math. Oxford Ser.* **1969**, *20*, 129–137. [CrossRef]
18. Wundrak, S.; Paul, J.; Ulrici, J.; Hell, E.; Rasche, V. A small surrogate for the golden angle in time-resolved radial MRI based on generalized fibonacci sequences. *IEEE Trans. Med Imaging* **2014**, *34*, 1262–1269. [CrossRef]
19. Bravo, J.J.; Gómez, C.A.G.; Luca, F. Powers of two as sums of two k-Fibonacci numbers. *Miskolc Math. Notes* **2016**, *17*, 85–100. [CrossRef]
20. Miles, E.P., Jr. Generalized Fibonacci numbers and associated matrices. *Am. Math. Mon.* **1960**, *67*, 745–752. [CrossRef]
21. Miller, M.D. On generalized Fibonacci numbers. *Am. Math. Mon.* **1971**, *78*, 1108–1109. [CrossRef]
22. Wolfram, D.A. Solving generalized Fibonacci recurrences. *Fibonacci Quart.* **1998**, *36*, 129–145.
23. Dresden, G.; Du, Z. A simplified Binet formula for k-generalized Fibonacci numbers. *J. Integer Seq.* **2014**, *17*, 14.
24. Bravo, J.J.; Luca, F. Powers of two in generalized Fibonacci sequences. *Rev. Colomb. Mat.* **2012**, *46*, 67–79.
25. Guzmán, S.; Luca, F. Linear combinations of factorials and S-units in a Binary Recurrence Sequence. *Annales Mathématiques du Québec* **2014**, *38*, 169–188.
26. Hensley, D. *Continued Fractions*; World Scientific Publishing Co. Pte. Ltd.: Hackensack, NJ, USA, 2006.
27. Sinha, S. The Fibonacci numbers and its amazing applications. *Int. J. Eng. Sci. Invent.* **2017**, *6*, 7–14.
28. Zou, J.; Ward, R.K.; Qi, D. The generalized Fibonacci transformations and application to image scrambling. In Proceedings of the 2004 IEEE International Conference on Acoustics, Speech, and Signal Processing, Montreal, QC, Canada, 17–21 May 2004; Volume 36, p. iii-385.
29. Davrieux, C.F.; Davrieux, J.A. Relationship between the Biliary Tree and the Fibonacci Sequence. *Gastro. Rev. Med.* **2019**, *3*, 1–7. [CrossRef]

30. Chan, R.W.; Ramsay, E.A.; Cunningham, C.H.; Plewes, D.B. Temporal stability of adaptive 3D radial MRI using multidimensional golden means. *Magn. Reson. Med.* **2019**, *61*, 354–363. [CrossRef]
31. Trapanese, E.; Tarro, G. PhiΦBreast & theory of spiral cancer new diagnostic techniques for breast cancer detection. *Transl. Med. Commun.* **2021**, *19*, 1–10.
32. Horadam, A.F. A generalized Fibonacci sequence. *Am. Math. Mon.* **1961**, *68*, 455–459. [CrossRef]
33. Fyrdahl, A.; Holst, K.; Caidahl, K.; Ugander, M.; Sigfridsson, A. Generalization of three-dimensional golden-angle radial acquisition to reduce eddy current artifacts in bSSFP CMR imaging. *Magn. Reson. Mater. Phys. Biol. Med.* **2021**, *34*, 109–118. [CrossRef]
34. Luca, F. Fibonacci and Lucas numbers with only one distinct digit. *Port. Math.* **2000**, *57*, 243–254.
35. Bednařík, D.; Trojovská, E. Repdigits as product of Fibonacci and Tribonacci numbers. *Mathematics* **2020**, *8*, 1720. [CrossRef]
36. Trojovský, P. On Terms of Generalized Fibonacci Sequences which are Powers of their Indexes. *Mathematics* **2019**, *7*, 700. [CrossRef]

Disclaimer/Publisher's Note: The statements, opinions and data contained in all publications are solely those of the individual author(s) and contributor(s) and not of MDPI and/or the editor(s). MDPI and/or the editor(s) disclaim responsibility for any injury to people or property resulting from any ideas, methods, instructions or products referred to in the content.

Article

Density of Some Special Sequences Modulo 1

Artūras Dubickas

Institute of Mathematics, Faculty of Mathematics and Informatics, Vilnius University, Naugarduko 24, LT-03225 Vilnius, Lithuania; arturas.dubickas@mif.vu.lt

Abstract: In this paper, we explicitly describe all the elements of the sequence of fractional parts $\{a^{f(n)}/n\}$, $n = 1, 2, 3, \ldots$, where $f(x) \in \mathbb{Z}[x]$ is a nonconstant polynomial with positive leading coefficient and $a \geq 2$ is an integer. We also show that each value $w = \{a^{f(n)}/n\}$, where $n \geq n_f$ and n_f is the least positive integer such that $f(n) \geq n/2$ for every $n \geq n_f$, is attained by infinitely many terms of this sequence. These results combined with some earlier estimates on the gaps between two elements of a subgroup of the multiplicative group $\mathbb{Z}_m^*$ of the residue ring $\mathbb{Z}_m$ imply that this sequence is everywhere dense in $[0,1]$. In the case when $f(x) = x$ this was first established by Cilleruelo et al. by a different method. More generally, we show that the sequence $\{a^{f(n)}/n^d\}$, $n = 1, 2, 3, \ldots$, is everywhere dense in $[0,1]$ if $f \in \mathbb{Z}[x]$ is a nonconstant polynomial with positive leading coefficient and $a \geq 2$, $d \geq 1$ are integers such that d has no prime divisors other than those of a. In particular, this implies that for any integers $a \geq 2$ and $b \geq 1$ the sequence of fractional parts $\{a^n/\sqrt[b]{n}\}$, $n = 1, 2, 3, \ldots$, is everywhere dense in $[0,1]$.

Keywords: fractional parts; density; powers modulo m; Euler's theorem

MSC: 11J71; 11B05; 11B50; 11B83

1. Introduction

Let $\xi \neq 0$ and $\alpha > 1$ be real numbers. The sequence of fractional parts of powers

$$\{\xi \alpha^n\}, \quad n = 1, 2, 3, \ldots, \tag{1}$$

have been studied starting with the papers of Weyl [1] and Koksma [2], where some metrical results have been obtained. In particular, their results imply that if $\xi \neq 0$ (resp. $\alpha > 1$) is fixed then for almost all $\alpha > 1$ (resp. for almost all real ξ) the sequence (1) is uniformly distributed in $[0,1]$.

However, for most specific pairs, say for $(\xi, \alpha) = (1, a/b)$, where $a/b > 1$ is a rational number that is not an integer, the results obtained (see, e.g., [3,4]) are very far from establishing even the density of the sequence

$$\{(a/b)^n\}, \quad n = 1, 2, 3, \ldots,$$

in $[0,1]$. (We say that a sequence S is *dense* or *everywhere dense* in an interval I if for any $c \in I$ and any $\varepsilon > 0$ the set $I \cap (c - \varepsilon, c + \varepsilon)$ contains infinitely many elements of the sequence S.) The most known conjecture concerning the fractional parts of powers of rational numbers is that of Mahler about the distribution of the sequence $\{\xi(3/2)^n\}$, $n = 1, 2, 3, \ldots$ [5]. The situation with transcendental α is even less described. For example, any kind of result for $(\xi, \alpha) = (1, e)$ is completely out of reach: e.g., disprove that $\{e^n\} \to 0$ as $n \to \infty$.

A special kind of sequences for which the density modulo 1 is confirmed are those of the form $\{a^n b^m \xi\}$, $m, n = 1, 2, 3, \ldots$, where $a, b \geq 2$ are two multiplicatively independent integers and ξ is irrational. See Furstenberg's theorem [6,7] and some more general results of this kind [8–14].

In [15], Cilleruelo, Kumchev, Luca, Rué and Shparlinski considered another interesting sequence
$$\{a^n/n\}, \ n = 1, 2, 3, \ldots, \tag{2}$$
where $a \geq 2$ is an integer. They proved that the sequence (2) is everywhere dense in $[0, 1]$ and obtained some other results on its distribution. A more general sequence $\{Q(\alpha^n)/n\}, \ n = 1, 2, 3, \ldots$, where $Q \in \mathbb{Z}[x]$ and α is a Pisot or a Salem number, has been considered by the author in [16].

In this paper, we will study some variations of the sequence (2) for a given integer $a \geq 2$. Specifically, we will investigate the sequence
$$\{a^{f(n)}/n^d\}, \ n = 1, 2, 3, \ldots, \tag{3}$$
where $a \geq 2, d \geq 1$ are integers and $f \in \mathbb{Z}[x]$ is a nonconstant polynomial with a positive leading coefficient.

Let $m \geq 2$ be an integer satisfying $\gcd(a, m) = 1$, and let $p_1, \ldots, p_k$ be the set of all prime divisors of a. Consider the set
$$S_a = \{p_1^{\alpha_1} \ldots p_k^{\alpha_k}, \text{ where } \alpha_1, \ldots \alpha_k \geq 0 \text{ are integers}\}$$
generated by the prime divisors of a. By $R_m(a)$ we denote the set S_a modulo m. In other words, $R_m(a)$ is a subgroup of $\mathbb{Z}_m^*$ generated by the prime divisors of a. Since each element of $R_m(a)$ is coprime to m, we have
$$|R_m(a)| \leq \varphi(m),$$
where φ stands for the Euler totient function.

Our first result gives a complete description of all possible values attained by the sequence (3) with $d = 1$:

Theorem 1. *Let $a \geq 2$ be a positive integer, and let $f \in \mathbb{Z}[x]$ be a nonconstant polynomial with positive leading coefficient. Suppose that n_f is the smallest positive integer such that $f(n) \geq n/2$ for each $n \geq n_f$, and $V_{a,f}$ is the set of values attained by the sequence of fractional parts*
$$\{a^{f(n)}/n\}, \ n \geq n_f, \ n \in \mathbb{N}.$$
Then, $w \in V_{a,f}$ if and only if $w = 0$ or $w = r/m$, where $m \geq 2$ is an integer coprime to a and $r \in R_m(a)$. Furthermore, each value w of $V_{a,f}$ is attained for infinitely many indices n.

The last claim of the theorem is an unusual one. It does not hold either for the sequence of fractional parts of powers (in fact, for (1) an opposite situation holds by the results in [17]) or, for example, for the sequence $\{2^n/n^2\}, n = 1, 2, 3, \ldots$, of type (3), where $a = d = 2$ and $f(x) = x$. In particular, by applying an old result of Hasse [18], we will show that infinitely many terms of the sequence $\{2^n/n^2\}, n = 1, 2, 3, \ldots$, are attained by a unique $n \in \mathbb{N}$. (The proof is given at the end of Section 5).

Note that we have $n_f = 1$ in the case when the coefficients of $f \in \mathbb{Z}[x]$ are all non-negative. The condition $n \geq n_f$ in Theorem 1 cannot be removed. Indeed, take, for example, $f(x) = x - 1$ and $a = 2$. Then, the value $1/2$ of the sequence $\{2^{n-1}/n\}, n = 1, 2, 3, \ldots$, is attained at $n = 1$ only. Since $x - 1 \geq x/2$ for $x \geq 2$, we have $n_f = 2$. Thus, Theorem 1 implies that each value of the sequence $\{2^{n-1}/n\}, n = 2, 3, 4, \ldots$, is attained infinitely many times.

Recall that the radical $\text{rad}(a)$ of an integer $a \geq 2$ is the product of its distinct prime divisors, and $\text{rad}(1) = 1$. Theorem 1 implies the following:

Corollary 1. *For any nonconstant $f \in \mathbb{Z}[x]$ with positive leading coefficient and any integers $a, a' \geq 2$ satisfying $\text{rad}(a) = \text{rad}(a')$ we have $V_{a,f} = V_{a',f}$.*

On the other hand, if $\operatorname{rad}(a) \neq \operatorname{rad}(a')$ then there is an integer $m \geq 2$ which is coprime to one of the numbers a, a' but not to the other. If, say $\gcd(a, m) = 1$ and $\gcd(a', m) > 1$, then, by Theorem 1, we find that $1/m \in V_{a,f}$, but $1/m \notin V_{a',f}$.

Let $f, g \in \mathbb{Z}[x]$ be two nonconstant polynomials with positive leading coefficients. Assume that $n_f \geq n_g$. Then, by Theorem 1, for any integer $a \geq 2$ we have $V_{a,f} \cap V_{a,g} = V_{a,f}$ and $V_{a,f} \cup V_{a,g} = V_{a,g}$.

We will also prove the following:

Theorem 2. *Let $f \in \mathbb{Z}[x]$ be a nonconstant polynomial with a positive leading coefficient, and let $a \geq 2$, $d \geq 1$ be integers satisfying $\operatorname{rad}(d) \mid \operatorname{rad}(a)$. Then, the sequence of fractional parts*

$$\{a^{f(n)}/n^d\}, \quad n = 1, 2, 3, \ldots,$$

is everywhere dense in $[0, 1]$.

The condition $\operatorname{rad}(d) \mid \operatorname{rad}(a)$ trivially holds for $d = 1$, which implies the density of $\{a^{f(n)}/n\}$, $n = 1, 2, 3, \ldots$. (Of course, Theorem 1 asserts much more than the density of this sequence in $[0, 1]$.)

Note that $\{a^{n^b}/n^d\}$, $n = 1, 2, 3, \ldots$, is a subsequence of the sequence $\{a^n/n^{d/b}\}$, $n = 1, 2, 3, \ldots$. So, Theorem 2 with $f(x) = x^b$, $b \in \mathbb{N}$, implies slightly more than what was proved in [15,16]:

Corollary 2. *For any integers $a \geq 2$, $b, d \geq 1$ satisfying $\operatorname{rad}(d) \mid \operatorname{rad}(a)$ the sequence of fractional parts*

$$\{a^n/n^{d/b}\} \quad n = 1, 2, 3, \ldots,$$

is everywhere dense in $[0, 1]$.

In particular, the sequence of fractional parts

$$\{a^n/\sqrt[b]{n}\} \quad n = 1, 2, 3, \ldots,$$

is everywhere dense in $[0, 1]$.

An important auxiliary result that we will use several times is the following:

Lemma 1. *For any integers $t \geq 1$, $u \geq 0$, $v \geq 1$, $a \geq 2$ and any $f \in \mathbb{Z}[x]$ with positive leading coefficient there are infinitely many positive integers n for which*

$$f(va^n) - n \equiv u \pmod{t}. \tag{4}$$

In the Section 2 we will show how Theorem 1 implies the density of the set $V_{a,f}$ in $[0, 1]$ and give some examples of $R_m(a)$. In Section 3 we will prove Lemma 1 and its generalization. The proofs of Theorems 1 and 2 are given in Section 4. Finally, in Section 5 we will show that the sequence $\{2^n/n^2\}$, $n = 1, 2, 3, \ldots$, contains infinitely many values that are attained only once and that it does not contain certain values r/m, where $m \geq 2$ is an integer coprime to a and $r \in R_m(a)$, at all.

2. Some Examples

Fix $a \geq 2$. Assume that $m = p$ is a prime number greater than $a + 1$. Clearly, $R_m(a)$ contains the multiplicative subgroup $\{1, a, a^2, \ldots, a^{\delta-1}\}$ of $\mathbb{Z}_p^*$, where $\delta = \delta_p$ is the order of a modulo p.

An unsolved Artin's conjecture asserts that $\delta_p = p - 1$ for infinitely many primes p if a is not a square. In [19], Erdős and Murty obtained a nontrivial lower bound on δ_p, which implies

$$\delta_p > p^{1/2} \tag{5}$$

for almost all primes p. See also [20]. On the other hand, under assumption (5), the largest gap between any two consecutive δ_p powers of a modulo p is less than

$$p^{437/480+o(1)} \text{ as } p \to \infty$$

(see Theorem 6.8 of [21]); some earlier bounds with slightly worse exponents have been established in [22–25]). Thus, for almost all prime numbers p, every subinterval of length $p^{-0.0896}$ of $[0, 1]$ contains the number r/p, with $r \in R_p(a)$. By Theorem 1, such r/p belongs to $V_{a,f}$, which implies the density of $V_{a,f}$ in $[0, 1]$. For infinitely many prime numbers p, the exponent 0.0896 can be improved by combining [19] with a subsequent result of Baker and Harman [26] which yields the exponent 0.677 for p in (5).

By a result of Heath-Brown (Corolary 2 of [27]), there are at most three primes a for which Artin's conjecture fails to hold. Suppose a has at least three distinct prime divisors. Then, for infinitely many prime numbers p, at least one of the factors of a is a primitive root modulo p, that is, the order of this prime factor of a is $\delta_p = p - 1$. This implies $R_p(a) = \{1, \ldots, p-1\}$ for each p. Hence, by Theorem 1, each fraction r/p, where $r = 0, 1, \ldots, p-1$, belongs to the set $V_{a,f}$ provided that a has at least three distinct prime divisors. (For example, this is true if $30 \mid a$.)

Let p be a Mersenne prime of the form $2^q - 1$, where $q \geq 2$ is a prime number. Then, for $a = 2$, the order δ_p of 2 modulo p is q. Hence, by Theorem 1, there are q positive rational numbers with denominator p that belong to V_2 (with, say $f(x) = x$ and $n_f = 1$), namely,

$$\frac{1}{p}, \frac{2}{p}, \frac{4}{p}, \frac{8}{p}, \ldots, \frac{2^{q-1}}{p}.$$

Note that $q - 1$ of them (all but the last one) belong to the interval $(0, 1/2)$.

Finally, assume that $A \geq 2$ and $d \geq 1$ are two fixed integers. Then, by the above-mentioned result [19], for almost all primes p the order of A modulo p is at least $p^{1/2}$. Thus, the order of the multiplicative group generated by A modulo p^d, where p is any of those almost all primes, is at least $p^{1/2}$ as well. The whole multiplicative group $\mathbb{Z}_{p^d}^*$ is of order $\varphi(p^d) = p^{d-1}(p-1)$. The distance between any two consecutive elements of the multiplicative group generated by A modulo p^d can be estimated using a corresponding exponential sum. (See, e.g., [28] (p. 12).) In our situation, using the main theorem in [29] or, more specifically, (Theorem 4.7 of [30]) we can record the following:

Lemma 2. *For any integers $A \geq 2$ and $d \geq 1$ there exist $\delta > 0$ and infinitely many prime numbers p such that the distance between any two consecutive elements of the multiplicative group generated by A modulo p^d is less than $p^{d-\delta}$.*

3. Proof of Lemma 1 and Its Generalization

Proof of Lemma 1. The claim is trivial if f is a constant, so assume that $\deg f \geq 1$. The proof is by induction on t. There is nothing to prove if $t = 1$. Assume that $t > 1$ and that the claim holds for all positive integers smaller than t. Suppose t_0 is the largest divisor of t which is coprime to a. Set

$$t' = t/t_0 \in \mathbb{N}.$$

Clearly, $1 \leq t_0 \leq t$, so $\varphi(t_0) < t$. By the induction hypothesis, there are infinitely many positive integers ℓ satisfying

$$f(va^\ell) - \ell \equiv u \pmod{\varphi(t_0)}. \tag{6}$$

Take any of those ℓ which is so large that

$$t' \mid va^\ell, \tag{7}$$

$f(va^\ell) > u + \ell$ and $f(x)$ is positive and increasing for $x \geq va^\ell$.

We will show that (4) holds for every n expressible as

$$n = f(va^\ell) - u.$$

Note that such n form an infinite set of positive integers, since so is the set of such ℓ.

Observe that for each n, we have

$$f(va^n) - n - u = f\big(va^{f(va^\ell)-u}\big) - f(va^\ell),$$

which is divisible by

$$va^{f(va^\ell)-u} - va^\ell = va^\ell\big(a^{f(va^\ell)-\ell-u} - 1\big),$$

because $f \in \mathbb{Z}[x]$ and $A - B$ divides $f(A) - f(B)$ for any $A, B \in \mathbb{Z}$, $A \neq B$. Hence, (4) is true provided that

$$t \mid va^\ell\big(a^{f(va^\ell)-\ell-u} - 1\big).$$

By (7) and $t = t't_0$, it remains to verify that

$$t_0 \mid a^{f(va^\ell)-\ell-u} - 1.$$

However, this holds by Euler's theorem in view of $\gcd(a, t_0) = 1$ and (6). □

In the proof of Theorem 1, we will also need the following generalization of Lemma 1. (Of course, similarly to the case of Lemma 1, the nontrivial case is when f is non-constant.)

Lemma 3. *For any $f \in \mathbb{Z}[x]$ with positive leading coefficient, any integers $t \geq 1, k \geq 1, m \geq 1$, $u_1, \ldots, u_k \geq 0$, $v_1, \ldots, v_k \geq 1$, $K \geq 1$ and any k positive integers $P_1, \ldots, P_k > 1$ there is a vector of positive integers $(n_1, \ldots, n_k)$ such that*

$$v_i f(mP_1^{n_1} \ldots P_k^{n_k}) - n_i \equiv u_i \pmod{t} \tag{8}$$

for $i = 1, \ldots, k$ and $\min_{1 \leq i \leq k} n_i \geq K$.

Proof. We can clearly assume that $\deg f \geq 1$. As before the proof is by induction on t. Assume that $t > 1$ and that the claim holds for all positive integers smaller than t. Introduce t_0 and t' similarly as in the proof of Lemma 1, namely, let t_0 be the largest divisor of t which is coprime to $P_1 \ldots P_k$, and $t' = t/t_0$.

This time, as $\varphi(t_0) < t$, by the induction hypothesis, there is a vector of positive integers $(\ell_1, \ldots, \ell_k)$ satisfying

$$v_i f(mP_1^{\ell_1} \ldots P_k^{\ell_k}) - \ell_i \equiv u_i \pmod{\varphi(t_0)} \tag{9}$$

for $i = 1, \ldots, k$, which is so large that

$$t' \mid P_1^{\ell_1} \ldots P_k^{\ell_k}, \tag{10}$$

$v_i f(mP_1^{\ell_1} \ldots P_k^{\ell_k}) - u_i \geq \ell_i + K$ for $i = 1, \ldots, k$, and $f(x)$ is increasing for $x \geq mP_1^{\ell_1} \ldots P_k^{\ell_k}$.

Set

$$n_i = v_i f(mP_1^{\ell_1} \ldots P_k^{\ell_k}) - u_i$$

for $i = 1, \ldots, k$. Then, $n_i > \ell_i$ and $\min_{1 \leq i \leq k} n_i \geq K$. Furthermore, with this choice of n_i, for every $i = 1, \ldots, k$ we obtain

$$v_i f(mP_1^{n_1} \ldots P_k^{n_k}) - n_i - u_i = v_i f(mP_1^{n_1} \ldots P_k^{n_k}) - v_i f(mP_1^{\ell_1} \ldots P_k^{\ell_k}),$$

which is divisible by

$$v_i(mP_1^{n_1}\ldots P_k^{n_k} - mP_1^{\ell_1}\ldots P_k^{\ell_k}) = v_i mP_1^{\ell_1}\ldots P_k^{\ell_k}(P_1^{n_1-\ell_1}\ldots P_k^{n_k-\ell_k} - 1).$$

By (10), t' divides $P_1^{\ell_1}\ldots P_k^{\ell_k}$. So, in order to prove (8) it suffices to show that

$$t_0 \mid P_1^{n_1-\ell_1}\ldots P_k^{n_k-\ell_k} - 1.$$

As $n_i > \ell_i$, this is the case if, for instance, each factor

$$P_i^{n_i-\ell_i} = P_i^{v_i f(mP_1^{\ell_1}\ldots P_k^{\ell_k}) - u_i - \ell_i},$$

where $i = 1,\ldots,k$, is 1 modulo t_0. However, the latter holds by Euler's theorem due to $\gcd(P_i, t_0) = 1$ and (9). □

4. Proofs of Theorems 1 and 2

Proof of Theorem 1. Note that $\{a^{f(n)}/n\} = 0$ for each $n = a^s$, where $s \in \mathbb{N}$ is large enough, so $0 \in V_{a,f}$, and the value 0 is attained for infinitely many indices n.

Now, assume that $w \neq 0$ is in $V_{a,f}$. Evidently, w must be a rational number lying in the interval $(0,1)$. Suppose that $w = \{a^{f(s)}/s\}$ for some $s \in \mathbb{N}$ satisfying $s \geq n_f$. We claim that $w = \{a^{f(n)}/n\}$ for infinitely many n of the form $n = sa^\ell$, where ℓ runs through an infinite set of positive integers. In order to prove this it suffices to show that the difference

$$\frac{a^{f(n)}}{n} - \frac{a^{f(s)}}{s} = \frac{a^{f(sa^\ell)}}{sa^\ell} - \frac{a^{f(s)}}{s} = \frac{a^{f(sa^\ell)-\ell} - a^{f(s)}}{s} = \frac{a^{f(s)}}{s}(a^{f(sa^\ell)-f(s)-\ell} - 1)$$

is an integer. Let s_0 be the largest divisor of s which is coprime to a. Set $s' = s/s_0 \in \mathbb{N}$. We will prove that

$$s' \mid a^{f(s)} \tag{11}$$

and

$$s_0 \mid a^{f(sa^\ell)-f(s)-\ell} - 1 \tag{12}$$

for infinitely many $\ell \in \mathbb{N}$.

Fix any prime p that divides s' (if any) and assume that the order of p in s' is $l \geq 1$. Then, $p^{2l} \mid a^s$, since the order of p in a^s is at least

$$s \geq s' \geq p^l \geq 2^l \geq 2l.$$

Applying this argument to each prime divisor p of s' we deduce $s'^2 \mid a^s$. Since $s \leq 2f(s)$ for $s \geq n_f$, this yields $s'^2 \mid a^{2f(s)}$, and (11) follows. (There is nothing to prove if $s' = 1$.)

To prove (12), by $\gcd(s_0, a) = 1$, $f(sa^\ell) - f(s) - \ell > 0$ and Euler's theorem, it suffices to show that

$$\varphi(s_0) \mid f(sa^\ell) - f(s) - \ell$$

for infinitely many $\ell \in \mathbb{N}$. This clearly follows by Lemma 1 with parameters $(t, u, v) = (\varphi(s_0), f(s), s)$. Consequently, each value $w = \{a^s/s\}$ of $V_{a,f}$ is attained for infinitely many indices $n = sa^\ell$ with certain $\ell \in \mathbb{N}$.

Next, assume that $w = r/m \in V_{a,f}$, where $m \geq 2$, $1 \leq r < m$, and $\gcd(r,m) = 1$. Then, for some $s \geq n_f$, we must have $r/m = \{a^{f(s)}/s\}$. Write s in the form $s's_0$, where s_0 is the largest divisor of s coprime to a. We claim that $s_0 = m$.

Indeed, by (11), we have $s' \mid a^{f(s)}$. So, setting $L = [a^{f(s)}/s]$, we find that $\{a^{f(s)}/s\}$ equals

$$\frac{r}{m} = \frac{a^{f(s)}}{s} - L = \frac{a^{f(s)}}{s's_0} - L = \frac{a^{f(s)}/s' - Ls_0}{s_0}.$$

Here, the numerator $a^{f(s)}/s' - Ls_0$ is coprime to s_0, which implies

$$r = a^{f(s)}/s' - Ls_0 \quad \text{and} \quad m = s_0.$$

In order to complete the proof of Theorem 1 it remains to show that only $r \in R_m(a)$ occur as numerators of the rational numbers $w = r/m \in V_{a,f}$ and that all $r \in R_m(a)$ indeed occur as numerators. The first assertion is clear, because $1 \leq r < m$ and $a^{f(s)}/s'$ is an integer in S_a, so that

$$r = a^{f(s)}/s' - Ls_0 = a^{f(s)}/s' - Lm \in R_m(a).$$

To prove the second assertion assume that $r \in R_m(a)$. Then, for some integers $u_1, \ldots, u_k, T \geq 0$, we have

$$r = p_1^{u_1} \ldots p_k^{u_k} - Tm. \tag{13}$$

(Recall that $p_1, \ldots, p_k$ are the prime divisors of a.)

Write

$$a = p_1^{v_1} \ldots p_k^{v_k},$$

with $v_1, \ldots, v_k \in \mathbb{N}$. Then, by Lemma 3 with $t = \varphi(m)$ and $P_i = p_i$, there is a vector of positive integers $(n_1, \ldots, n_k)$ satisfying

$$v_i f(m p_1^{n_1} \ldots p_k^{n_k}) - n_i \equiv u_i \pmod{\varphi(m)} \tag{14}$$

for $i = 1, \ldots, k$. Therefore, for

$$n = m p_1^{n_1} \ldots p_k^{n_k}, \tag{15}$$

we find that

$$\frac{a^{f(n)}}{n} = \frac{p_1^{v_1 f(n)} \ldots p_k^{v_k f(n)}}{m p_1^{n_1} \ldots p_k^{n_k}} = \frac{p_1^{v_1 f(m p_1^{n_1} \ldots p_k^{n_k}) - n_1} \ldots p_k^{v_k f(m p_1^{n_1} \ldots p_k^{n_k}) - n_k}}{m}.$$

In view of (14) and $\gcd(p_i, m) = 1$, $i = 1, 2, \ldots, k$, the numerator of the last fraction equals $p_1^{u_1} \ldots p_k^{u_k}$ modulo m, which is r modulo m by (13). Thus, $a^{f(n)}/n = r/m + B$ with some $B \in \mathbb{Z}$. Consequently, for every n as in (15), we obtain $\{a^{f(n)}/n\} = r/m$, which completes the proof of the theorem. □

Proof of Theorem 2. Write

$$f(x) = a_m x^m + \cdots + a_1 x + a_0 \in \mathbb{Z}[x], \quad m, a_m \in \mathbb{N},$$

and select a nonnegative integer c such that

$$d \mid a_0 - c.$$

In all what follows we will show that the sequence $\{a^{f(n)-c}/n^d\}$, $n \geq 1$, is everywhere dense in $[0,1]$. In particular, it is everywhere dense in $[0, a^{-c}]$. Since

$$\{a^{f(n)}/n^d\} - a^c \{a^{f(n)-c}/n^d\} \in \mathbb{Z},$$

this clearly implies that the original sequence $\{a^{f(n)}/n^d\}$, $n = 1, 2, 3, \ldots$, is everywhere dense in $[0, 1]$.

Let $p > a$ be a prime number. Consider the value of $a^{f(n)-c}/n^d$ at $n = pa^s$, where $s \geq 0$ is an integer:

$$\frac{a^{f(n)-c}}{n^d} = \frac{a^{f(pa^s)-c}}{(pa^s)^d} = \frac{a^{f(pa^s)-c-ds}}{p^d}. \tag{16}$$

We claim that for each $u \geq 0$ there are infinitely many positive integers s for which
$$p^d \mid a^{f(pa^s)-c-ds} - a^{du} = a^{du}(a^{f(pa^s)-c-ds-du} - 1). \tag{17}$$
If this is the case, then, by (16), each value
$$\frac{A^u \pmod{p^d}}{p^d},$$
where $A = a^d$ and $u \geq 0$ is an integer, is attained for infinitely many indices n of the sequence $\{a^{f(n)-c}/n^d\}$, $n = 1, 2, 3, \ldots$. Thus, this sequence is everywhere dense by Lemma 2.

In order to prove (17) we will apply Lemma 1 to the polynomial
$$g(x) = \frac{f(a^l x) - c}{d} = \frac{a_m (a^l x)^m + \cdots + a_1 a^l x}{d} + \frac{a_0 - c}{d} \in \mathbb{Z}[x]$$
with $v = p$, $t = \varphi(p^d)$ and $u + l$ in place of u, where $l \geq 0$ is a fixed integer satisfying $d \mid a^l$. (Here, we use the condition $\operatorname{rad}(d) \mid \operatorname{rad}(a)$.) Then, by (4) applied to the polynomial g, there are infinitely many integers $s > l$ satisfying
$$g(pa^{s-l}) - (s - l) \equiv u + l \pmod{\varphi(p^d)},$$
and hence
$$\varphi(p^d) \mid g(pa^{s-l}) - s - u.$$
Thus, from $dg(pa^{s-l}) = f(pa^s) - c$ it follows that
$$\varphi(p^d) \mid f(pa^s) - c - ds - du.$$
Also, $f(pa^s) - c - ds - du > 0$ for s sufficiently large. Since $\gcd(a, p^d) = 1$, this implies (17) by Euler's theorem, which completes the proof of Theorem 2. □

5. Fractional Parts of $2^n/n^2$ Behave Differently

First, we will show that the sequence $\{2^n/n^2\}$, $n = 1, 2, 3, \ldots$, attains the value $7/25$ for $n = 5$ only and does not attain the value, e.g., $2/25$ at all, although $2 \in R_{25}(2)$. This indicates that the behaviour of $\{2^n/n^2\}$, $n = 1, 2, 3, \ldots$, is different from that of $\{2^n/n\}$, $n = 1, 2, 3, \ldots$, as described in Theorem 1. (Note that $\{2^n/n^2\}$, $n = 1, 2, 3, \ldots$, is everywhere dense in $[0, 1]$ by Corollary 2).

Suppose that $\{2^n/n^2\} = r/25$, where r is a positive integer smaller than 25 and coprime to 5. Set $L = [2^n/n^2]$. Then,
$$\frac{rn^2}{25} = 2^n - n^2 L \in \mathbb{N}, \tag{18}$$
so $25 \mid n^2$. Hence, $n = 5^l m$ with $l, m \in \mathbb{N}$, $\gcd(m, 5) = 1$. Inserting this into (18) we obtain
$$5^{2l-2} rm^2 = 2^{5^l m} - 5^{2l} m^2 L.$$

The argument modulo 5 shows that $l = 1$ is the only possibility, and hence $rm^2 = 2^{5m} - 25m^2 L$. Now, the argument modulo m shows that $m = 2^\ell$, where ℓ is a nonnegative integer. It follows that
$$r + 25L = \frac{2^{5m}}{m^2} = 2^{5 \cdot 2^\ell - 2\ell},$$
and so
$$r \equiv 2^{5 \cdot 2^\ell - 2\ell} \pmod{25}.$$

Therefore, $r/25$, where $1 \leq r < 25$ and $\gcd(r,5) = 1$, occurs as the value of $\{2^n/n^2\}$ if and only if $r = r_\ell$, where
$$r_\ell = 2^{5 \cdot 2^\ell - 2\ell} \pmod{25}$$
for some integer $\ell \geq 0$.

Note that $2^{20} \equiv 1 \pmod{25}$. Hence, the sequence $r_2, r_3, r_4, \ldots$ is purely periodic with period 10, because for each $\ell \geq 2$ the difference
$$5 \cdot 2^{\ell+10} - 2(\ell+10) - 5 \cdot 2^\ell + 2\ell = 5 \cdot 1023 \cdot 2^\ell - 20$$
is divisible by 20.

For $\ell = 0, 1, \ldots, 11$ we have the following table.

ℓ	0	1	2	3	4	5	6	7	8	9	10	11
$5 \cdot 2^\ell - 2\ell$	5	8	16	34	72	150	308	626	1264	2542	5100	10,218
r_ℓ	7	6	11	9	21	24	6	14	16	4	1	19

Therefore, the fractional parts $\{2^n/n^2\}$, $n = 1, 2, 3, \ldots$, attain any value from the set
$$\left\{\frac{1}{25}, \frac{4}{25}, \frac{6}{25}, \frac{9}{25}, \frac{11}{25}, \frac{14}{25}, \frac{16}{25}, \frac{19}{25}, \frac{21}{25}, \frac{24}{25}\right\}$$
for infinitely many $n \in \mathbb{N}$. The value $7/25$ is taken for $n = 5$ only, since $r_\ell = 7$ for $\ell = 0$ only, while the values
$$\frac{2}{25}, \frac{3}{25}, \frac{8}{25}, \frac{12}{25}, \frac{13}{25}, \frac{17}{25}, \frac{18}{25}, \frac{22}{25}, \frac{23}{25} \tag{19}$$
are not attained.

The reason behind this is that, in general, for integers $t \geq 1$, $u \geq 0$, $v \geq 1$ we cannot claim that there are nonnegative integers n for which
$$v2^n - 2n \equiv u \pmod{t}. \tag{20}$$

(Compare to (4) in Lemma 1.) For $v = 5$ and $t = 20$ all possible u that can be obtained in (20) are either 5 (which happens for $n = 0$) or even. The values $u = 1, 3, 7, 9, 11, 13, 15, 17, 19$ are never attained in (20), which gives the corresponding numerators
$$2^u \pmod{25} = 2, 8, 3, 12, 23, 17, 18, 22, 13$$
in (19).

Finally, take any odd prime p such that the order δ_p of 2 modulo p is even. There are infinitely many of such p, and, by [18], the density of such primes is $17/24$. Consider the value $w = \{2^p/p^2\}$. We claim that the value w is unique, namely, attained by $n = p$ only.

Assume that $w = \{2^n/n^2\}$ for some $n \neq p$. Then, it is easy to see that n must be of the form $n = p2^k$ with some $k \in \mathbb{N}$. This happens if and only if
$$\frac{2^n}{n^2} - \frac{2^p}{p^2} = \frac{2^{p2^k}}{p^2 2^{2k}} - \frac{2^p}{p^2} = \frac{2^p}{p^2}(2^{p2^k - 2k - p} - 1)$$
is an integer. This is only possible if p divides $2^{p2^k - 2k - p} - 1$. Since the order δ_p of 2 modulo p is even, and δ_p divides the exponent $p2^k - 2k - p$, the latter integer must be even, which is not the case. This completes the proof of the fact that for each of those infinitely many primes p the value $w = \{2^p/p^2\}$ in the sequence $\{2^n/n^2\}$, $n = 1, 2, 3, \ldots$, is attained at $n = p$ only.

Funding: This research received no external funding.

Acknowledgments: The author thanks Igor Shparlinski, who explained the current state-of-the-art approaches related to the estimates for the gaps between elements of a multiplicative subgroup in a residue ring and supplied with corresponding references.

Conflicts of Interest: The author declares no conflict of interest.

References

1. Weyl, H. Über die Gleichverteilung von Zahlen modulo Eins. *Math. Ann.* **1916**, *77*, 313–352. [CrossRef]
2. Koksma, J.F. Ein mengen-theoretischer Satz über Gleichverteilung modulo eins. *Compos. Math.* **1935**, *2*, 250–258.
3. Dubickas, A. Arithmetical properties of powers of algebraic numbers. *Bull. Lond. Math. Soc.* **2006**, *38*, 70–80. [CrossRef]
4. Dubickas, A. On the distance from a rational power to the nearest integer. *J. Number Theory* **2006**, *117*, 222–239. [CrossRef]
5. Mahler, K. An unsolved problem on the powers of 3/2. *J. Aust. Math. Soc.* **1968**, *8*, 313–321. [CrossRef]
6. Boshernitzan, M.D. Elementary proof of Furstenberg's Diophantine result. *Proc. Am. Math. Soc.* **1994**, *122*, 67–70.
7. Furstenberg, H. Disjointness in ergodic theory, minimal sets, and a problem in Diophantine approximation. *Math. Syst. Theory* **1967**, *1*, 1–49. [CrossRef]
8. Abramoff, M.; Berend, D. A polynomial-exponential variation of Furstenberg's $\times 2 \times 3$ theorem. *Ergod. Theory Dyn. Syst.* **2020**, *40*, 1729–1737. [CrossRef]
9. Bourgain, J.; Lindenstrauss, E.; Michel, P.; Venkatesh, A. Some effective results for $\times a \times b$. *Ergod. Theory Dyn. Syst.* **2009**, *29*, 1705–1722. [CrossRef]
10. Gorodnik, A.; Kadyrov, S. Algebraic numbers, hyperbolicity, and density modulo one. *J. Number Theory* **2012**, *132*, 2499–2509. [CrossRef]
11. Katz, A. Generalizations of Furstenberg's Diophantine result. *Ergod. Theory Dyn. Syst.* **2018**, *38*, 1012–1024. [CrossRef]
12. Kra, B. A generalization of Furstenberg's diophantine theorem. *Proc. Am. Math. Soc.* **1999**, *127*, 1951–1956. [CrossRef]
13. Urban, R. Sequences of algebraic integers and density modulo 1. *J. Théor. Nombres Bordx.* **2007**, *19*, 755–762. [CrossRef]
14. Urban, R. Algebraic numbers and density modulo 1. *J. Number Theory* **2008**, *128*, 645–661. [CrossRef]
15. Cilleruelo, J.; Kumchev, A.; Luca, F.; Rué, J.; Shparlinski, I.E. On the fractional parts of a^n/n. *Bull. Lond. Math. Soc.* **2013**, *45*, 249–256. [CrossRef]
16. Dubickas, A. Density of some sequences modulo 1. *Colloq. Math.* **2012** *128*, 237–244. [CrossRef]
17. Dubickas, A. On the fractional parts of natural powers of a fixed number. *Sib. Math. J.* **2006**, *47*, 879–882. [CrossRef]
18. Hasse, H. Über die Dichte der Primzahlen p, für die eine vorgegebene ganzrationale Zahl $a \neq 0$ von gerader bzw. ungerader Ordnung mod.p ist. *Math. Ann.* **1966**, *166*, 19–23. [CrossRef]
19. Erdős, P.; Murty, M.R. On the order of $a \pmod{p}$. In *Number Theory*; CRM Proc. Lecture Notes; Ottawa, ON, Canada, 1996; pp. 87–97.
20. Pappalardi, F. On the order of finitely generated subgroups of $\mathbb{Q}^* \pmod{p}$ and divisors of $p-1$. *J. Number Theory* **1996**, *57*, 207–222. [CrossRef]
21. Murphy, B.; Rudnev, M.; Shkredov, I.; Shteinikov, Y. On the few products, many sums problem. *J. Théor. Nombres Bordx.* **2019**, *31*, 573–602. [CrossRef]
22. Bourgain, J.; Konyagin, S.V.; Shparlinski, I.E. Product sets of rationals, multiplicative translates of subgroups in residue rings, and fixed points of the discrete logarithm. *Int. Math. Res. Not.* **2008**, *2008*, rnn090.
23. Konyagin, S.V.; Shparlinski, I.E. *Character Sums with Exponential Functions and Their Applications*; Cambridge Tracts in Mathematics; Cambridge University Press: Cambridge, UK, 1999; Volume 136.
24. Shparlinski, I.E. Estimates for Gaussian sums. *Math. Notes* **1991**, *50*, 740–746. [CrossRef]
25. Shteinikov, Y. Estimates of trigonometric sums over subgroups and some of their applications. *Math. Notes* **2015**, *98*, 667–684. [CrossRef]
26. Baker, R.C.; Harman, G. Shifted primes without large prime factors. *Acta Arith.* **1998**, *83*, 331–361. [CrossRef]
27. Heath-Brown, D.R. Artin's conjecture for primitive roots. *Quart. J. Math. Oxf. Ser.* **1986**, *37*, 27–38. [CrossRef]
28. Konyagin, S.V.; Shparlinski, I.E. On the consecutive powers of a primitive root: Gaps and exponential sums. *Mathematika* **2012**, *58*, 11–20. [CrossRef]
29. Bourgain, J. Exponential sum estimates over subgroups of $\mathbb{Z}_q^*$, q arbitrary. *J. Anal. Math.* **2005**, *97*, 317–355. [CrossRef]
30. Bourgain, J.; Chang, M.-C. Exponential sum estimates over subgroups and almost subgroups of $\mathbb{Z}_Q^*$, where Q is composite with few prime factors. *Geom. Funct. Anal.* **2006**, *16*, 327–366. [CrossRef]

Disclaimer/Publisher's Note: The statements, opinions and data contained in all publications are solely those of the individual author(s) and contributor(s) and not of MDPI and/or the editor(s). MDPI and/or the editor(s) disclaim responsibility for any injury to people or property resulting from any ideas, methods, instructions or products referred to in the content.

Article

A Bound for a Sum of Products of Two Characters and Its Application

Teerapat Srichan

Department of Mathematics, Faculty of Science, Kasetsart University, Bangkok 10900, Thailand; fscitrp@ku.ac.th

Abstract: Using the exponent pair method, a bound is derived for the sum $\sum_{m^a n^b \leq x} \chi_1^a(m)\chi_2^b(n)$, where a, b are fixed positive integers, χ_1, χ_2 are primitive Dirichlet characters modulo q_1 and q_2, respectively, and χ_1^a, χ_2^b are not principal characters. As an application, an estimate for the error term in an asymptotic formula for the number of square-full integers simultaneously belonging to two arithmetic progressions is obtained.

Keywords: character sums; Dirichlet convolutions; exponent pair

MSC: 11A07; 11L40; 11N37

Citation: Srichan, T. A Bound for a Sum of Products of Two Characters and Its Application. *Mathematics* 2023, 11, 2507. https://doi.org/10.3390/math11112507

Academic Editors: Diana Savin, Nicusor Minculete, Vincenzo Acciaro, Jiyou Li and Abdelmejid Bayad

Received: 31 March 2023
Revised: 10 May 2023
Accepted: 26 May 2023
Published: 30 May 2023

Copyright: © 2023 by the author. Licensee MDPI, Basel, Switzerland. This article is an open access article distributed under the terms and conditions of the Creative Commons Attribution (CC BY) license (https://creativecommons.org/licenses/by/4.0/).

1. Introduction

The technique of character sums has proved useful in various fields of mathematics, particularly in dealing with counting problems in analytic number theory (see, for example, [1–4] (Chapter 8 in [3])). Character sums over products of more than one character have also proved useful in deriving a number of asymptotic estimates (see, for example, [5–11]). Because of such versatile applications, in [12], the problem of finding good bounds for character sums of the form

$$S_{\chi_1,\chi_2}(x) = \sum_{mn \leq x} \chi_1(m)\chi_2(n) \qquad (1)$$

were investigated. In the present work, we proceed further to derive a good bound for more general sums than those found in (1). As a possible application, we look at the problem of finding the number of square-full integers simultaneously belonging to two arithmetic progressions and use our main theorem to obtain a good bound for the error term for its asymptotic estimate.

Our main result is:

Theorem 1. *Let a, b be two fixed positive integers with $1 \leq a < b$. Let q_1, q_2 be two distinct positive integers. Let χ_1, χ_2 be two primitive Dirichlet characters modulo q_1 and q_2, respectively, which are subject to the condition that both χ_1^a and χ_2^b are not principal characters. For a positive real x, define*

$$V_{a,b}(\chi_1,\chi_2;x) = \sum_{m^a n^b \leq x} \chi_1(m^a)\chi_2(n^b). \qquad (2)$$

Then, for $2 \leq q_1 < q_2$ and $q_1^{-10/3} q_2^{13/3} < x^{1/(a+b)}$, we have

$$V_{a,b}(\chi_1,\chi_2;x) = \begin{cases} O\left(x^{2/(3a+3b)} q_1^{5/9} q_2^{7/9}\right) & \text{if } 2a > b, \\ O\left(x^{2/9a} q_1^{7/9} q_2^{5/9} \log x\right) & \text{if } 2a = b, \\ O\left(x^{2/(5a+2b)} q_1^{(3a+2b)/(5a+2b)} q_2^{5a/(5a+2b)}\right) & \text{if } 2a < b. \end{cases}$$

Before embarking upon the proof of Theorem 1, let us consider some of its special cases that indicate its origin and importance.
- The work in [12] deals with the case $a = b = 1$.
- When $\chi_1 = \chi_2 =: \chi$ is a character modulo q and $a = 1, b = 2$, Theorem 1 yields

$$V_{1,2}(\chi, \chi; x) = O(x^{2/9} q^{4/3} \log x),$$

which appears as a bound in Equation (64) of [2].
- When $\chi_1 = \chi_2 =: \chi$ is a character modulo q and $a = 2, b = 3$, Theorem 1 yields

$$V_{2,3}(\chi, \chi; x) = O(x^{2/15} q^{4/3}),$$

which is an improvement of the bound in Equation (15) of [4].

To begin our proof, let

$$\psi(x) = x - \lfloor x \rfloor - \frac{1}{2}.$$

We need the following lemmas.

Lemma 1. *Let χ be a primitive character modulo q, $q \geq 2$. For a real $z > 1$, we have*

$$\sum_{a \leq z} \chi(a) = \sum_{j \leq q} \chi(j) \left\lfloor \frac{z}{q} - \frac{j}{q} + 1 \right\rfloor.$$

Proof. From the periodicity of the primitive character modulo q, we find that

$$\sum_{a \leq z} \chi(a) = \sum_{j \leq q} \sum_{\substack{a \leq z \\ a \equiv j \bmod q}} \chi(a) = \sum_{j \leq q} \sum_{\substack{a \leq z \\ a \equiv j \bmod q}} \chi(j)$$

$$= \sum_{j \leq q} \chi(j) \sum_{\substack{a \leq z \\ a \equiv j \bmod q}} 1 = \sum_{j \leq q} \chi(j) \left\lfloor \frac{z}{q} - \frac{j}{q} + 1 \right\rfloor.$$

□

As elaborated in [13] (Section 2.3, Chapter 2), the notion of an exponent pair, which is crucial in our analysis, is defined as follows. Let $A > 1/2$, $B \geq 1$, $1 < h \leq B$, and suppose that

$$\sum_{B < n \leq B+h} e^{2\pi i f(n)} = O(A^\kappa B^\lambda)$$

for some pair (κ, λ) of real numbers satisfying $0 \leq \kappa \leq 1/2 \leq \lambda \leq 1$, and for any differentiable real-valued function f satisfying

$$A \ll |f'(x)| \ll A \quad \text{when } x \in [B, 2B].$$

Then, we call (κ, λ) an *exponent pair*.

The next lemma is Lemma 17 from [2].

Lemma 2. *Let x, η, α, ω be real numbers, j and q be positive integers with $x \geq 1, \alpha > 0, \eta \geq 1, 1 \leq j \leq q$, (k, ℓ) be an exponent pair with $k > 0$, and let*

$$R(x, \eta, \alpha; q, j; \omega) = \sum_{\substack{n \leq \eta \\ n \equiv j \bmod q}} \psi\left(\frac{x}{n^\alpha} + \omega\right),$$

where ω is independent of n. Then,

$$R(x,\eta,\alpha;q,j;\omega) = O(1) + O(x^{\frac{-1}{2}}\eta^{1+\frac{\alpha}{2}}q^{-1}) + \begin{cases} O(x^{\frac{k}{k+1}}\eta^{\frac{\ell-\alpha k}{k+1}}q^{\frac{-\ell}{k+1}}) & \text{if } \ell > \alpha k, \\ O(x^{\frac{k}{k+1}}\log\eta\, q^{\frac{-\alpha k}{k+1}}) & \text{if } \ell = \alpha k, \\ O((xq^{-\alpha})^{\frac{k}{1+(1+\alpha)k-\ell}}) & \text{if } \ell < \alpha k, \end{cases}$$

where the O-constants only depend on α.

2. Proof of Theorem 1

Proof. For $x > 1$, we have

$$V_{a,b}(\chi_1,\chi_2;x) = \sum_{m \le x^{1/(a+b)}} \chi_1(m^a) \sum_{n \le (x/m^a)^{1/b}} \chi_2(n^b) + \sum_{n \le x^{1/(a+b)}} \chi_2(n^b) \sum_{m \le (x/n^b)^{1/a}} \chi_1(m^a)$$
$$- \sum_{m \le x^{1/(a+b)}} \chi_1(m^a) \sum_{n \le x^{1/(a+b)}} \chi_2(n^b).$$

In view of Lemma 1, we obtain

$$V_{a,b}(\chi_1,\chi_2;x)$$
$$= \sum_{j \le q_2} \chi_2^b(j) \sum_{m \le x^{1/(a+b)}} \chi_1^a(m) \left\lfloor \frac{x^{1/b}}{q_2 m^{a/b}} - \frac{j}{q_2} + 1 \right\rfloor$$
$$+ \sum_{h \le q_1} \chi_1^a(h) \sum_{n \le x^{1/(a+b)}} \chi_2^b(n) \left\lfloor \frac{x^{1/a}}{q_1 n^{b/a}} - \frac{h}{q_1} + 1 \right\rfloor$$
$$- \sum_{h \le q_1} \sum_{j \le q_2} \chi_1^a(h)\chi_2^b(j) \left\lfloor \frac{x^{1/(a+b)}}{q_2} - \frac{j}{q_2} + 1 \right\rfloor \left\lfloor \frac{x^{1/(a+b)}}{q_1} - \frac{h}{q_1} + 1 \right\rfloor$$

Because $\lfloor x \rfloor = x - \psi(x) - \frac{1}{2}$, $\sum_{j \le q} \chi(j) = 0$ for non-principal characters χ and $\psi(x) = \psi(x+1)$, we have

$$V_{a,b}(\chi_1,\chi_2;x) = \sum_{j \le q_2} \chi_2^b(j) \sum_{m \le x^{1/(a+b)}} \chi_1^a(m) \left(\frac{x^{1/b}}{q_2 m^{a/b}} - \frac{j}{q_2} + \frac{1}{2} - \psi\left(\frac{x^{1/b}}{q_2 m^{a/b}} - \frac{j}{q_2}\right) \right)$$
$$+ \sum_{h \le q_1} \chi_1^a(h) \sum_{n \le x^{1/(a+b)}} \chi_2^b(n) \left(\frac{x^{1/a}}{q_1 n^{b/a}} - \frac{h}{q_1} + \frac{1}{2} - \psi\left(\frac{x^{1/a}}{q_1 n^{b/a}} - \frac{h}{q_1}\right) \right)$$
$$- \sum_{j \le q_2} \sum_{h \le q_1} \chi_1^a(h)\chi_2^b(j) \left(\frac{x^{1/(a+b)}}{q_2} - \frac{j}{q_2} + \frac{1}{2} - \psi\left(\frac{x^{1/(a+b)}}{q_2} - \frac{j}{q_2}\right) \right)$$
$$\times \left(\frac{x^{1/(a+b)}}{q_1} - \frac{h}{q_1} + \frac{1}{2} - \psi\left(\frac{x^{1/(a+b)}}{q_1} - \frac{h}{q_1}\right) \right)$$
$$= -\sum_{j \le q_2} \chi_2^b(j) \sum_{m \le x^{1/(a+b)}} \chi_1^a(m) \left(\frac{j}{q_2} + \psi\left(\frac{x^{1/b}}{q_2 m^{a/b}} - \frac{j}{q_2}\right) \right)$$
$$- \sum_{h \le q_1} \chi_1^a(h) \sum_{n \le x^{1/(a+b)}} \chi_2^b(n) \left(\frac{h}{q_1} + \psi\left(\frac{x^{1/a}}{q_1 n^{b/a}} - \frac{h}{q_1}\right) \right)$$
$$- \sum_{j \le q_2} \sum_{h \le q_1} \chi_1^a(h)\chi_2^b(j) \left(\frac{j}{q_2} + \psi\left(\frac{x^{1/(a+b)}}{q_2} - \frac{j}{q_2}\right) \right) \left(\frac{h}{q_1} + \psi\left(\frac{x^{1/(a+b)}}{q_1} - \frac{h}{q_1}\right) \right)$$
$$=: -T_1 - T_2 - T_3. \tag{3}$$

We separately analyze each of the three terms T_1, T_2, T_3, which appear in (3). It is easy to see that

$$T_3 = \sum_{j \leq q_2} \sum_{h \leq q_1} \chi_1^a(h)\chi_2^b(j)\left(\frac{j}{q_2} + \psi\left(\frac{x^{1/(a+b)}}{q_2} - \frac{j}{q_2}\right)\right)\left(\frac{h}{q_1} + \psi\left(\frac{x^{1/(a+b)}}{q_1} - \frac{h}{q_1}\right)\right)$$
$$= O(q_1 q_2).$$

As for T_1, by applying Lemma 1 to the first part of the second sum, and applying the periodicity of character to the second part, we get

$$T_1 = \sum_{j \leq q_2} \chi_2^b(j)\frac{j}{q_2} \sum_{h \leq q_1} \chi_1^a(h) \left\lfloor \frac{x^{1/(a+b)}}{q_1} - \frac{h}{q_1} + 1 \right\rfloor$$
$$+ \sum_{j \leq q_2} \chi_2^b(j) \sum_{h \leq q_1} \chi_1^a(h) \sum_{\substack{m \leq x^{1/(a+b)} \\ m \equiv h \bmod q_1}} \psi\left(\frac{x^{1/a}}{q_2 m^{a/b}} - \frac{j}{q_2}\right).$$

Repeating the above steps to the first part, i.e, replacing $\lfloor x \rfloor = x - \psi(x) - 1/2$, using $\sum_{j \leq q} \chi(j) = 0$ for non-principal characters, and $\psi(x) = \psi(x+m)$, $m \in \mathbb{Z}$, the first part is equal to

$$\sum_{j \leq q_2} \chi_2^b(j)\frac{j}{q_2} \sum_{h \leq q_1} \chi_1^a(h)\left(-\frac{h}{q_1} + \psi\left(\frac{x^{1/(a+b)}}{q_1} - \frac{h}{q_1}\right)\right) = O(q_1 q_2)$$

yielding

$$-T_1 = -\sum_{j \leq q_2} \chi_2^b(j) \sum_{h \leq q_1} \chi_1^a(h) \sum_{\substack{m \leq x^{1/(a+b)} \\ m \equiv h \bmod q_1}} \psi\left(\frac{x^{1/a}}{q_2 m^{a/b}} - \frac{j}{q_2}\right) + O(q_1 q_2).$$

Proceeding with T_2 in the same manner as that of T_1, we get

$$-T_2 = -\sum_{h \leq q_1} \chi_1^a(h) \sum_{j \leq q_2} \chi_2^b(j) \sum_{\substack{n \leq x^{1/(a+b)} \\ n \equiv j \bmod q_2}} \psi\left(\frac{x^{1/a}}{q_1 n^{b/a}} - \frac{h}{q_1}\right) + O(q_1 q_2).$$

Thus,

$$V_{a,b}(\chi_1, \chi_2; x) = -\sum_{j \leq q_2} \sum_{h \leq q_1} \chi_2^b(j)\chi_1^a(h) \sum_{\substack{m \leq x^{1/(a+b)} \\ m \equiv h \bmod q_1}} \psi\left(\frac{x^{1/b}}{q_2 m^{a/b}} - \frac{j}{q_2}\right)$$
$$- \sum_{j \leq q_2} \sum_{h \leq q_1} \chi_2^b(j)\chi_1^a(h) \sum_{\substack{n \leq x^{1/(a+b)} \\ n \equiv j \bmod q_2}} \psi\left(\frac{x^{1/a}}{q_1 n^{b/a}} - \frac{h}{q_1}\right) + O(q_1 q_2)$$
$$=: -S_1 - S_2 + O(q_1 q_2).$$

To estimate S_1 and S_2, we use the exponent pair $(k,\ell) = (2/7, 4/7)$ in Lemma 2; we note that from $a < b$ we have $ka/b = 2a/7b < 4/7 = \ell$ and keep in mind for the rest of the proof that $2 \leq q_1 < q_2 < q_1^{-10/3} q_2^{13/3} < x^{1/(a+b)}$. Using Lemma 2, we have

$$S_1 = \sum_{j \leq q_2} \sum_{h \leq q_1} \chi_2^b(j) \chi_1^a(h) R\left(\frac{x^{1/b}}{q_2}, x^{1/(a+b)}, \frac{a}{b}, q_1, h, \frac{-j}{q_2}\right)$$

$$\ll \sum_{j \leq q_2} \sum_{h \leq q_1} \left(x^{1/(2a+2b)} q_1^{-1} q_2^{1/2} + x^{2/(3a+3b)} q_1^{-4/9} q_2^{-2/9}\right) + O(q_1 q_2),$$

$$= O\left(x^{1/(2a+2b)} q_2^{3/2} + x^{2/(3a+3b)} q_1^{5/9} q_2^{7/9}\right) + O(q_1 q_2)$$

$$= O\left(x^{2/(3a+3b)} q_1^{5/9} q_2^{7/9}\right),$$

and

$$S_2 = \sum_{j \leq q_2} \sum_{h \leq q_1} \chi_2^b(j) \chi_1^a(h) R\left(\frac{x^{1/a}}{q_1}, x^{1/(a+b)}, \frac{b}{a}, q_2, j, \frac{-h}{q_1}\right)$$

$$\ll O(q_1 q_2) + O\left(x^{1/(2a+2b)} q_1^{3/2}\right) + \begin{cases} O\left(x^{2/(3a+3b)} q_1^{7/9} q_2^{5/9}\right) & \text{if } 2a > b, \\ O\left(x^{2/9a} q_1^{7/9} q_2^{5/9} \log x\right) & \text{if } 2a = b, \\ O\left(x^{2/(5a+2b)} q_1^{(3a+2b)/(5a+2b)} q_2^{5a/(5a+2b)}\right) & \text{if } 2a < b \end{cases}$$

$$= \begin{cases} O\left(x^{2/(3a+3b)} q_1^{7/9} q_2^{5/9}\right) & \text{if } 2a > b, \\ O\left(x^{2/9a} q_1^{7/9} q_2^{5/9} \log x\right) & \text{if } 2a = b, \\ O\left(x^{2/(5a+2b)} q_1^{(3a+2b)/(5a+2b)} q_2^{5a/(5a+2b)}\right) & \text{if } 2a < b. \end{cases}$$

Combining these estimates, the theorem follows. □

3. Application

In this section, we illustrate a possible use of our theorem to derive a good error term in the problem of finding an asymptotic estimate of the number of square-full integers belonging simultaneously to two arithmetic progressions. An integer $n > 1$ is called square-full if in its canonical prime representation each prime appears with exponent ≥ 2; the integer 1 is square-full by convention. For $n \in \mathbb{N}$, let

$$g(n) := \begin{cases} 1 & \text{if } n \text{ is square-full}, \\ 0 & \text{otherwise}, \end{cases}$$

denote the characteristic function of square-full integers. Let q_1, q_2 be two relatively prime positive integers and let $\ell_i \in \{1, 2, \ldots, q_i - 1\}$ with $\gcd(\ell_i, q_i) = 1$ $(i = 1, 2)$. For $x > 1$, define

$$G(x; \ell_1, \ell_2; q_1, q_2) := \sum_{\substack{n \leq x \\ n \equiv \ell_1 \bmod q_1 \\ n \equiv \ell_2 \bmod q_2}} g(n), \tag{4}$$

which counts the number of square-full integers ($\leq x$) simultaneously belonging to two arithmetic progressions. As evidenced from the proof of the Chinese remainder theorem ([14] Theorem 5.26), the set of solutions of the system of two congruences $n \equiv \ell_1 \bmod q_1$, $n \equiv \ell_2 \bmod q_2$ is contained in an arithmetic progression; as the number of square-full integers belonging to an arithmetic progression has a substantial proportion over $\mathbb{N}$ [1,4], the problem of seeking for an asymptotic estimate for $G(x; \ell_1, \ell_2; q_1, q_2)$ is non-trivial.

The orthogonality relation for Dirichlet characters mod q_1, q_2, Theorem 6.16 from [14] shows that

$$G(x; \ell_1, \ell_2; q_1, q_2) = \frac{1}{\phi(q_1)\phi(q_2)} \sum_{\chi_1 \bmod q_1} \sum_{\chi_2 \bmod q_2} \bar{\chi}_1(\ell_1) \bar{\chi}_2(\ell_2) \sum_{n \leq x} g(n) \chi_1(n) \chi_2(n). \quad (5)$$

For brevity, let

$$T(x; \chi_1, \chi_2) := \sum_{n \leq x} g(n) \chi_1(n) \chi_2(n).$$

Because each positive integer is square-full if and only if it can be written uniquely as $r^2 m^3$, with m being square-free ([3] Lemma 8.3.1), we have

$$T(x; \chi_1, \chi_2) = \sum_{r^2 m^3 \leq x} \mu^2(m) \chi_1(r^2 m^3) \chi_2(r^2 m^3).$$

Because $\mu^2(m) = \sum_{d^2 | m} \mu(d)$, we get

$$T(x; \chi_1, \chi_2) = \sum_{r^2 m^3 \leq x} \sum_{d^2 | m} \mu(d) \chi_1(r^2 m^3) \chi_2(r^2 m^3) = \sum_{r^2 (d^2 t)^3 \leq x} \mu(d) \chi_1(r^2 (d^2 t)^3) \chi_2(r^2 (d^2 t)^3)$$

$$= \sum_{d \leq x^{1/6}} \mu(d) \chi_1^6(d) \chi_2^6(d) \sum_{r^2 t^3 \leq x/d^6} \chi_1(r^2 t^3) \chi_2(r^2 t^3).$$

Using $\alpha(n)$ to denote the number of representations of each $n \in \mathbb{N}$ in the form $n = r^2 t^3$, we get

$$T(x; \chi_1, \chi_2) = \sum_{d \leq x^{1/6}} \mu(d) \chi_1^6(d) \chi_2^6(d) \sum_{n \leq x/d^6} \alpha(n) \chi_1(n) \chi_2(n). \quad (6)$$

Our immediate task now is to bound the sum $\sum_n \alpha(n) \chi_1(n) \chi_2(n)$. It is easily checked using the Euler product formula, of which the Dirichlet series of the function $\alpha(n) \chi_1(n) \chi_2(n)$ is

$$\sum_{n=1}^{\infty} \alpha(n) \chi_1(n) \chi_2(n) n^{-s} = L(2s, \chi_1^2 \chi_2^2) L(3s, \chi_1^3 \chi_2^3).$$

Perron's formula ([15] Theorem, p. 13) tells us that the main term of $\sum_{n \leq x} \alpha(n) \chi_1(n) \chi_2(n)$ is

$$\operatorname*{Res}_{s=1/2, 1/3} L(2s, \chi_1^2 \chi_2^2) L(3s, \chi_1^3 \chi_2^3) \frac{x^s}{s},$$

with contribution from the cases where either $\chi_1^2 \chi_2^2$ or $\chi_1^3 \chi_2^3$ is a principal character. The dominating error term of $\sum_{n \leq x} \alpha(n) \chi_1(n) \chi_2(n)$ is obtained by considering the cases where $\chi_1^2 \chi_2^2$ and $\chi_1^3 \chi_2^3$ are non-principal characters. As an example, let us complete the calculation when χ_1 is a cubic character mod q_1 and χ_2 is a quadratic character mod q_2. In this case, we obtain

$$\sum_{n=1}^{\infty} \alpha(n)\chi_1(n)\chi_2(n)n^{-s} = L(2s,\chi_1^2\chi_2^2)L(3s,\chi_1^3\chi_2^3)$$

$$= \prod_p (1-\chi_1^2(p)\chi_2^2(p)p^{-2s})^{-1}(1-\chi_1^3(p)\chi_2^3(p)p^{-3s})^{-1}$$

$$= \prod_{\substack{p \\ p \nmid q_1 q_2}} (1-\chi_1^2(p)p^{-2s})^{-1}(1-\chi_2^3(p)p^{-3s})^{-1}$$

$$= \left(\prod_p (1-\chi_1^2(p)p^{-2s})^{-1}(1-\chi_2^3(p)p^{-3s})^{-1}\right)\left(\prod_{\substack{p \\ p \mid q_1 q_2}} (1-\chi_1^2(p)p^{-2s})(1-\chi_2^3(p)p^{-3s})\right)$$

$$= L(2s,\chi_1^2)L(3s,\chi_2^3)C(q_1,q_2),$$

where

$$C(q_1,q_2) := \prod_{\substack{p \\ p \mid q_1 q_2}} (1-\chi_1^2(p)p^{-2s})(1-\chi_2^3(p)p^{-3s})$$

is a constant depending only on q_1, q_2. Putting

$$L(2s,\chi_1^2)L(3s,\chi_2^3) = \sum_{n=1}^{\infty} \beta(n)n^{-s},$$

we have

$$\beta(n) = \sum_{n=n_1^2 n_2^3} \chi_1^2(n_1)\chi_2^3(n_2).$$

Applying Theorem 1 with $a=2, b=3$, for $2 \leq q_1 < q_2 < q_1^{-10/3} q_2^{13/3} < x^{1/5}$, we have

$$\frac{1}{C(q_1,q_2)} \sum_{n \leq x} \alpha(n)\chi_1(n)\chi_2(n) = \sum_{n \leq x} \beta(n) = \sum_{n_1^2 n_2^3 \leq x} \chi_1^3(n_1)\chi_2^2(n_2) = O(x^{2/15} q_1^{5/9} q_2^{7/9}). \quad (7)$$

In view of (5)–(7), the error term in the estimation of $G(x; \ell_1, \ell_2; q_1, q_2)$ is $O(x^{1/6} q_1^{5/9} q_2^{7/9} / |C(q_1,q_2)|)$.

Funding: This research was supported by the Faculty of Science (International SciKU Branding, ISB), Kasetsart University, Thailand.

Data Availability Statement: The data that support the findings of this study are available from the corresponding author upon reasonable request.

Acknowledgments: The author would like to thank the support from the Faculty of Science (International SciKU Branding, ISB), Kasetsart University, Thailand.

Conflicts of Interest: The author declares no conflict of interest.

References

1. Munsch, M. Character sums over squarefree and squarefull numbers. *Arch. Math.* **2014**, *102*, 555–563. [CrossRef]
2. Richert, H.E. Uber die Anzahl Abelscher Gruppen gegebener Ordnung II. *Math. Z.* **1953**, *58*, 71–84. [CrossRef]
3. Shapiro, H.N. *Introduction to the Theory of Numbers*; Wiley: New York, NY, USA, 1983.
4. Srichan, T. Square-full and cube-full numbers in arithmetic progressions. *Šiaulai Math. Sem.* **2013**, *8*, 223–248.
5. Banks, W.D.; Shparlinski, I.E. Sums with convolutions of Dirichlet characters. *Manuscr. Math.* **2010**, *133*, 105–144. [CrossRef]
6. Friedlander, J.B.; Iwaniec, H. Summation formulae for coefficients of L-functions. *Canad. J. Math.* **2005**, *57*, 494–505. [CrossRef]
7. Iwaniec, H.; Kowalski, E. *Analytic Number Theory*; American Mathematical Society: Providence, RI, USA, 2004.

8. Laohakosol, V.; Srichan, T.; Tangsupphathawat, P. Square-full primitive roots in arithmetic progressions. *Mosc. J. Comb. Number Theory* **2020**, *9*, 187–202. [CrossRef]
9. Müller, C. Eine Formel der analytische Zahlentheorie. *Abh. Hambg. Univ.* **1954**, *19*, 62–65. [CrossRef]
10. Redmond, D. A generalization of a theorem of Ayoub and Chowla. *Proc. Am. Math. Soc. USA* **1982**, *88*, 574–580. [CrossRef]
11. Zhang, J.; Lv, X. On the primitive roots and the generalized Golomb's conjecture. *AIMS Math.* **2020**, *5*, 5654–5663. [CrossRef]
12. Srichan, T. A bound of sums with convolutions of Dirichlet characters. *Notes Number Theory Discret. Math.* **2020**, *26*, 70–74. [CrossRef]
13. Ivić, A. *The Theory of the Riemann Zeta Function*; Wiley: New York, NY, USA, 1985.
14. Apostol, T.M. *Introduction to Analytic Number Theory*; Springer: New York, NY, USA, 1976.
15. Karatsuba, A.A. *Complex Analysis in Number Theory*; CRC Press: Boca Raton, FL, USA, 1995.

Disclaimer/Publisher's Note: The statements, opinions and data contained in all publications are solely those of the individual author(s) and contributor(s) and not of MDPI and/or the editor(s). MDPI and/or the editor(s) disclaim responsibility for any injury to people or property resulting from any ideas, methods, instructions or products referred to in the content.

Article

A New Semi-Inner Product and p_n-Angle in the Space of p-Summable Sequences

Muh Nur [1,*], Mawardi Bahri [1], Anna Islamiyati [2] and Harmanus Batkunde [3]

[1] Department of Mathematics, Hasanuddin University, Makassar 90245, Indonesia; mawardi.bahri@unhas.ac.id
[2] Department of Statistics, Hasanuddin University, Makassar 90245, Indonesia; annaislamiyati@unhas.ac.id
[3] Department of Mathematics, Pattimura University, Ambon 97233, Indonesia; h.batkunde@fmipa.unpatti.ac.id
* Correspondence: muhammadnur@unhas.ac.id

Abstract: In this paper, we propose a definition for a semi-inner product in the space of p-summable sequences equipped with an n-norm. Using this definition, we introduce the concepts of p_n-orthogonality and the p_n-angle between two vectors in the space of p-summable sequences. For the special case $n = 1$, these concepts are identical to previous studies. We also introduce the notion of the p_n-angle between one-dimensional subspaces and arbitrary-dimensional subspaces. The authors believe that the results obtained in this paper are very significant, especially in the theory of n-normed space in functional analysis.

Keywords: semi-inner product; p_n-orthogonality; p_n-angle; n-norm

MSC: 15A03; 46B20; 46B45; 46C50

1. Introduction

Let X be the vector space. A *semi-inner product* on X is a mapping $[\cdot,\cdot] : X^2 \to \mathbb{R}$, which satisfies the following properties:

(1) $[x,x] \geq 0$ for every $x \in X$ and $[x,x] = 0$ if and only if $x = 0$;
(2) $[\alpha x, \beta y] = \alpha \beta \cdot [x,y]$ for every $x,y \in X$ and $\alpha, \beta \in \mathbb{R}$;
(3) $[x+y,z] = [x,z] + [y,z]$ for every $x,y,z \in X$;
(4) $|[x,y]| \leq [x,x]^{\frac{1}{2}} [y,y]^{\frac{1}{2}}$ for every $x,y \in X$.

The pair $(X, [\cdot,\cdot])$ is called a semi-inner product space. In this space, we can define a norm, that is, $\|\cdot\| = [\cdot,\cdot]^{\frac{1}{2}}$ [1].

Let $(X, \|\cdot\|)$ be a normed space. As it is known, not all normed spaces are inner product spaces, but we can define the semi-inner product. For instance, the space ℓ^p for $1 \leq p < \infty$, which is the space of all the p-summable sequences with norm $\|x\|_p = \left[\sum_{n=1}^{\infty} |x_n|^p\right]^{\frac{1}{p}}$, is not an inner product space, except for $p = 2$. Konca et al. [2] define a (weighted) inner product $\langle \cdot, \cdot \rangle_v$ and a weighted norm on ℓ^p. In this space with usual norm, we may check that

$$[x,y] = \|y\|_p^{2-p} \sum_j |y_j|^{p-1} \mathrm{sgn}(y_j) x_j, \quad x := (x_j), y := (y_j) \in l^p \qquad (1)$$

is a semi-inner product on $(\ell^p, \|\cdot\|_p)$ for $1 \leq p < \infty$ [3].

Next, the mapping $g : X^2 \to \mathbb{R}$ defined by the formula

$$g(x,y) := \frac{1}{2}\|x\|[\tau_+(x,y) + \tau_-(x,y)],$$

with
$$\tau_{\pm}(x,y) := \lim_{t \to \pm 0} \frac{\|x+ty\| - \|x\|}{t}$$
is the semi-inner product on X if $g(x,y)$ is linear in y.

Using the concept of semi-inner product g, Miličić [4] introduced the notions of g-orthogonality, namely $x \perp_y y$ if and only if $g(x,y) = 0$ and the g-angle, namely $A_g(x,y) := \arccos \frac{g(x,y)}{\|x\|\|y\|}$. Many researchers have studied the g-orthogonal and g-angle between two vectors and two subspaces in X; see, for example, [5–8]. In 2018, Nur et al. [9] developed the notion of the g-angle between two subspaces. If $V = \text{span}\{v\}$ and $W = \text{span}\{w_1, \cdots, w_m\}$ of X with $m \geq 1$, then the g-angle between V and W is defined by $A_g(V,W)$ with $\cos^2 A_g(V,W) = \frac{\|v_W\|^2}{\|v\|^2}$. Here, v_W denotes the g-orthogonal projection of v on W. Recently, Nur et al. [10] defined the standard n-norm using the (weighted) inner product and discussed the angle between two subspaces in the space of the p-summable.

In general, an n-norm on a real vector space X is a mapping $\|\cdot, \ldots, \cdot\| : X \times \cdots \times X \longrightarrow \mathbb{R}$, which satisfies the following four conditions:

(1) $\|x_1, \ldots, x_n\| = 0$ if and only if $x_1, \ldots, x_n$ are linearly dependent;
(2) $\|x_1, \ldots, x_n\|$ is invariant under permutation;
(3) $\|\alpha x_1, \ldots, x_n\| = |\alpha| \|x_1, \ldots, x_n\|$ for every $x_1, \ldots, x_n \in X$ and for every $\alpha \in \mathbb{R}$;
(4) $\|x_1, \ldots, x_{n-1}, y+z\| \leq \|x_1, \ldots, x_{n-1}, y\| + \|x_1, \ldots, x_{n-1}, z\|$ for every $x,y,z \in X$.

The pair $(X, \|\cdot, \ldots, \cdot\|)$ is called an n-normed space.

Geometrically, $\|x_1, \ldots, x_n\|$ may be interpreted as the volume of the n-dimensional parallelepiped spanned by $x_1, \ldots, x_n$. The theory of n-normed spaces for $n \geq 2$ was developed in the late 1960s [11–13]. Recent results can be found, for example, in [14–16]. On the space ℓ^p for $1 \leq p < \infty$, the following n-norm was defined by Gunawan in [17]:

$$\|x_1, \ldots, x_n\|_p := \left[\frac{1}{n!} \sum_{k_1} \cdots \sum_{k_n} \left(\text{abs} \begin{vmatrix} x_{1k_1} & \cdots & x_{1k_n} \\ \vdots & \ddots & \vdots \\ x_{nk_1} & \cdots & x_{nk_n} \end{vmatrix} \right)^p \right]^{\frac{1}{p}}. \tag{2}$$

The aim of this paper is to define a semi-inner product in an n-normed space $(\ell^p, \|\cdot, \ldots, \cdot\|_p)$ with $1 \leq p < \infty$. Using this result, we can introduce the p_n-orthogonal and the p_n-angle between two vectors. We also will discuss their properties. Moreover, we will define the p_n-angle between a one-dimensional subspace and an m-dimensional subspace in the n-normed space $(\ell^p, \|\cdot, \ldots, \cdot\|_p)$.

2. Main Results

2.1. Semi-Inner Product and p_n-Angle between Two Vectors

In this subsection, we shall begin with the new semi-inner product on ℓ^p spaces equipped with an n-norm. Let $(\ell^p, \|\cdot, \ldots, \cdot\|)$ be an n-normed space and $\{a_1, \ldots, a_n\}$ be a linearly independent set on ℓ^p. Now, we define the following mapping.

$$\|x\|_{p_n} := \left[\sum_{\{i_2, \ldots, i_n\} \subset \{1, \ldots, n\}} \|x, a_{i_2}, \ldots, a_{i_n}\|_p^p \right]^{\frac{1}{p}}, \tag{3}$$

for every $x \in \ell^p$. Next, we have the following proposition.

Proposition 1 ([17]). *The mapping $\|\cdot\|_{p_n}$ defines a norm on ℓ^p.*

Example 1. *For $p = 1, n = 3$. Let $\{a_1, a_2, a_3\}$ be the Schauder basis on ℓ^1, that is, $a_i = (\delta_{ij}), i = 1, 2, 3$ and $x = (2, 1, 3, 0, \ldots)$. We observe that*

$$\|x\|_{13} = \|x, a_1, a_2\|_1 + \|x, a_1, a_3\|_1 + \|x, a_2, a_3\|_1$$

$$= \frac{1}{6} \sum_{k_1} \sum_{k_2} \sum_{k_3} \left(\text{abs} \begin{vmatrix} x_{k_1} & x_{k_2} & x_{k_3} \\ a_{1k_1} & a_{1k_2} & a_{1k_3} \\ a_{2k_1} & a_{2k_2} & a_{2k_3} \end{vmatrix} \right) + \frac{1}{6} \sum_{k_1} \sum_{k_2} \sum_{k_3} \left(\text{abs} \begin{vmatrix} x_{k_1} & x_{k_2} & x_{k_3} \\ a_{1k_1} & a_{1k_2} & a_{1k_3} \\ a_{3k_1} & a_{3k_2} & a_{3k_3} \end{vmatrix} \right)$$

$$+ \frac{1}{6} \sum_{k_1} \sum_{k_2} \sum_{k_3} \left(\text{abs} \begin{vmatrix} y_{k_1} & y_{k_2} & y_{k_3} \\ a_{2k_1} & a_{2k_2} & a_{2k_3} \\ a_{3k_1} & a_{3k_2} & a_{3k_3} \end{vmatrix} \right) = 3 + 1 + 2 = 6.$$

Using the norm $\|\cdot\|_{p_n}$ with $a_i = (a_{ij})$ for $i = 1, \ldots, n$, we define a mapping $[\cdot, \cdot]_{p_n}$ on the n-normed space $(l^p, \|\cdot, \ldots, \cdot\|_p)$ with $1 \leq p < \infty$ by

$$[x, y]_{p_n} = \left[\frac{\left(\|x\|_{p_n}\right)^{2-p}}{n!} \sum_{\{i_2, \ldots, i_n\} \subset \{1, \ldots, n\}} \sum_{k_1} \cdots \sum_{k_n} \left(\text{abs} \begin{vmatrix} x_{1k_1} & \cdots & x_{1k_n} \\ a_{i_2 k_1} & \cdots & a_{i_2 k_n} \\ \vdots & \ddots & \vdots \\ a_{i_n k_1} & \cdots & a_{i_n k_n} \end{vmatrix} \right)^{p-1} \times \right.$$

$$\left. \times \text{sgn} \begin{vmatrix} x_{k_1} & \cdots & x_{k_n} \\ a_{i_2 k_1} & \cdots & a_{i_2 k_n} \\ \vdots & \ddots & \vdots \\ a_{i_n k_1} & \cdots & a_{i_n k_n} \end{vmatrix} \begin{vmatrix} y_{k_1} & \cdots & y_{k_n} \\ a_{i_2 k_1} & \cdots & a_{i_2 k_n} \\ \vdots & \ddots & \vdots \\ a_{i_n k_1} & \cdots & a_{i_n k_n} \end{vmatrix} \right]. \tag{4}$$

for every $x = (x_j), y = (y_j) \in \ell^p$.

Then we have the following result.

Theorem 1. *The mapping $[x, y]_{p_n}$ in (4) defines a semi-inner product on $(\ell^p, \|\cdot, \ldots \cdot\|_p)$.*

Proof. We will verify that $[x, y]_{p_n}$ satisfies the properties (1–4) of the semi-inner product.

1. Observe that

$$[x, x]_{p_n} = \left(\|x\|_{p_n}\right)^{2-p} \left[\sum_{\{i_2, \ldots, i_n\} \subset \{1, \ldots, n\}} \|x, a_{i_2}, \ldots, a_{i_n}\|_p^p \right]$$

$$= \left(\|x\|_{p_n}\right)^2.$$

2. Observe that

$$[\alpha x, \beta y]_{p_n} = \left[\frac{\left(\|\alpha x\|_{p_n}\right)^{2-p}}{n!} \sum_{\{i_2, \ldots, i_n\} \subset \{1, \ldots, n\}} \sum_{k_1} \cdots \sum_{k_n} \left(\text{abs} \begin{vmatrix} \alpha x_{1k_1} & \cdots & \alpha x_{1k_n} \\ a_{i_2 k_1} & \cdots & a_{i_2 k_n} \\ \vdots & \ddots & \vdots \\ a_{i_n k_1} & \cdots & a_{i_n k_n} \end{vmatrix} \right)^{p-1} \times \right.$$

$$\left. \times \text{sgn} \begin{vmatrix} \alpha x_{k_1} & \cdots & \alpha x_{k_n} \\ a_{i_2 k_1} & \cdots & a_{i_2 k_n} \\ \vdots & \ddots & \vdots \\ a_{i_n k_1} & \cdots & a_{i_n k_n} \end{vmatrix} \begin{vmatrix} \beta y_{k_1} & \cdots & \beta y_{k_n} \\ a_{i_2 k_1} & \cdots & a_{i_2 k_n} \\ \vdots & \ddots & \vdots \\ a_{i_n k_1} & \cdots & a_{i_n k_n} \end{vmatrix} \right]$$

$$= \alpha \beta [x, y]_{p_n}.$$

3. Using the properties of the determinant, we have

$$[x, y+y']_{p_n} = \left[\frac{\left(\|x\|_{p_n}\right)^{2-p}}{n!} \sum_{\{i_2,\ldots,i_n\} \subset \{1,\ldots,n\}} \sum_{k_1} \cdots \sum_{k_n} \left(\text{abs} \begin{vmatrix} x_{k_1} & \cdots & x_{k_n} \\ a_{i_2 k_1} & \cdots & a_{i_2 k_n} \\ \vdots & \ddots & \vdots \\ a_{i_n k_1} & \cdots & a_{i_n k_n} \end{vmatrix} \right)^{p-1} \right. \times$$

$$\left. \times \text{sgn} \begin{vmatrix} x_{k_1} & \cdots & x_{k_n} \\ a_{i_2 k_1} & \cdots & a_{i_2 k_n} \\ \vdots & \ddots & \vdots \\ a_{i_n k_1} & \cdots & a_{i_n k_n} \end{vmatrix} \begin{vmatrix} y_{k_1} + y'_{k_1} & \cdots & y_{k_n} + y'_{k_n} \\ a_{i_2 k_1} & \cdots & a_{i_2 k_n} \\ \vdots & \ddots & \vdots \\ a_{i_n k_1} & \cdots & a_{i_n k_n} \end{vmatrix} \right]$$

$$= [x, y]_{p_n} + [x, y']_{p_n}.$$

4. Observe that

$$|[x, y]_{p_n}| \leq \left[\frac{\left(\|x\|_{p_n}\right)^{2-p}}{n!} \sum_{\{i_2,\ldots,i_n\} \subset \{1,\ldots,n\}} \sum_{k_1} \cdots \sum_{k_n} \left(\text{abs} \begin{vmatrix} x_{k_1} & \cdots & x_{k_n} \\ a_{i_2 k_1} & \cdots & a_{i_2 k_n} \\ \vdots & \ddots & \vdots \\ a_{i_n k_1} & \cdots & a_{i_n k_n} \end{vmatrix} \right)^{p-1} \right. \times$$

$$\left. \times \text{abs} \begin{vmatrix} y_{k_1} & \cdots & y_{k_n} \\ a_{i_2 k_1} & \cdots & a_{i_2 k_n} \\ \vdots & \ddots & \vdots \\ a_{i_n k_1} & \cdots & a_{i_n k_n} \end{vmatrix} \right].$$

$$\leq \left[(\|x\|_{p_n})^{2-p} \left[\frac{1}{n!} \sum_{\{i_2,\ldots,i_n\} \subset \{1,\ldots,n\}} \sum_{k_1} \cdots \sum_{k_n} \left(\text{abs} \begin{vmatrix} x_{k_1} & \cdots & x_{k_n} \\ a_{i_2 k_1} & \cdots & a_{i_2 k_n} \\ \vdots & \ddots & \vdots \\ a_{i_n k_1} & \cdots & a_{i_n k_n} \end{vmatrix} \right)^p \right]^{\frac{p-1}{p}} \right. \times$$

$$\left. \times \left[\frac{1}{n!} \sum_{\{i_2,\ldots,i_n\} \subset \{1,\ldots,n\}} \sum_{k_1} \cdots \sum_{k_n} \left(\text{abs} \begin{vmatrix} y_{k_1} & \cdots & y_{k_n} \\ a_{i_2 k_1} & \cdots & a_{i_2 k_n} \\ \vdots & \ddots & \vdots \\ a_{i_n k_1} & \cdots & a_{i_n k_n} \end{vmatrix} \right)^p \right]^{\frac{1}{p}} \right].$$

$$= \|x\|_{p_n} \|y\|_{p_n}.$$

Therefore, $[x, y]_{p_n}$ defines a semi-inner product on ℓ^p. □

Example 2. For $p = 1, n = 3$. Let $\{a_1, a_2, a_3\}$ be the Schauder basis on ℓ^1, that is, $a_i = (\delta_{ij}), i = 1, 2, 3$ and $\|\cdot\|_{1_3}$ in Proposition 1. If $x = (2, 1, 3, 0, \ldots)$ and $y = (1, 2, -1, 0, \ldots)$ in ℓ^1, we have

$$\|x\|_{1_3} = \|x, a_1, a_2\|_1 + \|x, a_1, a_3\|_1 + \|x, a_2, a_3\|_1$$

$$= \frac{1}{6} \sum_{k_1} \sum_{k_2} \sum_{k_3} \left(\text{abs} \begin{vmatrix} x_{k_1} & x_{k_2} & x_{k_3} \\ a_{1 k_1} & a_{1 k_2} & a_{1 k_3} \\ a_{2 k_1} & a_{2 k_2} & a_{2 k_3} \end{vmatrix} \right) + \frac{1}{6} \sum_{k_1} \sum_{k_2} \sum_{k_3} \left(\text{abs} \begin{vmatrix} x_{k_1} & x_{k_2} & x_{k_3} \\ a_{1 k_1} & a_{1 k_2} & a_{1 k_3} \\ a_{3 k_1} & a_{3 k_2} & a_{3 k_3} \end{vmatrix} \right)$$

$$+ \frac{1}{6} \sum_{k_1} \sum_{k_2} \sum_{k_3} \left(\text{abs} \begin{vmatrix} y_{k_1} & y_{k_2} & y_{k_3} \\ a_{2 k_1} & a_{2 k_2} & a_{2 k_3} \\ a_{3 k_1} & a_{3 k_2} & a_{3 k_3} \end{vmatrix} \right) = 3 + 1 + 2 = 6.$$

and

$$\|y\|_{1_3} = \|y, a_1, a_2\|_1 + \|y, a_1, a_3\|_1 + \|y, a_2, a_3\|_1$$

$$= \frac{1}{6} \sum_{k_1} \sum_{k_2} \sum_{k_3} \left(abs \begin{vmatrix} y_{k_1} & y_{k_2} & y_{k_3} \\ a_{1k_1} & a_{1k_2} & a_{1k_3} \\ a_{2k_1} & a_{2k_2} & a_{2k_3} \end{vmatrix} \right) + \frac{1}{6} \sum_{k_1} \sum_{k_2} \sum_{k_3} \left(abs \begin{vmatrix} y_{k_1} & y_{k_2} & y_{k_3} \\ a_{1k_1} & a_{1k_2} & a_{1k_3} \\ a_{3k_1} & a_{3k_2} & a_{3k_3} \end{vmatrix} \right)$$

$$+ \frac{1}{6} \sum_{k_1} \sum_{k_2} \sum_{k_3} \left(abs \begin{vmatrix} y_{k_1} & y_{k_2} & y_{k_3} \\ a_{2k_1} & a_{2k_2} & a_{2k_3} \\ a_{3k_1} & a_{3k_2} & a_{3k_3} \end{vmatrix} \right) = 1 + 2 + 1 = 4$$

As a consequence,

$$[x, y]_{1_3} = \frac{(\|x\|_{1_3})}{3!} \sum_{\{i_2, i_3\} \subset \{1,2,3\}} \sum_{k_1} \sum_{k_2} \sum_{k_3} sgn \begin{vmatrix} x_{k_1} & x_{k_2} & x_{k_3} \\ a_{i_2k_1} & a_{i_2k_2} & a_{i_2k_3} \\ a_{i_3k_1} & a_{i_3k_2} & a_{i_3k_3} \end{vmatrix} \begin{vmatrix} y_{k_1} & y_{k_2} & y_{k_3} \\ a_{i_2k_1} & a_{i_2k_2} & a_{i_2k_3} \\ a_{i_3k_1} & a_{i_3k_2} & a_{i_3k_3} \end{vmatrix}$$

$$= -6 + 12 + 6 = 12$$

and

$$[y, x]_{1_3} = \frac{(\|y\|_{1_3})}{3!} \sum_{\{i_2, i_3\} \subset \{1,2,3\}} \sum_{k_1} \sum_{k_2} \sum_{k_3} sgn \begin{vmatrix} y_{k_1} & y_{k_2} & y_{k_3} \\ a_{i_2k_1} & a_{i_2k_2} & a_{i_2k_3} \\ a_{i_3k_1} & a_{i_3k_2} & a_{i_3k_3} \end{vmatrix} \begin{vmatrix} x_{k_1} & x_{k_2} & x_{k_3} \\ a_{i_2k_1} & a_{i_2k_2} & a_{i_2k_3} \\ a_{i_3k_1} & a_{i_3k_2} & a_{i_3k_3} \end{vmatrix}$$

$$= -18 + 6 + 12 = 0.$$

Remark 1. *The function $[x, y]_{1_3}$ does not satisfy commutative property. In the example above, we observe that $[x, y]_{1_3} = 12 \neq [y, x]_{1_3} = 0$.*

Specifically for $p = 2$, we observe that

$$[x, y]_{2_n} = \frac{1}{n!} \sum_{\{i_2,\ldots,i_n\} \subset \{1,\ldots,n\}} \sum_{k_1} \cdots \sum_{k_n} \begin{vmatrix} x_{k_1} & \cdots & x_{k_n} \\ a_{i_2k_1} & \cdots & a_{i_2k_1} \\ \vdots & \ddots & \vdots \\ a_{i_nk_1} & \cdots & a_{i_nk_1} \end{vmatrix} \begin{vmatrix} y_{k_1} & \cdots & y_{k_n} \\ a_{i_2k_1} & \cdots & a_{i_2k_1} \\ \vdots & \ddots & \vdots \\ a_{i_nk_1} & \cdots & a_{i_nk_1} \end{vmatrix}$$

$$= [y, x]_{2_n}.$$

As consequence, we have following corollary:

Corollary 1. *The mapping $[x, y]_{2_n}$ in (4) defines an inner product on $(\ell^2, \|\cdot, \ldots \cdot\|_2)$.*

Example 3. *For $n = 2$. Let $\{a_1, a_2\}$ be the Schauder basis on ℓ^2, that is, $a_i = (\delta_{ij}), i = 1, 2$. If $x = (2, 1, 0, 0, \ldots)$ and $y = (1, 2, 0, 0, \ldots)$ in ℓ^2, we have*

$$[x, y]_{2_2} = \frac{1}{2} \sum_{\{i_2\} \subset \{1,2\}} \sum_{k_1} \sum_{k_2} \begin{vmatrix} x_{k_1} & x_{k_2} \\ a_{i_2k_1} & a_{i_2k_2} \end{vmatrix} \begin{vmatrix} y_{k_1} & y_{k_2} \\ a_{i_2k_1} & a_{i_2k_2} \end{vmatrix}$$

$$= \frac{1}{2} \sum_{k_1} \sum_{k_2} \begin{vmatrix} x_{k_1} & x_{k_2} \\ a_{1k_1} & a_{1k_2} \end{vmatrix} \begin{vmatrix} y_{k_1} & y_{k_2} \\ a_{1k_1} & a_{1k_2} \end{vmatrix} + \frac{1}{2} \sum_{k_1} \sum_{k_2} \begin{vmatrix} x_{k_1} & x_{k_2} \\ a_{2k_1} & a_{2k_2} \end{vmatrix} \begin{vmatrix} y_{k_1} & y_{k_2} \\ a_{2k_1} & a_{2k_2} \end{vmatrix}$$

$$= 4.$$

By using the semi-inner product $[x, y]_{p_n}$, we define orthogonality in $(\ell^p, \|\cdot, \ldots \cdot\|_n)$ as follows:

Definition 1 (p_n-orthogonality). *Let $(\ell^p, \|\cdot, \ldots \cdot\|_n)$ be the n-normed space. Vector x is p_n-orthogonal to vector y, and we write $x \perp_{p_n} y$ if and only if $[x, y]_{p_n} = 0$.*

Example 4. For $p = 1, n = 3$. Let $\{a_1, a_2, a_3\}$ be the Schauder basis on ℓ^1, that is, $a_i = (\delta_{ij}), i = 1, 2, 3$. If $x = (1, 2, -1, 0, \dots)$ and $y = (2, 1, 3, 0, \dots)$ in ℓ^1, using Example 3, we have $[x, y]_{p_n} = 0$. Hence, x is 1_3-orthogonal to y.

Next, p_n-orthogonality has the following properties.

Proposition 2. *The p_n-orthogonality satisfies the following properties:*

(a) *Nondegeneracy property: If $x \perp_{p_n} x$, then $x = 0$.*
(b) *Homogeneity property: If $x \perp_{p_n} y$, then $\alpha x \perp_{p_n} \beta y$ for every $\alpha, \beta \in \mathbb{R}$.*
(c) *Right additive property: If $x \perp_{p_n} y$ and $x \perp_{p_n} z$, then $x \perp_g (y + z)$.*
(d) *Resolvability property: For every $x, y \in X$ there is $\gamma \in \mathbb{R}$ such that $x \perp_{p_n} (\gamma x + y)$.*

Proof. By using Theorem 1, the properties (a)–(c) are obviously true.

(d) Let $x, y \in \ell^p$. For case $x = 0$, the resolvability property is fulfilled. Next, for case $x \neq 0$, choose $\gamma = -\frac{[x,y]_{p_n}}{(\|x\|_{p_n})^2}$. Using Theorem 1, we have

$$[x, \gamma x + y]_{p_n} = \frac{1}{\gamma}[\gamma x, \gamma x + y]_{p_n}$$
$$= \frac{1}{\gamma}(\gamma \|x\|_{p_n}^2 + [\gamma x, y]_{p_n})$$
$$= \gamma \|x\|_{p_n}^2 + [x, y]_{p_n} = 0,$$

as desired. □

Remark 2. Note that for $n = 1$, the p_1-orthogonality coincides with the g-orthogonality in ℓ^p. Specifically for $p = 2$, the 2_n-orthogonality satisfies the symmetry and continuity property. Next, by using Remark 1, the p_n-orthogonality does not satisfy the symmetry property. The p_n-orthogonality also does not satisfy continuity property.

Example 5. For $p = 1$. Take $x_k = (\frac{1}{k}, 1, 0, \dots)$, $x = (0, 1, 0, \dots)$, and $y = (1, 1, 0, ..)$ in ℓ^1. Using inequality $\|x\|_1 \leq \|x\|_{1_n} \leq n\|x\|_1$ in [17], we have $x_k \to x$ (in norm $\|\cdot\|_{1_n}$). Next, we observe that $[x_k, y]_{1_n} = 0$ for every $k \in \mathbb{N}$, but $[x, y]_{1_n} \neq 0$.

Using a semi-inner product in (4), we define the angle between two nonzero vectors x and y on $(\ell^p, \|\cdot\|, \dots, \|\cdot\|_p)$ as follows:

$$A_{p_n}(x, y) := \arccos \frac{[y, x]_{p_n}}{\|x\|_{p_n}\|y\|_{p_n}}. \tag{5}$$

Note that $y \perp_{p_n} x$ if and only if $A_{p_n}(x, y) = \frac{1}{2}\pi$. We can observe that the angle $A_{p_n}(x, y)$ for $n = 1$ is identical with the g-angle $A_g(x, y)$ in [9].

Example 6. Let $(\ell^1, \|\cdot, \cdot, \cdot\|_1)$ be 3 normed space and $\{a_1, a_2, a_3\}$ be the Schauder basis on ℓ^1, that is, $a_i = (\delta_{ij}), i = 1, 2, 3$ and $\|\cdot\|_{1_3}$ in Proposition 1. If $x = (1, 2, -1, 0, \ldots)$ and $y = (2, 1, 3, 0, \ldots)$ in ℓ^1, we observe that

$$\|x\|_{1_3} = \|x, a_1, a_2\|_1 + \|x, a_1, a_3\|_1 + \|x, a_2, a_3\|_1$$

$$= \frac{1}{6} \sum_{k_1} \sum_{k_2} \sum_{k_3} \left(\text{abs} \begin{vmatrix} x_{k_1} & x_{k_2} & x_{k_3} \\ a_{1k_1} & a_{1k_2} & a_{1k_3} \\ a_{2k_1} & a_{2k_2} & a_{2k_3} \end{vmatrix} \right) + \frac{1}{6} \sum_{k_1} \sum_{k_2} \sum_{k_3} \left(\text{abs} \begin{vmatrix} x_{k_1} & x_{k_2} & x_{k_3} \\ a_{1k_1} & a_{1k_2} & a_{1k_3} \\ a_{3k_1} & a_{3k_2} & a_{3k_3} \end{vmatrix} \right)$$

$$+ \frac{1}{6} \sum_{k_1} \sum_{k_2} \sum_{k_3} \left(\text{abs} \begin{vmatrix} x_{k_1} & x_{k_2} & x_{k_3} \\ a_{2k_1} & a_{2k_2} & a_{2k_3} \\ a_{3k_1} & a_{3k_2} & a_{3k_3} \end{vmatrix} \right) = 1 + 2 + 1 = 4$$

and

$$\|y\|_{1_3} = \|y, a_1, a_2\|_1 + \|y, a_1, a_3\|_1 + \|y, a_2, a_3\|_1$$

$$= \frac{1}{6} \sum_{k_1} \sum_{k_2} \sum_{k_3} \left(\text{abs} \begin{vmatrix} y_{k_1} & y_{k_2} & y_{k_3} \\ a_{1k_1} & a_{1k_2} & a_{1k_3} \\ a_{2k_1} & a_{2k_2} & a_{2k_3} \end{vmatrix} \right) + \frac{1}{6} \sum_{k_1} \sum_{k_2} \sum_{k_3} \left(\text{abs} \begin{vmatrix} y_{k_1} & y_{k_2} & y_{k_3} \\ a_{1k_1} & a_{1k_2} & a_{1k_3} \\ a_{3k_1} & a_{3k_2} & a_{3k_3} \end{vmatrix} \right)$$

$$+ \frac{1}{6} \sum_{k_1} \sum_{k_2} \sum_{k_3} \left(\text{abs} \begin{vmatrix} y_{k_1} & y_{k_2} & y_{k_3} \\ a_{2k_1} & a_{2k_2} & a_{2k_3} \\ a_{3k_1} & a_{3k_2} & a_{3k_3} \end{vmatrix} \right) = 3 + 1 + 2 = 6.$$

As a consequence,

$$[y, x]_{1_3} = \frac{(\|y\|_{1_3})}{3!} \sum_{\{i_2, i_3\} \subset \{1,2,3\}} \sum_{k_1} \sum_{k_2} \sum_{k_3} \text{sgn} \begin{vmatrix} y_{k_1} & y_{k_2} & y_{k_3} \\ a_{i_2 k_1} & a_{i_2 k_2} & a_{i_2 k_3} \\ a_{i_3 k_1} & a_{i_3 k_2} & a_{i_3 k_3} \end{vmatrix} \begin{vmatrix} x_{k_1} & x_{k_2} & x_{k_3} \\ a_{i_2 k_1} & a_{i_2 k_2} & a_{i_2 k_3} \\ a_{i_3 k_1} & a_{i_3 k_2} & a_{i_3 k_3} \end{vmatrix}$$

$$= -6 + 12 + 6 = 12$$

Hence, $A_{1_3}(x, y) = \arccos(\frac{1}{2})$.

The angle $A_{p_n}(\cdot, \cdot)$ has the following properties.

Proposition 3. *Let $(\ell^p, \|\cdot, \ldots \cdot \|_n)$ be the n-normed space. The angle A_{p_n} between two nonzero vectors x and y on ℓ^p satisfies the following properties:*

(a) *If x and y are of the same direction, then $A_{p_n}(x, y) = 0$; if x and y are of the opposite direction, then $A_{p_n}(x, y) = \pi$ (part of parallelism property).*

(b) *$A_{p_n}(ax, by) = A_{p_n}(x, y)$ if $ab > 0$; $A_{p_n}(ax, by) = \pi - A_{p_n}(x, y)$ if $ab < 0$ (homogeneity property).*

(c) *If $x_n \to x$ (in norm $\|\cdot\|_{p_n}$), then $A_{p_n}(x_n, y) \to A_{p_n}(x, y)$ (part of continuity property).*

Proof.

(a) Let $y = kx$ for an arbitrary nonzero vector x in X and $k \in \mathbb{R} - \{0\}$. We have

$$A_{p_n}(x, y) = \arccos \frac{[kx, x]_{p_n}}{\|x\|_{p_n} \|kx\|_{p_n}} = \arccos \frac{k \cdot [x, x]_{p_n}}{|k| \|x\|_{p_n}^2} = \arccos \frac{k \|x\|_{p_n}^2}{|k| \|x\|_{p_n}^2}.$$

Hence, $A_{p_n}(x, y) = \arccos(1) = 0$ for $k > 0$ and $A_{p_n}(x, y) = \arccos(-1) = \pi$ for $k < 0$.

(b) Let α and $\beta \in \mathbb{R} - \{0\}$. Observe that

$$A_{p_n}(\alpha x, \beta y) = \arccos \frac{\alpha \beta \cdot [y, x]_{p_n}}{|\alpha \beta|(\|x\|_{p_n} \cdot \|y\|_{p_n})}.$$

If $\alpha\beta > 0$, then $A_{p_n}(\alpha x, \beta y) = \arccos \frac{[y,x]_{p_n}}{\|x\|_{p_n} \cdot \|y\|_{p_n}} = A_{p_n}(x,y)$. Likewise, if $\alpha\beta < 0$, then $A_{p_n}(\alpha x \beta b y) = \arccos \left(-\frac{[y,x]_{p_n}}{\|x\|_{p_n} \cdot \|y\|_{p_n}} \right) = \pi - A_{p_n}(x,y)$.

(c) If $x_k \to x$ (in norm $\|\cdot\|_{p_n}$), then

$$|[y, x_k - x]_{p_n}| \leq \|y\|_{p_n} \|x_n - x\|_{p_n} \longrightarrow 0.$$

Observe that $[y, x_k - x]_{p_n} = [y, x_k]_{p_n} - [y, x]_{p_n}$. We have $[y, x_k]_{p_n} \longrightarrow [y, x]_{p_n}$. Hence,

$$A_{p_n}(x_n, y) \to A_{p_n}(x, y),$$

as desired.

□

Remark 3. *Since the mapping $[\cdot, \cdot]_{p_n}$ in general is not commutative, the angle $A_{p_n}(\cdot, \cdot)$ does not satisfy the symmetry property. For example, we can see Remark 1. Likewise, the g-angle does not satisfy the continuity property.*

Example 7. *For $n=1$ and $p=1$. Take $x_k = (\frac{1}{k}, 1, 0, \dots)$, $x = (0, 1, 0, \dots)$, and $y = (1, 1, 0, ..)$ in ℓ^1. We observe that $\cos A_{1_1}(x_k, y) = 0$ for every $k \in \mathbb{N}$, but $\cos A_{1_1}(x, y) \neq 0$.*

2.2. p_n-Angle between Two Subspaces

In this section, we will discuss the p_n-angle between two subspaces in $(\ell^p, \|\cdot\|, \dots, \|\cdot\|_p)$. In particular, we define the p_n-angle between a one-dimensional subspace and an m-dimensional subspace for $m \geq 1$. Using $[\cdot, \cdot]_{p_n}$ in (4), we have the Gram determinant Γ_{p_n} as follows.

Definition 2. *Let $(\ell^p, \|\cdot\|, \dots, \|\cdot\|_p)$ be an n-normed space and $W = \text{span}\{w_1, \dots, w_m\}$ fo $1 \leq m \leq n$ is subspace of ℓ^p. The Gram determinant p_n of $\{w_1, \dots, w_m\}$, denoted by $\Gamma_{p_n}\{w_1, \dots, w_m\}$ is defined by*

$$\Gamma_{p_n}\{w_1, \dots, w_m\} := \begin{vmatrix} [w_1, w_1]_{p_n} & \cdots & [w_1, w_m]_{p_n} \\ \vdots & \ddots & \vdots \\ [w_m, w_1]_{p_n} & \cdots & [w_m, w_m]_{p_n} \end{vmatrix}.$$

Example 8. *For $p=1$ and $n=2$. Let $\{a_1, a_2\}$ be the Schauder basis on ℓ^1, that is, $a_i = (\delta_{ij}), i = 1, 2$ $w_1 = (1, 3, 0, \dots)$ and $w_2 = (3, 1, 0, \dots)$ in ℓ^1. We observe that $\|w_1\|_{1_2} = 4$ and $\|w_2\|_{1_2} = 4$. Using the semi-inner product in (4), we have*

$$[w_1, w_2]_{12} = \frac{(\|w_1\|_{1_2})^2}{2} \sum_{i=1}^{2} \sum_{k_1} \sum_{k_2} \text{sgn} \begin{vmatrix} w_{1k_1} & w_{1k_2} \\ a_{ik_1} & a_{ik_2} \end{vmatrix} \begin{vmatrix} w_{2k_1} & w_{2k_2} \\ a_{ik_1} & a_{ik_2} \end{vmatrix}$$
$$= 2(1+1+3+3) = 16$$

and

$$[w_2, w_1]_{12} = \frac{(\|w_2\|_{1_2})^2}{2} \sum_{i=1}^{2} \sum_{k_1} \sum_{k_2} \text{sgn} \begin{vmatrix} w_{2k_1} & w_{2k_2} \\ a_{ik_1} & a_{ik_2} \end{vmatrix} \begin{vmatrix} w_{1k_1} & w_{1k_2} \\ a_{ik_1} & a_{ik_2} \end{vmatrix}$$
$$= 2(3+3+1+1) = 16.$$

Hence, $\Gamma_{1_2}(w_1, w_2) = 0$.

We have the connection between the Gram determinant p_n of $\{w_1, \dots, w_m\}$ for $1 \leq m \leq n$ and the linearly independence set of $\{w_1, \dots, w_m\}$ as follows.

Theorem 2. *If $\Gamma_{p_n}(w_1, \ldots, w_m) \neq 0$, then $\{w_1, \ldots, w_m\}$ is a linearly independent set.*

Proof. Suppose by contradiction that $\{w_1, \ldots w_m\}$ is linearly dependent. Therefore, there is a i with $1 \leq i \leq m$ so that w_i is a linear combination of $w_1, \ldots, w_{i-1}, w_{i+1}, \ldots, w_m$. Using the properties of the determinant, we observe that the i-th column of Γ_{p_n} is a linear combination of the other columns. This implies $\Gamma_{p_n}(w_1, \ldots, w_m) = 0$, which is a contradiction. Hence, $\{w_1, \ldots, w_m\}$ is a linearly independent set. □

Example 9. *Suppose that $p = 1$, $n = 2$. Let $\{a_1, a_2\}$ be the Schauder basis on ℓ^1, that is, $a_i = (\delta_{ij})$, $i = 1, 2$ and $\|\cdot\|_{1_3}$ in Proposition 1. If $w_1 = (1, 0, 0, \ldots)$ and $w_2 = (0, 1, 0, 0, \ldots)$ in ℓ^1. We observe that $\|w_1\|_{1_2} = 1$ and $\|w_2\|_{1_2} = 1$. As a consequence,*

$$[w_1, w_2]_{1_2} = \frac{(\|w_1\|_{1_2})^2}{2} \sum_{i=1}^{2} \sum_j \sum_k \operatorname{sgn} \begin{vmatrix} w_{1j} & w_{1k} \\ a_{ij} & a_{ik} \end{vmatrix} \begin{vmatrix} w_{2j} & w_{2k} \\ a_{ij} & a_{ik} \end{vmatrix} = 0.$$

In a similar way is obtained $[w_2, w_1]_{1_2} = 0$. As a consequence, $\Gamma_{1_2}(w_1, w_2) = 1$. Hence, if $\Gamma_{p_n}(w_1, w_2) = 1 \neq 0$, then $\{w_1, w_2\}$ is a linearly independent set.

Remark 4. *The converse of the above theorem is not true. For instance, let $(\ell^1, \|\cdot, \cdot\|_1)$ be a 2-normed space with $a_1 = (1, 0, 0, \ldots)$ and $a_2 = (0, 1, 0, 0, \ldots)$. Take $w_1 = (1, 3, 0, \ldots)$ and $w_2 = (3, 1, 0, \ldots)$ in ℓ^1. We observe that $\|w_1\|_{1_2} = 4$ and $\|w_2\|_{1_2} = 4$. Using the semi-inner product in (4), we have*

$$\begin{aligned}[w_1, w_2]_{1_2} &= \frac{(\|w_1\|_{1_2})^2}{2} \sum_{i=1}^{2} \sum_{k_1} \sum_{k_2} \operatorname{sgn} \begin{vmatrix} w_{1k_1} & w_{1k_2} \\ a_{ik_1} & a_{ik_2} \end{vmatrix} \begin{vmatrix} w_{2k_1} & w_{2k_2} \\ a_{ik_1} & a_{ik_2} \end{vmatrix} \\ &= 2(1 + 1 + 3 + 3) = 16\end{aligned}$$

and

$$\begin{aligned}[w_2, w_1]_{1_2} &= \frac{(\|w_2\|_{1_2})^2}{2} \sum_{i=1}^{2} \sum_{k_1} \sum_{k_2} \operatorname{sgn} \begin{vmatrix} w_{2k_1} & w_{2k_2} \\ a_{ik_1} & a_{ik_2} \end{vmatrix} \begin{vmatrix} w_{1k_1} & w_{1k_2} \\ a_{ik_1} & a_{ik_2} \end{vmatrix} \\ &= 2(3 + 3 + 1 + 1) = 16.\end{aligned}$$

Hence, $\Gamma_{1_2}(w_1, w_2) = 0$ but w_1 and w_2 are linearly independent.

Next, we can discuss the p_n-orthogonal projection and the p_n-orthogonal complement as follows:

Definition 3. *Let v be a vector of ℓ^p and $W = \operatorname{span}\{w_1, \ldots, w_m\}$ be a subspace of ℓ^p with $\Gamma_{p_n}(w_1, \ldots, w_m) \neq 0$. The p_n-orthogonal projection of v on W, denoted by $v_{W_{p_n}}$, is defined by*

$$v_{W_{p_n}} := -\frac{1}{\Gamma_{p_n}(w_1, \ldots, w_m)} \begin{vmatrix} 0 & w_1 & \cdots & w_m \\ [w_1, v]_{p_n} & [w_1, w_1]_{p_n} & \cdots & [w_1, w_m]_{p_n} \\ \vdots & \vdots & \ddots & \vdots \\ [w_m, v]_{p_n} & [w_m, w_1]_{p_n} & \cdots & [w_m, w_m]_{p_n} \end{vmatrix},$$

and its p_n-orthogonal complement $v_{W_{p_n}}^\perp$ is given by

$$v_{W_{p_n}}^\perp := \frac{1}{\Gamma_{p_n}(w_1,\ldots,w_m)} \begin{vmatrix} v & w_1 & \cdots & w_m \\ [w_1,v]_{p_n} & [w_1,w_1]_{p_n} & \cdots & [w_1,w_m]_{p_n} \\ \vdots & \vdots & \ddots & \vdots \\ [w_m,v]_{p_n} & [w_m,w_1]_{p_n} & \cdots & [w_m,w_m]_{p_n} \end{vmatrix}.$$

Example 10. *Suppose that $p = 1$, $n = 2$ and $m = 2$. Let $\{a_1, a_2\}$ be the Schauder basis on ℓ^1, that is, $a_i = (\delta_{ij})$, $i = 1, 2$ and $\|\cdot\|_{1_3}$ in Proposition 1. If $v = (1,1,3,0,\ldots)$, $w_1 = (1,0,0,0,\ldots)$ and $w_2 = (0,1,0,0,\ldots)$, then $\Gamma_{1_2}(w_1, w_2) = 1$ by Example 9. Therefore,*

$$v_{W_{1_2}} = -\frac{1}{\Gamma_{1_2}(w_1,w_2)} \begin{vmatrix} 0 & w_1 & w_2 \\ [w_1,v]_{1_2} & [w_1,w_1]_{1_2} & [w_1,w_2]_{1_2} \\ [w_2,v]_{1_2} & [w_2,w_1]_{1_2} & [w_2,w_2]_{1_2} \end{vmatrix}$$

$$= -\begin{vmatrix} 0 & w_1 & w_2 \\ 1 & 1 & 0 \\ 1 & 0 & 1 \end{vmatrix} = w_1 + w_2 = (1,1,0,\ldots)$$

and

$$v_{W_{1_2}}^\perp = \frac{1}{\Gamma_{1_2}(w_1,w_2)} \begin{vmatrix} v & w_1 & w_2 \\ [w_1,v]_{1_2} & [w_1,w_1]_{1_2} & [w_1,w_2]_{1_2} \\ [w_2,v]_{1_2} & [w_2,w_1]_{1_2} & [w_2,w_2]_{1_2} \end{vmatrix}$$

$$= \begin{vmatrix} v & w_1 & w_2 \\ 1 & 1 & 0 \\ 1 & 0 & 1 \end{vmatrix} = v - w_1 - w_2 = (0,0,3,0,\ldots).$$

Using the properties of the determinant and the semi-inner product in (4), we obtain

$$[w_i, v_{W_{p_n}}^\perp]_{p_n} = \frac{1}{\Gamma_{p_n}(w_1,\ldots,w_m)} \begin{vmatrix} [w_i,v]_{p_n} & [w_i,w_1]_{p_n} & \cdots & [w_i,w_m]_{p_n} \\ [w_1,v]_{p_n} & [w_1,w_1]_{p_n} & \cdots & [w_1,w_m]_{p_n} \\ \vdots & \vdots & \ddots & \vdots \\ [w_m,v]_{p_n} & [w_m,w_1]_{p_n} & \cdots & [w_m,w_m]_{p_n} \end{vmatrix} = 0.$$

Hence, $w_i \perp_{p_n} v_{W_{p_n}}^\perp$ for every $i = 1,\ldots,n$.

The definition of the p_n-angle between $V = \text{span}\{v\}$ and $W = \text{span}\{w_1,\ldots,w_m\}$ of $(\ell^p, \|\cdot,\ldots,\cdot\|_p)$ is as follows.

Definition 4. *Let $(\ell^p, \|\cdot,\ldots,\cdot\|_p)$ be an n-normed space for $1 \leq p < \infty$. If $V = \text{span}\{v\}$ and $W = \text{span}\{w_1,\ldots,w_m\}$ are subspaces of ℓ^p with $\Gamma_{p_n}(w_1,\ldots,w_m) \neq 0$ dan $m \geq 1$ then the p_n-angle between subspaces V and W is denoted by $A_{p_n}(V,W)$ with*

$$\cos^2 A_{p_n}(V,W) = \frac{[v_{W_{p_n}}, v]_{p_n}^2}{(\|v\|_{p_n})^2 (\|v_{W_{p_n}}\|_{p_n})^2}. \tag{6}$$

where $v_{W_{p_n}}$ denotes the p_n-orthogonal projection of v on W.

Example 11. *Suppose that $p = 1$, $n = 2$ and $m = 2$ in Definition 4 Let $\{a_1, a_2\}$ be the Schauder basis on ℓ^1, that is, $a_i = (\delta_{ij})$, $i = 1, 2$ and $\|\cdot\|_{1_3}$ in Proposition 1. If $V = \text{span}\{v\}$ and*

$W = \text{span}\{w_1, w_2\}$ with $v = (1,1,3,0,\dots)$, $w_1 = (1,0,0,0,\dots)$ and $w_2 = (0,1,0,0,\dots)$ in ℓ^1, we observe that

$$\|v\|_{1_2} = \|v, a_1, a_2\|_1 + \|v, a_1, a_2\|_1$$

$$= \frac{1}{2}\sum_{k_1}\sum_{k_2}\left(abs\begin{vmatrix} v_{k_1} & v_{k_2} \\ a_{1k_1} & a_{1k_2}\end{vmatrix}\right) + \frac{1}{2}\sum_{k_1}\sum_{k_2}\left(abs\begin{vmatrix} v_{k_1} & v_{k_2} \\ a_{2k_1} & a_{2k_2}\end{vmatrix}\right)$$

$$= 4 + 4 = 8.$$

By using Example 9, we have $\Gamma_{1_2}(w_1, w_2) = 1$. Therefore,

$$v_{W_{1_2}} = -\frac{1}{\Gamma_{1_2}(w_1, w_2)}\begin{vmatrix} 0 & w_1 & w_2 \\ [w_1,v]_{1_2} & [w_1,w_1]_{1_2} & [w_1,w_2]_{1_2} \\ [w_2,v]_{1_2} & [w_2,w_1]_{1_2} & [w_2,w_2]_{1_2} \end{vmatrix}$$

$$= -\begin{vmatrix} 0 & w_1 & w_2 \\ 1 & 1 & 0 \\ 1 & 0 & 1 \end{vmatrix} = w_1 + w_2 = (1,1,0,\dots).$$

Moreover, we observe that $\left\|v_{W_{1_2}}\right\|_{1_2} = 2$ and $[v_{W_{1_2}}, v]_{1_2} = 4$. Hence,

$$\cos^2 A_{1_2}(V, W) = \frac{[v_{W_{1_2}}, v]_{1_2}^2}{(\|v\|_{1_2})^2 (\left\|v_{W_{1_2}}\right\|_{1_2})^2} = \frac{1}{16}.$$

Remark 5. If $W = \text{span}\{w\}$, then the p_n-orthogonal projection of v on W is

$$v_{W_{p_n}} = \frac{[w,v]_{p_n}}{\|w\|_{p_n}^2} w.$$

Using this p_n-orthogonal projection, the properties of the semi-inner product p_n and Definition 4, we have the p_n-angle between subspaces V and W, that is,

$$\cos^2 A_{p_n}(V, W) = \frac{[w,v]_{p_n}^2}{(\|v\|_{p_n})^2 (\|w\|_{p_n})^2}.$$

Hence, we can see that the p_n-angle between the two vectors is also the p_n-angle between these two vectors in the subspace spanned by them. Next, by using Definition 3, we have $v = v_{W_{p_n}} + v_{W_{p_n}}^\perp$. Therefore, Definition 4 may be rewritten as

$$\cos^2 A_{p_n}(V, W) = \frac{[v_{W_{p_n}}, v_{W_{p_n}} + v_{W_{p_n}}^\perp]_{p_n}^2}{(\|v\|_{p_n})^2 (\left\|v_{W_{p_n}}\right\|_{p_n})^2} = \frac{\left([v_{W_{p_n}}, v_{W_{p_n}}]_{p_n} + [v_{W_{p_n}}, v_{W_{p_n}}^\perp]_{p_n}\right)^2}{(\|v\|_{p_n})^2 (\left\|v_{W_{p_n}}\right\|_{p_n})^2}$$

$$= \frac{[v_{W_{p_n}}, v_{W_{p_n}}]_{p_n}^2}{(\|v\|_{p_n})^2 (\left\|v_{W_{p_n}}\right\|_{p_n})^2} = \frac{(\left\|v_{W_{p_n}}\right\|_{p_n})^2}{(\|v\|_{p_n})^2}.$$

This tells us that the value of $\cos A_{p_n}(V, W)$ is equal to the ratio between the norm $\|\cdot\|_{p_n}$ of the p_n-orthogonal projection of v on W and the norm $\|\cdot\|_{p_n}$ of v.

3. Further Results

Let X be a measured space with at least n disjoint subsets of positive measure. Our results also extend the n-normed space $(L^p(X), \|\cdot, \ldots, \cdot\|_{L^p})$ for $1 \leq p < \infty$ with a n-norm that was defined by Gunawan in [17]

$$\|f_1, \ldots, f_n\|_{L^p} = \frac{1}{n!} \int_X \cdots \int_X \left(\text{abs} \begin{vmatrix} f_1(x_1) & \cdots & f_n(x_n) \\ \vdots & \ddots & \vdots \\ f_n(x_1) & \cdots & f_n(x_n) \end{vmatrix} \right)^p dx_1 \ldots dx_2. \tag{7}$$

Next, Ekariani et al. [18] defines a norm on $L^p(X)$ by

$$\|f\|_{L^{p_n}} := \left[\sum_{\{i_2,\ldots,i_n\} \subset \{1,\ldots,n\}} \|f, a_{i_2}, \ldots, a_{i_n}\|_{L^p} \right]^{\frac{1}{p}},$$

where $\{a_1, \ldots, a_n\}$ is a linearly independent set in $L^p(X)$. Using the norm $\|\cdot\|_{L^{p_n}}$ with $a_i = (a_{ij})$ for $i = 1, \ldots, n$, we define a mapping $[\cdot, \cdot]_{L^{p_n}}$ with $1 \leq p < \infty$ by

$$[f, g]_{L^{p_n}} = \left[\frac{(\|f\|_{L^{p_n}})^{2-p}}{n!} \sum_{\{i_2,\ldots,i_n\} \subset \{1,\ldots,n\}} \int_X \cdots \int_X \text{abs} \begin{pmatrix} f(x_1) & \cdots & f(x_n) \\ a_{i_2}(x_1) & \cdots & a_{i_2}(x_n) \\ \vdots & \ddots & \vdots \\ a_{i_n}(x_1) & \cdots & a_{i_n}(x_n) \end{pmatrix}^{p-1} \times \right.$$

$$\left. \times \text{sgn} \begin{vmatrix} f(x_1) & \cdots & f(x_n) \\ a_{i_2}(x_1) & \cdots & a_{i_2}(x_n) \\ \vdots & \ddots & \vdots \\ a_{i_n}(x_1) & \cdots & a_{i_n}(x_n) \end{vmatrix} \begin{vmatrix} g(x_1) & \cdots & g(x_n) \\ a_{i_2}(x_1) & \cdots & a_{i_2}(x_n) \\ \vdots & \ddots & \vdots \\ a_{i_n}(x_1) & \cdots & a_{i_n}(x_n) \end{vmatrix} dx_1 \ldots dx_2 \right]. \tag{8}$$

and check $[f, g]_{L^{p_n}}$ defines a semi-inner product on $L^p(X)$. Next, the results are analogous to section main results.

4. Conclusions

In this article, we have introduced the semi-inner product in an n-normed space $(\ell^p, \|\cdot, \ldots, \cdot\|_p)$ with $1 \leq p < \infty$. We have introduced the p_n-orthogonal and the p_n-angle between two vectors. We have proven their properties. Moreover, we have introduced the notion of p_n-angle between one-dimensional subspaces and arbitrary-dimensional subspaces in the n-normed space $(\ell^p, \|\cdot, \ldots, \cdot\|_p)$.

Author Contributions: Conceptualization, M.N.; formal analysis, M.N.; funding acquisition, M.B. and M.N.; investigation and methodology, H.B. and A.I.; resources, M.B.; validation, A.I. and H.B.; writing review and editing, M.N. All authors have read and agreed to the published version of the manuscript.

Funding: This research is supported by PDUPT Program 2022 No. 956/UN4.22/PT.01.03/2022.

Institutional Review Board Statement: Not applicable.

Informed Consent Statement: Not applicable.

Data Availability Statement: Not applicable.

Conflicts of Interest: The authors declare no conflict of interest.

References

1. Dragomir, S. *Semi-Inner Products and Applications*; Victoria University of Technology: Melbourne, Australia, 1991.
2. Konca, S.; Idris, M.; Gunawan, H. p-summable sequence spaces with inner products. *Beu J. Sci. Technol.* **2015**, *5*, 37–41.
3. Giles, J.R. Classes of semi-inner-product spaces. *Trans. Am. Math. Soc.* **1967**, *129*, 436–446. [CrossRef]

4. Miličić, P.M. Sur le g-angle dans un espace norme. *Mat. Vesn.* **1993**, *45*, 43–48.
5. Miličić, P.M. On the B-angle and g-angle in normed Space. *J. Inequal. Pure Appl. Math.* **2007**, *8*, 1–9.
6. Nur, M.; Gunawan, H. A note on the g-angle between subspaces of a normed space. *Aequationes Math.* **2021**, *95*, 309–318. [CrossRef]
7. Balestro, V.; Horvàth, G.; Martini, H.; Teixeira, R. Angles in normed spaces. *Aequationes Math.* **2017**, *91*, 201–236. [CrossRef]
8. Chen, Z.-Z.; Lin, W.; Luo, L.-L. Projections, Birkhoff orthogonality and angles in normed spaces. *Comm. Math. Res.* **2011**, *27*, 378–384.
9. Nur, M.; Gunawan, H.; Neswan, O. A formula for the g-angle between two subspaces of a normed space. *Beitr. Algebra Geom.* **2018**, *59*, 133–143. [CrossRef]
10. Nur, M.; Idris, M.; Firman. Angle in the space of p-summable sequences. *AIMS Math.* **2022**, *7*, 2810–2819. [CrossRef]
11. Gähler, S. Untersuchungen über verallgemeinerte m-metrische räume. I. *Math. Nachr.* **1969**, *40*, 165–189. [CrossRef]
12. Gähler, S. Untersuchungen über verallgemeinerte m-metrische räume. II. *Math. Nachr.* **1969**, *40*, 229–264. [CrossRef]
13. Gähler, S. Untersuchungen über verallgemeinerte m-metrische räume. III. *Math. Nachr.* **1970**, *41*, 23–26. [CrossRef]
14. Gunawan, H. On n-inner products, n-norms, and the Cauchy-Schwarz inequality. *Sci. Math. Japan.* **2002**, *55*, 53–60.
15. Gunawan, H. Mashadi "On n-normed spaces". *Int. J. Math. Sci.* **2001**, *27*, 631–639. [CrossRef]
16. Huang, X.; Tan, A. Mappings of preserving n-distance one in n-normed spaces. *Aequationes Math.* **2018**, *92*, 401–413. [CrossRef]
17. Gunawan, H. The space of p-summable sequences and its natural n-norms. *Bull. Aust. Math. Soc.* **2001**, *64*, 137–147. [CrossRef]
18. Ekariani, S.; Gunawan, H.; Lindiarni, J. On the n-normed space of p-integrable functions. *Math. Aeterna* **2015**, *1*, 11–19.

Disclaimer/Publisher's Note: The statements, opinions and data contained in all publications are solely those of the individual author(s) and contributor(s) and not of MDPI and/or the editor(s). MDPI and/or the editor(s) disclaim responsibility for any injury to people or property resulting from any ideas, methods, instructions or products referred to in the content.

Article

Remarks on the Coefficients of Inverse Cyclotomic Polynomials

Dorin Andrica [1] and Ovidiu Bagdasar [2,3,*]

[1] Faculty of Mathematics and Computer Science, Babeș-Bolyai University, 400084 Cluj-Napoca, Romania; dandrica@math.ubbcluj.ro
[2] School of Computing and Engineering, University of Derby, Derby DE22 1GB, UK
[3] Department of Mathematics, Faculty of Exact Sciences, "1 Decembrie 1918" University of Alba Iulia, 510009 Alba Iulia, Romania
* Correspondence: o.bagdasar@derby.ac.uk

Abstract: Cyclotomic polynomials play an imporant role in discrete mathematics. Recently, inverse cyclotomic polynomials have been defined and investigated. In this paper, we present some recent advances related to the coefficients of inverse cyclotomic polynomials, including a practical recursive formula for their calculation and numerical simulations.

Keywords: cyclotomic polynomials; inverse cyclotomic polynomials; coefficients; recurrence formula; integral formula; Möbius function; Ramanujan sums

MSC: 51P99; 60A99

Citation: Andrica, D.; Bagdasar, O. Remarks on the Coefficients of Inverse Cyclotomic Polynomials. *Mathematics* **2023**, *11*, 3622. https://doi.org/10.3390/math11173622

Academic Editor: Diana Savin

Received: 30 July 2023
Revised: 16 August 2023
Accepted: 17 August 2023
Published: 22 August 2023

Copyright: © 2023 by the authors. Licensee MDPI, Basel, Switzerland. This article is an open access article distributed under the terms and conditions of the Creative Commons Attribution (CC BY) license (https://creativecommons.org/licenses/by/4.0/).

1. Introduction

For an integer $n \geq 1$, an nth root ζ of the unity is called primitive if $\zeta^n = 1$, but $\zeta^d \neq 1$ for all $1 \leq d < n$. By denoting $\zeta_n = \cos \frac{2\pi}{n} + i \sin \frac{2\pi}{n}$ as the first root of order n of the unity, the nth cyclotomic polynomial Φ_n is defined by the following:

$$\Phi_n(z) = \prod_{\substack{1 \leq k \leq n-1 \\ \gcd(k,n)=1}} (z - \zeta_n^k) = \sum_{j=0}^{\varphi(n)} c_j^{(n)} z^j, \qquad (1)$$

where φ is Euler's totient function, which is also the degree of the polynomial. It is known that Φ_n is palindromic (i.e., $c_j^{(n)} = c_{\varphi(n)-j}^{(n)}$, $j = 0, \ldots, \varphi(n)$). The term cyclotomic comes from the property of the nth roots of unity to divide the unit circle into n equal arcs, thereby forming a regular polygon inscribed in the unit circle.

The explicit calculation of the coefficients of cyclotomic polynomials is very difficult to perform (see, for instance, [1,2]), but many properties of these polynomials are known [3,4]. An explicit integral formula for the coefficients was established by the authors in [5].

For an integer $n \geq 2$, the nth inverse cyclotomic polynomial $\Psi_n(z)$ is defined by the following:

$$\Psi_n(z) = \frac{x^n - 1}{\Phi_n(z)} = \prod_{\substack{1 \leq k < n, \gcd(k,n) > 1}} \left(z - e^{\frac{2k\pi i}{n}}\right) = \sum_{j=0}^{n-\varphi(n)} d_j^{(n)} z^j. \qquad (2)$$

Notice that the nonprimitive nth roots of unity are the roots of this monic polynomial of the degree $n - \varphi(n)$. Here, we denote the coefficient of z^j in Ψ_n by $d_j^{(n)}$, $j = 0, \ldots, n - \varphi(n)$.

Using (2), the first inverse cyclotomic polynomials (discounting prime indices) are

$\Psi_1(z) = 1$, $\Psi_4(z) = z^2 - 1$, $\Psi_6(z) = z^4 + z^3 - z - 1$, $\Psi_8(z) = z^4 - 1$,
$\Psi_9(z) = z^3 - 1$, $\Psi_{10}(z) = z^6 + z^5 - z - 1$, $\Psi_{12}(z) = z^8 + z^6 - z^2 - 1$,
$\Psi_{14}(z) = z^8 + z^7 - z - 1$, $\Psi_{15}(z) = z^7 + z^6 + z^5 - z^2 - z - 1$,
$\Psi_{16}(z) = z^8 - 1$, $\Psi_{18}(z) = z^{12} + z^9 - z^3 - 1$, $\Psi_{20}(z) = z^{12} + z^{10} - z^2 - 1$,
$\Psi_{21}(z) = z^9 + z^8 + z^7 - z^2 - z - 1$, $\Psi_{22}(z) = z^{12} + z^{11} - z^2 - 1$.

The following properties of the polynomial Ψ_n are known, and we present them along with some sketches of proofs. More details can be found in [6,7].

Proposition 1. $1°$ *If p is a prime and $n = p^\alpha$ for $\alpha \geq 1$, then $\Psi_n(z) = z^{p^{\alpha-1}} - 1$.*
$2°$ *For $n = p_1 \cdots p_k$ to be square-free, $\deg(\Psi_n) = p_1 \cdots p_k - (p_1 - 1) \cdots (p_k - 1)$.*
$3°$ *If $p < q$ are primes, then, for $n = pq$, one has*

$$\Psi_n(z) = \frac{(z^p - 1)(z^q - 1)}{z - 1} = z^{p+q-1} + \cdots + z^{q+1} - z^{p-1} - \cdots - z^2 - z - 1.$$

$4°$ *If p, q, and r are different primes, then, for $n = pqr$, one has*

$$\Psi_n(z) = \frac{(z^{pq} - 1)(z^{qr} - 1)(z^{rp} - 1)(z - 1)}{(z^p - 1)(z^q - 1)(z^r - 1)}.$$

$5°$ $\Psi_{2n}(z) = (1 - z^n)\Psi_n(-z)$ *if n is odd.*
$6°$ $\Psi_{pn}(z) = \Psi_n(z^p)$ *if $p \mid n$.*
$7°$ $\Psi_{pn}(z) = \Psi_n(z^p)\Phi_n(z)$ *if $p \nmid n$.*
$8°$ Ψ_n *is antipalindromic (i.e., $d_j^{(n)} = -d_{n-\varphi(n)-j}^{(n)}$, $j = 0, \ldots, n - \varphi(n)$).*
$9°$ *The number of positive coefficients of Ψ_n is equal to the number of negative coefficients.*

Proof. For $1°$, note that, for this value of n, the only nonprimitive nth roots of unity are the ones having orders that divide $p^\alpha - 1$. These are the roots of the polynomial $z^{p^{\alpha-1}} - 1$, and the conclusion follows.

Property $2°$ follows immediately from the fact that $\varphi(n) = (p_1 - 1) \cdots (p_k - 1)$.

Let us prove $3°$. The only nonprimitive nth roots of unity have orders of 1, p, or q. Hence, these are the roots of the polynomials $z^p - 1$ and $z^q - 1$, respectively. Since the root 1 appears in both polynomials, we have that

$$\Psi_n(z) = \frac{(z^p - 1)(z^q - 1)}{z - 1}.$$

For $4°$, note that the nonprimitive pqrth roots of unity are the roots of unity of orders dividing pq, qr, or rp. By denoting U_k as the set of roots of unity which have orders dividing k, as well as by using the principle of inclusion and exclusion, we deduce that

$$|U_{pq} \cup U_{qr} \cup U_{rp}| = |U_{pq}| + |U_{qr}| + |U_{rp}| - |U_p| - |U_q| - |U_r| + |U_1|.$$

The elements of $U_{pq} \cup U_{qr} \cup U_{rp}$ are the roots of Ψ_n. The conclusion follows by identifying the roots of unity with the roots of the corresponding polynomials.

To prove $5°$, one just observes that the nonprimitive $2n$th roots of unity have orders dividing n or $2d$, where $d \mid n$, and $d < n$. The first ones are the roots of $1 - z^n$, whereas the second type can be found among the roots of $\Psi_n(-z)$. The statements $6°$ and $7°$ can be proved in a similar way. Then, $8°$ results from the definition and the fact that Φ_n is palindromic. From here, $9°$ follows directly. □

From the proposition above, we easily derive the following formulas. If p and q are distinct primes, then the cyclotomic polynomial satisfies the following:

$$\Phi_{pq}(z) = \frac{(z^{pq}-1)(z-1)}{(z^p-1)(z^q-1)}. \tag{3}$$

Moreover, if p, q, and r are distinct primes, then

$$\Phi_{pqr}(z) = \frac{(z^{pqr}-1)(z^p-1)(z^q-1)(z^r-1)}{(z^{pq}-1)(z^{qr}-1)(z^{rp}-1)(z-1)}. \tag{4}$$

The paper first presents some results on Ramanujan sums in Section 2, then it reviews some known formulae for the calculation of the coefficients of cyclotomic polynomials in Section 3. The paper's main results are contained in Section 4, where we derive new formulas for the coefficients of inverse cyclotomic polynomials in Theorems 4–6. These results are expressed in terms of Ramanujan sums and provide counterparts to similar formulae that were recently obtained in [6,8] for cyclotomic polynomials. The numerical experiments in Section 5 highlight the utility of the recursive formula in Theorem 6.

2. Preliminaries on Ramanujan Sums

Recall that the Möbius function μ is defined by

$$\mu(n) = \begin{cases} 1 & \text{if } n = 1, \\ (-1)^k & \text{if } n = p_1 p_2 \cdots p_k, \\ 0 & \text{if } n = p^2 m, \end{cases} \tag{5}$$

where $p, p_1, \ldots, p_k$ are prime numbers.

For every positive integer n and q, the Ramanujan sum $\rho(n,q)$ is defined as

$$\rho(n,q) = \sum_{\gcd(a,n)=1} e^{2\pi i \frac{a}{n} q}, \tag{6}$$

where the sum is taken over all a such that $1 \leq a \leq n$, and $\gcd(a,n) = 1$ (see [9,10]).

By fixing q or n, Ramanujan sums can be seen as arithmetic functions of the free variable. For a fixed $n \in \mathbb{N}^*$, the arithmetic function $\rho(n, \cdot) : \mathbb{N}^* \to \mathbb{C}$ is periodic, as $\rho(n, q+n) = \rho(n, q)$ for all $q \in \mathbb{N}$. By fixing q, the function $\rho(\cdot, q) : \mathbb{N}^* \to \mathbb{C}$ is also interesting. For example, $\rho(n, 0) = \varphi(n)$, and $n \in \mathbb{N}^*$ represents Euler's totient function.

For $q \in \mathbb{Z}$ and every positive integer n, we consider the function $\delta_q(n) = \sum_{a=1}^{n} e^{\frac{2\pi a}{n} iq}$.

The following straightforward identity (see, e.g., [6]) is useful in later computations.

$$\delta_q(n) = \begin{cases} n & \text{if } n \mid q \\ 0 & \text{if } n \nmid q \end{cases}. \tag{7}$$

Suppose that $q \in \mathbb{N}^*$ is fixed. By (7), we obtain that $\delta_q : \mathbb{N}^* \to \mathbb{N}$ is a multiplicative function. Indeed, if $m, n \in \mathbb{N}^*$ are coprime, then $nm \mid q$ if and only if $n \mid q$ and $m \mid q$. Hence,

$$\delta_q(nm) = \delta_q(n)\delta_q(m). \tag{8}$$

The following result of Kluyver is a direct consequence of the Möbius inversion formula and was obtained in 1906 [10]. If q is a fixed positive integer, then

$$\rho(n,q) = \sum_{d \mid \gcd(n,q)} d\mu\left(\frac{n}{d}\right) \text{ for all } n \in \mathbb{N}^*. \tag{9}$$

This result has an important consequence. As for any $n \in \mathbb{N}^*$, $\rho(n,q) = \sum_{d|n} \delta_q(d)\mu\left(\frac{n}{d}\right)$; the right-hand side is the convolution product $\delta_q * \mu$ of two multiplicative functions; hence, it follows that, for $q \in \mathbb{N}^*$ being fixed, the function $\rho(\cdot,q) : \mathbb{N}^* \to \mathbb{C}$ is multiplicative.

With the convention that $\mu\left(\frac{n}{d}\right) = 0$ if $d \nmid n$, we obtain the following explicit consequence of Formula (9) for $q = 1, \ldots, 17$, which is valid for all $n \in \mathbb{N}^*$.

$$\rho(n,1) = \mu(n);$$

$$\rho(n,2) = \sum_{d|\gcd(n,2)} d\mu\left(\frac{n}{d}\right) = \mu(n) + 2\mu(n/2);$$

$$\rho(n,3) = \sum_{d|\gcd(n,3)} d\mu\left(\frac{n}{d}\right) = \mu(n) + 3\mu(n/3);$$

$$\rho(n,4) = \sum_{d|\gcd(n,4)} d\mu\left(\frac{n}{d}\right) = \mu(n) + 2\mu(n/2) + 4\mu(n/4);$$

$$\rho(n,5) = \sum_{d|\gcd(n,5)} d\mu\left(\frac{n}{d}\right) = \mu(n) + 5\mu(n/5);$$

$$\rho(n,6) = \sum_{d|\gcd(n,6)} d\mu\left(\frac{n}{d}\right) = \mu(n) + 2\mu(n/2) + 3\mu(n/3) + 6\mu(n/6);$$

$$\rho(n,7) = \sum_{d|\gcd(n,7)} d\mu\left(\frac{n}{d}\right) = \mu(n) + 7\mu(n/7);$$

$$\rho(n,8) = \sum_{d|\gcd(n,8)} d\mu\left(\frac{n}{d}\right) = \mu(n) + 2\mu(n/2) + 4\mu(n/4) + 8\mu(n/8);$$

$$\rho(n,9) = \sum_{d|\gcd(n,9)} d\mu\left(\frac{n}{d}\right) = \mu(n) + 3\mu(n/3) + 9\mu(n/9);$$

$$\rho(n,10) = \sum_{d|\gcd(n,10)} d\mu\left(\frac{n}{d}\right) = \mu(n) + 2\mu(n/2) + 5\mu(n/5) + 10\mu(n/10);$$

$$\rho(n,11) = \sum_{d|\gcd(n,11)} d\mu\left(\frac{n}{d}\right) = \mu(n) + 11\mu(n/11);$$

$$\rho(n,12) = \sum_{d|\gcd(n,12)} d\mu\left(\frac{n}{d}\right)$$
$$= \mu(n) + 2\mu(n/2) + 3\mu(n/3) + 4\mu(n/4) + 6\mu(n/6) + 12\mu(n/12);$$

$$\rho(n,13) = \sum_{d|\gcd(n,13)} d\mu\left(\frac{n}{d}\right) = \mu(n) + 13\mu(n/13);$$

$$\rho(n,14) = \sum_{d|\gcd(n,14)} d\mu\left(\frac{n}{d}\right) = \mu(n) + 2\mu(n/2) + 7\mu(n/7) + 14\mu(n/14);$$

$$\rho(n,15) = \sum_{d|\gcd(n,15)} d\mu\left(\frac{n}{d}\right) = \mu(n) + 3\mu(n/3) + 5\mu(n/5) + 15\mu(n/15);$$

$$\rho(n,16) = \sum_{d|\gcd(n,16)} d\mu\left(\frac{n}{d}\right) = \mu(n) + 2\mu(n/2) + 4\mu(n/4) + 8\mu(n/8) + 16\mu(n/16);$$

$$\rho(n,17) = \sum_{d|\gcd(n,17)} d\mu\left(\frac{n}{d}\right) = \mu(n) + 17\mu(n/17).$$

When $n = p_1 p_2 \cdots p_k$ is a product of distinct k primes, $\gcd(n,q) = p_1 p_2 \cdots p_m$, and $m \leq k$, then by using the properties of the Möbius function, one obtains

$$\rho(n,q) = \sum_{i=1}^{m}(-1)^{k-i} S_i(p_1, p_2, \ldots, p_m), \tag{10}$$

where S_i is the ith fundamental symmetric polynomial in m variables.

The cases when n is a product of three or four distinct primes ($m = 3, 4$) present special interest in the study of cyclotomic and inverse cyclotomic polynomials.

2.1. Ramanujan Sums for $n = pqr$

With the convention that $\mu(\frac{n}{d}) = 0$ if $d \nmid n$, we obtain the following immediate consequences of Formula (9). These results are valid for all $n = pqr$ with $p < q < r$ odd primes and $j = 1\ldots, 17$:

$\rho(n,1) = \mu(n) = -1;$

$\rho(n,2) = \mu(n) + 2\mu(n/2) = -1;$

$\rho(n,3) = \mu(n) + 3\mu(n/3) = \begin{cases} 2 & \text{if } 3 \mid n \\ -1 & \text{if } 3 \nmid n \end{cases};$

$\rho(n,4) = \mu(n) + 2\mu(n/2) + 4\mu(n/4) = -1;$

$\rho(n,5) = \mu(n) + 5\mu(n/5) = \begin{cases} 4 & \text{if } 5 \mid n \\ -1 & \text{if } 5 \nmid n \end{cases};$

$\rho(n,6) = \mu(n) + 2\mu(n/2) + 3\mu(n/3) + 6\mu(n/6) = \begin{cases} 2 & \text{if } 3 \mid n \\ -1 & \text{if } 3 \nmid n \end{cases};$

$\rho(n,7) = \mu(n) + 7\mu(n/7) = \begin{cases} 6 & \text{if } 7 \mid n \\ -1 & \text{if } 7 \nmid n \end{cases}$

$\rho(n,8) = \mu(n) + 2\mu(n/2) + 4\mu(n/4) + 8\mu(n/8) = -1;$

$\rho(n,9) = \mu(n) + 3\mu(n/3) + 9\mu(n/9) = \begin{cases} 2 & \text{if } 3 \mid n \\ -1 & \text{if } 3 \nmid n. \end{cases}$

$\rho(n,10) = \mu(n) + 2\mu(n/2) + 5\mu(n/5) + 10\mu(n/10) = \begin{cases} 4 & \text{if } 5 \mid n \\ -1 & \text{if } 5 \nmid n. \end{cases};$

$\rho(n,11) = \mu(n) + 11\mu(n/11) = \begin{cases} 10 & \text{if } 11 \mid n \\ -1 & \text{if } 11 \nmid n. \end{cases};$

$\rho(n,12) = \mu(n) + 2\mu(n/2) + 3\mu(n/3) + 4\mu(n/4) + 6\mu(n/6) + 12\mu(n/12)$
$= \begin{cases} 2 & \text{if } 3 \mid n \\ -1 & \text{if } 3 \nmid n. \end{cases};$

$\rho(n,13) = \mu(n) + 13\mu(n/13) = \begin{cases} 12 & \text{if } 13 \mid n \\ -1 & \text{if } 13 \nmid n. \end{cases};$

$\rho(n,14) = \mu(n) + 2\mu(n/2) + 7\mu(n/7) + 14\mu(n/14) = \begin{cases} 6 & \text{if } 7 \mid n \\ -1 & \text{if } 7 \nmid n. \end{cases};$

$\rho(n,15) = \mu(n) + 3\mu(n/3) + 5\mu(n/5) + 15\mu(n/15) = \begin{cases} -8 & \text{if } 15 \mid n \\ 4 & \text{if } \gcd(n,15) = 5 \\ 2 & \text{if } \gcd(n,15) = 3 \\ -1 & \text{if } \gcd(n,15) = 1. \end{cases};$

$\rho(n,16) = \mu(n) + 2\mu(n/2) + 4\mu(n/4) + 8\mu(n/8) + 16\mu(n/16) = -1;$

$\rho(n,17) = \mu(n) + 17\mu(n/17) = \begin{cases} 16 & \text{if } 17 \mid n \\ -1 & \text{if } 17 \nmid n. \end{cases}$

Clearly, if $n = pqr$ with $p < q < r$ primes, then $\rho(n,j) = -1$ for $j = 1,\ldots,p-1$, while $\rho(n,p) = \mu(n) + p\mu(n/p) = p - 1$.

2.2. Ramanujan Sums for $n = pqrs$

For all $n = pqrs$ with $p < q < r < s$ odd primes and $j = 1\ldots, 17$, one obtains:

$\rho(n,1) = \mu(n) = 1;$

$\rho(n,2) = \mu(n) + 2\mu(n/2) = 1;$

$\rho(n,3) = \mu(n) + 3\mu(n/3) = \begin{cases} -2 & \text{if } 3 \mid n \\ 1 & \text{if } 3 \nmid n \end{cases};$

$\rho(n,4) = \mu(n) + 2\mu(n/2) + 4\mu(n/4) = 1;$

$\rho(n,5) = \mu(n) + 5\mu(n/5) = \begin{cases} -4 & \text{if } 5 \mid n \\ 1 & \text{if } 5 \nmid n \end{cases};$

$\rho(n,6) = \mu(n) + 2\mu(n/2) + 3\mu(n/3) + 6\mu(n/6) = \begin{cases} -2 & \text{if } 3 \mid n \\ 1 & \text{if } 3 \nmid n \end{cases};$

$\rho(n,7) = \mu(n) + 7\mu(n/7) = \begin{cases} -6 & \text{if } 7 \mid n \\ 1 & \text{if } 7 \nmid n \end{cases}$

$\rho(n,8) = \mu(n) + 2\mu(n/2) + 4\mu(n/4) + 8\mu(n/8) = 1;$

$\rho(n,9) = \mu(n) + 3\mu(n/3) + 9\mu(n/9) = \begin{cases} -2 & \text{if } 3 \mid n \\ 1 & \text{if } 3 \nmid n. \end{cases}$

$\rho(n,10) = \mu(n) + 2\mu(n/2) + 5\mu(n/5) + 10\mu(n/10) = \begin{cases} -4 & \text{if } 5 \mid n \\ 1 & \text{if } 5 \nmid n. \end{cases};$

$\rho(n,11) = \mu(n) + 11\mu(n/11) = \begin{cases} -10 & \text{if } 11 \mid n \\ 1 & \text{if } 11 \nmid n. \end{cases};$

$\rho(n,12) = \mu(n) + 2\mu(n/2) + 3\mu(n/3) + 4\mu(n/4) + 6\mu(n/6) + 12\mu(n/12)$
$= \begin{cases} -2 & \text{if } 3 \mid n \\ 1 & \text{if } 3 \nmid n. \end{cases};$

$\rho(n,13) = \mu(n) + 13\mu(n/13) = \begin{cases} -12 & \text{if } 13 \mid n \\ 1 & \text{if } 13 \nmid n. \end{cases};$

$\rho(n,14) = \mu(n) + 2\mu(n/2) + 7\mu(n/7) + 14\mu(n/14) = \begin{cases} -6 & \text{if } 7 \mid n \\ 1 & \text{if } 7 \nmid n. \end{cases};$

$\rho(n,15) = \mu(n) + 3\mu(n/3) + 5\mu(n/5) + 15\mu(n/15) = \begin{cases} 8 & \text{if } 15 \mid n \\ -4 & \text{if } \gcd(n,15) = 5 \\ -2 & \text{if } \gcd(n,15) = 3 \\ 1 & \text{if } \gcd(n,15) = 1. \end{cases};$

$\rho(n,16) = \mu(n) + 2\mu(n/2) + 4\mu(n/4) + 8\mu(n/8) + 16\mu(n/16) = 1;$

$\rho(n,17) = \mu(n) + 17\mu(n/17) = \begin{cases} -16 & \text{if } 17 \mid n \\ 1 & \text{if } 17 \nmid n. \end{cases}$

Clearly, if $n = pqrs$ with $p < q < r < s$ primes, then $\rho(n,j) = 1$ for $j = 1,\ldots, p-1$, while $\rho(n,p) = \mu(n) + p\mu(n/p) = 1 - p$.

3. Review of Some Results on the Coefficients of Cyclotomic Polynomials

The coefficients of cyclotomic polynomials have many interesting properties (see, for instance, [11–13]). For example, the polynomials Φ_n, $n = 1,\ldots, 104$, are flat (i.e., all the coefficients are 0, 1, or -1) and so are the polynomials obtained when $n = pq$, where p and

q are distinct primes. In 1883, Mignotti showed that Φ_{105} is not flat, as -2 is the coefficient of z^7, while 2 first appears as coefficient for $n = 165$.

In 1895, Bang proved that, for $n = pqr$ with $p < q < r$ odd primes, no coefficient of Φ_n can be larger than $p - 1$. Later on, Schur showed in 1931 that the coefficients of cyclotomic polynomials can be arbitrarily large in their absolute values [14]. In 1987, Suzuki [15] showed that any integer number can be a coefficient of some cyclotomic polynomial.

Under certain assumptions regarding the gap between consecutive primes [16], one can obtain more profound results. For example, Andrica's conjecture claims that for $n \geq 1$, one has $\sqrt{p_{n+1}} - \sqrt{p_n} < 1$, where p_n and p_{n+1} denote the nth and $(n+1)$th prime numbers, respectively, which still stands after over 40 years (see, for example, [17,18]). It was recently proven that Andrica's conjecture implies that every natural number occurs as the largest coefficient of some cyclotomic polynomial ([19], Theorem 16).

We state here the following conjecture.

Conjecture 1. *Every integer appears as a coefficient of infinitely many cyclotomic polynomials.*

By Möbius' inversion formula, one obtains a useful alternative form of (1) as follows:

$$\Phi_n(z) = \prod_{d|n}\left(z^d - 1\right)^{\mu(n/d)} = \prod_{d|n}\left(1 - z^d\right)^{\mu(n/d)}. \tag{11}$$

The last equality follows from

$$\Phi_n(z) = \prod_{d|n}(-1)^{\mu(n/d)} \cdot \left(1 - z^d\right)^{\mu(n/d)}$$

$$= (-1)^{\sum_{d|n}\mu(n/d)} \prod_{d|n}\left(1 - z^d\right)^{\mu(n/d)} = \prod_{d|n}\left(1 - z^d\right)^{\mu(n/d)},$$

since $\sum_{d|n}\mu(n/d) = \sum_{d|n} 1 \cdot \mu(n/d) = 1 * \mu(n) = \varepsilon(n) = 0$, where ε is the multiplicative unity in the convolution of the Dirichlet product, and $\varepsilon(n) = 0$ for every integer $n \geq 2$. By completing (11) with $\mu(n/d) = 0$, when n/d is not an integer, one can write

$$\Phi_n(z) = \prod_{d=1}^{\infty}\left(1 - z^d\right)^{\mu(n/d)}. \tag{12}$$

Hence, for a square-free n, the value $c_m^{(n)}$ depends only on the values of $\mu(n)$, $\mu(n/d)$, and on the prime divisors of n that are less than $m + 1$.

The following result was proven by Endo [20] using a fine mathematical induction argument and earlier results by Bloom [21] and Erdös [22]. A direct proof that allows for simplifications and extensions was given in [6].

Theorem 1. *The following formula holds*

$$c_m^{(n)} = \sum_{i_1 + 2i_2 + \cdots + mi_m = m}(-1)^{i_1 + \cdots + i_m}\binom{\mu(n)}{i_1}\binom{\mu(n/2)}{i_2}\cdots\binom{\mu(n/m)}{i_m}, \tag{13}$$

where the tuples $(i_1, \ldots, i_m)$ run over all the nonnegative integral solutions of the equation $i_1 + 2i_2 + \cdots + mi_m = m$ for m a positive integer.

A formula for the coefficients of Φ_n only in terms of the Ramanujan sums is given in ([8], Theorem 6):

Theorem 2. *We have*

$$c_k^{(n)} = \sum_{l_1+2l_2+\cdots+kl_k=k} (-1)^{l_1+l_2+\cdots+l_k} \frac{\rho(n,1)^{l_1}}{1^{l_1}l_1!} \cdot \frac{\rho(n,2)^{l_2}}{2^{l_2}l_2!} \cdots \frac{\rho(n,k)^{l_k}}{k^{l_k}l_k!}. \tag{14}$$

While the Formulae (13) and (14) are explicit, their practical applicability is limited for at least two reasons. First, large integers n cannot be factorised. Second, the sums are taken over all the solutions to the equation $i_1 + 2i_2 + \cdots + mi_m = m$, which requires the generation of all partitions of the positive integer m.

The following recursive formula for the coefficients of Φ_n in terms of the Ramanujan sums was obtained in ([8], Theorem 7), and this avoids the complication mentioned above related to the generation of partitions.

Theorem 3. *The following relation holds for every $k = 2, \ldots, \varphi(n)$:*

$$c_k^{(n)} = -\frac{1}{k}\left[\rho(n,k) + \rho(n,k-1)c_1^{(n)} + \cdots + \rho(n,1)c_{k-1}^{(n)}\right]. \tag{15}$$

4. The Coefficients of Ψ_n

Since Ψ_n is the division of the monic polynomial $z^n - 1$ and the cyclotomic polynomial Φ_n, both have integer coefficients; it follows that Ψ_n is monic with integer coefficients as well. As mentioned in the beginning of the section, Ψ_n is intimately connected to the cyclotomic polynomial Φ_n. This suggests that understanding the coefficients of Ψ_n is a challenging venture, as any knowledge about the coefficients of Ψ_n could be transferred to knowledge about the coefficients of Φ_n and vice versa.

If one knows the first few coefficients $c_k^{(n)}$, one can directly compute the coefficients $d_k^{(n)}$ of the inverse cyclotomic polynomial for small values of k. This can be achieved by identifying the coefficients in $\Phi_n(z) \cdot \Psi_n(z) = z^n - 1$. This is reduced to solving the following system:

$$\begin{cases} c_0^{(n)} d_0^{(n)} = -1 \\ c_0^{(n)} d_1^{(n)} + c_1^{(n)} d_0^{(n)} = 0 \\ c_0^{(n)} d_2^{(n)} + c_1^{(n)} d_1^{(n)} + c_2^{((n)} d_0^{(n)} = 0 \\ \vdots \end{cases},$$

where the coefficients $c_0^{(n)}, c_1^{(n)}, c_2^{(n)}, \ldots$, of Φ_n are the unknowns.

Many properties of the coefficients of inverse cyclotomic polynomials are presented in Moree [7]. For example, whenever $n = pq$ with p and q primes, Ψ_n is flat, as well as for the polynomials Ψ_{15r} or Ψ_{21r} when r is prime. The first nonflat inverse cyclotomic polynomial is Ψ_{561}. Analogous to Suzuki's Theorem, Moree [7] showed that every integer number can be a coefficient of some inverse cyclotomic polynomial Ψ_n.

Conjecture 2. *Every positive integer is the largest coefficient of an inverse cyclotomic polynomial.*

Considering the analogous aforementioned result concerning the coefficients of cyclotomic polynomials, it is possible that this property could be proved under the supplementary assumption that Andrica's conjecture holds.

Conjecture 3. *Every integer appears as a coefficient of infinitely inverse cyclotomic polynomials.*

4.1. The Analogous Formula for (13)

As $\mu(n) \in \{-1, 0, 1\}$, we get $\mu(n)^3 = \mu(n)$ and $n \geq 1$. For an integer $k \geq 2$, one has

$$\binom{\mu(n)}{k} = (-1)^k \binom{\mu(n)}{2}, \tag{16}$$

where we use the generalized binomial coefficient

$$\binom{\alpha}{j} = \frac{\alpha(\alpha-1)\cdots(\alpha-j+1)}{j!}, \quad \alpha \in \mathbb{R}, j \in \mathbb{N}.$$

Therefore, if $(i_1, \ldots, i_m)$ is a solution of the equation $i_1 + 2i_2 + \cdots + mi_m = m$ for a given $j = 1, \ldots, m$ one has $i_j \geq 2$; then the corresponding binomial coefficient in (13) with the form $(-1)^{i_j} \binom{\mu(n/j)}{i_j}$ can be replaced using Formula (16) by $\binom{\mu(n/j)}{2}$.

We can now establish a formula that is analogous to (13).

Theorem 4. *For every $m, n \in \mathbb{N}$, and $n \geq 1$, the following formula holds*

$$d_m^{(n)} = \sum_{i_1 + 2i_2 + \ldots + mi_m = m} (-1)^{i_1 + \cdots + i_m + 1} \binom{-\mu(n)}{i_1} \binom{-\mu(n/2)}{i_2} \cdots \binom{-\mu(n/m)}{i_m}. \tag{17}$$

Proof. We make use of the infinite product Formula (12) and observe that

$$\Psi_n(z) = \frac{z^n - 1}{\Phi_n(z)} = (z^n - 1) \prod_{d=1}^{\infty} (1 - z^d)^{-\mu(n/d)}$$

$$= (z^n - 1) \sum_{m=0}^{\infty} \left(\sum_{i_1 + 2i_2 + \cdots + mi_m = m} (-1)^{i_1 + \cdots + i_m} \binom{-\mu(n)}{i_1} \cdots \binom{-\mu(n/m)}{i_m} \right) z^m.$$

The formula follows by identifying coefficients of z^m on both sides. □

Let us emphasize how one can compute the first few coefficients of Ψ_n for every $n \in \mathbb{N}^*$ using the formula above.

- For $m = 1$, we have $i_1 = 1$; hence $d_1^{(n)} = \binom{-\mu(n)}{1} = -\mu(n)$.
- For $m = 2$, the equation $i_1 + 2i_2 = 2$ only has the solutions $(i_1, i_2) = (2, 0)$ and $(i_1, i_2) = (0, 1)$, so one obtains the relation

$$d_2^{(n)} = -\binom{-\mu(n)}{2} + \binom{-\mu(n/2)}{1} = -\frac{1}{2}\mu(n)(\mu(n) + 1) - \mu(n/2).$$

- For $m = 3$, the solutions to (l_1, l_2, l_3) of the equation $l_1 + 2l_2 + 3l_3 = 3$ are $(3, 0, 0)$, $(1, 1, 0)$, and $(0, 0, 1)$; therefore, by using $\mu^3 = \mu$, one obtains

$$d_3^{(n)} = \binom{-\mu(n)}{3} - \binom{-\mu(n)}{1}\binom{-\mu(n/2)}{1} + \binom{-\mu(n/3)}{1}$$

$$= -\frac{1}{2}\left(\mu(n)^2 + \mu(n)\right) - \mu(n)\mu(n/2) - \mu(n/3).$$

- For $m = 4$, the solutions (l_1, l_2, l_3, l_4) of the equation $l_1 + 2l_2 + 3l_3 + 4l_4 = 4$ are $(4, 0, 0, 0)$, $(2, 1, 0, 0)$, $(0, 2, 0, 0)$, $(1, 0, 1, 0)$, and $(0, 0, 0, 1)$. By using $\binom{-\mu(n)}{4} = \binom{-\mu(n)}{2}$, we obtain

$$d_4^{(n)} = -\binom{-\mu(n)}{4} + \binom{-\mu(n)}{2}\binom{-\mu(n/2)}{1} - \binom{-\mu(n)}{1}\binom{-\mu(n/3)}{1} +$$
$$+ \binom{-\mu(n/2)}{2} + \binom{-\mu(n/4)}{1}$$
$$= -\frac{\mu(n)(\mu(n)+1)}{2} - \frac{\mu(n)(\mu(n)+1)}{2}\mu(n/2) - \mu(n)\mu(n/3) +$$
$$+ \frac{\mu(n/2)(\mu(n/2)+1)}{2} - \mu(n/4).$$

4.2. The Analogous Formula for (14)

As in the case of cyclotomic polynomials, every coefficient $d_k^{(n)}$ of Ψ_n is a polynomial with rational coefficients with the variables given by the Ramanujan sums $\rho(n,k)$, where $k = 1, 2, \ldots, n - \varphi(n) - 1$. This property is illustrated in the following result.

Theorem 5. *We have*

$$d_k^{(n)} = -\sum_{l_1 + 2l_2 + \cdots + kl_k = k} \frac{\rho(n,1)^{l_1}}{1^{l_1} l_1!} \cdot \frac{\rho(n,2)^{l_2}}{2^{l_2} l_2!} \cdots \frac{\rho(n,k)^{l_k}}{k^{l_k} l_k!}. \tag{18}$$

Proof. Denote with P_j the j-th symmetric power polynomial evaluated at the $\varphi(n)$ roots of Φ_n (primitive roots of unity) and with P_j' for the jth symmetric power polynomial evaluated at the $n - \varphi(n)$ roots of Ψ_n. We then use the relations $P_j' = -\rho(n,j)$ and $S_k' = (-1)^{k+1} d_k^{(n)}$, and we then apply Theorem 7.3 from [6]. □

We compute the first four coefficients of Ψ_n, for every $n \in \mathbb{N}^*$, using Formula (18).

- For $k = 1$, we have $l_1 = 1$, hence $d_1^{(n)} = -\rho(n,1) = -\mu(n)$.
- For $k = 2$, the equation $i_1 + 2i_2 = 2$ only has the solutions $(i_1, i_2) = (2, 0)$ and $(i_1, i_2) = (0, 1)$, so one obtains

$$d_2^{(n)} = -\frac{1}{2}\rho(n,1)^2 - \frac{1}{2}\rho(n,2)$$
$$= -\frac{1}{2}\mu^2(n) - \frac{1}{2}(\mu(n) + 2\mu(n/2))$$
$$= -\frac{1}{2}\mu(n)(\mu(n)+1) - \mu(n/2).$$

- For $k = 3$, the solutions to (l_1, l_2, l_3) of the equation $l_1 + 2l_2 + 3l_3 = 3$ are $(3,0,0)$, $(1,1,0)$, and $(0,0,1)$; therefore, one obtains

$$d_3^{(n)} = -\frac{1}{6}\rho(n,1)^3 - \frac{1}{2}\rho(n,1)\rho(n,2) - \frac{1}{3}\rho(n,3)$$
$$= -\frac{1}{6}\mu^3(n) - \frac{1}{2}\mu(n)(\mu(n) + 2\mu(n/2)) - \frac{1}{3}(\mu(n) + 3\mu(n/3))$$
$$= -\frac{1}{2}(\mu^2(n) + \mu(n)) - \mu(n)\mu(n/2) - \mu(n/3),$$

where we used the relation $\mu^3 = \mu$.

- For $k = 4$, the solutions (l_1, l_2, l_3, l_4) of the equation $l_1 + 2l_2 + 3l_3 + 4l_4 = 4$ are $(4,0,0,0)$, $(2,1,0,0)$, $(0,2,0,0)$, $(1,0,1,0)$, and $(0,0,0,1)$; hence,

$$d_4^{(n)} = -\frac{1}{24}\rho(n,1)^4 - \frac{1}{4}\rho(n,1)^2\rho(n,2) - \frac{1}{3}\rho(n,1)\rho(n,3)$$
$$-\frac{1}{8}\rho(n,2)^2 - \frac{1}{4}\rho(n,4)$$
$$= -\frac{1}{24}\mu^4(n) - \frac{1}{4}\mu^2(n)(\mu(n)+2\mu(n/2))^2-$$
$$-\frac{1}{4}(\mu(n)+2\mu(n/2)+4\mu(n/4))$$
$$= -\frac{\mu(n)(\mu(n)+1)}{2} - \frac{\mu(n)(\mu(n)+1)}{2}\mu(n/2) - \mu(n)\mu(n/3)+$$
$$+\frac{\mu(n/2)(\mu(n/2)+1)}{2} - \mu(n/4).$$

In the relation above we repeatedly used the fact that $\mu^3 = \mu$.

A direct consequence is that for every $n \in \mathbb{N}^*$ and every $k \in \{1, 2, \ldots, n - \varphi(n)\}$, the anticyclotomic coefficient $d_k^{(n)}$ is a polynomial with rational coefficients in $\mu(n/d)$, where d is a divisor of n. Moreover, the degree of $\mu(n/d)$ in every monomial is at most 2.

4.3. A Recurrence Formula for the Coefficients $d_k^{(n)}$

The following recursive formula involving Ramanujan sums is analogous to (15).

Theorem 6. *The coefficients of Ψ_n satisfy the following relation:*

$$d_k^{(n)} = \frac{1}{k}\left[-\rho(n,k) + \rho(n,k-1)d_1^{(n)} + \cdots + \rho(n,1)d_{k-1}^{(n)}\right] \tag{19}$$

Proof. We use Newton's identities for Ψ_n to find a recurrence relation for $d_k^{(n)}$. Recall that we have $\delta_j(n) = \sum_{a=1}^{n}\left(e^{2\pi i \frac{a}{n}}\right)^j$, where $\delta_j(n) = \begin{cases} n \text{ if } n \mid j \\ 0 \text{ if } n \nmid j \end{cases}$.

In our notation, the symmetric power sum polynomials satisfy the relation $P_j + P'_j = \delta_j(n)$. However, for $j < n$, we have $n \nmid j$; hence, $P'_j = -P_j = -\rho(n,j)$, where ρ denotes the Ramanujan sum (6). The polynomial Ψ_n is antireciprocal; hence, we have the relations

$$S'_j = (-1)^j d_{n-\varphi(n)-j}^{(n)} = (-1)^{j+1}d_j^{(n)}, \; j = 1, 2, \ldots,$$

where S'_j is the evaluation of the jth fundamental symmetric polynomial at the $n - \varphi(n)$ roots of Ψ_n. The explanation above implies that the recurrence holds. □

We now apply the theorem to compute the first four coefficients of $d_k^{(n)}$, for every $n \in \mathbb{N}^*$, thereby recovering the results obtained right after Theorem 4.

- For $k = 1$, we have $d_1^{(n)} = -\rho(n,1) = -\mu(n)$.
- For $k = 2$, one obtains

$$d_2^{(n)} = \frac{1}{2}\left[-\rho(n,2) + \rho(n,1)d_1^{(n)}\right] = -\frac{1}{2}\left[\mu(n) + 2\mu(n/2) + \mu^2(n)\right]$$
$$= -\frac{\mu^2(n) + \mu(n)}{2} - \mu(n/2).$$

- For $k = 3$, using the identity $\mu^3 = \mu$, it follows that

$$d_3^{(n)} = \frac{1}{3}\left[-\rho(n,3) + \rho(n,2)d_1^{(n)} + \rho(n,1)d_2^{(n)}\right]$$

$$= \frac{1}{3}[-\mu(n) - 3\mu(n/3) - (\mu(n) + 2\mu(n/2))\mu(n) +$$

$$+ \mu(n)\left(-\frac{\mu(n)^2 + \mu(n)}{2} - \mu(n/2)\right)]$$

$$= -\frac{1}{2}\left(\mu(n)^2 + \mu(n)\right) - \mu(n)\mu(n/2) - \mu(n/3)$$

- For $k = 4$, again using the identity $\mu^3 = \mu$, we obtain

$$d_4^{(n)} = \frac{1}{4}\left[-\rho(n,4) + \rho(n,3)d_1^{(n)} + \rho(n,2)d_2^{(n)} + \rho(n,1)d_3^{(n)}\right]$$

$$= \frac{1}{4}[-\mu(n) - 2\mu(n/2) - 4\mu(n/4) - (\mu(n) + 3\mu(n/3))\mu(n) +$$

$$+ (\mu(n) + 2\mu(n/2))\left(\frac{\mu(n)^2 - \mu(n)}{2} - \mu(n/2)\right) +$$

$$+ \mu(n)\left(-\frac{1}{2}\left(\mu(n)^2 + \mu(n)\right) - \mu(n)\mu(n/2) - \mu(n/3)\right)]$$

$$= -\frac{\mu(n)(\mu(n) + 1)}{2} - \frac{\mu(n)(\mu(n) + 1)}{2}\mu(n/2) - \mu(n)\mu(n/3) +$$

$$+ \frac{\mu(n/2)(\mu(n/2) + 1)}{2} - \mu(n/4).$$

5. Numerical Simulations for the Recursive Formula

In this section, we apply the previous recursive formula to compute the coefficients of some ternary and quaternary inverse cyclotomic polynomials (i.e., n is a product of three or four distinct primes) for values of n that are inspired by the calculations from [7].

For numerical simulations, we will focus on some instances where Ψ_n is not flat. We have seen earlier that the first nonflat inverse cyclotomic polynomial is Ψ_{561}. As listed in Table 1 of [7], -3 first appears in Ψ_{1155} as the coefficient of z^{33}, while 4 first appears in Ψ_{2145} as the coefficient of z^{44}. These are the three cases we focus on, and we compute explicitly until we get the first coefficient which is not 0, 1, or -1.

5.1. Results for $n = 561 = 3 \cdot 11 \cdot 17$

From Table 1, the Ramanujan sums $\rho(n,j)$, $j = 1,\ldots,17$, take following values: $-1, -1, 2, -1, -1, 2, -1, -1, 2, -1, 10, 2, -1, -1, 2, -1, 16$.

Since $\mu(n) = -1$, from Formula (15) one obtains

$$d_1^{(n)} = -\mu(n) = 1;$$

$$d_2^{(n)} = \frac{1}{2}\left[-\rho(n,2) + \rho(n,1)d_1^{(n)}\right] = \frac{1}{2}[1 + (-1)] = 0;$$

$$d_3^{(n)} = \frac{1}{3}\left[-\rho(n,3) + \rho(n,2)d_1^{(n)} + \rho(n,1)d_2^{(n)}\right] = \frac{1}{3}[-2 - 1 + 0] = -1;$$

$$d_4^{(n)} = \frac{1}{4}\left[-\rho(n,4) + \rho(n,3)d_1^{(n)} + \rho(n,2)d_2^{(n)} + \rho(n,1)d_3^{(n)}\right]$$

$$= \frac{1}{4}[1 + 2 \cdot 1 + (-1) \cdot 0 + (-1) \cdot (-1)] = 1;$$

$$d_5^{(n)} = \frac{1}{5}\left[-\rho(n,5) + \rho(n,4)d_1^{(n)} + \rho(n,3)d_2^{(n)} + \rho(n,2)d_3^{(n)} + \rho(n,1)d_4^{(n)}\right]$$

$$= \frac{1}{5}[1 + (-1) \cdot 1 + 2 \cdot 0 + (-1) \cdot (-1) + (-1) \cdot 1] = 0.$$

Similarly, one obtains

$$d_6^{(n)} = \frac{1}{6}[-2 + (-1) \cdot 1 + (-1) \cdot 0 + 2 \cdot (-1) + (-1) \cdot 1 + (-1) \cdot 0] = -1;$$

$$d_7^{(n)} = \frac{1}{7}[1 + 2 \cdot 1 + (-1) \cdot 0 + (-1) \cdot (-1) + 2 \cdot 1 + (-1) \cdot 0 + (-1) \cdot (-1)] = 1;$$

$$d_8^{(n)} = \frac{1}{8}[1 + (-1) \cdot 1 + 2 \cdot 0 + (-1) \cdot (-1) + (-1) \cdot 1 + 2 \cdot 0 + (-1) \cdot (-1) + (-1) \cdot 1] = 0;$$

$$d_9^{(n)} = \frac{1}{9}[-2 + (-1) \cdot 1 + (-1) \cdot 0 + 2 \cdot (-1) + (-1) \cdot 1 + (-1) \cdot 0 + 2 \cdot (-1)] +$$
$$+ \frac{1}{9}[(-1) \cdot 1 + (-1) \cdot 0] = -1;$$

$$d_{10}^{(n)} = \frac{1}{10}[1 + 2 \cdot 1 + (-1) \cdot 0 + (-1) \cdot (-1) + 2 \cdot 1 + (-1) \cdot 0 + (-1) \cdot (-1)] +$$
$$+ \frac{1}{10}[2 \cdot 1 + (-1) \cdot 0 + (-1) \cdot (-1)] = 1;$$

$$d_{11}^{(n)} = \frac{1}{11}[-10 + (-1) \cdot 1 + 2 \cdot 0 + (-1) \cdot (-1) + (-1) \cdot 1 + 2 \cdot 0 + (-1) \cdot (-1)] +$$
$$+ \frac{1}{11}[(-1) \cdot 1 + 2 \cdot 0 + (-1) \cdot (-1) + (-1) \cdot 1] = -1;$$

Similar calculations result in $d_{12}^{(n)} = 0$, $d_{13}^{(n)} = 1$, $d_{14}^{(n)} = -1$, $d_{15}^{(n)} = 0$, $d_{16}^{(n)} = 1$, wherein

$$d_{17}^{(n)} = \frac{1}{17}[-16 + (-1) \cdot 1 + 2 \cdot 0 + (-1) \cdot (-1) + (-1) \cdot 1 + 2 \cdot 0 + 10 \cdot (-1)] +$$
$$+ \frac{1}{17}[(-1) \cdot 1 + 2 \cdot 0 + (-1) \cdot (-1) + (-1) \cdot 1 + 2 \cdot (-1) + (-1) \cdot 0] +$$
$$+ \frac{1}{17}[(-1) \cdot 1 + 2 \cdot (-1) + (-1) \cdot 0 + (-1) \cdot 1] = -2;$$

This confirms that -2 appears as the coefficient of z^{17} in

$$\Psi_{561}(z) = z^{241} - z^{240} + \cdots + 2z^{224} + \cdots + z^{18} +$$
$$- 2z^{17} + z^{16} - z^{14} + z^{13} - z^{11} + z^{10} - z^9 + z^7 - z^6 + z^4 - z^3 + z - 1.$$

One may notice that if $n = pqr$ with $p < q < r$ primes, then $\rho(n, j) = -1$ for $j = 1, \ldots, p-1$; hence, the first inverse cyclotomic coefficients are $d_1^{(n)} = -1$, $d_2^{(n)} = 1$, and $c_3^{(n)} = 1, \ldots, c_{p-1}^{(n)} = 1$. At the same time,

$$d_p^{(n)} = -\frac{1}{p}\left[\rho(n, p) + \rho(n, p-1)c_1^{(n)} + \cdots + \rho(n, 1)c_{p-1}^{(n)}\right]$$
$$= -\frac{1}{p}[(p-1) + (-1) + \cdots + (-1)] = 0.$$

This argument then allows for the calculation of further coefficients, and it suggests why the larger coefficients of inverse cyclotomic polynomials are moving towards the centre (also using the fact that the polynomial is an antipalindrome).

Table 1. Ramanujan sums $\rho(n,j)$ for $j = 1, \ldots, 17$ and $n = 561, 1155, 2145$.

n	$561 = 3 \cdot 11 \cdot 17$	$1155 = 3 \cdot 5 \cdot 7 \cdot 11$	$2145 = 3 \cdot 5 \cdot 11 \cdot 13$
$\rho(n,1)$	-1	1	1
$\rho(n,2)$	-1	1	1
$\rho(n,3)$	2	-2	-2
$\rho(n,4)$	-1	1	1
$\rho(n,5)$	-1	-4	-4
$\rho(n,6)$	2	-2	-2
$\rho(n,7)$	-1	-6	1
$\rho(n,8)$	-1	1	1
$\rho(n,9)$	2	-2	-2
$\rho(n,10)$	-1	-4	-4
$\rho(n,11)$	10	-10	-10
$\rho(n,12)$	2	-2	-2
$\rho(n,13)$	-1	1	-12
$\rho(n,14)$	-1	-6	1
$\rho(n,15)$	2	8	8
$\rho(n,16)$	-1	1	1
$\rho(n,17)$	16	1	1

5.2. Results for $n = 1155 = 3 \cdot 5 \cdot 7 \cdot 11$

From Table 1, the Ramanujan sums $\rho(n,j)$, $j = 1, \ldots, 17$ take the values

$$1, 1, -2, 1, -4, -2, -6, 1, -2, -4, -10, -2, 1, -6, 8, 1, 1.$$

By using $\mu(n) = -1$ and the second column in Table 1 in Formula (15), one obtains

$$d_1^{(n)} = -\mu(n) = -1;$$
$$d_2^{(n)} = \frac{1}{2}\left[-\rho(n,2) + \rho(n,1)d_1^{(n)}\right] = \frac{1}{2}[-1 + (-1)] = -1;$$
$$d_3^{(n)} = \frac{1}{3}\left[-\rho(n,3) + \rho(n,2)d_1^{(n)} + \rho(n,1)d_2^{(n)}\right] = \frac{1}{3}[2 - 1 - 1] = 0;$$
$$d_4^{(n)} = \frac{1}{4}\left[-\rho(n,4) + \rho(n,3)d_1^{(n)} + \rho(n,2)d_2^{(n)} + \rho(n,1)d_3^{(n)}\right]$$
$$= \frac{1}{4}[-1 + 2 - 1 + 0] = 0.$$

Similarly, one obtains

$$d_5^{(n)} = \frac{1}{5}[4 + 1 \cdot (-1) + (-2) \cdot (-1) + 1 \cdot 0 + (-1) \cdot 0] = 1;$$
$$d_6^{(n)} = \frac{1}{6}[2 + (-4) \cdot (-1) + 1 \cdot (-1) + (-2) \cdot 0 + 1 \cdot 0 + 1 \cdot 1] = 1;$$
$$d_7^{(n)} = \frac{1}{7}[6 + (-2) \cdot (-1) + (-4) \cdot (-1) + 1 \cdot 0 + (-2) \cdot 0 + 1 \cdot 1 + 1 \cdot 1] = \frac{14}{7} = 2.$$

This confirms that 2 appears as the coefficient of z^7 in

$$\Psi_{1155}(z) = z^{675} + z^{674} + z^{673} - z^{670} - z^{669} - 2z^{668} + \cdots + 3z^{642} + \cdots$$
$$- 3z^{33} + \cdots + z^8 + 2z^7 + z^6 + z^5 - z^2 - z - 1.$$

5.3. Results for $n = 2145 = 3 \cdot 5 \cdot 11 \cdot 13$

From Table 1, $\rho(n,j)$, $j = 1, \ldots, 17$ take the values

$$1, 1, -2, 1, -4, -2, 1, 1, -2, -4, -10, -2, -12, 1, 8, 1, 1.$$

Since $\mu(n) = -1$, from Formula (15), one obtains

$$d_1^{(n)} = -\mu(n) = -1;$$

$$d_2^{(n)} = \frac{1}{2}\left[-\rho(n,2) + \rho(n,1)d_1^{(n)}\right] = \frac{1}{2}[-1 + 1 \cdot (-1)] = -1;$$

$$d_3^{(n)} = \frac{1}{3}\left[-\rho(n,3) + \rho(n,2)d_1^{(n)} + \rho(n,1)d_2^{(n)}\right] = \frac{1}{3}[2 + 1 \cdot (-1) + 1 \cdot (-1)] = 0;$$

$$d_4^{(n)} = \frac{1}{4}\left[-\rho(n,4) + \rho(n,3)d_1^{(n)} + \rho(n,2)d_2^{(n)} + \rho(n,1)d_3^{(n)}\right]$$

$$= \frac{1}{4}[-1 + (-2) \cdot (-1) + 1 \cdot (-1) + 1 \cdot 0] = 0;$$

$$d_5^{(n)} = \frac{1}{5}\left[-\rho(n,5) + \rho(n,4)d_1^{(n)} + \rho(n,3)d_2^{(n)} + \rho(n,2)d_3^{(n)} + \rho(n,1)d_4^{(n)}\right]$$

$$= \frac{1}{5}[4 + 1 \cdot (-1) + (-2) \cdot (-1) + 1 \cdot 0 + 1 \cdot 0] = 1.$$

Similarly, one obtains

$$d_6^{(n)} = \frac{1}{6}[2 + (-4) \cdot (-1) + 1 \cdot (-1) + (-2) \cdot 0 + 1 \cdot 0 + 1 \cdot 1] = 1;$$

$$d_7^{(n)} = \frac{1}{7}[-1 + (-2) \cdot (-1) + (-4) \cdot (-1) + 1 \cdot 0 + (-2) \cdot 0 + 1 \cdot 1 + 1 \cdot 1] = 1;$$

$$d_8^{(n)} = \frac{1}{8}[-1 + 1 \cdot (-1) + (-2) \cdot (-1) + (-4) \cdot 0 + 1 \cdot 0 + (-2) \cdot 1 + 1 \cdot 1 + 1 \cdot 1] = 0;$$

$$d_9^{(n)} = \frac{1}{9}[2 + 1 \cdot (-1) + 1 \cdot (-1) + (-2) \cdot 0 + (-4) \cdot 0 + 1 \cdot 1]$$

$$+ \frac{1}{9}[(-2) \cdot 1 + 1 \cdot 1 + 1 \cdot 0] = 0;$$

$$d_{10}^{(n)} = \frac{1}{10}[4 + (-2) \cdot (-1) + 1 \cdot (-1) + 1 \cdot 0 + (-2) \cdot 0 + (-4) \cdot 1] +$$

$$+ \frac{1}{10}[1 \cdot 1 + (-2) \cdot 1 + 1 \cdot 0 + 1 \cdot 0] = 0;$$

$$d_{11}^{(n)} = \frac{1}{11}[10 + (-4) \cdot (-1) + (-2) \cdot (-1) + 1 \cdot 0 + 1 \cdot 0 + (-2) \cdot 1 + (-4) \cdot 1] +$$

$$+ \frac{1}{11}[1 \cdot 1 + (-2) \cdot 0 + 1 \cdot 0 + 1 \cdot 0] = 1;$$

$$d_{12}^{(n)} = \frac{1}{12}[2 + (-10) \cdot (-1) + (-4) \cdot (-1) + (-2) \cdot 0 + 1 \cdot 0 + 1 \cdot 1 + (-2) \cdot 1] +$$

$$+ \frac{1}{12}[(-4) \cdot 1 + 1 \cdot 0 + (-2) \cdot 0 + 1 \cdot 0 + 1 \cdot 1] = 1.$$

Finally, one obtains

$$d_{13}^{(n)} = \frac{1}{13}[12 + (-2) \cdot (-1) + (-10) \cdot (-1) + (-4) \cdot 0 + (-2) \cdot 0 + 1 \cdot 1 + 1 \cdot 1] +$$

$$+ \frac{1}{13}[(-2) \cdot 1 + (-4) \cdot 0 + 1 \cdot 0 + (-2) \cdot 0 + 1 \cdot 1 + 1 \cdot 1] = \frac{26}{13} = 2.$$

This confirms that 2 appears as the coefficient of z^{13} in

$$\Psi_{2145}(z) = z^{1185} + z^{1184} + z^{1183} - z^{1180} - z^{1179} - z^{1178} - z^{1174} - z^{1173} - 2z^{1172} + \cdots$$

$$+ 3z^{1152} + \cdots - 4z^{1141} + \cdots + 4z^{44} + \cdots - 3z^{33} + \cdots +$$

$$+ z^{14} + 2z^{13} + z^{12} + z^{11} + z^7 + z^6 + z^5 - z^2 - z - 1.$$

6. Conclusions

In this paper, we have studied properties of the coefficients of inverse cyclotomic polynomials, for which we have provided two explicit formulae, which involve the calculation of partitions, and a recursive formula (Theorem 6). The practicality of the latter approach was illustrated in Section 5 for some ternary and quaternary integers.

In future works, we aim to study the computational complexity of Formula (19) and to express the results in matrix language as has been calculated for polynomial sequences [23]. We also plan to explore practical applications, such as, for example, regarding difference equations [24].

Author Contributions: Conceptualizatio, D.A. and O.B.; methodology, D.A. and O.B.; software, O.B.; validation, D.A. and O.B.; formal analysis, D.A. and O.B.; investigation, D.A. and O.B.; resources, D.A. and O.B.; data curation, O.B.; writing—original draft preparation, D.A. and O.B.; writing—review and editing, D.A. and O.B.; project administration, D.A. and O.B. All authors have read and agreed to the published version of the manuscript.

Funding: This research received no funding.

Data Availability Statement: The calculations have been implemented in Matlab and Maple.

Acknowledgments: The authors are grateful to George-Cătălin Țurcaș for their helpful discussions and comments during the preparation of this work.

Conflicts of Interest: The authors declare no conflict of interest.

References

1. Bachman, G. *On the Coefficients of Cyclotomic Polynomials*; American Mathematical Society: Providence, RI, USA 1993; Volume 106.
2. Grytezuk, A.; Tropak, B. A numerical method for the determination of the cyclotomic polynomial coefficients. In *Computational Number Theory*; Pethö, A., Pohst, M.E., Williams, H.C., Zimmer, H.G., Eds.; De Gruyter: Berlin, Germany, 1991; pp. 15–20.
3. Lehmer, D.H. Some properties of the cyclotomic polynomial. *J. Math. Anal. Appl.* **1966**, *42*, 105–117. [CrossRef]
4. Sanna, C. A survey on coefficients of cyclotomic polynomials. *Expo. Math.* **2022**, *40*, 469–494. [CrossRef]
5. Andrica, D.; Bagdasar, O. On cyclotomic polynomial coefficients. *Malays. J. Math. Sci.* 2020, *14*, 389–402.
6. Andrica, D.; Bagdasar, O.; Țurcaș, G.-C. *Topics on Discrete Mathematics and Combinatorics*; Cluj University Press: Cluj, Romania, 2023; 318p.
7. Moree, P. Inverse cyclotomic polynomials. *J. Number Theory* **2009**, *129*, 667–680. [CrossRef]
8. Andrica, D.; Bagdasar, O. *Some Remarks on the Coefficients of Cyclotomic Polynomials*; Guàrdia, J., Minculete, M., Savin, D., Vela, M., Zekhnini, A., Eds.; Springer: Berlin/Heidelberg, Germany, 2023.
9. Hardy, G.H.; Wright, E.M. *An Introduction to the Theory of Numbers*, 5th ed.; Oxford University Press: Oxford, UK, 1979.
10. Hardy, G.H.; Seshu Aiyar, P.V.; Wilson, B.M. (Eds.) *Collected Papers of Srinivasa Ramanujan*; Cambridge University Press: Cambridge, UK, 2016; 355p.
11. Dresden, G.P. On the middle coefficient of a cyclotomic polynomial. *Am. Math. Mon.* **2004**, *111*, 531–533. [CrossRef]
12. Erdös, P.; Vaughan, R.C. Bounds for r-th coefficients of cyclotomic polynomials. *J. Lond. Math. Soc.* **1974**, *8*, 393–400. [CrossRef]
13. Ji, C.G.; Li, W.P. Values of coefficients of cyclotomic polynomials. *Discret. Math.* **2008**, *308*, 5860–5863. [CrossRef]
14. Lehmer, E. On the magnitude of the coefficients of the cyclotomic polynomial. *Bull. Am. Math. Soc.* **1936**, *42*, 389–392. [CrossRef]
15. Suzuki, J. On coefficients of cyclotomic polynomials. *Proc. Jpn. Acad. Ser. A Math. Sci.* **1987**, *63*, 279–280. [CrossRef]
16. Carneiro, E.; Milinovich, M.B.; Soundararajan, K. Fourier optimization and prime gaps. *Comment. Math. Helv.* **2019**, *94*, 533–568. [CrossRef] [PubMed]
17. Visser, M. Variants on Andrica's Conjecture with and without the Riemann Hypothesis. *Mathematics* **2018**, *6*, 289. [CrossRef]
18. Visser, M. Strong version of Andrica's conjecture. *Int. Math. Forum* **2019**, *14*, 181–188. [CrossRef]
19. Kosyak, A.; Moree, P.; Sofos, E.; Zhang, B. Cyclotomic polynomials with prescribed height and prime number theory. *Mathematika* **2021**, *67*, 214–234. [CrossRef]
20. Endo, M. On the coefficients of the cyclotomic polynomials. *Comment. Math. Univ. Sancti Pauli* **1974**, *23*, 121–126.
21. Bloom, D.M. On the coefficients of the cyclotomic polynomials. *Am. Math. Mon.* **1968**, *75*, 372–377. [CrossRef]
22. Erdös, P. On the coefficients of the cyclotomic polynomial. *Bull. Am. Math. Soc.* **1946**, *52*, 179–184. [CrossRef]
23. Luzón, A.; Morón, M.A. Recurrence relations for polynomial sequences via Riordan matrices. *Linear Algebra Its Appl.* **2010**, *433*, 1422–1446. [CrossRef]
24. Lyapin, A.P.; Akhtamova, S.S. Recurrence relations for the sections of the generating series of the solution to the multidimensional difference equation. *Vestn. Udmurtsk. Univ. Mat. Mekh.* **2021**, *31*, 414–423. [CrossRef]

Disclaimer/Publisher's Note: The statements, opinions and data contained in all publications are solely those of the individual author(s) and contributor(s) and not of MDPI and/or the editor(s). MDPI and/or the editor(s) disclaim responsibility for any injury to people or property resulting from any ideas, methods, instructions or products referred to in the content.

Article

On Indices of Septic Number Fields Defined by Trinomials $x^7 + ax + b$

Lhoussain El Fadil

Department of Mathematics, Faculty of Sciences Dhar El Mahraz-Fes, Sidi Mohamed Ben Abdellah University, Fez P.O. Box 1796, Morocco; lhoussain.elfadil@usmba.ac.ma

Abstract: Let K be a septic number field generated by a root, α, of an irreducible trinomial, $x^7 + ax + b \in \mathbb{Z}[x]$. In this paper, for every prime integer, p, we calculate $\nu_p(i(K))$; the highest power of p dividing the index, $i(K)$, of the number field, K. In particular, we calculate the index, $i(K)$. In application, when the index of K is not trivial, then K is not monogenic.

Keywords: power integral bases; theorem of Ore; prime ideal factorization; common index divisor

MSC: 11R04; 11Y40; 11R21

Citation: El Fadil, L. On Indices of Septic Number Fields Defined by Trinomials $x^7 + ax + b$. *Mathematics* 2023, 11, 4441. https://doi.org/10.3390/math11214441

Academic Editors: Diana Savin, Nicusor Minculete and Vincenzo Acciaro

Received: 11 September 2023
Revised: 18 October 2023
Accepted: 24 October 2023
Published: 26 October 2023

Copyright: © 2023 by the authors. Licensee MDPI, Basel, Switzerland. This article is an open access article distributed under the terms and conditions of the Creative Commons Attribution (CC BY) license (https://creativecommons.org/licenses/by/4.0/).

1. Introduction

Let K be a number field of degree n and $\mathbb{Z}_K$ its ring of integers. It is well known that $\mathbb{Z}_K$ is a free abelian group of rank n, and so, for every primitive integral element, $\theta \in \mathbb{Z}_K$, of K, the quotient group, $\mathbb{Z}_K/\mathbb{Z}[\theta]$, is finite. Let $\theta \in \mathbb{Z}_K$ be a primitive element of K and $ind(\theta) = (\mathbb{Z}_K : \mathbb{Z}[\theta])$ the cardinal order of $\mathbb{Z}_K/\mathbb{Z}[\theta]$. The index $ind(\theta)$ is called the index of θ. The index of the number field, K, denoted $i(K)$, is the greatest common divisor of all indices of all integral primitive elements of K. Namely, $i(K) = GCD((\mathbb{Z}_K : \mathbb{Z}[\theta]) \mid K = \mathbb{Q}(\theta)$ and $\theta \in \mathbb{Z}_K)$. A rational prime integer p dividing $i(K)$ is called a prime common index divisor of K. If, for some $\theta \in \mathbb{Z}_K$, $(1, \theta, \ldots, \theta^{n-1})$ is a $\mathbb{Z}$ basis of $\mathbb{Z}_K$, then the number field, K, is said to be monogenic and θ is a generator of a power integral basis of K. Otherwise, the number field, K, is said to be non-monogenic. Remark that, if K is monogenic, then $i(K) = 1$. It follows that, if a number field has a prime common index divisor, then it is non-monogenic. Monogenity of number fields is a classical problem of algebraic number fields, going back to Dedekind, Hasse and Hensel; see for instance [1–3] for the present state of this area. Let $\theta \in \mathbb{Z}_K$ be a primitive element of K, d_K the absolute discriminant of K, and $\triangle(\theta)$ the discriminant of the minimal polynomial of θ over $\mathbb{Q}$. A well-known relation linking the discriminant and the index says that:

$$|\triangle(\theta)| = ind(\theta)^2 \cdot |d_K|$$

(see [3]).

Clearly, $(1, \theta, \ldots, \theta^{n-1})$ is a power integral basis of $\mathbb{Z}_K$ for some primitive element $\theta \in \mathbb{Z}_K$ of K if and only if $ind(\theta) = 1$.

The problem of studying monogenity of a number field and constructing all possible generators of power integral bases have been intensively studied during the last decades, mainly by Gaál, Nakahara, Pohst, and their collaborators (see for instance [4–6]). In 1871, Dedekind gave an example of a number field with a non-trivial index. He considered the cubic number field, K, generated by a root of $x^3 - x^2 - 2x - 8$, and he showed that the rational prime integer 2 splits completely in K ([7], § 5, page 30). In 1930, for every number field, K, of a degree less than 8 and for every prime integer $p \leq n$, Engstrom linked the p-index, $\nu_p(i(K))$, of the number field, K, and the prime ideal factorization of $p\mathbb{Z}_K$ [8]. He gave an an explicit formula linking the value of $\nu_p(i(K))$ and the factorization of $p\mathbb{Z}_K$ into powers of prime ideals of K for every positive rational prime integer $p \leq n$. This motivated Narkiewicz to ask a very important question, stated as problem 22 in Narkiewicz's book ([9], Problem 22), which asks for an explicit formula of the highest power, $\nu_p(i(K))$, for a given rational prime p dividing $i(K)$. In [10], Nakahara characterized the index of abelian biquadratic number fields. Also in [11], Gaál et al. studied the indices of biquadratic number fields. Recently, many authors have focused on monogenity of number fields defined by trinomials. Based on the calculation of the p-index form of K using p-integral bases of K given in [12], Davis and Spearman [13] characterized the index of any quartic number field, K, generated by a root of an irreducible quartic irreducible trinomial, $F(x) = x^4 + ax + b \in \mathbb{Z}[x]$. In [14], based on Newton's polygon techniques, we reformulated Davis' and Spearman's results. In [15], El Fadil and Gaál characterized the index of quartic number fields, K, generated by a root of a quadratic irreducible trinomial of the form $F(x) = x^4 + ax^2 + b \in \mathbb{Z}[x]$. They gave necessary and sufficient conditions on a and b, which characterize when a prime, $p \in \{2, 3\}$, is a common index divisor of K. In [16], for a sextic number field, K, defined by a trinomial, $F(x) = x^6 + ax^3 + b \in \mathbb{Z}[x]$, Gaál calculated all possible generators of power integral bases of K. In [17], we extended Gaál's studies by providing all cases where K is not monogenic. Also in [18], we characterized when a prime integer, $p \in \{2, 3\}$, is a common index divisor of K, where K is a number field defined by an irreducible trinomial, $F(x) = x^5 + ax^2 + b \in \mathbb{Z}[x]$. In [19], for a number field defined by an irreducible trinomial, $F(x) = x^n + ax^m + b \in \mathbb{Z}[x]$, we provided some cases where $i(K)$ is not trivial, and so K is not monogenic. In this paper, for a septic number field generated by a root of an irreducible trinomial, $F(x) = x^7 + ax + b \in \mathbb{Z}[x]$, and for every prime integer, p, we calculate $\nu_p(i(K))$, the highest power of p dividing the index $i(K)$ of the septic field, K. Our study key is based on prime ideal factorization in number fields, which is carried out in [20,21] and in the thesis of Montes (1999). The author warmly thanks Professor Enric Nart who provided him with a copy of Montes' thesis.

2. Main Results

Let K be a septic number field generated by a root, α, of an irreducible trinomial, $F(x) = x^7 + ax + b \in \mathbb{Z}[x]$. Without loss of generality, we can assume that for every rational prime integer, p, $\nu_p(a) \leq 5$ or $\nu_p(b) \leq 6$. Let $a \in \mathbb{Z}$ be a rational integer and a prime integer, p. Along this paper, let $a_p = \dfrac{a}{p^{\nu_p(a)}}$.

Our first main result characterizes when is $\mathbb{Z}[\alpha]$ the ring of integers of K?

Theorem 1. *The ring, $\mathbb{Z}[\alpha]$, is the ring of integers of K if and only if every prime integer, p, satisfies one of the following conditions:*

1. *If $p|a$ and $p|b$, then $\nu_p(b) = 1$.*
2. *If $p = 2$, p divides b and does not divide a, then $(a, b) \in \{(1, 0), (3, 2)\} \pmod 4$.*
3. *If $p = 3$, p divides b and $a \equiv -1 \pmod 3$, then $(a, b) \in \{(2, 0), (8, 3), (8, 6)\} \pmod 9$.*
4. *If $p = 3$, p divides b and $a \equiv 1 \pmod 3$, then $(a, b) \not\equiv (1, 0) \pmod 9$.*
5. *If $p = 7$, p divides a and does not divide b, then $\nu_7(1 - a - b^6) = 1$.*
6. *If $p \notin \{2, 3, 7\}$, p does not divide both a and b, then $\nu_p(7^7 b^6 + 6^6 a^7) \leq 1$.*

The following is an example of a monogenic septic number field defined by a non-monogenic irreducible trinomial.

Example 1. *Let K be the number field generated by a root, α, of $F(x) = x^7 + 16x + 16 \in \mathbb{Z}[x]$. Then $F(x)$ is irreducible over $\mathbb{Q}$, which is a non-monogenic polynomial, and K is a monogenic number field.*

Indeed, since $\triangle(F) = -2^{24} \cdot 977 \cdot 1607$ is the discriminant of $F(x)$, and $\overline{F(x)} = x^7$ in $\mathbb{F}_2[x]$, then according to the notations of Section 3, let $\phi = x$ and $N_\phi(F)$ be the ϕ-Newton polygon of $F(x)$ with respect to $p = 2$. Then, $N_\phi(F) = S$ has a single side of degree 1. Thus by Remark 2 (2) of [22], $F(x)$ is irreducible over $\mathbb{Q}$. Let θ be a root of $F(x)$. Since the height $h(S) = 4$, by Theorem 5, $\nu_2(ind(\theta)) \geq ind_\phi(F) = 9$. Therefore, $F(x)$ is a non-monogenic polynomial. Let $\alpha = \dfrac{\theta^2}{2}$. Then $G(x) = x^7 + 4x^4 + 4x - 2$ is the minimal polynomial of α over $\mathbb{Q}$. So α is a primitive integral element of K. Therefore, in order to show that $\mathbb{Z}_K = \mathbb{Z}[\alpha]$, we need to show that $\nu_2(ind(\alpha)) = 0$. Since $\triangle(F) = -2^6 \cdot 977 \cdot 1607$ is the discriminant of $G(x)$, then thanks to the formula

$$|\triangle(\theta)| = ind(\theta)^2 \cdot |d_K|,$$

the unique prime candidate to divide $ind(\alpha)$ is 2. Let $N_\phi(G)$ be the ϕ-Newton polygon of $G(x)$ with respect to $p = 2$. Then $N_\phi(G) = T$ has a single side of height 1, by Theorem 6, $\nu_2(ind(\alpha)) = 0$. Thus K is monogenic and α generates a power integral basis of K.

For every $(a, b) \in \mathbb{Z}^2$, such that $x^7 + ax + b$ is irreducible over $\mathbb{Q}$, let $\triangle = -(6^6 a^7 + 7^7 b^6)$ be the discriminant of $F(x)$. Let p be a prime integer and $\triangle_p = \dfrac{\triangle}{p^{\nu_p(\triangle)}}$. In the remainder of this section, for every prime integer, p, and for every value of a and b, we calculate $\nu_p(i(K))$.

Theorem 2. *The following table provides the value of $\nu_2(i(K))$.*

conditions	$\nu_2(i(K))$
$a \equiv 28 \pmod{32}$ and $b \equiv 0 \pmod{32}$	1
$a \equiv 112 \pmod{128}$ and $b \equiv 0 \pmod{128}$	1
$a \equiv 1 \pmod{8}$ and $b \equiv 2 \pmod 4$ $\nu_2(\triangle)$ even and $\triangle_2 \equiv 3 \pmod 4$	1
$a \equiv 3 \pmod 8$ and $b \equiv 4 \pmod 8$	1
$a \equiv 3 \pmod 4$ and $b \equiv 0 \pmod 8$	3
$(a, b) \in \{(5, 2), (5, 6), (13, 2), (13, 14)\} \pmod{16}$	1
Otherwise	0

Theorem 3. *The following table provides the value of $\nu_3(i(K))$.*

conditions	$\nu_3(i(K))$
$a \equiv 5 \pmod 9$ and $b \in \{3, 6\} \pmod 9$	1
$a \equiv 8 \pmod 9$ and $b \equiv 0 \pmod 9$	2
$a \equiv 2 \pmod 9$ and $b \in \{3, 6\} \pmod 9$ $\nu_3(\triangle) = 2k$ and $k \geq 5$	1
$a \equiv 2 \pmod 9$ and $b \in \{3, 6\} \pmod 9$ $\nu_3(\triangle) = 2k + 1$, $k \geq 5$ and $\triangle_3 \equiv 1 \pmod 3$	2
Otherwise	0

Theorem 4. *Let $p \geq 5$ be a prime integer and $(a, b) \in \mathbb{Z}^2$, such that $F(x) = x^7 + ax + b$ is irreducible over $\mathbb{Q}$. Let K be the number field generated by a root, α, of $F(x)$. Then p does not divide $i(K)$.*

Corollary 1. *Let $(a, b) \in \mathbb{Z}^2$, such that $F(x) = x^7 + ax + b$ is an irreducible polynomial over $\mathbb{Q}$. Then $i(K) \in \{1, 2, 3, 6, 8, 9, 18, 24, 72\}$.*

Remark 1.

(1) The field K can be non monogenic even if the index $i(K) = 1$.
(2) The unique method that characterises the monogenity of K is to calculate the solutions of the index form equation of K (see for instance [3,23]).

3. A Short Introduction to Newton's Polygon Techniques Applied on Prime Ideal Factorization

For a number field, K, generated by a root of a monic irreducible polynomial, $F(x) \in \mathbb{Q}[x]$, and for every prime integer, p, in 1894, Hensel developed a powerful technique by establishing a one–one correspondence between maximal ideals of $\mathbb{Z}_K$ containing p and monic irreducible factors of $F(x)$ with a coefficient in $\mathbb{Q}_p$. For every prime ideal corresponding to any irreducible factor, the ramification index and the residue degree together are the same as those of the local field defined by the associated irreducible factor [24]. Since then, to factorize $p\mathbb{Z}_K$, one needs to factorize $F(x)$ in $\mathbb{Q}_p[x]$. Newton's polygon techniques can be used to refine the factorization of $F(x)$. We have introduced the corresponding concepts in several former papers. Here, we only give a brief introduction, which makes our proofs understandable. For a detailed description, we refer to Ore's Paper [25] and Guardia, Montes, and Nart's paper [26]. For every prime integer, p, let ν_p be the p-adic valuation of $\mathbb{Q}_p$ and $\mathbb{Z}_p$ the ring of p-adic integers. Let $F(x) \in \mathbb{Z}_p[x]$ be a monic polynomial and $\phi \in \mathbb{Z}_p[x]$ a monic lift of an irreducible factor of $\overline{F(x)}$ modulo p. Let $F(x) = a_0(x) + a_1(x)\phi(x) + \cdots + a_n(x)\phi(x)^l$ be the ϕ-expansion of $F(x)$, $N_\phi(F)$ the ϕ-Newton polygon of $F(x)$, and $N_\phi^+(F)$ its principal part. Let $\mathbb{F}_\phi$ be the field $\mathbb{F}_p[x]/(\overline{\phi})$. For every side, S, of $N_\phi^+(F)$ with length l and initial point (s, u_s), for every $i = 0, \ldots, l$, let $c_i \in \mathbb{F}_\phi$ be the residue coefficient, defined as follows:

$$c_i = \begin{cases} 0, & \text{if } (s+i, u_{s+i}) \text{ lies strictly above } S, \\ \left(\dfrac{a_{s+i}(x)}{p^{u_{s+i}}}\right) \mod (p, \phi(x)), & \text{if } (s+i, u_{s+i}) \text{ lies on } S. \end{cases}$$

Let $-\lambda = -h/e$ be the slope of S, where h and e are two positive coprime integers. Then $d = l/e$ is the degree of S. Let $R_1(F)(y) = t_d y^d + t_{d-1} y^{d-1} + \cdots + t_1 y + t_0 \in \mathbb{F}_\phi[y]$ be the residual polynomial of $F(x)$ attached to the side S, where for every $i = 0, \ldots, d$, $t_i = c_{ie}$. If $R_1(F)(y)$ is square free for each side of the polygon, $N_\phi^+(F)$, then we say that $F(x)$ is ϕ-regular.

Let $\overline{F(x)} = \prod_{i=1}^{r} \overline{\phi_i}^{l_i}$ be the factorization of $F(x)$ into powers of monic irreducible coprime polynomials over $\mathbb{F}_p$, and we say that the polynomial $F(x)$ is p-regular if $F(x)$ is a ϕ_i-regular polynomial with respect to p for every $i = 1, \ldots, r$. Let $N_{\phi_i}^+(F) = S_{i1} + \cdots + S_{ir_i}$ be the ϕ_i-principal Newton polygon of $F(x)$ with respect to p. For every $j = 1, \ldots, r_i$, let $R_{1_{ij}}(F)(y) = \prod_{s=1}^{s_{ij}} \psi_{ijs}^{a_{ijs}}(y)$ be the factorization of $R_{1_{ij}}(F)(y)$ in $\mathbb{F}_{\phi_i}[y]$, where $R_{1_{ij}}(F)(y)$ is the residual polynomial of $F(x)$ attached to the side S_{ij}. Then we have the following theorem of index of Ore:

Theorem 5 (Theorems 1.7 and 1.9 of [12]).

1.
$$\nu_p((\mathbb{Z}_K : \mathbb{Z}[\alpha])) \geq \sum_{i=1}^{r} \text{ind}_{\phi_i}(F).$$

The equality holds if $F(x)$ is p-regular.

2. If $F(x)$ is p-regular, then
$$p\mathbb{Z}_K = \prod_{i=1}^{r} \prod_{j=1}^{t_i} \prod_{s=1}^{s_{ij}} \mathfrak{p}_{ijs}^{e_{ij}},$$

where $\mathfrak{p}_{ijs}$ is a prime ideal of $\mathbb{Z}_K$ lying above p, e_{ij} is the smallest positive integer satisfying $e_{ij}\lambda_{ij} \in \mathbb{Z}$, and the residue degree of $\mathfrak{p}_{ijs}$ over p is given by $f_{ijs} = \deg(\phi_i) \times \deg(\psi_{ijs})$ for every (i, j, s).

The Dedekind's criterion can be reformulated as follows:

Theorem 6 (Theorem 1.1 of [27]). *Let $\overline{F(x)} = \prod_{i=1}^{r} \overline{\phi_i}^{l_i}$ be the factorization of $F(x)$ into powers of monic irreducible coprime polynomials over $\mathbb{F}_p$. For every $i = 1, \ldots, r$, let $R_i(x)$ be the remainder of the Euclidean division of $F(x)$ by $\phi_i(x)$. Then $\nu_p(ind(\alpha)) = 0$ if and only if $l_i = 1$ or $\nu_p(R_i(x)) = 1$ for every $i = 1, \ldots, r$.*

When the theorem of Ore fails, that is, $F(x)$ is not p-regular, then in order to complete the factorization of $F(x)$, Guardia, Montes, and Nart introduced the notion of *higher order Newton's polygons*. Analogous to the first order, for each order, r, the authors of [26] introduced the valuation, ω_r, of order r, the key polynomial, $\phi_r(x)$, of such a valuation, $N_r(F)$ the Newton polygon of any polynomial, $F(x)$, with respect to ω_r and $\phi_r(x)$, and for every side of $N_r(F)$ the residual polynomial $R_r(F)$, and the index of $F(x)$ in order r. For more details, we refer to [26].

4. Proofs of Our Main Results

Proof of Theorem 1.

1. If p divides a and b, then, by Theorem 6, p does not divide $(\mathbb{Z}_K : \mathbb{Z}[\alpha])$ if and only if $\nu_p(b) = 1$.
2. For $p = 2$, 2 divides b and does not divide a, we have $\overline{F(x)} = x(x-1)^2(x^2+x+1)^2$. Let $\phi_1 = x - 1$ and $\phi_2 = x^2 + x + 1$. Since $F(x) = \cdots - (4x-2)\phi_2 + (a+1)x + b$ and $F(x) = \cdots + (a+7)\phi_1 + (a+1+b)$, by Theorem 6, 2 does not divide $(\mathbb{Z}_K : \mathbb{Z}[\alpha])$ if and only if $\nu_2(b+a+1) = 1$ and $\nu_2((a+1)x+b) = 1$, which means $b \equiv 1 - a \pmod{4}$ and $a \equiv 1 \pmod 4$ or $b \equiv 2 \pmod 4$. That is, $(a, b) \in \{(1, 0), (3, 2)\} \pmod 4$.
3. For $p = 3$, 3 divides b and $a \equiv 1 \pmod 3$, we have $\overline{F(x)} = x(x^2+1)^3$. Let $\phi = x^2 + 1$. Since $F(x) = x\phi^3 - 3x\phi^2 + 3x\phi + (a-1)x + b$, by Theorem 6, 3 does not divide $(\mathbb{Z}_K : \mathbb{Z}[\alpha])$ if and only if $\nu_3((a-1)x + b) = 1$, which means that $a \not\equiv 1 \pmod 9$ or $b \not\equiv 0 \pmod 9$. That is, $(a, b) \not\equiv (1, 0) \pmod 9$.
4. For $p = 3$, 3 divides b and $a \equiv -1 \pmod 3$, we have $\overline{F(x)} = x(x-1)^3(x+1)^2$. Let $\phi_1 = x - 1$ and $\phi_2 = x + 1$. Since $F(x) = \phi_1^7 + 7\phi_1^6 + 21\phi_1^5 + 35\phi_1^4 + 35\phi_1^3 + 21\phi_1^2 + (a+7)\phi_1 + (a+1+b)$ and $F(x) = \phi_2^7 - 7\phi_2^6 + 21\phi_2^5 - 35\phi_2^4 + 35\phi_2^3 - 21\phi_2^2 + (a+7)\phi_2 + (b-a-1)$, by Theorem 6, 3 does not divide $(\mathbb{Z}_K : \mathbb{Z}[\alpha])$ if and only if $\nu_2(a+1+b) = 1$ and $\nu_3(b-a-1) = 1$. That is, $(a, b) \in \{(2, 0), (8, 3), (8, 6)\} \pmod 9$.
5. For $p = 7$, if 7 divides a and 7 does not divide b, then $\overline{F(x)} = (x+b)^7$. Let $\phi = x + b$. Then $F(x) = \phi^7 - 7b\phi^6 + 21b^2\phi^5 - 35b^3\phi^4 + 35b^4\phi^3 - 21b^5\phi^2 + (a+7b^6)\phi + (b - ab - b^7)$, by Theorem 6, 7 does not divide $(\mathbb{Z}_K : \mathbb{Z}[\alpha])$ if and only if $\nu_7(1 - a - b^6) = 1$.
6. For $p \notin \{2, 3, 7\}$ such that p does not divide both a and b, if p^2 does not divide $6^6 a^7 + 7^7 b^6$, then, by the formula $\triangle = (\mathbb{Z}_K : \mathbb{Z}[\alpha])^2 d_K$, p does not divide $(\mathbb{Z}_K : \mathbb{Z}[\alpha])$. If p^2 divides $6^6 a^7 + 7^7 b^6$, then let t be an integer such that $6at \equiv -7b \pmod{p^2}$. Then $(6a)^6 F'(t) = 7(-7b)^6 + 6^6 a^7 \equiv 0 \pmod{p^2}$ and $(6a)^7 F(t) \equiv 0 \pmod{p^2}$. Thus $(x - t)^2$ divides $\overline{F(x)}$ in $\mathbb{F}_p[x]$. As $F(t)$ is the remainder of the Euclidean division of $F(x)$ by $x - t$, by Theorem 6, p divides the index $(\mathbb{Z}_K : \mathbb{Z}[\alpha])$.

The proofs of Theorems 2 and 3 are based on Engstrom's results [28]. □

Proof of Theorem 2. By virtue of Engstrom's results [28], the proof is achieved if we provide the factorization of $2\mathbb{Z}_K$ into powers of prime ideals of $\mathbb{Z}_K$. Based on Theorem 1, we deal with the cases: $2 | a$ and $4 | b$ or $(a, b) \in \{(1, 2), (3, 0)\} \pmod 4$.

1. If 2 divides a and 4 divides b, then, for $\phi = x$, we have $\overline{F(x)} = \phi^7$ in $\mathbb{F}_2[x]$.
   (a) If $N_\phi(F) = S$ has a single side, that is, $\nu_2(a) \geq \nu_2(b)$, then the side, S, is of degree 1. Thus there is a unique prime ideal of $\mathbb{Z}_K$ lying above 2.
   (b) If $N_\phi(F) = S_1 + S_2$ has two sides joining $(0, \nu_2(b))$, $(1, \nu_2(a))$, and $(7, 0)$, that is, $\nu_2(a) + 1 \leq \nu_2(b)$, then S_1 is of degree 1, and so it provides a unique prime ideal of $\mathbb{Z}_K$ lying above 2 with residue degree 1. Let d be the degree of S_2.

i. If $v_2(a) \notin \{2,3,4\}$, then S_2 is of degree 1, and so there are exactly two prime ideals of $\mathbb{Z}_K$ lying above 2 with residue degree 1 each.

ii. If $v_2(a) = 2$, then the slope of S_2 is $\dfrac{-1}{3}$ and $R_1(F)(y) = (y+1)^2$ is the residual polynomial of $F(x)$ attached to S_2. Thus, we have to use second order Newton polygon techniques. Let ω_2 be the valuation of a second order Newton polygon; defined by $\omega_2(P(x)) = \min\{3v_2(p_i) + ih, \beta = 0, \ldots, n\}$ for every non-zero polynomial $P = \sum_{i=0}^{n} p_i x^i$. Let ϕ_2 be the key polynomial of ω_2 and let $N_2(F)$ be the ϕ_2-Newton polygon of $F(x)$ with respect to the valuation ω_2. It follows that:
if $v_2(b) = 3$, then for $\phi_2 = x^3 + 2x + 2$, we have $F(x) = x\phi_2^2 + (4 - 4x - 4x^2)\phi_2 + 8x^2 + (a-4)x + b - 8$. It follows that, if $v_2(a-4) = 3$, then $N_2(F) = T$ has a single side joining $(0,10)$ and $(2,7)$. Thus T is of degree 1, and so S_2 provides a unique prime ideal of $\mathbb{Z}_K$ lying above 2. If $v_2(a-4) \geq 4$ and $v_2(b-8) \geq 4$, then $N_2(F) = T$ has a single side joining $(0,11)$, $(1,9)$, and $(2,7)$, with $R_2(F)(y) = y^2 + y + 1$, which is irreducible over $\mathbb{F}_2 = \mathbb{F}_0$. Thus, S_2 provides a unique prime ideal of $\mathbb{Z}_K$ lying above 2 with residue degree 2. Hence 2 is not a common index divisor of K.
If $v_2(b) \geq 4$ and $v_2(a+4) = 3$, then, for $\phi_2 = x^3 + 2$, we have $F(x) = x\phi_2^2 - 4x\phi_2 + (a+4)x + b$ is the ϕ_2-expansion of $F(x)$, and so $N_2(F) = T$ has a single side joining $(0,10)$ and $(2,7)$. In this case the side T is of degree 1 and S_2 provides a unique prime ideal of $\mathbb{Z}_K$ lying above 2. If $v_2(b) = 4$ and $v_2(a+4) \geq 4$, then for $\phi_2 = x^3 + 2$, $N_2(F) = T$ has a single side joining $(0,12)$ and $(2,7)$. Thus T is of degree 1, and so S_2 provides a unique prime ideal of $\mathbb{Z}_K$ lying above 2. If $v_2(b) \geq 5$ and $v_2(a+4) = 4$, then, for $\phi_2 = x^3 + 2$, we have $F(x) = x\phi_2^2 - 4x\phi_2 + (a+4)x + b$ as the ϕ_2-expansion of $F(x)$, and $N_2(F) = T$ has a single side joining $(0,13)$, $(1,10)$, and $(2,7)$. So, T is of degree 2 with attached residual polynomial $R_2(F) = y^2 + y + 1$ irreducible over $\mathbb{F}_2 = \mathbb{F}_0$. Thus, S_2 provides a unique prime ideal of $\mathbb{Z}_K$ lying above 2 with residue degree 2.
If $v_2(b) \geq 5$ and $v_2(a+4) \geq 5$, then, for $\phi_2 = x^3 + 2$, $N_2(F) = T_1 + T_2$ has two sides joining $(0,v)$, $(1,10)$, and $(2,7)$ with $v \geq 15$. So, each T_i has degree 1, and so S_2 provides two prime ideals of $\mathbb{Z}_K$ lying above 2 with residue degree 1 each. As S_1 provides a prime ideal of $\mathbb{Z}_K$ lying above 2 with residue degree 1, we conclude that there are three prime ideals of $\mathbb{Z}_K$ lying above 2 with residue degree 1 each, and so 2 is a common index divisor of K. In this last case, $2\mathbb{Z}_K = \mathfrak{p}_{111}\mathfrak{p}_{121}^3\mathfrak{p}_{131}^3$ with residue degree 1 each prime ideal factor. Based on Engstrom's result, we conclude that $v_2(i(K)) = 1$.

iii. For $v_2(a) = 3$, we have $R_1(F)(y) = y^3 + 1 = (y^2 + y + 1)(y + 1)$ as the residual polynomial of $F(x)$ attached to T_1. Thus, T_1 provides a unique prime ideal of $\mathbb{Z}_K$ lying above 2, with residue degree 1 and a unique prime ideal of $\mathbb{Z}_K$ lying above 2 with residue degree 2. Thus, $v_2(i(K)) = 0$.

iv. The case $v_2(a) = 4$ is similar to the case $v_2(a) = 2$. In this case, $v_2(i(K)) \geq 1$ if and only if $v_2(b) \geq 7$ and $v_2(a+16) \geq 7$. In this case, $2\mathbb{Z}_K = \mathfrak{p}_{111}\mathfrak{p}_{121}^3\mathfrak{p}_{131}^3$ with residue degree 1 each factor. Based on Engstrom's result, we conclude that $v_2(i(K)) = 1$.

2. $(a,b) \in \{(1,2),(3,0)\} \pmod 4$. In this case, $\overline{F(x)} = x(x-1)^2(x^2+x+1)^2$ modulo 2. Let $\phi = x-1$, $g(x) = x^2+x+1$, $F(x) = \cdots - 21\phi^2 + (7+a)\phi + (b+a+1)$, and $F(x) = (x-3)g^3 + (5+3x)g^2 - (4x+2)g + (a+1)x + b$. Since x provides a unique

prime ideal of $\mathbb{Z}_K$ lying above 2, we conclude that 2 is a common index divisor of K if and only if ϕ provides two prime ideals of $\mathbb{Z}_K$ lying above 2 of degree 1 each or ϕ provides a unique prime ideal of $\mathbb{Z}_K$ lying above 2 of degree 2, and g provides at least one prime ideal of $\mathbb{Z}_K$ lying above 2 of degree 2 or also g provides two prime ideals of $\mathbb{Z}_K$ lying above 2 of degree 2 each. That is if and only if one of the following conditions holds:

(a) If $a \equiv 1 \pmod 4$ and $b \equiv 2 \pmod 4$, then $v_2(\triangle) \geq 7$ and $N_g^+(F)$ has a single side of height 1, and so g provides a unique prime ideal $\mathfrak{p}_{311}$ of $\mathbb{Z}_K$ lying above 2 with residue degree 2. For $N_\phi^+(F)$, let $u = \dfrac{-7b_2}{3a}$. Then $u \in \mathbb{Z}_2$. Let $F(x+u) = x^7 + \cdots + 21u^5 x^2 + Ax + B$, where $A = 7u^6 + a = \dfrac{-\triangle}{6^6 a^6}$ and $B = u^7 + au + b = \dfrac{b\triangle}{6^7 a^7}$. It follows that $v_2(A) = v_2(B) = v_2(\triangle) - 6$, and so $N_\phi^+(F) = S_1$ has a single side joining $(0, v_2(\triangle) - 6)$ and $(2, 0)$. Thus, if $v_2(\triangle)$ is odd, then ϕ provides a unique prime ideal $\mathfrak{p}_{211}$ of $\mathbb{Z}_K$ lying above 2 with residue degree 1. If $v_2(\triangle) = 2(k+3)$ for some positive integer, k, then let $F(x + u + 2^k) = x^7 + \cdots + 21(u+2^k)^5 x^2 + A_1 x + B_1$, where $A_1 = 7u^6 + a + 3 \cdot 2^{k+1} u^5 + 2^{2k} D = A + 3 \cdot 2^{k+1} u^5 + 2^{2k} D$ and $B_1 = B + A \cdot 2^k + 2^{2k} \cdot 21 u^5 + 2^{3k} H = 2^{2k} (\dfrac{b_2 \triangle_2}{3^7 a^7} + 21 u^5) + 2^{3k} H$ for some $D \in \mathbb{Z}_2$ and $H \in \mathbb{Z}_2$. Thus, $B_1 = 2^{2k}(3 \cdot a \cdot b_2 \triangle_2 + 3 \cdot a \cdot b_2) + 2^{2k+3} L$ for some $L \in \mathbb{Z}_2$. Hence if $k \geq 2$, then $v_2(A_1) = k+1$ and $v_2(B_1) \geq 2k+1$. More precisely, if $\triangle_2 \equiv 1 \pmod 4$, then $v_2(B_1) = 2k+1$, and so ϕ provides a unique prime ideal $\mathfrak{p}_{211}$ of $\mathbb{Z}_K$ lying above 2 with residue degree 1. If $\triangle_2 \equiv 3 \pmod 4$, then $v_2(B_1) \geq 2k+2$. It follows that, if $v_2(B_1) = 2k+2$, and so ϕ provides a unique prime ideal $\mathfrak{p}_{211}$ of $\mathbb{Z}_K$ lying above 2 with residue degree 2. If $v_2(B_1) \geq 2k+3$, then $v_2(B_1) \geq 2k+3$, and so ϕ provides two prime ideals of $\mathbb{Z}_K$ lying above 2 with residue degree 1 each. In these last two cases, we have 2 divides $i(K)$ and $v_2(i(K)) = 1$. For $k = 1$, we have $v_2(\triangle) = 8$ and $a \equiv 5 \pmod 8$. In this case, $\overline{F(x)} = x(x-1)^2(x^2+x+1)^2$ modulo 2. Let $\phi = x - 1$, $g(x) = x^2 + x + 1$, $F(x) = \cdots - 21\phi^2 + (7+a)\phi + (b+a+1)$, and $F(x) = (x-3)g^3 + (5+3x)g^2 - (4x+2)g + (a+1)x + b$. Since x provides a unique prime ideal of of $\mathbb{Z}_K$ lying above 2 with residue degree 1 and g provides a unique prime ideal of of $\mathbb{Z}_K$ lying above 2 with residue degree 2, we conclude that $v_2(i(K)) \geq 1$ if and only if ϕ provides a unique prime ideal of of $\mathbb{Z}_K$ lying above 2 with residue degree 2 or ϕ provides two distinct prime ideals of of $\mathbb{Z}_K$ lying above 2 with residue degree 1 each. If $(a, b) \in \{(5, 10), (13, 2)\} \pmod{16}$, then ϕ provides a unique prime ideal of $\mathbb{Z}_K$ lying above 2 with residue degree 2, and so $v_2(i(K)) = 1$. If $(a, b) \in \{(5, 10), (13, 10)\} \pmod{16}$, then ϕ provides a unique prime ideal of $\mathbb{Z}_K$ lying above 2 with residue degree 1, and so $v_2(i(K)) = 0$. For $(a, b) \in \{(5, 6), (5, 14), (13, 6), (13, 14)\} \pmod{16}$, let us replace ϕ by $\phi' = x - 3$ and consider the ϕ'-Newton polygon of $F(x)$ with respect to v_2. It follows that, if $(a, b) \in \{(5, 6), (13, 14)\} \pmod{16}$, then ϕ' provides two prime ideals of $\mathbb{Z}_K$ lying above 2 with residue degree 1 each, and so $v_2(i(K)) = 1$. If $(a, b) \in \{(5, 14), (13, 6)\} \pmod{16}$, then ϕ' provides a unique prime ideal of $\mathbb{Z}_K$ lying above 2 with residue degree 1, and so $v_2(i(K)) = 0$.

(b) $a \equiv 3 \pmod 4$ and $b \equiv -(a+1) \pmod 8$ because $N_\phi^+(F)$ has two sides.

(c) If $a \equiv 3 \pmod 8$ and $b \equiv 0 \pmod 8$, then ϕ provides a unique prime ideal of $\mathbb{Z}_K$ lying above 2 with residue degree 2 and g provides two prime ideals of $\mathbb{Z}_K$ lying above 2 with residue degree 2 each because $N_g^+(F)$ has a single side of degree 2 with $(1+x)y^2 + y + x = (x+1)(y-1)(y-x)$ its attached residual polynomial of $F(x)$. In this case, $2\mathbb{Z}_K = \mathfrak{p}_{111}\mathfrak{p}_{211}\mathfrak{p}_{311}\mathfrak{p}_{312}$ with residue degrees $f_{111} = 1$ and $f_{211} = f_{311} = f_{312} = 2$, and so $v_2(i(K)) = 3$.

(d) $a \equiv 7 \pmod{8}$ and $b \equiv 0 \pmod{8}$. In this case, ϕ provides a unique prime ideal of $\mathbb{Z}_K$ lying above 2 with residue degree 2 and $N_g^+(F)$ has two sides. More precisely, $2\mathbb{Z}_K = \mathfrak{p}_{111}\mathfrak{p}_{211}\mathfrak{p}_{311}\mathfrak{p}_{321}$ with residue degrees $f_{111} = 1$ and $f_{211} = f_{311} = f_{312} = 2$, and so $\nu_2(i(K)) = 3$.

(e) If $a \equiv 5 \pmod{8}$ and $b \equiv -(a+1) \pmod{16}$ because if $b \equiv -(a+1) \pmod{32}$, then $N_\phi^+(F)$ has two sides, and if $b \equiv -(a+1) + 16 \pmod{32}$, then $N_\phi^+(F)$ has a single side of degree 2, which provides a single prime ideal of $\mathbb{Z}_K$ lying above 2 with residue degree 2 and $N_g^+(F)$ has a single side of degree 1. Thus, there are 2 prime ideals of $\mathbb{Z}_K$ lying above 2 with residue degree 2 each.

(f) If $a \equiv 5 \pmod{8}$ and $\nu_2(b + (a+1)) = 2$, then $\nu_2(b - (a+1)) \geq 3$. If $\nu_2(b - (a+1)) = 3$, then, for $\phi = x + 1$, $N_\phi^+(F)$ has a single side of degree 1. Since $\nu_2(a+1) = 1$, then $N_g^+(F)$ has a single side of height 1. Thus, there are two prime ideals of $\mathbb{Z}_K$ lying above 2 with residue degree 1 each and one prime ideal with residue degree 2. If $\nu_2(b - (a+1)) = 4$, then, for $\phi = x + 1$, $N_\phi^+(F)$ has a single side of degree 2, and its attached residual polynomial of F is $R_1(F)(y) = y^2 + y + 1$. Since $b \equiv 6 \pmod{8}$, we conclude that $N_g^+(F)$ has a single side of degree 1, and then there are 2 prime ideals of $\mathbb{Z}_K$ lying above 2 with residue degree 2 each, and so 2 divides $i(K)$. If $\nu_2(b - (a+1)) \geq 5$, then, for $\phi = x + 1$, $N_\phi^+(F)$ has two sides of degree 1 each, and so there are 3 prime ideals of $\mathbb{Z}_K$ lying above 2 with residue degree 1 each, and so 2 divides $i(K)$.

□

Proof of Theorem 3. By virtue of Engstrom's results [28], the proof is achieved if we provide the factorization of $3\mathbb{Z}_K$ into powers of prime ideals of $\mathbb{Z}_K$. Based on Theorem 1, we deal with the cases:

1. $3 \mid a$ and $9 \mid b$.
2. $(a, b) \not\equiv \{(2,0), (8,3), (8,6)\} \pmod{9}$.
3. $(a, b) \equiv (1, 0) \pmod{9}$.

1. $3 \mid a$ and $9 \mid b$, then for $\phi = x$, $\overline{F(x)} = \phi^7$ in $\mathbb{F}_3[x]$. It follows that:

    (a) If $\nu_3(a) \geq \nu_3(b)$, then $N_\phi(F)$ has a single side of degree 1, and so there is a unique prime ideal of $\mathbb{Z}_K$ lying above 3.

    (b) If $\nu_3(a) + 1 \leq \nu_3(b)$, then $N_\phi(F) = S_1 + S_2$ has two sides joining $(0, \nu_3(b))$, $(1, \nu_3(a))$, and $(7, 0)$. Since S_1 is of degree 1, S_1 provides a unique prime ideal of $\mathbb{Z}_K$ lying above 3 with residue degree 1. Thus, $\nu_3(i(K)) \geq 1$ if and only if S_2 provides at least three prime ideals of $\mathbb{Z}_K$ lying above 3, with residue degree 1 each. If $\nu_3(a) \notin \{2, 3, 4\}$, then S_2 is of degree 1, and so S_2 provides exactly one prime ideal of $\mathbb{Z}_K$ lying above 3, with residue degree 1 each. If $\nu_3(a) \in \{2, 4\}$, then S_2 is of degree 2, and so S_2 provides at most two prime ideal of $\mathbb{Z}_K$ lying above 3. Hence 3 is not a common index divisor of K. If $\nu_3(a) = 3$, then S_2 is of degree 3 and its attached residual polynomial of $F(x)$ is $R_1(F)(y) = y^3 + a_3 = (y + a_3)^3$. So, we have to use a second order Newton polygon. Let ω_2 be the valuation of the second order Newton polygon. ω_2 is defined by $\omega_2(P) = \min\{2\nu_3(p_i) + i, i = 0, \ldots, n\}$ for every non-zero polynomial $p = \sum_{i=0}^{n} p_i x^i$ of $\mathbb{Q}_3[x]$. Let $\phi_2 = x^2 + 3a_3$ be a key polynomial of ω_2 and $N_2(F)$ the ϕ_2-Newton polygon of $F(x)$ with respect to ω_2. It follows that: if $a_3 \equiv 1 \pmod{3}$, then, for $\phi_2 = x^2 + 3$, we have $F(x) = x\phi_2^3 - 9x\phi_2^2 + 27x\phi_2 + (a - 27)x + b$ as the ϕ_2-expansion of $F(x)$. We have the following cases:

    i. If $\nu_3(b) = 4$, then $N_2(F) = T$ has a single side joining $(0, 8)$ and $(3, 7)$. Thus, T is of degree 1 and S_2 provides a unique prime ideal of $\mathbb{Z}_K$ lying above 3 with residue degree 1.

ii. If $v_3(b) \geq 5$ and $v_3(a - 27) = 4$, then $N_2(F) = T$ has a single side joining $(0,9)$ and $(3,7)$. Thus, T is of degree 1 and S_2 provides a unique prime ideal of $\mathbb{Z}_K$ lying above 3 with residue degree 1.

iii. If $v_3(b) = 5$ and $v_3(a - 27) \geq 5$, then $N_2(F) = T$ has a single side joining $(0,10)$ and $(3,7)$ and its attached residual polynomial of F is $R_2(F)(y) = xy^3 + xy + b_3$, which is irreducible over $\mathbb{F}_2 = \mathbb{F}_\phi$ because ϕ is of degree 1. Thus, S_2 provides a unique prime ideal of $\mathbb{Z}_K$ lying above 3 with residue degree 3.

iv. If $v_3(b) \geq 6$ and $v_3(a - 27) \geq 5$, then $N_2(F) = T_1 + T_2$ has two sides joining $(0,v)$, $(2,9)$, and $(3,7)$ with $v \geq 11$. Thus, T_1 is of degree 1, T_2 of degree 2, and $R_2(F)(y) = xy^2 + x$ is its attached residual polynomial of $F(x)$, which is irreducible over $\mathbb{F}_2 = \mathbb{F}_\phi$. Thus, S_2 provides a unique prime ideal of $\mathbb{Z}_K$ lying above 3, with residue degree 1 and a unique prime ideal of $\mathbb{Z}_K$ lying above 3 with residue degree 2.

Similarly, for $a_3 \equiv -1 \pmod 3$, let $\phi_2 = x^2 - 3$. Then, $F(x) = x\phi_2^3 + 9x\phi_2^2 + 27x\phi_2 + (a + 27)x + b$ is the ϕ_2-expansion of $F(x)$. Analogous to the case $a_3 \equiv 1 \pmod 3$, in every case 3 does not divide $i(K)$. If $a \equiv 1 \pmod 3$, then $\overline{F(x)} = x(x^2 + 1)^3$ in $\mathbb{F}_3[x]$. So, there is exactly a unique prime ideal of $\mathbb{Z}_K$ lying above 3 with residue degree 1, and the other prime ideals of $\mathbb{Z}_K$ lying above 3 are of residue degrees at least 2 each prime ideal factor. Hence, $v_3(i(K)) = 0$.

(c) If $a \equiv -1 \pmod 3$, then $\overline{F(x)} = x(x-1)^3(x+1)^3$ in $\mathbb{F}_3[x]$. Let $\phi_1 = x - 1$, $\phi_2 = x + 1$, $F(x) = \phi_1^7 + 7\phi_1^6 + 21\phi_1^5 + 35\phi_1^4 + 35\phi_1^3 + 21\phi_1^2 + (7+a)\phi_1 + (b+a+1)$, and $F(x) = \phi_2^7 - 7\phi_2^6 + 21\phi_2^5 - 35\phi_2^4 + 35\phi_2^3 - 21\phi_2^2 + (7+a)\phi_2 + (b - (a+1))$. It follows that:

i. If $a \equiv 8 \pmod 9$ and $b \equiv 0 \pmod 9$, then $v_3(b + (1 + a)) \geq 2$ and $v_3(b - (1 + a)) \geq 2$. Thus, x a provides a unique prime ideal of $\mathbb{Z}_K$ lying above 3 with residue degree 1, and each ϕ_i provides two prime ideals of $\mathbb{Z}_K$ lying above 3 with residue degree 1 each prime ideal factor. In these two cases, $v_3(i(K)) = 2$.

ii. If $a \equiv 5 \pmod 9$ and $b \equiv 3 \pmod 9$, then $v_3(b + (1 + a)) \geq 2$ and $v_3(b - (1 + a)) = 1$. Thus, x and ϕ_2 each provide a unique prime ideal of $\mathbb{Z}_K$ lying above 3 with residue degree 1, and ϕ_1 provides two prime ideals of $\mathbb{Z}_K$ lying above 3 with residue degree 1 each. Similarly, if $a \equiv 5 \pmod 9$ and $b \equiv 6 \pmod 9$, then $v_3(b - (1 + a)) \geq 2$ and $v_3(b + (1 + a)) = 1$. Thus, x and ϕ_1 each provide a unique prime ideal of $\mathbb{Z}_K$ lying above 3 with residue degree 1, and ϕ_2 provides two prime ideals of $\mathbb{Z}_K$ lying above 3 with residue degree 1 each. In these two cases, $v_3(i(K)) = 1$.

iii. If $a \equiv 2 \pmod 9$ and $b \equiv (1+a) \pm 9 \pmod{27}$, then $N_{\phi_2}^+(F)$ has a single side joining $(0,2)$ and $(3,0)$, and $N_{\phi_1}^+(F)$ has a single side joining $(0,1)$ and $(3,0)$. Thus, there are 3 prime ideals of $\mathbb{Z}_K$ lying above 3 with residue degree 1 each, and so $v_3(i(K)) = 0$.

iv. Similarly, if $a \equiv 2 \pmod 9$ and $b \equiv -(1+a) \pm 9 \pmod{27}$, then there are 3 prime ideals of $\mathbb{Z}_K$ lying above 3 with residue degree 1 each, and so $v_3(i(K)) = 0$.

v. If $a \equiv 2 \pmod 9$ and $v_3(b) = 1$, then $v_3(\triangle) \geq 8$. Let $u = \dfrac{-7b_3}{2a}$. Then $u \in \mathbb{Z}_3$. Let $\phi = x - u$ and $F(x + u) = x^7 + \cdots + 35u^4x^3 + 21u^5x^2 + Ax + B$, where $A = 7u^6 + a = \dfrac{-\triangle}{6^6 a^6}$ and $B = u^7 + au + b = \dfrac{b\triangle}{6^7 a^7}$. It follows that $v_3(A) = v_3(B) = v_3(\triangle) - 6$, and so $N_\phi^+(F) = S_1$ has a single side joining $(0, v_3(\triangle) - 6)$ and $(3,0)$. Remark that, since $v_3(b) = 1$ and $v_3(B) \geq 2$, $v_3(-u^7 - au + b) = 1$, and so $(x + u)$ provides a unique prime ideal of $\mathbb{Z}_K$ lying above 3 with residue degree 1. Thus,

$v_3(i(K)) \geq 1$ if and only if ϕ provides at least two prime ideals of $\mathbb{Z}_K$ lying above 3 with residue degree 1 each prime ideal factor.

A. If $v_3(\triangle) = 8$, then $N_\phi^+(F)$ has a single side of degree 1, and so ϕ provides a unique prime ideal of $\mathbb{Z}_K$ lying above 3 with residue degree 1.

B. If $v_3(\triangle) = 9$, then $N_\phi^+(F) = S$ has a single side joining $(0,3)$ and $(3,0)$, with $R_1(F)(y) = -u^4 y^3 + u^5 y^2 + B_3$ its attached residual polynomial of $F(x)$. Since $a \equiv -1 \pmod{3}$ and $B = \frac{b\triangle}{6^7 a^7}$, we have $u \equiv -b_3 \pmod{3}$ and $B_3 \equiv b_3 \triangle_3 \pmod{3}$. Thus, $R_1(F)(y) = -y^3 - b_3 y^2 + b_3 \triangle_3$. Since $R_1(F)(y)$ is square free and $R_1(F)(0) \neq 0$, then $R_1(F)(y)$ has at most one root in $\mathbb{F}_\phi$. Thus, S provides at most a unique prime ideal of $\mathbb{Z}_K$ lying above 3 with residue degree 1. Therefore, $v_3(i(K)) = 0$.

C. If $v_3(\triangle) \geq 10$, then $N_\phi^+(F) = S_1 + S_2$ has two sides joining $(0, v-6)$ and $(3,1)$. It follows that, since S_2 is of degree 1, it provides a unique prime ideal of $\mathbb{Z}_K$ lying above 3 with residue degree 1. Moreover, if $v_3(\triangle)$ is even, then S_1 is of degree 1, and so ϕ provides two prime ideals of $\mathbb{Z}_K$ lying above 3 with residue degree 1 each. In this case, $v_3(i(K)) = 1$. If $v_3(\triangle) = 2(k+3) + 1$, then S_1 is of degree 2, with residual polynomial $R_1(F)(y) = uy^2 + b_3 \triangle_3$. Since $a \equiv -1 \pmod{3}$, we have $2a \equiv 1 \pmod{3}$ and $u \equiv -b_3 \pmod{3}$. Thus, $R_1(F)(y) = -b_3(y^2 - \triangle_3)$. It follows that, if $(\frac{\triangle_3}{3}) = 1$, then $R_1(F)(y)$ has two different factors of degree 1 each, and so S_1 provides two prime ideals of $\mathbb{Z}_K$ lying above 3 with residue degree 1 each. In this case, there are exactly five prime ideals of $\mathbb{Z}_K$ lying above 3 with residue degree 1 each and, according to Engstrom's results, $v_3(i(K)) = 2$. But, if $(\frac{\triangle_3}{3}) = -1$, then $R_1(F)(y)$ is irreducible over $\mathbb{F}_\phi = \mathbb{F}_3$, and so S_1 provides a unique prime ideal of $\mathbb{Z}_K$ lying above 3 with residue degree 2. In this last case, there are exactly three prime ideals of $\mathbb{Z}_K$ lying above 3 with residue degree 1 each, and so $v_3(i(K)) = 0$.

$\square$

Proof of Theorem 4. We start by showing that 5 does not divide $i(K)$ for every integer of a and b, such that $x^7 + ax + b$ is irreducible. By virtue of Engstrom's results [28], the proof is achieved if we provide the factorization of $5\mathbb{Z}_K$ into powers of prime ideals of $\mathbb{Z}_K$. Using the index formula $\triangle = (\mathbb{Z}_K : \mathbb{Z}[\alpha])^2 d_K$, if 5^2 does not divide $\triangle$, then $v_5(i(K)) = 0$. So, we assume that 5^2 divides $\triangle$.

1. So, $6^6 a^7 + 7^7 b^6 \equiv 0 \pmod{5}$. Since $a^5 \equiv a \pmod{5}$ and $b^5 \equiv b \pmod{5}$, then $a^3 \equiv 2b^2 \pmod{5}$, which means $(a, b) \in \{(0,0), (3,1), (2,2), (2,3), (3,4)\} \pmod{5}$. In order to show that $v_5(i(K)) = 0$, it suffices to show that for every value $(a, b) \in \mathbb{Z}^2$, such that $x^7 + ax + b$ is irreducible and $(a, b) \in \{(0,0), (2,1), (3,2), (3,3), (2,34)\} \pmod{5}$, there are at most four prime ideals of $\mathbb{Z}_K$ lying above 5 with residue degree 1, where K is the number field generated by a complex root of $x^7 + ax + b$.

   (a) For $(a, b) \equiv (0, 0) \pmod{5}$, if $v_5(a) \geq v_5(b)$, then $N_\phi(F) = S$ has a single side and it is of degree 1. Thus, there is a unique prime ideal, $\mathfrak{p}$, of $\mathbb{Z}_K$ lying above 5 with residue degree 1. More precisely, $5\mathbb{Z}_K = \mathfrak{p}^7$.
   If $v_5(a) + 1 \leq v_5(b)$, then $N_\phi(F) = S_1 + S_2$ has two sides. More precisely, S_1 is of degree 1. Let d be degree of S_2. Since 6 is the length of S_2, then $d \in \{1, 2, 3\}$. Thus, S_1 provides a unique prime ideal, $\mathfrak{p}$, of $\mathbb{Z}_K$ lying above 5 with residue

(b) For $(a,b) \equiv (3,1) \pmod 5$, since $\overline{F(x)} = (x+4)^2(x+3)(x^4+4x^3+x^2+x+2)$ in $\mathbb{F}_5[x]$, there are at most three prime ideals, $\mathfrak{p}$, of $\mathbb{Z}_K$ lying above 5 with residue degree 1 each.

(c) For $(a,b) \equiv (2,2) \pmod 5$, since $\overline{F(x)} = (x^4+2x^3+4x^2+2x+2)(x+4)(x+2)^2$ in $\mathbb{F}_5[x]$, there are at most three prime ideals, $\mathfrak{p}$, of $\mathbb{Z}_K$ lying above 5 with residue degree 1 each.

(d) For $(a,b) \equiv (2,3) \pmod 5$, since $\overline{F(x)} = (x+1)(x+3)^2(x^4+3x^3+4x^2+3x+2)$ in $\mathbb{F}_5[x]$, there are at most three prime ideals $\mathfrak{p}$ of $\mathbb{Z}_K$ lying above 5 with residue degree 1 each.

(e) For $(a,b) \equiv (3,4) \pmod 5$, since $\overline{F(x)} = (x^4+x^3+x^2+4x+2)(x+1)^2(x+2)$ in $\mathbb{F}_5[x]$, there are at most three prime ideals, $\mathfrak{p}$, of $\mathbb{Z}_K$ lying above 5 with residue degree 1 each.

We conclude that in all cases $\nu_5(i(K)) = 0$.

For $p \geq 7$, since the field K is of degree 7, there are at most 7 prime ideals of $\mathbb{Z}_K$ lying above p. The fact that there at least $p \geq 7$ monic irreducible polynomials of degree f in $\mathbb{F}_p[x]$ for every positive integer $f \in \{1,2,3\}$, we conclude that p does not divide $i(K)$. □

5. Examples

Let $F = x^7 + ax + b \in \mathbb{Z}[x]$ be a monic irreducible polynomial and K a number field generated by a root, α, of $F(x)$. In the following examples, we calculate the index of the field K. First based on Theorem 4, $\nu_p(i(K)) = 0$ for every prime integer $p \geq 5$. Thus, we need only to calculate $\nu_p(i(K))$ for $p = 2,3$.

1. For $a = 6$ and $b = 6$, since $F(x)$ is p-Eisenstein for every $p = 2,3$, we conclude that $F(x)$ is irreducible over $\mathbb{Q}$, and 2 (resp. 3) does not divide $(\mathbb{Z}_K : \mathbb{Z}[\alpha])$. Thus, 2 (resp. 3) does not divide $i(K)$), and so $i(K) = 1$.

2. For $a = 28$ and $b = 32$, since $\overline{F(x)}$ is irreducible over $\mathbb{F}_5$, $F(x)$ is irreducible over $\mathbb{Q}$. By the first item of Theorem 2, we have $\nu_2(i(K)) = 1$. By Theorem 3, $\nu_3(i(K)) = 0$. Thus, $i(K) = 2$.

3. For $a = 3$ and $b = 8$, since $\overline{F(x)}$ is irreducible over $\mathbb{F}_5$, $F(x)$ is irreducible over $\mathbb{Q}$. Again, since $a \equiv 3 \pmod 4$ and $b \equiv 0 \pmod 8$, by Theorem 2, $\nu_2(i(K)) = 3$. By Theorem 3, $\nu_3(i(K)) = 0$. Thus, $i(K) = 8$.

4. For $a = -1$ and $b = 9$, since $\overline{F(x)}$ is irreducible over $\mathbb{F}_2$, $F(x)$ is irreducible over $\mathbb{Q}$. Since $2\mathbb{Z}_K$ is a prime ideal of $\mathbb{Z}_K$, $\nu_2(i(K)) = 0$. Also, since $a \equiv 8 \pmod 9$ and $b \equiv 0 \pmod 9$, by Theorem 3, $\nu_3(i(K)) = 2$. Thus, $i(K) = 9$.

5. For $a = 803$ and $b = 2112$, since $\overline{F(x)}$ is irreducible over $\mathbb{F}_5$, $F(x)$ is irreducible over $\mathbb{Q}$. Since $a \equiv 3 \pmod 4$ and $b \equiv 0 \pmod 8$, by Theorem 2, $\nu_2(i(K)) = 3$. Similarly, since $a \equiv 5 \pmod 9$ and $b \equiv 6 \pmod 9$, by Theorem 3, $\nu_3(i(K)) = 1$. Thus, $i(K) = 24$.

6. For $a = 35$ and $b = 72$, since $\overline{F(x)}$ is irreducible over $\mathbb{F}_{11}$, $F(x)$ is irreducible over $\mathbb{Q}$. Since $a \equiv 3 \pmod 4$ and $b \equiv 0 \pmod 8$, by Theorem 2, $\nu_2(i(K)) = 3$. Similarly, since $a \equiv 8 \pmod 9$ and $b \equiv 0 \pmod 9$, by Theorem 3, $\nu_3(i(K)) = 2$. Thus, $i(K) = 72$.

Funding: This research received no external funding.

Data Availability Statement: Data sharing not applicable to this article as no datasets were generated or analyzed during the current study.

Acknowledgments: The author is deeply grateful to the anonymous referees whose valuable comments and suggestions have tremendously improved the quality of this paper. As well as to István Gaál for his encouragement and advice and to Enric Nart who introduced him to Newton polygon techniques.

Conflicts of Interest: There are non-financial competing interests to report.

References

1. Hasse, H. *Zahlentheorie*; Akademie-Verlag: Berlin, Germany, 1963.
2. Hensel, K. *Theorie der Algebraischen Zahlen*; Teubner Verlag: Leipzig, Germany, 1908.
3. Gaál, I. *Diophantine Equations and Power Integral Bases, Theory and Algorithm*, 2nd ed.; Birkhäuser: Boston, MA, USA, 2019.
4. Ahmad, S.; Nakahara, T.; Hameed, A. On certain pure sextic fields related to a problem of Hasse. *Int. J. Alg. Comput.* **2016**, *26*, 577–583. [CrossRef]
5. Gaál, I.; Györy, K. Index form equations in quintic fields. *Acta Arith.* **1999**, 89, 379–396. [CrossRef]
6. Pethö, A.; Pohst, M. On the indices of multiquadratic number fields. *Acta Arith.* **2012**, *153*, 393–414. [CrossRef]
7. Dedekind, R. Über den Zusammenhang zwischen der Theorie der Ideale und der Theorie der höheren Kongruenzen. *Göttingen Abh.* **1878**, *23*, 1–23.
8. Endler, O. *Valuation Theory*; Springer: Berlin, Germany, 1972.
9. Narkiewicz, W. *Elementary and Analytic Theory of Algebraic Numbers*; Springer: Berlin/Heidelberg, Germany, 2004.
10. Nakahara, T. On the indices and integral bases of non-cyclic but abelian biquadratic fields. *Arch. Der Math.* **1983**, *41*, 504–508. [CrossRef]
11. Gaál, I.; Pethö, A.; Pohst, M. On the indices of biquadratic number fields having Galois group V_4. *Arch. Math.* **1991**, *57*, 357–361. [CrossRef]
12. El Fadil, L.; Montes, J.; Nart, E. Newton polygons and p-integral bases of quartic number fields. *J. Algebra Appl.* **2012**, *11*, 1250073. [CrossRef]
13. Davis, C.T.; Spearman, B.K. The index of a quartic field defined by a trinomial $x^4 + ax + b$. *Alg. Its Appl.* **2018**, *17*, 1850197. [CrossRef]
14. El Fadil, L. A note on Indices of Quartic Number Fields Defined by Trinomials $x^4 + ax + b$. *Commun. Algebra.* **2023**. [CrossRef]
15. El Fadil, L.; Gaál, I. On non-monogenity of certain number fields defined by trinomials $x^4 + ax^2 + b$. *Mathematics* 2022, submitted.
16. Gaál, I. An experiment on the monogenity of a family of trinomials. *J. Algebra Number Theory Appl.* **2021**, *51*, 97–111.
17. El Fadil, L. On non monogenity of certain number fields defined by a trinomial $x^6 + ax^3 + b$. *J. Number Theory* **2022**, *239*, 489–500. [CrossRef]
18. El Fadil, L. On common index divisor and monogenity of certain number fields defined by a trinomial $x^5 + ax^2 + b$. *Commun. Algebra* **2022**, *50*, 3102–3112. [CrossRef]
19. El Fadil, L. On index and monogenity of certain number fields defined by trinomials. *Math. Slovaca* **2023**, *73*, 861–870. [CrossRef]
20. Guardia, J.; Montes, J.; Nart, E. Higher Newton polygons in the computation of discriminants and prime ideal decomposition in number fields. *J. ThÉorie Des Nombres Bordeaux* **2011**, *23*, 3667–3696. [CrossRef]
21. LlOrente, P.; Nart, E.; Vila, N. Decomposition of primes in number fields defined by trinomials. *Séminaire Théorie Des Nombres Bordeaux* **1991**, *3*, 27–41. [CrossRef]
22. El Fadil, L. A generalization of Eisenstein-Shonemann's irreducibility criterion. *Tatra Mt. Math. Publ.* **2023**, *83*, 51–56.
23. Gaál, I.; Remete, L. Power integral bases and monogenity of pure fields. *J. Number Theory* **2017**, *173*, 129–146. [CrossRef]
24. Hensel, K. Untersuchung der Fundamentalgleichung einer Gattung für eine reelle Primzahl als Modul und Bestimmung der Theiler ihrer Discriminante. *J. FüR Die Reine Und Angew. Math.* **1894**, *113*, 61–83.
25. Ore, O. Newtonsche Polygone in der Theorie der algebraischen Korper. *Math. Ann.* **1928**, *99*, 84–117. [CrossRef]
26. Guardia, J.; Montes, J.; Nart, E. Newton polygons of higher order in algebraic number theory. *Trans. Amer. Math. Soc.* **2012**, *364*, 361–416. [CrossRef]
27. Deajim, A.; El Fadil, L. On the integral closednessof $R[\alpha]$. *Math. Rep.* **2022**, *24*, 571–581.
28. Engstrom, H.T. On the common index divisors of an algebraic field. *Trans. Am. Math. Soc.* **1930**, *32*, 223–237. [CrossRef]

Disclaimer/Publisher's Note: The statements, opinions and data contained in all publications are solely those of the individual author(s) and contributor(s) and not of MDPI and/or the editor(s). MDPI and/or the editor(s) disclaim responsibility for any injury to people or property resulting from any ideas, methods, instructions or products referred to in the content.

Article

Generalized Fibonacci Sequences for Elliptic Curve Cryptography

Zakariae Cheddour, Abdelhakim Chillali and Ali Mouhib *

LSI Laboratory, Department of Mathematics, Polydisciplinary Faculty of Taza, University of Sidi Mohamed Ben Abdellah, Taza B.P. 1223, Morocco; zakariae.cheddour@usmba.ac.ma (Z.C.); abdelhakim.chillali@usmba.ac.ma (A.C.)
* Correspondence: ali.mouhib@usmba.ac.ma

Abstract: The Fibonacci sequence is a well-known sequence of numbers with numerous applications in mathematics, computer science, and other fields. In recent years, there has been growing interest in studying Fibonacci-like sequences on elliptic curves. These sequences have a number of exciting properties and can be used to build new encryption systems. This paper presents a further generalization of the Fibonacci sequence defined on elliptic curves. We also describe an encryption system using this sequence which is based on the discrete logarithm problem on elliptic curves.

Keywords: cryptosystem; elliptic curve; elliptic curve discrete logarithm problem; Fibonacci sequence; fully homomorphic encryption; matrices

MSC: 11G05; 14H52; 11B39; 11T71

Citation: Cheddour, Z.; Chillali, A.; Mouhib, A. Generalized Fibonacci Sequences for Elliptic Curve Cryptography. *Mathematics* 2023, 11, 4656. https://doi.org/10.3390/math11224656

Academic Editors: Li Guo, Diana Savin, Nicusor Minculete and Vincenzo Acciaro

Received: 21 September 2023
Revised: 29 October 2023
Accepted: 13 November 2023
Published: 15 November 2023

Copyright: © 2023 by the authors. Licensee MDPI, Basel, Switzerland. This article is an open access article distributed under the terms and conditions of the Creative Commons Attribution (CC BY) license (https://creativecommons.org/licenses/by/4.0/).

1. Introduction

The Fibonacci sequence, represented by the $\{F_n\}$ sequence, is a well-known and widely studied number series in mathematics. With applications in a variety of fields, it has fascinated researchers for centuries. Recently, interest in exploring Fibonacci-type sequences on elliptic curves has grown, leading to the discovery of exciting properties and new possibilities in cryptography. This article discusses the concept of the modified Multinacci sequence on an elliptic curve, a generalization of the classical Fibonacci sequence, and presents a new encryption system based on the discrete logarithm problem on elliptic curves. The classical Fibonacci sequence is defined by the recurrence relation

$$F_n = F_{n-1} + F_{n-2} \text{ for } n \geq 2,$$

with initial values $F_0 = 0$ and $F_1 = 1$. Various generalizations and extensions of this sequence have been proposed and studied by different authors over the years. Falcon and Plaza [1] introduced the k-Fibonacci sequence, while Edson and Yayenie [2] generalized the Fibonacci sequence and explored related identities.

The study of repeating sequences in algebraic structures began with the early work of Wall, who studied regular Fibonacci sequences in cyclic groups. Several authors followed his example and extended the theory to specific linear repeating sequences, see, for example, refs. [3–9]. These include the extensions by Deveci and Shannon [10,11], who studied quaternions and introduced the complex Fibonacci sequence with various applications.

In this article, we want to take the study a step further and explore the concept of Fibonacci sequences for groups generated by points on an elliptic curve. We present a modified Fibonacci sequence operating on an elliptic curve that extends the theory beyond traditional algebraic structures. On the other hand, elliptic curve cryptography (ECC) is an approach to public key cryptography based on the algebraic properties of elliptic curves over finite fields. Here, we present an innovative approach that combines ECC with the Fibonacci sequence. The resulting secure protocol is based on the elliptic curve discrete logarithm problem (ECDLP), which plays a crucial role in elliptic curve coding and adaptive coding. The proposed new encryption system uses the modified Fibonacci sequence on an elliptic curve as its basis. By exploiting the complexity of the discrete logarithm problem on elliptic curves, we believe this scheme offers greater security and represents a promising avenue in the field of cryptography. The theoretical properties of numbers obtained from homogeneous linear repetition relations relevant to our research context have been extensively studied by various authors, see, for example, refs. [12–22]. Their work has shed light on key aspects of this topic and provided valuable insights into the properties of Fibonacci-type sequences on elliptic curves.

2. The Modified Fibonacci Sequence

In this section, we will define the generalized Fibonacci sequence over elliptic curves.

Definition 1 (The generalized Fibonacci sequence [2]). *For $n \in \mathbb{N}$ such that $n \geq 2$, the generalized Fibonacci sequence $\{G_k\}_k \geq 0$ of order n is given by*

$$G_{k+n} = G_k + G_{k+1} + G_{k+2} + \ldots + G_{k+n-1}$$

where $G_0 = G_1 = \ldots = G_{n-2} = 0$ and $G_{n-1} = 1$. The generalized Fibonacei sequence $\{G_k\}_{k \geq 0}$ is called the multinacci sequence.

In the following definition, we generalize our previous results on Fibonacci-like sequences on elliptic curves [23]. We introduce a modified multinacci sequence defined on an elliptic curve.

Definition 2. *Let $\mathbb{F}_q$ be a finite field and $E/\mathbb{F}_q$ an elliptic curve, take a point of order g, ϕ over E and $G = <\phi>$. So, for $k, n \in \mathbb{N}$ and $\chi_0, \chi_1, \ldots, \chi_{n-1} \in G$, the elliptic multinacci sequence $\{N_{k,n}\}$ is defined by the recurrence relation*

$$N_{k+n} = N_k + N_{k+1} + \ldots + N_{k+n-1} \text{ for } n \geq 2,$$

with $N_k = \chi_0, N_{k+1} = \chi_1, \ldots, N_{k+n-1} = \chi_{n-1}$.
The first few elliptic multinacci points are

$$N_n = \chi_0 + \chi_1 + \ldots + \chi_{n-1},$$
$$N_{n+1} = \chi_0 + 2\chi_1 + 2\chi_2 + \ldots + 2\chi_{n-1},$$
$$N_{n+2} = 2\chi_0 + 3\chi_1 + 4\chi_2 + 4\chi_3 \ldots + 4\chi_{n-1}.$$

For choosing the points $\chi_0, \chi_1, \ldots, \chi_{n-1}$ on a well-defined elliptic curve. We will use a private key exchange protocol to generate a sequence of points on an elliptic curve.

2.1. Sequence of Private Points

In this section, we study the problem of choosing points on an elliptic curve. We generalize our previous results on the elliptic matrix [24] to an elliptic matrix of order n. We also use a generalized approach that we used in our previous work [24]. The problem of choosing points on an elliptic curve is important in cryptography applications. In our previous work [23], we showed that the elliptic matrix can be used to generate a sequence of points on an elliptic curve. In this section, we generalize this result to an elliptic matrix of order n. We also show that our generalized approach is more efficient than the previous one.

Let $\mathbb{F}_q$ be a finite field and $E/\mathbb{F}_q$ an elliptic curve, take a point of order g, ϕ over E and $G = <\phi>$. In this part, we present the theoretical concept for our encryption scheme by using the matrix-ring $\aleph$, with the following form,

$$\aleph = \left\{ \begin{pmatrix} a_1 & P_{1,2} & \cdots & P_{1,n} \\ Q_{2,1} & a_2 & \cdots & P_{2,n} \\ \vdots & \vdots & \ddots & \vdots \\ Q_{n,1} & Q_{n,2} & \cdots & a_n \end{pmatrix} \mid a_i \in \mathbb{Z}/g\mathbb{Z}, P_{i,j}, Q_{i,j} \in G, i,j \in \{1,2,\cdots,n\} \right\}$$

2.2. The Ring $\aleph$

Let $X = \begin{pmatrix} a_1 & P_{1,2} & \cdots & P_{1,n} \\ Q_{2,1} & a_2 & \cdots & P_{2,n} \\ \vdots & \vdots & \ddots & \vdots \\ Q_{n,1} & Q_{n,2} & \cdots & a_n \end{pmatrix}$ and $Y = \begin{pmatrix} b_1 & P'_{1,2} & \cdots & P'_{1,n} \\ Q'_{2,1} & b_2 & \cdots & P'_{2,n} \\ \vdots & \vdots & \ddots & \vdots \\ Q'_{n,1} & Q'_{n,2} & \cdots & b_n \end{pmatrix}$ be two elements in $\aleph$. So,

$$X + Y = \begin{pmatrix} a_1 + b_1 & P_{1,2} + P'_{1,2} & \cdots & P_{1,n} + P'_{1,n} \\ Q_{2,1} + Q'_{2,1} & a_2 + b_2 & \cdots & P_{2,n} + P'_{2,n} \\ \vdots & \vdots & \ddots & \vdots \\ Q_{n,1} + Q'_{n,1} & Q_{n,2} + Q'_{n,2} & \cdots & a_n + b_n \end{pmatrix},$$

$$X \star Y = \begin{pmatrix} a_1 b_1 & b_2 P_{1,2} + a_1 P'_{1,2} & \cdots & b_n P_{1,n} + a_1 P'_{1,n} \\ b_1 Q_{2,1} + a_2 Q'_{2,1} & a_2 b_2 & \cdots & b_n P_{2,n} + a_2 P'_{2,n} \\ \vdots & \vdots & \ddots & \vdots \\ b_1 Q_{n,1} + a_n Q'_{n,1} & b_2 Q_{n,2} + a_n Q'_{n,2} & \cdots & a_n b_n \end{pmatrix}.$$

Lemma 1. $(\aleph, +, \star)$ *is a unitary non-commutative ring with identities,*

$$1_\aleph = \begin{pmatrix} 1 & (0:1:0) & \cdots & (0:1:0) \\ (0:1:0) & 1 & \cdots & (0:1:0) \\ \vdots & \vdots & \ddots & \vdots \\ (0:1:0) & (0:1:0) & \cdots & 1 \end{pmatrix}$$

and

$$0_\aleph = \begin{pmatrix} 0 & (0:1:0) & \cdots & (0:1:0) \\ (0:1:0) & 0 & \cdots & (0:1:0) \\ \vdots & \vdots & \ddots & \vdots \\ (0:1:0) & (0:1:0) & \cdots & 0 \end{pmatrix},$$

where $(0:1:0)$ is the point of the elliptic at infinity.

Proof. Let

$$X = \begin{pmatrix} a_1 & P_{1,2} & \cdots & P_{1,n} \\ Q_{2,1} & a_2 & \cdots & P_{2,n} \\ \vdots & \vdots & \ddots & \vdots \\ Q_{n,1} & Q_{n,2} & \cdots & a_n \end{pmatrix}, Y = \begin{pmatrix} b_1 & P'_{1,2} & \cdots & P'_{1,n} \\ Q'_{2,1} & b_2 & \cdots & P'_{2,n} \\ \vdots & \vdots & \ddots & \vdots \\ Q'_{n,1} & Q'_{n,2} & \cdots & b_n \end{pmatrix}$$

and

$$Z = \begin{pmatrix} c_1 & P''_{1,2} & \cdots & P''_{1,n} \\ Q''_{2,1} & c_2 & \cdots & P''_{2,n} \\ \vdots & \vdots & \ddots & \vdots \\ Q''_{n,1} & Q''_{n,2} & \cdots & c_n \end{pmatrix}$$

be elements in $\aleph$, then

- Associative laws,

  We start with the product law "$\star$",

$$(X \star Y) \star Z =$$

$$= \begin{pmatrix} a_1b_1 & b_2P_{1,2}+a_1P'_{1,2} & \cdots & b_nP_{1,n}+a_1P'_{1,n} \\ b_1Q_{2,1}+a_2Q'_{2,1} & a_2b_2 & \cdots & b_nP_{2,n}+a_2P'_{2,n} \\ \vdots & \vdots & \ddots & \vdots \\ b_1Q_{n,1}+a_nQ'_{n,1} & b_2Q_{n,2}+a_nQ'_{n,2} & \cdots & a_nb_n \end{pmatrix} \star \begin{pmatrix} c_1 & P''_{1,2} & \cdots & P''_{1,n} \\ Q''_{2,1} & c_2 & \cdots & P''_{2,n} \\ \vdots & \vdots & \ddots & \vdots \\ Q''_{n,1} & Q''_{n,2} & \cdots & c_n \end{pmatrix}$$

$$= \begin{pmatrix} a_1b_1c_1 & b_2c_2P_{1,2}+a_1c_2P'_{1,2}+a_1b_1P''_{1,2} & \cdots & b_nc_nP_{1,n}+a_1c_nP'_{1,n}+a_1b_1P''_{1,n} \\ b_1c_1Q_{2,1}+a_2c_1Q'_{2,1}+a_2b_2Q''_{2,1} & a_2b_2c_2 & \cdots & b_nc_nP_{2,n}+a_2c_nP'_{2,n}+a_2b_2P''_{2,n} \\ \vdots & \vdots & \ddots & \vdots \\ b_1c_1Q_{n,1}+a_nc_1Q'_{n,1}+a_nb_nQ''_{n,1} & b_2c_2Q_{n,2}+a_nc_2Q'_{n,2}+a_nb_nQ''_{n,2} & \cdots & a_nb_nc_n \end{pmatrix}$$

and,

$$X \star (Y \star Z) =$$

$$= \begin{pmatrix} a_1 & P_{1,2} & \cdots & P_{1,n} \\ Q_{2,1} & a_2 & \cdots & P_{2,n} \\ \vdots & \vdots & \ddots & \vdots \\ Q_{n,1} & Q_{n,2} & \cdots & a_n \end{pmatrix} \star \begin{pmatrix} b_1c_1 & c_2P'_{1,2}+b_1P''_{1,2} & \cdots & c_nP'_{1,n}+b_1P''_{1,n} \\ c_1Q'_{2,1}+b_2Q''_{2,1} & b_2c_2 & \cdots & c_nP'_{2,n}+b_2P''_{2,n} \\ \vdots & \vdots & \ddots & \vdots \\ c_1Q'_{n,1}+b_nQ''_{n,1} & c_2Q'_{n,2}+b_nQ''_{n,2} & \cdots & b_nc_n \end{pmatrix}$$

$$= \begin{pmatrix} a_1b_1c_1 & b_2c_2P_{1,2}+a_1c_2P'_{1,2}+a_1b_1P''_{1,2} & \cdots & b_nc_nP_{1,n}+a_1c_nP'_{1,n}+a_1b_1P''_{1,n} \\ b_1c_1Q_{2,1}+a_2c_1Q'_{2,1}+a_2b_2Q''_{2,1} & a_2b_2c_2 & \cdots & b_nc_nP_{2,n}+a_2c_nP'_{2,n}+a_2b_2P''_{2,n} \\ \vdots & \vdots & \ddots & \vdots \\ b_1c_1Q_{n,1}+a_nc_1Q'_{n,1}+a_nb_nQ''_{n,1} & b_2c_2Q_{n,2}+a_nc_2Q'_{n,2}+a_nb_nQ''_{n,2} & \cdots & a_nb_nc_n \end{pmatrix}$$

Hence, $(X \star Y) \star Z = X \star (Y \star Z)$.
On the other hand, in the same way, we find that $(X + Y) + Z = X + (Y + Z)$.

- Distributive laws, we shall prove that $(X + Y) \star Z = X \star Z + Y \star Z$ and $\star Z \star (X + Y) = Z \star X + Z \star Y$.

  So, for the first equality $(X + Y) \star Z = X \star Z + Y \star Z$, we have

$$(X+Y) \star Z = \begin{pmatrix} a_1+b_1 & P_{1,2}+P'_{1,2} & \cdots & P_{1,n}+P'_{1,n} \\ Q_{2,1}+Q'_{2,1} & a_2+b_2 & \cdots & P_{2,n}+P'_{2,n} \\ \vdots & \vdots & \ddots & \vdots \\ Q_{n,1}+Q'_{n,1} & Q_{n,2}+Q'_{n,2} & \cdots & a_n+b_n \end{pmatrix} \star \begin{pmatrix} c_1 & P''_{1,2} & \cdots & P''_{1,n} \\ Q''_{2,1} & c_2 & \cdots & P''_{2,n} \\ \vdots & \vdots & \ddots & \vdots \\ Q''_{n,1} & Q''_{n,2} & \cdots & c_n \end{pmatrix}$$

$$= \begin{pmatrix} (a_1+b_1)c_1 & c_2(P_{1,2}+P'_{1,2})+(a_1+b_1)P''_{1,2} & \cdots & c_n(P_{1,n}+P'_{1,n})+(a_1+b_1)P''_{1,n} \\ c_1(Q_{2,1}+Q'_{2,1})+(a_2+b_2)Q''_{2,1} & (a_2+b_2)c_2 & \cdots & c_n(P_{2,n}+P'_{2,n})+(a_2+b_2)P''_{2,n} \\ \vdots & \vdots & \ddots & \vdots \\ c_1(Q_{n,1}+Q'_{n,1})+(a_n+b_n)Q''_{n,1} & c_2(Q_{n,2}+Q'_{n,2})+(a_n+b_n)Q''_{n,2} & \cdots & (a_n+b_n)c_n \end{pmatrix},$$

and,

$$X \star Z + Y \star Z = \begin{pmatrix} a_1c_1+b_1c_1 & c_2P_{1,2}+c_2P'_{1,2}+(a_1+b_1)P''_{1,2} & \cdots & c_nP_{1,n}+c_nP'_{1,n}+(a_1+b_1)P''_{1,n} \\ c_1Q_{2,1}+c_1Q'_{2,1}+(a_2+b_2)Q''_{2,1} & a_2c_2+b_2c_2 & \cdots & c_nP_{2,n}+c_nP'_{2,n}+(a_2+b_2)P''_{2,n} \\ \vdots & \vdots & \ddots & \vdots \\ c_1Q_{n,1}+c_1Q'_{n,1}+(a_n+b_n)Q''_{n,1} & c_2Q_{n,2}+c_2Q'_{n,2}+(a_n+b_n)Q''_{n,2} & \cdots & a_nc_n+b_nc_n \end{pmatrix}$$

Hence, $(X + Y) \star Z = X \star Z + Y \star Z$.
Similarly for the second equality.

- Additive inverses, for all $X = \begin{pmatrix} a_1 & P_{1,2} & \cdots & P_{1,n} \\ Q_{2,1} & a_2 & \cdots & P_{2,n} \\ \vdots & \vdots & \ddots & \vdots \\ Q_{n,1} & Q_{n,2} & \cdots & a_n \end{pmatrix} \in \aleph$, we have $X + (-X) = 0_\aleph$,

with $(-X) = \begin{pmatrix} -a_1 & -P_{1,2} & \cdots & -P_{1,n} \\ -Q_{2,1} & -a_2 & \cdots & -P_{2,n} \\ \vdots & \vdots & \ddots & \vdots \\ -Q_{n,1} & -Q_{n,2} & \cdots & -a_n \end{pmatrix}$ is called the additive inverse of X.

□

The following proposition describes the collection of invertible elements within $\aleph$.

Proposition 1. *Let* $X = \begin{pmatrix} a_1 & P_{1,2} & \cdots & P_{1,n} \\ Q_{2,1} & a_2 & \cdots & P_{2,n} \\ \vdots & \vdots & \ddots & \vdots \\ Q_{n,1} & Q_{n,2} & \cdots & a_n \end{pmatrix} \in \aleph$, X *is invertible if only if* $\gcd(g, a_i) = 1$ *for all* $i \in \{1, 2, \ldots, n\}$, *in this case we have,*

$$X^{\star(-1)} = \begin{pmatrix} a_1^{-1} & -a_1^{-1}a_2^{-1}P_{1,2} & \cdots & -a_1^{-1}a_n^{-1}P_{1,n} \\ -a_1^{-1}a_2^{-1}Q_{2,1} & a_2^{-1} & \cdots & -a_2^{-1}a_n^{-1}P_{2,n} \\ \vdots & \vdots & \ddots & \vdots \\ -a_1^{-1}a_n^{-1}Q_{n,1} & -a_2^{-1}a_n^{-1}Q_{n,2} & \cdots & a_n^{-1} \end{pmatrix} \in \aleph.$$

Proof. Let $Y = \begin{pmatrix} b_1 & P'_{1,2} & \cdots & P'_{1,n} \\ Q'_{2,1} & b_2 & \cdots & P'_{2,n} \\ \vdots & \vdots & \ddots & \vdots \\ Q'_{n,1} & Q'_{n,2} & \cdots & b_n \end{pmatrix}$ the inverse of X, we have:

$$X \star Y = Y \star X = 1_\aleph$$

So, $X \star Y = \begin{pmatrix} a_1b_1 & b_2P_{1,2} + a_1P'_{1,2} & \cdots & b_nP_{1,n} + a_1P'_{1,n} \\ b_1Q_{2,1} + a_2Q'_{2,1} & a_2b_2 & \cdots & b_nP_{2,n} + a_2P'_{2,n} \\ \vdots & \vdots & \ddots & \vdots \\ b_1Q_{n,1} + a_nQ'_{n,1} & b_2Q_{n,2} + a_nQ'_{n,2} & \cdots & a_nb_n \end{pmatrix}$

$= \begin{pmatrix} 1 & (0:1:0) & \cdots & (0:1:0) \\ (0:1:0) & 1 & \cdots & (0:1:0) \\ \vdots & \vdots & \ddots & \vdots \\ (0:1:0) & (0:1:0) & \cdots & 1 \end{pmatrix},$

and

$Y \star X = \begin{pmatrix} a_1b_1 & b_1P_{1,2} + a_2P'_{1,2} & \cdots & b_1P_{1,n} + a_nP'_{1,n} \\ b_2Q_{2,1} + a_1Q'_{2,1} & a_2b_2 & \cdots & b_2P_{2,n} + a_nP'_{2,n} \\ \vdots & \vdots & \ddots & \vdots \\ b_nQ_{n,1} + a_1Q'_{n,1} & b_nQ_{n,2} + a_2Q'_{n,2} & \cdots & a_nb_n \end{pmatrix}$

$= \begin{pmatrix} 1 & (0:1:0) & \cdots & (0:1:0) \\ (0:1:0) & 1 & \cdots & (0:1:0) \\ \vdots & \vdots & \ddots & \vdots \\ (0:1:0) & (0:1:0) & \cdots & 1 \end{pmatrix},$

it follows that, for all $i, j \in \{1, 2, \ldots, n\}$ we have $a_i b_i \equiv 1 \pmod{g}$ and

$$b_i P_{j,i} + a_j P'_{j,i} = (0:1:0), i \neq j,$$
$$b_j Q_{i,j} + a_i Q'_{i,j} = (0:1:0), i \neq j.$$

Therefore, X is invertible if only if $\gcd(g, a_i) = 1$ for all $i \in \{1, 2, \ldots, n\}$, in this case we have, $b_i = a_i^{-1}$ for all $i \in \{1, 2, \ldots, n\}$ and

$$P'_{i,j} = -a_i^{-1} a_j^{-1} P_{i,j}, i \neq j,$$
$$Q'_{i,j} = -a_i^{-1} a_j^{-1} Q_{i,j}, i \neq j.$$

So,

$$X^{\star(-1)} = \begin{pmatrix} a_1^{-1} & -a_1^{-1}a_2^{-1}P_{1,2} & \cdots & -a_1^{-1}a_n^{-1}P_{1,n} \\ -a_1^{-1}a_2^{-1}Q_{2,1} & a_2^{-1} & \cdots & -a_2^{-1}a_n^{-1}P_{2,n} \\ \vdots & \vdots & \ddots & \vdots \\ -a_1^{-1}a_n^{-1}Q_{n,1} & -a_2^{-1}a_n^{-1}Q_{n,2} & \cdots & a_n^{-1} \end{pmatrix} \in \aleph.$$

□

Lemma 2. *Let $k \in \mathbb{N}$. Then the k-power of* $X = \begin{pmatrix} a_1 & P_{1,2} & \cdots & P_{1,n} \\ Q_{2,1} & a_2 & \cdots & P_{2,n} \\ \vdots & \vdots & \ddots & \vdots \\ Q_{n,1} & Q_{n,2} & \cdots & a_n \end{pmatrix} \in \aleph$, *is given by*

$$X^{\star k} = \begin{pmatrix} a_1^k & \lambda_{1,2}^k P_{1,2} & \cdots & \lambda_{1,n}^k P_{1,n} \\ \lambda_{1,2}^k Q_{2,1} & a_2^k & \cdots & \lambda_{2,n}^k P_{2,n} \\ \vdots & \vdots & \ddots & \vdots \\ \lambda_{1,n}^k Q_{n,1} & \lambda_{2,n}^k Q_{n,2} & \cdots & a_n^k \end{pmatrix},$$

where

$$\lambda_{e,f}^k = \sum_{i+j=k-1} a_e^i a_f^j, \text{ for } e \in \{1, \ldots, n-1\} \text{ and } f \in \{2, \ldots, n\}$$

Proof. For $k = 1$, we have $\lambda_{e,f}^1 = 1$ for all $e \in \{1, \ldots, n-1\}$ and $f \in \{2, \ldots, n\}$, then $X^{\star 1} = X$.

Let $k \geq 1$. Assuming that $\lambda_{e,f}^k = \sum_{i+j=k-1} a_e^i a_f^j$ is true, we prove that we have,

$$\lambda_{e,f}^{k+1} = \sum_{i+j=k} a_e^i a_f^j.$$

So, we have

$$X^{\star(k+1)} = \begin{pmatrix} a_1^k & \lambda_{1,2}^k P_{1,2} & \cdots & \lambda_{1,n}^k P_{1,n} \\ \lambda_{1,2}^k Q_{2,1} & a_2^k & \cdots & \lambda_{2,n}^k P_{2,n} \\ \vdots & \vdots & \ddots & \vdots \\ \lambda_{1,n}^k Q_{n,1} & \lambda_{2,n}^k Q_{n,2} & \cdots & a_n^k \end{pmatrix} \star \begin{pmatrix} a_1 & P_{1,2} & \cdots & P_{1,n} \\ Q_{2,1} & a_2 & \cdots & P_{2,n} \\ \vdots & \vdots & \ddots & \vdots \\ Q_{n,1} & Q_{n,2} & \cdots & a_n \end{pmatrix}$$

Then,

$$X^{\star(k+1)} = \begin{pmatrix} a_1^{k+1} & (a_1^k + a_2\lambda_{1,2}^k)P_{1,2} & \cdots & (a_1^k + a_n\lambda_{1,n}^k)P_{1,n} \\ (a_2^k + a_1\lambda_{1,2}^k)Q_{2,1} & a_2^{k+1} & \cdots & (a_2^k + a_n\lambda_{2,n}^k)P_{2,n} \\ \vdots & \vdots & \ddots & \vdots \\ (a_n^k + a_1\lambda_{1,n}^k)Q_{n,1} & (a_n^k + a_2\lambda_{2,n}^k)Q_{n,2} & \cdots & a_n^{k+1} \end{pmatrix}$$

Thus, for $e \in \{1, \ldots, n-1\}$ and $f \in \{2, \ldots, n\}$ we have

$$\lambda_{e,f}^{k+1} = a_e^k + a_f \lambda_{e,f}^k = a_e^k + a_f \sum_{i+j=k-1} a_e^i a_f^j.$$

We conclude that, for all $k \geq 1$,

$$\lambda_{e,f}^k = \sum_{i+j=k-1} a_e^i a_f^j.$$

Hence, the result. □

Given the non-commutative nature of the $\star$ operation, in the upcoming proposition, we will define the set $C_\aleph(X)$, which consists of matrices in $\aleph$ that commute with the mentioned matrix.

$$X = \begin{pmatrix} a_1 & g_{1,2}\phi & \cdots & g_{1,n}\phi \\ m_{2,1}\phi & a_2 & \cdots & g_{2,n}\phi \\ \vdots & \vdots & \ddots & \vdots \\ m_{n,1}\phi & m_{n,2}\phi & \cdots & a_n \end{pmatrix}.$$

Proposition 2. *Using the same notation as above, we have*

$$Y = \begin{pmatrix} b_1 & e_{1,2}\phi & \cdots & e_{1,n}\phi \\ f_{2,1}\phi & b_2 & \cdots & e_{2,n}\phi \\ \vdots & \vdots & \ddots & \vdots \\ f_{n,1}\phi & f_{n,2}\phi & \cdots & b_n \end{pmatrix} \in C_\aleph(X)$$

if and only if
$$\begin{cases} (b_j - b_i)g_{i,j} = (a_j - a_i)e_{i,j} \pmod{g}, & \text{for } i \neq j; \\ (b_j - b_i)m_{j,i} = (a_j - a_i)f_{j,i} \pmod{g}, & \text{for } i \neq j. \end{cases}$$

Proof. Since,

$$X \star Y = \begin{pmatrix} a_1 b_1 & (b_2 g_{1,2} + a_1 e_{1,2})\phi & \cdots & (b_n g_{1,n} + a_1 e_{1,n})\phi \\ (b_1 m_{2,1} + a_2 f_{2,1})\phi & a_2 b_2 & \cdots & (b_n g_{2,n} + a_2 e_{2,n})\phi \\ \vdots & \vdots & \ddots & \vdots \\ (b_1 m_{n,1} + a_n f_{n,1})\phi & (b_2 m_{n,2} + a_n f_{n,2})\phi & \cdots & a_n b_n \end{pmatrix}$$

and

$$Y \star X = \begin{pmatrix} a_1 b_1 & (b_1 g_{1,2} + a_2 e_{1,2})\phi & \cdots & (b_1 g_{1,n} + a_n e_{1,n})\phi \\ (b_2 m_{2,1} + a_1 f_{2,1})\phi & a_2 b_2 & \cdots & (b_2 g_{2,n} + a_n e_{2,n})\phi \\ \vdots & \vdots & \ddots & \vdots \\ (b_n m_{n,1} + a_1 f_{n,1})\phi & (b_n m_{n,2} + a_2 f_{n,2})\phi & \cdots & a_n b_n \end{pmatrix}.$$

We can then check the result by making comparative calculations. □

3. Encryption Scheme

In this section, we will use the Fibonacci sequence $N_{k,n}$ and the matrix $M(B_1, B_2, B_3) = \begin{pmatrix} B_1 & B_2 \\ 0 & B_3 \end{pmatrix}$ to build a cryptosystem, where $B_i \in \aleph$ for all $i \in \{1,2,3\}$.

3.1. Cryptographic Protocols

3.1.1. Public-Key Encryption

Let $\mathbb{F}_q$ be a finite field where q is a power of a prime number p, and ϕ a point on an elliptic curve $E/\mathbb{F}_q$ of order g (Public).

Initially, Allice and Boob perform the following steps:

- Select an integer "e" satisfying $2^e \geq order(\phi)$.
- Construct encryption and decryption tables for the alphabetical letters, as illustrated in Table 1
- Allice chooses two matrices A and $S_1 \in \aleph$ such that $S_1 \notin C_\aleph(A)$ and publishes the pair $(A, C_\aleph(S_1))$.
- Boob chooses two matrices B and $B_2 \in \aleph$ such that $B_2 \notin C_\aleph(B)$ and publishes the pair $(B, C_\aleph(B_2))$.
- Allice chooses private keys: $r \in \mathbb{N}^*$ and $S_2 \in C_\aleph(B_2) \setminus C_\aleph(A)$. She computed the matrix

$$(M(S_1, A+B, S_2))^{\star r} = \begin{pmatrix} S_1^{\star r} & V_r \\ 0 & S_2^{\star r} \end{pmatrix},$$

and send $V_r = \sum_{j=0}^{r-1} S_1^{r-1-j}(A+B)S_2^j$ to Boob.

- Boob chooses private keys, $t \in \mathbb{N}^*$ and $B_1 \in C_\aleph(S_1) \setminus C_\aleph(B)$. He computed the matrix

$$(M(B_1, A+B, B_2))^{\star t} = \begin{pmatrix} B_1^{\star t} & W_t \\ 0 & B_2^{\star t} \end{pmatrix},$$

and sends $W_t = \sum_{i=0}^{t-1} B_1^{t-1-i}(A+B)B_2^i$ to Allice.

Using their respective private keys r and t,

$$\text{Allice calculates the matrix}: M(S_1, W_t, S_2)^{\star r} = \begin{pmatrix} S_1^{\star r} & W_{t,r} \\ 0 & S_2^{\star r} \end{pmatrix}.$$

$$\text{Boob calculates the matrix}: M(B_1, V_r, B_2)^{\star t} = \begin{pmatrix} B_1^{\star t} & V_{r,t} \\ 0 & B_2^{\star t} \end{pmatrix}.$$

Table 1. Table of codes.

m	Symbol	N_{k+m-1}	Code
1	a	(235935:268849:1)	0011100110011001111101000001101000110001
2	b	(389657:135909:1)	0101111100100001100100100001001011100101
3	c	(77635:277268:1)	0001001011110100001101000011101100010100
4	d	(731184:813740:1)	1011001010000011000011000110101010101100
5	e	(276883:380201:1)	0100001110011001001101011100110100101001
6	f	(45356:13835:1)	0000101100010010110000000011011000001011
7	g	(594378:213743:1)	1001000100011100101000110100001011101111
8	h	(769911:70637:1)	1011101111110111011100010001001111101101
9	i	(91429:614433:1)	0001011001010010010110010110000000100001
10	j	(727719:560865:1)	1011000110101010011111000100011101100001
11	k	(798495:460116:1)	1100001011110001111101110000010101010100
12	l	(228759:663560:1)	0011011110110010111010001000000001000
13	m	(140564:784634:1)	0010001001010001010010111111100011111010
14	n	(206051:230879:1)	0011001001001110001100111000010111011111

Table 1. Cont.

m	Symbol	N_{k+m-1}	Code
15	o	(493299:599363:1)	01111000011011110011100100100101010000011
16	p	(119068:314376:1)	00011101000100011100010011001100000001000
17	q	(343828:667652:1)	01010011111100010100101000110000000000100
18	r	(440735:296723:1)	01101011100110011111101001000011100010011
19	s	(600806:253674:1)	10010010101011100110001110111011011101010
20	t	(576171:209834:1)	10001100101010101011001100110011010101010
21	u	(799322:20471:1)	11000011001001011010000001001111111110111
22	v	(480331:755394:1)	01110101010001001011101110000110110000010
23	w	(11625:186679:1)	00000010110101101001001011011001001101111
24	x	(703147:653544:1)	10101011101010101011100111111100011101000
25	y	(86566:248985:1)	00010101001000100110001111001100010011001
26	z	(803203:590888:1)	11000100000110000011100100000010000101000
27	0	(253297:647609:1)	00111011101011100011001111000011101110011
28	1	(638352:140976:1)	10011011110110010000001000100110101101100
29	2	(325216:589272:1)	01001110110011000001000111111011111011100
30	3	(290526:188929:1)	01000110111011011110001011100010000000001
31	4	(442462:359536:1)	01101100000000101110010101111110011110000
32	5	(235154:97923:1)	00111001011010010010000010111111010000011
33	6	(831595:598381:1)	11001011000001101011100100100000101101101
34	7	(501957:121621:1)	01111010100011000101000111011011000100101
35	8	(423213:594366:1)	01100111010100101101100100010001100111110
36	9	(469008:24502:1)	01110010100000010000000001011111101110110
37	+	(57173:619400:1)	00001101111101010101010101011001110001000
38	,	(68386:767724:1)	00010000110010001010111011011011110100
39	=	(836347:26992:1)	11001100001011110110000011010010101110000
40	space	(546050:89480:1)	10000101010100000100000101011011000011000
⋮	⋮	⋮	⋮
⋮	⋮	⋮	⋮

Lemma 3. *Using the same notations as above, we obtain* $W_{t,r} = V_{r,t}$.

Proof. We have,

$$V_{r,t} = \sum_{i=0}^{t-1} B_1^{t-i-1} V_r B_2^i$$

$$= \sum_{i=0}^{t-1} B_1^{t-i-1} \left(\sum_{j=0}^{r-1} S_1^{r-1-j} (A+B) S_2^j \right) B_2^i$$

$$= \sum_{i=0}^{t-1} \sum_{j=0}^{r-1} B_1^{t-i-1} S_1^{r-1-j} (A+B) S_2^j B_2^i$$

and

$$W_{t,r} = \sum_{j=0}^{r-1} S_1^{r-j-1} W_t S_2^j$$

$$= \sum_{j=0}^{r-1} S_1^{r-j-1} \left(\sum_{i=0}^{t-1} B_1^{t-1-i} (A+B) B_2^i \right) S_2^j$$

$$= \sum_{j=0}^{r-1} \sum_{i=0}^{t-1} S_1^{r-j-1} B_1^{t-1-i} (A+B) B_2^i S_2^j.$$

Or, $B_1 \in C_\aleph(S_1)$ and $S_2 \in C_\aleph(B_2)$, it follows that

$$\Phi = V_{r,t} = W_{t,r} = \begin{pmatrix} \alpha_1 & \chi_{1,2} & \cdots & \chi_{1,n} \\ \psi_{2,1} & \alpha_2 & \cdots & \chi_{2,n} \\ \vdots & \vdots & \ddots & \vdots \\ \psi_{n,1} & \psi_{n,2} & \cdots & \alpha_n \end{pmatrix}.$$

□

3.1.2. The Secret Fibonacci Sequence

At present, we have the secret matrix Φ. Next, we will introduce the Fibonacci sequence, an essential element in the implementation of our protocol. The Fibonacci sequence is defined by:

$$N_{k+n} = N_k + N_{k+1} + \ldots + N_{k+n-1} \text{ for } n \geq 2,$$

$$N_i = \alpha_{i-k+1} \chi_{i-k+1,i-k+2} + \Sigma_{j=1}^{i-k} \psi_{i-k+1,j} + \Sigma_{j=i-k+3}^{n} \chi_{i-k+1,j} \text{ for } k \leq i \leq n+k-1.$$

where $k \in \mathbb{N}$. Therefore, we derive the secret key between Allice and Boob, represented by the elliptic Fibonacci sequence.

Let

$$G = <\phi> = \{1_\aleph, \phi, 2\phi, 3\phi, \ldots, (m-1)\phi\},$$

with $m = ord(G)$. For $l \leq m$, we code $l\phi$ by $l\phi \to N_{n+l}$ and $1_\aleph \to N_{n+m}$. Then we get $\phi \to N_{n+1}, 2\phi \to N_{n+2}, \ldots, i\phi \to N_{n+i}, \ldots$

3.2. Encrypt and Decrypt Messages

If the secret key Φ shared between Boob and Allice is invertible, and ∇ represents the message that Boob intends to transmit to Allice, note that ∇ is a matrix of the same size as Φ. This leads to the encrypted message

$$\triangle = e_\Phi(\nabla) = \Phi \star \nabla \star \Phi^{-1}$$

We repeat the above procedure if Φ is not invertible

After receiving the encrypted message $\triangle$ from Boob, Allice uses a decryption process to decrypt it. This decryption function, called d_Φ, is defined as follows

$$d_\Phi(\triangle) = \Phi^{-1} \star \nabla \star \Phi.$$

It follows that $d_\Phi \circ e_\Phi(\nabla) = \nabla$.

Lemma 4. *Given two messages, ∇_1 and ∇_2, then for any invertible key Φ, the following condition applies:*

$$e_\Phi(\nabla_1 + \nabla_2) = e_\Phi(\nabla_1) + e_\Phi(\nabla_2)$$
$$e_\Phi(\nabla_1 \star \nabla_2) = e_\Phi(\nabla_1) \star e_\Phi(\nabla_2)$$

3.3. Discussion and Analysis

In this section, we will look at the security aspects of the system and make a comparative analysis with other systems.

Considering that ECLDP (Elliptic Curve Discrete Logarithm Problem) is notably more challenging to solve in comparison to the Discrete Logarithm Problem (DLP) on finite fields, we can assert that our cryptosystem implemented over elliptic curves offers enhanced security when juxtaposed with cryptosystems operating on finite fields. It is worth noting that there are sub-exponential algorithms available for resolving the DLP over fields, which affects the security landscape.

Nonetheless, the cryptographic primitive underpinning our scheme is fundamentally rooted in the difficulty of solving the DLP. Consequently, to achieve a sufficient level of security, it becomes imperative to operate within the domain of large fields. However, this choice comes at the cost of increased transmission overhead, implementation complexity, and computational time.

Conversely, our cryptosystem presents advantages over schemes based on finite fields due to the fact that (ECDLP) is an exponential problem. To ensure the highest level of security within our cryptographic system, careful selection of the elliptic curve becomes crucial. Additionally, solving the ECLDP is more formidable compared to the Integer Factorization Problem (IFP), further solidifying the security of our elliptic curve-based approach in comparison to the RSA cryptosystem.

Furthermore, it is important to highlight that ECLDP provides a heightened level of security even with relatively smaller key sizes, surpassing the security levels of the RSA or DSA cryptosystems in terms of key size.

Digital Signature Algorithm [25]. The following table shows the key length required to achieve an adequate security level of k-bits.

Security Level	Elliptic Curve Algorithms	Asymmetric Algorithms RSA, DSA and El Gamal	Symmetric Algorithms
128	160	1024	80
1024	256	2048	128

In conclusion, the memory consumption in our elliptic curve-based cryptosystem is significantly lower compared to the Cramer–Shoup signature scheme relying on strong RSA [26].

4. Numerical Example

Let $\mathbb{F}_{357347}$ be a finite field, and the $\phi = (231025:130838:1)$ point of order $g = 358438$ over the elliptic curve

$$E : y^2 = x^3 + 5x + 3 \pmod{357347}.$$

Initially, Allice and Boob perform the following steps:

- Select an integer "$e = 19$" satisfying $2^e \geq order(\phi) = 358438$.
- Construct encryption and decryption tables for the alphabetical letters, as illustrated in Table 1.

Our objective in this example is to encrypt the message "a new encryption scheme". We will take matrices of size 4.

First Allice chooses two matrices in $\aleph$,

$$A = \begin{pmatrix} 0 & (231025:130838:1) & (231025:130838:1) & (209305:158310:1) \\ (313039:156928:1) & 3 & (313039:156928:1) & (325271:280330:1) \\ (209305:158310:1) & (4959:212177:1) & 2 & (167587:100994:1) \\ (209305:158310:1) & (325271:280330:1) & (167587:100994:1) & 10 \end{pmatrix},$$

$$S_1 = \begin{pmatrix} 5 & (4959:212177:1) & (167587:100994:1) & (231025:130838:1) \\ (0:1:0) & 3 & (231025:130838:1) & (313039:156928:1) \\ (0:1:0) & (0:1:0) & 2 & (204268:290591:1) \\ (0:1:0) & (0:1:0) & (0:1:0) & 1 \end{pmatrix}$$

and publish the pair $(A, C_\aleph(S_1))$, in the same way, Boob chooses two matrices in $\aleph$,

$$B = \begin{pmatrix} 1 & (231025{:}130838{:}1) & (313039{:}156928{:}1) & (231025{:}130838{:}1) \\ (209305{:}158310{:}1) & 3 & (325271{:}280330{:}1) & (209305{:}158310{:}1) \\ (4959{:}212177{:}1) & (204268{:}290591{:}1) & 9 & (325271{:}280330{:}1) \\ (154308{:}310813{:}1) & (130516{:}286691{:}1) & (260212{:}57983{:}1) & 6 \end{pmatrix},$$

$$B_2 = \begin{pmatrix} 9 & (325271{:}280330{:}1) & (231025{:}130838{:}1) & (130516{:}286691{:}1) \\ (204268{:}290591{:}1) & 4 & (209305{:}158310{:}1) & (313039{:}156928{:}1) \\ (154308{:}310813{:}1) & (260212{:}57983{:}1) & 5 & (325271{:}280330{:}1) \\ (313039{:}156928{:}1) & (231025{:}130838{:}1) & (4959{:}212177{:}1) & 3 \end{pmatrix}$$

and publish the pair $(B, C_\aleph(B_2))$.

Allice choose a private keys, $r = 9$, and a matrix

$$S_2 = \begin{pmatrix} 7 & (325271{:}280330{:}1) & (231025{:}130838{:}1) & (130516{:}286691{:}1) \\ (204268{:}290591{:}1) & 2 & (209305{:}158310{:}1) & (313039{:}156928{:}1) \\ (154308{:}310813{:}1) & (260212{:}57983{:}1) & 3 & (325271{:}280330{:}1) \\ (313039{:}156928{:}1) & (231025{:}130838{:}1) & (4959{:}212177{:}1) & 1 \end{pmatrix}$$

$\in C_\aleph(B_2)$. She calculated the matrix

$$(M(S_1, A + B, S_2))^{\star 9} = \begin{pmatrix} S_1^{\star 9} & V_9 \\ 0 & S_2^{\star 9} \end{pmatrix},$$

where
$V_9 = \sum_{i=0}^{8} S_1^{\star(8-i)}(A + B)S_2^{\star i}$
$$= \begin{pmatrix} 260850 & (284421{:}77961{:}1) & (46354{:}273053{:}1) & (253036{:}363{:}1) \\ (141069{:}328577{:}1) & 115026 & (169368{:}225949{:}1) & (233261{:}218998{:}1) \\ (215911{:}142203{:}1) & (19315{:}277743{:}1) & 210881 & (19698{:}226465{:}1) \\ (274056{:}81341{:}1) & (120373{:}104427{:}1) & (49922{:}87765{:}1) & 144 \end{pmatrix}$$
and send it to Boob.

In turn, Boob chooses a private keys, $t = 15$, and a matrix

$$B_1 = \begin{pmatrix} 8 & (4959{:}212177{:}1) & (167587{:}100994{:}1) & (231025{:}130838{:}1) \\ (0{:}1{:}0) & 6 & (231025{:}130838{:}1) & (313039{:}156928{:}1) \\ (0{:}1{:}0) & (0{:}1{:}0) & 5 & (204268{:}290591{:}1) \\ (0{:}1{:}0) & (0{:}1{:}0) & (0{:}1{:}0) & 4 \end{pmatrix} \in C_\aleph(S_1).$$

He calculates the matrix

$$(M(B_1, A + B, B_2))^{\star 15} = \begin{pmatrix} B_1^{\star 15} & W_{15} \\ 0 & B_2^{\star 15} \end{pmatrix}$$

where
$W_{15} = \sum_{i=0}^{14} B_1^{\star(14-i)}(A + B)B_2^{\star i}$
$$= \begin{pmatrix} 121580 & (345221{:}60330{:}1) & (316655{:}87844{:}1) & (308469{:}221497{:}1) \\ (328166{:}88484{:}1) & 113055 & (130888{:}226438{:}1) & (241759{:}227219{:}1) \\ (282529{:}104352{:}1) & (177632{:}285982{:}1) & 117214 & (60282{:}99805{:}1) \\ (66269{:}6336{:}1) & (293187{:}236446{:}1) & (238123{:}156971{:}1) & 246421 \end{pmatrix}$$
and send it to Allice.

Using their respective private keys r and t,

$$\text{Allice calculates the matrix}: M(S_1, W_{15}, S_2)^{\star 9} = \begin{pmatrix} S_1^{\star 9} & W_{15,9} \\ 0 & S_2^{\star 9} \end{pmatrix} \quad (1)$$

$$\text{Boob calculates the matrix}: M(B_1, V_9, B_2)^{\star 15} = \begin{pmatrix} B_1^{\star 15} & V_{9,15} \\ 0 & B_2^{\star 15} \end{pmatrix}, \quad (2)$$

where,
$$W_{15,9} = \begin{pmatrix} 311444 & (241211:319426:1) & (212029:332425:1) & (339654:338816:1) \\ (7202:167718:1) & 67850 & (66389:270022:1) & (347520:94766:1) \\ (55034:223659:1) & (271929:140762:1) & 111658 & (5192:291054:1) \\ (254981:166477:1) & (58713:332732:1) & (194215:179039:1) & 73707 \end{pmatrix}$$

and,
$$V_{9,15} = \begin{pmatrix} 311444 & (241211:319426:1) & (212029:332425:1) & (339654:338816:1) \\ (7202:167718:1) & 67850 & (66389:270022:1) & (347520:94766:1) \\ (55034:223659:1) & (271929:140762:1) & 111658 & (5192:291054:1) \\ (254981:166477:1) & (58713:332732:1) & (194215:179039:1) & 73707 \end{pmatrix}$$

Hence, $W_{15,9} = V_{9,15}$.

So,
$$\phi = \begin{pmatrix} \alpha_1 & \chi_{1,2} & \chi_{1,3} & \chi_{1,4} \\ \psi_{2,1} & \alpha_2 & \chi_{2,3} & \chi_{2,4} \\ \psi_{3,1} & \psi_{3,2} & \alpha_3 & \chi_{3,4} \\ \psi_{4,1} & \psi_{4,2} & \chi_{4,3} & \alpha_4 \end{pmatrix} \tag{3}$$

$$= \begin{pmatrix} 311444 & (241211:319426:1) & (212029:332425:1) & (339654:338816:1) \\ (7202:167718:1) & 67850 & (66389:270022:1) & (347520:94766:1) \\ (55034:223659:1) & (271929:140762:1) & 111658 & (5192:291054:1) \\ (254981:166477:1) & (58713:332732:1) & (194215:179039:1) & 73707 \end{pmatrix} \tag{4}$$

Then, the secret Fibonacci sequence is defined by

$$N_{k+3} = N_k + N_{k+1} + N_{k+2} + N_{k+3},$$

$$N_k = \alpha_1 \chi_{1,2} + \chi_{1,3} + \chi_{1,4},$$

$$N_{k+1} = \psi_{2,1} + \alpha_2 \chi_{2,3} + \chi_{2,4},$$

$$N_{k+2} = \psi_{3,1} + \psi_{3,2} + \alpha_3 \chi_{3,4}.$$

$$N_{k+3} = \psi_{4,1} + \psi_{4,2} + \chi_{4,3}$$

where $k \in \mathbb{N}$. Therefore, we derive the secret key between Allice and Boob, represented by the elliptic Fibonacci sequence.

Let
$$G = <\phi> = \{1_{\aleph}, \phi, 2\phi, 3\phi, ..., (m-1)\phi\},$$

with $m = ord(G)$. For $1 \leq m$, we code $l\phi$ by $l\phi \to N_{n+l}$ and $1_{\aleph} \to N_{n+m}$. Then we get $\phi \to N_{n+1}, 2\phi \to N_{n+2}, ..., i\phi \to N_{n+i}, ...$

Step 1. Then, referring to the Table 1, the message "a new encryption scheme" is translated into the following binary code:
0011100110011001111101000001101000110001100001010101000001000010101111011000
1000001100100100111000110011100001011101111101000011100110010011010111001101
0010100100000101101011010010010110100100110111100001010101000001000010101
1101100010000100001110011001001101011001101001010010011001001001111000110011
1000010111011111000100101111010000110100001110110001010001101011100110011111
0100100001110001001100010101001000100110001111001100100110001110100010001
1100010011001100000100010001100101010101011001100110011101010100001011001 01
00100101100101100000010000101110000110111100110010010010100001100110010
0100111000110011100001011101 1111

Step 2. After receiving the above series of bits, Boob converts it into a pair of points $(x, y) = N_{k+m}$ and calculates the corresponding value using the description function.

5. Analysis of the Security and Complexity of Our Protocol

5.1. Complexity

In the context of our cryptographic protocol, it is essential to consider both temporal and spatial complexity. While the focus is traditionally on temporal complexity due to its impact on the efficiency and speed of the protocol, we cannot ignore the importance of spatial complexity, particularly in scenarios where we encounter a large centralizer of the private element.

The centralizer, which is a set of elements that switch with the private element, can grow to a considerable size depending on the specific cryptographic operations and algorithms employed. When the centralizer becomes large, it poses significant problems of spatial complexity. The centralizer can contain a large number of elements that need to be stored and manipulated during protocol execution.

By increasing the number of switched elements, it becomes more difficult for potential adversaries to decipher the private element. This enhanced security can be particularly advantageous in scenarios where robust security is paramount, even if it involves greater spatial complexity.

In what follows, however, we will approximate the computation time required to run (ECDLP).

- The multiplication of two matrices of order n requires $\delta\epsilon$ operations with $\delta \in \mathbb{N}$ and ϵ is the number of operations required to add two points on an elliptic curve.
- The calculation of A^t requires $\delta\epsilon \log(g)$ bit operations.
- The calculation of $V_k = \sum_{j=0}^{k-1} S_1^{k-1-j} B S_2^j$ therefore requires $2k\delta\epsilon(\log(g)+1)$ of operations
- Hence, to calculate $V_{k,t} = \sum_{i=0}^{t-1} B_1^{t-i-1} V_k B_2^i$, we need $2\delta\epsilon t(k+1)(\log(g)+1)$ operations.
- So, the overall number of bit operations needed to compute ϕ is $O(2\delta\epsilon t(k+1)(\log(g)+1))$ which is proportional to $O(2\delta\epsilon t(k+1)\log(g))$.

In Diffie–Hellman (KE), we have the commutative group $\mathbb{F}_p^*$ as a platform and so, keys are elements of $\mathbb{F}_p^*$ and the key computation complexity is $O\left((\log_2 p)^3\right)$. In our protocol, the keys are $n \times n$ matrices over $\aleph$. To compute the shared key, five matrices of this type are multiplied. As a result, the computational complexity for key generation is $O(2\delta\epsilon t(k+1)\log(g))$. On the other hand, the complexity of exhaustive search is proportional to $O(\eta p)$, where η represents the cardinality of the ring $\aleph$ and the exponents are chosen from $\mathbb{Z}/g\mathbb{Z}$.

5.2. Security

The protocol's security, as explained in Section 3, relies on the complexity of a computational problem. Specifically, it assumes that it is difficult to compute the shared key using the public information A, B, V_k, and W_t. This is the protocol's computational assumption, and a stronger version of which is the decisional assumption, which states that distinguishing ϕ from a random element $M_1(A+B)M_2$ is also hard.

In the following security analysis, we examine our protocol's resistance to different types of attacks found in the literature [27–29].

Attacks through matrix properties:

Our (ECDLP) problem is impervious to Cayley–Hamilton [28] as well as eigenvalue [27] attacks.

- Cayley–Hamilton attack
  We must know S_1, A, B and $S_2 \in \mathbb{F}_q[\aleph]$ such that $S_1^k B S_2^t = g(S_1)h(A+B)f(S_2)$, for $g(x), h(x)$ and $f(x) \in (\mathbb{F}_q[\aleph])[x]$ with

  $$g(S_1) = \sum_{i=0}^{m-1} a_i S_1^i, \quad h(A+B) = \sum_{i=0}^{m-1} b_i (A+B)^i \quad \text{and} \quad f(S_2) = \sum_{i=0}^{m-1} c_i S_2^i.$$

  since we do not know S_1 and S_2, it is not possible to find $g(x)$ and $f(x)$ so using the Cayley–Hamilton attack to solve the (ECDLP) is a bad choice
- Eigenvalues attack
  Here, the eigenvalues of $S_1^k(A+B)S_2^t$ are not known and those of A and B are. This attack is therefore not applicable.

Attacks on (ECDLP):

There are several methods to solve (ECDLP) like Pollard Rho, Pohling–Hellman, and Baby-Step Giant-Step, but without modifying this protocol, the adversary cannot apply these methods directly, because in these methods he knows an element T and a power T^t, but here S_1^k and S_2^j are hidden, that is, $V_k = \sum_{j=0}^{k-1} S_1^{k-1-j}(A+B)S_2^j$.

Linear algebra attack:

An adversary can attack our protocol with a linear algebra attack discussed in [29] only if the following conditions are satisfied:

- Find V such that $VS_1 = S_1V$.
- Find W such that $WS_2 = S_2W$.
- $W_t = V(A+B)W$.

If we can find V, W with the previous conditions, then we can compute the exchanged key:

$$VV_kW = V\sum_{j=0}^{k-1} S_1^{k-1-j}(A+B)S_2^jW \qquad (5)$$

$$= \sum_{j=0}^{k-1} VS_1^{k-1-j}(A+B)S_2^jW \qquad (6)$$

$$= \sum_{j=0}^{k-1} S_1^{k-1-j}V(A+B)WS_2^j \qquad (7)$$

$$= \sum_{j=0}^{k-1} S_1^{k-1-j}W_tS_2^j \qquad (8)$$

$$= \phi. \qquad (9)$$

Since the underlying structure is non-commutative, the first and second conditions cannot be written as a system of linear equations on the ring $\aleph$. Thus, the choice of our platform prevents anyone from expressing $VS_1 = S_1V$ or $WS_2 = S_2W$ as a system of linear equations. It is therefore not possible to find V and W by this method. Furthermore, since we consider that $S_1, S_2 \notin C_\aleph(A)$ and $B_1, B_2 \notin C_\aleph(B)$ as shown in Section 3, we can say that these conditions allow us to avoid this linear algebra attack.

Explanation with the Random Oracle Model:

In the Random Oracle Model, we treat the elliptic curve operations as idealized mathematical operations, much like the random oracle itself. In this model, computing Q from A^sB is a straightforward mathematical operation. However, the difficulty in the (ECDLP) arises from the fact that, given Q and A^sB, it is extremely challenging to compute s and B efficiently, even with knowledge of the curve parameters. Here's why:

Multiplication is a random oracle operation:

We can think of the multiplication A^sB as an interrogation of a random oracle that generates points on the curve. The oracle takes AB and applies a random transformation s times to generate Q. Each query to this random oracle produces a matrix in $\aleph$, in the same way that the random oracle model produces random values in other cryptographic scenarios.

Infeasibility of reversing the oracle:

(ECDLP) is difficult in this model, as the inversion of the oracle to find s and B is infeasible. The difficulty stems from the fact that the transformations applied in the oracle are essentially random and unpredictable. There is no known efficient algorithm that can reverse this process, and finding s and B would require an exhaustive search of all possible values, which is computationally infeasible for large elliptic curves.

6. Conclusions

In summary, the Fibonacci sequence and its generalizations have proved to be a rich area of research with applications in a variety of fields. By extending this theory to elliptic curve sequences, we have explored new possibilities in cryptography. The proposed encryption scheme, based on the modified Fibonacci sequence, combines the power of elliptic curve cryptography with the elegance of Fibonacci numbers. A notable advantage of this new approach lies in its ability to generate a large number of points with a smaller prime number, p. To this end, a matrix of order n is used. While this may potentially increase the complexity of the Elliptic Curve Discrete Logarithm Problem (ECDLP) (which could weaken security), the use of the Fibonacci sequence allows the derivation of a single point with several private variables. As a result, the reduction in security that might otherwise occur is circumvented.

Author Contributions: Writing—original draft, Z.C.; Supervision, A.C. and A.M. All authors have read and agreed to the published version of the manuscript.

Funding: This research received no external funding.

Data Availability Statement: Data sharing not applicable to this article as no datasets were generated or analyzed during the current study.

Acknowledgments: The authors are thankful to the anonymous referees for their helpful comments.

Conflicts of Interest: The authors declare no conflict of interest.

References

1. Falcon, S.; Plaza, A. The k-Fibonacci sequence and the Pascal 2-triangle. *Chaos Solitons Fractals* **2007**, *33*, 38–49. [CrossRef]
2. Edson, M.; Yayenie, O. A new generalization of Fibonacci sequences and extended Binet's formula. *Integers* **2009**, *9*, 639–654. [CrossRef]
3. Deveci, O.; Karaduman, E.; Campbell, C.M. On the k-Fibonacci sequences in finite binary polyhedral groups. *Algebra Colloq* **2011**, *18*, 945–954. [CrossRef]
4. Edson, M.; Lewis, S.; Yayenie, O. The k-periodic Fibonacci sequence and an extended Binet's formula. *Integers* **2011**, *11*. [CrossRef]
5. Falcon, S.; Plaza, Á. k-Fibonacci sequences modulo m. *Chaos Solitons Fract.* **2009**, *41*, 497–504. [CrossRef]
6. Karaduman, E.; Aydin, H. k-Fibonacci sequences in some special groups of finite order. *Math. Comput. Modell.* **2009**, *50*, 53–58. [CrossRef]
7. Ozkan, E.; Aydin, H.; Dikici, R. 3-step Fibonacci series modulo m. *Appl. Math. Comput.* **2003**, *143*, 165–172.
8. Prasad, K.; Mahato, H. Cryptography using generalized Fibonacci matrices with Affine-Hill cipher. *J. Discrete Math. Sci. Cryptogr.* **2022**, *25*, 2341–2352. [CrossRef]
9. Wall, D.D. Fibonacci series modulo m. *Am. Math. Mon.* **1960**, *67*, 525–532. [CrossRef]
10. Deveci, O.; Shannon, A.G. The quaternion-Pell sequence. *Commun. Algebra* **2018**, *46*, 5403–5409. [CrossRef]
11. Deveci, O.; Shannon, A.G. The complex-type k-Fibonacci sequences and their applications. *Commun. Algebra* **2018**, *49*, 1352–1367. [CrossRef]
12. Deveci, O.; Karaduman, E.; Campbell, C.M. The Fibonacci-circulant sequences and their applications. *Iran. J. Sci. Technol. Trans. Sci.* **2017**, *41*, 1033–1038. [CrossRef]
13. Kilic, E. The Binet formula, sums and representations of generalized Fibonacci p-numbers. *Eur. J. Combin.* **2008**, *29*, 701–711. [CrossRef]
14. Kilic, E.; Tasci, D. On the generalized order-k Fibonacci and Lucas numbers. *Rocky Mt. J. Math.* **2006**, *36*, 1915–1926. [CrossRef]
15. Kilic, E.; Tasci, D. On the permanents of some tridiagonal matrices with applications to the Fibonacci and Lucas numbers. *Rocky Mt. J. Math.* **2007**, *37*, 1953–1969. [CrossRef]
16. Kwon, Y. A note on the modified k-Fibonacci-Like sequence. *Commun. Korean Math. Soc.* **2016**, *31*, 1–16. [CrossRef]
17. Lagheliel, S.; Chillali, A.; Ait-Mokhtar, A. New encryption scheme using k-Fibonacci-like sequence. *Asian-Eur. J. Math.* **2022**, *15*, 2250037. [CrossRef]
18. Ozgur, N.Y. On the sequences related to Fibonacci and Lucas numbers. *J. Korean Math. Soc.* **2005**, *42*, 135–151. [CrossRef]
19. Stakhov, A.P.; Rozin, B. Theory of Binet formulas for Fibonacci and Lucas p-numbers. *Chaos Solitons Fract.* **2006**, *27*, 1162–1177. [CrossRef]
20. Stakhov, A.P.; Rozin, B. The continuous functions for the Fibonacci and Lucas p-numbers. *Chaos Solitons Fract.* **2006**, *28*, 1014–1025. [CrossRef]
21. Tasci, D.; Firengiz, M.C. Incomplete Fibonacci and Lucas p-numbers. *Math. Comput. Modell.* **2010**, *52*, 1763–1770. [CrossRef]
22. Yayenie, O. A note on generalized Fibonacci sequences. *Appl. Math. Comput.* **2011**, *217*, 5603–5611. [CrossRef]
23. Cheddour, Z.; Chillali, A.; Mouhib, A. Elliptic curve and k-Fibonacci-like sequence. *Sci. Afr.* **2023**, *20*, e01734. [CrossRef]

24. Cheddour, Z.; Chillali, A.; Mouhib, A. The "Elliptic" matrices and a new kind of cryptography. *Bol. Soc. Parana. Mat.* **2023**, *2023*, 1–12. [CrossRef]
25. Odlyzko, A. Discrete logarithms: The past and the future. *Des. Codes Cryptogr.* **2000**, *19*, 129–145. [CrossRef]
26. Cramer, R.; Shoup, V. Signature Schemes Based on the Strong RSA Assumption. *ACM Trans. Inf. Syst. Secur.* **2000**, *3*, 161–185. [CrossRef]
27. Eftekhari, M. Cryptanalysis of some protocols using matrices over group rings. In Proceedings of the International Conference on Cryptology in Africa—AFRICACRYPT 2017, Dakar, Senegal, 24–26 May 2017.
28. Micheli, G. Cryptanalysis of a non-commutative (KEP). *Adv. Math. Commun.* **2015**, *9*, 247–253. [CrossRef]
29. Shpilrain, V. Cryptanalysis of Stickels key exchange scheme. In Proceedings of the 3rd International Computer Science Symposium in Russia, Moscow, Russia, 7–12 June 2008; pp. 283–288.

Disclaimer/Publisher's Note: The statements, opinions and data contained in all publications are solely those of the individual author(s) and contributor(s) and not of MDPI and/or the editor(s). MDPI and/or the editor(s) disclaim responsibility for any injury to people or property resulting from any ideas, methods, instructions or products referred to in the content.

Article

A New Class of Leonardo Hybrid Numbers and Some Remarks on Leonardo Quaternions over Finite Fields

Elif Tan [1,*], Diana Savin [2] and Semih Yılmaz [3]

[1] Department of Mathematics, Faculty of Science, Ankara University, 06100 Ankara, Turkey
[2] Department of Mathematics and Computer Science, Transilvania University of Brasov, 500091 Brasov, Romania; diana.savin@unitbv.ro
[3] Department of Actuarial Sciences, Kırıkkale University, 71450 Kırıkkale, Turkey; syilmaz@kku.edu.tr
* Correspondence: etan@ankara.edu.tr

Abstract: In this paper, we present a new class of Leonardo hybrid numbers that incorporate quantum integers into their components. This advancement presents a broader generalization of the q-Leonardo hybrid numbers. We explore some fundamental properties associated with these numbers. Moreover, we study special Leonardo quaternions over finite fields. In particular, we determine the Leonardo quaternions that are zero divisors or invertible elements in the quaternion algebra over the finite field $\mathbb{Z}_p$ for special values of prime integer p.

Keywords: hybrid numbers; quaternions; Fibonacci numbers; Leonardo numbers; quantum integer; zero divisor; finite fields

MSC: 11B37; 11B39; 11R52; 16G30

1. Introduction

The study of second-order linear recurrence relations has various applications in mathematics, computer science, physics, engineering, and other fields where the behavior of sequences is of interest. For some recent studies, see [1–5]. The general second-order linear recurrence $\{W_n\}$ is defined by

$$W_n = sW_{n-1} + tW_{n-2}, \quad n \geq 2$$

with arbitrary initial values W_0, W_1 and nonzero integers s, t. The Binet formula of the sequence $\{W_n\}$ is

$$W_n = \frac{(W_1 - W_0\delta)\gamma^n - (W_1 - W_0\gamma)\delta^n}{\gamma - \delta},$$

where γ, δ are the roots of the characteristic polynomial $x^2 - sx - t$. Many well-known second-order linear recurrences arise as a special case of the sequence $\{W_n\}$. The well-known Fibonacci sequence $\{F_n\}$ arises by taking $s = t = 1$ and $W_0 = 0, W_1 = 1$ in the sequence $\{W_n\}$. In addition, if we take $s = t = 1$ with initial values $W_0 = 2, W_1 = 1$ in the sequence $\{W_n\}$, it gives the classical Lucas sequence $\{L_n\}$. Thus, the Binet formulas of the Fibonacci and Lucas sequences are $F_n = \frac{\alpha^n - \beta^n}{\alpha - \beta}$ and $L_n = \alpha^n + \beta^n$, respectively, where $\alpha = \frac{1+\sqrt{5}}{2}$ and $\beta = \frac{1-\sqrt{5}}{2}$. For further information regarding the general second-order linear recurrences, we refer to [6–9].

There are several nonhomogeneous extensions of the Fibonacci recurrence relation. One among them is the Leonardo sequence $\{\mathcal{L}_n\}$, which is defined by the following nonhomogenous recurrence relation:

$$\mathcal{L}_n = \mathcal{L}_{n-1} + \mathcal{L}_{n-2} + 1, \quad n \geq 2 \tag{1}$$

with initial values $\mathcal{L}_0 = \mathcal{L}_1 = 1$. The Leonardo sequence finds applications in various fields, including mathematics, computer science, and cryptography. It appears in problems involving tiling, divisibility, and combinatorial counting, among others. The sequence has been the subject of mathematical research and exploration, leading to the discovery of intriguing patterns and connections with other sequences and mathematical concepts. In 1981, Dijkstra [10] used these numbers as an integral part of his smoothsort algorithm. For the properties of Leonardo numbers and related studies, we refer to [11–16], and for the history of Leonardo sequences, see [A001595] in the On-Line Encyclopedia of Integer Sequences [17].

Recently, Kuhapatanakul and Chobsorn [18] have defined the generalized Leonardo sequence $\{\mathcal{L}_{k,n}\}$ by the following nonhomogenous relation:

$$\mathcal{L}_{k,n} = \mathcal{L}_{k,n-1} + \mathcal{L}_{k,n-2} + k, \ n \geq 2 \qquad (2)$$

with initial values $\mathcal{L}_{k,0} = \mathcal{L}_{k,1} = 1$. The parameter k is a fixed positive integer. It is clear to see that when $k = 1$, it reduces to the classical Leonardo sequence $\{\mathcal{L}_n\}$. Shattuck [19] gave a combinatorial interpretation for the generalized Leonardo sequence in terms of colored linear tilings. In particular, the generalized Leonardo number $\mathcal{L}_{k,n}$ counts the number of all linear colored tilings of length n by using squares, dominoes, and the k-tiles where a square covers a single cell, a domino covers two consecutive cells, and a k-tile is a rectangular piece coming in one of k colors, which must occur as the first piece in a tiling, if it occurs at all, and has an arbitrary length greater than or equal to two. For more on linear tilings, we refer to [19,20].

On the other hand, quaternions can be viewed as an extension of complex numbers and have been explored in various fields, including computer science, physics, differential geometry, and quantum physics, as extensively documented by researchers. Let F be a field with characteristic not 2. The generalized quaternion algebra over a field F is defined as:

$$Q_F(a,b) = \left\{ x + y\mathbf{i} + z\mathbf{j} + t\mathbf{k} \mid x,y,z,t \in F, \mathbf{i}^2 = a, \mathbf{j}^2 = b, \mathbf{ij} = -\mathbf{ji} = \mathbf{k} \right\} \qquad (3)$$

where a,b are nonzero invertible elements of field F. It is clear to see that the algebra $Q_\mathbb{R}(-1,-1)$ reduces to the real quaternion algebra. We recall that a generalized quaternion algebra is a division algebra if and only if a quaternion with a norm of zero is necessarily the zero quaternion. In other words, for $X = x + y\mathbf{i} + z\mathbf{j} + t\mathbf{k} \in Q_F(a,b)$, the norm of X, denoted as $N(X)$ and defined as $N(X) = x^2 - ay^2 - bz^2 + abt^2$, equals zero if and only if $X = 0$. Otherwise, the algebra is called a split algebra. It is known that real quaternion algebra is a division algebra and the quaternion algebra over finite field $\mathbb{Z}_p$, denoted as $Q_{\mathbb{Z}_p}(-1,-1)$, is a split algebra, where p is an odd prime integer, see [21]. In [22], the author studied special elements in quaternion algebras over finite fields. For more information related to quaternion algebras, we refer to [22] and the references therein.

Similar to real quaternions, hybrid number multiplication is also noncommutative. The concept of hybrid numbers was introduced by Ozdemir [23] as a generalization of complex, hyperbolic, and dual numbers. They are defined as

$$\mathbb{H} = \left\{ x + y\mathbf{i} + z\epsilon + t\mathbf{h} \mid x,y,z,t \in \mathbb{R}, \mathbf{i}^2 = -1, \epsilon^2 = 0, \mathbf{h}^2 = 1, \mathbf{ih} = -\mathbf{hi} = \epsilon + \mathbf{i} \right\}. \qquad (4)$$

The addition and the subtraction of two hybrid numbers are defined component-wise, and the product of two hybrid numbers is defined according to the rule specified in (4). For more details on the hybrid numbers, we refer to [23].

Many authors have extensively researched different types of quaternions and hybrid numbers, where their components are derived from terms found in special integer sequences. In particular, Leonardo hybrid quaternions were studied in [24], Leonardo sedenions were studied in [25], Szynal [26] studied Horadam hybrid numbers, which generalize the classical Fibonacci hybrid numbers and the classical Lucas hybrid numbers. Polynomial versions of Fibonacci and Lucas hybrid numbers were studied in [27]. Tan and

Ait-Amrane [28] introduced the bi-periodic Horadam hybrid numbers. Alp and Kocer [29] bring together hybrid numbers and Leonardo numbers and defined the hybrid Leonardo numbers as:

$$\mathbb{HL}_n = \mathcal{L}_n + \mathcal{L}_{n+1}i + \mathcal{L}_{n+2}\epsilon + \mathcal{L}_{n+3}h \tag{5}$$

where $\mathcal{L}_n$ is the nth Leonardo number. We note that throughout this paper, we call the sequence $\{\mathbb{HL}_n\}$ as the Leonardo hybrid sequence. By considering the relation between Leonardo numbers and Fibonacci numbers, $\mathcal{L}_n = 2F_{n+1} - 1$, Ozimamoglu [30] expressed the coefficient of Leonardo hybrid numbers in terms of q-integers as

$$\begin{aligned}\mathbb{HL}_n(\alpha;q) &= \left(2\alpha^n[n+1]_q - 1\right) + \left(2\alpha^{n+1}[n+2]_q - 1\right)i \\ &+ \left(2\alpha^{n+2}[n+3]_q - 1\right)\epsilon + \left(2\alpha^{n+3}[n+4]_q - 1\right)h\end{aligned} \tag{6}$$

and called them as q-Leonardo hybrid numbers. It is clear to see that by taking $q = \frac{-1}{\alpha^2}$, the q-Leonardo hybrid numbers reduce to the classical Leonardo hybrid numbers in (5). To express the coefficients of the Leonardo hybrid numbers in terms of quantum integers, it is essential to recall the definition of quantum integers. Quantum integers are mathematical objects that generalize the concept of integers and emerge in the field of quantum physics, particularly in the study of quantum groups and their representations. For positive integer n, the quantum integer (q-integer) n is defined by

$$[n]_q = \frac{1-q^n}{1-q} = 1 + q + q^2 + \cdots + q^{n-1} \tag{7}$$

where q is a complex number with $q \neq 1$. For details on the theory of quantum calculus, we refer to the book by Kac and Cheung [31]. We also note that in [32], the authors established the concept of Fibonacci quaternions with coefficients from quantum integers. By using a similar approach, Kizilates [33] defined the Fibonacci and Lucas hybrid numbers with quantum integers as

$$\mathbb{HF}_n(\gamma;q) = \gamma^{n-1}[n]_q + \gamma^n[n+1]_q i + \gamma^{n+1}[n+2]_q \epsilon + \gamma^{n+2}[n+3]_q h \tag{8}$$

and

$$\mathbb{HL}_n(\gamma;q) = \gamma^n \frac{[2n]_q}{[n]_q} + \gamma^{n+1}\frac{[2n+2]_q}{[n+1]_q}i + \gamma^{n+2}\frac{[2n+4]_q}{[n+2]_q}\epsilon + \gamma^{n+3}\frac{[2n+6]_q}{[n+3]_q}h, \tag{9}$$

respectively.

In this paper, we introduce the concept of generalized Leonardo hybrid numbers, which generalize the classical Leonardo hybrid numbers. Different from the papers [29,30], we define a new family of hybrid numbers that reflects the generalized Leonardo numbers $\mathcal{L}_{k,n}$. Additionally, we define a new class of Leonardo hybrid numbers, called q-generalized Leonardo hybrid numbers, that incorporate quantum integers into their components. We derive several fundamental properties of these numbers including recurrence relations, the exponential generating function, the Binet formula, Vajda's identity, and summation formulas. We should note that this new class of Leonardo hybrid numbers is even more general than the one studied in [29,30]. Considering the extensive usage of quantum integers in physics, quantum hybrid numbers are expected to garner wider interest and find various applications. The major innovation point of the paper is that we study certain special Leonardo quaternions in quaternion algebras over finite fields. In particular, we consider the quaternion algebra $Q_{\mathbb{Z}_p}(-1,-1)$, and we determine the Leonardo quaternions, which are zero divisors or invertible elements in the quaternion algebra over finite field $\mathbb{Z}_p$ for special values of prime integer p.

To conclude this section, we recall some basic identities associated with the generalized Leonardo numbers, which can be found in [18]:

$$\mathcal{L}_{k,n} = (k+1)F_{n+1} - k, \tag{10}$$

$$\mathcal{L}_{k,n} = (k+1)(L_n - F_{n-1}) - k, \tag{11}$$

$$\sum_{j=0}^{n} \mathcal{L}_{k,j} = \mathcal{L}_{k,n+2} - k(n+1) - 1. \tag{12}$$

2. q-Generalized Leonardo Hybrid Numbers

In this section, we give the definitions of generalized Leonardo hybrid numbers and q-generalized Leonardo hybrid numbers. We explore the fundamental properties of these sequences. Throughout this section, we adopt the notation $I := 1 + i + \epsilon + h$. Since we take $\alpha = \frac{1+\sqrt{5}}{2}$, we use the notations $\mathbb{H}F_n^q$ and $\mathbb{H}L_n^q$ instead of $\mathbb{H}F_n(\alpha; q)$ and $\mathbb{H}L_n(\alpha; q)$ in (8) and (9), respectively.

Definition 1. *The nth generalized Leonardo hybrid number is defined by*

$$\mathbb{H}\mathcal{L}_{k,n} = \mathcal{L}_{k,n} + \mathcal{L}_{k,n+1}i + \mathcal{L}_{k,n+2}\epsilon + \mathcal{L}_{k,n+3}h,$$

where i, ϵ, and h satisfy the multiplication rules in (4).

In the following theorem, we establish certain relations concerning the generalized Leonardo hybrid numbers that yield analogous results to those in Equations (1), (11) and (12), respectively.

Theorem 1. *For generalized Leonardo hybrid numbers, we have the following*

(i) $\mathbb{H}\mathcal{L}_{k,n} = \mathbb{H}\mathcal{L}_{k,n-1} + \mathbb{H}\mathcal{L}_{k,n-2} + kI$, $n \geq 2$,

(ii) $\mathbb{H}\mathcal{L}_{k,n} = (k+1)(\mathbb{H}L_n - \mathbb{H}F_{n-1}) - kI$,

(iii) $\sum_{j=0}^{n} \mathbb{H}\mathcal{L}_{k,j} = \mathbb{H}\mathcal{L}_{k,n+2} - k(n+1)I - I - (k+1)(i + 2\epsilon + 4h)$.

Proof. (i) For $n \geq 2$, by using Definition 1 and Equation (2), the generalized Leonardo hybrid numbers satisfy the following recurrence relation

$$\begin{aligned}
\mathbb{H}\mathcal{L}_{k,n} &= \mathcal{L}_{k,n} + \mathcal{L}_{k,n+1}i + \mathcal{L}_{k,n+2}\epsilon + \mathcal{L}_{k,n+3}h \\
&= (\mathcal{L}_{k,n-1} + \mathcal{L}_{k,n-2} + k) + (\mathcal{L}_{k,n} + \mathcal{L}_{k,n-1} + k)i \\
&\quad + (\mathcal{L}_{k,n+1} + \mathcal{L}_{k,n} + k)\epsilon + (\mathcal{L}_{k,n+2} + \mathcal{L}_{k,n-1} + k)h \\
&= (\mathcal{L}_{k,n-1} + \mathcal{L}_{k,n}i + \mathcal{L}_{k,n+1}\epsilon + \mathcal{L}_{k,n+2}h) \\
&\quad + (\mathcal{L}_{k,n-2} + \mathcal{L}_{k,n-1}i + \mathcal{L}_{k,n}\epsilon + \mathcal{L}_{k,n-1}h) \\
&\quad + k(1 + i + \epsilon + h) \\
&= \mathbb{H}\mathcal{L}_{k,n-1} + \mathbb{H}\mathcal{L}_{k,n-2} + kI.
\end{aligned}$$

(ii) By using Definition 1 and Equation (11), the generalized Leonardo hybrid numbers can be expressed in terms of Fibonacci hybrid numbers and Lucas hybrid numbers as:

$$\begin{aligned}
\mathbb{HL}_{k,n} &= \mathcal{L}_{k,n} + \mathcal{L}_{k,n+1}i + \mathcal{L}_{k,n+2}\epsilon + \mathcal{L}_{k,n+3}h \\
&= ((k+1)(L_n - F_{n-1}) - k) + ((k+1)(L_{n+1} - F_n) - k)i \\
&\quad + ((k+1)(L_{n+2} - F_{n+1}) - k)\epsilon + ((k+1)(L_{n+3} - F_{n+2}) - k)h \\
&= (k+1)((L_n + L_{n+1}i + L_{n+2}\epsilon + L_{n+3}h) - (F_{n-1} + F_n i + F_{n12}\epsilon + F_{n+2}h)) \\
&\quad - k(1 + i + \epsilon + h) \\
&= (k+1)(\mathbb{HL}_n - \mathbb{HF}_{n-1}) - kI.
\end{aligned}$$

(iii) By using Definition 1 and Equation (12), we have a sum formula for generalized Leonardo hybrid numbers as:

$$\begin{aligned}
\sum_{j=0}^n \mathbb{HL}_{k,j} &= \sum_{j=0}^n \mathcal{L}_{k,j} + \sum_{j=0}^n \mathcal{L}_{k,j+1}i + \sum_{j=0}^n \mathcal{L}_{k,j+2}\epsilon + \sum_{j=0}^n \mathcal{L}_{k,j+3}h \\
&= (\mathcal{L}_{k,n+2} - k(n+1) - 1) + (\mathcal{L}_{k,n+3} - k(n+2) - 1 - \mathcal{L}_{k,0})i \\
&\quad + (\mathcal{L}_{k,n+4} - k(n+3) - 1 - \mathcal{L}_{k,0} - \mathcal{L}_{k,1})\epsilon \\
&\quad + (\mathcal{L}_{k,n+5} - k(n+4) - 1 - \mathcal{L}_{k,0} - \mathcal{L}_{k,1} - \mathcal{L}_{k,2})h \\
&= \mathbb{HL}_{k,n+2} - k(n+1)I - I - (k+1)(i + 2\epsilon + 4h).
\end{aligned}$$

□

Remark 1. *If we take $k = 1$ in Theorem 1 (i), we obtain the recurrence relation for the classical Leonardo hybrid numbers*

$$\mathbb{HL}_n = \mathbb{HL}_{n-1} + \mathbb{HL}_{n-2} + I, \ n \geq 2,$$

which was given in [29]. If we take $k = 1$ in Theorem 1 (iii), we obtain

$$\sum_{j=0}^n \mathbb{HL}_j = \mathbb{HL}_{n+2} - (n+2)I - (2i + 4\epsilon + 8h),$$

which can be found in ([29] Theorem 2.5).

Definition 2. *The nth q-generalized Leonardo hybrid number is defined by*

$$\begin{aligned}
\mathbb{HL}_{k,n}^q &= \left((k+1)\alpha^n[n+1]_q - k\right) + \left((k+1)\alpha^{n+1}[n+2]_q - k\right)i \\
&\quad + \left((k+1)\alpha^{n+2}[n+3]_q - k\right)\epsilon + \left((k+1)\alpha^{n+3}[n+4]_q - k\right)h,
\end{aligned}$$

where $i, \epsilon,$ and h satisfy the multiplication rules in (4).

Some special cases of q-generalized Leonardo hybrid numbers can be given as follows:

1. If we take $q = \frac{-1}{\alpha^2}$ in Definition 2, we obtain the generalized Leonardo hybrid numbers $\mathbb{HL}_{k,n}$ in Definition 1.
2. If we take $k = 1$ in Definition 2, we obtain the q-Leonardo hybrid numbers $\mathbb{HL}_n(\alpha; q)$ in (6).
3. If we take $k = 1$ and $q = \frac{-1}{\alpha^2}$ in Definition 2, we obtain the classical Leonardo hybrid numbers $\mathbb{HL}_n$ in (5).

The following result gives a relation between q-generalized Leonardo hybrid numbers and q-Fibonacci hybrid numbers.

Theorem 2. *For $n > 0$, we have*

$$\mathbb{HL}_{k,n}^q = (k+1)\mathbb{H}F_{n+1}^q - kI,$$

where $\mathbb{H}F_n^q$ is the nth q-Fibonacci hybrid number.

Proof. By using the definitions of q-Fibonacci hybrid numbers and q-generalized Leonardo hybrid numbers, we obtain the desired result. □

Remark 2. *If we take $k = 1$ in Theorem 2, we obtain the identity in ([30] Corollary 3.1).*

Next, we state the Binet formula for the q-generalized Leonardo hybrid numbers.

Theorem 3. *The Binet formula for the q-generalized Leonardo hybrid numbers is*

$$\mathbb{HL}_{k,n}^q = (k+1)\left(\frac{\alpha^{n+1}\alpha^* - (\alpha q)^{n+1}\beta^*}{\alpha(1-q)}\right) - kI,$$

where $\alpha^* = 1 + \alpha i + \alpha^2 \epsilon + \alpha^3 h$ and $\beta^* = 1 + (\alpha q)i + (\alpha q)^2 \epsilon + (\alpha q)^3 h$.

Proof. From Theorem 2 and the Binet formula of q-Fibonacci hybrid numbers in ([33] Theorem 2), we obtain

$$\mathbb{HL}_{k,n}^q = (k+1)\mathbb{H}F_{n+1}^q - kI = (k+1)\left(\frac{\alpha^{n+1}\alpha^* - (\alpha q)^{n+1}\beta^*}{\alpha(1-q)}\right) - kI.$$

□

Theorem 4. *The exponential generating function of the q-generalized Leonardo hybrid numbers is*

$$\sum_{n=0}^{\infty} \mathbb{HL}_{k,n}^q \frac{x^n}{n!} = (k+1)\left(\frac{\alpha^* e^{\alpha x} - q\beta^* e^{\alpha q x}}{1-q}\right) - kIe^x,$$

where $\alpha^* = 1 + \alpha i + \alpha^2 \epsilon + \alpha^3 h$ and $\beta^* = 1 + (\alpha q)i + (\alpha q)^2 \epsilon + (\alpha q)^3 h$.

Proof. From the Binet formula of q-generalized Leonardo hybrid numbers in Theorem 3, we obtain

$$\sum_{n=0}^{\infty} \mathbb{HL}_{k,n}^q \frac{x^n}{n!} = \sum_{n=0}^{\infty}\left((k+1)\left(\frac{\alpha^{n+1}\alpha^* - (\alpha q)^{n+1}\beta^*}{\alpha(1-q)}\right) - kI\right)\frac{x^n}{n!}$$

$$= (k+1)\sum_{n=0}^{\infty}\left(\frac{\alpha^{n+1}\alpha^* - (\alpha q)^{n+1}\beta^*}{\alpha(1-q)}\right)\frac{x^n}{n!} - kI\sum_{n=0}^{\infty}\frac{x^n}{n!}$$

$$= (k+1)\frac{\alpha^*}{1-q}\sum_{n=0}^{\infty}\frac{(\alpha x)^n}{n!} - (k+1)\frac{q\beta^*}{1-q}\sum_{n=0}^{\infty}\frac{(\alpha q x)^n}{n!} - kI\sum_{n=0}^{\infty}\frac{x^n}{n!}$$

$$= (k+1)\left(\frac{\alpha^* e^{\alpha x} - q\beta^* e^{\alpha q x}}{1-q}\right) - kIe^x.$$

□

We have the following summation formula for the q-generalized Leonardo hybrid numbers.

Theorem 5. For $n \geq 0$, we have

$$\sum_{j=0}^{n} \mathbb{HL}_{k,j}^q = (k+1)\left(\frac{\mathbb{H}F_1^q - q\alpha^2\mathbb{H}F_0^q - \mathbb{H}F_{n+2}^q + q\alpha^2\mathbb{H}F_{n+1}^q}{(1-\alpha)(1-\alpha q)}\right) - kI(n+1).$$

Proof. First, we give a summation formula for the q-Fibonacci hybrid numbers.

$$\sum_{j=0}^{n} \mathbb{H}F_{j+1}^q = \sum_{j=0}^{n} \frac{\alpha^{j+1}\alpha^* - (\alpha q)^{j+1}\beta^*}{\alpha(1-q)}$$

$$= \frac{1}{1-q}\sum_{j=0}^{n} \alpha^j \alpha^* - q(\alpha q)^j \beta^* = \frac{\alpha^*}{1-q}\sum_{j=0}^{n}\alpha^j - \frac{q\beta^*}{1-q}\sum_{j=0}^{n}(\alpha q)^j$$

$$= \frac{1}{1-q}\left(\frac{\alpha^*(1-\alpha^{n+1})}{1-\alpha} - \frac{q\beta^*(1-(\alpha q)^{n+1})}{1-\alpha q}\right)$$

$$= \frac{1}{1-q}\left(\frac{\alpha^*(1-\alpha^{n+1})(1-\alpha q) - q\beta^*(1-(\alpha q)^{n+1})(1-\alpha)}{(1-\alpha)(1-\alpha q)}\right)$$

$$= \frac{\alpha^*(1-\alpha q - \alpha^{n+1} + q\alpha^{n+2}) - q\beta^*(1-\alpha - (\alpha q)^{n+1} + \alpha^{n+2}q^{n+1})}{(1-q)(1-\alpha)(1-\alpha q)}$$

$$= \frac{(\alpha^* - q\beta^*) - (\alpha^*\alpha q - \alpha q\beta^*) - (\alpha^*\alpha^{n+1} - q\beta^*(\alpha q)^{n+1}) + (\alpha^* q\alpha^{n+2} - \beta^*(\alpha q)^{n+2})}{(1-q)(1-\alpha)(1-\alpha q)}$$

$$= \frac{1}{(1-\alpha)(1-\alpha q)} \times$$

$$\left(\frac{\alpha\alpha^* - \alpha q\beta^*}{\alpha(1-q)} - \frac{q\alpha^2(\alpha^* - \beta^*)}{\alpha(1-q)} - \frac{\alpha^{n+2}\alpha^* - (\alpha q)^{n+2}\beta^*}{\alpha(1-q)} + \frac{q\alpha^2(\alpha^{n+1}\alpha^* - (\alpha q)^{n+1}\beta^*)}{\alpha(1-q)}\right).$$

By using the Binet formula of q-Fibonacci hybrid numbers in ([33] Theorem 2), we obtain

$$\sum_{j=0}^{n}\mathbb{H}F_{j+1}^q = \frac{\mathbb{H}F_1^q - q\alpha^2\mathbb{H}F_0^q - \mathbb{H}F_{n+2}^q + q\alpha^2\mathbb{H}F_{n+1}^q}{(1-\alpha)(1-\alpha q)}. \tag{13}$$

On the other hand, from Theorem 2, we have

$$\sum_{j=0}^{n}\mathbb{HL}_{k,j}^q = \sum_{j=0}^{n}\left((k+1)\mathbb{H}F_{j+1}^q - kI\right)$$

$$= (k+1)\sum_{j=0}^{n}\mathbb{H}F_{j+1}^q - kI\sum_{j=0}^{n}1$$

$$= (k+1)\sum_{j=0}^{n}\mathbb{H}F_{j+1}^q - kI(n+1). \tag{14}$$

By using the sum Formula (13) in Equation (14), we obtain the desired result. □

In the following theorem, we provide Vajda's identity for the q-generalized Leonardo hybrid numbers. As a corollary of this theorem, we express Catalan's identity, Cassini's identity, and d'Ocagne's identity in terms of q-integers. It should be noted that Vajda's identity for the classical Fibonacci numbers can be found in ([34] Identity (20a)). It is also worth noting that setting $q = \frac{-1}{\alpha^2}$ where $\alpha = \frac{1+\sqrt{5}}{2}$ in the following identities yields the corresponding results for the generalized Leonardo hybrid numbers.

Theorem 6. *For nonnegative integers n, r, and s, we have*

$$\mathbb{HL}^q_{k,n+r}\mathbb{HL}^q_{k,n+s} - \mathbb{HL}^q_{k,n}\mathbb{HL}^q_{k,n+r+s} = \frac{(k+1)^2\alpha^{2n+r+s}}{(1-q)^2}(1-q^r)q^{n+1}(\beta^*\alpha^* - \alpha^*\beta^*q^s)$$
$$+k\left(\left(\mathbb{HL}^q_{k,n} - \mathbb{HL}^q_{k,n+r}\right)I + I\left(\mathbb{HL}^q_{k,n+r+s} - \mathbb{HL}^q_{k,n+s}\right)\right).$$

Proof. From the Binet formula of q-generalized Leonardo hybrid numbers, we have

$$\mathbb{HL}^q_{k,n+r}\mathbb{HL}^q_{k,n+s} - \mathbb{HL}^q_{k,n}\mathbb{HL}^q_{k,n+r+s}$$

$$= \frac{(k+1)^2}{\alpha^2(1-q)^2}\left(\left(\left(\alpha^{n+r+1}\alpha^* - (\alpha q)^{n+r+1}\beta^*\right)\left(\alpha^{n+s+1}\alpha^* - (\alpha q)^{n+s+1}\beta^*\right)\right)\right.$$
$$\left. - \left(\alpha^{n+1}\alpha^* - (\alpha q)^{n+1}\beta^*\right)\left(\alpha^{n+r+s+1}\alpha^* - (\alpha q)^{n+r+s+1}\beta^*\right)\right)$$
$$- \frac{(k+1)}{\alpha(1-q)}\left(\alpha^{n+r+1}\alpha^* - (\alpha q)^{n+r+1}\beta^* - \alpha^{n+1}\alpha^* + (\alpha q)^{n+1}\beta^*\right)kI$$
$$- \frac{(k+1)}{\alpha(1-q)}kI\left(\alpha^{n+s+1}\alpha^* - (\alpha q)^{n+s+1}\beta^* - \alpha^{n+r+s+1}\alpha^* + (\alpha q)^{n+r+s+1}\beta^*\right)$$

$$= \frac{(k+1)^2\alpha^{2n+r+s}}{(1-q)^2}(1-q^r)q^{n+1}(\beta^*\alpha^* - \alpha^*\beta^*q^s)$$
$$+ \frac{k(k+1)}{(1-q)}\left(\left(\alpha^{n+1}\alpha^* - (\alpha q)^{n+1}\beta^*\right) - \left(\alpha^{n+r+1}\alpha^* - (\alpha q)^{n+r+1}\beta^*\right)\right)I$$
$$+ \frac{k(k+1)}{(1-q)}I\left(\left(\alpha^{n+r+s+1}\alpha^* - (\alpha q)^{n+r+s+1}\beta^*\right) - \left(\alpha^{n+s+1}\alpha^* - (\alpha q)^{n+s+1}\beta^*\right)\right)$$

$$= \frac{(k+1)^2\alpha^{2n+r+s}}{(1-q)^2}(1-q^r)q^{n+1}(\beta^*\alpha^* - \alpha^*\beta^*q^s)$$
$$+k\left(\left(\mathbb{HL}^q_{k,n} - \mathbb{HL}^q_{k,n+r}\right)I + I\left(\mathbb{HL}^q_{k,n+r+s} - \mathbb{HL}^q_{k,n+s}\right)\right).$$

□

The following identity corresponds to Catalan's identity for the q-generalized Leonardo hybrid numbers.

Corollary 1. *For nonnegative integers n and m with $n \geq m$, we have*

$$\mathbb{HL}^q_{k,n-m}\mathbb{HL}^q_{k,n+m} - \left(\mathbb{HL}^q_{k,n}\right)^2 = -\frac{(k+1)^2\alpha^{2n}}{(1-q)^2}(1-q^m)q^{n+1}(\beta^*\alpha^*q^{-m} - \alpha^*\beta^*)$$
$$+k\left(\left(\mathbb{HL}^q_{k,n} - \mathbb{HL}^q_{k,n-m}\right)I + I\left(\mathbb{HL}^q_{k,n} - \mathbb{HL}^q_{k,n+m}\right)\right).$$

Proof. If we take $r, s \to m$ and $n \to n - m$ in Theorem 6, we obtain

$$\mathbb{HL}^q_{k,n}\mathbb{HL}^q_{k,n} - \mathbb{HL}^q_{k,n-m}\mathbb{HL}^q_{k,n+m} = \frac{(k+1)^2\alpha^{2n}}{(1-q)^2}(1-q^m)q^{n-m+1}(\beta^*\alpha^* - \alpha^*\beta^*q^m)$$
$$+k\left(\left(\mathbb{HL}^q_{k,n-m} - \mathbb{HL}^q_{k,n}\right)I + I\left(\mathbb{HL}^q_{k,n+m} - \mathbb{HL}^q_{k,n}\right)\right).$$

Thus, we obtain the desired result. □

The following identity corresponds to Cassini's identity for the q-generalized Leonardo hybrid numbers.

Corollary 2. *For positive integer n, we have*

$$\mathbb{HL}^q_{k,n-1}\mathbb{HL}^q_{k,n+1} - \left(\mathbb{HL}^q_{k,n}\right)^2 = -\frac{(k+1)^2\alpha^{2n}}{1-q}q^n(\beta^*\alpha^* - \alpha^*\beta^*q)$$
$$+ k\left(\left(\mathbb{HL}^q_{k,n} - \mathbb{HL}^q_{k,n-1}\right)I + I\left(\mathbb{HL}^q_{k,n} - \mathbb{HL}^q_{k,n+1}\right)\right).$$

Proof. If we take $r = s = 1$ and $n \to n-1$ in Theorem 6, we obtain

$$\mathbb{HL}^q_{k,n}\mathbb{HL}^q_{k,n} - \mathbb{HL}^q_{k,n-1}\mathbb{HL}^q_{k,n+1} = \frac{(k+1)^2\alpha^{2n}}{1-q}q^n(\beta^*\alpha^* - \alpha^*\beta^*q)$$
$$+ k\left(\left(\mathbb{HL}^q_{k,n-1} - \mathbb{HL}^q_{k,n}\right)I + I\left(\mathbb{HL}^q_{k,n+1} - \mathbb{HL}^q_{k,n}\right)\right).$$

Thus, we obtain the desired result. □

The following identity corresponds to d'Ocagne's identity for the q-generalized Leonardo hybrid numbers.

Corollary 3. *For nonnegative integers n and m with $m \geq n$, we have*

$$\mathbb{HL}^q_{k,m}\mathbb{HL}^q_{k,n+1} - \mathbb{HL}^q_{k,n}\mathbb{HL}^q_{k,m+1} = \frac{(k+1)^2\alpha^{n+m+1}}{(1-q)^2}(1-q^{m-n})q^{n+1}(\beta^*\alpha^* - \alpha^*\beta^*q)$$
$$+ k\left(\left(\mathbb{HL}^q_{k,n} - \mathbb{HL}^q_{k,m}\right)I + I\left(\mathbb{HL}^q_{k,m+1} - \mathbb{HL}^q_{k,n+1}\right)\right).$$

Proof. If we take $r = m - n$ and $s = 1$ in Theorem 6, we obtain the desired result. □

Remark 3. *It should be noted that Theorem 6 is more general than the results given in [30]. If we take $k = 1$ in the above corollaries, we obtain the identities for the q-Leonardo hybrid numbers in ([30] Theorem 3.6, Theorem 3.7, Corollary 3.2).*

Theorem 7. *Let $\Delta := (\alpha - \alpha q)^2$. For nonnegative integers n and r, the following hold:*

(i) $\sum_{i=0}^{n} \binom{n}{i}(-\alpha^2 q)^{n-i}\mathbb{HL}^q_{k,2i+r} = \begin{cases} (k+1)\sqrt{\Delta}^n \mathbb{H}F^q_{n+r+1} - k(1-\alpha^2 q)^n I, & \text{if } n \text{ is even,} \\ (k+1)\sqrt{\Delta}^{n-1}\mathbb{H}L^q_{n+r+1} - k(1-\alpha^2 q)^n I, & \text{if } n \text{ is odd.} \end{cases}$

(ii) $\sum_{i=0}^{n} \binom{n}{i}(-1)^i(-\alpha^2 q)^{n-i}\mathbb{HL}^q_{k,2i+r} = (k+1)(-\alpha[2]_q)^n \mathbb{H}F^q_{n+r+1} + (-1)^{n+1}k\left(1+\alpha^2 q\right)^n I.$

Proof. (i) From the Binet formulas of q-generalized Leonardo hybrid numbers, we have

$$\sum_{i=0}^{n} \binom{n}{i} \left(-\alpha^2 q\right)^{n-i} \mathbb{H}\mathcal{L}_{k,2i+r}^{q}$$

$$= \sum_{i=0}^{n} \binom{n}{i} \left(-\alpha^2 q\right)^{n-i} \left((k+1) \left(\frac{\alpha^{2i+r+1}\alpha^* - (\alpha q)^{2i+r+1}\beta^*}{\sqrt{\Delta}} \right) - kI \right)$$

$$= \frac{k+1}{\sqrt{\Delta}} \left(\alpha^{r+1}\alpha^* \sum_{i=0}^{n} \binom{n}{i} \left(-\alpha^2 q\right)^{n-i} \alpha^{2i} - (\alpha q)^{r+1}\beta^* \sum_{i=0}^{n} \binom{n}{i} \left(-\alpha^2 q\right)^{n-i} (\alpha q)^{2i} \right)$$

$$- kI \sum_{i=0}^{n} \binom{n}{i} \left(-\alpha^2 q\right)^{n-i}$$

$$= \frac{k+1}{\sqrt{\Delta}} \left(\alpha^{r+1}\alpha^* \left(\alpha^2 - \alpha^2 q\right)^n - (\alpha q)^{r+1}\beta^* \left(\alpha^2 q^2 - \alpha^2 q\right)^n \right) - kI\left(1 - \alpha^2 q\right)^n$$

$$= \frac{k+1}{\sqrt{\Delta}} \left(\alpha^{r+1}\alpha^* \left(\alpha\sqrt{\Delta}\right)^n - (\alpha q)^{r+1}\beta^* \left(-\alpha q\sqrt{\Delta}\right)^n \right) - kI\left(1 - \alpha^2 q\right)^n.$$

For even n, we have

$$\sum_{i=0}^{n} \binom{n}{i} \left(-\alpha^2 q\right)^{n-i} \mathbb{H}\mathcal{L}_{k,2i+r}^{q}$$

$$= (k+1)\sqrt{\Delta}^n \frac{\alpha^{n+r+1}\alpha^* - (\alpha q)^{n+r+1}\beta^*}{\sqrt{\Delta}} - k\left(1 - \alpha^2 q\right)^n I$$

$$= (k+1)\sqrt{\Delta}^n \mathbb{H}F_{n+r+1}^{q} - k\left(1 - \alpha^2 q\right)^n I.$$

For odd n, we have

$$\sum_{i=0}^{n} \binom{n}{i} \left(-\alpha^2 q\right)^{n-i} \mathbb{H}\mathcal{L}_{k,2i+r}^{q}$$

$$= (k+1) \frac{\left(\alpha^{r+1}\alpha^* \left(\alpha\sqrt{\Delta}\right)^n + (\alpha q)^{r+1}\beta^* \left(\alpha q\sqrt{\Delta}\right)^n\right)}{\sqrt{\Delta}} - k\left(1 - \alpha^2 q\right)^n I$$

$$= (k+1)\sqrt{\Delta}^n \frac{\alpha^{n+r+1}\alpha^* + (\alpha q)^{n+r+1}\beta^*}{\sqrt{\Delta}} - k\left(1 - \alpha^2 q\right)^n I$$

$$= (k+1)\sqrt{\Delta}^{n-1} \mathbb{H}L_{n+r+1}^{q} - k\left(1 - \alpha^2 q\right)^n I.$$

The identity (ii) can be proven similarly. □

Remark 4. *If we take $k = 1$ in Theorem 7, we obtain the identities for the q-Leonardo hybrid numbers in ([30] Theorem 3.3).*

3. Leonardo Quaternions over Finite Fields

In this section, we consider the quaternion algebra $Q_{\mathbb{Z}_p}(-1,-1)$, for simplicity $Q_{\mathbb{Z}_p}$. Since $Q_{\mathbb{Z}_p}$ is a split algebra, it is natural to ask about the zero divisors within this quaternion algebra. Now we determine the Leonardo quaternions, which are zero divisors in the quaternion algebra $Q_{\mathbb{Z}_p}$ for $p = 3$ and $p = 5$. Additionally, we identify certain Leonardo quaternions that are invertible in the quaternion algebra $Q_{\mathbb{Z}_p}$ for prime integer p with $p \geq 7$.

It should be noted that determining the Leonardo quaternions that are zero divisors and invertible elements is a more challenging task compared to the Fibonacci quaternions, which was studied by Savin in [22], due to the increased complexity of the norm associated with Leonardo quaternions. Therefore, we restrict our focus to the conventional Leonardo quaternions case.

Let QL_n be the nth Leonardo quaternion [24] defined as

$$QL_n = \mathcal{L}_n + \mathcal{L}_{n+1}\mathbf{i} + \mathcal{L}_{n+2}\mathbf{j} + \mathcal{L}_{n+3}\mathbf{k},$$

where the basis $\{1, \mathbf{i}, \mathbf{j}, \mathbf{k}\}$ satisfies the multiplication rules $\mathbf{i}^2 = \mathbf{j}^2 = \mathbf{k}^2 = \mathbf{ijk} = -1$. By using the definition of Leonardo quaternion and the relations $F_n + F_{n+2} = L_{n+1}$, $F_n^2 + F_{n+1}^2 = F_{2n+1}$ and $F_n + F_{n+4} = 3F_{n+2}$, the norm of Leonardo quaternion can be obtained as follows:

$$\begin{aligned}
N(QL_n) &= \mathcal{L}_n^2 + \mathcal{L}_{n+1}^2 + \mathcal{L}_{n+2}^2 + \mathcal{L}_{n+3}^2 \\
&= (2F_{n+1} - 1)^2 + (2F_{n+2} - 1)^2 + (2F_{n+3} - 1)^2 + (2F_{n+4} - 1)^2 \\
&= 4\left(F_{n+1}^2 + F_{n+2}^2 + F_{n+3}^2 + F_{n+4}^2\right) - 4(F_{n+1} + F_{n+2} + F_{n+3} + F_{n+4}) + 4 \\
&= 4(F_{2n+3} + F_{2n+7}) - 4(F_{n+3} + F_{n+5}) + 4 \\
&= 4(3F_{2n+5} - L_{n+4} + 1). \quad (15)
\end{aligned}$$

Proposition 1. *A Leonardo quaternion QL_n is a zero divisor in quaternion algebra $Q_{\mathbb{Z}_3}$ if and only if $n \equiv 0, 5, 7 \pmod{8}$. Moreover, in $Q_{\mathbb{Z}_3}$, there are 3 Leonardo quaternions that are zero divisors.*

Proof. We recall that the cycle of Lucas numbers modulo 3 is

$$2, 1, 0, 1, 1, 2, 0, 2.$$

Therefore, the cycle length of Lucas numbers modulo 3 is 8.

A Leonardo quaternion QL_n is a zero divisor in quaternion algebra $Q_{\mathbb{Z}_3}$ if and only if $N(QL_n) = \bar{0}$ in $\mathbb{Z}_3$. By using Equation (15), we have

$$L_{n+4} \equiv 1 \pmod{3} \Leftrightarrow n + 4 \equiv 1, 3, 4 \pmod{8} \Leftrightarrow n \equiv 0, 5, 7 \pmod{8}.$$

There are 81 elements in the quaternion algebra $Q_{\mathbb{Z}_3}$. From [35], the number of zero divisors in $Q_{\mathbb{Z}_p}$ is $p^3 + p^2 - p$. Thus, from 81 quaternions, 33 quaternions are zero divisors in $Q_{\mathbb{Z}_3}$. From those, only 3 quaternions are zero divisor Leonardo quaternions, namely:

$$\begin{aligned}
QL_0 &= \bar{\mathcal{L}}_0 + \bar{\mathcal{L}}_1\mathbf{i} + \bar{\mathcal{L}}_2\mathbf{j} + \bar{\mathcal{L}}_3\mathbf{k} = \bar{1} + \mathbf{i} + \bar{2}\mathbf{k}, \\
QL_5 &= \bar{\mathcal{L}}_5 + \bar{\mathcal{L}}_6\mathbf{i} + \bar{\mathcal{L}}_7\mathbf{j} + \bar{\mathcal{L}}_8\mathbf{k} = \mathbf{i} + \bar{2}\mathbf{j} + \mathbf{k}, \\
QL_7 &= \bar{\mathcal{L}}_7 + \bar{\mathcal{L}}_8\mathbf{i} + \bar{\mathcal{L}}_9\mathbf{j} + \bar{\mathcal{L}}_{10}\mathbf{k} = \bar{2} + \mathbf{i} + \mathbf{j}.
\end{aligned}$$

□

Proposition 2. *A Leonardo quaternion QL_n is a zero divisor in quaternion algebra $Q_{\mathbb{Z}_5}$ if and only if $n \equiv 2, 5, 7, 16 \pmod{20}$.*

Proof. We recall that the cycle of Fibonacci numbers modulo 5 is

$$0, 1, 1, 2, 3, 0, 3, 3, 1, 4, 0, 4, 4, 3, 2, 0, 2, 2, 4, 1.$$

Therefore, the cycle length of Fibonacci numbers modulo 5 is 20. See ([17] A082116).

A Leonardo quaternion QL_n is a zero divisor in quaternion algebra $Q_{\mathbb{Z}_5}$ if and only if $N(QL_n) = \bar{0}$ in $\mathbb{Z}_5$. By using Equation (15), we have

$$F_{n+3} + F_{n+5} + 2F_{2n+5} \equiv 1 \pmod{5}. \quad (16)$$

To find n such that the congruence (16) is satisfied, we need to consider the following five cases:

Case 1: If $n \equiv 0 \pmod 5$, then $F_{n+5} \equiv 0 \pmod 5$, $F_{2n+5} \equiv 0 \pmod 5$. Therefore, we obtain that the congruence (16) is true if and only if $F_{n+3} \equiv 1 \pmod 5 \Leftrightarrow n+3 \equiv 8 \pmod{20} \Leftrightarrow n \equiv 5 \pmod{20}$.

Case 2: If $n \equiv 1 \pmod 5$, then we have four subcases:

- If $n \equiv 1 \pmod{20}$, then $F_{n+3} \equiv 3 \pmod 5$, $F_{n+5} \equiv 3 \pmod 5$, $F_{2n+5} \equiv 3 \pmod 5$. It results $F_{n+3} + F_{n+5} + 2F_{2n+5} \equiv 2 \pmod 5$, therefore, the congruence (16) is not satisfied.
- If $n \equiv 6 \pmod{20}$, then $F_{n+3} \equiv 4 \pmod 5$, $F_{n+5} \equiv 4 \pmod 5$, $F_{2n+5} \equiv 2 \pmod 5$. It results $F_{n+3} + F_{n+5} + 2F_{2n+5} \equiv 2 \pmod 5$, therefore, the congruence (16) is not satisfied.
- If $n \equiv 11 \pmod{20}$, then $F_{n+3} \equiv 2 \pmod 5$, $F_{n+5} \equiv 2 \pmod 5$, $F_{2n+5} \equiv 3 \pmod 5$. It results $F_{n+3} + F_{n+5} + 2F_{2n+5} \equiv 0 \pmod 5$, therefore, the congruence (16) is not satisfied.
- If $n \equiv 16 \pmod{20}$, then $F_{n+3} \equiv 1 \pmod 5$, $F_{n+5} \equiv 1 \pmod 5$, $F_{2n+5} \equiv 2 \pmod 5$. It results $F_{n+3} + F_{n+5} + 2F_{2n+5} \equiv 1 \pmod 5$, therefore, the congruence (16) is satisfied.

Therefore, in Case 2, we have $N(Q\mathcal{L}_n) = \overline{0} \Leftrightarrow n \equiv 16 \pmod{20}$.

Case 3: If $n \equiv 2 \pmod 5$, then we have four subcases:

- If $n \equiv 2 \pmod{20}$, then $F_{n+3} \equiv 0 \pmod 5$, $F_{n+5} \equiv 3 \pmod 5$, $F_{2n+5} \equiv 4 \pmod 5$. It results $F_{n+3} + F_{n+5} + 2F_{2n+5} \equiv 1 \pmod 5$, therefore, the congruence (16) is satisfied.
- If $n \equiv 7 \pmod{20}$, then $F_{n+3} \equiv 0 \pmod 5$, $F_{n+5} \equiv 4 \pmod 5$, $F_{2n+5} \equiv 1 \pmod 5$. It results $F_{n+3} + F_{n+5} + 2F_{2n+5} \equiv 1 \pmod 5$, therefore, the congruence (16) is satisfied.
- If $n \equiv 12 \pmod{20}$, then $F_{n+3} \equiv 0 \pmod 5$, $F_{n+5} \equiv 2 \pmod 5$, $F_{2n+5} \equiv 4 \pmod 5$. It results $F_{n+3} + F_{n+5} + 2F_{2n+5} \equiv 0 \pmod 5$, therefore, the congruence (16) is not satisfied.
- If $n \equiv 17 \pmod{20}$, then $F_{n+3} \equiv 0 \pmod 5$, $F_{n+5} \equiv 1 \pmod 5$, $F_{2n+5} \equiv 1 \pmod 5$. It results $F_{n+3} + F_{n+5} + 2F_{2n+5} \equiv 3 \pmod 5$, therefore, the congruence (16) is not satisfied.

Therefore, in Case 3, we have $N(Q\mathcal{L}_n) = \overline{0} \Leftrightarrow n \equiv 2, 7 \pmod{20}$.

Case 4: If $n \equiv 3 \pmod 5$, then we have four subcases:

- If $n \equiv 3 \pmod{20}$, then $F_{n+3} \equiv 3 \pmod 5$, $F_{n+5} \equiv 1 \pmod 5$, $F_{2n+5} \equiv 4 \pmod 5$. It results $F_{n+3} + F_{n+5} + 2F_{2n+5} \equiv 2 \pmod 5$, therefore, the congruence (16) is not satisfied.
- If $n \equiv 8 \pmod{20}$, then $F_{n+3} \equiv 4 \pmod 5$, $F_{n+5} \equiv 3 \pmod 5$, $F_{2n+5} \equiv 1 \pmod 5$. It results $F_{n+3} + F_{n+5} + 2F_{2n+5} \equiv 4 \pmod 5$, therefore, the congruence (16) is not satisfied.
- If $n \equiv 13 \pmod{20}$, then $F_{n+3} \equiv 2 \pmod 5$, $F_{n+5} \equiv 4 \pmod 5$, $F_{2n+5} \equiv 4 \pmod 5$. It results $F_{n+3} + F_{n+5} + 2F_{2n+5} \equiv 4 \pmod 5$, therefore, the congruence (16) is not satisfied.
- If $n \equiv 18 \pmod{20}$, then $F_{n+3} \equiv 1 \pmod 5$, $F_{n+5} \equiv 2 \pmod 5$, $F_{2n+5} \equiv 1 \pmod 5$. It results $F_{n+3} + F_{n+5} + 2F_{2n+5} \equiv 0 \pmod 5$, therefore, the congruence (16) is not satisfied.

Therefore, in Case 4, we have $N(Q\mathcal{L}_n) \neq \overline{0}$.

Case 5: If $n \equiv 4 \pmod 5$, then we have four subcases:

- If $n \equiv 4 \pmod{20}$, then $F_{n+3} \equiv 3 \pmod 5$, $F_{n+5} \equiv 4 \pmod 5$, $F_{2n+5} \equiv 3 \pmod 5$. It results $F_{n+3} + F_{n+5} + 2F_{2n+5} \equiv 3 \pmod 5$, therefore, the congruence (16) is not satisfied.
- If $n \equiv 9 \pmod{20}$, then $F_{n+3} \equiv 4 \pmod 5$, $F_{n+5} \equiv 2 \pmod 5$, $F_{2n+5} \equiv 2 \pmod 5$. It results $F_{n+3} + F_{n+5} + 2F_{2n+5} \equiv 0 \pmod 5$, therefore, the congruence (16) is not satisfied.
- If $n \equiv 14 \pmod{20}$, then $F_{n+3} \equiv 2 \pmod 5$, $F_{n+5} \equiv 1 \pmod 5$, $F_{2n+5} \equiv 3 \pmod 5$. It results $F_{n+3} + F_{n+5} + 2F_{2n+5} \equiv 4 \pmod 5$, therefore, the congruence (16) is not satisfied.
- If $n \equiv 19 \pmod{20}$, then $F_{n+3} \equiv 1 \pmod 5$, $F_{n+5} \equiv 3 \pmod 5$, $F_{2n+5} \equiv 2 \pmod 5$. It results $F_{n+3} + F_{n+5} + 2F_{2n+5} \equiv 3 \pmod 5$, therefore, the congruence (16) is not satisfied.

Therefore, in Case 5, we have $N(Q\mathcal{L}_n) \neq \overline{0}$.

Thus, we obtain the desired result. □

Proposition 3. *The Leonardo quaternion $Q\mathcal{L}_{p-4}$ is invertible in quaternion algebra $Q_{\mathbb{Z}_p}$ for prime integer p with $p \geq 7$.*

Proof. Recall that $p \nmid F_{2p-3}$ for prime integer p with $p \geq 7$. (Since the proof involved many calculations, we skip it.) From (15), in $\mathbb{Z}_p$, we have

$$N(Q\mathcal{L}_{p-4}) = \overline{4}\left(\overline{3}\overline{F}_{2p-3} - \overline{L}_p + \overline{1}\right).$$

Since $L_p \equiv 1 \pmod{p}$ and $F_{2p-3} \not\equiv 0 \pmod{p}$, we have $N(Q\mathcal{L}_{p-4}) \neq \overline{0}$ in $\mathbb{Z}_p$. Thus, $Q\mathcal{L}_{p-4}$ is an invertible element in $Q_{\mathbb{Z}_p}$. □

4. Conclusions

We can summarize the results obtained in this paper under two main headings. Firstly, we introduce a new class of Leonardo hybrid numbers and investigate some of their properties. The main advantage of the proposed family of hybrid numbers that reflect the generalized Leonardo numbers is that it allows the derivation of several hybrid number classes as a special case. In particular, different from the work [30], where the Leonardo hybrid numbers in [29] are obtained by taking $q = -1/\alpha^2$ with $\alpha = \frac{1+\sqrt{5}}{2}$, in this paper, by taking $q = -1/\alpha^2$ with $\alpha = \frac{1+\sqrt{5}}{2}$, we obtain the generalized Leonardo hybrid numbers, which are firstly defined here. Secondly, we study the Leonardo quaternions that are zero divisors and invertible elements in the quaternion algebra $Q_{\mathbb{Z}_p}$ for special values of prime integer p. This part can be seen as an application of Leonardo quaternions over finite fields, and it marks the first instance in the literature of determining Leonardo quaternions that are zero divisors or invertible elements. To provide a brief summary of our findings:

- We introduce the generalized Leonardo hybrid numbers, which are reduced to the conventional Leonardo hybrid numbers in [29] when $k = 1$.
- We derive a new class of Leonardo hybrid numbers, referred to as the q-generalized Leonardo hybrid numbers. When $k = 1$, the q-generalized Leonardo hybrid numbers reduce to the conventional q-Leonardo hybrid numbers in [30].
- We obtain Vajda's identity for q-generalized Leonardo numbers, which generalizes Catalan's identity, Cassini's identity, and d'Ocagne's identity automatically. Thus, this result is even more general than the ones in [30].
- We obtain that a Leonardo quaternion $Q\mathcal{L}_n$ is a zero divisor in quaternion algebra $Q_{\mathbb{Z}_3}$ if and only if $n \equiv 0, 5, 7 \pmod{8}$.
- We obtain that a Leonardo quaternion $Q\mathcal{L}_n$ is a zero divisor in quaternion algebra $Q_{\mathbb{Z}_5}$ if and only if $n \equiv 2, 5, 7, 16 \pmod{20}$.
- We show that the Leonardo quaternion $Q\mathcal{L}_{p-4}$ is invertible in quaternion algebra $Q_{\mathbb{Z}_p}$ for prime $p \geq 7$.

Author Contributions: Conceptualization, E.T., D.S. and S.Y.; methodology, E.T., D.S. and S.Y.; validation, E.T., D.S. and S.Y.; formal analysis, E.T., D.S. and S.Y.; investigation, E.T., D.S. and S.Y.; resources, E.T., D.S. and S.Y.; writing—original draft preparation, E.T.; writing—review and editing, E.T.; project administration, E.T. All authors have read and agreed to the published version of the manuscript.

Funding: This research received no external funding.

Data Availability Statement: Data are contained within the article.

Acknowledgments: We would like to thank an anonymous referee for constructive comments that have led to a great improvement of the paper.

Conflicts of Interest: The authors declare no conflict of interest.

References

1. Wang, W.; Zhang, H.; Jiang, X.; Yang, X. A high-order and efficient numerical technique for the nonlocal neutron diffusion equation representing neutron transport in a nuclear reactor. *Ann. Nucl. Energy* **2024**, *195*, 110163. [CrossRef]
2. Yang, X.; Wu, L.; Zhang, H. A space-time spectral order sinc-collocation method for the fourth-order nonlocal heat model arising in viscoelasticity. *Appl. Math. Comput.* **2023**, *457*, 128192. [CrossRef]
3. Zhang, H.; Liu, Y.; Yang, X. An efficient ADI difference scheme for the nonlocal evolution problem in three-dimensional space. *J. Appl. Math. Comput.* **2023**, *69*, 651–674. [CrossRef]
4. Zhang, H.; Yang, X.; Tang, Q.; Xu, D. A robust error analysis of the OSC method for a multi-term fourth-order sub-diffusion equation. *Comput. Math. Appl.* **2022**, *109*, 180–190.
5. Zhou, Z.; Zhang, H.; Yang, X. H^1-norm error analysis of a robust ADI method on graded mesh for three-dimensional subdiffusion problems. *Numer. Algorithms* **2023**, 1–19. [CrossRef]

6. Horadam, A.F. Basic properties of a certain generalized sequence of numbers. *Fibonacci Q.* **1965**, *3*, 161–176.
7. Tan, E. Some properties of the bi-periodic Horadam sequences. *Notes Number Theory Discret. Math.* **2017**, *23*, 56–65.
8. Tan, E.; Dagli, M.; Belkhir, A. Bi-periodic incomplete Horadam numbers. *Turk. J. Math.* **2023**, *47*, 554–564. [CrossRef]
9. Tan, E.; Leung, H.H. Some results on Horadam quaternions. *Chaos Solitons Fractals* **2020**, *138*, 109961. [CrossRef]
10. Dijkstra, E.W. Archive: Fibonacci Numbers and Leonardo Numbers. (EWD 797). July 1981. Available online: www.cs.utexas.edu/users/EWD/ewd07xx/EWD797.PDF (accessed on 16 November 2023).
11. Alp, Y.; Kocer, E.G. Some properties of Leonardo numbers. *Konuralp J. Math.* **2021**, *9*, 183–189.
12. Catarino, P.; Borges, A. On Leonardo numbers. *Acta Math. Univ. Comen.* **2019**, *89*, 75–86.
13. Catarino, P.; Borges, A. A note on incomplete Leonardo numbers. *Integers* **2020**, *20*, 1–7.
14. Nurkan, S.K.; Güven, I.A. Ordered Leonardo Quadruple Numbers. *Symmetry* **2023**, *15*, 149. [CrossRef]
15. Shannon, A.G. A note on generalized Leonardo numbers. *Notes Number Theory Discret. Math.* **2019**, *25*, 97–101. [CrossRef]
16. Tan, E.; Leung, H.H. On Leonardo p-numbers. *Integers* **2023**, *23*, 1–11.
17. Sloane, N.J.A. The On-Line Encyclopedia of Integers Sequences, The OEIS Foundation Inc. Available online: https//oeis.org/ (accessed on 16 November 2023).
18. Kuhapatanakul, K.; Chobsorn, J. On the generalized Leonardo numbers. *Integers* **2022**, *22*, 1–7.
19. Shattuck, M. Combinatorial proofs of identities for the generalized Leonardo numbers. *Notes Number Theory Discret. Math.* **2022**, *28*, 778–790. [CrossRef]
20. Benjamin, A.T.; Quinn, J.J. *Proofs That Really Count: The Art of Combinatorial Proof*; Mathematical Association of America: Washington, DC, USA, 2003.
21. Grau, J.M.; Miguel, C.; Oller-Marcen, A.M. On the structure of quaternion rings over $\mathbb{Z}/n\mathbb{Z}$. *Adv. Appl. Clifford Algebr.* **2015**, *25*, 875–887. [CrossRef]
22. Savin, D. About Special Elements in Quaternion Algebras Over Finite Fields. *Adv. Appl. Clifford Algebr.* **2017**, *27*, 1801–1813. [CrossRef]
23. Ozdemir, M. Introduction to Hybrid Numbers. *Adv. Appl. Clifford Algebr.* **2016**, *26*, 441–447. [CrossRef]
24. Mangueira, M.C.S.; Alves, F.R.V.; Catarino, P.M.M.C. Hybrid Quaternions of Leonardo. *Trends Comput. Appl. Math.* **2022**, *23*, 51–62. [CrossRef]
25. Ozimamoglu, H. On Leonardo sedenions. *Afr. Mat.* **2023**, *34*, 26. [CrossRef]
26. Szynal-Liana, A. The Horadam hybrid numbers. *Discuss. Math.-Gen. Algebra Appl.* **2018**, *38*, 91–98. [CrossRef]
27. Szynal-Liana, A.; Włoch I. Introduction to Fibonacci and Lucas hybrinomials. *Complex Var. Elliptic Equ.* **2020**, *65*, 1736–1747. [CrossRef]
28. Tan, E.; Ait-Amrane, N.R. On a new generalization of Fibonacci hybrid numbers. *Indian J. Pure Appl. Math.* **2023**, *54*, 428–438. [CrossRef]
29. Alp, Y.; Kocer, E.G. Hybrid Leonardo numbers. *Chaos Solitons Fractals* **2021**, *150*, 111128. [CrossRef]
30. Ozimamoglu, H. A new generalization of Leonardo hybrid numbers with q-integers. *Indian J. Pure Appl. Math.* **2023**. [CrossRef]
31. Kac, V.G.; Cheung, P. *Quantum Calculus*; Springer: New York, NY, USA, 2002; Volume 113.
32. Akkus, I.; Kizilaslan, G. Quaternions: Quantum calculus approach with applications. *Kuwait J. Sci.* **2019**, *46*, 1–13.
33. Kızılates, C. A new generalization of Fibonacci hybrid and Lucas hybrid numbers. *Chaos Solitons Fractals* **2020**, *130*, 109449. [CrossRef]
34. Vajda, S. *Fibonacci and Lucas Numbers, and the Golden Section: Theory and Applications*; Ellis Horwood: London, UK, 1989.
35. Miguel, C.J.; Serodio, R. On the structure of quaternion rings Over $\mathbb{Z}_p$. *Int. J. Algebra* **2011**, *5*, 1313–1325.

Disclaimer/Publisher's Note: The statements, opinions and data contained in all publications are solely those of the individual author(s) and contributor(s) and not of MDPI and/or the editor(s). MDPI and/or the editor(s) disclaim responsibility for any injury to people or property resulting from any ideas, methods, instructions or products referred to in the content.